SEVENTH EDITION

READINGS FOR
SOCIOLOGY

EDITED BY

Garth Massey

W. W. Norton & Company ■ New York ■ London

W. W. Norton & Company has been independent since its founding in 1923, when William Warder Norton and Mary D. Herter Norton first published lectures delivered at the People's Institute, the adult education division of New York City's Cooper Union. The firm soon expanded its program beyond the Institute, publishing books by celebrated academics from America and abroad. By midcentury, the two major pillars of Norton's publishing program—trade books and college texts—were firmly established. In the 1950s, the Norton family transferred control of the company to its employees, and today—with a staff of four hundred and a comparable number of trade, college, and professional titles published each year—W. W. Norton & Company stands as the largest and oldest publishing house owned wholly by its employees.

Manufacturing by QuadGraphics—Fairfield, PA.
Composition by Innodata Isogen.
Book design by JoAnn Simony.
Project editor: Kathleen Feighery.
Production manager: Benjamin Reynolds.

Library of Congress Cataloging-in-Publication Data

Readings for Sociology / edited by Garth Massey. — 7th ed.
    p. cm.
  Includes bibliographical references.
  ISBN 978-0-393-91270-8 (pbk.)
1. Sociology.   I. Massey, Garth.
  HM585.R427 2012
  301—dc22
                                2010051749

W. W. Norton & Company, Inc., 500 Fifth Avenue, New York, N.Y. 10110-0017
www.wwnorton.com

W. W. Norton & Company Ltd., Castle House, 75/76 Wells Street, London W1T 3QT

  2   3   4   5   6   7   8   9

CONTENTS

PART 4 SOCIAL INTERACTION AND IDENTITY

PART 5 SOCIAL INEQUALITY AND LABOR

PART 6 SOCIAL CONTROL AND ORGANIZATIONAL POWER

PART 7 SOCIAL INSTITUTIONS

PART 8 SOCIAL CHANGE

PREFACE

I recently walked by a yard sale and spotted an old book, *Readings for Sociology* by Edgar Schuler and his colleagues from Wayne State and Michigan State Universities. It was published fifty years ago (1960) at $4.25. I bought it for twenty-five cents. The book's 909 pages of 111 readings are grouped into ten sections and an appendix, Sociologists at Work. Not all the authors are sociologists or even social scientists: e.g., George Orwell, Bruno Bettelheim, Theodore White, John Houseman, John Steinbeck, J. Robert Oppenheimer, Julian Huxley, Jawaharlal Nehru. The order of readings move from Environmental Factors to Persons and Groups, Social Organization, Social Processes, and Social and Cultural Change. Social Organization has five subsections and accounts for sixty-one (fifty-five percent) of the readings.

For a sociologist, this is all very interesting. As I composed this new, Seventh edition of *Readings for Sociology*, I couldn't help thinking about the Schuler reader. So much has changed in American society—the world, the university, and the discipline of sociology. And some things have changed very little.

An introductory reader should include works that are well written and tell a story. That hasn't changed. The Schuler reader is full of things I want to read or reread. The titles are exciting, inviting, intriguing, and involve matters of importance. Sociology has always aspired to be these things, and not infrequently it has succeeded. I am proud to be part of an academic discipline that isn't afraid to engage in public issues, as Burawoy's essay, "Public Sociologies" urges. Should we do more of it? Of course. There is so much to make sense of, clarify, and contribute to public discussion and policy. Can we do it better? Indeed, that is the only way we can be credible and actually make a positive contribution.

I and many of my peers were drawn to sociology because we didn't know what we wanted to do when we grew up. Sociology had a breadth that let us delay the dreaded decision. The range of subjects in Schuler's reader is very broad: The Scopes trial, the social order of chickens, life in India, lynching, gossip and snobbery, National Merit scholars, Japanese peasants, toothpaste, Stone Age axes, the atomic bomb, and diesel trains. Sociology finds significance in even the most mundane features of social life and certainly should have something to say about important matters as well.

In this edition of *Readings for Sociology*, Lorna Rhodes takes the reader into a maximum security prison, Michael Pollan, Bob Glennon, and Bill McKibben confront problems of food and the environment, Herb Kelman and Lee Hamilton explore the My Lai massacre, William Adler tells a story of jobs lost, and Elijah Anderson examines the roots of gang violence. The topic of race was in the reader sixty years ago and it is very much in this reader. Social class, work, and inequality are more represented here, but it was there as well. So are bureaucracy, family dynamics, religion, crime, deviance, and socialization. These have remained important sociological topics. And, yes, there are essays that explore the mundane.

Jimm Myers, an igneous petrologist and professor of geology, once explained to me the dilemma of undergraduate geology education. He lamented that students, excited to be geologists, hit a (stone?) wall their third year when their classes begin to require strong mathematical skills. No longer does the identification of rocks and the mystery of geological time and motion dominate their coursework. It's all about numbers. Could the same be said of sociology? Fortunately not, but it is curious that introductory readers contain so little statistical analysis, while the discipline thrives on it. I'm not sure the Schuler reader has a single table or graph, and neither does this edition of *Readings for Sociology*.

Am I guilty of luring students into a discipline by misrepresenting it? Hardly! Empirical, if not quantitative, sociology is no less represented here than in the *American Journal of Sociology*. Many of the articles are based on extensive statistical work, and all of them rely on what is known to be the facts, not on wishful thinking or uninformed opinion. Ethnographic fieldwork, analysis of existing documents, and interviews based on small samples predominate. These are the data-collection approaches most undergraduates will use in doing their own research projects and, frankly, are among the methods used in the very best work in sociology.

What has most changed between 1960 and today is that sociology is a more critical discipline and more self-consciously tries to explain what is problematic in the world. The emphasis on social organization in the Schuler reader has been replaced with sociologies that emphasize process, conflict, asymmetry, and power. Both readers appear to treat social change as an afterthought, but this *Readings for Sociology* implicitly examines social change from the first essay to the last. Gender, identity, the body, and global inequality had no place in 1960. Now they do.

Globalization, lives in flux, social transitions, divergent trajectories, and the construction and abandonment of cultural forms are the themes of many of the selections. Given its continuing emphasis on political economy, *Readings for Sociology* tells many stories of the challenges people are experiencing and the struggles that make up so much of social life today.

I don't know why it's taken until now to include a reading by Georg Simmel. One of the greatest early sociologists, his work has had a tremendous impact on the discipline, beginning with Lewis Coser's and Theodore Caplow's explications and, given its centrality, in Erving Goffman's sociology. Simmel's language may be a bit stilted for some students, but "The Stranger" is an essay to ponder and discuss at length. Both the structural analysis of social interaction and the contradictions inherent in social life are beautifully expressed in this essay.

Three readings were added in the previous edition of *Readings for Sociology* that moved the discussion of socialization and the life cycle into some very interesting areas: Beth Montemurro's "Deviance and Liminality" from her book *Something Old, Something Bold*; Julie Bettie's "Women Without Class"; and Annette Lareau's "Concerted Cultivation and the Accomplishment of Natural Growth" from her *Unequal Childhoods*. When I read Allison Pugh's *Longing and Belonging*, I knew it had to join them. This is smart sociology based on extensive fieldwork, and finely written. The reading here, "Care and Belonging in the Market" gives a taste of what her book offers.

For years Elizabeth and Robert Fernea's "A Look Behind the Veil" was included in *Readings for Sociology*. Amid the controversy over veiling in England, France, and elsewhere, and the obvious need to confront issues surrounding Islam in the United States, I decided to exchange the Fernea essay for an article originally published in *Gender and Society*. Jen'nan Ghazal Read and John Bartkowski's "To Veil or Not to Veil" speaks more directly to students about issues of faith and identity and makes a nice companion to Mary Waters's classic essay, "Optional Ethnicities."

Katherine Benton-Cohen's 2009 social history, *Borderline Americans*, provides an analysis of labor strife (control of the labor process), power, and social inequality that reveals in new and insightful ways the social construction of ethnicity. The story of immigration and citizenship Benton-Cohen tells, set in Cochise County, Arizona, exemplifies the use of history to shed light on the present.

I have substituted the earlier reading by William Julius Wilson—from *When Work Disappears*—with a chapter from his newest book, *More than Just Race: Being Black and Poor in the Inner City*. "The Economic Plight of Inner-City Black Males" can be read as an example of sociological eclecticism, combining structural and cultural analysis to answer a question of major importance. It can also be read as a summary of decades of intellectual debate and social policy that offers a window on sociology and its role in public policy, to say nothing of how its work can be abused. Less sociological analysis and more a personal expression of the idea of race is Barack Obama's 2008 Philadelphia speech, "A More Perfect Union." On hearing it, I was struck by its honesty and candor. Reading it more recently, I see the many ways it can inform sociological questions and stimulate a discussion of race all of us so badly need.

The inclusion of a chapter by Stephanie Coontz, "The Radical Idea of Marrying for Love" from her *Marriage, a History*, is especially satisfying to me. A social historian, Coontz has for many years provided lively, well written, and insightful discussions of marriage and the family. Her *The Way We Never Were* and *The Way We Really Are* have given me more of what Peter Berger calls that "Aha" experience than anything I can think of. Her work shows students what sociology can reveal with a historical and comparative perspective, and a sense of humor.

As I was finishing the revision of *Readings for Sociology*, an old friend reminded me of a recent article in the *American Sociological Review* by a young sociologist who is looking at contemporary social movements generated from above: Not grassroots but Astroturf. In his essay "Industry-Driven Activism" Edward Walker provides a more accessible discussion of the topic covered in his *ASR* article. These movements seemed to dominate the last midterm elections, with huge sums of money from unidentified donors. Walker's is a disquieting glimpse into the future of social movements and political life.

The Schuler reader is 909 pages! Were students expected to read all of it? At the front of the book is a table, "Correlation of this Book with Introductory Sociology Texts," that lists fifteen sociology texts then in print. Were students expected to read the book *and* a text? In honesty, I don't expect students to read all forty-nine essays in my *Readings for Sociology*, but I wish they would. Instructors can pick and choose, and they can add a text or other book to the assigned readings. I have tried to provide quality works that meet the needs of faculty who will teach a course that works for them.

One final mea culpa. In adding new readings I have eliminated others. [Decisions of what to keep and what to drop are more and more guided by publishers' pricing of permissions to reprint articles and chapters.] In the Great Recession this has become acute, with new prices for some selections taking them out of reach. It's important to support authors and publishers, so I'm not grumbling. If there is a favorite reading that doesn't appear here, don't grumble. Let me know.

GARTH MASSEY
Portland, Oregon
gmmassey@uwyo.edu

TO THE INSTRUCTOR

Sociological Principles	Corresponding Readings
1. Introduction to Theory	1, 2, 3, 4, 5, 7, 9, 13, 24, 30, 31, 35
2. Methods	1, 3, 6, 8, 21, 23
3. Culture and Society	9, 10, 11, 12, 13, 16, 30, 37, 38, 39, 40, 41, 44
4. Socialization and the Life Cycle	11, 14, 15, 16, 17, 20, 25, 28, 37
5. Social Interaction and Everyday Life	4, 9, 11, 18, 19, 20, 21, 22, 27, 32, 33, 36, 42, 43
6. Groups, Networks, and Organizations	5, 10, 14, 16, 20, 32, 33, 34, 35, 39, 41, 42, 48
7. Deviance and Crime	17, 25, 29, 33, 36
8. Stratification and Inequality	11, 15, 20, 23, 24, 28, 29, 30, 31
9. Globalization and Global Inequality	13, 24, 42, 46, 49
10. Gender and Gender Inequality	9, 14, 17, 19, 20, 21, 23, 28
11. Ethnicity and Race	8, 9, 11, 20, 21, 22, 26, 28, 45
12. Aging	19, 37, 44
13. Government, Power, and Social Movements	5, 24, 26, 33, 34, 47, 48
14. Work and Economics	23, 24, 25, 26, 27, 30, 31, 35, 36, 40, 41, 42, 46
15. Family and Intimate Relationships	4, 15, 16, 19, 21, 37, 38, 39, 41
16. Education and the Mass Media	13, 21, 28, 29
17. Religion	9, 37, 40, 43, 44
18. Health and the Body	8, 9, 12, 19, 24, 49
19. Population and the Environment	26, 34, 35, 44, 47, 49

PART ONE

THE STUDY
OF SOCIOLOGY

1

Sociology as an Individual Pastime

<small>FROM</small> *Invitation to Sociology*

PETER L. BERGER

What does it mean to "think sociologically"? In this selection from his book Invitation to Sociology, *Peter Berger explains why sociologists are so annoying to the powers that be, the purveyors of conventional wisdom, advertisers, politicians, and others with a vested interest in your going along with their view of things. Sociologists have a reputation for stirring up the waters and occasionally making trouble. For Berger, this is just part of the way sociologists see the world.*

It is gratifying from certain value positions (including some of this writer's) that sociological insights have served in a number of instances to improve the lot of groups of human beings by uncovering morally shocking conditions or by clearing away collective illusions or by showing that socially desired results could be obtained in more humane fashion. One might point, for example, to some applications of sociological knowledge in the penological practice of Western countries. Or one might cite the use made of sociological studies in the Supreme Court decision of 1954 on racial segregation in the public schools. Or one could look at the applications of other sociological studies to the humane planning of urban redevelopment. Certainly the sociologist who is morally and politically sensitive will derive gratification from such instances. But, once more, it will be well to keep in mind that what is at issue here is not sociological understanding as such but certain applications of this understanding. It is not difficult to see how the same understanding could be applied with opposite intentions. Thus the sociological understanding of the dynamics of racial prejudice can be applied effectively by those promoting intragroup hatred as well as by those wanting to spread tolerance. And the sociological understanding of the nature of human solidarity can be employed in the service of both totalitarian and democratic regimes.

* * *

One [more recent] image [of the sociologist is that of] a gatherer of statistics about human behavior. The sociologist is here seen essentially as an aide-de-camp to an IBM machine. He* goes out with a questionnaire, interviews

---

*Berger wrote this in 1963, using gendered language (preferring *he* to the now-standard *he/she*). Today more than half of all sociology students are women. [*Editor's note*].

people selected at random, then goes home, enters his tabulations onto innumerable punch cards, which are then fed into a machine. In all of this, of course, he is supported by a large staff and a very large budget. Included in this image is the implication that the results of all this effort are picayune, a pedantic re-statement of what everybody knows anyway. As one observer remarked pithily, a sociologist is a fellow who spends $100,000 to find his way to a house of ill repute.

This image of the sociologist has been strengthened in the public mind by the activities of many agencies that might well be called parasociological, mainly agencies concerned with public opinion and market trends. The pollster has become a well-known figure in American life, importuning people about their views from foreign policy to toilet paper. Since the methods used in the pollster business bear close resemblance to sociological research, the growth of this image of the sociologist is understandable. The Kinsey studies of American sexual behavior have probably greatly augmented the impact of this image. The fundamental sociological question, whether concerned with premarital petting or with Republican votes or with the incidence of gang knifings, is always presumed to be "how often?" or "how many?"

* * *

Now it must be admitted, albeit regretfully, that this image of the sociologist and his trade is not altogether a product of fantasy. Beginning shortly after World War I, American sociology turned rather resolutely away from theory to an intensive preoccupation with narrowly circumscribed empirical studies. In connection with this turn, sociologists increasingly refined their research techniques. Among these, very naturally, statistical techniques figured prominently. Since about the mid 1940s there has been a revival of interest in sociological theory, and there are good indications that this tendency away from a narrow empiricism is continuing to gather momentum. It remains true, however, that a goodly part of the sociological enterprise in this country continues to consist of little studies of obscure fragments of social life, irrelevant to any broader theoretical concern. One glance at the table of contents of the major sociological journals or at the list of papers read at sociological conventions will confirm this statement.

* * *

Statistical data by themselves do not make sociology. They become sociology only when they are sociologically interpreted, put within a theoretical frame of reference that is sociological. Simple counting, or even correlating different items that one counts, is not sociology. There is almost no sociology in the Kinsey reports. This does not mean that the data in these studies are not true or that they cannot be relevant to sociological understanding. They are, taken by themselves, raw materials that can be used in sociological interpretation. The interpretation, however, must be broader than the data themselves. So the sociologist cannot arrest himself at the frequency tables of premarital petting or extramarital pederasty. These enumerations are meaningful to him only in terms of their much broader implications for an understanding of institutions and values in our society. To arrive at such understanding the sociologist will often have to apply statistical techniques, especially when he is dealing with the mass phenomena of modern social life. But sociology consists of statistics as little as philology consists of conjugating irregular verbs or chemistry of making nasty smells in test tubes.

Sociology has, from its beginnings, understood itself as a science. There has been much controversy about the precise meaning of this self-definition. * * * But the allegiance of sociologists to the scientific ethos has meant everywhere a willingness to be bound by certain scientific canons of procedure. If the sociologist remains faithful to his calling, his statements must be arrived at through the observation of certain rules of evidence that allow others to check on or to repeat or to develop his findings further. It is this scientific discipline that often supplies the motive for reading a sociological work as against, say, a novel on the same topic that might describe matters in much more impressive and convincing language. As sociologists tried to develop their scientific rules of evidence, they were compelled to reflect upon methodological problems. This is why methodology is a necessary and valid part of the sociological enterprise.

At the same time it is quite true that some sociologists, especially in America, have become so preoccupied with methodological questions that they have ceased to be interested in society at all. As a result, they have found out nothing of significance about any aspect of social life, since in science as in love a concentration on technique is quite likely to lead to impotence. Much of this fixation on methodology can be explained in terms of the urge of a relatively new discipline to find acceptance on the academic scene. Since science is an almost sacred entity among Americans in general and American academicians in particular, the desire to emulate the procedures of the older natural sciences is very strong among the newcomers in the marketplace of erudition.

* * *

As they become more secure in their academic status, it may be expected that this methodological inferiority complex will diminish even further.

The charge that many sociologists write in a barbaric dialect must also be admitted with similar reservations. Any scientific discipline must develop a terminology. This is self-evident for a discipline such as, say, nuclear physics that deals with matters unknown to most people and for which no words exist in common speech. However, terminology is possibly even more important for the social sciences, just because their subject matter *is* familiar and just because words *do* exist to denote it. Because we are well acquainted with the social institutions that surround us, our perception of them is imprecise and often erroneous. In very much the same way most of us will have considerable difficulty giving an accurate description of our parents, husbands or wives, children or close friends. Also, our language is often (and perhaps blessedly) vague and confusing in its references to social reality. Take for an example the concept of *class,* a very important one in sociology. There must be dozens of meanings that this term may have in common speech—income brackets, races, ethnic groups, power cliques, intelligence ratings, and many others. It is obvious that the sociologist must have a precise, unambiguous definition of the concept if his work is to proceed with any degree of scientific rigor. In view of these facts, one can understand that some sociologists have been tempted to invent altogether new words to avoid the semantic traps of the vernacular usage.

Finally, we would look at an image of the sociologist not so much in his professional role as in his being, supposedly, a certain kind of person. This is the image of the sociologist as a detached, sardonic observer, and a cold manipulator of men. Where this image prevails, it may represent an ironic triumph of the sociologist's own efforts to be accepted as a genuine scientist. The sociologist here becomes the self-appointed superior man, standing off from the warm vitality of common existence, finding his satisfactions not in living but in coolly appraising the lives of others, filing them away in little categories, and thus presumably missing the real significance of what he is observing. Further, there is the notion that, when he involves himself in social processes at all, the sociologist does so as an uncommitted technician, putting his manipulative skills at the disposal of the powers that be.

This last image is probably not very widely held. * * * As a general portrait of the contemporary sociologist it is certainly a gross distortion. It fits very few individuals that anyone is likely to meet in this country today. The problem of the political role of the social scientist is, nevertheless, a very genuine one. For instance, the employment of sociologists by certain branches of industry and government raises moral questions that ought to be faced more widely than they have been so far. These are, however, moral questions that concern all men in positions of responsibility in modern society. The image of the sociologist as an observer without compassion and a manipulator without conscience need not detain us further here. * * * As for contemporary sociologists, most of them would lack the emotional equipment for such a role, even if they should aspire to it in moments of feverish fantasy.

How then are we to conceive of the sociologist? In discussing the various images of him that abound in the popular mind we have already brought out certain elements that would have to go into our conception.

* * *

The sociologist, then, is someone concerned with understanding society in a disciplined way. The nature of this discipline is scientific. This means that what the sociologist finds and says about the social phenomena he studies occurs within a certain rather strictly defined frame of reference. One of the main characteristics of this scientific frame of reference is that operations are bound by certain rules of evidence. As a scientist, the sociologist tries to be objective, to control his personal preferences and prejudices, to perceive clearly rather than to judge normatively. This restraint, of course, does not embrace the totality of the sociologist's existence as a human being, but is limited to his operations *qua* sociologist. Nor does the sociologist claim that his frame of reference is the only one within which society can be looked at. For that matter, very few scientists in any field would claim today that one should look at the world only scientifically. The botanist looking at a daffodil has no reason to dispute the right of the poet to look at the same object in a very different manner. There are many ways of playing. The point is not that one denies other people's games but that one is clear about the rules of one's own. The game of the sociologist, then, uses scientific rules. As a result, the sociologist must be clear in his own mind as to the meaning of these rules. That is, he must concern himself with methodological questions. Methodology does not constitute his goal. The latter, let us recall once more, is the attempt to understand society. Methodology helps in reaching this goal. In order to understand society, or that segment of it that he is studying at the moment, the sociologist will use a variety of means. Among these are statistical techniques. Statistics can be very useful in answering certain sociological questions. But statistics does not constitute sociology. As a scientist, the sociologist will have to be concerned with the exact significance of the terms he is using. That is, he will have to be careful about terminology. This does not have to mean that he must invent a new language of his own, but it does mean that he cannot naively use the language of everyday discourse. Finally, the interest of the sociologist is primarily theoretical. That is, he is interested in understanding for its own sake. He may be aware of or even concerned with the practical applicability and consequences of his findings, but at that point he leaves the sociological frame of reference as such and moves into realms of values, beliefs and ideas that he shares with other men who are not sociologists.

* * *

[THE MOTIVATION TO DO SOCIOLOGY]

[W]e would like to go a little bit further here and ask a somewhat more personal (and therefore, no doubt, more controversial) question. We would like to ask not only what it is that the sociologist is doing but also what it is that drives him to it. Or, to use the phrase Max Weber used in a similar connection, we want to inquire a little into the nature of the sociologist's demon. In doing so, we shall evoke an image that is not so much ideal-typical in the above sense but more confessional in the sense of personal commitment. Again, we are not interested in excommunicating anyone. The game of sociology goes on in a spacious playground. We are just describing a little more closely those we would like to tempt to join our game.

We would say then that the sociologist (that is, the one we would really like to invite to our game) is a person intensively, endlessly, shamelessly interested in the doings of men. His natural habitat is all the human gathering places of the world, wherever men come together. The sociologist may be interested in many other things. But his consuming interest remains in the world of men, their institutions, their history, their passions. And since he is interested in men, nothing that men do can be altogether tedious for him. He will naturally be interested in the events that engage men's ultimate beliefs, their moments of tragedy and grandeur and ecstasy. But he will also be fascinated by the common place, the everyday. He will know reverence, but this reverence will not prevent him from wanting to see and to understand. He may sometimes feel revulsion or contempt. But this also will not deter him from wanting to have his questions answered. The sociologist, in his quest for understanding, moves through the world of men without respect for the usual lines of demarcation. Nobility and degradation, power and obscurity, intelligence and folly—these are equally *interesting* to him, however unequal they may be in his personal values or tastes. Thus his questions may lead him to all possible levels of society, the best and the least known places, the most respected and the most despised. And, if he is a good sociologist, he will find himself in all these places because his own questions have so taken possession of him that he has little choice but to seek for answers.

It would be possible to say the same things in a lower key. We could say that the sociologist, but for the grace of his academic title, is the man who must listen to gossip despite himself, who is tempted to look through keyholes, to read other peoples mail, to open closed cabinets. Before some otherwise unoccupied psychologist sets out now to construct an aptitude test for sociologists on the basis of sublimated voyeurism, let us quickly say that we are speaking merely by way of analogy. Perhaps some little boys consumed with curiosity to watch their maiden aunts in the bathroom later become inveterate sociologists. This is quite uninteresting. What interests us is the curiosity that grips any sociologist in front of a closed door behind which there are human voices. If he is a good sociologist, he will want to open that door, to understand these voices. Behind each closed door he will anticipate some new facet of human life not yet perceived and understood.

The sociologist will occupy himself with matters that others regard as too sacred or as too distasteful for dispassionate investigation. He will find rewarding the company of priests or of prostitutes, depending not on his personal preferences but on the questions he happens to be asking at the moment. He will also concern himself with matters that others may find much too boring. He will be interested in the human interaction that goes with warfare or with great intellectual discoveries, but also in the relations between people employed in a restaurant or between a group of little girls playing with their dolls. His main focus of attention is not the ultimate significance of what men do, but the action in itself, as another example of the infinite richness of human conduct. So much for the image of our playmate.

In these journeys through the world of men the sociologist will inevitably encounter other professional Peeping Toms. Sometimes these will resent his presence, feeling that he is poaching on their preserves. In some places the sociologist will meet up with the economist, in others with the political scientist, in yet others with the psychologist or the ethnologist. Yet chances are that the questions that have brought him to these same places are different from the ones that propelled his fellow-trespassers. The sociologist's questions always remain essentially the same: "What are people doing with each other here?" "What are their relationships to each other?" "How are these relationships organized in institutions?" "What are the collective ideas that move men and institutions?" In trying to answer these questions in specific instances, the sociologist will, of course, have to deal with economic or political matters, but he will do so in a way rather different from that of the economist or the political scientist. The scene that he contemplates is the same human scene that these other scientists concern themselves with. But the sociologist's angle of vision is different. When this is understood, it becomes clear that it makes little sense to try to stake out a special enclave within which the sociologist will carry on business in his own right. * * * There is, however, one traveler whose path the sociologist will cross more often than anyone else's on his journeys. This is the historian. Indeed, as soon as the sociologist turns from the present to the past, his preoccupations are very hard indeed to distinguish from those of the historian. However, we shall leave this relationship to a later part of our considerations. Suffice it to say here that the sociological journey will be much impoverished unless it is punctuated frequently by conversation with that other particular traveler.

Any intellectual activity derives excitement from the moment it becomes a trail of discovery. In some fields of learning this is the discovery of worlds previously unthought and unthinkable. This is the excitement of the astronomer or of the nuclear physicist on the antipodal boundaries of the realities that man is capable of conceiving. But it can also be the excitement of bacteriology or geology. In a different way it can be the excitement of the linguist discovering new realms of human expression or of the anthropologist exploring human customs in faraway countries. In such discovery, when undertaken with passion, a widening of awareness, sometimes a veritable transformation of consciousness, occurs. The universe turns out to be much more wonderful than one had ever dreamed. The excitement of sociology is usually of a different sort. Sometimes, it is true, the sociologist penetrates into worlds that had previously been quite unknown to him—for instance, the world of crime, or the world of some bizarre religious sect, or the world fashioned by the exclusive concerns of some group such as medical specialists or military leaders or advertising executives. However, much of the time the sociologist moves in sectors of experience that are familiar to him and to most people in his society. He investigates communities, institutions and activities that one can read about every day in the newspapers. Yet there is another excitement of discovery beckoning in his investigations. It is not the excitement of coming upon the totally unfamiliar, but rather the excitement of finding the familiar becoming transformed in its meaning. The fascination of sociology lies in the fact that its perspective makes us see in a new light the very world in which we have lived all our lives. This also constitutes a transformation of conscious-ness. Moreover, this transformation is more relevant existentially than that of many other intellectual disciplines, because it is more difficult to segregate in some special compartment of the mind. The astronomer does not live in the remote galaxies, and the nuclear physicist can, outside his laboratory, eat and laugh and marry and vote without thinking about the insides of the atom. The geologist looks at rocks only at appropriate times, and the linguist speaks English with his wife. The sociologist lives in society, on the job and off it. His own life, inevitably, is part of his subject matter. Men being what they are, sociologists too manage to segregate their professional insights from their everyday affairs. But it is a rather difficult feat to perform in good faith.

The sociologist moves in the common world of men, close to what most of them would call real. The categories he employs in his analyses are only refinements of the categories by which other men live—power, class, status, race, ethnicity. As a result, there is a deceptive simplicity and obviousness about some sociological investigations. One reads them, nods at the familiar scene, remarks that one has heard all this before and don't people have bet-ter things to do than to waste their time on truisms—until one is suddenly brought up against an insight that radically questions everything one had previously assumed about this familiar scene. This is the point at which one begins to sense the excitement of sociology.

Let us take a specific example. Imagine a sociology class in a Southern col-lege where almost all the students are white Southerners. Imagine a lecture on the subject of the racial system of the South. The lecturer is talking here of matters that have been familiar to his students from the time of their infancy. Indeed, it may be that they are much more familiar with the minutiae of this system than he is. They are quite bored as a result. It seems to them that he is only using more pretentious words to describe what they already know. Thus he may use the term "caste," one commonly used now by American sociologists to describe the Southern racial system. But in explaining the term he shifts to traditional Hindu society, to make it clearer. He then goes on to analyze the magical beliefs inherent in caste tabus, the social dynamics of commensalism and connubium, the economic interests concealed within the system, the way in which religious beliefs relate to the tabus, the effects of the caste system upon the industrial development of the society and vice versa—all in India. But suddenly India is not very far away at all. The lecture then goes back to its Southern theme. The familiar now seems not quite so familiar any more.

Questions are raised that are new, perhaps raised angrily, but raised all the same. And at least some of the students have begun to understand that there are functions involved in this business of race that they have not read about in the newspapers (at least not those in their hometowns) and that their parents have not told them—partly, at least, because neither the newspapers nor the parents knew about them.

It can be said that the first wisdom of sociology is this—things are not what they seem. This too is a deceptively simple statement. It ceases to be simple after a while. Social reality turns out to have many layers of meaning. The discovery of each new layer changes the perception of the whole.

Anthropologists use the term "culture shock" to describe the impact of a totally new culture upon a newcomer. In an extreme instance such shock will be experienced by the Western explorer who is told, halfway through dinner, that he is eating the nice old lady he had been chatting with the previous day—a shock with predictable physiological if not moral consequences. Most explorers no longer encounter cannibalism in their travels today. However, the first encounters with polygamy or with puberty rites or even with the way some nations drive their automobiles can be quite a shock to an American visitor. With the shock may go not only disapproval or disgust but a sense of excitement that things can *really* be that different from what they are at home. To some extent, at least, this is the excitement of any first travel abroad. The experience of sociological discovery could be described as "culture shock" minus geographical displacement. In other words, the sociologist travels at home—with shocking results. He is unlikely to find that he is eating a nice old lady for dinner. But the discovery, for instance, that his own church has considerable money invested in the missile industry or that a few blocks from his home there are people who engage in cultic orgies may not be drastically different in emotional impact. Yet we would not want to imply that sociological discoveries are always or even usually outrageous to moral sentiment. Not at all. What they have in common with exploration in distant lands, however, is the sudden illumination of new and unsuspected facets of human existence in society. This is the excitement and, as we shall try to show later, the humanistic justification of sociology.

People who like to avoid shocking discoveries, who prefer to believe that society is just what they were taught in Sunday School, who like the safety of the rules and the maxims of what Alfred Schuetz has called the "world-taken-for-granted," should stay away from sociology. People who feel no temptation before closed doors, who have no curiosity about human beings, who are content to admire sceneiy without wondering about the people who live in those houses on the other side of that river, should probably also stay away from sociology. They will find it unpleasant or, at any rate, unrewarding. People who are interested in human beings only if they can change, convert or reform them should also be warned, for they will find sociology much less useful than they hoped. And people whose interest is mainly in their own conceptual constructions will do just as well to turn to the study of little white mice. Sociology will do just as well to turn to the study of little mice. Sociology will be satisfying, in the long run, only to those who can think of nothing more entrancing than to watch men and to understand things human.

* * *

To be sure, sociology is an individual pastime in the sense that it interests some men and bores others. Some like to observe human beings, others to experiment with mice. The world is big enough to hold all kinds and there is no logical priority for one interest as against another. But the word "pastime" is weak in describing what we mean. Sociology is more like a passion. The sociological perspective is more like a demon that possesses one, that drives one compellingly, again and again, to the questions that are its own. An introduction to sociology is, therefore, an invitation to a very special kind of passion.

2

Personal Experiences and Public Issues

FROM *The Sociological Imagination*

C. WRIGHT MILLS

C. Wright Mills wrote of his own work, "I have tried to be objective; I do not claim to be detached." He argues that sociologists' questions come from the same sources as the important questions everyone asks: their own experiences and the things that perplex, confuse, and inspire them. To be effective, sociology must make a connection between the individual and the social. It must allow the individual to see the larger social context in which his or her life is lived, and in this way give both understanding and meaning to personal experiences.

Nowadays men often feel that their private lives are a series of traps. They sense that within their everyday worlds, they cannot overcome their troubles, and in this feeling, they are often quite correct: What ordinary men are directly aware of and what they try to do are bounded by the private orbits in which they live; their visions and their powers are limited to the close-up scenes of job, family, neighborhood; in other milieux, they move vicariously and remain spectators. And the more aware they become, however vaguely, of ambitions and of threats which transcend their immediate locales, the more trapped they seem to feel.

Underlying this sense of being trapped are seemingly impersonal changes in the very structure of continent-wide societies. The facts of contemporary history are also facts about the success and the failure of individual men and women. When a society is industrialized, a peasant becomes a worker; a feudal lord is liquidated or becomes a businessman. When classes rise or fall, a man is employed or unemployed; when the rate of investment goes up or down, a man takes new heart or goes broke. When wars happen, an insurance salesman becomes a rocket launcher; a store clerk, a radar man; a wife lives alone; a child grows up without a father. Neither the life of an individual nor the history of a society can be understood without understanding both.

Yet men do not usually define the troubles they endure in terms of historical change and institutional contradiction. The well-being they enjoy, they do not usually impute to the big ups and downs of the societies in which they live. Seldom aware of the intricate connection between the patterns of their own lives and the course of world history, ordinary men do not usually know what this connection means for the kinds of men they are becoming and for the kinds of history-making in which they might take part. They do not possess the quality of mind essential to grasp the interplay of man and society, of biography and history, of self and world. They cannot cope with their personal troubles in such ways as to control the structural transformations that usually lie behind them.

Surely it is no wonder. In what period have so many men been so totally exposed at so fast a pace to such earthquakes of change? That Americans have not known such catastrophic changes as have the men and women of other societies is due to historical facts that are now quickly becoming 'merely history.' The history that now affects every man is world history. Within this scene and this period, in the course of a single generation, one sixth of mankind is transformed from all that is feudal and backward into all that is modern, advanced, and fearful. Political colonies are freed; new and less visible forms of imperialism installed. Revolutions occur; men feel the intimate grip of new kinds of authority. Totalitarian societies rise, and are smashed to bits—or succeed fabulously. After two centuries of ascendancy, capitalism is shown up as only one way to make society into an industrial apparatus. After two centuries of hope, even formal democracy is restricted to a quite small portion of mankind. Everywhere in the underdeveloped world, ancient ways of life are broken up and vague expectations become urgent demands. Everywhere in the overdeveloped world, the means of authority and of violence become total in scope and bureaucratic in form. Humanity itself now lies before us, the super-nation at either pole concentrating its most coordinated and massive efforts upon the preparation of World War Three.

The very shaping of history now outpaces the ability of men to orient themselves in accordance with cherished values. And which values? Even when they do not panic, men often sense that older ways of feeling and thinking have collapsed and that newer beginnings are ambiguous to the point of moral stasis. Is it any wonder that ordinary men feel they cannot cope with the larger worlds with which they are so suddenly confronted? That they cannot understand the meaning of their epoch for their own lives? That—in defense of selfhood—they become morally insensible, trying to remain altogether private men? Is it any wonder that they come to be possessed by a sense of the trap?

It is not only information that they need—in this Age of Fact, information often dominates their attention and overwhelms their capacities to assimilate it. It is not only the skills of reason that they need—although their struggles to acquire these often exhaust their limited moral energy.

What they need, and what they feel they need, is a quality of mind that will help them to use information and to develop reason in order to achieve lucid summations of what is going on in the world and of what may be happening within themselves. It is this quality, I am going to contend, that journalists and scholars, artists and publics, scientists and editors are coming to expect of what may be called the sociological imagination.

1

The sociological imagination enables its possessor to understand the larger historical scene in terms of its meaning for the inner life and the external career of a variety of individuals. It enables him to take into account how individuals, in the welter of their daily experience, often become falsely conscious of their social positions. Within that welter, the framework of modern society is sought, and within that framework the psychologies of a variety of men and women are formulated. By such means the personal uneasiness of individuals is focused upon explicit troubles and the indifferences of publics is transformed into involvement with public issues.

The first fruit of this imagination—and the first lesson of the social science that embodies it—is the idea that the individual can understand his own experience and gauge his own fate only by locating himself within his period, that he can know his own chances in life only by becoming aware of those of all individuals in his circumstances. In many ways it is a terrible lesson; in many ways a magnificent one. We do not know the limits of man's capacities for supreme effort or willing degradation, for agony or glee, for pleasurable brutality or the sweetness of reason. But in our time we have come to know that the limits of 'human nature' are frighteningly broad. We have come to know that every individual lives, from one generation to the next, in some society; that he lives out a biography, and that he lives it out within some historical sequence. By the fact of his living he contributes, however minutely, to the shaping of this society and to the course of its history, even as he is made by society and by its historical push and shove.

The sociological imagination enables us to grasp history and biography and the relations between the two within society. That is its task and its promise. To recognize this task and this promise is the mark of the classic social analyst. And it is the signal of what is best in contemporary studies of man and society.

No social study that does not come back to the problems of biography, of history and of their intersections within a society has completed its intellectual journey. Whatever the specific problems of the classic social analysts, however limited or however broad the features of social reality they have examined, those who have been imaginatively aware of the promise of their work have consistently asked three sorts of questions:

1. What is the structure of this particular society as a whole? What are its essential components, and how are they related to one another? How does it differ from other varieties of social order? Within it, what is the meaning of any particular feature for its continuance and for its change?
2. Where does this society stand in human history? What are the mechanics by which it is changing? What is its place within and its meaning for the development of humanity as a whole? How does any

particular feature we are examining affect, and how is it affected by, the historical period in which it moves? And this period—what are its essential features? How does it differ from other periods? What are its characteristic ways of history-making?

3. What varieties of men and women now prevail in this society and in this period? And what varieties are coming to prevail? In what ways are they selected and formed, liberated and repressed, made sensitive and blunted? What kinds of 'human nature' are revealed in the conduct and character we observe in this society in this period? And what is the meaning for 'human nature' of each and every feature of the society we are examining?

Whether the point of interest is a great power state or a minor literary mood, a family, a prison, a creed—these are the kinds of questions the best social analysts have asked. They are the intellectual pivots of classic studies of man in society—and they are the questions inevitably raised by any mind possessing the sociological imagination. For that imagination is the capacity to shift from one perspective to another—from the political to the psychological; from examination of a single family to comparative assessment of the national budgets of the world; from the theological school to the military establishment; from considerations of an oil industry to studies of contemporary poetry. It is the capacity to range from the most impersonal and remote transformations to the most intimate features of the human self—and to see the relations between the two. Back of its use there is always the urge to know the social and historical meaning of the individual in the society and in the period in which he has his quality and his being.

That, in brief, is why it is by means of the sociological imagination that men now hope to grasp what is going on in the world, and to understand what is happening in themselves as minute points of the intersections of biography and history within society. In large part, contemporary man's self-conscious view of himself as at least an outsider, if not a permanent stranger, rests upon an absorbed realization of social relativity and of the transformative power of history. The sociological imagination is the most fruitful form of this self-consciousness. By its use men whose mentalities have swept only a series of limited orbits often come to feel as if suddenly awakened in a house with which they had only supposed themselves to be familiar. Correctly or incorrectly, they often come to feel that they can now provide themselves with adequate summations, cohesive assessments, comprehensive orientations. Older decisions that once appeared sound now seem to them products of a mind unaccountably dense. Their capacity for astonishment is made lively again. They acquire a new way of thinking, they experience a transvaluation of values: in a word, by their reflection and by their sensibility, they realize the cultural meaning of the social sciences.

2

Perhaps the most fruitful distinction with which the sociological imagination works is between 'the personal troubles of milieu' and 'the public issues of social structure.' This distinction is an essential tool of the sociological imagination and a feature of all classic work in social science.

Troubles occur within the character of the individual and within the range of his immediate relations with others; they have to do with his self and with those limited areas of social life of which he is directly and personally aware. Accordingly, the statement and the resolution of troubles properly lie within the individual as a biographical entity and within the scope of his immediate milieu—the social setting that is directly open to his personal experience and to some extent his willful activity. A trouble is a private matter: values cherished by an individual are felt by him to be threatened.

Issues have to do with matters that transcend these local environments of the individual and the range of his inner life. They have to do with the organization of many such milieux into the institutions of an historical society as a whole, with the ways in which various milieux overlap and interpenetrate to form the larger structure of social and historical life. An issue is a public matter: some value cherished by publics is felt to be threatened. Often there is a debate about what that value really is and about what it is that really threatens it. This debate is often without focus if only because it is the very nature of an issue, unlike even widespread trouble, that it cannot very well be defined in terms of the immediate and everyday environments of ordinary men. An issue, in fact, often involves a crisis in institutional arrangements, and often too it involves what Marxists call 'contradictions' or 'antagonisms.'

In these terms, consider unemployment. When, in a city of 100,000, only one man is unemployed, that is his personal trouble, and for its relief we properly look to the character of the man, his skills, and his immediate opportunities. But when in a nation of 50 million employees, 15 million men are unemployed, that is an issue, and we may not hope to find its solution within the range of opportunities open to any one individual. The very structure of opportunities has collapsed. Both the correct statement of the problem and the range of possible solutions require us to consider the economic and political institutions of the society, and not merely the personal situation and character of a scatter of individuals.

Consider war. The personal problem of war, when it occurs, may be how to survive it or how to die in it with honor; how to make money out of it; how to climb into the higher safety of the military apparatus; or how to contribute to the war's termination. In short, according to one's values, to find a set of milieux and within it to survive the war or make one's death in it meaningful. But the structural issues of war have to do with its causes; with what types of men it throws up into command; with its effects upon economic and political, family and religious institutions, with the unorganized irresponsibility of a world of nation-states.

Consider marriage. Inside a marriage a man and a woman may experience personal troubles, but when the divorce rate during the first four years of marriage is 250 out of every 1,000 attempts, this is an indication of a structural issue having to do with the institutions of marriage and the family and other institutions that bear upon them.

Or consider the metropolis—the horrible, beautiful, ugly, magnificent sprawl of the great city. For many upper-class people, the personal solution to 'the problem of the city' is to have an apartment with private garage under it in the heart of the city, and forty miles out, a house by Henry Hill, garden by Garrett Eckbo, on a hundred acres of private land. In these two controlled environments—with a small staff at each end and a private helicopter connection—most people could solve many of the problems of personal milieux caused by the facts of the city. But all this, however splendid, does not solve the public issues that the structural fact of the city poses. What should be done with this wonderful monstrosity? Break it all up into scattered units, combining residence and work? Refurbish it as it stands? Or, after evacuation, dynamite it and build new cities according to new plans in new places? What should those plans be? And who is to decide and to accomplish whatever choice is made? These are structural issues; to confront them and to solve them requires us to consider political and economic issues that affect innumerable milieux.

In so far as an economy is so arranged that slumps occur, the problem of unemployment becomes incapable of personal solution. In so far as war is inherent in the nation-state system and in the uneven industrialization of the world, the ordinary individual in his restricted milieu will be powerless—with or without psychiatric aid—to solve the troubles this system or lack of system imposes upon him. In so far as the family as an institution turns women into darling little slaves and men into their chief providers and unweaned dependents, the problem of a satisfactory marriage remains incapable of purely private solution. In so far as the overdeveloped megalopolis and the overdeveloped automobile are built-in features of the overdeveloped society, the issues of urban living will not be solved by personal ingenuity and private wealth.

What we experience in various and specific milieux, I have noted, is often caused by structural changes. Accordingly, to understand the changes of many personal milieux we are required to look beyond them. And the number and variety of such structural changes increase as the institutions within which we live become more embracing and more intricately connected with one another. To be aware of the idea of social structure and to use it with sensibility is to be capable of tracing such linkages among a great variety of milieux. To be able to do that is to possess the sociological imagination.

3

What Makes Sociology Different?

FROM *The Rules of Sociological Method*

ÉMILE DURKHEIM

Along with Karl Marx and Max Weber, Émile Durkheim (1858–1917) is considered a founder of modern sociology. In this essay he presents his most important contribution to the discipline: that social facts should be the subject matter for the study of social life and can provide explanations for human thinking and behavior. In more modern times, we describe social facts as "social structure" or the tangible features or characteristics of socially ordered human affairs. For many people, Durkheim provides a key to unlocking the mystery of why we do what we do.

Before beginning the search for the method appropriate to the study of social facts it is important to know what are the facts termed 'social.'

The question is all the more necessary because the term is used without much precision. It is commonly used to designate almost all the phenomena that occur within society, however little social interest of some generality they present. Yet under this heading there is, so to speak, no human occurrence that cannot be called social. Every individual drinks, sleeps, eats, or employs his reason, and society has every interest in seeing that these functions are regularly exercised. If therefore these facts were social ones, sociology would possess no subject matter peculiarly its own, and its domain would be confused with that of biology and psychology.

However, in reality there is in every society a clearly determined group of phenomena separable, because of their distinct characteristics, from those that form the subject matter of other sciences of nature.

When I perform my duties as a brother, a husband or a citizen and carry out the commitments I have entered into, I fulfill obligations which are defined in law and custom and which are external to myself and my actions. Even when they conform to my own sentiments and when I feel their reality within me, that reality does not cease to be objective, for it is not I who have prescribed these duties; I have received them through education. Moreover, how often does it happen that we are ignorant of the details of the obligations that we must assume, and that, to know them, we must consult the legal code and its authorized interpreters! Similarly the believer has discovered from birth, ready fashioned, the beliefs and practices of his religious life; if they existed before he did, it follows that they exist outside him. The system of signs that I employ to express my thoughts, the monetary system I use to pay my debts, the credit instruments I utilise in my commercial relationships, the practices I follow in my profession, etc., all function independently of the use I make of them. Considering in turn each member of society, the foregoing remarks can be repeated for each single one of them. Thus there are ways of acting, thinking and feeling which possess the remarkable property of existing outside the consciousness of the individual.

Not only are these types of behaviour and thinking external to the individual, but they are endowed with a compelling and coercive power by virtue of which, whether he wishes it or not, they impose themselves upon him. Undoubtedly when I conform to them of my own free will, this coercion is not felt or felt hardly at all, since it is unnecessary. None the less it is intrinsically a characteristic of these facts; the proof of this is that it asserts itself as soon as I try to resist. If I attempt to violate the rules of law they react against me so as to forestall my action, if there is still time. Alternatively, they annul it or make my action conform to the norm if it is already accomplished but capable of being reversed; or they cause me to pay the penalty for it if it is irreparable. If purely moral rules are at stake, the public conscience restricts any act which infringes them by the surveillance it exercises over the conduct of citizens and by the special punishments it has at its disposal. In other cases the constraint is less violent; nevertheless, it does not cease to exist. If I do not conform to ordinary conventions, if in my mode of dress I pay no heed to what is customary in my country and in my social class, the laughter I provoke, the social distance at which I am kept, produce, although in a more mitigated form, the same results as any real penalty. In other cases, although it may be indirect, constraint is no less effective. I am not forced to speak French with my compatriots, nor to use the legal currency, but it is impossible for me to do otherwise. If I tried to escape the necessity, my attempt would fail miserably. As an industrialist nothing prevents me from working with the processes and methods of the previous century, but if I do I will most certainly ruin myself. Even when in fact I can struggle free from these rules and successfully break them, it is never without being forced to fight against them. Even if in the end they are overcome, they make their constraining power sufficiently felt in the resistance that they afford. There is no innovator, even a fortunate one, whose ventures do not encounter opposition of this kind.

Here, then, is a category of facts which present very special characteristics: they consist of manners of acting, thinking and feeling external to the individual, which are invested with a coercive power by virtue of which they exercise control over him. Consequently, since they consist of representations and actions, they cannot be confused with organic phenomena, nor with psychical phenomena, which have no existence save in and through the individual consciousness. Thus they constitute a new species and to them must be exclusively assigned the term *social*. It is appropriate, since it is clear that, not having the individual as their substratum, they can have none other than society, either political society in its entirety or one of the partial groups that it includes—religious denominations, political and literary schools, occupational corporations, etc. Moreover, it is for such as these alone that the term is fitting, for the word 'social' has the sole meaning of designating those phenomena which fall into none of the categories of facts already constituted and labeled. They are consequently the proper field of sociology. It is true that this word 'constraint,' in terms of which we define them, is in danger of infuriating those who zealously uphold out-and-out individualism. Since they maintain that the individual is completely autonomous, it seems to them that he is diminished every time he is made aware that he is not dependent on himself alone. Yet since it is indisputable today that most of our ideas and tendencies are not developed by ourselves, but come to us from outside, they can only penetrate us by imposing themselves upon us. This is all that our definition implies. Moreover, we know that all social constraints do not necessarily exclude the individual personality.

Yet since the examples just cited (legal and moral rules, religious dogmas, financial systems, etc.) consist wholly of beliefs and practices already well established, in view of what has been said it might be maintained that no social fact can exist except where there is a well defined social organization. But there are other facts which do not present themselves in this already crystallised form but which also possess the same objectivity and ascendancy over the individual. These are what are called social 'currents.' Thus in a public gathering the great waves of enthusiasm, indignation and pity that are produced have their seat in no one individual consciousness. They come to each one of us from outside and can sweep us along in spite of ourselves. If perhaps I abandon myself to them I may not be conscious of the pressure that they are exerting upon me, but that pressure makes its presence felt immediately I attempt to struggle against them. If an individual tries to pit himself against one of these collective manifestations, the sentiments that he is rejecting will be turned against him. Now if this external coercive power asserts itself so acutely in cases of resistance, it must be because it exists in the other instances cited above without our being conscious of it. Hence we are the victims of an illusion which leads us to believe we have ourselves produced what has been imposed upon us externally. But if the willingness with which we let ourselves be carried along disguises the pressure we have undergone, it does not eradicate it. Thus air does not cease to have weight, although we no longer feel that weight. Even when we have individually and spontaneously shared in the common emotion, the impression we have experienced is utterly different from what we would have felt if we had been alone. Once the assembly has broken up and these social influences have ceased to act upon us, and we are once more on our own, the emotions we have felt seem an alien phenomenon, one in which we no longer recognize ourselves. It is then we perceive that we have undergone the emotions much more than generated them. These emotions may even perhaps fill us with horror, so much do they go against the grain. Thus individuals who are normally perfectly harmless may, when gathered together in a crowd, let themselves be drawn into acts of atrocity. And what we assert about these transitory outbreaks likewise applies to those more lasting movements of opinion which relate to religious, political, literary and artistic matters, etc., and which are constantly being produced around us, whether throughout society or in a more limited sphere.

Moreover, this definition of a social fact can be verified by examining an experience that is characteristic. It is sufficient to observe how children are brought up. If one views the facts as they are and indeed as they have always been, it is patently obvious that all education consists of a continual effort to impose upon the child ways of seeing, thinking and acting which he himself would not have arrived at spontaneously. From his earliest years we oblige him to eat, drink and sleep at regular hours, and to observe cleanliness, calm and obedience; later we force him to learn how to be mindful of others, to respect customs and conventions, and to work, etc. If this constraint in time ceases to be felt it is because it gradually gives rise to habits, to inner tendencies which render it superfluous; but they supplant the constraint only because they are derived from it. It is true that, in [English social theorist Herbert] Spencer's view, a rational education should shun such means and allow the child complete freedom to do what he will. Yet as this educational theory has never been put into practice among any known people, it can only be the personal expression of a *desideratum* and not a fact which can be established in contradiction to the other facts given above. What renders these latter facts particularly illuminating is that education sets out precisely with the object of creating a social being. Thus there can be seen, as in an abbreviated form, how the social being has been fashioned historically. The pressure to which the child is subjected unremittingly is the same pressure of the social environment which seeks to shape him in its own image, and in which parents and teachers are only the representatives and intermediaries.

Thus it is not the fact that they are general which can serve to characterize sociological phenomena. Thoughts to be found in the consciousness of each individual and movements which are repeated by all individuals are not for this reason social facts. If some have been content with using this characteristic in order to define them it is because they have been confused, wrongly, with what might be termed their individual incarnations. What constitutes social facts are the beliefs, tendencies and practices of the group taken collectively. But the forms that these collective states may assume when they are 'refracted' through individuals are things of a different kind. What irrefutably demonstrates this duality of kind is that these two categories of facts frequently are manifested dissociated from each other. Indeed some of these ways of acting or thinking acquire, by dint of repetition, a sort of consistency which, so to speak, separates them out, isolating them from the particular events which reflect them. Thus they assume a shape, a tangible form peculiar to them and constitute a reality *sui generis* vastly distinct from the individual facts which manifest that reality. Collective custom does not exist only in a state of immanence in the successive actions which it determines but, by a privilege without example in the biological kingdom, expresses itself once and for all in a formula repeated by word of mouth, transmitted by education and even enshrined in the written word. Such are the origins and nature of legal and moral rules, aphorisms and popular sayings, articles of faith in which religious or political sects epitomise their beliefs, and standards of taste drawn up by literary schools, etc. None of these modes of acting and thinking are to be found wholly in the application made of them by individuals, since they can even exist without being applied at the time.

Undoubtedly this state of dissociation does not always present itself with equal distinctiveness. It is sufficient for dissociation to exist unquestionably in the numerous important instances cited, for us to prove that the social fact exists separately from its individual effects. Moreover, even when the dissociation is not immediately observable, it can often be made so with the help of certain methodological devices. Indeed it is essential to embark on such procedures if one wishes to refine out the social fact from any amalgam and so observe it in its pure state. Thus certain currents of opinion, whose intensity varies according to the time and country in which they occur, impel us, for example, towards marriage or suicide, towards higher or lower birth-rates, etc. Such currents are plainly social facts. At first sight they seem inseparable from the forms they assume in individual cases. But statistics afford us a means of isolating them. They are indeed not inaccurately represented by rates of births, marriages and suicides, that is, by the result obtained after dividing the average annual total of marriages, births, and voluntary homicides by the number of persons of an age to marry, produce children, or commit suicide. Since each one of these statistics includes without distinction all individual cases, the individual circumstances which may have played some part in producing the phenomenon cancel each other out and consequently do not contribute to determining the nature of the phenomenon. What it expresses is a certain state of the collective mind.

That is what social phenomena are when stripped of all extraneous elements. As regards their private manifestations, these do indeed having something social about them, since in part they reproduce the collective model. But to a large extent each one depends also upon the psychical and organic constitution of the individual, and on the particular circumstances in which he is placed. Therefore they are not phenomena which are in the strict sense sociological. They depend on both domains at the same time, and could be termed socio-psychical. They are of interest to the sociologist without constituting the immediate content of sociology. The same characteristic is to be found in the organisms of those mixed phenomena of nature studied in the combined sciences such as biochemistry.

It may be objected that a phenomenon can only be collective if it is common to all the members of society, or at the very least to a majority, and consequently, if it is general. This is doubtless the case, but if it is general it is because it is collective (that is, more or less obligatory); but it is very far from being collective because it is general. It is a condition of the group repeated in individuals because it imposes itself upon them. It is in each part because it is in the whole, but far from being in the whole because it is in the parts. This is supremely evident in those beliefs and practices which are handed down to us ready fashioned by previous generations. We accept and adopt them because, since they are the work of the collectivity and one that is centuries old, they are invested with a special authority that our education has taught us to recognize and respect. It is worthy of note that the vast majority of social phenomena come to us in this way. But even when the social fact is partly due to our direct co-operation, it is no different in nature. An outburst of collective emotion in a gathering does not merely express the sum total of what individual feelings share in common, but is something of a very different order, as we have demonstrated. It is a product of shared existence, of actions and reactions called into play between the consciousness of individuals. If it is echoed in each one of them it is precisely by virtue of the special energy derived from its collective origins. If all hearts beat in unison, this is not as a consequence of a spontaneous, preestablished harmony; it is because one and the same force is propelling them in the same direction. Each one is borne along by the rest.

We have therefore succeeded in delineating for ourselves the exact field of sociology. It embraces one single, well defined group of phenomena. A social fact is identifiable through the power of external coercion which it exerts or is capable of exerting upon individuals. The presence of this power is in turn recognizable because of the existence of some pre-determined sanction, or through the resistance that the fact opposes to any individual action that may threaten it. However, it can also be defined by ascertaining how widespread it is within the group, provided that, as noted above, one is careful to add a second essential characteristic; this is, that it exists independently of the particular forms that it may assume in the process of spreading itself within the group. In certain cases this latter criterion can even be more easily applied than the former one. The presence of constraint is easily ascertainable when it is manifested externally through some direct reaction of society, as in the case of law, morality, beliefs, customs and even fashions. But when constraint is merely indirect, as with that exerted by an economic organization, it is not always so clearly discernible. Generality combined with objectivity may then be easier to establish. Moreover, this second definition is simply another formulation of the first one: if a mode of behaviour existing outside the consciousness of individuals becomes general, it can only do so by exerting pressure upon them.

However, one may well ask whether this definition is complete. Indeed the facts which have provided us with its basis are all *ways of functioning:* they are 'physiological' in nature. But there are also collective *ways of being,* namely, social facts of an 'anatomical' or morphological nature. Sociology cannot dissociate itself from what concerns the substratum of collective life. Yet the number and nature of the elementary parts which constitute society, the way in which they are articulated, the degree of coalescence they have attained, the distribution of population over the earth's surface, the extent and nature of the network of communications, the design of dwellings, etc., do not at first sight seem relatable to ways of acting, feeling or thinking.

Yet, first and foremost, these various phenomena present the same characteristic which has served us in defining the others. These ways of being impose themselves upon the individual just as do the ways of acting we have dealt with. In fact, when we wish to learn how a society is divided up politically, in what its divisions consist and the degree of solidarity that exists between them, it is not through physical inspection and geographical observation that we may come to find this out: such divisions are social, although they may have some physical basis. It is only through public law that we can study such political organization, because this law is what determines its nature, just as it determines our domestic and civic relationships. The organization is no less a form of compulsion. If the population clusters together in our cities instead of being scattered over the rural areas, it is because there exists a trend of opinion, a collective drive which imposes this concentration upon individuals. We can no more choose the design of our houses than the cut of our clothes at least, the one is as much obligatory as the other. The communication network forcibly prescribes the direction of internal migrations or commercial exchanges, etc., and even their intensity. Consequently, at the most there are grounds for adding one further category to the list of phenomena already enumerated as bearing the distinctive stamp of a social fact. But as that enumeration was in no wise strictly exhaustive, this addition would not be indispensable.

Moreover, it does not even serve a purpose, for these ways of being are only ways of acting that have been consolidated. A society's political structure is only the way in which its various component segments have become accustomed to living with each other. If relationships between them are traditionally close, the segments tend to merge together; if the contrary, they tend to remain distinct. The type of dwelling imposed upon us is merely the way in which everyone around us and, in part, previous generations, have customarily built their houses. The communication network is only the channel which has been cut by the regular current of commerce and migrations, etc., flowing in the same direction. Doubtless if phenomena of a morphological kind were the only ones that displayed this rigidity, it might be thought that they constituted a separate species. But a legal rule is no less permanent an arrangement than an architectural style, and yet it is a 'physiological' fact. A simple moral maxim is certainly more malleable, yet it is cast in forms much more rigid than a mere professional custom or fashion. Thus there exists a whole range of gradations which, without any break in continuity, join the most clearly delineated structural facts to those free currents of social life which are not yet caught in any definite mould. This therefore signifies that the differences between them concern only the degree to which they have become consolidated. Both are forms of life at varying stages of crystallisation. It would undoubtedly be advantageous to reserve the term 'morphological' for those social facts which relate to the social substratum, but only on condition that one is aware that they are of the same nature as the others. Our definition will therefore subsume all that has to be defined it if states:

A social fact is any way of acting, whether fixed or not, capable of exerting over the individual an external constraint;

or:

which is general over the whole of a given society whilst having an existence of its own, independent of its individual manifestations.

4

The Stranger

GEORG SIMMEL

Most students can name the cliques in their high school, but few admit to being in one, at least full time. They were both inside and outside, involved but detached. Why does this seem like a good way to be? Georg Simmel (1858–1918) suggests it allows for intimacies and "confidences," in part because the stranger is not so completely "bound up" with the group itself. In this sketch of the stranger, and in his other sketches of social types (e.g., the poor, the miser, the adventurer), Simmel is presenting sociology as the study of relationships and the possibilities—often contradictory—for different types of interaction. His studies of dyads and triads (two- and three-person groups) have the same playful but insightful examination of bonds, networks, and strategies that make society appear to be almost a dance or a game of chess.

If wandering, considered as a state of detachment from every given point in space, is the conceptual opposite of attachment to any point, then the sociological form of "the stranger" presents the synthesis, as it were, of both of these properties. (This is another indication that spatial relations not only are determining conditions of relationships among men, but are also symbolic of those relationships.) The stranger will thus not be considered here in the usual sense of the term, as the wanderer who comes today and goes tomorrow, but rather as the man who comes today and stays tomorrow—the potential wanderer, so to speak, who, although he has gone no further, has not quite got over the freedom of coming and going. He is fixed within a certain spatial circle—or within a group whose boundaries are analogous to spatial boundaries—but his position within it is fundamentally affected by the fact that he does not belong in it initially and that he brings qualities into it that are not, and cannot be, indigenous to it.

In the case of the stranger, the union of closeness and remoteness involved in every human relationship is patterned in a way that may be succinctly formulated as follows: the distance within this relation indicates that one who is close by is remote, but his strangeness indicates that one who is remote is near. The state of being a stranger is of course a completely positive relation; it is a specific form of interaction. * * *

The following statements about the stranger are intended to suggest how factors of repulsion and distance work to create a form of being together, a form of union based on interaction.

In the whole history of economic activity the stranger makes his appearance everywhere as a trader, and the trader makes his as a stranger. As long as production for one's own needs is the general rule, or products are exchanged within a relatively small circle, there is no need for a middleman within the group. A trader is required only for goods produced outside the group. Unless there are people who wander out into foreign lands to buy these necessities, in which case they are themselves "strange" merchants in this other region, the trader *must* be a stranger; there is no opportunity for anyone else to make a living at it.

This position of the stranger stands out more sharply if, instead of leaving the place of his activity, he settles down there. In innumerable cases even this is possible only if he can live by trade as a middleman. Any closed economic group where land and handicrafts have been apportioned in a way that satisfies local demands will still support a livelihood for the trader. For trade alone makes possible unlimited combinations, and through it intelligence is constantly extended and applied in new areas, something that is much harder for the primary producer with his more limited mobility and his dependence on a circle of customers that can be expanded only very slowly. Trade can always absorb more men than can primary production. It is therefore the most suitable activity for the stranger, who intrudes as a supernumerary, so to speak, into a group in which all the economic positions are already occupied. The classic example of this is the history of European Jews. The stranger is by his very nature no owner of land—land not only in the physical sense but also metaphorically as a vital substance which is fixed, if not in space, then at least in an ideal position within the social environment.

Although in the sphere of intimate personal relations the stranger may be attractive and meaningful in many ways, so long as he is regarded as a stranger he is no "landowner" in the eyes of the other. Restriction to intermediary trade and often (as though sublimated from it) to pure finance gives the stranger the specific character of *mobility*. The appearance of this mobility within a bounded group occasions that synthesis of nearness and remoteness which constitutes the formal position of the stranger. The purely mobile person comes incidentally into contact with *every* single element but is not bound up organically, through established ties of kinship, locality, or occupation, with any single one.

Another expression of this constellation is to be found in the objectivity of the stranger. Because he is not bound by roots to the particular constituents and partisan dispositions of the group, he confronts all of these with a distinctly "objective" attitude, an attitude that does not signify mere detachment and nonparticipation, but is a distinct structure composed of remoteness and nearness, indifference and involvement. I refer to my analysis of the dominating positions gained by aliens, in the discussion of superordination and subordination, typified by the practice in certain Italian cities of recruiting their judges from outside, because no native was free from entanglement in family interests and factionalism.

Connected with the characteristic of objectivity is a phenomenon that is found chiefly, though not exclusively, in the stranger who moves on. This is that he often receives the most surprising revelations and confidences, at times reminiscent of a confessional, about matters which are kept carefully hidden from everybody with whom one is close. Objectivity is by no means nonparticipation, a condition that is altogether outside the distinction between subjective and objective orientations. It is rather a positive and definite kind of participation, in the same way that the objectivity of a theoretical observation clearly does not mean that the mind is a passive tabula rasa on which things inscribe their qualities, but rather signifies the full activity of a mind working according to its own laws, under conditions that exclude accidental distortions and emphases whose individual and subjective differences would produce quite different pictures of the same object.

Objectivity can also be defined as freedom. The objective man is not bound by ties which could prejudice his perception, his understanding, and his assessment of data. This freedom, which permits the stranger to experience and treat even his close relationships as though from a bird's-eye view, contains many dangerous possibilities. From earliest times, in uprisings of all sorts the attacked party has claimed that there has been incitement from the outside, by foreign emissaries and agitators. Insofar as this has happened, it represents an exaggeration of the specific role of the stranger: he is the freer man, practically and theoretically; he examines conditions with less prejudice; he assesses them against standards that are more general and more objective; and his actions are not confined by custom, piety, or precedent.

Finally, the proportion of nearness and remoteness which gives the stranger the character of objectivity also finds practical expression in the more *abstract* nature of the relation to him. That is, with the stranger one has only certain *more general* qualities in common, whereas the relation with organically connected persons is based on the similarity of just those specific traits which differentiate them from the merely universal. In fact, all personal relations whatsoever can be analyzed in terms of this scheme. They are not determined only by the existence of certain common characteristics which the individuals share in addition to their individual differences, which either influence the relationship or remain outside of it. Rather, the kind of effect which that commonality has on the relation essentially depends on whether it exists only among the participants themselves, and thus, although general within the relation, is specific and incomparable with respect to all those on the outside, or whether the participants feel that what they have in common is so only because it is common to a group, a type, or mankind in general. In the latter case, the effect of the common features becomes attenuated in proportion to the size of the group bearing the same characteristics. The commonality provides a basis for unifying the members, to be sure; but it does not specifically direct *these* particular persons to one another. A similarity so widely shared could just as easily unite each person with every possible other. This, too, is evidently a way in which a relationship includes both nearness and remoteness simultaneously. To the extent to which the similarities assume a universal nature, the warmth of the connection based on them will acquire an element of coolness, a sense of the contingent nature of precisely *this* relation—the connecting forces have lost their specific, centripetal character.

In relation to the stranger, it seems to me, this constellation assumes an extraordinary preponderance in principle over the individual elements peculiar to the relation in question. The stranger is close to us insofar as we feel between him and ourselves similarities of nationality or social position, of occupation or of general human nature. He is far from us insofar as these similarities extend beyond him and us, and connect us only because they connect a great many people.

A trace of strangeness in this sense easily enters even the most intimate relationships. In the stage of first passion, erotic relations strongly reject any thought of generalization. A love such as this has never existed before; there is nothing to compare either with the person one loves or with our feelings for that person. An estrangement is wont to set in (whether as cause or effect is hard to decide) at the moment when this feeling of uniqueness disappears from the relationship. A skepticism regarding the intrinsic value of the relationship and its value for us adheres to the very thought that in this relation, after all, one is only fulfilling a general human destiny, that one has had an experience that has occurred a thousand times before, and that, if one had not accidentally met this precise person, someone else would have acquired the same meaning for us.

Something of this feeling is probably not absent in any relation, be it ever so close, because that which is common to two is perhaps never common *only* to them but belongs to a general conception which includes much else besides, many *possibilities* of similarities. No matter how few of these possibilities are realized and how often we may forget about them, here and there, nevertheless, they crowd in like shadows between men, like a mist eluding every designation, which must congeal into solid corporeality for it to be called jealousy. Perhaps this is in many cases a more general, at least more insurmountable, strangeness than that due to differences and obscurities. It is strangeness caused by the fact that similarity, harmony, and closeness are accompanied by the feeling that they are actually not the exclusive property of this particular relation, but stem from a more general one—a relation that potentially includes us and an indeterminate number of others, and therefore prevents that relation which alone was experienced from having an inner and exclusive necessity.

On the other hand, there is a sort of "strangeness" in which this very connection on the basis of a general quality embracing the parties is precluded.

The relation of the Greeks to the barbarians is a typical example; so are all the cases in which the general characteristics one takes as peculiarly and merely human are disallowed to the other. But here the expression "the stranger" no longer has any positive meaning. The relation with him is a nonrelation; he is not what we have been discussing here: the stranger as a member of the group itself.

As such, the stranger is near and far *at the same time*, as in any relationship based on merely universal human similarities. Between these two factors of nearness and distance, however, a peculiar tension arises, since the consciousness of having only the absolutely general in common has exactly the effect of putting a special emphasis on that which is not common. For a stranger to the country, the city, the race, and so on, what is stressed is again nothing individual, but alien origin, a quality which he has, or could have, in common with many other strangers. For this reason strangers are not really perceived as individuals, but as strangers of a certain type. Their remoteness is no less general than their nearness.

This form appears, for example, in so special a case as the tax levied on Jews in Frankfurt and elsewhere during the Middle Ages. Whereas the tax paid by Christian citizens varied according to their wealth at any given time, for every single Jew the tax was fixed once and for all. This amount was fixed because the Jew had his social position as a *Jew*, not as the bearer of certain objective contents. With respect to taxes every other citizen was regarded as possessor of a certain amount of wealth, and his tax could follow the fluctuations of his fortune. But the Jew as taxpayer was first of all a Jew, and thus his fiscal position contained an invariable element. This appears most forcefully, of course, once the differing circumstances of individual Jews are no longer considered, limited though this consideration is by fixed assessments, and all strangers pay exactly the same head tax.

Despite his being inorganically appended to it, the stranger is still an organic member of the group. Its unified life includes the specific conditioning of this element. Only we do not know how to designate the characteristic unity of this position otherwise than by saying that it is put together of certain amounts of nearness and of remoteness. Although both these qualities are found to some extent in all relationships, a special proportion and reciprocal tension between them produce the specific form of the relation to the "stranger."

5

The My Lai Massacre: A Crime of Obedience?

FROM *Crimes of Obedience: Toward a Social Psychology*
of Authority and Responsibility

HERBERT C. KELMAN AND V. LEE HAMILTON

Understanding why people do what they do is never easy. It is especially difficult when behaviors are contrary to what anyone would expect or want people to do, as in the case of heinous crimes. In this account of the murder of hundreds of innocent people—perhaps the most painful episode of a long and unpopular war—Kelman and Hamilton depart from psychological explanations and focus on the sociology of men in war. They make a compelling case that the social conditions of these men dramatically weakened the moral inhibitions that otherwise would have prevented their doing the unthinkable.

March 16, 1968, was a busy day in U.S. history. Stateside, Robert F. Kennedy announced his presidential candidacy, challenging a sitting president from his own party—in part out of opposition to an undeclared and disastrous war. In Vietnam, the war continued. In many ways, March 16 may have been a typical day in that war. We will probably never know. But we do know that on that day a typical company went on a mission—which may or may not have been typical—to a village called Son (or Song) My. Most of what is remembered from that mission occurred in the subhamlet known to Americans as My Lai 4.

The My Lai massacre was investigated and charges were brought in 1969 and 1970. Trials and disciplinary actions lasted into 1971. Entire books have been written about the army's year-long cover-up of the massacre (for example, Hersh, 1972), and the cover-up was a major focus of the army's own investigation of the incident. Our central concern here is the massacre itself—a crime of obedience—and public reactions to such crimes, rather than the lengths to which many went to deny the event. Therefore this account concentrates on one day: March 16, 1968.[1]

Many verbal testimonials to the horrors that occurred at My Lai were available. More unusual was the fact that an army photographer, Ronald Haeberle, was assigned the task of documenting the anticipated military engagement at

---

1. In reconstructing the events of that day, we consulted Hammer (1970), in addition to the sources cited in the text. Schell (1968) provided information on the region around My Lai. Concerning Vietnam and peasant rebellions, we consulted FitzGerald (1972), Paige (1975), Popkin (1979), and Wolf (1969).

My Lai—and documented a massacre instead. Later, as the story of the massacre emerged, his photographs were widely distributed and seared the public conscience. What might have been dismissed as unreal or exaggerated was depicted in photographs of demonstrable authenticity. The dominant image appeared on the cover of *Life*: piles of bodies jumbled together in a ditch along a trail—the dead all apparently unarmed. All were Oriental, and all appeared to be children, women, or old men. Clearly there had been a mass execution, one whose image would not quickly fade.

So many bodies (over twenty in the cover photo alone) are hard to imagine as the handiwork of one killer. These were not. They were the product of what we call a crime of obedience. Crimes of obedience begin with orders. But orders are often vague and rarely survive with any clarity the transition from one authority down a chain of subordinates to the ultimate actors. The operation at Son My was no exception.

"Charlie" Company, Company C, under Lt. Col. Frank Barker's command, arrived in Vietnam in December of 1967. As the army's investigative unit, directed by Lt. Gen. William R. Peers, characterized the personnel, they "contained no significant deviation from the average" for the time. Seymour S. Hersh (1970) described the "average" more explicitly: "Most of the men in Charlie Company had volunteered for the draft; only a few had gone to college for even one year. Nearly half were black, with a few Mexican-Americans. Most were eighteen to twenty-two years old. The favorite reading matter of Charlie Company, like that of other line infantry units in Vietnam, was comic books" (p. 18). The action at My Lai, like that throughout Vietnam, was fought by a cross-section of those Americans who either believed in the war or lacked the social resources to avoid participating in it. Charlie Company was indeed average for that time, that place, and that war.

Two key figures in Charlie Company were more unusual. The company's commander, Capt. Ernest Medina, was an upwardly mobile Mexican-American who wanted to make the army his career, although he feared that he might never advance beyond captain because of his lack of formal education. His eagerness had earned him a nickname among his men: "Mad Dog Medina." One of his admirers was the platoon leader Second Lt. William L. Calley, Jr., an undistinguished, five-foot-three-inch junior-college dropout who had failed four of the seven courses in which he had enrolled his first year. Many viewed him as one of those "instant officers" made possible only by the army's then-desperate need for manpower. Whatever the cause, he was an insecure leader whose frequent claim was "I'm the boss." His nickname among some of the troops was "Surfside 5½," a reference to the swashbuckling heroes of a popular television show, "Surfside 6."

The Son My operation was planned by Lieutenant Colonel Barker and his staff as a search-and-destroy mission with the objective of rooting out the Forty-eighth Viet Cong Battalion from their base area of Son My village. Apparently no written orders were ever issued. Barker's superior, Col. Oran

Henderson, arrived at the staging point the day before. Among the issues he reviewed with the assembled officers were some of the weaknesses of prior operations by their units, including their failure to be appropriately aggressive in pursuit of the enemy. Later briefings by Lieutenant Colonel Barker and his staff asserted that no one except Viet Cong was expected to be in the village after 7 A.M. on the following day. The "innocent" would all be at the market. Those present at the briefings gave conflicting accounts of Barker's exact orders, but he conveyed at least a strong suggestion that the Son My area was to be obliterated. As the army's inquiry reported: "While there is some conflict in the testimony as to whether LTC Barker ordered the destruction of houses, dwellings, livestock, and other foodstuffs in the Song My area, the preponderance of the evidence indicates that such destruction was implied, if not specifically directed, by his orders of 15 March" (Peers Report, in Goldstein et al., 1976, p. 94).

Evidence that Barker ordered the killing of civilians is even more murky. What does seem clear, however, is that—having asserted that civilians would be away at the market—he did not specify what was to be done with any who might nevertheless be found on the scene. The Peers Report therefore considered it "reasonable to conclude that LTC Barker's minimal or nonexistent instructions concerning the handling of noncombatants created the potential for grave misunderstandings as to his intentions and for interpretation of his orders as authority to fire, without restriction, on all persons found in target area" (Goldstein et al., 1976, p. 95). Since Barker was killed in action in June 1968, his own formal version of the truth was never available.

Charlie Company's Captain Medina was briefed for the operation by Barker and his staff. He then transmitted the already vague orders to his own men. Charlie Company was spoiling for a fight, having been totally frustrated during its months in Vietnam—first by waiting for battles that never came, then by incompetent forays led by inexperienced commanders, and finally by mines and booby traps. In fact, the emotion-laden funeral of a sergeant killed by a booby trap was held on March 15, the day before My Lai. Captain Medina gave the orders for the next day's action at the close of that funeral. Many were in a mood for revenge.

It is again unclear what was ordered. Although all participants were still alive by the time of the trials for the massacre, they were either on trial or probably felt under threat of trial. Memories are often flawed and self-serving at such times. It is apparent that Medina relayed to the men at least some of Barker's general message—to expect Viet Cong resistance, to burn, and to kill livestock. It is not clear that he ordered the slaughter of the inhabitants, but some of the men who heard him thought he had. One of those who claimed to have heard such orders was Lt. William Calley.

As March 16 dawned, much was expected of the operation by those who had set it into motion. Therefore a full complement of "brass" was present in helicopters overhead, including Barker, Colonel Henderson, and their superior,

Major General Koster (who went on to become commandant of West Point before the story of My Lai broke). On the ground the troops were to carry with them one reporter and one photographer to immortalize the anticipated battle.

The action for Company C began at 7:30 as their first wave of helicopters touched down near the subhamlet of My Lai 4. By 7:47 all of Company C was present and set to fight. But instead of the Viet Cong Forty-eighth Battalion, My Lai was filled with the old men, women, and children who were supposed to have gone to market. By this time, in their version of the war, and with whatever orders they thought they had heard, the men from Company C were nevertheless ready to find Viet Cong everywhere. By nightfall, the official tally was 128 VC killed and three weapons captured, although later unofficial body counts ran as high as 500. The operation at Son My was over. And by night-fall, as Hersh reported: "the Viet Cong were back in My Lai 4, helping the survivors bury the dead. It took five days. Most of the funeral speeches were made by the Communist guerrillas. Nguyen Bat was not a Communist at the time of the massacre, but the incident changed his mind. 'After the shooting,' he said, 'all the villagers became Communists'" (1970, p. 74). To this day, the memory of the massacre is kept alive by markers and plaques designating the spots where groups of villagers were killed, by a large statue, and by the My Lai Museum, established in 1975 (Williams, 1985).

But what could have happened to leave American troops reporting a vic-tory over Viet Cong when in fact they had killed hundreds of noncombatants? It is not hard to explain the report of victory; that is the essence of a cover-up. It is harder to understand how the killings came to be committed in the first place, making a cover-up necessary.

MASS EXECUTIONS AND THE DEFENSE OF SUPERIOR ORDERS

Some of the atrocities on March 16, 1968, were evidently unofficial, spontane-ous acts: rapes, tortures, killings. For example, Hersh (1970) describes Charlie Company's Second Platoon as entering "My Lai 4 with guns blazing" (p. 50); more graphically, Lieutenant "Brooks and his men in the second platoon to the north had begun to systematically ransack the hamlet and slaughter the people, kill the livestock, and destroy the crops. Men poured rifle and machine-gun fire into huts without knowing—or seemingly caring—who was inside" (pp. 49–50).

Some atrocities toward the end of the action were part of an almost casual "mopping-up," much of which was the responsibility of Lieutenant LaCross's Third Platoon of Charlie Company. The Peers Report states: "The entire 3rd Platoon then began moving into the western edge of My Lai (4), for the mop-up operation. . . . The squad . . . began to burn the houses in the southwestern portion of the hamlet" (Goldstein et al., 1976, p. 133). They became mingled with other platoons during a series of rapes and killings of survivors for which it was impossible to fix responsibility. Certainly to a Vietnamese all GIs would by this point look alike: "Nineteen-year-old Nguyen Thi Ngoc Tuyet watched a baby trying to open her slain mother's blouse to nurse. A soldier shot the infant while it was struggling with the blouse, and then slashed it with his bayonet." Tuyet also said she saw another baby hacked to death by GIs wielding their bayonets. "Le Tong, a twenty-eight-year-old rice farmer, reported seeing one woman raped after GIs killed her children. Nguyen Khoa, a thirty-seven-year-old peasant, told of a thirteen-year-old girl who was raped before being killed. GIs then attacked Khoa's wife, tearing off her clothes. Before they could rape her, however, Khoa said, their six-year-old son, riddled with bullets, fell and saturated her with blood. The GIs left her alone" (Hersh, 1970, p. 72). All of Company C was implicated in a pattern of death and destruction throughout the hamlet, much of which seemingly lacked rhyme or reason.

But a substantial amount of the killing was *organized* and traceable to one authority: the First Platoon's Lt. William Calley. Calley was originally charged with 109 killings, almost all of them mass executions at the trail and other locations. He stood trial for 102 of these killings, was convicted of 22 in 1971, and at first received a life sentence. Though others—both superior and subordinate to Calley—were brought to trial, he was the only one convicted for the My Lai crimes. Thus, the only actions of My Lai for which *anyone* was ever convicted were mass executions, ordered and committed. We suspect that there are common sense reasons why this one type of killing was singled out. In the midst of rapidly moving events with people running about, an execution of stationary targets is literally a still life that stands out and whose participants are clearly visible. It can be proven that specific people committed specific deeds. An execution, in contrast to the shooting of someone on the run, is also more likely to meet the legal definition of an act resulting from intent—with malice aforethought. Moreover, American military law specifically forbids the killing of unarmed civilians or military prisoners, as does the Geneva Convention between nations. Thus common sense, legal standards, and explicit doctrine all made such actions the likeliest target for prosecution.

When Lieutenant Calley was charged under military law it was for violation of the Uniform Code of Military Justice (UCMJ) Article 118 (murder). This article is similar to civilian codes in that it provides for conviction if an accused:

1. without justification or excuse, unlawfully kills a human being, when he—
2. has a premeditated design to kill;
3. intends to kill or inflict great bodily harm;
4. is engaged in an act which is inherently dangerous to others and evinces a wanton disregard of human life; or
5. is engaged in the perpetration or attempted perpetration of burglary, sodomy, rape, robbery, or aggravated arson. (Goldstein et al., 1976, p. 507)

For a soldier, one legal justification for killing is warfare; but warfare is subject to many legal limits and restrictions, including, of course, the inadmissibility of killing unarmed noncombatants or prisoners whom one has disarmed. The pictures of the trail victims at My Lai certainly portrayed one or the other of these. Such an action would be illegal under military law; ordering another to commit such an action would be illegal; and following such an order would be illegal.

But following an order may provide a second and pivotal justification for an act that would be murder when committed by a civilian. * * * American military law assumes that the subordinate is inclined to follow orders, as that is the normal obligation of the role. Hence, legally, obedient subordinates are protected from unreasonable expectations regarding their capacity to evaluate those orders:

> An order requiring the performance of a military duty may be inferred to be legal. An act performed manifestly beyond the scope of authority, or pursuant to an order that a man of ordinary sense and understanding would know to be illegal, or in a wanton manner in the discharge of a lawful duty, is not excusable. (Par. 216, Subpar. *d*, Manual for Courts Martial, United States, 1969 Rev.)

Thus what *may* be excusable is the good-faith carrying out of an order, as long as that order appears to the ordinary soldier to be a legal one. In military law, invoking superior orders moves the question from one of the action's consequences—the body count[2]—to one of evaluating the actor's motives and good sense.

In sum, if anyone is to be brought to justice for a massacre, common sense and legal codes decree that the most appropriate targets are those who make themselves executioners. This is the kind of target the government selected in prosecuting Lieutenant Calley with the greatest fervor. And in a military context, the most promising way in which one can redefine one's undeniable deeds into acceptability is to invoke superior orders. This is what Calley did in attempting to avoid conviction. Since the core legal issues involved points of mass execution—the ditches and trail where America's image of My Lai was formed—we review these events in greater detail.

The day's quiet beginning has already been noted. Troops landed and swept unopposed into the village. The three weapons eventually reported as the haul from the operation were picked up from three apparent Viet Cong who fled the village when the troops arrived and were pursued and killed by helicopter gunships. Obviously the Viet Cong did frequent the area. But it appears that by about 8:00 A.M. no one who met the troops was aggressive, and no one was armed. By the laws of war Charlie Company had no argument with such people.

---

2. During the Vietnam War, the success of a military action was often measured by the number of "enemy" killed, relative to allied casualties. [*Editor's note*].

As they moved into the village, the soldiers began to gather its inhabitants together. Shortly after 8:00 A.M. Lieutenant Calley told Pfc. Paul Meadlo that "you know what to do with" a group of villagers Meadlo was guarding. Estimates of the numbers in the group ranged as high as eighty women, children, and old men, and Meadlo's own estimate under oath was thirty to fifty people. As Meadlo later testified, Calley returned after ten or fifteen minutes: "He [Calley] said, 'How come they're not dead?' I said, 'I didn't know we were supposed to kill them.' He said, 'I want them dead.' He backed off twenty or thirty feet and started shooting into the people—the Viet Cong—shooting automatic. He was beside me. He burned four or five magazines. I burned off a few, about three. I helped shoot 'em" (Hammer, 1971, p. 155). Meadlo himself and others testified that Meadlo cried as he fired; others reported him later to be sobbing and "all broke up." It would appear that to Lieutenant Calley's subordinates something was unusual, and stressful, in these orders.

At the trial, the first specification in the murder charge against Calley was for this incident; he was accused of premeditated murder of "an unknown number, not less than 30, Oriental human beings, males and females of various ages, whose names are unknown, occupants of the village of My Lai 4, by means of shooting them with a rifle" (Goldstein et al., 1976, p. 497).

Among the helicopters flying reconnaissance above Son My was that of CWO Hugh Thompson. By 9:00 or soon after Thompson had noticed some horrifying events from his perch. As he spotted wounded civilians, he sent down smoke markers so that soldiers on the ground could treat them. They killed them instead. He reported to headquarters, trying to persuade someone to stop what was going on. Barker, hearing the message, called down to Captain Medina. Medina, in turn, later claimed to have told Calley that it was "enough for today." But it was not yet enough.

At Calley's orders, his men began gathering the remaining villagers—roughly seventy-five individuals, mostly women and children—and herding them toward a drainage ditch. Accompanied by three or four enlisted men, Lieutenant Calley executed several batches of civilians who had been gathered into ditches. Some of the details of the process were entered into testimony in such accounts as Pfc. Dennis Conti's: "A lot of them, the people, were trying to get up and mostly they was just screaming and pretty bad shot up. . . . I seen a woman tried to get up. I seen Lieutenant Calley fire. He hit the side of her head and blew it off" (Hammer, 1971, p. 125).

Testimony by other soldiers presented the shooting's aftermath. Specialist Four Charles Hall, asked by Prosecutor Aubrey Daniel how he knew the people in the ditch were dead, said: "There was blood coming from them. They were just scattered all over the ground in the ditch, some in piles and some scattered out 20, 25 meters perhaps up the ditch. . . . They were very old people, very young children, and mothers. . . . There was blood all over them" (Goldstein et al., 1976, pp. 501–02). And Pfc. Gregory Olson corroborated the general picture of the victims: "They were—the majority were women and children, some babies. I distinctly remember one middle-aged Vietnamese male dressed in white right at my feet as I crossed. None of the bodies were mangled in any way. There was blood. Some appeared to be dead, others followed me with their eyes as I walked across the ditch" (Goldstein et al., 1976, p. 502).

The second specification in the murder charge stated that Calley did "with premeditation, murder an unknown number of Oriental human beings, not less than seventy, males and females of various ages, whose names are unknown, occupants of the village of My Lai 4, by means of shooting them with a rifle" (Goldstein et al., 1976, p. 497). Calley was also charged with and tried for shootings of individuals (an old man and a child); these charges were clearly supplemental to the main issue at trial—the mass killings and how they came about.

It is noteworthy that during these executions more than one enlisted man avoided carrying out Calley's orders, and more than one, by sworn oath, directly refused to obey them. For example, Pfc. James Joseph Dursi testified, when asked if he fired when Lieutenant Calley ordered him to: "No. I just stood there. Meadlo turned to me after a couple of minutes and said 'Shoot! Why don't you shoot! Why don't you fire! He was crying and yelling. I said, 'I can't I won't!' And the people were screaming and crying and yelling. They kept firing for a couple of minutes, mostly automatic and semi-automatic" (Hammer, 1971, p. 143).

Specialist Four Ronald Grzesik reported an even more direct confrontation with Calley, although under oath he hedged about its subject:

GRZESIK: Well, Lieutenant Calley—I walked past the ditch. I was called back by someone, I don't recall who. I had a discussion with Lieutenant Calley. He said to take the fire team back into the village and help the second platoon search.
DANIEL: Did Lieutenant Calley say anything before he gave you that order?
GRZESIK: He said, "Finish them off." I refused.
DANIEL: What did you refuse to do?
GRZESIK: To finish them off.
DANIEL: What did he mean? Who did he mean to finish off?
GRZESIK: I don't know what he meant or who he meant by them. (Hammer, 1971, p. 150)

In preceding months, not under oath, Grzesik had indicated that he had a good idea what was meant but that he simply would not comply. It is likely that the jury at Calley's trial did not miss the point.

Disobedience of Lieutenant Calley's own orders to kill represented a serious legal and moral threat to a defense *based* on superior orders, such as Calley was attempting. This defense had to assert that the orders seemed reasonable enough to carry out, that they appeared to be legal orders. Even if the orders in question were not legal, the defense had to assert that an ordinary individual could not and should not be expected to see the distinction. In short, if what happened was "business as usual," even though it might be bad business, then the defendant stood a chance of acquittal. But under direct command from "Surfside 5 1/2," some ordinary enlisted men managed to refuse, to avoid, or at least to stop doing what they were ordered to do. As "reasonable men" of "ordinary sense and understanding," they had apparently found something awry that morning; and it would have been hard for an officer to plead successfully that he was more ordinary than his men in his capacity to evaluate the reasonableness of orders.

Even those who obeyed Calley's orders showed great stress. For example, Meadlo eventually began to argue and cry directly in front of Calley. Pfc. Herbert Carter shot himself in the foot, possibly because he could no longer take what he was doing. We were not destined to hear a sworn version of the incident, since neither side at the Calley trial called him to testify.

The most unusual instance of resistance to authority came from the skies. CWO Hugh Thompson, who had protested the apparent carnage of civilians, was Calley's inferior in rank but was not in his line of command. He was also watching the ditch from his helicopter and noticed some people moving after the first round of slaughter—chiefly children who had been shielded by their mothers' bodies. Landing to rescue the wounded, he also found some villagers hiding in a nearby bunker. Protecting the Vietnamese with his own body, Thompson ordered his men to train their guns on the Americans and to open fire if the Americans fired on the Vietnamese. He then radioed for additional rescue helicopters and stood between the Vietnamese and the Americans under Calley's command until the Vietnamese could be evacuated. He later returned to the ditch to unearth a child buried, unharmed, beneath layers of bodies. In October 1969, Thompson was awarded the Distinguished Flying Cross for heroism at My Lai, specifically (albeit inaccurately) for the rescue of children hiding in a bunker "between Viet Cong forces and advancing friendly forces" and for the rescue of a wounded child "caught in the intense crossfire" (Hersh, 1970, p. 119). Four months earlier, at the Pentagon, Thompson had identified Calley as having been at the ditch.

By about 10:00 A.M., the massacre was winding down. The remaining actions consisted largely of isolated rapes and killings, "clean-up" shootings of the wounded, and the destruction of the village by fire. We have already seen some examples of these more indiscriminate and possibly less premeditated acts. By the 11:00 A.M. lunch break, when the exhausted men of Company C were relaxing, two young girls wandered back from a hiding place only to be invited to share lunch. This surrealist touch illustrates the extent to which the soldiers' action had become dissociated from its meaning. An hour earlier, some of these men were making sure that not even a child would escape the executioner's bullet. But now the job was done and it was time for lunch—and in this new context it seemed only natural to ask the children who had managed to escape execution to join them. The massacre had ended. It remained only for the Viet Cong to reap the political rewards among the survivors in hiding.

The army command in the area knew that something had gone wrong. Direct commanders, including Lieutenant Colonel Barker, had firsthand reports, such as Thompson's complaints. Others had such odd bits of evidence as the claim of 128 Viet Cong dead with a booty of only three weapons. But the cover-up of My Lai began at once. The operation was reported as a victory over a stronghold of the Viet Cong Forty-eighth.

My Lai might have remained a "victory" but for another odd twist. A soldier who had not even been at the massacre, Ronald Ridenhour, talked to several friends and acquaintances who had been. As he later wrote: "It was late in April, 1968 that I first heard of 'Pinkville' [a nickname reflecting the villagers' reputed Communist sympathies] and what allegedly happened there. I received that first report with some skepticism, but in the following months I was to hear similar stories from such a wide variety of people that it became impossible for me to disbelieve that something rather dark and bloody did indeed occur sometime in March, 1968 in a village called 'Pinkville' in the Republic of Viet Nam" (Goldstein et al., 1976, p. 34). Ridenhour's growing conviction that a massacre—or something close to it—had occurred was reinforced by his own travel over the area by helicopter soon after the event. My Lai was desolate. He gradually concluded that someone was covering up the incident within the army and that an independent investigation was needed.

At the end of March 1969, he finally wrote a letter detailing what he knew about "Pinkville." The letter, beginning with the paragraph quote above, was sent to thirty individuals—the president, Pentagon officials, and some members of the Senate and House. Ridenhour's congressman, fellow Arizonian Morris Udall, gave it particular heed. The slow unraveling of the cover-up began. During the following months, the army in fact initiated an investigation but carried it out in strict secrecy. Ridenhour, convinced that the cover-up was continuing, sought journalistic help and finally, by coincidence, connected with Seymour Hersh. Hersh followed up and broke the story, which eventually brought him a Pulitzer Prize and other awards for his investigative reporting. The cover-up collapsed, leaving only the question of the army's resolve to seek justice in the case: Against whom would it proceed, with how much speed and vigor, and with what end in mind?

William Calley was not the only man tried for the events at My Lai. The actions of over thirty soldiers and civilians were scrutinized by investigators; over half of these had to face charges or disciplinary action of some sort. Targets of investigation included Captain Medina, who was tried, and various higher-ups, including General Koster. But Lieutenant Calley was the only person convicted, the only person to serve time.

* * *

SANCTIONED MASSACRES

The slaughter at My Lai is an instance of a class of violent acts that can be described as sanctioned massacres (Kelman, 1973): acts of indiscriminate, ruthless, and often systematic mass violence, carried out by military or paramilitary personnel while engaged in officially sanctioned campaigns, the victims of which are defenseless and unresisting civilians, including old men, women, and children. Sanctioned massacres have occurred throughout history. Within American history, My Lai had its precursors in the Philippine war around the turn of the century (Schirmer, 1971) and in the massacres of American Indians. Elsewhere in the world, one recalls the Nazis' "final solution" for European Jews, the massacres and deportations of Armenians by Turks, the liquidation of the kulaks and the great purges in the Soviet Union, and more recently the massacres in Indonesia and Bangladesh, in Biafra and Burundi, in South Africa and Mozambique, in Cambodia and Afghanistan, in Syria and Lebanon. Sanctioned massacres may vary on a number of dimensions. For present purposes, however, we want to focus on features they share. Two of these are the *context* and the *target* of the violence.

Sanctioned massacres tend to occur in the context of an overall policy that is explicitly or implicitly genocidal: designed to destroy all or part of a category of people defined in ethnic, national, racial, religious, or other terms. Such a policy may be deliberately aimed at the systematic extermination of a population group as an end in itself, as was the case with the Holocaust during World War II. In the Nazis' "final solution" for European Jewry, a policy aimed at exterminating millions of people was consciously articulated and executed (see Levinson, 1973), and the extermination was accomplished on a mass-production basis through the literal establishment of a well-organized, efficient death industry. Alternatively, such a policy may be aimed at an objective other than extermination—such as the pacification of the rural population of South Vietnam, as was the case in U.S. policy for Indochina—but may include the deliberate decimation of large segments of a population as an acceptable means to that end.

We agree with Bedau's (1974) conclusion from his carefully reasoned argument that the charge of U.S. genocide in Vietnam has not been definitively proven, since such a charge requires evidence of a specific genocidal *intent*. Although the evidence suggests that the United States committed war crimes and crimes against humanity in Indochina (see Sheehan, 1971; Browning and Forman, 1972), it does not show that extermination was the conscious purpose of U.S. policy. The evidence reviewed by Bedau, however, suggests that the United States did commit genocidal acts in Vietnam as a means to other ends. Central to U.S. strategy in South Vietnam were such actions as unrestricted air and artillery bombardments of peasant hamlets, search-and-destroy missions by ground troops, crop destruction programs, and mass deportation of rural populations. These actions (and similar ones in Laos and Cambodia) were clearly and deliberately aimed at civilians and resulted in the death, injury, and/or uprooting of large numbers of that population and in the destruction of their countryside, their source of livelihood, and their social structure. These consequences were anticipated by policymakers and indeed were intended as part of their pacification effort; the actions were designed to clear the countryside and deprive guerrillas of their base of operations, even if this meant destroying the civilian population. Massacres of the kind that occurred at My Lai were not deliberately planned, but they took place in an atmosphere in which the rural Vietnamese population was viewed as expendable and actions that resulted in the killing of large numbers of that population as strategic necessities.

A second feature of sanctioned massacres is that their targets have not themselves threatened or engaged in hostile actions toward the perpetrators of the violence. The victims of this class of violence are often defenseless civilians, including old men, women, and children. By all accounts, at least after the first moments at My Lai, the victims there fit this description, although in guerrilla warfare there always remains some ambiguity about the distinction between armed soldiers and unarmed civilians. * * *

There are, of course, historical and situational reasons particular groups become victims of sanctioned massacres, but these do not include their own immediate harmfulness or violence toward the attackers. Rather, their selection as targets for massacre at a particular time can ultimately be traced to their relationship to the pursuit of larger policies. Their elimination may be seen as a useful tool[3] of their continued existence as an irritating obstacle in the execution of policy.

* * *

In searching for a psychological explanation for mass violence under these conditions, one's first inclination is to look for forces that might impel people toward such murderous acts. Can we identify, in massacre situations, psychological forces so powerful that they outweigh the moral restraints that would normally inhibit unjustifiable violence?

The most obvious approach—searching for psychological dispositions within those who perpetrate these acts—does not yield a satisfactory explanation of the phenomenon, although it may tell us something about the types of individuals most readily recruited for participation. For example, any explanation involving the attackers' strong sadistic impulses is inadequate. There is no evidence that the majority of those who participate in such killings are sadistically inclined. Indeed, speaking of the participants in the Nazi slaughters, Arendt (1964) points out that they "were not sadists or killers by nature; on the contrary, a systematic effort was made to weed out all those who

---

3. Committing violence against innocents as a tool to achieve political goals is the hallmark of terrorism. [*Editor's note*].

derived physical pleasure from what they did" (p. 105). To be sure, some of the commanders and guards of concentration camps could clearly be described as sadists, but what has to be explained is the existence of concentration camps in which these individuals could give play to their sadistic fantasies. These opportunities were provided with the participation of large numbers of individuals to whom the label of sadist could not be applied.

A more sophisticated type of dispositional approach seeks to identify certain characterological themes that are dominant within a given culture. An early example of such an approach is Fromm's (1941) analysis of the appeals of Nazism in terms of the prevalence of sadomasochistic strivings, particularly among the German lower middle class. It would be important to explore whether similar kinds of characterological dispositions can be identified in the very wide range of cultural contexts in which sanctioned massacres have occurred. However general such dispositions turn out to be, it seems most likely that they represent states of readiness to participate in sanctioned massacres when the opportunity arises rather than major motivating forces in their own right. Similarly, high levels of frustration within a population are probably facilitators rather than instigators of sanctioned massacres. * * *

Could participation in sanctioned massacres be traced to an inordinately intense hatred toward those against whom the violence is directed? The evidence does not seem to support such an interpretation. Indications are that many of the active participants in the extermination of European Jews, such as Adolf Eichmann (Arendt, 1964), did not feel any passionate hatred of Jews. There is certainly no reason to believe that those who planned and executed American policy in Vietnam felt a profound hatred of the Vietnamese population, although deeply rooted racist attitudes may conceivably have played a role.

To be sure, hatred and rage *play a part* in sanctioned massacres. Typically there is a long history of profound hatred against the groups targeted for violence—the Jews in Christian Europe, the Chinese in Southeast Asia, the Ibos in northern Nigeria—which helps establish them as suitable victims. Hostility also plays an important part at the point at which the killings are actually perpetrated, even if the official planning and the bureaucratic preparations that ultimately lead up to this point are carried out in a passionless and businesslike atmosphere. For example, Lifton's (1973) descriptions of My Lai, based on eyewitness reports, suggest that the killings were accompanied by generalized rage and by expressions of anger and revenge toward the victims. Hostility toward the target, however, does not seem to be the *instigator* of these violent actions. The expressions of anger in the situation itself can more properly be viewed as outcomes rather than causes of the violence. They serve to provide the perpetrators with an explanation and rationalization for their violent actions and appropriate labels for their emotional state. They also help reinforce, maintain, and intensify the violence, but the anger is not the primary source of the violence. Hostility toward the target, historically rooted or situationally induced, contributes heavily toward the violence, but it does so largely by dehumanizing the victims rather than by motivating violence against them in the first place.

In sum, the occurrence of sanctioned massacres cannot be adequately explained by the existence of psychological forces—whether these be characterological dispositions to engage in murderous violence or profound hostility against the target—so powerful that they must find expression in violent acts unhampered by moral restraints. Instead, the major instigators for this class of violence derive from the policy process. The question that really calls for psychological analysis is why so many people are willing to formulate, participate in, and condone policies that call for the mass killings of defenseless civilians. Thus it is more instructive to look not at the motives for violence but at the conditions under which the usual moral inhibitions against violence become weakened. Three social processes that tend to create such conditions can be identified: authorization, routinization, and dehumanization. Through authorization, the situation becomes so defined that the individual is absolved of the responsibility to make personal moral choices. Through routinization, the action becomes so organized that there is no opportunity for raising moral questions. Through dehumanization, the actors' attitudes toward the target and toward themselves become so structured that it is neither necessary nor possible for them to view the relationship in moral terms.

AUTHORIZATION

Sanctioned massacres by definition occur in the context of an authority situation, a situation in which, at least for many of the participants, the moral principles that generally govern human relationships do not apply. Thus, when acts of violence are explicitly ordered, implicitly encouraged, tacitly approved, or at least permitted by legitimate authorities, people's readiness to commit or condone them is enhanced. That such acts are authorized seems to carry automatic justification for them. Behaviorally, authorization obviates the necessity of making judgments or choices. Not only do normal moral principles become inoperative, but—particularly when the actions are explicitly ordered—a different kind of morality linked to the duty to obey superior orders, tends to take over.

In an authority situation, individuals characteristically feel obligated to obey the orders of the authorities, whether or not these correspond with their personal preferences. They see themselves as having no choice as long as they accept the legitimacy of the orders and of the authorities who give them. Individuals differ considerably in the degree to which—and the conditions under which—they are prepared to challenge the legitimacy of an order on the grounds that the order itself is illegal, or that those giving it have overstepped their authority, or that it stems from a policy that violates fundamental societal values. Regardless of subtle individual differences, however, the basic structure of a situation of legitimate authority requires subordinates to respond in terms of their role obligations rather than their personal preferences; they can openly disobey only by challenging the legitimacy of the authority. Often people obey without question even though the behavior they engage in may entail great personal sacrifice or great harm to others.

An important corollary of the basic structure of the authority situation is that actors often do not see themselves as personally responsible for the consequences of their actions. Again, there are individual differences, depending on actors' capacity and readiness to evaluate the legitimacy of orders received. Insofar as they see themselves as having had no choice in their actions, however, they do not feel personally responsible for them. They were not personal agents, but merely extensions of the authority. Thus, when their actions cause harm to others, they can feel relatively free of guilt. A similar mechanism operates when a person engages in antisocial behavior that was not ordered by the authorities but was tacitly encouraged and approved by them—even if only by making it clear that such behavior will not be punished. In this situation, behavior that was formerly illegitimate is legitimized by the authorities' acquiescence.

In the My Lai massacre, it is likely that the structure of the authority situation contributed to the massive violence in both ways—that is, by conveying the message that acts of violence against Vietnamese villagers were *required*, as well as the message that such acts, even if not ordered, were *permitted* by the authorities in charge. The actions at My Lai represented, at least in some respects, responses to explicit or implicit orders. Lieutenant Calley indicated, by orders and by example, that he wanted large numbers of villagers killed. Whether Calley himself had been ordered by his superiors to "waste" the whole area, as he claimed, remains a matter of controversy. Even if we assume, however, that he was not explicitly ordered to wipe out the village, he had reason to believe that such actions were expected by his superior officers. Indeed, the very nature of the war conveyed this expectation. The principal measure of military success was the "body count"—the number of enemy soldiers killed—and any Vietnamese killed by the U.S. military was commonly defined as a "Viet Cong." Thus, it was not totally bizarre for Calley to believe that what he was doing at My Lai was to increase his body count, as any good officer was expected to do.

Even to the extent that the actions at My Lai occurred spontaneously, without reference to superior orders, those committing them had reason to assume that such actions might be tacitly approved of by the military authorities. Not only had they failed to punish such acts in most cases, but the very strategies and tactics that the authorities consistently devised were based on the proposition that the civilian population of South Vietnam—whether "hostile" or "friendly"—was expendable. Such policies as search-and-destroy missions, the establishment of free-shooting zones, the use of antipersonnel weapons, the bombing of entire villages if they were suspected of harboring guerrillas, the forced migration of masses of the rural population, and the defoliation of vast forest areas helped legitimize acts of massive violence of the kind occurring at My Lai.

Some of the actions at My Lai suggest an orientation to authority based on unquestioning obedience to superior orders, no matter how destructive the actions these orders call for. Such obedience is specifically fostered in the course of military training and reinforced by the structure of the military authority situation. It also reflects, however, an ideological orientation that may be more widespread in the general population. * * *

ROUTINIZATION

Authorization processes create a situation in which people become involved in an action without considering its implications and without really making a decision. Once they have taken the initial step, they are in a new psychological and social situation in which the pressures to continue are powerful. As Lewin (1947) has pointed out, many forces that might originally have kept people out of a situation reverse direction once they have made a commitment (once they have gone through the "gate region") and now serve to keep them in the situation. For example, concern about the criminal nature of an action, which might originally have inhibited a person from becoming involved, may now lead to deeper involvement in efforts to justify the action and to avoid negative consequences.

Despite these forces, however, given the nature of the actions involved in sanctioned massacres, one might still expect moral scruples to intervene; but the likelihood of moral resistance is greatly reduced by transforming the action into routine, mechanical, highly programmed operations. Routinization fulfills two functions. First, it reduces the necessity of making decisions, thus minimizing the occasions in which moral questions may arise. Second, it makes it easier to avoid the implications of the action, since the actor focuses on the details of the job rather than on its meaning. The latter effect is more readily achieved among those who participate in sanctioned massacres from a distance—from their desks or even from the cockpits of their bombers.

Routinization operates both at the level of the individual actor and at the organizational level. Individual job performance is broken down into a series of discrete steps, most of them carried out in automatic, regularized fashion. It becomes easy to forget the nature of the product that emerges from this process. When Lieutenant Calley said of My Lai that it was "no great deal," he probably implied that it was all in a day's work. Organizationally, the task is divided among different offices, each of which has responsibility for a small portion of it. This arrangement diffuses responsibility and limits the amount and scope of decision making that is necessary. There is no expectation that the moral implications will be considered at any of these points, nor is there any opportunity to do so. The organizational processes also help further legitimize the actions of each participant. By proceeding in routine fashion—processing papers, exchanging memos, diligently carrying out their assigned tasks—the different units mutually reinforce each other in the view that what is going on must be perfectly normal, correct, and legitimate. The shared illusion that they are engaged in a legitimate enterprise helps the participants assimilate their activities to other purposes, such as the efficiency of their performance, the productivity of their unit, or the cohesiveness of their group (see Janis, 1972).

Normalization of atrocities is more difficult to the extent that there are constant reminders of the true meaning of the enterprise. Bureaucratic inventiveness in the use of language helps to cover up such meaning. For example, the SS had a set of *Sprachregelungen*, or "language rules," to govern descriptions of their extermination program. As Arendt (1964) points out, the term *language rule* in itself was "a code name; it meant what in ordinary language would be called a lie" (p. 85). The code names for killing and liquidation were "final solution," "evacuation," and "special treatment." The war in Indochina produced its own set of euphemisms, such as "protective reaction," "pacification," and "forced-draft urbanization and modernization." The use of euphemisms allows participants in sanctioned massacres to differentiate their actions from ordinary killing and destruction and thus to avoid confronting their true meaning.

DEHUMANIZATION

Authorization processes override standard moral considerations; routinization processes reduce the likelihood that such considerations will arise. Still, the inhibitions against murdering one's fellow human beings are generally so strong that the victims must also be stripped of their human status if they are to be subjected to systematic killing. Insofar as they are dehumanized, the usual principles of morality no longer apply to them.

Sanctioned massacres become possible to the extent that the victims are deprived in the perpetrators' eyes of the two qualities essential to being perceived as fully human and included in the moral compact that governs human relationships: *identity*—standing as independent, distinctive individuals, capable of making choices and entitled to live their own lives—and *community*—fellow membership in an interconnected network of individuals who care for each other and respect each other's individuality and rights (Kelman, 1973; see also Bakan, 1966, for a related distinction between "agency" and "communion"). Thus, when a group of people is defined entirely in terms of a category to which they belong, and when this category is excluded from the human family, moral restraints against killing them are more readily overcome.

Dehumanization of the enemy is a common phenomenon in any war situation. Sanctioned massacres, however, presuppose a more extreme degree of dehumanization, insofar as the killing is not in direct response to the target's threats or provocations. It is not what they have done that marks such victims for death but who they are—the category to which they happen to belong. They are the victims of policies that regard their systematic destruction as a desirable end or an acceptable means. Such extreme dehumanization becomes possible when the target group can readily be identified as a separate category of people who have historically been stigmatized and excluded by the victimizers; often the victims belong to a distinct racial, religious, ethnic, or political group regarded as inferior or sinister. The traditions, the habits, the images, and the vocabularies for dehumanizing such groups are already well established and can be drawn upon when the groups are selected for massacre. Labels help deprive the victims of identity and community, as in the epithet "gooks" that was commonly used to refer to Vietnamese and other Indochinese peoples.

The dynamics of the massacre process itself further increase the participants' tendency to dehumanize their victims. Those who participate as part of the bureaucratic apparatus increasingly come to see their victims as bodies to be counted and entered into their reports, as faceless figures that will determine their productivity rates and promotions. Those who participate in the massacre directly—in the field, as it were—are reinforced in their perception of the victims as less than human by observing their very victimization. The only way they can justify what is being done to these people—both by others and by themselves—and the only way they can extract some degree of meaning out of the absurd events in which they find themselves participating (see Litton, 1971, 1973) is by coming to believe that the victims are subhuman and deserve to be rooted out. And thus the process of dehumanization feeds on itself.

* * *

REFERENCES

Arendt, H. (1964). *Eichmann in Jerusalem: A report on the banality of evil.* New York: Viking Press.

Bakan, D. (1966). *The duality of human existence.* Chicago: Rand McNally.

Browning, F., & Forman, D. (Eds.). (1972). *The wasted nations: Report of the International Commission of Enquiry into United States Crimes in Indochina, June 20–25, 1971.* New York: Harper & Row.

FitzGerald, F. (1972). *Fire in the lake: The Vietnamese and the Americans in Vietnam.* Boston: Atlantic-Little, Brown.

Fromm, E. (1941). *Escape from freedom.* New York: Rinehart.

Goldstein, J.; Marshall, B.; & Schwartz, J. (Eds.). (1976). *The My Lai massacre and its cover-up: Beyond the reach of law?* (The Peers report with a supplement and introductory essay on the limits of law.) New York: Free Press.

Hammer, R. (1970). *One morning in the war.* New York: Coward-McCann.

_____. (1971). *The court-martial of Lt. Calley.* New York: Coward, McCann, & Geoghegan.

Hersh, S. (1970). *My Lai 4: A report on the massacre and its aftermath.* New York: Vintage Books.

Janis, I. L. (1972). *Victims of groupthink: A psychological study of foreign-policy decisions and fiascoes.* Boston: Houghton Mifflin.

Kelman, H. C. (1958). Compliance, identification, and internalization: Three processes of attitude change. *Journal of Conflict Resolution, 2,* 51–60.

_____. (1972). The rights of the subject in social research: An analysis in terms of relative power and legitimacy. *American Psychologist, 27,* 989–1016.

_____. (1973). Violence without moral restraint: Reflections on the dehumanization of victims and victimizers. *Journal of Social Issues,* 29(4), 25–61.

Levinson, S. (1973). Responsibility for crimes of war. *Philosophy and Public Affairs, 2,* 244–273.

Lifton, R. J. (1971). Existential evil. In N. Sanford, C. Comstock, & Associates, *Sanctions for evil: Sources of social destructiveness.* San Francisco: Jossey-Bass.

_____. (1973). *Home from the war—Vietnam veterans: Neither victims nor executioners.* New York: Simon & Schuster.

Paige, J. (1975). *Agrarian revolution: Social movements and export agriculture in the underdeveloped world.* New York: Free Press.

Popkin, S. L. (1979). *The rational peasant: The political economy of rural society in Vietnam.* Berkeley: University of California Press.

Schell, J. (1968). *The military half.* New York: Vintage Books.

Schirmer, D. B. (1971, April 24). My Lai was not the first time. *New Republic,* pp. 18–21.

Sheehan, N. (1971, March 28). Should we have war crime trials? *The New York Times Book Review,* pp. 1–3, 30–34.

Williams, B. (1985, April 14–15). "I will never forgive," says My Lai survivor. *Jordan Times* (Amman), p. 4.

Wolf, E. (1969). *Peasant wars of the twentieth century.* New York: Harper & Row.

6

Telling the Truth about Damned Lies and Statistics

JOEL BEST

Many people feel they live in a world of information overload. Statistics are a big part of this feeling, continually thrown about to impress, sell, or convince. In many cases the statistics are not accurate, leading to distrust of all statistics. But as Joel Best explains, we need good statistics, and he shows why. Part of the "sociological imagination" is the capacity to think critically about information, including statistics, in order to answer questions and solve problems. As you read this essay, think of the last time you heard someone misuse a statistic. Better yet, think of the last time you did.

The dissertation prospectus began by quoting a statistic—a "grabber" meant to capture the reader's attention. The graduate student who wrote this prospectus undoubtedly wanted to seem scholarly to the professors who would read it; they would be supervising the proposed research. And what could be more scholarly than a nice, authoritative statistic, quoted from a professional journal in the student's field?

So the prospectus began with this (carefully footnoted) quotation: "Every year since 1950, the number of American children gunned down has doubled." I had been invited to serve on the student's dissertation committee. When I read the quotation, I assumed the student had made an error in copying it. I went to the library and looked up the article the student had cited. There, in the journal's 1995 volume, was exactly the same sentence: "Every year since 1950, the number of American children gunned down has doubled."

This quotation is my nomination for a dubious distinction: I think it may be the worst—that is, the most inaccurate—social statistic ever.

What makes this statistic so bad? Just for the sake of argument, let's assume that "the number of American children gunned down" in 1950 was one. If the number doubled each year, there must have been two children gunned down in 1951, four in 1952, eight in 1953, and so on. By 1960, the number would have been 1,024. By 1965, it would have been 32,768 (in 1965, the F.B.I. identified only 9,960 criminal homicides in the entire country, including adult as well as child victims). By 1970, the number would have passed one million; by 1980, one billion (more than four times the total U.S. population in that year). Only three years later, in 1983, the number of American children gunned down would have been 8.6 billion (nearly twice the earths population at the time). Another milestone would have been passed in 1987, when the number of gunned-down American children (137 billion) would have surpassed the best estimates for the total human population throughout history (110 billion). By 1995, when the article was published, the annual number of victims would have been over 35 trillion—a really big number, of a magnitude you rarely encounter outside economics or astronomy.

Thus my nomination: estimating the number of American child gunshot victims in 1995 at 35 trillion must be as far off—as hilariously, wildly wrong—as a social statistic can be. (If anyone spots a more inaccurate social statistic, I'd love to hear about it.)

Where did the article's author get this statistic? I wrote the author, who responded that the statistic came from the Children's Defense Fund, a well-known advocacy group for children. The C.D.F.'s *The State of America's Children Yearbook 1994* does state: "The number of American children killed each year by guns has doubled since 1950." Note the difference in the wording—the C.D.F. claimed there were twice as many deaths in 1994 as in 1950; the article's author reworded that claim and created a very different meaning.

It is worth examining the history of this statistic. It began with the C.D.F. noting that child gunshot deaths had doubled from 1950 to 1994. This is not quite as dramatic an increase as it might seem. Remember that the U.S. population also rose throughout this period; in fact, it grew about 73 percent—or nearly double. Therefore, we might expect all sorts of things—including the number of child gunshot deaths—to increase, to nearly double, just because the population grew. Before we can decide whether twice as many deaths indicates that things are getting worse, we'd have to know more. The C.D.F. statistic raises other issues as well: Where did the statistic come from? Who counts child gunshot deaths, and how? What is meant by a "child" (some C.D.F. statistics about violence include everyone under age 25)? What is meant by "killed by guns" (gunshot-death statistics often include suicides and accidents, as well as homicides)? But people rarely ask questions of this sort when they encounter statistics. Most of the time, most people simply accept statistics without question.

Certainly, the article's author didn't ask many probing, critical questions about the C.D.F.'s claim. Impressed by the statistic, the author repeated it—well, meant to repeat it. Instead, by rewording the C.D.F.'s claim, the author created a mutant statistic, one garbled almost beyond recognition.

But people treat mutant statistics just as they do other statistics—that is, they usually accept even the most implausible claims without question. For example, the journal editor who accepted the author's article for publication did not bother to consider the implications of child victims doubling each year. And people repeat bad statistics: The graduate student copied the garbled statistic and inserted it into the dissertation prospectus. Who knows whether still other readers were impressed by the author's statistic and remembered it or repeated it? The article remains on the shelf in hundreds of libraries, available to anyone who needs a dramatic quote. The lesson should be clear: Bad statistics live on; they take on lives of their own.

Some statistics are born bad—they aren't much good from the start, because they are based on nothing more than guesses or dubious data. Other statistics mutate; they become bad after being mangled (as in the case of the author's creative rewording). Either way, bad statistics are potentially important: They can be used to stir up public outrage or fear; they can distort our understanding of our world; and they can lead us to make poor policy choices.

The notion that we need to watch out for bad statistics isn't new. We've all heard people say, "You can prove anything with statistics." The title of my book, *Damned Lies and Statistics,* comes from a famous aphorism (usually attributed to Mark Twain or Benjamin Disraeli): "There are three kinds of lies: lies, damned lies, and statistics." There is even a useful little book, still in print after more than 40 years, called *How to Lie With Statistics.*

Statistics, then, have a bad reputation. We suspect that statistics may be wrong, that people who use statistics may be "lying"—trying to manipulate us by using numbers to somehow distort the truth. Yet, at the same time, we need statistics; we depend upon them to summarize and clarify the nature of our complex society. This is particularly true when we talk about social problems. Debates about social problems routinely raise questions that demand statistical answers: Is the problem widespread? How many people—and which people—does it affect? Is it getting worse? What does it cost society? What will it cost to deal with it? Convincing answers to such questions demand evidence, and that usually means numbers, measurements, statistics.

But can't you prove anything with statistics? It depends on what "prove" means. If we want to know, say, how many children are "gunned down" each year, we can't simply guess—pluck a number from thin air: 100, 1,000, 10,000, 35 trillion, whatever. Obviously, there's no reason to consider an arbitrary guess "proof" of anything. However, it might be possible for someone—using records kept by police departments or hospital emergency rooms or coroners—to keep track of children who have been shot; compiling careful, complete records might give us a fairly accurate idea of the number of gunned-down children. If that number seems accurate enough, we might consider it very strong evidence—or proof.

The solution to the problem of bad statistics is not to ignore all statistics, or to assume that every number is false. Some statistics are bad, but others are pretty good, and we need statistics—good statistics—to talk sensibly about social problems. The solution, then, is not to give up on statistics, but to become better judges of the numbers we encounter. We need to think critically about statistics—at least critically enough to suspect that the number of children gunned down hasn't been doubling each year since 1950.

A few years ago, the mathematician John Allen Paulos wrote *Innumeracy,* a short, readable book about "mathematical illiteracy." Too few people, he argued, are comfortable with basic mathematical principles, and this makes them poor judges of the numbers they encounter. No doubt this is one reason we have so many bad statistics. But there are other reasons, as well.

Social statistics describe society, but they are also products of our social arrangements. The people who bring social statistics to our attention have reasons for doing so; they inevitably want something, just as reporters and the other media figures who repeat and publicize statistics have their own goals. Statistics are tools, used for particular purposes. Thinking critically about statistics requires understanding their place in society.

While we may be more suspicious of statistics presented by people with whom we disagree—people who favor different political parties or have different beliefs—bad statistics are used to promote all sorts of causes. Bad statistics come from conservatives on the political right and liberals on the left, from wealthy corporations and powerful government agencies, and from advocates of the poor and the powerless.

In order to interpret statistics, we need more than a checklist of common errors. We need a general approach, an orientation, a mind-set that we can use to think about new statistics that we encounter. We ought to approach statistics thoughtfully. This can be hard to do, precisely because so many people in our society treat statistics as fetishes. We might call this the mind-set of the Awestruck—the people who don't think critically, who act as though statistics have magical powers. The awestruck know they don't always understand the statistics they hear, but this doesn't bother them. After all, who can expect to understand magical numbers? The reverential fatalism of the awestruck is not thoughtful—it is a way of avoiding thought. We need a different approach.

One choice is to approach statistics critically. Being critical does not mean being negative or hostile—it is not cynicism. The critical approach statistics thoughtfully; they avoid the extremes of both naive acceptance and cynical rejection of the numbers they encounter. Instead, the critical attempt to evaluate numbers, to distinguish between good statistics and bad statistics.

The critical understand that, while some social statistics may be pretty good, they are never perfect. Every statistic is a way of summarizing complex information into relatively simple numbers. Inevitably, some information, some of the complexity, is lost whenever we use statistics. The critical recognize that this is an inevitable limitation of statistics. Moreover, they realize that every statistic is the product of choices—the choice between defining a category broadly or narrowly, the choice of one measurement over another, the choice of a sample. People choose definitions, measurements, and samples for all sorts of reasons: Perhaps they want to emphasize some aspect of a problem; perhaps it is easier or cheaper to gather data in a particular way— many considerations can come into play. Every statistic is a compromise among choices. This means that every definition—and every measurement and every sample—probably has limitations and can be criticized.

Being critical means more than simply pointing to the flaws in a statistic. Again, every statistic has flaws. The issue is whether a particular statistic's flaws are severe enough to damage its usefulness. * * * Similarly, how do the choices of measurements and samples affect the statistic? What would happen if different measures or samples were chosen? And how is the statistic used? Is it being interpreted appropriately, or has its meaning been mangled to create a mutant statistic? Are the comparisons that are being made appropriate, or are apples being confused with oranges? How do different choices produce the conflicting numbers found in stat wars? These are the sorts of questions the critical ask.

As a practical matter, it is virtually impossible for citizens in contemporary society to avoid statistics about social problems. Statistics arise in all sorts of ways, and in almost every case the people promoting statistics want to persuade us. Activists use statistics to convince us that social problems are serious and deserve our attention and concern. Charities use statistics to encourage donations. Politicians use statistics to persuade us that they understand society's problems and that they deserve our support. The media use statistics to make their reporting more dramatic, more convincing, more compelling. Corporations use statistics to promote and improve their products. Researchers use statistics to document their findings and support their conclusions. Those with whom we agree use statistics to reassure us that we're on the right side, while our opponents use statistics to try and convince us that we are wrong. Statistics are one of the standard types of evidence used by people in our society.

It is not possible simply to ignore statistics, to pretend they don't exist. That sort of head-in-the-sand approach would be too costly. Without statistics, we limit our ability to think thoughtfully about our society; without statistics, we have no accurate ways of judging how big a problem may be, whether it is getting worse, or how well the policies designed to address that problem actually work. And awestruck or naive attitudes toward statistics are no better than ignoring statistics; statistics have no magical properties, and it is foolish to assume that all statistics are equally valid. Nor is a cynical approach the answer; statistics are too widespread and too useful to be automatically discounted.

It would be nice to have a checklist, a set of items we could consider in evaluating any statistic. The list might detail potential problems with definitions, measurements, sampling, mutation, and so on. These are, in fact, common sorts of flaws found in many statistics, but they should not be considered a formal, complete checklist. It is probably impossible to produce a complete list of statistical flaws—no matter how long the list, there will be other possible problems that could affect statistics.

The goal is not to memorize a list, but to develop a thoughtful approach. Becoming critical about statistics requires being prepared to ask questions about numbers. When encountering a new statistic in, say, a news report, the critical try to assess it. What might be the sources for this number? How could one go about producing the figure? Who produced the number, and what interests might they have? What are the different ways key terms might have been defined, and which definitions have been chosen? How might the phenomena be measured, and which measurement choices have been made? What sort of sample was gathered, and how might that sample affect the result? Is the statistic being properly interpreted? Are comparisons being made, and if so, are the comparisons appropriate? Are there competing statistics? If so, what stakes do the opponents have in the issue, and how are those stakes likely to affect their use of statistics? And is it possible to figure out why the statistics seem to disagree, what the differences are in the ways the competing sides are using figures?

At first, this list of questions may seem overwhelming. How can an ordinary person—someone who reads a statistic in a magazine article or hears it on a news broadcast—determine the answers to such questions? Certainly news reports rarely give detailed information on the process by which statistics are created. And few of us have time to drop everything and investigate the background of some new number we encounter. Being critical, it seems, involves an impossible amount of work.

In practice, however, the critical need not investigate the origin of every statistic. Rather, being critical means appreciating the inevitable limitations that affect all statistics, rather than being awestruck in the presence of numbers. It means not being too credulous, not accepting every statistic at face value. But it also means appreciating that statistics, while always imperfect, can be useful. Instead of automatically discounting every statistic, the critical reserve judgment. When confronted with an interesting number, they may try to learn more, to evaluate, to weigh the figure's strengths and weaknesses.

Of course, this critical approach need not—and should not—be limited to statistics. It ought to apply to all the evidence we encounter when we scan a news report, or listen to a speech—whenever we learn about social problems. Claims about social problems often feature dramatic, compelling examples; the critical might ask whether an example is likely to be a typical case or an extreme, exceptional instance. Claims about social problems often include quotations from different sources, and the critical might wonder why those sources have spoken and why they have been quoted: Do they have particular expertise? Do they stand to benefit if they influence others? Claims about social problems usually involve arguments about the problem's causes and potential solutions. The critical might ask whether these arguments are convincing. Are they logical? Does the proposed solution seem feasible and appropriate? And so on. Being critical—adopting a skeptical, analytical stance when confronted with claims—is an approach that goes far beyond simply dealing with statistics.

Statistics are not magical. Nor are they always true—or always false. Nor need they be incomprehensible. Adopting a critical approach offers an effective way of responding to the numbers we are sure to encounter. Being critical requires more thought, but failing to adopt a critical mind-set makes us powerless to evaluate what others tell us. When we fail to think critically, the statistics we hear might just as well be magical.

7

Public Sociologies:
Contradictions, Dilemmas, and Possibilities

MICHAEL BURAWOY

Since the middle of the nineteenth century, social scientists have been asking about the influence of their work on society. Should it contribute to social order and stability? Should it address problems and seek to devise solutions? Or should it promote social change that could lead to a new and more progressive form of society? One view of science is that the best research is guided by idle curiosity, while another argues that necessity and crisis spur the greatest discoveries. Some scholars embrace their work with personal passion, while others believe scientific objectivity is compromised by too much emotional investment. Sociology is not immune to these debates. This article, a version of the presidential address to the American Sociological Association, again raises the question the great sociologist Howard Becker asked years ago, "Whose side are you on?"

In 2003 the members of the American Sociological Association (ASA) were asked to vote on a member resolution opposing the war in Iraq. The resolution included the following justification: "[F]oreign interventions that do not have the support of the world community create more problems than solutions . . . Instead of lessening the risk of terrorist attacks, this invasion could serve as the spark for multiple attacks in years to come." It passed by a two-thirds majority (with 22% of voting members abstaining) and became the association's official position. In an opinion poll on the same ballot, 75% of the members who expressed an opinion were opposed to the war. To assess the ethos of sociologists today, it is worthwhile comparing these results with those of 1968 when a similar double item was presented to the membership with respect to the Vietnam war. Then two-thirds of the votes cast *opposed* the ASA adopting a resolution against the war and only 54% were individually opposed to the war (Rhoades 1981:60).

It is complicated to interpret this apparent shift in political orientation, given the different national and military contexts within which the voting took place, given the different wording of the questions. Still two hypotheses present themselves. First, the membership of the ASA, always leaning toward the liberal end of the political spectrum, has moved much further to the left. In 1968 the opinion of sociologists was close to the rest of the population (54% of sociologists opposed the war as compared to between 46% and 54% of the general public), whereas in 2003 the two distributions were the inverse of each other—75% of voting sociologists opposed the war at the end of April, 2003, while at the same time 75% of the public supported the war. One might conjecture that in 1968 a very different generation dominated the profession—a postwar generation celebratory of the U.S. and its "victory over fascism," among them pioneers of professional sociology. Today's post-Vietnam generations are more accustomed to criticizing the U.S. government and in particular its foreign policy. They are also less concerned about the purity of sociology as science and more likely to assume that our accumulated knowledge should be put to public use, whether in the form of member resolutions or policy interventions.

Second, the world itself is different. In 1968 the world seemed ripe for change for the better. The civil rights movements, the women's movement, student movements around the world, antiwar marches and sit-ins captured the imagination of a new generation of sociologists who saw conventional sociology as lagging behind the most progressive movements; whereas today the world is lagging behind sociology, unapologetic about its drift into political and economic fundamentalism. Sociologists shift their critical eye ever more away from sociology toward the world it describes, a shift reflected in the insurgent interest in public sociology. In short, over the last 35 years there has been a scissors movement. The political context and the sociological conscience have moved in opposite directions, so that the world we inhabit is increasingly in conflict with the ethos and principles that animate sociologists—an ethos opposed to inequality, to the erosion of civil liberties, to the destruction of public life, and to discrimination and exclusion.

This shift in sociological ethos is not uncontroversial. It has, indeed, generated its own opposition. Dissatisfied with the political winds, 102 ASA members signed a petition, sent to the association's Committee on Professional Ethics, charging that the anti-Iraq-war resolution violated the ASA's code of conduct. Why? Because it did not rely on "scientifically and professionally derived knowledge." The complaint did not get far because, unlike other professional associations, there are no clear rules that limit the types of resolutions the ASA can endorse. Nonetheless, the 102 (and presumably many others) did take a principled position: scientific sociologists have no business making moral or political pronouncements. Taking a moral or political position is incompatible with scientific objectivity. Opposition to the resolution also took a more pragmatic form, fears that such a visible and public stance against the war (and I have not found another association to have taken such a stance) would undermine what legitimacy we have as sociologists, conceivably threaten research funding, and even prompt political reprisals. Alas, this is not so far fetched. * * *

The "pure science" position that research must be completely insulated from politics is untenable since antipolitics is no less political than *public engagement*. The more usual "abstentionist" position limits politics to *professional self-defense*: that we should enter the political arena only to defend our immediate professional interests. Thus, we might mobilize resources to oppose the defunding of research into sexual behavior (as was attempted in Congress recently), or to protest the closure or dramatic cuts in a sociology department (as in Germany today), or to protect the human rights of an individual (e.g., Egyptian sociologist, Saad Eddin Ibrahim), or, most recently, to defend a journal's right to review and edit articles from "enemy" countries. In all these instances we enter the political arena, but solely to defend the integrity of our professional activities.

Between professional self-defense and public engagement there is a compromise position that moves from the defense of professional interests to *policy interventions*. Here the association takes a political position on the basis of an accumulated body of evidence whose validity is widely accepted and whose interpretation is unambiguous. One such example is the ASA's recent statement that summarized the sociological literature on race: race exists, it has social causes, and it has social consequences. An extension of this was the ASA's Amicus Curiae brief to the Supreme Court in the 2003 Michigan Law School affirmative action case, *Grutter* v. *Bollinger*. Again a body of sociological research was mobilized to show that racial discrimination exists and that efforts to diversify the student body would improve the educational experience of all.

So far, then, we have three possible political stances: "professional self-defense," "policy intervention" and "public engagement." There is, however, a fourth stance. The association is a political venue unto itself—a place to debate the stances we might adopt. We cannot advocate democracy for others if we are not internally democratic, if we do not attempt to arrive at public stances through maximal participation in collective deliberation. It is just such a critical debate that we are involved in today. The resolution against the Iraq War is but a dramatic instance of the broader issue we are discussing: what should be our involvement in the world beyond the academy? Recognizing we are part of the world we study, we must take some *stance* with respect to that world. To fail to do so is to take a stance by default.

We can problematize our place in society by asking two questions. The first was posed by Alfred McClung Lee in his 1976 Presidential Address to the American Sociological Association: "Knowledge for Whom?" As sociologists are we just talking to ourselves? Are we to remain locked up in the antechambers of society, never really entering its tumultuous currents, hiding behind the barricades of professional insularity? Or can we, ever cautious, ever vigilant, wade forth into society, armed with our sociological expertise? If we are going to talk to others, which others and how shall we do it? This leads directly to the second question, famously posed by Robert Lynd (1939): Knowledge for What? Do we take the values and goals of our research for granted, handed down to us by some external (funding or policy) agency? Should we only concentrate on providing solutions to predefined problems, focusing on the means to achieve predetermined ends, on what Weber called technical rationality and what I call *instrumental knowledge?* In other words, should we repress the question of ends and pretend that knowledge and laws spring spontaneously from the data, if only we can develop the right methods? Or should we be concerned explicitly with the goals for which our research may be mobilized, and with the values that underpin and guide our research? Going further afield, should sociologists be in the business of stimulating public discussions about the possible meanings of the "good society"? Like Weber, I believe that without value commitments there can be no sociology, no basis for the questions that guide our research programs. Without values social science is blind. * * * Thus, empirical science can only take us so far: it can help us understand the consequences of our value commitments and inform our value discussions, but it cannot determine those values. Determining values should take place through democratic and collective deliberation.

* * * Professional and policy sociology are forms of instrumental knowledge focusing respectively on academic and extra-academic audiences. Critical and public sociology are forms of reflexive knowledge focusing respectively on academic and extra-academic audiences. Let me consider each in turn.

Public sociology engages publics beyond the academy in dialogue about matters of political and moral concern. It has to be relevant to such publics without being faddish, that is subservient to publics. * * *

* * *

Public sociology should be distinguished from *policy sociology.* While public sociology generates conversation or debate between sociologist and public on a terrain of reciprocal engagement, policy sociology focuses on solutions to specific problems defined by clients. The relation between sociologist and client is often of a contractual character in which expertise is sold for a fee. The sociologist, thereby, cedes independence to the client. All manner of organizations may contract sociological expertise, from business to state, from multilateral organization to the small NGO [nongovernmental organization]. What makes the relation instrumental is that the research terrain is not defined by the sociologist. It is defined narrowly in the case of a "client" or broadly in the case of a "patron."

* * *

Public and policy sociologies could not exist without *professional sociology,* which provides legitimacy, expertise, distinctive problem definitions, relevant bodies of knowledge, and techniques for analyzing data. An effective public or policy sociology is not hostile to, but depends upon the professional sociology that lies at the core of our disciplinary field. Why do I call our disciplinary knowledge instrumental? As professional sociologists we are located in research traditions, sometimes going back to founding fathers (Weber, Durkheim, and Marx) and otherwise of a more recent pedigree (feminism, poststructuralism). These research traditions may be elaborated into self-conscious research programs—structural functionalism, stratification theory, sex-gender systems, experimental social psychology—with their grounding assumptions, distinctive questions, exemplary models and appropriate techniques of research. Research programs (Lakatos 1978) advance by resolving internal contradictions and absorbing anomalies (discrepancies between theoretical expectation and empirical observations). They require a community of scientists committed to working on the important (collectively defined) *puzzles* that the research program generates. Flourishing public and policy sociologies increase the stakes of our knowledge and thus makes the vigilant pursuit of coherent research programs all the more important.

In the world of normal science we cannot push forward the frontiers of knowledge and at the same time question its foundations. The latter task is the province of *critical sociology*. In much the same way that public sociology interrogates the value assumptions of policy sociology, so in a similar and more direct way critical sociology is the conscience of professional sociology.

* * *

As sociology grew, its institutional base differentiated, so that today sociologists work both inside and outside academia. Those outside tend to occupy positions in government agencies, such as the census bureau or the department of corrections; in consulting companies for human resource management; or in international NGOs. Then, there are sociologists who are employed in professional schools—business schools, public administration, educational schools, agricultural extension, and so forth—where they may engage nonacademic audiences. Equally important is the complex hierarchy of the university system which ranges from elite private universities, to the different tiers of state university systems, liberal arts colleges, and two-year community colleges. The configuration of the division of sociological labor will vary with a departments location in this system. Thus, in state colleges where teaching takes up so much of one's time, research has a public or policy dimension, often driven by local issues. Based on my attendance at the meetings of state associations, such as the North Carolina Sociological Association, I have found public sociology to be both more widely practiced and more highly valued in state colleges than in most elite departments. I have found projects ranging from research on displaced workers, toxic waste, housing inequalities, and educational reform, to advocacy for public health campaigns around HIV-AIDS or needle exchange to training community organizers to deal with the media. Sadly, all too often, this public (and policy) sociology, widespread though it may be, remains invisible and unrecognized because its practitioners lack the time or incentive to write it up.

History and hierarchy give one sense of the possible variation in the configuration of the disciplinary field, international comparisons give another. When one travels the world talking about public sociology, one quickly learns just how distinctively American the concept is, marking the unique strength of professional sociology in the U.S. In many countries it is taken for granted that sociology has a public face. Why else be a sociologist? The career of sociology in many Third World countries reflects the succession of different political regimes. One of the first acts of the Pinochet regime in Chile was to abolish sociology. In South Africa sociology flourished in the late 1970s and 1980s as the anti-apartheid movement grew in strength, just as it has suffered amalgamation and budgetary cuts in the postapartheid period. Soviet sociology, nonexistent under Stalinism, reappeared in the 1950s as an ideological and surveillance arm of the party state. Sociological opinion research was deployed as a weapon of critique, revealing public discontent in order to justify swings in policy. This instrumental use of sociology comes home to roost in the post-Soviet period where, increasingly, it has become a form of market research. If it is not co-opted or repressed by authoritarian regimes, sociology's reflexive side may sustain critical opposition, as was often the case in Eastern Europe. In the social democratic countries of Scandinavia, by contrast, it is the policy dimension that often stands out. Although when conservative parties assume power, the sociological winds shift direction from policy to public.

Here then are just a few hints at national variation, underlining once again just how peculiar is U.S. sociology. It is not just peculiar, it is also very powerful, dominating the world scene. Accordingly in the international division of sociological labor, professional sociology is concentrated in the resource rich United States, and to a lesser extent in Western Europe, while public sociology has relatively greater strength in the poorer countries—a distribution that mirrors the hierarchy within the U.S.

* * *

Finally, we come to the critical question: what are the grounds for claiming sociology's affinity to the public? If political science's distinctive object of study is the state and its value the protection of political order, and if economics has as it distinctive object the economy and its value is the expansion of the market, then sociology's distinctive object is civil society and its value is the resilience and autonomy of the social. Sociology is born with civil society and dies with civil society. The classical sociology of Weber, Durkheim, Simmel, and Pareto arose with the expansion of trade unions, political parties, mass education, voluntary associations at the end of the nineteenth century, just as U.S. sociology was born amidst reform and religious organizations. Sociology disappears with the eclipse of civil society as in fascism, Stalinism or Pinochet's Chile, just as it quickly bubbles to the surface with the unfurling of perestroika in the Soviet Union or the civic and labor associations of South Africa's anti-apartheid movement.

* * *

The burgeoning interest in public sociology and the unanticipated vote against the war in Iraq suggest to me that the stakes are indeed becoming clearer. In a world tending toward market tyranny and state unilateralism, civil society is at once threatened with extinction and at the same time a major possible hold-out against deepening inequalities and multiplying threats to all manner of human rights. The interest of sociology in the very existence, let alone expansion, of civil society (even with all its warts) becomes the interest of humanity—locally, nationally and globally. If we can transcend our parochialism and recognize our distinctive relation to diverse publics within and across borders, sociologists could yet create the fulcrum around which a critical social science might evolve, one responsive to public issues while at the same time committed to professional excellence.

REFERENCES

Lakatos, Imre. 1978. *The Methodology of Scientific Research Programmes.* Cambridge University Press.

Lee, Alfred McClung. 1976. "Sociology for Whom?" *American Sociological Review* 44: 925–36.

Lynd, Robert. 1939. *Knowledge for What? The Place of Social Sciences in American Culture.* Princeton University Press.

Rhoades, Lawrence. 1981. *A History of the American Sociological Association, 1905–1980.* American Sociological Association, Washington D.C.

8

Racism and Research:
The Case of the Tuskegee Syphilis Study

ALLAN M. BRANDT

Was it scientific zeal and the search for medical knowledge? Or was it a callous disregard for the lives and suffering of persons thought to be inferior in a racist society? Probably both, and the lessons remain important for everyone. This tragic study has become a classic example of how to do unethical research. Perhaps the lessons to be learned from it can somehow begin to make amends for the harm it did.

In 1932 the U.S. Public Health Service (USPHS) initiated an experiment in Macon County, Alabama, to determine the natural course of untreated, latent syphilis in black males. The test comprised 400 syphilitic men, as well as 200 uninfected men who served as controls. The first published report of the study appeared in 1936 with subsequent papers issued every four to six years, through the 1960s. When penicillin became widely available by the early 1950s as the preferred treatment for syphilis, the men did not receive therapy. In fact on several occasions, the USPHS actually sought to prevent treatment. Moreover, a committee at the federally operated Center for Disease Control decided in 1969 that the study should be continued. Only in 1972, when accounts of the study first appeared in the national press, did the Department of Health, Education, and Welfare halt the experiment. At that time seventy-four of the test subjects were still alive; at least twenty-eight, but perhaps more than 100, had died directly from advanced syphilitic lesions. In August 1972, HEW appointed an investigatory panel, which issued a report the following year. The panel found the study to have been "ethically unjustified," and argued that penicillin should have been provided to the men.

This article attempts to place the Tuskegee Study in a historical context and to assess its ethical implications. Despite the media attention which the study received, the HEW *Final Report,* and the criticism expressed by several professional organizations, the experiment has been largely misunderstood. The most basic questions of *how* the study was undertaken in the first place and *why* it continued for forty years were never addressed by the HEW investigation. Moreover, the panel misconstrued the nature of the experiment, failing to consult important documents available at the National Archives which bear significantly on its ethical assessment. Only by examining the specific ways in which values are engaged in scientific research can the study be understood.

RACISM AND MEDICAL OPINION

A brief review of the prevailing scientific thought regarding race and heredity in the early twentieth century is fundamental for an understanding of the Tuskegee Study. By the turn of the century, Darwinism had provided a new rationale for American racism. Essentially primitive peoples, it was argued, could not be assimilated into a complex, white civilization. Scientists speculated that in the struggle for survival the Negro in America was doomed. Particularly prone to disease, vice, and crime, black Americans could not be helped by education or philanthropy. Social Darwinists analyzed census data to predict the virtual extinction of the Negro in the twentieth century, for they believed the Negro race in America was in the throes of a degenerative evolutionary process.

The medical profession supported these findings of late nineteenth- and early twentieth-century anthropologists, ethnologists, and biologists. Physicians studying the effects of emancipation on health concluded almost universally that freedom had caused the mental, moral, and physical deterioration of the black population. They substantiated this argument by citing examples in the comparative anatomy of the black and white races. As Dr. W. T. English wrote: "A careful inspection reveals the body of the negro a mass of minor defects and imperfections from the crown of the head to the soles of the feet. . . ." Cranial structures, wide nasal apertures, receding chins, projecting jaws, all typed the Negro as the lowest species in the Darwinian hierarchy.

Interest in racial differences centered on the sexual nature of blacks. The Negro, doctors explained, possessed an excessive sexual desire, which threatened the very foundations of white society. As one physician noted in the *Journal of the American Medical Association,* "The negro springs from a southern race, and as such his sexual appetite is strong; all of his environments stimulate this appetite, and as a general rule his emotional type of religion certainly does not decrease it." Doctors reported a complete lack of morality on the part of blacks:

> Virtue in the negro race is like angels' visits—few and far between. In a practice
> of sixteen years I have never examined a virgin negro over fourteen years of age.

A particularly ominous feature of this overzealous sexuality, doctors argued, was the black males' desire for white women. "A perversion from which most races are exempt," wrote Dr. English, "prompts the negro's inclination towards white women, whereas other races incline towards females of their own." Though English estimated the "gray matter of the negro brain" to be at least a thousand years behind that of the white races, his genital organs were overdeveloped. As Dr. William Lee Howard noted:

> The attacks on defenseless white women are evidences of racial instincts that
> are about as amenable to ethical culture as is the inherent odor of the race. . . .

When education will reduce the size of the negro's penis as well as bring about the sensitiveness of the terminal fibers which exist in the Caucasian, then will it also be able to prevent the African's birth-right to sexual madness and excess.

One southern medical journal proposed "Castration Instead of Lynching," as retribution for black sexual crimes. "An impressive trial by a ghost-like kuklux klan [sic] and a 'ghost' physician or surgeon to perform the operation would make it an event the 'patient' would never forget," noted the editorial.

According to these physicians, lust and immorality, unstable families, and reversion to barbaric tendencies made blacks especially prone to venereal diseases. One doctor estimated that over 50 percent of all Negroes over the age of twenty-five were syphilitic. Virtually free of disease as slaves, they were now overwhelmed by it, according to informed medical opinion. More-over, doctors believed that treatment for venereal disease among blacks was impossible, particularly because in its latent stage the symptoms of syphilis become quiescent. As Dr. Thomas W. Murrell wrote:

> They come for treatment at the beginning and at the end. When there are visible manifestations or when harried by pain, they readily come, for as a race they are not averse to physic; but tell them not, though they look well and feel well, that they are still diseased. Here ignorance rates science a fool . . .

Even the best-educated black, according to Murrell, could not be convinced to seek treatment for syphilis. Venereal disease, according to some doctors, threatened the future of the race. The medical profession attributed the low birth rate among blacks to the high prevalence of venereal disease, which caused stillbirths and miscarriages. Moreover, the high rates of syphilis were thought to lead to increased insanity and crime. One doctor writing at the turn of the century estimated that the number of insane Negroes had increased thirteen-fold since the end of the Civil War. Dr. Murrell's conclusion echoed the most informed anthropological and ethnological data:

> So the scourge sweeps among them. Those that are treated are only half cured, and the effort to assimilate a complex civilization driving their diseased minds until the results are criminal records. Perhaps here, in conjunction with tuber-culosis, will be the end of the negro problem. Disease will accomplish what man cannot do.

This particular configuration of ideas formed the core of medical opinion concerning blacks, sex, and disease in the early twentieth century. Doctors generally discounted socioeconomic explanations of the state of black health, arguing that better medical care could not alter the evolutionary scheme. These assumptions provide the backdrop for examining the Tuskegee Syphilis Study.

THE ORIGINS OF THE EXPERIMENT

In 1929, under a grant from the Julius Rosenwald Fund, the USPHS conducted studies in the rural South to determine the prevalence of syphilis among blacks and explore possibilities for mass treatment. The USPHS found Macon County, Alabama, in which the town of Tuskegee is located, to have the highest syphilis rate of the six counties surveyed. The Rosenwald Study concluded that mass treatment could be successfully implemented among rural blacks. Although it is doubtful that the necessary funds would have been allocated even in the best economic conditions, after the economy collapsed in 1929, the findings were ignored. It is, however, ironic that the Tuskegee Study came to be based on findings of the Rosenwald Study that demonstrated the possibilities of mass treatment.

Three years later, in 1932, Dr. Taliaferro Clark, Chief of the USPHS Venereal Disease Division and author of the Rosenwald Study report, decided that conditions in Macon County merited renewed attention. Clark believed the high prevalence of syphilis offered an "unusual opportunity" for observation. From its inception, the USPHS regarded the Tuskegee Study as a classic "study in nature,"[1] rather than an experiment. As long as syphilis was so prevalent in Macon and most of the blacks went untreated throughout life, it seemed only natural to Clark that it would be valuable to observe the consequences. He described it as a "ready-made situation." Surgeon General H. S. Cumming wrote to R. R. Moton, Director of the Tuskegee Institute:

> The recent syphilis control demonstration carried out in Macon County, with the financial assistance of the Julius Rosenwald Fund, revealed the presence of an unusually high rate in this county and, what is more remarkable, the fact that 99 percent of this group was entirely without previous treatment. This combination, together with the expected cooperation of your hospital, offers an unparalleled opportunity for carrying on this piece of scientific research which probably cannot be duplicated anywhere else in the world.

Although no formal protocol appears to have been written, several letters of Clark and Cumming suggest what the USPHS hoped to find. Clark indicated that it would be important to see how disease affected the daily lives of the men:

---

1. In 1865, Claude Bernard, the famous French physiologist, outlined the distinction between a "study in nature" and experimentation. A study in nature required simple observation, an essentially passive act, while experimentation demanded intervention which altered the original condition. The Tuskegee Study was thus clearly not a study in nature. The very act of diagnosis altered the original conditions. "It is on this very possibility of acting or not acting on a body," wrote Bernard, "that the distinction will exclusively rest between sciences called sciences of observation and sciences called experimental."

The results of these studies of case records suggest the desirability of making a further study of the effect of untreated syphilis on the human economy among people now living and engaged in their daily pursuits.

It also seems that the USPHS believed the experiment might demonstrate that antisyphilitic treatment was unnecessary. As Cumming noted: "It is expected the results of this study may have a marked bearing on the treatment, or conversely the non-necessity of treatment, of cases of latent syphilis. . . ."

SELECTING THE SUBJECTS

Clark sent Dr. Raymond Vonderlehr to Tuskegee in September 1932 to assemble a sample of men with latent syphilis for the experiment. The basic design of the study called for the selection of syphilitic black males between the ages of twenty-five and sixty, a thorough physical examination including x-rays, and finally, a spinal tap to determine the incidence of neuro-syphilis. They had no intention of providing any treatment for the infected men. The USPHS originally scheduled the whole experiment to last six months; it seemed to be both a simple and inexpensive project.

The task of collecting the sample, however, proved to be more difficult than the USPHS had supposed. Vonderlehr canvassed the largely illiterate, poverty-stricken population of sharecroppers and tenant farmers in search of test subjects. If his circulars requested only men over twenty-five to attend his clinics, none would appear, suspecting he was conducting draft physicals. Therefore, he was forced to test large numbers of women and men who did not fit the experiments specifications. This involved considerable expense since the USPHS had promised the Macon County Board of Health that it would treat those who were infected, but not included in the study. Clark wrote to Vonderlehr about the situation: "It never once occured to me that we would be called upon to treat a large part of the county as return for the privilege of making this study. . . . I am anxious to keep the expenditures for treatment down to the lowest possible point because it is the one item of expenditure in connection with the study most difficult to defend despite our knowledge of the need therefor." Vonderlehr responded: "If we could find from 100 to 200 cases . . . we would not have to do another Wassermann on useless individuals. . . ."

Significantly, the attempt to develop the sample contradicted the prediction the USPHS had made initially regarding the prevalence of the disease in Macon County. Overall rates of syphilis fell well below expectations; as opposed to the USPHS projection of 35 percent, 20 percent of those tested were actually diseased. Moreover, those who had sought and received previous treatment far exceeded the expectations of the USPHS. Clark noted in a letter to Vonderlehr:

I find your report of March 6th quite interesting but regret the necessity for Wassermanning [sic] . . . such a large number of individuals in order to uncover this relatively limited number of untreated cases.

Further difficulties arose in enlisting the subjects to participate in the experiment, to be "Wassermanned," and to return for a subsequent series of examinations. Vonderlehr found that only the offer of treatment elicited the cooperation of the men. They were told they were ill and were promised free care. Offered therapy, they became willing subjects. The USPHS did not tell the men that they were participants in an experiment; on the contrary, the subjects believed they were being treated for "bad blood"—the rural South's colloquialism for syphilis. They thought they were participating in a public health demonstration similar to the one that had been conducted by the Julius Rosenwald Fund in Tuskegee several years earlier. In the end, the men were so eager for medical care that the number of defaulters in the experiment proved to be insignificant.

To preserve the subjects' interest, Vonderlehr gave most of the men mercurial ointment, a noneffective drug, while some of the younger men apparently received inadequate dosages of neoarsphenamine. This required Vonderlehr to write frequently to Clark requesting supplies. He feared the experiment would fail if the men were not offered treatment.

* * *

The readiness of the test subjects to participate of course contradicted the notion that blacks would not seek or continue therapy.

The final procedure of the experiment was to be a spinal tap to test for evidence of neuro-syphilis. The USPHS presented this purely diagnostic exam, which often entails considerable pain and complications, to the men as a "special treatment." Clark explained to Moore:

> We have not yet commenced the spinal punctures. This operation will be deferred to the last in order not to unduly disturb our field work by any adverse reports by the patients subjected to spinal puncture because of some disagreeable sensations following this procedure. These negroes are very ignorant and easily influenced by things that would be of minor significance in a more intelligent group.

The letter to the subjects announcing the spinal tap read:

> Some time ago you were given a thorough examination and since that time we hope you have gotten a great deal of treatment for bad blood. You will now be given your last chance to get a second examination. This examination is a very special one and after it is finished you will be given a special treatment if it is believed you are in a condition to stand it. . . .
>
> REMEMBER THIS IS YOUR LAST CHANCE FOR SPECIAL FREE TREATMENT. BE SURE TO MEET THE NURSE.

The HEW investigation did not uncover this crucial fact: the men participated in the study under the guise of treatment.

Despite the fact that their assumption regarding prevalence and black attitudes toward treatment had proved wrong, the USPHS decided in the summer of 1933 to continue the study. Once again, it seemed only "natural" to
pursue the research since the sample already existed, and with a depressed
economy, the cost of treatment appeared prohibitive—although there is no
indication it was ever considered. Vonderlehr first suggested extending the
study in letters to Clark and Wenger:

> At the end of this project we shall have a considerable number of cases present-
> ing various complications of syphilis, who have received only mercury and may
> still be considered untreated in the modern sense of therapy. Should these cases
> be followed over a period of from five to ten years many interesting facts could
> be learned regarding the course and complications of untreated syphilis.

"As I see it," responded Wenger, "we have no further interest in these
patients *until they die.*" Apparently, the physicians engaged in the experiment
believed that only autopsies could scientifically confirm the findings of the
study.

Bringing the men to autopsy required the USPHS to devise a further series
of deceptions and inducements. Wenger warned Vonderlehr that the men
must not realize that they would be autopsied:

> There is one danger in the latter plan and that is if the colored population be-
> come aware that accepting free hospital care means a postmortem; every dar-
> key will leave Macon County and it will hurt [Dr. Eugene] Dibble's hospital.

The USPHS offered several inducements to maintain contact and to pro-
cure the continued cooperation of the men. Eunice Rivers, a black nurse, was
hired to follow their health and to secure approval for autopsies. She gave the
men non-effective medicines—"spring tonic" and aspirin—as well as transportation and hot meals on the days of their examinations. More important,
Nurse Rivers provided continuity to the project over the entire forty-year
period. By supplying "medicinals," the USPHS was able to continue to deceive
the participants, who believed that they were receiving therapy from the government doctors. Deceit was integral to the study. When the test subjects
complained about spinal taps one doctor wrote:

> They simply do not like spinal punctures. A few of those who were tapped are
> enthusiastic over the results but to most, the suggestion causes violent shaking
> of the head; others claim they were robbed of their procreative powers (regard-
> less of the fact that I claim it stimulates them).

Letters to the subjects announcing an impending USPHS visit to Tuskegee
explained: "[The doctor] wants to make a special examination to find out how

you have been feeling and whether the treatment has improved your health." In fact, after the first six months of the study, the USPHS had furnished no treatment whatsoever.

Finally, because it proved difficult to persuade the men to come to the hospital when they became severely ill, the USPHS promised to cover their burial expenses. The Milbank Memorial Fund provided approximately $50 per man for this purpose beginning in 1935. This was a particularly strong inducement as funeral rites constituted an important component of the cultural life of rural blacks. One report of the study concluded. "Without this suasion it would, we believe, have been impossible to secure the cooperation of the group and their families."

Reports of the study's findings, which appeared regularly in the medical press beginning in 1936, consistently cited the ravages of untreated syphilis. The first paper, read at the 1936 American Medical Association annual meeting, found "that syphilis in this period [latency] tends to greatly increase the frequency of manifestations of cardiovascular disease." Only 16 percent of the subjects gave no sign of morbidity as opposed to 61 percent of the controls. Ten years later, a report noted coldly, "The fact that nearly twice as large a proportion of the syphilitic individuals as of the control group has died is a very striking one." Life expectancy, concluded the doctors, is reduced by about 20 percent.

A 1955 article found that slightly more than 30 percent of the test group autopsied had died *directly* from advanced syphilitic lesions of either the cardiovascular or the central nervous system. Another published account stated, "Review of those still living reveals that an appreciable number have late complications of syphilis which probably will result, for some at least, in contributing materially to the ultimate cause of death." In 1950, Dr. Wenger had concluded, "We now know, where we could only surmise before, that we have contributed to their ailments and shortened their lives." As black physician Vernal Cave, a member of the HEW panel, later wrote, "They proved a point, then proved a point, then proved a point."

During the forty years of the experiment the USPHS had sought on several occasions to ensure that the subjects did not receive treatment from other sources. To this end, Vonderlehr met with groups of local black doctors in 1934, to ask their cooperation in not treating the men. Lists of subjects were distributed to Macon County physicians along with letters requesting them to refer these men back to the USPHS if they sought care. The USPHS warned the Alabama Health Department not to treat the test subjects when they took a mobile VD unit into Tuskegee in the early 1940s. In 1941, the Army drafted several subjects and told them to begin antisyphilitic treatment immediately. The USPHS supplied the draft board with a list of 256 names they desired to have excluded from treatment, and the board complied.

In spite of these efforts, by the early 1950s many of the men had secured some treatment on their own. By 1952, almost 30 percent of the test subjects had received some penicillin, although only 7.5 percent had received what could be considered adequate doses. Vonderlehr wrote to one of the participating physicians, "I hope that the availability of antibiotics has not interfered too much with this project." A report published in 1955 considered whether the treatment that some of the men had obtained had "defeated" the study. The article attempted to explain the relatively low exposure to penicillin in an age of antibiotics, suggesting as a reason: "the stoicism of these men as a group; they still regard hospitals and medicines with suspicion and prefer an occasional dose of time-honored herbs or tonics to modern drugs." The authors failed to note that the men believed they already were under the care of the government doctors and thus saw no need to seek treatment elsewhere. Any treatment which the men might have received, concluded the report, had been insufficient to compromise the experiment.

When the USPHS evaluated the status of the study in the 1960s they continued to rationalize the racial aspects of the experiment. For example, the minutes of a 1965 meeting at the Center for Disease Control recorded:

> Racial issue was mentioned briefly. Will not affect the study. Any questions can be handled by saying these people were at the point that therapy would no longer help them. They are getting better medical care than they would under any other circumstances.

A group of physicians met again at the CDC in 1969 to decide whether or not to terminate the study. Although one doctor argued that the study should be stopped and the men treated, the consensus was to continue. Dr. J. Lawton Smith remarked, "You will never have another study like this; take advantage of it." A memo prepared by Dr. James B. Lucas, Assistant Chief of the Venereal Disease Branch, stated: "Nothing learned will prevent, find, or cure a single case of infectious syphilis or bring us closer to our basic mission of controlling veneral disease in the United States." He concluded, however, that the study should be continued "along its present lines." When the first accounts of the experiment appeared in the national press in July 1972, data were still being collected and autopsies performed.

THE NEW FINAL REPORT

HEW finally formed the Tuskegee Syphilis Study Ad Hoc Advisory Panel on August 28, 1972, in response to criticism that the press descriptions of the experiment had triggered. The panel, composed of nine members, five of them black, concentrated on two issues. First, was the study justified in 1932 and had the men given their informed consent? Second, should penicillin have been provided when it became available in the early 1950s? The panel was also charged with determining if the study should be terminated and assessing current policies regarding experimentation with human subjects. The group issued their report in June 1973.

By focusing on the issues of penicillin therapy and informed consent, the *Final Report* and the investigation betrayed a basic misunderstanding of the experiment's purposes and design. The HEW report implied that the failure to provide penicillin constituted the study's major ethical misjudgment; implicit was the assumption that no adequate therapy existed prior to penicillin. Nonetheless medical authorities firmly believed in the efficacy of arsenotherapy for treating syphilis at the time of the experiments inception in 1932. The panel further failed to recognize that the entire study had been predicated on nontreatment. Provision of effective medication would have violated the rationale of the experiment—to study the natural course of the disease until death. On several occasions, in fact, the USPHS had prevented the men from receiving proper treatment. Indeed, there is no evidence that the USPHS ever considered providing penicillin.

The other focus of the *Final Report*—informed consent—also served to obscure the historical facts of the experiment. In light of the deceptions and exploitations which the experiment perpetrated, it is an understatement to declare, as the *Report* did, that the experiment was "ethically unjustified," because it failed to obtain informed consent from the subjects. The *Final Report's* statement, "Submitting voluntarily is not informed consent," indicated that the panel believed that the men had volunteered *for the experiment.* The records in the National Archives make clear that the men did not submit voluntarily to an experiment; they were told and they believed that they were getting free treatment from expert government doctors for a serious disease. The failure of the HEW *Final Report* to expose this critical fact—that the USPHS lied to the subjects—calls into question the thoroughness and credibility of their investigation.

Failure to place the study in a historical context also made it impossible for the investigation to deal with the essentially racist nature of the experiment. The panel treated the study as an aberration, well-intentioned but misguided. Moreover, concern that the *Final Report* might be viewed as a critique of human experimentation in general seems to have severely limited the scope of the inquiry. The *Final Report* is quick to remind the reader on two occasions: "The position of the Panel must not be construed to be a general repudiation of scientific research with human subjects." The *Report* assures as that a better-designed experiment could have been justified:

> It is possible that a scientific study in 1932 of untreated syphilis, properly conceived with a clear protocol and conducted with suitable subjects who fully understood the implications of their involvement, might have been justified in the pre-penicillin era. This is especially true when one considers the uncertain nature of the results of treatment of late latent syphilis and the highly toxic nature of therapeutic agents then available.

This statement is questionable in view of the proven dangers of untreated syphilis known in 1932.

Since the publication of the HEW *Final Report,* a defense of the Tuskegee Study has emerged. These arguments, most clearly articulated by Dr. R. H. Kampmeier in the *Southern Medical Journal,* center on the limited knowledge of effective therapy for latent syphilis when the experiment began. Kampmeier argues that by 1950, penicillin would have been of no value for these men. Others have suggested that the men were fortunate to have been spared the highly toxic treatments of the earlier period. Moreover, even these contemporary defenses assume that the men never would have been treated anyway. As Dr. Charles Barnett of Stanford University wrote in 1974, "The lack of treatment was not contrived by the USPHS but was an established fact of which they proposed to take advantage." Several doctors who participated in the study continued to justify the experiment. Dr. J. R. Heller, who on one occasion had referred to the test subjects as the "Ethiopian population," told reporters in 1972:

> I don't see why they should be shocked or horrified. There was no racial side to this. It just happened to be in a black community. I feel this was a perfectly straightforward study, perfectly ethical, with controls. Part of our mission as physicians is to find out what happens to individuals with disease and without disease.

These apologies, as well as the HEW *Final Report,* ignore many of the essential ethical issues which the study poses. The Tuskegee Study reveals the persistence of beliefs within the medical profession about the nature of blacks, sex, and disease—beliefs that had tragic repercussions long after their alleged "scientific" bases were known to be incorrect. Most strikingly, the entire health of a community was jeopardized by leaving a communicable disease untreated. There can be little doubt that the Tuskegee researchers regarded their subjects as less than human. As a result, the ethical canons of experimenting on human subjects were completely disregarded.

The study also raises significant questions about professional self-regulation and scientific bureaucracy. Once the USPHS decided to extend the experiment in the summer of 1933, it was unlikely that the test would be halted short of the men's deaths. The experiment was widely reported for forty years without evoking any significant protest within the medical community. Nor did any bureaucratic mechanism exist within the government for the periodic reassessment of the Tuskegee experiment's ethics and scientific value. The USPHS sent physicians to Tuskegee every several years to check on the study's progress, but never subjected the morality or usefulness of the experiment to serious scrutiny. Only the press accounts of 1972 finally punctured the continued rationalizations of the USPHS and brought the study to an end. Even the HEW investigation was compromised by fear that it would be considered a threat to future human experimentation.

In retrospect the Tuskegee Study revealed more about the pathology of racism than it did about the pathology of syphilis; more about the nature of scientific inquiry than the nature of the disease process. The injustice committed by the experiment went well beyond the facts outlined in the press and the HEW *Final Report*. The degree of deception and damages have been seriously underestimated. As this history of the study suggests, the notion that science is a value-free discipline must be rejected. The need for greater vigilance in assessing the specific ways in which social values and attitudes affect professional behavior is clearly indicated.*

---

*In the summer of 2010 Susan Reverby, history professor at Wellesley College, revealed that from 1946 to 1948 doctors from the United States deliberately infected Guatemalans with venereal diseases, ostensibly to study the use of penicillin as a preventative as well as a curative for syphilis. Dr. John C. Cutler, involved in the Tuskegee experiments, led the experiment in Guatemala. It is unclear if the Guatemalan subjects were effectively treated once they were infected with venereal diseases. See Donald G. McNeil's article, "U.S. Infected Guatemalans with Syphilis in '40s" in *The New York Times*, October 1, 2010, page A1 and A6. [*Editor's note*].

PART TWO

CULTURE AND SOCIETY

9

To Veil or Not to Veil? A Case Study of Identity Negotiation Among Muslim Women in Austin, Texas*

JEN'NAN GHAZAL READ AND JOHN P. BARTKOWSKI

There is much controversy in England, France, and other European countries about the clothes Muslim women wear. Some people object to the scarf (in Arabic, hijab) worn to cover women's hair. As a cultural object, Orthodox Jewish women, too, cover their natural hair. Many women in traditional groups (e.g., Mennonites, Amish) and fundamentalist Mormons do the same. Catholic nuns until a few years ago wore a habit that covered all but their faces. Interestingly, millions of Muslim women worldwide do not wear the hijab, *in Indonesia, Malaysia, Turkey, Tunisia, Senegal, and elsewhere. In the United States it is a choice that carries both social implications and personal meanings, for those who wear the* hijab *and those who do not.*

In light of expanded social opportunities for women in Western industrialized countries, scholars have turned their attention to the status of women in other parts of the world. This burgeoning research literature has given rise to a debate concerning the social standing of Muslim women in the Middle East. On one hand, some scholars contend that Muslim women occupy a subordinate status within many Middle Eastern countries. Some empirical evidence lends support to this view, as many researchers have highlighted the traditional and gendered customs prescribed by Islam—most notably, the veiling and shrouding of Muslim women.

On the other hand, a growing number of scholars now argue that claims about the oppression and subjugation of veiled Muslim women may, in many regards, be overstated. Scholars who have generated insider portraits of Islamic gender relations have revealed that Muslim women's motivations for veiling can vary dramatically. Some Muslim women veil to express their strongly held convictions about gender difference, others are motivated to do so more as a means of critiquing Western colonialism in the Middle East. It is this complexity surrounding the veil that leads Elizabeth Fernea (1993, 122) to conclude that the veil (or *hijab***) "means different things to different people

---

*Footnotes and references can be found in the article by the same name published in *Gender and Society*, June 2000.
**The *hijab* is called a veil but is, in fact, a hair covering, usually a scarf. It "screens" (the literal meaning of *hijab*) the beauty of a woman's hair from the untoward gaze of males. The face covering, *niqab*, comes to mind when the word "veil" is used but is not the subject of this essay. Curious students can Google "images" to see the variety of forms of the *hijab*. [*Editor's note*].

within [Muslim] society, and it means different things to Westerners than it does to Middle Easterners."

Our study takes as its point of departure the conflicting meanings of the veil among both Muslim religious elites and rank-and-file Islamic women currently living in the United States. In undertaking this investigation, we supplement the lone study (published in Arabic) that compares the gender attitudes of veiled and unveiled women. That study, based largely on survey data collected from university women living in the Middle East, demonstrates that while veiled women evince somewhat conservative gender attitudes, the vast majority of them support women's rights in public life and a substantial proportion subscribe to marital equality. We seek to extend these suggestive findings by using in-depth, personal interviews, because data from such interviews are more able to capture the negotiation of cultural meanings by veiled and unveiled respondents, as well as the nuances of these women's gender identities.

The importance of our study is further underscored by the influx of Muslims into the United States during recent decades and the increasing prominence of Muslim Americans and Islamic women on the domestic scene. Although population estimates of Muslim Americans vary (ranging from 5 to 8 million), many observers consider Islam to be one of the fastest growing religions in the United States. Moreover, recent research indicates that a majority of Muslims in the United States are university graduates firmly situated within the American middle class. Yet, even as this religious subculture has enjoyed such rapid growth and economic privilege throughout much of the West, Muslims in the United States and abroad have become the target of pejorative stereotypes. Caricatures that portray Islamic women as submissive and backward have become more pervasive within recent years, but recent research on Muslim women living in the United States has called such unflattering depictions into question. Such research has revealed that Muslim American women creatively negotiate their gender, religious, and ethnic identities in light of dominant U.S. social norms and modernist discourses that often define these women as "other."

Our investigation therefore aims to enrich this growing research literature, while critically evaluating negative stereotypes about Muslim women. After outlining our theoretical perspective, we review the debates that currently characterize Muslim elite discourse concerning the veil. Then, to discern the impact of these broad cultural disputes on the gender identities of women of Islam located in the United States, we analyze interview data collected from a sample of religiously active Muslim women—both veiled and unveiled—currently living in Austin, Texas. Our analysis highlights salient points of ideological divergence, as well as unanticipated points of congruence, between these veiled and unveiled Muslim women concerning this controversial cultural practice.

THEORY AND CONTEXT: DISCOURSE, IDENTITY, AND THE LANDSCAPE OF ISLAM

How can scholars effectively explore the interconnections between broad-based cultural constructions of gender on one hand and the more circumscribed (inter)subjective (i.e., personal) negotiation of gender relations on the other? In an effort to address these issues, a large number of contemporary feminist theorists and gender scholars have begun to examine discourse as one important medium through which gender is constructed. Our study is informed by these theoretical insights and by feminist standpoint theories and notions of subjectivity that take seriously women's agency, as well as their bodily practices and everyday experiences, in the negotiation of their gender identities.

Theories of discourse suggest that cultural forms (e.g., gender, religion, ethnicity) are best understood as *constructed*, *contested*, and *intersecting* social phenomena. First, the meanings attributed to the Muslim veil are not endemic to the veil itself; rather, they are produced through cultural discourse and vast networks of social relationships. Social practices that imbue the veil with cultural significance include the rhetoric of religious elites who equate veiling with religious devotion, as well as the actual ostracism of unveiled Muslim women from some Islamic institutions. Second, theories of discourse call attention to the contested character of cultural forms. Cultural symbols are capable of being interpreted in a variety of different ways and often become a site of struggle and contestation. Divergent interpretations of the same cultural practice may be advanced by groups who share a common religious heritage. As evidenced in our analysis below, various factions of Muslim elites offer strikingly different interpretations of the veil and the Qur'anic passages pertaining to this cultural practice. Finally, theories of discourse attune researchers to the multidimensional and overlapping character of cultural forms. Discourses are not discrete ideologies; rather, they are culturally specific modes of understanding the world that intersect with competing viewpoints. As we reveal below, religiously active Muslim women living in the United States are exposed not only to the internecine gender debates waged within Islamic circles mentioned above. These women also construct their gender identities in light of non-Muslim discourses of gender and ethnicity prevalent in late-twentieth-century America.

As noted, we complement these insights with feminist notions of standpoint, subjectivity, and bodily practice. Taken together, these theoretical perspectives suggest that discursive regimes provide social actors with important symbolic resources for identity negotiation and for the legitimation of everyday social and bodily practices. Current gender scholarship construes identity negotiation as a *process* and everyday *practice* that is fraught with ambiguity, contradiction, and struggle. These perspectives stand in bold contrast to more static psychological conceptualizations of *personality* as divorced from lived experience and bodily practice. Therefore, we are careful to recognize

how competing discourses of the veil enable veiled Muslim women to legitimate their decision to veil on a variety of grounds—from explicitly antifemi-
nist rationales to feminist justifications for veiling. Yet, at the same time, we
reveal how the respondents use their everyday experiences to lend a practical
edge to their understanding of the veil and their perceptions of themselves as
Muslim women.

The most germane aspects of Muslim theology for this study concern two
sets of Islamic sacred texts, the Qur'an and the hidiths. The Qur'an is held
in high esteem by virtually all Muslims. Not unlike the "high view" of the
Bible embraced by various conservative Christian groups, many contemporary Muslims believe that the Qur'an is the actual Word of God that was ably
recorded by Muhammed during the early portion of the seventh century. In
addition to the Qur'an, many Muslims also look to the hidiths for moral and
spiritual guidance in their daily lives. The hidiths, second-hand reports of
Muhammed's personal traditions and lifestyle, began to be collected shortly
after his death because of the difficulty associated with applying the dictates
of the Qur'an to changing historical circumstances. The full collection of these
hidiths has come to be known as the *sunna.* Along with the Qur'an, the hidiths
constitute the source of law that has shaped the ethics and values of many
Muslims.

Within Islam, the all-male Islamic clergy (variously called *faghihs, imams,*
[*maribors*], *muftis, mullahs,* or *ulumas*) often act as interpretive authorities who
are formally charged with distilling insights from the Qur'an or hidiths and
with disseminating these scriptural interpretations to the Muslim laity. Given
that such positions of structural privilege are set aside for Muslim men, Islam
is a patriarchal religious institution. Yet, patriarchal institutions do not necessarily produce homogeneous gender ideologies, a fact underscored by the
discursive fissures [arguments] that divide Muslim religious authorities and
elite commentators concerning the veil.

COMPETING DISCOURSES OF THE VEIL
IN CONTEMPORARY ISLAM

Many Muslim clergy and Islamic elites currently prescribe veiling as a custom in which "good" Muslim women should engage. Proponents of veiling
often begin their defense of this cultural practice by arguing that men are
particularly vulnerable to corruption through unregulated sexual contact
with women. These experts contend that the purpose of the hijab or veil is the
regulation of such contact:

> The society that Islam wants to establish is not a sensate, sex-ridden society. . . .
> The Islamic system of *Hijab* is a wide-ranging system which protects the fam-
> ily and closes those avenues that lead toward illicit sex relations or even indis-
> criminate contact between the sexes in society. . . . To protect her virtue and to

safeguard her chastity from lustful eyes and covetous hands, Islam has provided for purdah which sets norms of dress, social get-together ... and going out of the four walls of one's house in hours of need. (Siddiqi 1983, vii–viii)

Many expositors of the pro-veiling discourse call attention to the uniquely masculine penchant for untamed sexual activity and construe the veil as a God-ordained solution to the apparent disparities in men's and women's sexual appetites. Women are therefore deemed responsible for the management of men's sexuality. Some contend that the Muslim woman who veils should be sure that the hijab covers her whole body (including the palms of her hands), should be monotone in color ("so as not to be attractive to draw the attentions to"), and should be opaque and loose so as not to reveal "the woman's shape or what she is wearing underneath" (Al-Swailem 1995, 24–25).

Pro-veiling Muslim luminaries also defend veiling on a number of non-sexual grounds. The veil, according to these commentators, serves as (1) a demonstration of the Muslim woman's unwavering obedience to the tenets of Islam; (2) a clear indication of the essential differences distinguishing men from women; (3) a reminder to women that their proper place is in the home rather than in pursuing public-sphere activities; and (4) a sign of the devout Muslim woman's disdain for the profane, immodest, and consumerist cultural customs of the West. In this last regard, veiling is legitimated as an anti-imperialist statement of ethnic and cultural distinctiveness.

Nevertheless, the most prominent justifications for veiling entail, quite simply, the idea that veiling is prescribed in the Qur'an. Several Muslim clergy place a strong interpretive emphasis on a Qur'anic passage (S. 24:31) that urges women "not [to] display their beauty and adornments" but rather to "draw their head cover over their bosoms and not display their ornament." Many of these same defenders of the veil marshal other Qur'anic passages that bolster their proveiling stance: "And when you ask them [the Prophet's wives] for anything you want ask them from before a screen (*hijab*); that makes for greater purity for your hearts and for them" (S. 33:53); "O Prophet! Tell your wives and daughters and the believing women that they should cast their outer garments over themselves, that is more convenient that they should be known and not molested" (S. 33:59).

In addition to these Qur'anic references, pro-veiling Muslim clergy highlight hadiths intended to support the practice of veiling. Many pro-veiling Muslim clergy maintain that the veil verse was revealed to Muhammad at a wedding five years before the Prophet's death. As the story goes, three tactless guests overstayed their welcome after the wedding and continued to chat despite the Prophet's desire to be alone with his new wife. To encourage their departure, Muhammad drew a curtain between the nuptial chamber and one of his inconsiderate companions while ostensibly uttering "the verse of the hijab" (S. 33:53, cited above). A second set of hadiths claim that the verse of hijab was prompted when one of the Prophet's companions accidentally touched the hand of one of Muhammad's wives while eating dinner. Yet a third set of hadiths suggests that the verse's objective was to stop the visits of an unidentified man who tarried with the wives of the Prophet, promising them marriage after Muhammad's death.

In stark contrast to the pro-veiling apologias discussed above, an oppositional discourse against veiling has emerged within Islamic circles in recent years. Most prominent among these opponents of veiling are Islamic feminists. Although Islamic feminists are marginalized from many of the institutional apparatuses available to the all-male Muslim clergy, they nevertheless exercise considerable influence via the dissemination of dissident publications targeted at Islamic women and through grassroots social movements. Fatima Mernissi, arguably the most prominent Muslim feminist, is highly critical of dominant gender conceptualizations that construe veiling as the ultimate standard by which the spiritual welfare and religious devoutness of Muslim women should be judged. In *The Veil and the Male Elite: A Feminist Interpretation of Women's Rights in Islam*, Mernissi (1991, 194) queries her readers:

> What a strange fate for Muslim memory, to be called upon in order to censure and punish [Islamic women]! What a strange memory, where even dead men and women do not escape attempts at assassination, if by chance they threaten to raise the *hijab* [veil] that covers the mediocrity and servility that is presented to us [Muslim women] as tradition. How did the tradition succeed in transforming the Muslim woman into that submissive, marginal creature who buries herself and only goes out into the world timidly and huddled in her veils? Why does the Muslim man need such a mutilated companion?

Mernissi and other Muslim commentators who oppose veiling do so on a number of grounds. First, Mernissi seeks to reverse the sacralization of the veil by linking the hijab with oppressive social hierarchies and male domination. She argues that the veil represents a tradition of "mediocrity and servility" rather than a sacred standard against which to judge Muslim women's devotion to Allah. Second, antiveiling Muslim commentators are quick to highlight the historical fact that veiling is a cultural practice that originated from outside of Islamic circles. Although commonly assumed to be of Muslim origin, historical evidence reveals that veiling was actually practiced in the ancient Near East and Arabia long before the rise of Islam. Using this historical evidence to bolster their antiveiling stance, some Muslim feminists conclude that because the veil is not a Muslim invention, it cannot be held up as the standard against which Muslim women's religiosity is to be gauged.

Finally, Islamic feminists such as Mernissi point to the highly questionable scriptural interpretations on which Muslim clergy often base their pro-veiling edicts. Dissident Islamic commentators call attention to the fact that the Qur'an refers cryptically to a "curtain" and never directly instructs women to wear a veil. Although proponents of veiling interpret Qur'anic edicts as

Allah's directive to all Muslim women for all time, Islamic critics of veiling counter this interpretive strategy by placing relatively greater weight on the "occasions of revelation" (*asbab nuzul al-Qur'an*)—that is, the specific social circumstances under which key Qur'anic passages were revealed. It is with this interpretive posture that many Islamic feminists believe the veil verse (S. 33:53) to be intended solely for the wives of Muhammad. Muslim critics of veiling further counter many of the pro-veiling hadith citations by arguing that they are interpretations of extrascriptural texts whose authenticity is highly questionable. Finally, critics of hijab point to select verses in the Qur'an that invoke images of gender egalitarianism, including one passage that refers to the "vast reward" Allah has prepared for both "men who guard their modesty and women who guard their modesty" (S. 33:35).

THE VEIL AND GENDER IDENTITY NEGOTIATION AMONG MUSLIM WOMEN IN AUSTIN

To this point, we have drawn comparisons between pro-veiling edicts that link devout, desexualized Muslim womanhood to the practice of veiling and anti-veiling discourses that reject this conflation of hijab and women's religious devotion. We now attempt to gauge the impact of these debates on the gender identities of a sample of 24 Muslim women—12 of whom veil, 12 of whom do not. All women in our sample define themselves as devout Muslims (i.e., devoted followers of Muhammad who actively practice their faith). These women were recruited through a combination of snowball and purposive sampling. Taken together, the respondents identify with a range of different nationalities (e.g., Iranian, Pakistani, Kuwaiti) and Muslim sects. Nineteen women have lived 10 or more years in the United States, while five women in our sample have immigrated in the past 5 years. Their ages range from 21 to 55 years old, and they occupy a range of social roles (e.g., college students, professional women, homemakers). Consistent with the demographic characteristics of U.S. Muslim immigrants at large, our sample is composed of middle-class women with some postsecondary education (either a college degree or currently attending college). Class homogeneity among the respondents is also partly a product of the locale from which the sample was drawn, namely, a university town. Consequently, this study extends cross-cultural scholarship on the intersection of veiling, ethnicity, and nationality for middle-class Muslim women living in Western and largely modernized societies.

In-depth interviews with these Muslim women were conducted by the first author during 1996 and 1997. The interview questionnaire covered a range of topics, including the women's practical experiences with veiling, the meaning of the veil to them, their reasons for wearing or not wearing the veil and the impact of this decision on their social relationships, their perceptions about the significance of the veil in their country of origin, and the importance of Islamic beliefs and devotional activities (e.g., prayer, scriptural study) to these women. In light of our topic's sensitivity, as well as cultural differences between our respondents and the first author (a non-Muslim unveiled woman), the interviews were not audiotaped. Because many of the women were forthright about their opposition to participating in a study based on tape-recorded interviews, the tenor, depth, and candor of these interviews would have been seriously inhibited if conversations were tape-recorded. Consequently, with the women's consent, handwritten notes were recorded during the course of each interview. Immediately after the interview, these notes were then elaborated into a more detailed set of transcripts. Each transcript was initially evaluated as an independent conversation concerning the significance of the veil and its relationship to the respondent's religious and gender identity. Emergent themes from each interview were flagged and coded during this stage of the analysis. Then, during a second stage of analysis, we compared the themes that emerged from interviews conducted with each of the two different subgroups of Muslim women (veiled and unveiled).

Interview data collected from these women, identified below by pseudonyms, are designed to address several interrelated issues: What does the veil itself and the practice of veiling mean to these women? Among the women who veil, why do they do so? Among the women who do not veil, how have they arrived at the decision to remain unveiled? Finally, how does each group of our respondents feel about women who engage in the "opposite" cultural practice?

VEILED CONTRADICTIONS: PERCEPTIONS OF HIJAB AND GENDER PRACTICES AMONG VEILED MUSLIM WOMEN

Religious Edicts and Social Bonds

In several respects, the veiled respondents' accounts of wearing hijab conform to the pro-veiling gender discourse explicated above. Many of the veiled women invoke various sorts of religious imagery and theological edicts when asked about their motivations for veiling. One respondent in her early twenties, Huneeya, states flatly: "I wear the hijab because the Qur'an says it's better [for women to be veiled]." Yet another veiled woman, Najette, indicates that hijab "makes [her] more special" because it symbolizes her commitment to Islam. Mona says outright: "The veil represents submission to God," and Masouda construes the veil as a "symbol of worship" on the part of devout Muslim women to Allah and the teachings of the Prophet Muhammad. Not surprisingly, many veiled women contend that veiling is commanded in the Qur'an.

Of course, this abundance of theological rationales is not the only set of motivations that the veiled women use to justify this cultural practice. For many of the veiled respondents, the scriptural edicts and the religious symbolism surrounding the veil are given palpable force through their everyday gender practices and the close-knit social networks that grow out of this distinctive cultural practice. Indeed, narratives about some women's deliberate choice to begin veiling at a particular point in their lives underscore how religious edicts stand in tension with the women's strategic motivations. Several women recount that they began to veil because they had friends who did so or because they felt more closely connected to significant others through this cultural practice. Aisha, for example, longed to wear the veil while she attended high school in the Middle East approximately three decades ago. Reminiscent of issues faced by her teen counterparts in the United States, Aisha's account suggests that high school was a crucial time for identity formation and the cultivation of peer group relationships. The veil served Aisha as a valuable resource in resolving many of the dilemmas she faced 30 years ago as a maturing high school student. She decided to begin veiling at that time after hearing several prominent Muslim speakers at her school "talk[ing] about how good veiling is." The veil helped Aisha not only to form meaningful peer relationships at that pivotal time in her life (i.e., adolescence) but also continues to facilitate for her a feeling of connectedness with a broader religious community of other veiled Muslim women. During her recent trip to Egypt during the summer, Aisha says that the veil helped her "to fit in" there in a way that she would not have if she were unveiled.

Several other respondents also underscore the significance of Islamic women's friendship networks that form around the veil, which are particularly indispensable because they live in a non-Muslim country (i.e., the United States). In recounting these friendship circles that are cultivated around hijab in a "foreign" land, our veiled respondents point to an important overlay between their gender identities (i.e., good Muslim women veil) and their ethnic identities (i.e., as Middle Easterners). The common foundation on which these twin identities are negotiated is distinctively religious in nature. Hannan touts the personal benefits of veiling both as a *woman*—"the veil serves as an identity for [Islamic] women"—and as a *Muslim*: "[Because I veil,] Muslim people know I am Muslim, and they greet me in Arabic." This interface between gender and ethnicity is also given voice by Aisha, whose initial experiences with the veil were noted above. Aisha maintains, "The veil differentiates Muslim women from other women. When you see a woman in hijab, you know she's a Muslim." Much like the leading Muslim commentators who encourage Islamic women to "wear" their religious convictions (literally, via the veil) for all to see, these veiled respondents find comfort in the cultural and ethnic distinctiveness that the veil affords them. In this way, hijab is closely connected with their overlapping religious-gender-ethnic identities and links them to the broader community (*ummah*) of Islamic believers and Muslim women.

Gender Difference and Women's "Emancipation"

In addition to providing religious rationales for wearing the veil, many of the women who wear hijab also invoke the discourse of masculine-feminine

difference to defend the merits of veiling. For several women, the idea of masculine hypersexuality and feminine vulnerability to the male sex drive is crucial to this essentialist rationale for veiling. Despite the fact that veiled women
were rather guarded in their references to sex, their nods in that direction are
difficult to interpret in any other fashion. In describing the veil's role in Islam
and in the lives of Muslim men and women (such as herself), Sharadda states,
"Islam is natural and men need some things naturally. If we abide by these
needs [and veil accordingly], we will all be happy." She continues, "If the veil
did not exist, many evil things would happen. Boys would mix with girls, which
will result in evil things."

Similarly, Hannan describes what she perceives to be women's distinctive
attributes and their connection to the veil: "Women are like diamonds; they are
so precious. They should not be revealed to everyone—just to their husbands
and close kin." Like Qur'anic references to women's "ornaments," Hannan is
contrasting the "precious" diamond-like feminine character to the ostensibly
less refined, less distinctive masculine persona. Interestingly, it is by likening
women to diamonds that Hannan rhetorically inverts traditional gender hierarchies that privilege "masculine" traits over their "feminine" counterparts. In
the face of those who would denigrate feminine qualities, Hannan reinterprets
the distinctiveness of womanhood as more "precious" (i.e., more rare and valuable) than masculine qualities. Women's inherent difference from men, then, is
perceived to be a source of esteem rather than denigration.

It is important to recognize, however, that the respondents who invoke
this rhetoric of gender difference are not simply reproducing the pro-veiling
discourse advanced by Muslim elites [clerics]. Despite their essentialist convictions, many of the veiled respondents argue that the practice of wearing
hijab actually liberates them from men's untamed, potentially explosive sexuality and makes possible for them various sorts of public-sphere pursuits. So,
whereas pro-veiling Islamic elites often reason that women's sexual vulnerability (and, literally, their fragile bodily "ornaments") should restrict them to the
domestic sphere, many of the veiled women in this study simply do not support
this view of domesticated femininity. To the contrary, these women—many of
whom are themselves involved in occupational or educational pursuits—argue
that the veil is a great equalizer that enables women to work alongside of men.
In the eyes of Hannan, women's "preciousness" should not be used to cajole
them to remain in the home: "Women who wear the hijab are not excluded
from society. They are freer to move around in society because of it."

Rabbab, who attends to various public-sphere pursuits, offers a similar
appraisal. She argues that the veil (hijab) is an invaluable aid for Muslim
women who engage in extradomestic pursuits. In advancing this claim,
Rabbab uses women who veil their whole bodies (such body garments are
called *abaya*) as a counterpoint of excessive traditionalism. When asked what
the veil means to her personally, as well as to Muslim women and Islamic
culture at large, she says,

It depends on the extent of the hijab [that is worn]. . . . Women who wear face veils and cover their whole bodies [with abaya] are limited to the home. They are too dependent on their husbands. How can they interact when they are so secluded? . . . [However,] taking away the hijab would make women have to fight to be taken seriously [in public settings]. . . . With hijab, men take us more seriously.

This hijab-as-liberator rationale for veiling was repeated by many of the veiled women who pursued educational degrees in schools and on college campuses where young predatorial men ostensibly rove in abundance. Aisha, a 41-year-old former student, recounts how the veil emancipated her from the male gaze during her school years:

There was a boy who attended my university. He was very rude to all of the girls, always whistling and staring at them. One day, I found myself alone in the hallway with him. I was very nervous because I had to walk by him. But because I was wearing the hijab, he looked down when I walked past. He did not show that respect to the unveiled girls.

Drawing on experiences such as these, Aisha concludes succinctly: "The veil gives women advantages. . . . They can go to coeducational schools and feel safe." A current student, Najette, says that the veil helps her to "feel secure" in going about her daily activities. Finally, the account of a young female student who is 22 years of age sheds further light on the hijab's perceived benefits in the face of men's apparent propensity to objectify women: "If you're in hijab, then someone sees you and treats you accordingly. I feel more free. Especially men, they don't look at your appearance—they appreciate your intellectual abilities. They respect you." For many of the veiled women in this study, the respect and protection afforded them by the hijab enables them to engage in extradomestic pursuits that would ironically generate sharp criticism from many pro-veiling Muslim elites.

The Discontents of Hijab and Tolerance for the Unveiled

While the foregoing statements provide clear evidence of these women's favorable feelings about hijab, many of the veiled women also express mixed feelings about this controversial cultural symbol. It was not uncommon for the veiled respondents to recount personal difficulties that they have faced because of their decision to wear hijab. Some dilemmas associated with the veil emanate from the fact that these women live in a secular society inhabited predominantly by Christians rather than Muslims. Najette, the same respondent who argued that veiling makes her feel "special," was quick to recognize that this esteem is purchased at the price of being considered "weird" by some Americans who do not understand her motivations for veiling. For women like her, engaging in a dissident cultural practice underscores Najette's cultural distinctiveness in a way that some people find refreshing and others find threatening.

Such points of tension surrounding the veil are evident not only in cross-cultural encounters such as that mentioned above. Even within Muslim circles, the practice of veiling has generated enough controversy to produce rifts among relatives and friends when some of the veiled respondents appear publicly in hijab. Huneeya, a student who veils because she wishes to follow Qur'anic edicts and enjoys being treated as an intellectual equal by her male peers, highlighted just this point of friction with her family members, all of whom except her are "against hijab. [My family members] think it is against modernity."

For some women, the tensions produced within intimate relationships by the veil move beyond the realm of intermittent family squabbles. One veiled respondent, Asma, revealed that extended family difficulties surrounding the veil have caused her to alter the practice of veiling itself, if only temporarily. Her recent experiences underscore the complex machinations of power involved in the contested arenas of family relations and friendships where veiling is concerned. Asma moved to the United States with her husband only two years ago. Asma was quite conscientious about veiling. She relished the sense of uniqueness and cultural distinctiveness afforded to her by the hijab while living in a non-Muslim country. Yet, recent summer-long visits from her mother-in-law presented her with a dilemma. Asma's mother-in-law had arranged the marriage between her son and daughter-in-law. At the time, the mother-in-law greatly appreciated the conservative religious values embraced by her future daughter-in-law, evidenced in Asma's attentiveness to wearing the veil. Yet, since that time, Asma's mother-in-law had undergone a conversion of sorts concerning the practice of veiling. Quite recently, Asma's mother-in-law stopped wearing the veil and wanted her daughter-in-law to follow suit by discarding the veil as well. Indeed, this mother-in-law felt that Asma was trying to upstage her by using the veil to appear more religiously devout than her elder. Asma's short-term solution to this dilemma is to submit to the wishes of her mother-in-law during her summer visits to the United States. Consequently, for two months each summer, Asma discards her veil. Yet, this solution is hardly satisfactory to her and does not placate Asma's veiled friends who think less of her for unveiling:

> I feel very uncomfortable without the veil. The veil keeps us [Muslim women] from getting mixed up in American culture. But I don't want to make my mother-in-law feel inferior, so I take it off while she is here. I know my friends think I am a hypocrite.

Although Asma is sanctioned by her friends for unveiling temporarily during her mother-in-law's visit, our interview data suggest that the preponderance of veiled women in this study harbor no ill will toward their Muslim sisters who choose not to veil. Despite these veiled women's enthusiastic defenses of hijab, they are willing to define what it means to be a good Muslim broadly enough to include Islamic women who do not veil. When asked, for instance, what she thought being a good Muslim entails, one of our veiled respondents (Najette) states simply: "You must be a good person and always be honest." Echoing these sentiments, Masouda suggests, "Your attitude towards God is most important for being a good Muslim—your personality. You must be patient, honest, giving." Even when asked point-blank if veiling makes a woman a good Muslim, another veiled respondent answers, "Hijab is not so important for being a good Muslim. Other things are more important, like having a good character and being honest." One respondent even took on a decidedly ecumenical tone in detaching veiling from Islamic devotion: "Being a good Muslim is the same as being a good Christian or a good Jew—treat others with respect and dignity. Be considerate and open-minded." In the end, then, these women in hijab are able to distinguish between what veiling means to them at a personal level (i.e., a sign of religious devotion) versus what the veil says about Muslim women in general (i.e., a voluntary cultural practice bereft of devotional significance). These veiled women's heterogeneous lived experiences with the hijab—both comforting and uncomfortable, affirming and tension producing, positive and negative—seem to provide them with a sensitivity to cultural differences that often seems lacking in the vitriolic debates about veiling currently waged by leading Muslims.

ISLAMIC FEMINISM MODIFIED: PERCEPTIONS OF HIJAB AND GENDER PRACTICES AMONG THE UNVEILED

Patriarchal Oppression and Religious Fanaticism

Just as veiled women draw on the pro-veiling discourse to defend the wearing of hijab, the unveiled women in this study often justify their abstention from this cultural practice by invoking themes from the antiveiling discourse. Several of these unveiled women argue quite straightforwardly that the veil reinforces gender distinctions that work to Muslim women's collective disadvantage. According to many of the unveiled women, the veil was imposed on Muslim women because of Middle Eastern men's unwillingness to tame their sexual caprice and because of their desire to dominate women. Rabeeya, for example, contends that Muslim women are expected to veil because "Middle Eastern men get caught up in beauty. The veil helps men control themselves." Offering a strikingly similar response, Najwa argues that "men can't control themselves, so they make women veil." Using the same critical terminology—that is, *control*—to make her point, Fozia has an even less sanguine view of the veil's role in Islam. When asked about the significance of the veil in Muslim societies, she states flatly: "The veil is used to control women." In short, many of the unveiled respondents view hijab in much the same way as elite Islamic feminists; that is, as a mechanism of patriarchal control.

Comments such as these suggest points of congruence between the veiled and unveiled respondents' understandings of hijab. Both groups of women seem to agree that hijab is closely related to men's sexuality. Recall that some of the veiled women contrast masculine hypersexuality to a desexualized view of femininity. Such women conclude that the veil is the God-ordained corrective for men's inability to control their own sexual impulses. Likewise, as evidenced in several statements from unveiled women, they link the veil to men's apparent inability (or, better, unwillingness) to contain their sexual desires. However, whereas several of the veiled women see masculine hypersexuality as natural and view the veil as a divine remedy for such sexual differences, many of the unveiled women reject these views. The unveiled respondents seem less willing to accept the notion that categorical gender differences should translate into a cultural practice that (literally and figuratively) falls on the shoulders of women. In a key point of departure from their sisters who wear hijab, the unveiled women in this study trace the origin of the veil not to God but rather to men's difficulties in managing their sexuality (again, "men can't control themselves, so they make women veil"). In men's attempt to manage their sexual impulses, so the account goes, they have foisted the veil on women. Very much in keeping with feminist discourses that take issue with such gendered double standards, the unveiled women conclude that it is unfair to charge women with taming men's sexuality.

Apart from these issues of social control and sexuality, several of the unveiled respondents also invoke themes of religious devotion and ethnic identity when discussing the significance of the veil for Muslims in general and for themselves (as unveiled Islamic women) in particular. Recall that leading Muslims who support veiling often highlight the religious and ethnic distinctiveness of hijab; however, prominent Muslim feminists counter that veiling did not originate with Islam and should not be understood as central to women's religious devoutness or ethnic identities (as non-Westerners). Echoing these Muslim feminist themes, several of the unveiled respondents seek to sever the veil from its religious and ethnic moorings. Fozia says that Muslim "women are made to believe that the veil is religious. In reality, it's all political," while Fatima asserts, "The veil is definitely political. It is used by men as a weapon to differentiate us from Westerners." Yet another respondent, Mah'ha, argues that it is only "fanatical" and "strict" Muslims who use the veil to draw sharp distinctions between Middle Easterners and Westerners. These remarks and others like them are designed to problematize the conflation of religious devotion, ethnic distinctiveness, and hijab evidenced in the pro-veiling discourse. Whereas the dominant discourse of veiling measures women's devotion to Islamic culture against hijab, many of the unveiled respondents imply—again, via strategic terms such as *political, fanatical,* and *strict*—that religious devotion and ethnic identification are good only in proper measure.

This rhetorical strategy allows these unveiled women to claim more moderate (and modern) convictions over and against those whose devotion to

Allah has in their view been transmogrified into political dogmatism, religious extremism, and racial separatism. The unveiled women in our study do not eschew religious commitment altogether, nor are they in any way ashamed of their ethnic heritage. To the contrary, the unveiled respondents champion religious commitment (again, in good measure) and are proud to count themselves among the followers of Muhammad. Yet, they are quick to illustrate that their devotion to Allah and their appreciation of their cultural heritage are manifested through means that do not include the practice of veiling. Amna, for example, says, "Religious education makes me feel like a more pious Muslim. I read the Qur'an weekly and attend Friday prayer sermons," while Rabeeya states, "Being a good Muslim means believing in one God; no idolatry; following the five pillars of Islam; and believing in Muhammad." Concerning the issue of ethnoreligious identity, the basic message articulated by many of the unveiled women can be stated quite succinctly: A Muslim women can be true to her cultural and religious heritage without the veil. Samiya, a 38-year-old unveiled woman, says as much: "Muslim society doesn't exist on the veil. Without the veil, you would still be Muslim." Therefore, many of the unveiled women believe that the veil is of human (actually, male) origin rather than of divine making. And it is this very belief about the veil's this-worldly origins that enables many of the unveiled women to characterize themselves as devout followers of Muhammad who honor their cultural heritage even though they have opted not to veil.

Standing on Common Ground:
Tolerance for the Other among Unveiled Women

Finally, we turn our attention to the subjective contradictions that belie the prima facie critical reactions of our unveiled respondents toward the veil. Interestingly, just as the veiled women are reluctant to judge harshly their unveiled counterparts, these unveiled women who eschew hijab at a personal level nevertheless express understanding and empathy toward their Middle Eastern sisters who veil. At several points during interview encounters, the unveiled respondents escape the polemical hold of the antiveiling discourse by building bridges to their sisters who engage in a cultural practice that they themselves eschew.

First, several respondents imply that it would be wrong to criticize veiled women for wearing hijab when it is men—specifically, male Muslim elites—who are to blame for the existence and pervasiveness of the veil in Islamic culture. Amna, who does not veil, takes on a conciliatory tone toward women who do so by conceding that "the veil helps women in societies where they want to be judged solely on their character and not on their appearances." How is it that such statements, which sound so similar to the justifications for wearing hijab invoked by veiled women, emanate from the unveiled respondents? The strongly antipatriarchal sentiments of the unveiled women (described in the preceding section) seem to exonerate veiled women from charges of gender traitorism. Recall that many of the unveiled respondents, in fact, locate the origin of the veil in *men*'s sexual indiscretion and in *men*'s desire to control women: "Middle Eastern *men* get caught up in beauty. The veil helps *men* control *themselves*" (Rabeeya); "*Men* can't control *themselves*, so *they* make women veil" (Najwa); "The veil is *used to control women*. The women are *made to believe* that the veil is religious" (Fozia) (emphasis added). Ironically, it is the very antipatriarchal character of these statements that simultaneously enables the unveiled women to express their stinging criticism of the veil itself while proclaiming tolerance and respect for Islamic women who wear the veil. Indeed, since many of the unveiled respondents construe hijab to be a product of *patriarchal* oppression and assorted *masculine* hang-ups (e.g., struggles with sexuality, a preoccupation with domination and control), veiled women cannot legitimately be impugned for wearing hijab.

Second, many of the unveiled respondents are willing to concede that despite their own critical views of the veil, hijab serves an important cultural marker for Islamic women other than themselves. When asked about the role of the veil among Muslim women she knows in the United States, Rabeeya recognizes that many of her veiled Islamic sisters who currently live in America remain "very, very tied to their culture. Or they are trying to be. They [veil because they] want to feel tied to their culture even when they are far away from home." Because she herself is a devout Islamic woman living in a religiously pluralistic and publicly secularized society, Rabeeya is able to empathize with other Muslim women residing in the United States who veil in order to shore up their cultural identity. Similarly, Sonya draws noteworthy distinctions between her personal antipathy toward veiling and veiled women's attraction to hijab: "Some Muslim women need the veil to identify themselves with the Muslim culture. I don't feel that way."

Finally, several of the unveiled women in our study seem to express tolerance and empathy for their sisters in hijab because, at one time or another in the past, they themselves have donned the veil. Two of the unveiled respondents, for example, are native Iranians who are currently living in the United States. When these women return to Iran, they temporarily don the veil. Najwa, one of these women, explains, "As soon as we cross the Iranian border, I go to the bathroom on the airplane and put on the hijab." The experiences of our other native-born Iranian woman, Fatima, speak even more directly to the practical nuances that undergird unveiled women's tolerance for their veiled counterparts. On one hand, Fatima is highly critical of the veil, which has been the legally required dress for women in Iran during the past two decades. Referring to this fact, she impugns the veil as a "political . . . weapon" used by religious elites to reinforce invidious distinctions between Westerners and Middle Easterners. Yet, on the other hand, her personal experiences with hijab lead her to reject the stereotype that women who veil are "backward": "Progress has nothing to do with veiling. Countries without veiling can be very backwards . . . I have nothing against veiling. I feel very modern [in not veiling], but I respect those who veil." Like so many of her unveiled sisters, then, Rabeeya is critical of the veil as a religious icon but is unwilling to look down on Islamic women who wear hijab.

CONCLUSION AND DISCUSSION

This study has examined how a sample of Muslim women living in Austin, Texas, negotiate their gender identities in light of ongoing Islamic disputes about the propriety of veiling. Interview data with 12 veiled and 12 unveiled women reveal that many of them draw upon the pro-veiling and antiveiling discourses of Muslim elites, respectively, to justify their decisions about the veil. At the same time, the women highlight various subjective contradictions manifested in many of their accounts of veiling. Women who veil are not typically disdainful toward their unveiled Muslim sisters, and unveiled women in our sample seem similarly reluctant to impugn their veiled counterparts. Such findings were unanticipated in light of elite Muslim debates about the propriety of veiling.

What are we to make of the fact that the acrimony manifested between elite Muslim proponents and opponents of veiling is largely absent from these women's accounts of the veil? Several possible answers to this question emerge from our investigation. First, both the veiled and unveiled women in our study clearly exercise agency in crafting their gender identities. Drawing on themes of individualism and tolerance for diversity, the women are able to counterpose their own "choice" to veil or to remain unveiled on one hand with the personal inclinations of their sisters who might choose a path that diverges from their own. In this way, the respondents fashion gender identities that are malleable and inclusive enough to navigate through the controversy surrounding the veil. Second, the social context within which the women are situated seems to provide them with resources that facilitate these gender innovations. As noted above, our sample is composed of middle-class, well-educated Muslim women. We suspect that the progressive, multicultural climate of Austin and the human capital enjoyed by the women foster greater empathy between the veiled respondents and their unveiled counterparts. This degree of tolerance between veiled and unveiled Muslim women evinced in our study may be decidedly different for Islamic women living in other parts of the United States, other Western nations, or particular countries in the Middle East where the veil is a more publicly contested symbol.

Consequently, this study lends further credence to the insight that culture is not simply produced from "above" through the rhetoric of elites to be consumed untransformed by social actors who are little more than judgmental dopes. While the pro-veiling and antiveiling discourses have carved out distinctive positions for veiled Muslim women and their unveiled counterparts within the late twentieth century, the respondents in our study are unique and indispensable contributors to contemporary Islamic culture. It is these women, rather than the often combative elite voices within Islamic circles, who creatively build bridges across the contested cultural terrain of veiling; who forge ties of tolerance with their sisters, veiled and unveiled; and who help foster the sense of community (*ummah*) that is so esteemed by Muslims around the world. Convictions about Islamic culture and community take on new meaning as they are tested in the crucible of Muslim women's everyday experiences. These findings parallel those that have emerged from other studies of politicized issues in the contemporary United States, including debates about abortion, family decision making, and women's paid labor force participation. These studies have revealed that the contemporary "culture wars" over gender are often waged by a select few—namely, elite ideologists and vanguard activists—whose views do not wholly correspond with the local standpoints of actual women at whom such rhetoric is targeted. * * *

Finally, there are some telling points of convergence between gender relations in contemporary Islam, Orthodox Judaism, and conservative Protestantism. Given the spate of recent studies which suggest that gender is negotiated by conservative Protestants and Orthodox Jews, what parallels might exist between the gendered experiences of Muslim women and their conservative Protestant or Orthodox Jewish counterparts? And, in what ways might the gender practices and the enactment of specific definitions of the religiously "devout woman" (whether Muslim, evangelical, or Orthodox Jew) diverge? No research of which we are aware has compared the processes of identity negotiation among Muslim women with those manifested in other conservative religious contexts. When interpreted in light of the emerging literature on gender negotiation within conservative Protestantism and Orthodox Judaism, our findings suggest that there is much to be gained by drawing more detailed cross-cultural comparisons between the gendered experiences of such women, as well as the culturally specific "patriarchal bargains" (Kandiyoti 1988) with which these groups of women are confronted. In the end, arriving at a richer understanding of gender negotiation in those contexts where we might least expect to find it can shed new light on the transformation of gender relations as we begin the millennium.

REFERENCES

Al-Swailem, Sheikh Abdullah Ahmed. 1995. Introduction. In *A comparison between veiling and unveiling,* by Halah bint Abdullah. Riyadh, Saudi Arabia: Dar-us-Salam.

Fernea, Elizabeth W. 1993. The veiled revolution. In *Everyday life in the Muslim Middle East,* edited by D. L. Bowen and E. A. Early. Bloomington: Indiana University Press.

Kandiyoti, Deniz. 1988. Bargaining with patriarchy. *Gender & Society* 2:274–90.

Mernissi, Fatima. 1991. *The veil and the male elite: A feminist interpretation of women's rights in Islam.* Translated by Mary Jo Lakeland. New York: Addison-Wesley.

Siddiqi, Muhammad Iqbal. 1983. *Islam forbids free mixing of men and women.* Lahore, Pakistan: Kazi.

10

McDonald's in Hong Kong: Consumerism, Dietary Change, and the Rise of a Children's Culture

FROM *Golden Arches East*

JAMES L. WATSON

McDonald's has not only become the symbol of globalization. It is emblematic of the influence of the West, and particularly the United States, on the rest of the world. Many people question the value of this bequest, seeing fast food as a corrosive and crude intrusion on traditional practices, to say nothing of its questionable nutritional value. James Watson takes exception, not because he necessarily loves fast food and wants to speed up the erosion of local practices, but because he finds in those who are encouraged to take up Western practices—in this case the McDonald's "experience"—more selectivity and creativity than is usually supposed. Although South Koreans openly oppose and reject McDonald's, many in Hong Kong have redefined McDonald's in ways that reveal the human capacity to shape culture and find compatibility between the old and the new.

TRANSNATIONALISM AND THE FAST FOOD INDUSTRY

Does the roaring success of McDonald's and its rivals in the fast food industry mean that Hong Kong's local culture is under siege? Are food chains helping to create a homogeneous, "global" culture better suited to the demands of a capitalist world order? Hong Kong would seem to be an excellent place to test the globalization hypothesis, given the central role that cuisine plays in the production and maintenance of a distinctive local identity. Man Tso-chuen's great-grandchildren are today avid consumers of Big Macs, pizza, and Coca-Cola; does this somehow make them less "Chinese" than their grandfather?

It is my contention that the cultural arena in places like Hong Kong is changing with such breathtaking speed that the fundamental assumptions underlining such questions are themselves questionable. Economic and social realities make it necessary to construct an entirely new approach to global issues, one that takes the consumers' own views into account. Analyses based on neomarxian and dependency (center/periphery) models that were popular in the 1960s and 1970s do not begin to capture the complexity of emerging transnational systems.

This chapter represents a conscious attempt to bring the discussion of globalism down to earth, focusing on one local culture. The people of Hong Kong have embraced American-style fast foods, and by so doing they might appear to be in the vanguard of a worldwide culinary revolution. But they have not been stripped of their cultural traditions, nor have they become

"Americanized" in any but the most superficial of ways. Hong Kong in the late 1990s constitutes one of the world's most heterogeneous cultural environments. Younger people, in particular, are fully conversant in transnational idioms, which include language, music, sports, clothing, satellite television, cyber-communications, global travel, and—of course—cuisine. It is no longer possible to distinguish what is local and what is not. In Hong Kong, as I hope to show in this chapter, the transnational *is* the local.

EATING OUT: A SOCIAL HISTORY OF CONSUMPTION

By the time McDonald's opened its first Hong Kong restaurant in 1975, the idea of fast food was already well established among local consumers. Office workers, shop assistants, teachers, and transport workers had enjoyed various forms of take-out cuisine for well over a century; an entire industry had emerged to deliver mid-day meals direct to workplaces. In the 1960s and 1970s thousands of street vendors produced snacks and simple meals on demand, day or night. Time has always been money in Hong Kong; hence, the dual keys to success in the catering trade were speed and convenience. Another essential characteristic was that the food, based primarily on rice or noodles, had to be hot. Even the most cosmopolitan or local consumers did not (and many still do not) consider cold foods, such as sandwiches and salads, to be acceptable meals. Older people in South China associate cold food with offerings to the dead and are understandably hesitant to eat it.

The fast food industry in Hong Kong had to deliver hot items that could compete with traditional purveyors of convenience foods (noodle shops, dumpling stalls, soup carts, portable grills). The first modern chain to enter the fray was Café de Coral, a local corporation that began operation in 1969 and is still a dominant player in the Hong Kong fast food market (with 109 outlets and a 25 percent market share, compared to McDonald's 20 percent market share in 1994).* Café de Coral's strategy was simple: It moved Hong Kong's street foods indoors, to a clean, well-lighted cafeteria that offered instant service and moderate prices; popular Cantonese items were then combined with (sinicized) "Western" foods that had been popular in Hong Kong for decades. Café de Coral's menu reads like the *locus classicus* of Pacific Rim cuisine: deep-fried chicken wings, curry on rice, hot dogs, roast pork in soup noodles, spaghetti with meat balls, barbecued ribs, red bean sundaes, Oval-tine, Chinese tea, and Coca-Cola (with lemon, hot or cold). The formula was so successful it spawned dozens of imitators, including three full-scale chains.

* * *

---

*Seven of the world's ten busiest McDonald's restaurants are located in Hong Kong. When McDonald's first opened in 1975, few thought it would survive more than a few months. By January 1, 1997, Hong Kong had 125 outlets, which means that there was one McDonald's for every 51,200 residents, compared to one for every 30,000 people in the United States.

McDonald's mid-1970s entry also corresponded to an economic boom associated with Hong Kong's conversion from a low-wage, light-industrial outpost to a regional center for financial services and high-technology industries. McDonald's' takeoff thus paralleled the rise of a new class of highly educated, affluent consumers who thrive in Hong Kong's ever-changing urban environment—one of the most stressful in the world. These new consumers eat out more often than their parents and have created a huge demand for fast, convenient foods of all types. In order to compete in this market, McDonald's had to offer something different. That critical difference, at least during the company's first decade of operation, was American culture packaged as all-American, middle-class food.

* * *

MENTAL CATEGORIES: SNACK VERSUS MEAL

As in other parts of East Asia, McDonald's faced a serious problem when it began operation in Hong Kong: Hamburgers, fries, and sandwiches were perceived as snacks (Cantonese *siu sihk,* literally "small eats"); in the local view these items did not constitute the elements of a proper meal. This perception is still prevalent among older, more conservative consumers who believe that hamburgers, hot dogs, and pizza can never be "filling." Many students stop at fast food outlets on their way home from school; they may share hamburgers and fries with their classmates and then eat a full meal with their families at home. This is not considered a problem by parents, who themselves are likely to have stopped for tea and snacks after work. Snacking with friends and colleagues provides a major opportunity for socializing (and transacting business) among southern Chinese. Teahouses, coffee shops, bakeries, and ice cream parlors are popular precisely because they provide a structured yet informal setting for social encounters. Furthermore, unlike Chinese restaurants and banquet halls, snack centers do not command a great deal of time or money from customers.

Contrary to corporate goals, therefore, McDonald's entered the Hong Kong market as a purveyor of snacks. Only since the late 1980s has its fare been treated as the foundation of "meals" by a generation of younger consumers who regularly eat non-Chinese food. Thanks largely to McDonald's, hamburgers and fries are now a recognized feature of Hong Kong's lunch scene. The evening hours remain, however, the weak link in McDonald's marketing plan; the real surprise was breakfast, which became a peak traffic period.

The mental universe of Hong Kong consumers is partially revealed in the everyday use of language. Hamburgers are referred to, in colloquial Cantonese, as *han bou bao*—*han* being a homophone for "ham" and *bao* the common term for stuffed buns or bread rolls. *Bao* are quintessential snacks, and however excellent or nutritious they might be, they do not constitute the basis of a satisfying (i.e., filling) meal. In South China that honor is reserved for culinary arrangements that rest, literally, on a bed of rice (*fan*). Foods that accompany rice are referred to as *sung,* probably best translated as "toppings" (including meat, fish, and vegetables). It is significant that hamburgers are rarely categorized as meat (*yuk*); Hong Kong consumers tend to perceive anything that is served between slices of bread (Big Macs, fish sandwiches, hot dogs) as *bao.* In American culture the hamburger is categorized first and foremost as a meat item (with all the attendant worries about fat and cholesterol content), whereas in Hong Kong the same item is thought of primarily as bread.

FROM EXOTIC TO ORDINARY: MCDONALD'S BECOMES LOCAL

Following precedents in other international markets, the Hong Kong franchise promoted McDonald's basic menu and did not introduce items that would be more recognizable to Chinese consumers (such as rice dishes, tropical fruit, soup noodles). Until recently the food has been indistinguishable from that served in Mobile, Alabama, or Moline, Illinois. There are, however, local preferences: the best-selling items in many outlets are fish sandwiches and plain hamburgers; Big Macs tend to be the favorites of children and teenagers. Hot tea and hot chocolate outsell coffee, but Coca-Cola remains the most popular drink.

McDonald's conservative approach also applied to the breakfast menu. When morning service was introduced in the 1980s, American-style items such as eggs, muffins, pancakes, and hash brown potatoes were not featured. Instead, the local outlets served the standard fare of hamburgers and fries for breakfast. McDonald's initial venture into the early morning food market was so successful that Mr. Ng hesitated to introduce American-style breakfast items, fearing that an abrupt shift in menu might alienate consumers who were beginning to accept hamburgers and fries as a regular feature of their diet. The transition to eggs, muffins, and hash browns was a gradual one, and today most Hong Kong customers order breakfasts that are similar to those offered in American outlets. But once established, dietary preferences change slowly: McDonald's continues to feature plain hamburgers (but not the Big Mac) on its breakfast menu in most Hong Kong outlets.

Management decisions of the type outlined above helped establish McDonald's as an icon of popular culture in Hong Kong. From 1975 to approximately 1985, McDonald's became the "in" place for young people wishing to associate themselves with the laid-back, nonhierarchical dynamism they perceived American society to embody. The first generation of consumers patronized McDonald's precisely because it was *not* Chinese and was *not* associated with Hong Kong's past as a backward-looking colonial outpost where (in their view) nothing of consequence ever happened. Hong Kong was changing and, as noted earlier, a new consumer culture was beginning to take shape. McDonald's caught the wave of this cultural movement and has been riding it ever since.

* * *

Today, McDonald's restaurants in Hong Kong are packed—wall-to-wall—with people of all ages, few of whom are seeking an American cultural experience. Twenty years after Mr. Ng opened his first restaurant, eating at McDonald's has become an ordinary, everyday experience for hundreds of thousands of Hong Kong residents. The chain has become a local institution in the sense that it has blended into the urban landscape; McDonalds outlets now serve as rendezvous points for young and old alike.

* * *

WHAT'S IN A SMILE? FRIENDLINESS AND PUBLIC SERVICE

American consumers expect to be served "with a smile" when they order fast food, but this is not true in all societies. In Hong Kong people are suspicious of anyone who displays what is perceived to be an excess of congeniality, solicitude, or familiarity. The human smile is not, therefore, a universal symbol of openness and honesty. "If you buy an apple from a hawker and he smiles at you," my Cantonese tutor once told me, "you know you're being cheated."

Given these cultural expectations, it was difficult for Hong Kong management to import a key element of the McDonald's formula—service with a smile—and make it work. Crew members were trained to treat customers in a manner that approximates the American notion of "friendliness." Prior to the 1970s, there was not even an indigenous Cantonese term to describe this form of behavior. The traditional notion of friendship is based on loyalty to close associates, which by definition cannot be extended to strangers. Today the concept of *public* friendliness is recognized—and verbalized—by younger people in Hong Kong, but the term many of them use to express this quality is "friendly," borrowed directly from English. McDonald's, through its television advertising, may be partly responsible for this innovation, but to date it has had little effect on workers in the catering industry.

During my interviews it became clear that the majority of Hong Kong consumers were uninterested in public displays of congeniality from service personnel. When shopping for fast food, most people cited convenience, cleanliness, and table space as primary considerations; few even mentioned service except to note that the food should be delivered promptly. Counter staff in Hong Kong's fast food outlets (including McDonald's) rarely make great efforts to smile or to behave in a manner Americans would interpret as friendly. Instead, they project qualities that are admired in the local culture: competence, directness, and unflappability. In a North American setting the facial expression that Hong Kong employees use to convey these qualities would likely be interpreted as a deliberate attempt to be rude or indifferent. Workers who smile on the job are assumed to be enjoying themselves at the consumer's (and management's) expense: In the words of one diner I overheard while standing in a queue, "They must be playing around back there. What are they laughing about?"

CONSUMER DISCIPLINE?

[A] hallmark of the American fast food business is the displacement of labor costs from the corporation to the consumers. For the system to work, consumers must be educated—or "disciplined"—so that they voluntarily fulfill their side of an implicit bargain: We (the corporation) will provide cheap, fast service, if you (the customer) carry your own tray, seat yourself, and help clean up afterward. Time and space are also critical factors in the equation: Fast service is offered in exchange for speedy consumption and a prompt departure, thereby making room for others. This system has revolutionized the American food industry and has helped to shape consumer expectations in other sectors of the economy. How has it fared in Hong Kong? Are Chinese customers conforming to disciplinary models devised in Oak Brook, Illinois?

The answer is both yes and no. In general Hong Kong consumers have accepted the basic elements of the fast food formula, but with "localizing" adaptations. For instance, customers generally do not bus their own trays, nor do they depart immediately upon finishing. Clearing one's own table has never been an accepted part of local culinary culture, owing in part to the low esteem attaching to this type of labor. During McDonald's' first decade in Hong Kong, the cost of hiring extra cleaners was offset by low wages. A pattern was thus established, and customers grew accustomed to leaving without attending to their own rubbish. Later, as wages escalated in the late 1980s and early 1990s McDonald's tried to introduce self-busing by posting announcements in restaurants and featuring the practice in its television advertisements. As of February 1997, however, little had changed. Hong Kong consumers * * * have ignored this aspect of consumer discipline.

What about the critical issues of time and space? Local managers with whom I spoke estimated that the average eating time for most Hong Kong customers was between 20 and 25 minutes, compared to 11 minutes in the United States fast food industry. This estimate confirms my own observations of McDonald's consumers in Hong Kong's central business district (Victoria and Tsimshatsui). A survey conducted in the New Territories city of Yuen Long—an old market town that has grown into a modern urban center—revealed that local McDonalds consumers took just under 26 minutes to eat.

Perhaps the most striking feature of the American-inspired model of consumer discipline is the queue. Researchers in many parts of the world have reported that customers refuse, despite "education" campaigns by the chains involved, to form neat lines in front of cashiers. Instead, customers pack themselves into disorderly scrums and jostle for a chance to place their orders. Scrums of this nature were common in Hong Kong when McDonalds opened in 1975. Local managers discouraged this practice by stationing queue monitors near the registers during busy hours and, by the 1980s, orderly lines were the norm at McDonald's. The disappearance of the scrum corresponds to a general change in Hong Kong's public culture as a new generation of residents, the children of refugees, began to treat the territory as their home. Courtesy toward strangers was largely unknown in the 1960s: Boarding a bus during rush hour could be a nightmare and transacting business at a bank teller's window required brute strength. Many people credit McDonald's with being the first public institution in Hong Kong to enforce queuing, and thereby helping to create a more "civilized" social order. McDonald's did not, in fact, introduce the queue to Hong Kong, but this belief is firmly lodged in the public imagination.

HOVERING AND THE NAPKIN WARS

Purchasing one's food is no longer a physical challenge in Hong Kong's McDonald's but finding a place to sit is quite another matter. The traditional practice of "hovering" is one solution: Choose a group of diners who appear to be on the verge of leaving and stake a claim to their table by hovering nearby, sometimes only inches away. Seated customers routinely ignore the intrusion; it would, in fact, entail a loss of face to notice. Hovering was the norm in Hong Kong's lower- to middle-range restaurants during the 1960s and 1970s, but the practice has disappeared in recent years. Restaurants now take names or hand out tickets at the entrance; warning signs, in Chinese and English, are posted: "Please wait to be seated." Customers are no longer allowed into the dining area until a table is ready.

Fast food outlets are the only dining establishments in Hong Kong where hovering is still tolerated, largely because it would be nearly impossible to regulate. Customer traffic in McDonald's is so heavy that the standard restaurant design has failed to reproduce American-style dining routines: Rather than ordering first and finding a place to sit afterward, Hong Kong consumers usually arrive in groups and delegate one or two people to claim a table while someone else joins the counter queues. Children make ideal hoverers and learn to scoot through packed restaurants, zeroing in on diners who are about to finish. It is one of the wonders of comparative ethnography to witness the speed with which Hong Kong children perform this reconnaissance duty. Foreign visitors are sometimes unnerved by hovering, but residents accept it as part of everyday life in one of the worlds most densely populated cities. It is not surprising, therefore, that Hong Kong's fast food chains have made few efforts to curtail the practice.

Management is less tolerant of behavior that affects profit margins. In the United States fast food companies save money by allowing (or requiring) customers to collect their own napkins, straws, plastic flatware, and condiments. Self-provisioning is an essential feature of consumer discipline, but it only works if the system is not abused. In Hong Kong napkins are dispensed, one at a time, by McDonalds crew members who work behind the counter; customers who do not ask for napkins do not receive any. This is a deviation from the corporations standard operating procedure and adds a few seconds to each transaction, which in turn slows down the queues. Why alter a well-tested routine? The reason is simple: napkins placed in public dispensers disappear faster than they can be replaced.

* * *

Buffets, like fast food outlets, depend upon consumers to perform much of their own labor in return for reduced prices. Abuse of the system—wasting food or taking it home—is taken for granted and is factored into the price of buffet meals. Fast food chains, by contrast, operate at lower price thresholds where consumer abuse can seriously affect profits.

Many university students of my acquaintance reported that they had frequently observed older people pocketing wads of paper napkins, three to four inches thick, in restaurants that permit self-provisioning. Management efforts to stop this behavior are referred to, in the Cantonese-English slang of Hong Kong youth, as the "Napkin Wars." Younger people were appalled by what they saw as the waste of natural resources by a handful of customers. As they talked about the issue, however, it became obvious that the Napkin Wars represented more—in their eyes—than a campaign to conserve paper. The sight of diners abusing public facilities reminded these young people of the bad old days of their parents and grandparents, when Hong Kong's social life was dominated by refugees who had little stake in the local community. During the 1960s and 1970s, economic insecurities were heightened by the very real prospect that Red Guards might take over the colony at any moment. The game plan was simple during those decades: Make money as quickly as possible and move on. In the 1980s a new generation of local-born youth began treating Hong Kong as home and proceeded to build a public culture better suited to their vision of life in a cosmopolitan city. In this new Hong Kong, consumers are expected to be sophisticated and financially secure, which means that it would be beneath their dignity to abuse public facilities. Still, McDonalds retains control of its napkins.

CHILDREN AS CONSUMERS

During the summer of 1994, while attending a business lunch in one of Hong Kong's fanciest hotels, I watched a waiter lean down to consult with a customer at an adjoining table. The object of his attention was a six-year-old child who studied the menu with practiced skill. His parents beamed as their prodigy performed; meanwhile, sitting across the table, a pair of grandparents sat bolt upright, scowling in obvious disapproval. Twenty years ago the sight of a child commanding such attention would have shocked the entire restaurant into silence. No one, save the immediate party (and this observer), even noticed in 1994.

Hong Kong children rarely ate outside their home until the late 1970s, and when they did, they were expected to eat what was put in front of them. The idea that children might actually order their own food or speak to a waiter would have outraged most adults; only foreign youngsters (notably the offspring of British and American expatriates) were permitted to make their preferences known in public. Today, Hong Kong children as young as two or three participate in the local economy as full-fledged consumers, with their own tastes and brand loyalties. Children now have money in their pockets and they spend it on personal consumption, which usually means snacks. In response, new industries and a specialized service sector has emerged to "feed" these discerning consumers. McDonald's was one of the first corporations to recognize the potential of the children's market; in effect, the company started a revolution by making it possible for even the youngest consumers to *choose* their own food.

* * *

Many Hong Kong children of my acquaintance are so fond of McDonald's that they refuse to eat with their parents or grandparents in Chinese-style restaurants or *dim sam* teahouses. This has caused intergenerational distress in some of Hong Kong's more conservative communities. In 1994, a nine-year-old boy, the descendant of illustrious ancestors who settled in the New Territories eight centuries ago, talked about his concerns as we consumed Big Macs, fries, and shakes at McDonald's: "A-bak [uncle], I like it here better than any place in the world. I want to come here every day." His father takes him to McDonald's at least twice a week, but his grandfather, who accompanied them a few times in the late 1980s, will no longer do so. "I prefer to eat *dim sam,*" the older man told me later. "That place [McDonald's] is for kids." Many grandparents have resigned themselves to the new consumer trends and take their preschool grandchildren to McDonald's for midmorning snacks—precisely the time of day that local teahouses were once packed with retired people. Cantonese grandparents have always played a prominent role in child minding, but until recently the children had to accommodate to the proclivities of their elders. By the 1990s grandchildren were more assertive and the mid-morning *dim sam* snack was giving way to hamburgers and Cokes.

* * *

RONALD MCDONALD AND THE INVENTION
OF BIRTHDAY PARTIES

Until recently most people in Hong Kong did not even know, let alone celebrate, their birthdates in the Western calendrical sense; dates of birth according to the lunar calendar were recorded for divinatory purposes but were not noted in annual rites. By the late 1980s, however, birthday parties, complete with cakes and candles, were the rage in Hong Kong. Any child who was anyone had to have a party, and the most popular venue was a fast food restaurant, with McDonald's ranked above all competitors. The majority of Hong Kong people live in overcrowded flats, which means that parties are rarely held in private homes.

Except for the outlets in central business districts, McDonald's restaurants are packed every Saturday and Sunday with birthday parties, cycled through at the rate of one every hour. A party hostess, provided by the restaurant, leads the children in games while the parents sit on the sidelines, talking quietly among themselves. For a small fee celebrants receive printed invitation cards, photographs, a gift box containing toys and a discount coupon for future trips to McDonald's. Parties are held in a special enclosure, called the Ronald Room, which is equipped with low tables and tiny stools—suitable only for children. Television commercials portray Ronald McDonald leading birthday celebrants on exciting safaris and expeditions. The clown's Cantonese name, Mak Dong Lou Suk-Suk ("Uncle McDonald"), plays on the intimacy of kinship and has helped transform him into one of Hong Kong's most familiar cartoon figures.

* * *

MCDONALD'S AS A YOUTH CENTER

Weekends may be devoted to family dining and birthday parties for younger children, but on weekday afternoons, from 3:00 to 6:00 P.M., McDonald's restaurants are packed with teenagers stopping for a snack on their way home from school. In many outlets 80 percent of the late afternoon clientele appear in school uniforms, turning the restaurants into a sea of white frocks, light blue shirts, and dark trousers. The students, aged between 10 and 17, stake out tables and buy snacks that are shared in groups. The noise level at this time of day is deafening; students shout to friends and dart from table to table. Few adults, other than restaurant staff, are in evidence. It is obvious that

McDonald's is treated as an informal youth center, a recreational extension of school where students can unwind after long hours of study.

* * *

In contrast to their counterparts in the United States, where fast food chains have devised ways to discourage lingering, McDonald's in Hong Kong does not set a limit on table time. When I asked the managers of several Hong Kong outlets how they coped with so many young people chatting at tables that might otherwise be occupied by paying customers, they all replied that the students were "welcome." The obvious strategy is to turn a potential liability into an asset: "Students create a good atmosphere which is good for our business," said one manager as he watched an army of teenagers—dressed in identical school uniforms—surge into his restaurant. Large numbers of students also use McDonald's as a place to do homework and prepare for exams, often in groups. Study space of any kind, public or private, is hard to find in overcrowded Hong Kong. * * *

CONCLUSIONS: WHOSE CULTURE IS IT?

In concluding this chapter, I would like to return to the questions raised in my opening remarks: In what sense, if any, is McDonald's involved in these cultural transformations (the creation of a child-centered consumer culture, for instance)? Has the company helped to create these trends, or merely followed the market? Is this an example of American-inspired, transnational culture crowding out indigenous cultures?

* * *

The deeper I dig into the lives of consumers themselves, in Hong Kong and elsewhere, the more complex the picture becomes. Having watched the processes of culture change unfold for nearly thirty years, it is apparent to me that the ordinary people of Hong Kong have most assuredly *not* been stripped of their cultural heritage, nor have they become the uncomprehending dupes of transnational corporations. Younger people— including many of the grandchildren of my former neighbors in the New Territories—are avid consumers of transnational culture in all of its most obvious manifestations: music, fashion, television, and cuisine. At the same time, however, Hong Kong has itself become a major center for the *production* of transnational culture, not just a sinkhole for its *consumption*. Witness, for example, the expansion of Hong Kong popular culture into China, Southeast Asia, and beyond: "Cantopop" music is heard on radio stations in North China, Vietnam, and Japan; the Hong Kong fashion industry influences clothing styles in Los Angeles, Bangkok, and Kuala Lumpur; and, perhaps most significant of all, Hong Kong is emerging as a center for the production and dissemination of satellite television programs throughout East, Southeast, and South Asia.

A lifestyle is emerging in Hong Kong that can best be described as post-modern, postnationalist, and flamboyantly transnational. The wholesale acceptance and appropriation of Big Macs, Ronald McDonald and birthday parties are small but significant aspects of this redefinition of Chinese cultural identity. In closing, therefore, it seems appropriate to pose an entirely new set of questions: Where does the transnational end and the local begin? Whose culture is it, anyway? In places like Hong Kong the postcolonial periphery is fast becoming the metropolitan center, where local people are consuming and simultaneously producing new cultural systems.

* * *

11

The Code of the Street

ELIJAH ANDERSON

The capacity of sociology to look beyond the headlines is captured in this ethnographic account of a culture of respect, violence, and control on urban streets. Anderson describes this as "a cultural adaptation" to poverty, discrimination in public services, and social marginality. The "presentation of self" examined in this essay is a fascinating social construction and one with deadly serious consequences for everyone, not only for those who embrace the code of the street. The rich complexity of social life is revealed in Anderson's account, as is the difficulty in altering cultural practices without changing the circumstances of those who live the code.

Of all the problems besetting the poor inner-city black community, none is more pressing than that of interpersonal violence and aggression. It wreaks havoc daily with the lives of community residents and increasingly spills over into downtown and residential middle-class areas. Muggings, burglaries, carjackings, and drug-related shootings, all of which may leave their victims or innocent bystanders dead, are now common enough to concern all urban and many suburban residents. The inclination to violence springs from the circumstances of life among the ghetto poor—the lack of jobs that pay a living wage, the stigma of race, the fallout from rampant drug use and drug trafficking, and the resulting alienation and lack of hope for the future.

Simply living in such an environment places young people at special risk of falling victim to aggressive behavior. Although there are often forces in the community which can counteract the negative influences, by far the most powerful being a strong, loving, "decent" (as inner-city residents put it) family committed to middle-class values, the despair is pervasive enough to have spawned an oppositional culture, that of "the streets," whose norms are often consciously opposed to those of mainstream society. These two orientations—decent and street—socially organize the community, and their coexistence has important consequences for residents, particularly children growing up in the inner city. Above all, this environment means that even youngsters whose home lives reflect mainstream values—and the majority of homes in the community do—must be able to handle themselves in a street-oriented environment.

This is because the street culture has evolved what may be called a code of the streets, which amounts to a set of informal rules governing interpersonal public behavior, including violence. The rules prescribe both a proper comportment and a proper way to respond if challenged. They regulate the use of violence and so allow those who are inclined to aggression to precipitate violent encounters in an approved way. The rules have been established and are enforced mainly by the street-oriented, but on the streets the distinction between street and decent is often irrelevant; everybody knows that if the rules are violated, there are penalties. Knowledge of the code is thus largely defensive; it is literally necessary for operating in public. Therefore, even though families with a decency orientation are usually opposed to the values of the code, they often reluctantly encourage their children's familiarity with it to enable them to negotiate the inner-city environment.

At the heart of the code is the issue of respect—loosely defined as being treated "right," or granted the deference one deserves. However, in the troublesome public environment of the inner city, as people increasingly feel buffeted by forces beyond their control, what one deserves in the way of respect becomes more and more problematic and uncertain. This in turn further opens the issue of respect to sometimes intense interpersonal negotiation. In the street culture, especially among young people, respect is viewed as almost an external entity that is hard-won but easily lost, and so must constantly be guarded. The rules of the code in fact provide a framework for negotiating respect. The person whose very appearance—including his clothing, demeanor, and way of moving—deters transgressions feels that he possesses, and may be considered by others to possess, a measure of respect. With the right amount of respect, for instance, he can avoid "being bothered" in public. If he is bothered, not only may he be in physical danger but he has been disgraced or "dissed" (disrespected). Many of the forms that dissing can take might seem petty to middle-class people (maintaining eye contact for too long, for example), but to those invested in the street code, these actions become serious indications of the other person's intentions. Consequently, such people become very sensitive to advances and slights, which could well serve as warnings of imminent physical confrontation.

This hard reality can be traced to the profound sense of alienation from mainstream society and its institutions felt by many poor inner-city black people, particularly the young. The code of the streets is actually a cultural adaptation to a profound lack of faith in the police and the judicial system. The police are most often seen as representing the dominant white society and not caring to protect inner-city residents. When called, they may not respond, which is one reason many residents feel they must be prepared to take extraordinary measures to defend themselves and their loved ones against those who are inclined to aggression. Lack of police accountability has in fact been incorporated into the status system: the person who is believed capable of "taking care of himself" is accorded a certain deference, which translates into a sense of physical and psychological control. Thus the street code emerges where the influence of the police ends and personal responsibility for one's safety is felt to begin. Exacerbated by the proliferation of drugs and easy access to guns, this volatile situation results in the ability of the street-oriented minority (or those who effectively "go for bad") to dominate the public spaces.

DECENT AND STREET FAMILIES

Although almost everyone in poor inner-city neighborhoods is struggling financially and therefore feels a certain distance from the rest of America, the decent and the street family in a real sense represent two poles of value orientation, two contrasting conceptual categories. The labels "decent" and "street," which the residents themselves use, amount to evaluative judgments that confer status on local residents. The labeling is often the result of a social contest among individuals and families of the neighborhood. Individuals of the two orientations often coexist in the same extended family. Decent residents judge themselves to be so while judging others to be of the street, and street individuals often present themselves as decent, drawing distinctions between themselves and other people. In addition, there is quite a bit of circumstantial behavior—that is, one person may at different times exhibit both decent and street orientations, depending on the circumstances. Although these designations result from so much social jockeying, there do exist concrete features that define each conceptual category.

Generally, so called decent families tend to accept mainstream values more fully and attempt to instill them in their children. Whether married couples with children or single-parent (usually female) households, they are generally "working poor" and so tend to be better off financially than their street-oriented neighbors. They value hard work and self-reliance and are willing to sacrifice for their children. Because they have a certain amount of faith in mainstream society, they harbor hopes for a better future for their children, if not for themselves. Many of them go to church and take a strong interest in their children's schooling. Rather than dwelling on the real hardships and inequities facing them, many such decent people, particularly the increasing number of grandmothers raising grandchildren, see their difficult situation as a test from God and derive great support from their faith and from the church community.

Extremely aware of the problematic and often dangerous environment in which they reside, decent parents tend to be strict in their child-rearing practices, encouraging children to respect authority and walk a straight moral line. They have an almost obsessive concern about trouble of any kind and remind their children to be on the lookout for people and situations that might lead to it. At the same time, they are themselves polite and considerate of others, and teach their children to be the same way. At home, at work, and in church, they strive hard to maintain a positive mental attitude and a spirit of cooperation.

So-called street parents, in contrast, often show a lack of consideration for other people and have a rather superficial sense of family and community.

Though they may love their children, many of them are unable to cope with the physical and emotional demands of parenthood, and find it difficult to reconcile their needs with those of their children. These families, who are more fully invested in the code of the streets than the decent people are, may aggressively socialize their children into it in a normative way. They believe in the code and judge themselves and others according to its values.

In fact the overwhelming majority of families in the inner-city community try to approximate the decent-family model, but there are many others who clearly represent the worst fears of the decent family. Not only are their financial resources extremely limited, but what little they have may easily be misused. The lives of the street-oriented are often marked by disorganization. In the most desperate circumstances people frequently have a limited understanding of priorities and consequences, and so frustrations mount over bills, food, and, at times, drink, cigarettes, and drugs. Some tend toward self-destructive behavior; many street-oriented women are crack-addicted ("on the pipe"), alcoholic, or involved in complicated relationships with men who abuse them. In addition, the seeming intractability of their situation, caused in large part by the lack of well-paying jobs and the persistence of racial discrimination, has engendered deep-seated bitterness and anger in many of the most desperate and poorest blacks, especially young people. The need both to exercise a measure of control and to lash out at somebody is often reflected in the adults' relations with their children. At the least, the frustrations of persistent poverty shorten the fuse in such people—contributing to a lack of patience with anyone, child or adult, who irritates them.

In these circumstances a woman—or a man, although men are less consistently present in children's lives—can be quite aggressive with children, yelling at and striking them for the least little infraction of the rules she has set down. Often little if any serious explanation follows the verbal and physical punishment. This response teaches children a particular lesson. They learn that to solve any kind of interpersonal problem one must quickly resort to hitting or other violent behavior. Actual peace and quiet, and also the appearance of calm, respectful children conveyed to her neighbors and friends, are often what the young mother most desires, but at times she will be very aggressive in trying to get them. Thus she may be quick to beat her children, especially if they defy her law, not because she hates them but because this is the way she knows to control them. In fact, many street-oriented women love their children dearly. Many mothers in the community subscribe to the notion that there is a "devil in the boy" that must be beaten out of him or that socially "fast girls need to be whupped." Thus much of what borders on child abuse in the view of social authorities is acceptable parental punishment in the view of these mothers.

Many street-oriented women are sporadic mothers whose children learn to fend for themselves when necessary, foraging for food and money any way they can get it. The children are sometimes employed by drug dealers or become addicted themselves. These children of the street, growing up with little supervision, are said to "come up hard." They often learn to fight at an early age, sometimes using short-tempered adults around them as role models. The street-oriented home may be fraught with anger, verbal disputes, physical aggression, and even mayhem. The children observe these goings-on, learning the lesson that might makes right. They quickly learn to hit those who cross them, and the dog-eat-dog mentality prevails. In order to survive, to protect oneself, it is necessary to marshal inner resources and be ready to deal with adversity in a hands-on way. In these circumstances physical prowess takes on great significance. * * *

CAMPAIGNING FOR RESPECT

These realities of inner-city life are largely absorbed on the streets. At an early age, often even before they start school, children from street-oriented homes gravitate to the streets, where they "hang"—socialize with their peers. Children from these generally permissive homes have a great deal of latitude and are allowed to "rip and run" up and down the street. They often come home from school, put their books down, and go right back out the door. On school nights eight- and nine-year-olds remain out until nine or ten o'clock (and teenagers typically come in whenever they want to). On the streets they play in groups that often become the source of their primary social bonds. Children from decent homes tend to be more carefully supervised and are thus likely to have curfews and to be taught how to stay out of trouble.

When decent and street kids come together, a kind of social shuffle occurs in which children have a chance to go either way. Tension builds as a child comes to realize that he must choose an orientation. The kind of home he comes from influences but does not determine the way he will ultimately turn out—although it is unlikely that a child from a thoroughly street-oriented family will easily absorb decent values on the streets. Youths who emerge from street-oriented families but develop a decency orientation almost always learn those values in another setting—in school, in a youth group, in church. Often it is the result of their involvement with a caring "old head" (adult role model).

In the street, through their play, children pour their individual life experiences into a common knowledge pool, affirming, confirming, and elaborating on what they have observed in the home and matching their skills against those of others. And they learn to fight. Even small children test one another, pushing and shoving, and are ready to hit other children over circumstances not to their liking. In turn, they are readily hit by other children, and the child who is toughest prevails. Thus the violent resolution of disputes, the hitting and cursing, gains social reinforcement. The child in effect is initiated into a system that is really a way of campaigning for respect.

In addition, younger children witness the disputes of older children, which are often resolved through cursing and abusive talk, if not aggression or

and the trophy—extrinsic or intrinsic, tangible or intangible—identifies the current winner.

An important aspect of this often violent give-and-take is its zero-sum quality. That is, the extent to which one person can raise himself up depends on his ability to put another person down. This underscores the alienation that permeates the inner-city ghetto community. There is a generalized sense that very little respect is to be had, and therefore everyone competes to get what affirmation he can of the little that is available. The craving for respect that results gives people thin skins. Shows of deference by others can be highly soothing, contributing to a sense of security, comfort, self-confidence, and self-respect. Transgressions by others which go unanswered diminish these feelings and are believed to encourage further transgressions. Hence one must be ever vigilant against the transgressions of others or even *appearing* as if transgressions will be tolerated. Among young people, whose sense of self-esteem is particularly vulnerable, there is an especially heightened concern with being disrespected. Many inner-city young men in particular crave respect to such a degree that they will risk their lives to attain and maintain it.

The issue of respect is thus closely tied to whether a person has an inclination to be violent, even as a victim. In the wider society people may not feel required to retaliate physically after an attack, even though they are aware that they have been degraded or taken advantage of. They may feel a great need to defend themselves *during* an attack, or to behave in such a way as to deter aggression (middle-class people certainly can and do become victims of street-oriented youths), but they are much more likely than street-oriented people to feel that they can walk away from a possible altercation with their self-esteem intact. Some people may even have the strength of character to flee, without any thought that their self-respect or esteem will be diminished.

In impoverished inner-city black communities, however, particularly among young males and perhaps increasingly among females, such flight would be extremely difficult. To run away would likely leave one's self-esteem in tatters. Hence people often feel constrained not only to stand up and at least attempt to resist during an assault but also to "pay back"—to seek revenge—after a successful assault on their person. This may include going to get a weapon or even getting relatives involved. Their very identity and self-respect, their honor, is often intricately tied up with the way they perform on the streets during and after such encounters. This outlook reflects the circumscribed opportunities of the inner-city poor. Generally people outside the ghetto have other ways of gaining status and regard, and thus do not feel so dependent on such physical displays.

BY TRIAL OF MANHOOD

On the street, among males these concerns about things and identity have come to be expressed in the concept of "manhood." Manhood in the inner city means taking the prerogatives of men with respect to strangers, other men, and women—being distinguished as a man. It implies physicality and a certain ruthlessness. Regard and respect are associated with this concept in large part because of its practical application: if others have little or no regard for a person's manhood, his very life and those of his loved ones could be in jeopardy. But there is a chicken-and-egg aspect to this situation: one's physical safety is more likely to be jeopardized in public *because* manhood is associated with respect. In other words, an existential link has been created between the idea of manhood and one's self-esteem, so that it has become hard to say which is primary. For many inner-city youths, manhood and respect are flip sides of the same coin; physical and psychological well-being are inseparable, and both require a sense of control, of being in charge.

The operating assumption is that a man, especially a real man, knows what other men know—the code of the streets. And if one is not a real man, one is somehow diminished as a person, and there are certain valued things one simply does not deserve. There is thus believed to be a certain justice to the code, since it is considered that everyone has the opportunity to know it. Implicit in this is that everybody is held responsible for being familiar with the code. If the victim of a mugging, for example, does not know the code and so responds "wrong," the perpetrator may feel justified even in killing him and may feel no remorse. He may think, "Too bad, but it's his fault. He should have known better."

So when a person ventures outside, he must adopt the code—a kind of shield, really—to prevent others from "messing with" him. In these circumstances it is easy for people to think they are being tried or tested by others even when this is not the case. For it is sensed that something extremely valuable is at stake in every interaction, and people are encouraged to rise to the occasion, particularly with strangers. For people who are unfamiliar with the code—generally people who live outside the inner city—the concern with respect in the most ordinary interactions can be frightening and incomprehensible. But for those who are invested in the code, the clear object of their demeanor is to discourage strangers from even thinking about testing their manhood. And the sense of power that attends the ability to deter others can be alluring even to those who know the code without being heavily invested in it—the decent inner-city youths. Thus a boy who has been leading a basically decent life can, in trying circumstances, suddenly resort to deadly force.

Central to the issue of manhood is the widespread belief that one of the most effective ways of gaining respect is to manifest "nerve." Nerve is shown when one takes another persons possessions (the more valuable the better), "messes with" someone's woman, throws the first punch, "gets in someone's face," or pulls a trigger. Its proper display helps on the spot to check others who would violate one's person and also helps to build a reputation that works to prevent future challenges. But since such a show of nerve is a forceful expression of disrespect toward the person on the receiving end, the victim may be greatly offended and seek to retaliate with equal or greater force. A display of nerve, therefore, can easily provoke a life-threatening response, and the background knowledge of that possibility has often been incorporated into the concept of nerve.

True nerve exposes a lack of fear of dying. Many feel that it is acceptable to risk dying over the principle of respect. In fact, among the hard-core street-oriented, the clear risk of violent death may be preferable to being "dissed" by another. The youths who have internalized this attitude and convincingly display it in their public bearing are among the most threatening people of all, for it is commonly assumed that they fear no man. As the people of the community say, "They are the baddest dudes on the street." They often lead an existential life that may acquire meaning only when they are faced with the possibility of imminent death. Not to be afraid to die is by implication to have few compunctions about taking another's life. Not to be afraid to die is the quid pro quo of being able to take somebody else's life—for the right reasons, if the situation demands it. When others believe this is one's position, it gives one a real sense of power on the streets. Such credibility is what many inner-city youths strive to achieve, whether they are decent or street-oriented, both because of its practical defensive value and because of the positive way it makes them feel about themselves. The difference between the decent and the street-oriented youth is often that the decent youth makes a conscious decision to appear tough and manly; in another setting—with teachers, say, or at his part-time job—he can be polite and deferential. The street-oriented youth, on the other hand, has made the concept of manhood a part of his very identity; he has difficulty manipulating it—it often controls him.

GIRLS AND BOYS

Increasingly, teenage girls are mimicking the boys and trying to have their own version of "manhood." Their goal is the same—to get respect, to be recognized as capable of setting or maintaining a certain standard. They try to achieve this end in the ways that have been established by the boys, including posturing, abusive language, and the use of violence to resolve disputes, but the issues for the girls are different. Although conflicts over turf and status exist among the girls, the majority of disputes seem rooted in assessments of beauty (which girl in a group is "the cutest"), competition over boyfriends, and attempts to regulate other people's knowledge of and opinions about a girl's behavior or that of someone close to her, especially her mother.

A major cause of conflicts among girls is "he say, she say." This practice begins in the early school years and continues through high school. It occurs when "people," particularly girls, talk about others, thus putting their "business in the streets." Usually one girl will say something negative about another in the group, most often behind the person's back. The remark will then get back to the person talked about. She may retaliate or her friends may feel required to "take up for" her. In essence this is a form of group gossiping in which individuals are negatively assessed and evaluated. As with much gossip, the things said may or may not be true, but the point is that such imputations can cast aspersions on a person's good name. The accused is required to defend herself against the slander, which can result in arguments and fights, often over little of real substance. Here again is the problem of low self-esteem, which encourages youngsters to be highly sensitive to slights and to be vulnerable to feeling easily "dissed." To avenge the dissing, a fight is usually necessary.

Because boys are believed to control violence, girls tend to defer to them in situations of conflict. Often if a girl is attacked or feels slighted, she will get a brother, uncle, or cousin to do her fighting for her. Increasingly, however, girls are doing their own fighting and are even asking their male relatives to teach them how to fight. Some girls form groups that attack other girls or take things from them. A hard-core segment of inner-city girls inclined toward violence seems to be developing. As one thirteen-year-old girl in a detention center for youths who have committed violent acts told me, "To get people to leave you alone, you gotta fight. Talking don't always get you out of stuff." One major difference between girls and boys: girls rarely use guns. Their fights are therefore not life-or-death struggles. Girls are not often willing to put their lives on the line for "manhood." The ultimate form of respect on the male-dominated inner-city street is thus reserved for men.

"GOING FOR BAD"

In the most fearsome youths such a cavalier attitude toward death grows out of a very limited view of life. Many are uncertain about how long they are going to live and believe they could die violently at any time. They accept this fate; they live on the edge. Their manner conveys the message that nothing intimidates them; whatever turn the encounter takes, they maintain their attack—rather like a pit bull, whose spirit many such boys admire. The demonstration of such tenacity "shows heart" and earns their respect.

This fearlessness has implications for law enforcement. Many street-oriented boys are much more concerned about the threat of "justice" at the hands of a peer than at the hands of the police. Moreover, many feel not only that they have little to lose by going to prison but that they have something to gain. The toughening-up one experiences in prison can actually enhance one's reputation on the streets. Hence the system loses influence over the hard core who are without jobs, with little perceptible stake in the system. If mainstream society has done nothing *for* them, they counter by making sure it can do nothing *to* them.

At the same time, however, a competing view maintains that true nerve consists in backing down, walking away from a fight, and going on with one's business. One fights only in self-defense. This view emerges from the decent philosophy that life is precious, and it is an important part of the socialization process common in decent homes. It discourages violence as the primary means of resolving disputes and encourages youngsters to accept nonviolence and talk as confrontational strategies. But "if the deal goes down," self-defense is greatly encouraged. When there is enough positive support for this orientation, either in the home or among one's peers, then nonviolence has a chance to prevail. But it prevails at the cost of relinquishing a claim to being bad and tough, and therefore sets a young person up as at the very least alienated from street-oriented peers and quite possibly a target of derision or even violence.

Although the nonviolent orientation rarely overcomes the impulse to strike back in an encounter, it does introduce a certain confusion and so can prompt a measure of soul-searching, or even profound ambivalence. Did the person back down with his respect intact or did he back down only to be judged a "punk"—a person lacking manhood? Should he or she have acted? Should he or she have hit the other person in the mouth? These questions beset many young men and women during public confrontations. What is the "right" thing to do? In the quest for honor, respect, and local status—which few young people are uninterested in—common sense most often prevails, which leads many to opt for the tough approach, enacting their own particular versions of the display of nerve. The presentation of oneself as rough and tough is very often quite acceptable until one is tested. And then that presentation may help the person pass the test, because it will cause fewer questions to be asked about what he did and why. It is hard for a person to explain why he lost the fight or why he backed down. Hence many will strive to appear to "go for bad," while hoping they will never be tested. But when they are tested, the outcome of the situation may quickly be out of their hands, as they become wrapped up in the circumstances of the moment.

AN OPPOSITIONAL CULTURE

The attitudes of the wider society are deeply implicated in the code of the streets. Most people in inner-city communities are not totally invested in the code, but the significant minority of hard-core street youths who are have to maintain the code in order to establish reputations, because they have—or feel they have—few other ways to assert themselves. For these young people the standards of the street code are the only game in town. The extent to which some children—particularly those who through upbringing have become most alienated and those lacking in strong and conventional social support—experience, feel, and internalize racist rejection and contempt from mainstream society may strongly encourage them to express contempt for the more conventional society in turn. In dealing with this contempt and rejection, some youngsters will consciously invest themselves and their considerable mental resources in what amounts to an oppositional culture to preserve themselves and their self-respect. Once they do, any respect they might be able to garner in the wider system pales in comparison with the respect available in the local system; thus they often lose interest in even attempting to negotiate the mainstream system.

At the same time, many less alienated young blacks have assumed a street-oriented demeanor as a way of expressing their blackness while really embracing a much more moderate way of life; they, too, want a nonviolent setting in which to live and raise a family. These decent people are trying hard to be part of the mainstream culture, but the racism, real and perceived, that they encounter helps to legitimate the oppositional culture. And so on occasion they adopt street behavior. In fact, depending on the demands of the situation, many people in the community slip back and forth between decent and street behavior.

A vicious cycle has thus been formed. The hopelessness and alienation many young inner-city black men and women feel, largely as a result of endemic joblessness and persistent racism, fuels the violence they engage in. This violence serves to confirm the negative feelings many whites and some middle-class blacks harbor toward the ghetto poor, further legitimating the oppositional culture and the code of the streets in the eyes of many poor young blacks. Unless this cycle is broken, attitudes on both sides will become increasingly entrenched, and the violence, which claims victims black and white, poor and affluent, will only escalate.

12

America's National Eating Disorder

FROM *The Omnivore's Dilemma: A Natural History of Four Meals*

MICHAEL POLLAN

One of the most popular and talked-about books of recent years, The Omnivore's Dilemma, *includes this essay, which asks, What should I eat? In an affluent society where grocery items come from all over the world, everything is available. Or, I can skip the grocery store and just eat out. But in either case, I may not know what I'm eating. Michael Pollan has tapped the root of food insecurity and come up with a critique of both American culture and corporate capitalism. It is certainly food for thought.*

All the customs and rules culture has devised to mediate the clash of human appetite and society probably bring greater comfort to us as eaters than as sexual beings. Freud and others lay the blame for many of our sexual neuroses at the door of an overly repressive culture, but that doesn't appear to be the principal culprit in our neurotic eating. To the contrary, it seems as though our eating tends to grow more tortured as our culture's power to manage our relationship to food weakens.

This seems to me precisely the predicament we find ourselves in today as eaters, particularly in America. America has never had a stable national cuisine; each immigrant population has brought its own foodways to the American table, but none has ever been powerful enough to hold the national diet very steady. We seem bent on reinventing the American way of eating every generation, in great paroxysms of neophilia and neophobia. That might explain why Americans have been such easy marks for food fads and diets of every description.

This is the country, after all, where at the turn of the last century Dr. John Harvey Kellogg persuaded great numbers of the country's most affluent and best educated to pay good money to sign themselves into his legendarily nutty sanitarium at Battle Creek, Michigan, where they submitted to a regime that included all-grape diets and almost hourly enemas. Around the same time millions of Americans succumbed to the vogue for "Fletcherizing"—chewing each bite of food as many as one hundred times—introduced by Horace Fletcher, also known as the Great Masticator.

This period marked the first golden age of American food faddism, though of course its exponents spoke not in terms of fashion but of "scientific eating," much as we do now. Back then the best nutritional science maintained that carnivory promoted the growth of toxic bacteria in the colon; to battle these evildoers Kellogg vilified meat and mounted a two-fronted assault on his patients' alimentary canals, introducing quantities of Bulgarian yogurt at both ends. It's easy to make fun of people who would succumb to such fads, but it's not at all clear that we're any less gullible. It remains to be seen whether the current Atkins school theory of ketosis—the process by which the body resorts to burning its own fat when starved of carbohydrates—will someday seem as quaintly quackish as Kellogg's theory of colonic autointoxication.

What is striking is just how little it takes to set off one of these applecart-toppling nutritional swings in America; a scientific study, a new government guideline, a lone crackpot with a medical degree can alter this nation's diet overnight. One article in the *New York Times Magazine* in 2002 almost single-handedly set off the recent spasm of carbophobia in America. But the basic pattern was fixed decades earlier, and suggests just how vulnerable the lack of stable culinary traditions leaves us to the omnivore's anxiety, and the companies and quacks who would prey on it. So every few decades some new scientific research comes along to challenge the prevailing nutritional orthodoxy; some nutrient that Americans have been happily chomping for decades is suddenly found to be lethal; another nutrient is elevated to the status of health food; the industry throws its weight behind it; and the American way of dietary life undergoes yet another revolution.

Harvey Levenstein, a Canadian historian who has written two fascinating social histories of American foodways, neatly sums up the beliefs that have guided the American way of eating since the heyday of John Harvey Kellogg: "that taste is not a true guide to what should be eaten; that one should not simply eat what one enjoys; that the important components of food cannot be seen or tasted, but are discernible only in scientific laboratories; and that experimental science has produced rules of nutrition that will prevent illness and encourage longevity." The power of any orthodoxy resides in its ability not to seem like one and, at least to a 1906 or 2006 genus American, these beliefs don't seem in the least bit strange or controversial.

It's easy, especially for Americans, to forget just how novel this nutritional orthodoxy is, or that there are still cultures that have been eating more or less the same way for generations, relying on such archaic criteria as taste and tradition to guide them in their food selection. We Americans are amazed to learn that some of the cultures that set their culinary course by the lights of habit and pleasure rather than nutritional science and marketing are actually healthier than we are—that is, suffer a lower incidence of diet-related health troubles.

The French paradox is the most famous such case, though as Paul Rozin points out, the French don't regard the matter as paradoxical at all. We Americans resort to that term because the French experience—a population of wine-swilling cheese eaters with lower rates of heart disease and obesity—confounds our orthodoxy about food. That orthodoxy regards certain tasty foods as poisons (carbs now, fats then), failing to appreciate that how we eat, and even how we feel about eating, may in the end be just as important as what we eat. The French eat all sorts of supposedly unhealthy foods, but they do it according to a strict and stable set of rules: They eat small portions and don't go back for seconds; they don't snack; they seldom eat alone; and communal meals are long, leisurely affairs. In other words, the French culture of food successfully negotiates the omnivore's dilemma, allowing the French to enjoy their meals without ruining their health.

Perhaps because we have no such culture of food in America almost every question about eating is up for grabs. Fats or carbs? Three squares or continuous grazing? Raw or cooked? Organic or industrial? Veg or vegan? Meat or mock meat? Foods of astounding novelty fill the shelves of our supermarket, and the line between a food and a "nutritional supplement" has fogged to the point where people make meals of protein bars and shakes. Consuming these neo-pseudo-foods alone in our cars, we have become a nation of antinomian eaters, each of us struggling to work out our dietary salvation on our own. Is it any wonder Americans suffer from so many eating disorders? In the absence of any lasting consensus about what and how and where and when to eat, the omnivore's dilemma has returned to America with an almost atavistic force.

This situation suits the food industry just fine, of course. The more anxious we are about eating, the more vulnerable we are to the seductions of the marketer and the expert's advice. Food marketing in particular thrives on dietary instability and so tends to exacerbate it. Since it's difficult to sell more food to such a well-fed population (though not, as we're discovering, impossible), food companies put their efforts into grabbing market share by introducing new kinds of highly processed foods, which have the virtue of being both highly profitable and infinitely adaptable. Sold under the banner of "convenience," these processed foods are frequently designed to create whole new eating occasions, such as in the bus on the way to school (the protein bar or Pop-Tart) or in the car on the way to work (Campbell's recently introduced a one-handed microwaveable microchunked soup in a container designed to fit a car's cup holder).

The success of food marketers in exploiting shifting eating patterns and nutritional fashions has a steep cost. Getting us to change how we eat over and over again tends to undermine the various social structures that surround and steady our eating, institutions like the family dinner, for example, or taboos on snacking between meals and eating alone. In their relentless pursuit of new markets, food companies (with some crucial help from the microwave oven, which made "cooking" something even small children could do) have broken Mom's hold over the American menu by marketing to every conceivable demographic—and especially to children.

A vice president of marketing at General Mills once painted for me a picture of the state of the American family dinner, courtesy of video cameras that the company's consulting anthropologists paid families to let them install in the ceiling above the kitchen and dining room tables. Mom, perhaps feeling sentimental about the dinners of her childhood, still prepares a dish and a salad that she usually winds up eating by herself. Meanwhile, the kids, and Dad, too, if he's around, each fix something different for themselves, because Dad's on a low-carb diet, the teenager's become a vegetarian, and the eight-year-old is on a strict ration of pizza that the shrink says it's best to indulge (lest she develop eating disorders later on in life). So over the course of a half hour or so each family member roams into the kitchen, removes a single-portion entrée from the freezer, and zaps it in the microwave. (Many of these entrées have been helpfully designed to be safely "cooked" by an eight-year-old.) After the sound of the beep each diner brings his microwaveable dish to the dining room table, where he or she may or may not cross paths with another family member at the table for a few minutes. Families who eat this way are among the 47 percent of Americans who report to pollsters that they still sit down to a family meal every night.

Several years ago, in a book called *The Cultural Contradictions of Capitalism*, sociologist Daniel Bell called attention to the tendency of capitalism, in its single-minded pursuit of profit, to erode the various cultural underpinnings that steady a society but often impede the march of commercialization. The family dinner, and more generally a cultural consensus on the subject of eating, appears to be the latest such casualty of capitalism. These rules and rituals stood in the way of the food industry's need to sell a well-fed population more food through ingenious new ways of processing, packaging, and marketing it. Whether a stronger set of traditions would have stood up better to this relentless economic imperative is hard to say; today America's fast-food habits are increasingly gaining traction even in places like France.

So we find ourselves as a species almost back where we started: anxious omnivores struggling once again to figure out what it is wise to eat. Instead of relying on the accumulated wisdom of a cuisine, or even on the wisdom of our senses, we rely on expert opinion, advertising, government food pyramids, and diet books, and we place our faith in science to sort out for us what culture once did with rather more success. Such has been the genius of capitalism, to re-create something akin to a state of nature in the modern supermarket or fast-food outlet, throwing us back on a perplexing, nutritionally perilous landscape deeply shadowed again by the omnivore's dilemma.

13

From *Nike Culture: The Sign of the Swoosh*

ROBERT GOLDMAN AND STEPHEN PAPSON

Modern society is based on industrial production; postmodern society is based on information, including advertising. No one entity has taken advertising's central role in the creation of modern culture as far and as effectively as the Nike Corporation. Nike's swoosh is everywhere, and its larger cultural themes, such as the "love of the game," provide an inspirational image delivered with no restrictions of time and space. In this excerpt from their book the authors use sociological concepts of the sacred and profane and the ideas of Bellah and his colleagues (reading 43) to examine Nike's creation of a spiritual message of universal humanity that transcends class, power, and ethnic divides. Inspiring, yes, but designed first and foremost to sell a product.

THE COMMUNITY OF SPORT AND PLAY

The contradiction between the desire for individual glory and the desire to be a part of an egalitarian and democratic community of others plays itself out throughout American culture. In *Habits of the Heart,* Robert Bellah and his associates addressed this tension between unbridled individualism and the desire for community. Bellah argued that American cosmology celebrates individual success to such a degree that it fails to give adequate voice to the need for communal belongingness. Without an historically grounded community, decisions, values, and moral codes are driven by privatized self-interests and personal feelings and desires. With the disappearance of real communities of memory, the desire for community becomes expressed as nostalgia. Nevertheless, the yearning for community remains.[1]

While much of *Nike* advertising addresses the autonomous individual, a surprising number of sports also dwell on the social character of sporting activity. In recent years, *Nike* ads about rugby in the snow, tennis in a NY City street intersection, and kids' street hockey have pivoted on the social side of sport. A car horn beeps and a kid hollers "Car!" Thus begins a street hockey commercial patterned after the Dr. Seuss story *And To Think That I Saw It On Mulberry Street.* The kids clear the goal nets off the street to let the car pass and then resume playing. Moments later a kid yells "Motorcycle gang!" and a group of bikers pass through. Next a kid yells "Marathon," and a marathon passes by.

---

1. Robert Bellah, Richard Madsen, William M. Sullivan, Ann Swidler, and Steven M. Tipton, *Habits of the Heart: Individualism and Commitment in American Life (Harper, New York, 1985).*

This is followed by "Parade!" complete with marching band, floats, cheerleaders, and a beauty queen blowing kisses. Finally, a kid yells "Stampede" and a black frame appears with "Just do it" bouncing up and down to the ground-shaking stampede in the background. The musical background is lively and upbeat, punctuated by the "whack! whack!" of slapping the puck. The ad's humor is based on exaggerating the social experience of kids' informal play. Though the ad speaks to kids, it also nostalgically engages older audiences about that time in their lives when the spontaneous community of childhood games battled cars for control of the street. Most importantly, the spontaneity of play transcends social conventions. Similarly, a Sampras–Agassi tennis commercial plays on this social control of the street. Sampras instructs a NYC cab driver, "Looks pretty good. Stop right here." He and Agassi hop out, stop traffic and set up a net. With punk music defining the background they aggressively overhit balls at one another on their hastily-assembled street court. A crowd gathers and cheers them on. In this ad the pleasure of sport takes place as a form of transgression. Play transcends the socially proscribed use of urban traffic space, and an instant community is born. City workers, pedestrians, automobiles all stop, taking a moment to share the pleasure of disobeying the repressive order of everyday routines, until a city bus comes barreling through the net, ending the break and restoring order. Rather than view these as merely amusing yarns, we take these to be parables reflecting *Nike's* philosophy. These ads portray space and time as social constructs that can be overcome by the will to play. The spirit of sport restructures social space, carving out conviviality in the most unlikely places—marking off a rugby field by spray-painting red lines on a blanket of snow; children's informal play communities carving out space for play wherever the opportunity presents itself; or the forcible seizure of a traffic intersection governed by laws and regulations to create a fugitive tennis court as a theater for the passion of play. The latter of course assembles not a community of players, but a community of spectators brought together by the staging of *Nike's* guerilla theater.

Celebrating the Game

"The game" refers to that which is sacred in sport. The game is pure and simple. At its basic level it is a set of rules that govern relationships and performance. Within this set of rules everyone is equal. It does not matter who you are but what you do. As soon as one enters the circle of the game, one's ability and determination magically displace class, race, gender, and age. The game is the pure form of sociality—play. Like society, the game has a history and a future which transcends the individual. On playgrounds, in parks, in school yards, in stadiums, and on TV the game not only empowers the individual but also represents a space in which community still exists. The "love" for the game recognizes a world greater than the individual.

In our society there are two recognized threats to the game—commodification and spectacularization, or more concretely, money and the media. These forces are seen as intrusions into the essence of the game, the pure form of sociality. Here, there is an odd congruity between *Nike's* position and the sociological approach of Robert Bellah. Both "theories"—Bellah's and *Nike's*—disregard capital as a force that structures privatized lives. And yet, each in its own way recognizes the pernicious impact of markets on culture and community life. Like Bellah, *Nike's* solution to this dilemma is idealist. Bellah speaks to desires for secular re-spiritualization. *Nike* similarly poses the activity of sport as highly spiritualized: the means of finding oneself and belonging to a community of others.

The celebrity athlete embodies the conflict between the sacred (the game) and the secular (commercialization). Representations of the super athlete signify human transcendence, but those representations are constructed by media, sport corporations, and advertisers to serve their own materialistic ends. The athlete as a celebrity is a threat to the pure form of the game. Bigger contracts and proliferating endorsements prompt fans to suspect that money rather than the love of the game is the prime motivation. Consequently, the athlete must be regularly purified of his/her materialistic motives. When Michael Jordan retired from basketball to play minor league baseball, *Nike* used the opportunity to celebrate Jordan's purity of soul and motives by humorously casting his retirement as a consequence of his desire to preserve his deep love for the essence of basketball, the game. The tongue in cheek comments on Jordan's retirement made by members of the professional basketball sports fraternity provide the narration for the ad which tracks Jordan in various disguises—wearing a beard, a wig, goggles, a trenchcoat—as he plays basketball with minor league teams like Las Cruces, Gary, Billings, and the Crawfish.

JOHN THOMPSON: If Michael is out there still playing, the message is clear. Here is the guy who is the greatest player of all times letting nothing stand in his way doing what he loves to do. And that's just play basketball.

MARV ALBERT: I think he had to get away from everything. It all overwhelmed him. I can understand Michael playing in disguise.

MICHAEL IRVIN: You can't blame the man. This man just wants to play the game.

AHMAD RASHAD: I think that he got so tired of the hype and so tired of the media that he wanted to find a place that he could play and really have fun.

DAN MAJERLE: I think that he's a little bored. I think he wants to come back for the competition. And he wants a chance to come out and score some points and play against his old friends again.

DAVID ROBINSON: I think that Mike is doing this just to get away from the insanity of pro basketball—the hype.

B.J. ARMSTRONG: The pressure.

MARV ALBERT: The media.

DENNIS RODMAN: The refs.

SPIKE LEE: The commercials.

CHRIS WEBBER: Nah! I think he's scared of me.

HAROLD MINER: Or maybe Mike is doing this just because he wants to be a player again.

Nike encourages an exaggerated self-awareness when these commentators speak directly to the camera (to us) as they speculate on why Jordan retired from the *NBA*—because of the hype, the media, the commercials, the pressure, all answers that focus on the commercialization and the spectacular-ization of sport. When Spike Lee holds up a pair of shoes and blames commercials for Jordan's retirement, *Nike* playfully critiques itself. By poking fun at itself and its role in creating the hype and spectacle that drove Jordan from the *NBA*, *Nike* hails the cynical viewer and then deflates both criticism and cynicism by humor. This is another example of the knowing wink. Throughout the commercial *Nike's* icon remains pure. Jordan, the king of sign value, is shown transcending the hype because his love for the game remains strong. What does Jordan want to do? Just play the game, to be a player again. What motivates him? His love for the game. In spite of the spectacle, Jordan and his fellow players remain pure at heart in their love of the game. Here at the center of sports, lies something which cannot be commodified, our love of the game. The commercial also permits us backstage among a fraternity of men who play the game, and who share a sense of camaraderie, respect, and shared purpose. *Nike* constructs the relationship of these athletes to their work in a way that reproduces C. Wright Mills' ideals of craftsmanship—internal motivation, a unity of work and leisure, and work as play.

Like the Michael Jordan retirement commercial, the "Play ball" commercial uses a similar structural form to celebrate the sociability of an athletic community held together by the shared culture of the game. Sociability is expressed by the cut up dialogue in which players complete each others sentences and finish jokes, suggesting a shared intertextual culture (knowledge of the game's history as well as contemporary events linked to athletes) organized around baseball.

CAL RIPKEN: I believe that hitting a round ball with a round bat

KIRBY PUCKETT: is the hardest thing to do in all sports.

RAUL MONDESI: I believe that Roberto Clemente is the patron saint of baseball . . .

KURT GIBSON: I believe in the designated hitter.

DON MATTINGLY: I believe that Lou Gehrig's birthday should be a national holiday . . .

KEN GRIFFEY: I believe walls are hard.

DON MATTINGLY: I believe that no one is bigger than the game

MATT WILLIAMS: except maybe Boog Powell.

DON MATTINGLY: I believe somebody,

KIRBY PUCKETT: somewhere,

KURT GIBSON: understands the infield fly rule.

KEN GRIFFEY: I believe it's time to sing.

DON MATTINGLY: Take me out to the ball game (he sings)

MATT WILLIAMS: I believe that even I sing better than Don Mattingly.

MIKE PIAZZA: I believe that.

KIRBY PUCKETT: And I believe that every player should have a day off after 2160 games.

MATT WILLIAMS: I believe that dome stadiums are great
KEN GRIFFEY: for tractor pulls.
KURT GIBSON: I believe that the two greatest words
DON MATTINGLY: in the English language
MATT WILLIAMS: are play ball . . .
DON MATTINGLY: I believe if Shoeless Joe Jackson were playing today he'd have a shoe contract.

This culture has a history (references to Lou Gehrig, Boog Powell, Shoeless Joe Jackson) and a sense of the sacred with its patron saint Roberto Clemente. Players joke about one another (Don Mattingly "can't sing," Tony Gwynn "sleeps with his bat") and make self-referential jokes about themselves and the game (Ken Griffey's comment about playing in the Seattle Kingdome plagued by falling tiles), while also speaking with admiration about each other (Kirby Puckett's bow to Cal Ripken's record of consecutive games played). Insider jokes signify a shared culture. Any game or team that has continuity develops a comparable culture. This shared culture and bonding mechanism parallels that constructed in everyday life by those who have played on a softball team (*Nike's* other commercial about the octogenarian Kubs), noon-time basketball, or playground basketball. In a social world that has become, by and large, privatized, this *Nike* ad invites viewers to share in this sports community through knowledge of the game, or more importantly, through knowledge of the ad itself—being able to identify the players and knowing the background to the joking references. Recognizing players and their intertextual banter serves as the criterion for admission to the baseball fraternity.

After the screen has gone to the *Nike* logo, the camera returns to Don Mattingly saying, "I believe if Shoeless Joe Jackson were playing today he'd have a shoe contract." Mattingly's banter has now turned on our host as he jokes about *Nike's* habit of signing the stars of the game. The reference to Shoeless Joe Jackson demands some minimal knowledge of baseball legend and lore. To fully appreciate the insider's joke shared by Mattingly with *Nike* we need to know that Shoeless Joe was an old-time ballplayer. Legend has it that Shoeless Joe was just a good ol' country boy who purely loved to play baseball. But he got caught up in the Chicago Black Sox scandal in the 1919 World Series and betrayed the integrity of the game. Shoeless Joe thus became a fallen celebrity of some interest because he represented the cultural tension between playing for the love of sport and the immorality of money. The story has been revived and romanticized by the baseball film *Field of Dreams,* and more recently has been a subject of attention in Ken Burns's epic history of baseball and in John Sayles' cinematic rendering of the Black Sox scandal. At any rate, with the last barb flung back at itself, *Nike* pokes fun at itself, thus including itself into the community of *Nike* athletes.

Ads like this celebrate the community organized around the game itself. The All-Star Game is the perfect venue not just because it has celebrity athletes but because the game celebrates the sport itself. References to the love of the game abound in commercials. *Reebok* depicted its celebrity athletes playing pick-up ball in gyms to demonstrate that "you gotta have the love" and, of course, *NBA* promos use the slogan "I love this game." Though the latter is but a hollow tagline that celebrates the commercialization of basketball when it is positioned adjacent to a series of spectacular images of players and fans displaying intense emotion, the simple reference to "the game" legitimizes *NBA* practices. In a society inundated by commercialism, references to a mythical essence of sport provide an imaginary core of meaning. The litany of "I believe" in *Nike's* All-Star Game "Play ball" commercial resembles a religious service. Ironically, the commercial has two endings: love for the game and a *Nike* shoe contract. After all, are the two greatest words in the English language "play ball" or "shoe contract"?

Joining the Nike Community

The meanings of sports have anchored male public culture for much of the twentieth century. During the previous century, male culture revolved more around tools and making things, or politics. *Nike* and *Wieden & Kennedy* recognize that sport has slowly replaced work, religion and community as the glue of collective consciousness in latter twentieth century America. To be sure, *Nike's* advertising is not unique in extolling the therapeutic merits of ministering to body and spirit through athletic activity. Such ads have become so prolific that a 1995 public service style ad for a religious organization mimics the look and feel of *Soloflex* ads as a lure to enjoining viewers to attend that other "temple" this weekend. As secular religion, few ads have more explicitly caught the metaphor of your body as a temple than the *Nike* "Don't rush" ad campaign for their women's fitness products. *Nike's* men's ads have been less likely to express this blend of therapeutic narcissism, stressing instead sociability. Male sports banter lies at the heart of this advertising—banter similar to that which once shaped, for both better and worse, a proletarian public sphere; and banter that we today associate, thanks to the media, with trash-talking in black urban culture.

Nike ads create a community of athletes who share the *Nike* philosophy: they play intensely because they love the game. While the Jordan retirement ad emphasizes that philosophy, it also constructs a *Nike* community based on sports talk. This includes media hype, advertising discourse, shop talk—strategies, evaluation of players, statistics, and predictions. Media discourse and informal conversation intermix. These stars have become part of the sports fan's family and he/she part of theirs—at least within the spectacle. But there is also an informal discourse that defines the community—trash-talking, jiving, and teasing. For example, when Webber suggests that Jordan quit because he is scared of playing against him, Mullins shares with us a look of humorous disbelief. Viewers are positioned as part of this camaraderie. We are included in the playful exchanges. We are invited into the conversation, and into the community.

* * *

TRANSCENDENCE IN THE HUMAN COMMUNITY

An aesthetic referent for classic humanism is *The Family of Man,* an exhibition created by Edward Steichen for the Museum of Modern Art in 1955. Composed of 503 photographs from 68 countries covering approximately a 100-year period, it was organized around universals—death, gestures (smiles, tears), family relations, play, work, war. *The Family of Man* constructed human essence based on participation in these experiences. We are born, we work, we play, we cry, we laugh, and we die. Ergo we are human.

As corporations like *Nike* participate in the global order they search for both new markets and new resources of production (cheaper labor). In this context, advertising cannot just sell products, it must also legitimate the corporate sponsor as a source of meaning. Classical humanism modeled after *The Family of Man* exhibition offers a stylistic look which positions the corporation as global, as pan-human, as multicultural. *Wieden & Kennedy* has embellished the *Nike* philosophy around this look and the philosophy of classical humanism. In the P.L.A.Y. and "Time of Hope" ad campaigns, differences between people in *Nike's* world are reduced to representations of the common ability in all of us to prevail over our circumstances. *Nike* enjoins viewers not to capitulate to the injustices of circumstance and difference (being poor, black, a woman, or confined to a wheelchair).

The "Time of Hope" ad compiled images drawn from *Nike's* stock of commercials that mix age, gender, race, amateur and professional athletes. A medley of sports activities compose the ad—baseball, track, volleyball, soccer, basketball, wheelchair marathon, and bicycling. The ad's first sequence of images is kinetic, each scene an action waiting to be completed—a boy preparing to swing a bat, a playground basketball player about to dunk, runners starting a race. The concluding sequence of cuts offers corresponding finishing actions—a dunk, Ken Griffey hitting a baseball, a wheelchair athlete crossing the finish line. Children tend to be shown in less organized play activities, while adults are involved in organized games. "A Time of Hope" celebrates a social democracy where there exists no apparent hierarchy of importance. Parity is created between the amateur and the professional, the child and the adult—each represented as equally important. For example, the match cut shown here pairs Barkley pulling down a rebound with a young girl trying to momentarily balance a basketball on her head.

Amid the flow of images shown in this inspirational sequence, a *Nike* shoe appears but once, approximately 20 seconds into the ad. Hence, this does not register as a product ad, but as *Nike's* celebration of the true meanings of sports etched across faces and bodies—meanings of intensity and determination, of awe and enjoyment. Using a telephoto lens to blur the background heightens the expressivity of the human face and eyes with their expressions of pleasure, determination, and intensity. Because the ad represents a celebration of the human will, the background doesn't matter; it disappears, whether it is a stadium or the street or a ghetto. The black and white ad uses hyperreal techniques including jump cuts, swish pans, and staccato editing to intermix these poignant images with frames of heavily scratched high contrast film that momentarily burst between the images. As noted earlier, these scratches were intended to signify the opposite of soft drink ads that imply the acquisition of traits magically through the product image. The scratches signify a "rawer, edgier" tone and visually provoke and amplify the ad's feeling of intensity. The music, cobbled together from several cuts by a band called Buffalo Tom, supports this feeling and builds throughout. The copy that appears across the screen celebrates these moments:

> *When all that is BETTER*
> *is before us.*
> *A time of HOPE.*
> *HOPE fastened to a GAME.*
> *HOPE not so much to be*
> *the Best to ever play the Game,*
> *But simply to stay in the game.*
> *And RIDE it*
> *WHEREVER it goes.*
> *JUST DO IT.*

Throughout, *Nike* celebrates participation over success. Yet make no mistake, this ad continues to build *Nike's* sign value, by maintaining a tension between the *Nike* stable of star athletes (Barkley, Griffey, Jordan) and the everyday player. Just as the screen reads "Hope not so much to be the Best to ever play the game, But simply to stay in the game," "the Best" appears across a closeup of Michael Jordan.

The emotional texture of *Nike's* inspirational ads separates them from competitors. This ad overflows with a sense of genuine humanity. *Nike* hails each viewer personally through the mix of images, music, and technique that inspires the viewer to feel as if he or she can "just do it." Although *Nike* commercials encourage viewers to identify with its celebrity athletes, they also hail viewers as potentially sharing the same heroic traits of determination, hard work, and desire to go beyond one's personal limits. *Nike* advertising hails us to be part of the universal community of athletes. They include anyone who perceives her/himself as an athlete or a potential athlete. The *Nike* community is for everyone who demonstrates athletic determination. It is not the athlete that *Nike* so well signifies but the athletic spirit. In this sense *Nike* has tapped into the mythology of sport in ways which its competitors have at best occasionally imitated. This appellation method is populist and inclusive. Depicting HOPE fastened to a GAME suggests a better future when we allow people to realize themselves through sport. While *Nike* preaches an anti-elitist humanism, it also appeals to an almost-Nietzschean will to power as a route to an emergent self—is this everyman a superman or is this superman in everyman?

It's nice to be addressed this way, particularly in an advertising and celebrity culture which continually positions viewers in terms of "abuse value, cynical seduction and chronic humiliation.[2] Throughout the ad, the faces of children register the joys of sport. Images such as a small boy wearing a miniature Detroit Tigers uniform or a Dominican child with his arm around a pal's shoulder connote a classic humanism or *Nike's* version of *The Family of Man*. This ad provides viewers with the space in which to feel good about one another without actually having to socialize with others. The mixture of realism and romance in this video album tugs at deeply frustrated desires to realize our species being—our essence realized socially. The ad closes on this utopian desire.

A recurrent theme in *Nike* ads is this decontextualized humanism—the stress placed on an abstract, but universal right of men, women, and children to sports and play. This resonates with Phil Knight's view that "Access to play should be a kid's inalienable right." If celebration of this utopian moment is *Nike's* primary ideological achievement, so also then, its central tendency to abstract rather than contextualize highlights the greatest weakness of *Nike's* social and cultural philosophy of sports. For what good is a guarantee of an abstract right in a society governed by the full commodification of resources?

To universalize an experience it must be decontextualized—removed from time and place, disconnected from socio-historical context—and then recontextualized around "chosen" universals. *The Family of Man* removed dates. The activity in each frame was given meaning by its shared similarity with adjacent photographs. Biblical, Native American, and literary quotes, also decontextualized, helped construct the overall themes of the exhibit. Universality was reduced to a maxim. The photographic traces of historical detail were made to signify the universal existential qualities of being human.

* * *

Nike uses a photographic style which idealizes individuals. It mixes realism with classicism—ghetto landscapes with low-angle shots of soaring basketball players, wheelchair athletes racing down a curved hill, impoverished children smiling to the pleasure of play. Alienation and affliction are the background for the celebration of the human spirit. Subjectivity is removed from existential conditions (time and place) and reframed in relation to a human essence—signifiers of alienation plus signifiers of determination equals transcendence. And it is sport (play) which is the activity which provides the space for transcendence. As long as one stays in the game, life has meaning. One participates in the human community defined by the characteristic that makes us human, the ability to transcend.

2. Arthur Kroker and Michael Weinstein, *Data Trash: The Theory of the Virtual Class* (St. Martin's Press, New York, 1994).

PART THREE

GROWING UP SOCIAL

14

Boyhood, Organized Sports, and the Construction of Masculinities

MICHAEL A. MESSNER

Though young women are now participating in sports in unprecedented numbers, the influence of sports activity on boys' identity and socialization experience remains a major interest in gender studies. Michael Messner, one of the pioneers and most prominent researchers of this topic, examines the way sports focus and define what it is to be masculine, the variations in sports' influence across social classes, and some unsuspected lessons sports participation imparts for relationships beyond the gym, pool, and fields of play. In reading this article, you might want to ask yourself: What would this article be saying if the subject was young women?

In this study I explore and interpret the meanings that males themselves attribute to their boyhood participation in organized sport. In what ways do males construct masculine identities within the institution of organized sports? In what ways do class and racial differences mediate this relationship and perhaps lead to the construction of different meanings, and perhaps different masculinities? And what are some of the problems and contradictions within these constructions of masculinity?

DESCRIPTION OF RESEARCH

Between 1983 and 1985, I conducted interviews with 30 male former athletes. Most of the men I interviewed had played the (U.S.) "major sports"—football, basketball, baseball, track. At the time of the interview, each had been retired from playing organized sports for at least five years. Their ages ranged from 21 to 48, with the median, 33; 14 were black, 14 were white, and two were Hispanic; 15 of the 16 black and Hispanic men had come from poor or working-class families, while the majority (9 of 14) of the white men had come from middle-class or professional families. All had at some time in their lives based their identities largely on their roles as athletes and could therefore be said to have had "athletic careers." Twelve had played organized sports through high school, 11 through college, and seven had been professional athletes. Though the sample was not randomly selected, an effort was made to see that the sample had a range of difference in terms of race and social class backgrounds, and that there was some variety in terms of age, types of sports played and levels of success in athletic careers. Without exception each man contacted agreed to be interviewed.

The tape-recorded interviews were semi-structured and took from one and one-half to six hours, with most taking about three hours. I asked each man to talk about four broad eras in his life: (1) his earliest experiences with sports in boyhood, (2) his athletic career, (3) retirement or disengagement from the athletic career, and (4) life after the athletic career. In each era, I focused the interview on the meanings of "success and failure," and on the boy's/man's relationships with family, with other males, with women, and with his own body.

In collecting what amounted to life histories of these men, my overarching purpose was to use feminist theories of masculine gender identity to explore how masculinity develops and changes as boys and men interact within the socially constructed world of organized sports. In addition to using the data to move toward some generalizations about the relationship between "masculinity and sport," I was also concerned with sorting out some of the variations among boys, based on class and racial inequalities, that led them to relate differently to athletic careers. I divided my sample into two comparison groups. The first group was made up of 10 men from higher-status backgrounds, primarily white, middle-class, and professional families. The second group was made up of 20 men from lower status backgrounds, primarily minority, poor, and working-class families.

BOYHOOD AND THE PROMISE OF SPORTS

Zane Grey once said, "All boys love baseball. If they don't they're not real boys" (as cited in Kimmel 1990). This is, of course, an ideological statement; in fact, some boys do *not* love baseball, or any other sports, for that matter. There are millions of males who at an early age are rejected by, become alienated from, or lose interest in organized sports. Yet all boys are, to a greater or lesser extent, judged according to their ability, or lack of ability, in competitive sports (Eitzen, 1975; Sabo, 1985). In this study I focus on those males who did become athletes—males who eventually poured thousands of hours into the development of specific physical skills. It is in boyhood that we can discover the roots of their commitment to athletic careers.

How did organized sports come to play such a central role in these boy's lives? When asked to recall how and why they initially got into playing sports, many of the men interviewed for this study seemed a bit puzzled: after all, playing sports was "just the thing to do." A 42-year-old black man who had played college basketball put it this way:

> It was just what you did. It's kind of like, you went to school, you played athletics, and if you didn't, there was something wrong with you. It was just like brushing your teeth: it's just what you did. It's part of your existence.

Spending one's time playing sports with other boys seemed as natural as the cycle of the seasons: baseball in the spring and summer, football in the fall, basketball in the winter—and then it was time to get out the old baseball glove and begin again. As a black 35-year-old former professional football star said:

> I'd say when I wasn't in school, 95% of the time was spent in the park playing. It was the only thing to do. It just came as natural.

And a black, 34-year-old professional basketball player explained his early experiences in sports:

> My principal and teacher said, "Now if you work at this you might be pretty damned good." So it was more or less a community thing—everybody in the community said, "Boy, if you work hard and keep your nose clean, you gonna be good." 'Cause it was natural instinct.

"It was natural instinct." "I was a natural." Several athletes used words such as these to explain their early attraction to sports. But certainly there is nothing "natural" about throwing a ball through a hoop, hitting a ball with a bat, or jumping over hurdles. A boy, for instance, may have amazingly dexterous inborn hand-eye coordination, but this does not predispose him to a career of hitting baseballs any more than it predisposes him to a life as a brain surgeon. When one listens closely to what these men said about their early experiences in sports, it becomes clear that their adoption of the self-definition of "natural athlete" was the result of what Connell (1990) has called "a collective practice" that constructs masculinities. The boyhood development of masculine identity and status—truly problematic in a society that offers no official rite of passage into adulthood—results from a process of interaction with people and social institutions. Thus, in discussing early motivations in sports, men commonly talk of the importance of relationships with family members, peers, and the broader community.

FAMILY INFLUENCES

Though most of the men in this study spoke of their mothers with love, respect, even reverence, their descriptions of their earliest experiences in sports are stories of an exclusively male world. The existence of older brothers or uncles who served as teachers and athletic role models—as well as sources of competition for attention and status within the family—was very common. An older brother, uncle, or even close friend of the family who was a successful athlete appears to have acted as a sort of standard of achievement against whom to measure oneself. A 34-year-old black man who had been a three-sport star in high school said:

> My uncles—my Uncle Harold went to the Detroit Tigers, played pro ball—all of 'em, everybody played sports, so I wanted to be better than anybody else. I knew

that everybody in this town knew them—their names were something. I wanted my name to be just like theirs.

Similarly, a black 41-year-old former professional football player recalled:

I was the younger of three brothers and everybody played sports, so consequently I was more or less forced into it. 'Cause one brother was always better than the next brother and then I came along and had to show them that I was just as good as them. My oldest brother was an all-city ballplayer, then my other brother comes along he's all-city and all-state, and then I have to come along.

For some, attempting to emulate or surpass the athletic accomplishments of older male family members created pressures that were difficult to deal with. A 33-year-old white man explained that he was a good athlete during boyhood, but the constant awareness that his two older brothers had been better made it difficult for him to feel good about himself, or to have fun in sports:

I had this sort of reputation that I followed from the playgrounds through grade school, and through high school. I followed these guys who were all-conference and all-state.

Most of these men, however, saw their relationships with their athletic older brothers and uncles in a positive light; it was within these relationships that they gained experience and developed motivations that gave them a competitive "edge" within their same-aged peer group. As a 33-year-old black man describes his earliest athletic experiences:

My brothers were role models. I wanted to prove—especially to my brothers— that I had heart, you know, that I was a man.

When asked, "What did it mean to you to be 'a man' at that age?" he replied:

Well, it meant that I didn't want to be a so-called scaredy-cat. You want to hit a guy even though he's bigger than you to show that, you know, you've got this macho image. I remember that at that young an age, that feeling was exciting to me. And that carried over, and as I got older, I got better and I began to look around me and see, well hey! I'm competitive with these guys, even though I'm younger, you know? And then of course all the compliments come—and I began to notice a change, even in my parents— especially in my father—he was proud of that, and that was very important to me. He was extremely important . . . he showed me more affection, now that I think of it.

As this man's words suggest, if men talk of their older brothers and uncles mostly as role models, teachers, and "names" to emulate, their talk of their relationships with their fathers is more deeply layered and complex. Athletic skills and competition for status may often be learned from older brothers, but it is in boys' relationships with fathers that we find many of the keys to the emotional salience of sports in the development of masculine identity.

RELATIONSHIPS WITH FATHERS

The fact that boys' introductions to organized sports are often made by fathers who might otherwise be absent or emotionally distant adds a power-ful emotional charge to these early experiences (Osherson 1986). Although playing organized sports eventually came to feel "natural" for all of the men interviewed in this study, many needed to be "exposed" to sports, or even gently "pushed" by their fathers to become involved in activities like Little League baseball. A white, 33-year-old-man explained:

> I still remember it like it was yesterday—Dad and I driving up in his truck, and I had my glove and my hat and all that—and I said, "Dad, I don't want to do it." He says, "What?" I says, "I don't want to do it." I was nervous. That I might fail. And he says, "Don't be silly. Lookit: There's Joey and Petey and all your friends out there." And so Dad says, "You're gonna do it, come on." And in my memory he's never said that about anything else; he just knew I needed a little kick in the pants and I'd do it. And once you're out there and you see all the other kids making errors and stuff, and you know you're better than those guys, you know: Maybe I *do* belong here. As it turned out, Little League was a good experience.

Some who were similarly "pushed" by their fathers were not so successful as the aforementioned man had been in Little League baseball, and thus the experience was not altogether a joyous affair. One 34-year-old white man, for instance, said he "inherited" his interest in sports from his father, who started playing catch with him at the age of four. Once he got into Little League, he felt pressured by his father, one of the coaches, who expected him to be the star of the team:

> I'd go 0-for-four sometimes, strike out three times in a Little League game, and I'd dread the ride home. I'd come home and he'd say, "Go in the bathroom and swing the bat in the mirror for an hour," to get my swing level . . . It didn't help much, though, I'd go out and strike out three or four times again the next game too [laughs ironically].

When asked if he had been concerned with having his father's approval, he responded:

Failure in his eyes? Yeah, I always thought that he wanted me to get some kind of [athletic] scholarship. I guess I was afraid of him when I was a kid. He didn't hit that much, but he had a rage about him—he'd rage, and that voice would just rattle you.

Similarly, a 24-year-old black man described his awe of his father's physical power and presence, and his sense of inadequacy in attempting to emulate him:

My father had a voice that sounded like rolling thunder. Whether it was intentional on his part or not, I don't know, but my father gave me a sense, an image of him being the most powerful being on earth, and that no matter what I ever did I would never come close to him . . . There were definite feelings of physical inadequacy that I couldn't work around.

It is interesting to note how these feelings of physical inadequacy relative to the father lived on as part of this young man's permanent internalized image. He eventually became a "feared" high school football player and broke school records in weight-lifting, yet,

As I grew older, my mother and friends told me that I had actually grown to be a larger man than my father. Even though in time I required larger clothes than he, which should have been a very concrete indication, neither my brother nor I could ever bring ourselves to say that I was bigger. We simply couldn't conceive of it.

Using sports activities as a means of identifying with and "living up to" the power and status of one's father was not always such a painful and difficult task for the men I interviewed. Most did not describe fathers who "pushed" them to become sports stars. The relationship between their athletic strivings and their identification with their fathers was more subtle. A 48-year-old black man, for instance, explained that he was not pushed into sports by his father, but was aware from an early age of the community status his father had gained through sports. He saw his own athletic accomplishments as a way to connect with and emulate his father:

I wanted to play baseball because my father had been quite a good baseball player in the Negro leagues before baseball was integrated, and so he was kind of a model for me. I remember, quite young, going to a baseball game he was in—this was before the war and all—I remember being in the stands with my mother and seeing him on first base, and being aware of the crowd . . . I was aware of people's confidence in him as a serious baseball player. I don't think my father ever said anything to me like "play sports" . . . [But] I knew he would like it if I did well. His admiration was important . . . he mattered.

Similarly, a 24-year-old white man described his father as a somewhat distant "role model" whose approval mattered:

> My father was more of an example . . . he definitely was very much in touch with and still had very fond memories of being an athlete and talked about it, bragged about it. . . . But he really didn't do that much to teach me skills, and he didn't always go to every game I played like some parents. But he approved and that was important, you know. That was important to get his approval. I always knew that playing sports was important to him, so I knew implicitly that it was good and there was definitely a value on it.

First experiences in sports might often come through relationships with brothers or older male relatives, and the early emotional salience of sports was often directly related to a boy's relationship with his father. The sense of commitment that these young boys eventually made to the development of athletic careers is best explained as a process of development of masculine gender identity and status in relation to same-sex peers.

MASCULINE IDENTITY AND EARLY COMMITMENT TO SPORTS

When many of the men in this study said that during childhood they played sports because "it's just what everybody did," they of course meant that it was just what *boys* did. They were introduced to organized sports by older brothers and fathers, and once involved, found themselves playing within an exclusively male world. Though the separate (and unequal) gendered worlds of boys and girls came to appear as "natural," they were in fact socially constructed. Thorne's observations of children's activities in schools indicated that rather than "naturally" constituting "separate gendered cultures," there is considerable interaction between boys and girls in classrooms and on playgrounds. When adults set up legitimate contact between boys and girls, Thorne observed, this usually results in "relaxed interactions." But when activities in the classroom or on the playground are presented to children as sex-segregated activities and gender is marked by teachers and other adults ("boys line up here, girls over there"), "gender boundaries are heightened, and mixed-sex interaction becomes an explicit arena of risk" (Thorne 1986; 70). Thus sex-segregated activities such as organized sports as structured by adults, provide the context in which gendered identities and separate "gendered cultures" develop and come to appear natural. For the boys in this study, it became "natural" to equate masculinity with competition, physical strength, and skills. Girls simply did not (could not, it was believed) participate in these activities.

Yet it is not simply the separation of children, by adults, into separate activities that explains why many boys came to feel such a strong connection with sports activities, while so few girls did. As I listened to men recall their earliest experiences in organized sports, I heard them talk of insecurity, lone-liness, and especially a need to connect with other people as a primary moti-vation in their early sports strivings. As a 42-year-old white man stated, "The most important thing was just being out there with the rest of the guys—being friends." Another 32-year-old interviewee was born in Mexico and moved to the United States at a fairly young age. He never knew his father, and his mother died when he was only nine years old. Suddenly he felt rootless, and threw himself into sports. His initial motivations, however, do not appear to be based on a need to compete and win:

> Actually, what I think sports did for me is it brought me into kind of an instant family. By being on a Little League team, or even just playing with all kinds of different kids in the neighborhood, it brought what I really wanted, which was some kind of closeness. It was just being there, and being friends.

Clearly, what these boys needed and craved was that which was most problematic for them: connection and unity with other people. But why do these young males find *organized sports* such an attractive context in which to establish "a kind of closeness" with others? Comparative observations of young boys' and girls' game-playing behaviors yield important insights into this question. Piaget (1965) and Lever (1976) both observed that girls tend to have more "pragmatic" and "flexible" orientations to the rules of games; they are more prone to make exceptions and innovations in the middle of a game in order to make the game more "fair." Boys, on the other hand, tend to have a more firm, even inflexible orientation to the rules of a game; to them, the rules are what protects any fairness. This difference, according to Gilligan (1982), is based on the fact that early developmental experiences have yielded deeply rooted differences between males' and females' developmental tasks, needs, and moral reasoning. Girls, who tend to define themselves primar-ily through connection with others, experience highly competitive situations (whether in organized sports or in other hierarchical institutions) as threats to relationships, and thus to their identities. For boys, the development of gender identity involves the construction of positional identities, where a sense of self is solidified through separation from others (Chodorow 1978). Yet feminist psychoanalytic theory has tended to oversimplify the internal lives of men (Lichterman 1986). Males do appear to develop positional iden-tities, yet despite their fears of intimacy, they also retain a human need for closeness and unity with others. This ambivalence toward intimate relation-ships is a major thread running through masculine development throughout the life course. Here we can conceptualize what Craib (1987) calls the "elec-tive affinity" between personality and social structure: For the boy who both seeks and fears attachment with others, the rule-bound structure of orga-nized sports can promise to be a safe place in which to seek nonintimate attachment with others within a context that maintains clear boundaries, distance, and separation.

COMPETITIVE STRUCTURES AND CONDITIONAL SELF-WORTH

Young boys may initially find that sports gives them the opportunity to experience "some kind of closeness" with others, but the structure of sports and athletic careers often undermines the possibility of boys learning to transcend their fears of intimacy, thus becoming able to develop truly close and intimate relationships with others (Kidd 1990; Messner 1987). The sports world is extremely hierarchical, and an incredible amount of importance is placed on winning, on "being number one." For instance, a few years ago I observed a basketball camp put on for boys by a professional basketball coach and his staff. The youngest boys, about eight years old (who could barely reach the basket with their shots) played a brief scrimmage. Afterwards, the coaches lined them up in a row in front of the older boys who were sitting in the grandstands. One by one, the coach would stand behind each boy, put his hand on the boy's head (much in the manner of a priestly benediction), and the older boys in the stands would applaud and cheer, louder or softer, depending on how well or poorly the young boy was judged to have performed. The two or three boys who were clearly the exceptional players looked confident that they would receive the praise they were due. Most of the boys, though, had expressions ranging from puzzlement to thinly disguised terror on their faces as they awaited the judgments of the older boys.

This kind of experience teaches boys that it is not "just being out there with the guys—being friends," that ensures the kind of attention and connection that they crave; it is being *better* than the other guys—*beating* them—that is the key to acceptance. Most of the boys in this study did have some early successes in sports, and thus their ambivalent need for connection with others was met, at least for a time. But the institution of sport tends to encourage the development of what Schafer (1975) has called "conditional self-worth" in boys. As boys become aware that acceptance by others is contingent upon being good—a "winner"—narrow definitions of success, based upon performance and winning become increasingly important to them. A 33-year-old black man said that by the time he was in his early teens:

> It was expected of me to do well in all my contests—I mean by my coaches, my peers, and my family. So I in turn expected to do well, and if I didn't do well, then I'd be very disappointed.

The man from Mexico, discussed above, who said that he had sought "some kind of closeness" in his early sports experiences began to notice in his early teens that if he played well, was a *winner,* he would get attention from others:

> It got to the point where I started realizing, noticing that people were always there for me, backing me all the time—sports got to be really fun because I always had some people there backing me. Finally my oldest brother started going to all my games, even though I had never really seen who he was [laughs]—after the game, you know, we never really saw each other, but he was at all my baseball games, and it seemed like we shared a kind of closeness there, but only in those situations. Off the field, when I wasn't in uniform, he was never around.

By high school, he said, he felt "up against the wall." Sports hadn't delivered what he had hoped it would, but he thought if he just tried harder, won one more championship trophy, he would get the attention he truly craved. Despite his efforts, this attention was not forthcoming. And, sadly, the pressures he had put on himself to excel in sports had taken most of the fun out of playing.

For many of the men in this study, throughout boyhood and into adolescence, this conscious striving for successful achievement became the primary means through which they sought connection with other people (Messner 1987). But it is important to recognize that young males' internalized ambivalences about intimacy do not fully determine the contours and directions of their lives. Masculinity continues to develop through interaction with the social world—and because boys from different backgrounds are interacting with substantially different familial, educational, and other institutions, these differences will lead them to make different choices and define situations in different ways. Next, I examine the differences in the ways that boys from higher- and lower-status families and communities related to organized sports.

STATUS DIFFERENCES AND COMMITMENTS TO SPORTS

In discussing early attractions to sports, the experiences of boys from higher- and lower-status backgrounds are quite similar. Both groups indicate the importance of fathers and older brothers in introducing them to sports. Both groups speak of the joys of receiving attention and acceptance among family and peers for early successes in sports. Note the similarities, for instance, in the following descriptions of boyhood athletic experiences of two men. First, a man born in a white, middle-class family:

> I loved playing sports so much from a very early age because of early exposure. A lot of the sports came easy at an early age, and because they did, and because you were successful at something, I think that you're inclined to strive for that gratification. It's like, if you're good, you like it, because it's instant gratification. I'm doing something that I'm good at and I'm gonna keep doing it.

Second, a black man from a poor family:

> Fortunately I had some athletic ability, and, quite naturally, once you start do-
> ing good in whatever it is—I don't care if it's jacks—you show off what you do.
> That's your ability, that's your blessing, so you show it off as much as you can.

For boys from both groups, early exposure to sports, the discovery that
they had some "ability," shortly followed by some sort of family, peer, and
community recognition, all eventually led to the commitment of hundreds
and thousands of hours of playing, practicing, and dreaming of future stardom. Despite these similarities, there are also some identifiable differences
that begin to explain the tendency of males from lower-status backgrounds
to develop higher levels of commitment to sports careers. The most clear-cut
differences was that while men from higher-status backgrounds are likely to
describe their earliest athletic experiences and motivations almost exclusively
in terms of immediate family, men from lower-status backgrounds more commonly describe the importance of a broader community context. For instance,
a 46-year-old man who grew up in a "poor working class" black family in a
small town in Arkansas explained:

> In that community, at the age of third or fourth grade, if you're a male, they
> expect you to show some kind of inclination, some kind of skill in football or bas-
> ketball. It was an expected thing, you know? My mom and my dad, they didn't
> push at all. It was the general environment.

A 48-year-old man describes sports activities as a survival strategy in his
poor black community:

> Sports protected me from having to compete in gang stuff, or having to be good
> with my fists. If you were an athlete and got into the fist world, that was your
> business, and that was okay—but you didn't have to if you didn't want to. People
> would generally defer to you, give you your space away from trouble.

A 35-year-old man who grew up in "a poor black ghetto" described his boyhood relationship to sports similarly:

> Where I came from, either you were one of two things: you were in sports or
> you were out on the streets being a drug addict, or breaking into places. The
> guys who were in sports, we had it a little easier, because we were accepted by
> both groups. . . . So it worked out to my advantage, cause I didn't get into a lot of
> trouble—some trouble, but not a lot.

The fact that boys in lower-status communities faced these kinds of realities
gave salience to their developing athletic identities. In contrast, sports were

important to boys from higher-status backgrounds, yet the middle-class environment seemed more secure, less threatening, and offered far more options. By the time most of these boys got into junior high or high school, many had made conscious decisions to shift their attentions away from athletic careers to educational and (nonathletic) career goals. A 32-year-old white college athletic director told me that he had seen his chance to pursue a pro baseball career as "pissing in the wind," and instead, focused on education. Similarly, a 33-year-old white dentist who was a three-sport star in high school, decided not to play sports in college, so he could focus on getting into dental school. As he put it,

> I think I kind of downgraded the stardom thing. I thought it was small potatoes. And sure, that's nice in high school and all that, but on a broad scale, I didn't think it amounted to all that much.

This statement offers an important key to understanding the construction of masculine identity within a middle-class context. The status that this boy got through sports had been *very* important to him, yet he could see that "on a broad scale," this sort of status was "small potatoes." This sort of early recognition is more than a result of the oft-noted middle-class tendency to raise "future-oriented" children (Rubin 1976; Sennett and Cobb 1973). Perhaps more important, it is that the *kinds* of future orientations developed by boys from higher-status backgrounds are consistent with the middle-class context. These men's descriptions of their boyhoods reveal that they grew up immersed in a wide range of institutional frameworks, of which organized sports was just one. And—importantly—they could see that the status of adult males around them was clearly linked to their positions within various professions, public institutions, and bureaucratic organizations. It was clear that access to this sort of institutional status came through educational achievement, not athletic prowess. A 32-year-old black man who grew up in a professional-class family recalled that he had idolized Wilt Chamberlain and dreamed of being a pro basketball player, yet his father discouraged his athletic strivings:

> He knew I liked the game. I *loved* the game. But basketball was not recommended; my dad would say, "That's a stereotyped image for black youth. . . . When your basketball is gone and finished, what are you gonna do? One day, you might get injured. What are you gonna look forward to?" He stressed education.

Similarly, a 32-year-old man who was raised in a white, middle-class family, had found in sports a key means of gaining acceptance and connection in his peer group. Yet he was simultaneously developing an image of himself as a "smart student," and becoming aware of a wide range of nonsport life options:

My mother was constantly telling me how smart I was, how good I was, what a nice person I was, and giving me all sorts of positive strokes, and those positive strokes became a self-motivating kind of thing. I had this image of myself as smart, and I lived up to that image.

It is not that parents of boys in lower-status families did not also encourage their boys to work hard in school. Several reported that their parents "stressed books first, sports second." It's just that the broader social context—education, economy, and community—was more likely to *narrow* lower-status boys' perceptions of real-life options, while boys from higher-status backgrounds faced an expanding world of options. For instance, with a different socioeconomic background, one 35-year-old black man might have become a great musician instead of a star professional football running back. But he did not. When he was a child, he said, he was most interested in music:

> I wanted to be a drummer. But we couldn't afford drums. My dad couldn't go out and buy me a drum set or a guitar even—it was just one of those things; he was just trying to make ends meet.

But he *could* afford, as could so many in his socioeconomic condition, to spend countless hours at the local park, where he was told by the park supervisor

> that I was a natural—not only in gymnastics or baseball—whatever I did, I was a natural. He told me I shouldn't waste this talent, and so I immediately started watching the big guys then.

In retrospect, this man had potential to be a musician or any number of things, but his environment limited his options to sports, and he made the best of it. Even within sports, he, like most boys in the ghetto, was limited:

> We didn't have any tennis courts in the ghetto—we used to have a lot of tennis balls, but no racquets. I wonder today how good I might be in tennis if I had gotten a racquet in my hands at an early age.

It is within this limited structure of opportunity that many lower-status young boys found sports to be *the* place, rather than *a* place, within which to construct masculine identity, status, the relationships. A 36-year-old white man explained that his father left the family when he was very young and his mother faced a very difficult struggle to make ends meet. As his words suggest, the more limited a boy's options, and the more insecure his family situation, the more likely he is to make an early commitment be an athletic career.

I used to ride my bicycle to Little League practice—if I'd waited for someone to pick me up and take me to the ball park I'd have never played. I'd get to the ball park and all the other kids would have their dad bring them to practice or games. But I'd park my bike to the side and when it was over I'd get on it and go home. Sports was the way for me to move everything to the side—family problems, just all the embarrassments—and think about one thing, and that was sports . . . In the third grade, when the teacher went around the classroom and asked everybody, "What do you want to be when you grow up?," I said, "I want to be a major league baseball player," and everybody laughed their heads off.

This man eventually did enjoy a major league baseball career. Most boys from lower-status backgrounds who make similar early commitments to athletic careers are not so successful. As stated earlier, the career structure of organized sports is highly competitive and hierarchical. In fact, the chances of attaining professional status in sports are approximately 4:100,000 for a white man, 2:100,000 for a black man, and 3:1 million for a Hispanic man in the United States (Leonard and Reyman 1988). Nevertheless, the immediate rewards (fun, status, attention), along with the constricted (nonsports) structure of opportunity, attract disproportionately large numbers of boys from lower-status backgrounds to athletic careers as their major means of constructing a masculine identity. These are the boys who later, as young men, had to struggle with "conditional self-worth," and, more often than not, occupational dead ends. Boys from higher-status backgrounds, on the other hand, bolstered their boyhood, adolescent, and early adult status through their athletic accomplishments. Their wider range of experiences and life chances led to an early shift away from sports careers as the major basis of identity (Messner 1989).

CONCLUSION

The conception of the masculinity-sports relationship developed here begins to illustrate the idea of an "elective affinity" between social structure and personality. Organized sports is a "gendered institution"—an institution constructed by gender relations. As such, its structure and values (rules, formal organization, sex composition, etc.), reflect dominant conceptions of masculinity and femininity. Organized sports is also a "gendering institution"—an institution that helps to construct the current gender order. Part of this construction of gender is accomplished through the "masculinizing" of male bodies and minds.

Yet boys do not come to their first experiences in organized sports as "blank slates," but arrive with already "gendering" identities due to early developmental experiences and previous socialization. I have suggested here that an important thread running through the development of masculine identity is males' ambivalence toward intimate unity with others.

Those boys who experience early athletic successes find in the structure of organized sport an affinity with this masculine ambivalence toward intimacy: The rule-bound, competitive, hierarchical world of sport offers boys an attractive means of establishing an emotionally distant (and thus "safe") connection with others. Yet as boys begin to define themselves as "athletes," they learn that in order to be accepted (to have connection) through sports, they must be winners. And in order to be winners, they must construct relationships with others (and with themselves) that are consistent with the competitive and hierarchical values and structure of the sports world. As a result, they often develop a "conditional self-worth" that leads them to construct more instrumental relationships with themselves and others. This ultimately exacerbates their difficulties in constructing intimate relationships with others. In effect, the interaction between the young male's preexisting internalized ambivalence toward intimacy with the competitive hierarchical institution of sport has resulted in the construction of a masculine personality that is characterized by instrumental rationality, goal-orientation, and difficulties with intimate connection and expression (Messner 1987).

This theoretical line of inquiry invites us not simply to examine how social institutions "socialize" boys, but also to explore the ways that boys' already-gendering identities interact with social institutions (which, like organized sport, are themselves the product of gender relations). This study has also suggested that it is not some singular "masculinity" that is being constructed through athletic careers. It may be correct, from a psychoanalytic perspective, to suggest that all males bring ambivalences toward intimacy to their interactions with the world, but "the world" is a very different place for males from different racial and socioeconomic backgrounds. Because males have substantially different interactions with the world, based on class, race, and other differences and inequalities, we might expect the construction of masculinity to take on different meanings for boys and men from differing backgrounds (Messner 1989). Indeed, this study has suggested that boys from higher-status backgrounds face a much broader range of options than do their lower-status counterparts. As a result, athletic careers take on different meanings for these boys. Lower-status boys are likely to see athletic careers as *the* institutional context for the construction of their masculine status and identities, while higher-status males make an early shift away from athletic careers toward other institutions (usually education and nonsports careers). A key line of inquiry for future studies might begin by exploring this irony of sports careers: Despite the fact that "the athlete" is currently an example of an exemplary form of masculinity in public ideology, the vast majority of boys who become most committed to athletic careers are never well-rewarded for their efforts. The fact that class and racial dynamics lead boys from higher-status backgrounds, unlike their lower status counterparts to move into non-sports careers illustrates how

this, a robust sense of entitlement takes root in the children. This sense of entitlement plays an especially important role in institutional settings, where middle-class children learn to question adults and address them as relative equals.

Only twenty minutes away, in blue-collar neighborhoods, and slightly farther away, in public housing projects, childhood looks different. Mr. Yanelli, a white working-class father, picks up his son Little Billy, a fourth-grader, from an after-school program. They come home and Mr. Yanelli drinks a beer while Little Billy first watches television, then rides his bike and plays in the street. Other nights, he and his Dad sit on the sidewalk outside their house and play cards. At about 5:30 P.M. Billys mother gets home from her job as a house cleaner. She fixes dinner and the entire family sits down to eat together. Extended family are a prominent part of their lives. Ms. Yanelli touches base with her "entire family every day" by phone. Many nights Little Billy's uncle stops by, sometimes bringing Little Billy's youngest cousin. In the spring, Little Billy plays baseball on a local team. Unlike for Garrett and Alexander, who have at least four activities a week, for Little Billy, baseball is his only organized activity outside of school during the entire year. Down the road, a white working-class girl, Wendy Driver, also spends the evening with her girl cousins, as they watch a video and eat popcorn, crowded together on the living room floor.

Farther away, a Black fourth-grade boy, Harold McAllister, plays outside on a summer evening in the public housing project in which he lives. His two male cousins are there that night, as they often are. After an afternoon spent unsuccessfully searching for a ball so they could play basketball, the boys had resorted to watching sports on television. Now they head outdoors for a twilight water balloon fight. Harold tries to get his neighbor, Miss Latifa, wet. People sit in white plastic lawn chairs outside the row of apartments. Music and television sounds waft through the open windows and doors.

The adults in the lives of Billy, Wendy, and Harold want the best for them. Formidable economic constraints make it a major life task for these parents to put food on the table, arrange for housing, negotiate unsafe neighborhoods, take children to the doctor (often waiting for city buses that do not come), clean children's clothes, and get children to bed and have them ready for school the next morning. But unlike middle-class parents, these adults do not consider the concerted development of children, particularly through organized leisure activities, an essential aspect of good parenting. Unlike the Tallingers and Williamses, these mothers and fathers do not focus on concerned cultivation. For them, the crucial responsibilities of parenthood do not lie in eliciting their children's feelings, opinions, and thoughts. Rather, they see a clear boundary between adults and children. Parents tend to use directives: they tell their children what to do rather than persuading them with reasoning. Unlike their middle-class counterparts, who have a steady diet of adult organized activities, the working-class and poor children have more control over the character of their leisure activities. Most children are free to go out and play with friends and relatives who typically live close by. Their parents and guardians facilitate the *accomplishment of natural growth*. Yet these children and their parents interact with central institutions in the society, such as schools, which firmly and decisively promote strategies of concerted cultivation in child rearing. For working-class and poor families, the cultural logic of child rearing at home is out of synch with the standards of institutions. As a result, while children whose parents adopt strategies of concerted cultivation appear to gain a sense of entitlement, children such as Billy Yanelli, Wendy Driver, and Harold McAllister appear to gain an emerging sense of distance, distrust, and constraint in their institutional experiences.

CULTURAL REPERTOIRES

Professionals who work with children, such as teachers, doctors, and counselors, generally agree about how children should be raised. Of course, from time to time they may disagree on the ways standards should be enacted for an individual child or family. For example, teachers may disagree about whether or not parents should stop and correct a child who mispronounces a word while reading. Counselors may disagree over whether a mother is being too protective of her child. Still, there is little dispute among professionals on the broad principles for promoting educational development in children through proper parenting. These standards include the importance of talking with children, developing their educational interests, and playing an active role in their schooling. Similarly, parenting guidelines typically stress the importance of reasoning with children and teaching them to solve problems through negotiation rather than with physical force. Because these guidelines are so generally accepted, and because they focus on a set of practices concerning how parents should raise children, they form a *dominant set of cultural repertoires* about how children should be raised. This widespread agreement among professionals about the broad principles for child rearing permeates our society. A small number of experts thus potentially shape the behavior of a large number of parents.

Professionals' advice regarding the best way to raise children has changed regularly over the last two centuries. From strong opinions about the merits of bottle feeding, being stern with children, and utilizing physical punishment (with dire warnings of problematic outcomes should parents indulge children), there have been shifts to equally strongly worded recommendations about the benefits of breast feeding, displaying emotional warmth toward children, and using reasoning and negotiation as mechanisms of parental control. Middle-class parents appear to shift their behaviors in a variety of spheres more rapidly and more thoroughly than do working-class or poor parents. As professionals have shifted their recommendations from bottlefeeding to breast feeding, from stern approaches to warmth and empathy, and from spanking to time-outs, it is middle-class parents who have responded most promptly. Moreover, in recent decades, middle-class children in the United

States have had to face the prospect of "declining fortunes." Worried about how their children will get ahead, middle-class parents are increasingly determined to make sure that their children are not excluded from any opportunity that might eventually contribute to their advancement.

Middle-class parents who comply with current professional standards and engage in a pattern of concerted cultivation deliberately try to stimulate their children's development and foster their cognitive and social skills. The commitment among working-class and poor families to provide comfort, food, shelter, and other basic support requires ongoing effort, given economic challenges and the formidable demands of child rearing. But it stops short of the deliberate cultivation of children and their leisure activities that occurs in middle-class families. For working-class and poor families, sustaining children's natural growth is viewed as an accomplishment.

What is the outcome of these different philosophies and approaches to child rearing? Quite simply, they appear to lead to the *transmission of differential advantages* to children. In this study, there was quite a bit more talking in middle-class homes than in working-class and poor homes, leading to the development of greater verbal agility, larger vocabularies, more comfort with authority figures, and more familiarity with abstract concepts. Importantly, children also developed skill differences in interacting with authority figures in institutions and at home. Middle-class children such as Garrett Tallinger and Alexander "Williams learn, as young boys, to shake the hands of adults and look them in the eye. In studies of job interviews, investigators have found that potential employees have less than one minute to make a good impression. Researchers stress the importance of eye contact, firm handshakes, and displaying comfort with bosses during the interview. In poor families like Harold McAllister's, however, family members usually do not look each other in the eye when conversing. In addition, as Elijah Anderson points out, they live in neighborhoods where it can be dangerous to look people in the eye too long. The types of social competence transmitted in the McAllister family are valuable, but they are potentially less valuable (in employment interviews, for example) than those learned by Garrett Tallinger and Alexander Williams.

The white and Black middle-class children in this study also exhibited an emergent version of the *sense of entitlement* characteristic of the middle-class. They acted as though they had a right to pursue their own individual preferences and to actively manage interactions in institutional settings. They appeared comfortable in these settings; they were open to sharing information and asking for attention. Although some children were more outgoing than others, it was common practice among middle-class children to shift interactions to suit *their* preferences. Alexander Williams knew how to get the doctor to listen to his concerns (about the bumps under his arm from his new deodorant). His mother explicitly trained and encouraged him to speak up with the doctor. Similarly, a Black middle-class girl, Stacey Marshall, was taught by her mother to expect the gymnastics teacher to accommodate her individual learning style. Thus, middle-class children were trained in "the rules of the game" that govern interactions with institutional representatives. They were not conversant in other important social skills, however, such as organizing their time for hours on end during weekends and summers, spending long periods of time away from adults, or hanging out with adults in a nonobtrusive, subordinate fashion. Middle-class children also learned (by imitation and by direct training) how to make the rules work in their favor. Here, the enormous stress on reasoning and negotiation in the home also has a potential advantage for future institutional negotiations. Additionally, those in authority responded positively to such interactions. Even in fourth grade, middle-class children appeared to be acting on their own behalf to gain advantages. They made special requests of teachers and doctors to adjust procedures to accommodate their desires.

The working-class and poor children, by contrast, showed an emerging *sense of constraint* in their interactions in institutional settings. They were less likely to try to customize interactions to suit their own preferences. Like their parents, the children accepted the actions of persons in authority (although at times they also covertly resisted them). Working-class and poor parents sometimes were not as aware of their children's school situation (as when their children were not doing homework). Other times, they dismissed the school rules as unreasonable. For example, Wendy Driver's mother told her to "punch" a boy who was pestering her in class; Billy Yanelli's parents were proud of him when he "beat up" another boy on the playground, even though Billy was then suspended from school. Parents also had trouble getting "the school" to respond to their concerns. When Ms. Yanelli complained that she "hates" the school, she gave her son a lesson in powerlessness and frustration in the face of an important institution. Middle-class children such as Stacey Marshall learned to make demands on professionals, and when they succeeded in making the rules work in their favor they augmented their "cultural capital" (i.e., skills individuals inherit that can then be translated into different forms of value as they move through various institutions) for the future. When working-class and poor children confronted institutions, however, they generally were unable to make the rules work in their favor nor did they obtain capital for adulthood. Because of these patterns of legitimization, children raised according to the logic of concerted cultivation can gain advantages, in the form of an emerging sense of entitlement, while children raised according to the logic of natural growth tend to develop an emerging sense of constraint.

In this study, the research assistants and I followed a small number of families around in an intensive fashion to get a sense of the rhythms of their everyday lives. On the basis of the data collected, I develop the claim that common economic position in the society, defined in terms of social class membership, is closely tied to differences in the cultural logic of child-rearing. Following a well-established Western European tradition, I provide a categorical analysis, grouping families into the social categories of middle class, working class, and

TABLE I. TYPOLOGY OF DIFFERENCES
IN CHILD REARING

	Child-Rearing Approach	
	Concerted Cultivation	*Accomplishment of Natural Growth*
Key Elements	Parent actively fosters and assesses child's talents, opinions, and skills	Parent cares for child and allows child to grow
Organization of Daily Life	Multiple child leisure activities orchestrated by adults	"Hanging out," particularly with kin, by child
Language Use	Reasoning/directives Child contestation of adult statements Extended negotiations between parents and child	Directives Rare questioning or challenging of adults by child General acceptance by child of directives
Interventions in Institutions	Criticisms and interventions on behalf of child Training of child to take on this role	Dependence on institutions Sense of powerlessness and frustration Conflict between child-rearing practices at home and at school
Consequences	Emerging sense of entitlement on the part of the child	Emerging sense of constraint on the part of the child

poor. * * * I see this approach as more valuable than the gradational analysis often adopted by American scholars. In addition, I demonstrate that class differences in family life cut across a number of different and distinct spheres, which are usually not analyzed together by social scientists.

In particular, I delineate a pattern of concerted cultivation in middle-class families and a pattern of the accomplishment of natural growth in working-class and poor families. Table I provides an overview of the main points of the book. It indicates that concerted cultivation entails an emphasis on children's structured activities, language development and reasoning in the home, and active intervention in schooling. By contrast, the accomplishment of natural growth describes a form of child rearing in which children "hang out" and play, often with relatives, are given clear directives from parents with limited negotiation, and are granted more autonomy to manage their own affairs in institutions outside of the home. These patterns help us unpack the mechanisms through which social class conveys an advantage in daily life.

* * *

Social class differences in children's life experiences can be seen in the details of life. In our study, the pace of life was different for middle-class families compared to working-class and poor families. In the middle class, life was hectic. Parents were racing from activity to activity. In families with more than one child, parents often juggled conflicts between children's activities. In these families, economic resources for food, clothing, shelter, transportation, children's activities, and other routine expenses were in ample supply. Of course, some parents often *felt* short of money. At times they were not able to enjoy the vacations that they would have liked. But, as I show, families routinely spent hundreds and even thousands of dollars per year promoting children's activities.

Because there were so many children's activities, and because they were accorded so much importance, children's activities determined the schedule for the entire family. Siblings tagged along, sometimes willingly and sometimes not. Adults' leisure time was absorbed by children's activities. Children also spent much of their time in the company of adults or being directed by adults. They also had informal free time, but generally it was sandwiched between structured activities. In the organization of daily life, children's interests and activities were treated as matters of consequence.

In working-class and poor families, the organization of daily life differed from that of middle-class families. Here, there was economic strain not felt by many middle-class families. Particularly in poor families, it took enormous labor to get family members through the day, as mothers scrimped to make food last until they were able to buy more, waited for buses that didn't come, carried children's laundry out to public washers, got young children up, fed, dressed, and ready for school and oversaw children's daily lives. Children were aware of the economic strain. Money matters were frequently discussed.

Although money was in short supply, children's lives were more relaxed and, more importantly, the pace of life was slower. Children played with other children outside of the house. They frequently played with their cousins. Some children had organized activities, but they were far fewer than in middle-class families. Other times, children wanted to be in organized activities, but economic constraints, compounded by lack of transportation, made participation prohibitive. When children sought to display their budding talents and pursue activities more informally around the house, adults often treated children's interests as inconsequential. In addition, since they were not riding around in cars with parents going to organized activities or being directed by adults in structured activities, children in working-class and poor families had more autonomy from adults. Working-class and poor children had long stretches of free time during which they watched television and played with relatives and friends in the neighborhood, creating ways to occupy themselves. In these activities, there was more of a separation between adults' worlds and children's worlds.

In sum, there were social class differences in the number of organized activities, pace of family life, economic strain of family life, time spent in informal play, interest on the part of adults in children's activities, domination by children's activities of adult lives, and the amount of autonomy children had from adults. To be sure, other things also mattered in addition to social class. Gender differences were particularly striking. Girls and boys enjoyed different types of activities. Girls had more sedentary lives compared to boys. They also played closer to home. Race also played a role, particularly as racial segregation of residential neighborhoods divided children into racially segregated informal play groups (although race did not influence the number of activities children had).

THE POWER OF SOCIAL CLASS

In the United States, people disagree about the importance of social class in daily life. Many Americans believe that this country is fundamentally *open.* They assume the society is best understood as a collection of individuals. They believe that people who demonstrate hard work, effort, and talent are likely to achieve upward mobility. Put differently, many Americans believe in the American Dream. In this view, children should have roughly equal life chances. The extent to which life chances vary can be traced to differences in aspirations, talent, and hard work on the part of individuals. This perspective rejects the notion that parents' social location systematically shapes children's life experiences and outcomes. Instead, outcomes are seen as resting more in the hands of individuals.

In a distinctly different but still related vein, some social scientists acknowledge that there are systemic forms of inequality, including, for example, differences in parents' educational levels, occupational prestige, and income, as well as in their child-rearing practices. These scholars, however, see such differences within society as a matter of *graduation.* To explain unequal life outcomes, they see it as helpful to look at, for example, differences in mothers' years of education or the range of incomes by households in a particular city. These different threads are interwoven in an intricate and often baffling pattern. Scholars who take this perspective on inequality typically focus on the ways specific patterns are related (e.g., the number of years of mothers' schooling and the size of children's vocabularies, or the number of years of mothers' education and parental involvement in schooling). Implicitly and explicitly, social scientists who share this perspective do not accept the position that there are identifiable, categorical differences in groups. They do not believe that the differences that do exist across society cohere into patterns recognizable as social classes.

* * * I have challenged both views. Rather than seeing society as a collection of individuals, I stressed the importance of individuals' social structural location in shaping their daily lives. Following a well-established European tradition, I rejected analyses that see differences in American families as best interpreted as a matter of fine gradations. Instead, I see as more valuable a

categorical analysis, wherein families are grouped into social categories such as poor, working class, and middle class. I argued that these categories are helpful in understanding the behavior of family members, not simply in one particular aspect but across a number of spheres. Family practices cohere by social class. Social scientists who accept this perspective may disagree about the number and type of categories and whether there should be, for example, an upper-middle-class category as well as a lower-middle-class one. Still, they agree that the observed differences in how people act can be meaningfully and fruitfully grouped into categories, without violating the complexity of daily life. My own view is that seeing selected aspects of family life as differentiated by social class is simply a better way to understand the reality of American family life. I also believe that social location at birth can be very important in shaping the routines of daily life, even when family members are not particularly conscious of the existence of social classes.

Thus, I have stressed how social class dynamics are woven into the texture and rhythm of children and parents' daily lives. Class position influences critical aspects of family life: time use, language use, and kin ties. Working-class and middle-class mothers may express beliefs that reflect a similar notion of "intensive mothering," but their behavior is quite different.

When children and parents move outside the home into the world of social institutions, they find that these cultural practices are not given equal value. There are signs that middle-class children benefit, in ways that are invisible to them and to their parents, from the degree of similarity between the cultural repertoires in the home and those standards adopted by institutions. * * *

CONCERTED CULTIVATION AND THE ACCOMPLISHMENT OF NATURAL GROWTH

* * * [S]ocial class made a significant difference in the routines of children's daily lives. The white and Black middle-class parents engaged in practices of *concerted cultivation.* In these families, parents actively fostered and assessed their children's talents, opinions, and skills. They scheduled their children for activities. They reasoned with them. They hovered over them and outside the home they did not hesitate to intervene on the children's behalf. They made a deliberate and sustained effort to stimulate children's development and to cultivate their cognitive and social skills. The working-class and poor parents viewed children's development as unfolding spontaneously, as long as they were provided with comfort, food, shelter, and other basic support. I have called this cultural logic of child rearing the *accomplishment of natural growth.* As with concerted cultivation, this commitment, too, required ongoing effort; sustaining children's natural growth despite formidable life challenges is properly viewed as accomplishment. Parents who relied on natural growth generally organized their children's lives so they spent time in and around home, in informal play with peers, siblings, and cousins. As a result,

the children had more autonomy regarding leisure time and more opportunities for child-initiated play. They also were more responsible for their lives outside the home. Unlike in middle-class families, adult-organized activities were uncommon. Instead of the relentless focus on reasoning and negotiation that took place in middle-class families, there was less speech (including less whining and badgering) in working-class and poor homes. Boundaries between adults and children were clearly marked; parents generally used language not as an aim in itself but more as a conduit for social life. Directives were common. In their institutional encounters, working-class and poor parents turned over responsibility to professionals; when parents did try to intervene, they felt that they were less capable and less efficacious than they would have liked. While working-class and poor children differed in important ways, particularly in the stability of their lives, surprisingly there was not a major difference between them in their cultural logic of child rearing. Instead, in this study the cultural divide appeared to be between the middle class and everyone else.

16

Care and Belonging in the Market*

FROM *Longing and Belonging: Parents, Children, and Consumer Culture*

ALLISON J. PUGH

Everyone laments the targeting of children by advertisers, the tens of thousands of commercial messages children see even before their first day of school, the unhealthy foods they are encouraged to eat, and the public temper tantrums at being told they can't have the latest toy. Allison Pugh goes beyond these things with a keen sociological eye, to examine the meaning of desiring and possessing things. In the tradition of Erving Goffman (author of reading 18) and in the best tradition of symbolic interactionism, Pugh develops concepts, naming strategic interactions and face-saving gestures used by children to obtain entrance and membership in the peer groups of their lives. Not incidentally, she has a great deal of insightful things to say about parenting and adults navigating the world of material consumption.

It is a few days before Halloween at the Sojourner Truth after-school center in Oakland, California, and I am sitting with some children at a table where they are supposed to be doing their homework. Instead, the children, all of them from low-income families and who attend this center for free or almost no cost, are talking about the upcoming holiday. Aleta, an African-American third grader, is holding forth about her costume.

"I'm going to be a vampire," she announces, gleefully, almost cackling. Already she has the outfit: the teeth, the cape, the shoes. Her mom bought it at Target, she says offhandedly, tossing her head and making the beads in her hair rattle. Simon and Marco, two recent immigrant children about seven years old, are listening closely without smiling, eyeing her like dancers memorizing an audition routine, and occasionally filling in their homework sheets. Thinking to include them in Aleta's fantastic reverie, I ask them what they will be for Halloween, but they find the question difficult.

"I'm not going to be anything," Simon, a recent African immigrant, says flatly, his eyebrows arched high in a disdain he appears to be trying on for size. "I only care about the candy."

Marco, who arrived from Mexico last year, agrees, but then he pauses. "I'm just going to go as me," he says, with a studied casualness. "The humans were the scariest part of [the horror movie] *Dawn of the Dead.*"

---

*Footnotes and references can be found in Allison Pugh's *Longing and Belonging.*

Neither Simon's nor Marco's parents had been in the country more than two years; later, Simon's proud mother tells me Halloween is as meaningless to them as the Tooth Fairy. To Simon's parents, refugees who have been working three jobs to save for a home, a Halloween costume is the height of frivolity, a potent symbol of the children's peer culture to which they, with the bemused confidence born of certainty, turn a deaf ear.

But later on that same day at Sojourner Truth, when another classmate comes up to the table and asks the same question, Simon is prepared, ready to manage the commercial demands of the peer culture in which he has found himself. "I am going as me," I overhear him saying, his high, clear voice piercing the din of children's voices as they get ready for snack. "The humans were the scary ones in *Dawn of the Dead.*"

A few days later, on a quiet, leafy street whose elegant homes seem farther away than the short, seven-minute drive from Sojourner Truth, Judy Berger put her elbows on her teak dining table and sighed when I asked her whether she had ever regretted buying anything for her eight-year-old son Max. A quiet and reflective woman, Judy was nonetheless clearly pained when she described how the popular electronic handheld Game Boy had affected her family's life. They finally bought Max the gaming system for his birthday, after two years of his intense lobbying, in which he pointed out that all of his friends had them, and that "that is what they do for fun, [and] that is what they talk about over lunch and stuff like that," Judy said. The fight had gone on so long he had given up hope that they would buy him one, contenting himself with a magazine featuring Game Boy lore, which he pored over again and again, acquiring a certain Game Boy fluency if not possession. Judy laughed wryly about his absorption, saying, "At least he had something to do on the plane to Australia." When he actually unwrapped the Game Boy on his birthday, Judy recalled, "I have to say I don't think that I have ever seen him so happy before or after that."

But the good feeling didn't last. "It really strained our relationship," she said. "Max was doing it [playing games] every day, every single morning before school we were really fighting about turning it off, and how important—you know, what is more important, finishing this level or going to school on time?" She grimaced at the memory. "So now one of the rules we have is that when it is time to go to school or time to go to violin lesson or camp, when we really have to leave, he just has to turn it off no matter what." After too many arguments about whether or not he could stop in the middle of a game, Judy even called the manufacturer to see if her son was right, was there no way to save his progress, did he have to keep playing until he was past a certain level, could he not just put it down when she wanted him to? When Judy talked about the Game Boy, it was as if she was talking about a teenager's alarming girlfriend, one who distracted her son from making wise choices, one who was outside her control, but also one who, because of her son's intense attachment, could not simply be turned away.

She instituted other rules to control Max's playing. He could play it in the morning only when he had his backpack on, his breakfast eaten, his teeth brushed. He could play for only a half hour a day, and they set a kitchen timer to keep track. He could not play it in the car, even though she knew other families found that convenient. "I am not buying this as a babysitter, you know," she said. "I am buying it for—because I gave in."

Thus when I asked Judy if she regretted a particular purchase, it would not have been surprising if she had named the Game Boy. But she demurred. It is not that she rued buying the Game Boy for Max, she insisted. "I guess I felt almost like it wasn't really, like I couldn't have not bought it, because now we are there in our life," she said, her normally smooth syntax turning convoluted to express her certain ambivalence, the contradictions she was straddling between her distaste for what she considered the Game Boy's addictive, violent, and sedentary properties, and her desire to make Max happy. Most important, the gaming system had so saturated the social lives of eight-year-old boys they knew that she did not think she could relegate Max to that kind of invisibility, that kind of social pathos. "It *is* kind of sad that it feels like it is a given that you will have one," she conceded. "It is too bad that that is where we are." Judy did not regret buying the Game Boy, she regretted *having* to buy it.

THE HIDDEN CRISES OF CHILDHOOD CONSUMPTION

Commodity consumption for children has exploded, with fully $670 billion annually spent on or by children in the United States by 2004. Many moments of childhood now involve the act of buying, from daily experiences to symbolic rituals, from transportation to lunches to birthdays. As market researcher James McNeal has crowed, "precisely all those activities that we call consumer behavior are performed by millions of . . . children . . . every day in virtually every aspect of life." The U.S. government calculated that the cost of raising a child to age seventeen, adjusted for inflation, climbed by 12.8 percent from 1960 to 2000, but many experts believe even these measures are far too low: a recalculation in an article in the *Wall Street Journal* entitled "The Million-Dollar Kid" *tripled* the most recent government estimates for the richest families. The "commodity frontier" is advancing in child rearing, the sociologist Arlie Hochschild warns, as "companies . . . expand the number of market niches for goods and services covering activities that, in yesteryear, formed part of unpaid 'family life.'"

Many social commentators blame consumer culture for a burgeoning crisis of childhood. Television advertising and overindulgent parents have led to epidemics of children's materialism, depression, hyperactivity, obesity, and other problems, these analysts contend. Books and editorials with titles such as "Parenting, Inc.," *Consuming Kids: The Hostile Takeover of Childhood,* and "Reclaiming Childhood" lament the commodification of children's lives, arguing that childhood in the United States and other advanced economies is in danger of being overrun by the market, with children's lives tethered to the corporate bottom line.

These stories reflect real concerns about children's lives, and how parents and children are responding to new pressures and tensions embedded in the task of growing up. They usefully draw our attention to the billion-dollar industry bent on using whatever works to capture children's attention and allegiance. Yet underlying their critique of corporate capitalism is an acute discomfort with children's desire generally. Is it that children should not be consuming at all (surely next to impossible in this world), or is it rather that children want the wrong things (too adult, too tacky, or just too much), or they want them in the wrong way (too intensely)? Perhaps widespread uneasiness with the often unsubtle, uninhibited nature of children's consumer desire is distracting us from other, more fundamental, concerns: the hidden crises of consumption.

I argue the question we should be asking is this: How is the commercialization of childhood shaping what it means to care, and what it means to belong? An analogy to divorce helps clarify the issue: some family scholars have argued that high divorce rates affect not just the families that break apart, but even those that stay together, through the spread of a "divorce culture" and its weakened assumptions about mutual trust and obligation. In the same way, perhaps rising consumption, by its sheer domination of childhood today, establishes a new cultural environment, with new expectations about what parents should provide, what children should have, and what having, or not having, signifies. The market suffuses childhood today, but it does not do so in the aggregate, like so much liquid poison pouring into one individual child after another, as some critics would have it. Instead, it permeates the relationships in which children are embedded. What role does the market play in these relationships? What meanings do children and parents impart to particular commodities? How does commercial culture thread its way through children's emotional connections, with peers and with parents?

I investigated these questions through an ethnography of childhood consumer culture, involving observations of children at school and with their families, and interviews with parents and other caregivers. I spent three years with the children of Sojourner Truth, and six months with children in more affluent settings, a private school I call Arrowhead, and an elite public school I call Oceanview. I sat at "circle time" with the children, read to them, tied their shoes, knitted with them, threw footballs, jumped rope, and went to birthday parties and on field trips. I listened to their jokes and stories, eavesdropped on their conversations, taped their songs and games, took them shopping, to the car wash, to the library. I also listened to parents from fifty-four families, in interviews generally lasting two to four hours, sometimes over several visits. I talked to teachers and other school staff and attended neighborhood meetings, award ceremonies, fundraisers, and festivals. * * * Through these efforts, I immersed myself in the childhoods and parenthoods of people grappling every day with the exigencies of consuming for children, its practices and meanings. I found that the hidden crises of consumption for children lurk in the convergence of inequality, care, and the market, which enables consumer culture to saturate children's emotional connections to others.

THE ECONOMY OF DIGNITY

I argue that the key to children's consumer culture, to the explosion of parent buying and the question of what things mean to children, lies in social experiences much like the incidents described at the beginning of this chapter, the exchange about costumes and movies among Simon, Marco, and Aleta at the Sojourner Truth center, and Max's lunch-table discussions about Game Boys as recounted by his mother, Judy. I observed similar conversations among affluent and poor children alike, in private schools and public, on playgrounds, at birthday parties—wherever children gathered. Everywhere children claim, contest, and exchange among themselves the terms of their social belonging, or just what it would take to be able to participate among their peers. I came to call this system of social meanings the "economy of dignity."

The "economy of dignity" echoes a phrase coined by Arlie Hochschild, who dubbed the exchange of recognition between spouses—for gifts of time, work, or feeling—the "economy of gratitude." Couples negotiating who would do the laundry or make dinner owed or banked gratitude, depending on how their behavior measured up against their sometimes unstable bargain about who should be responsible for what. Similarly, I argue, children collect or confer dignity among themselves, according to their (shifting) consensus about what sort of objects or experiences are supposed to count for it.

The dictionary defines *dignity* as "the quality or state of being worthy," but we might reasonably ask, worthy of what? I suggest that for children a vital answer is "worthy of belonging." I use "dignity" to mean the most basic sense of children's participation in their social world, what the Nobel Prize–winning economist Amartya Sen called an "absolute capability . . . to take part in the life of the community." With dignity, children are visible to their peers, and granted the aural space, the very right to speak in their own community's conversation.

By focusing on dignity, I am not talking about a particularly common view of why people buy: competitive status-seeking behavior. Buyers buy, according to this tradition, in order to establish themselves as better than those to whom they compare themselves, to "gain the esteem and envy of one's fellow-men," as Veblen put it more than a hundred years ago. While inducing jealousy is certainly part of the emotional landscape of consumption, my use of "dignity" refers less to "envy" than to the "esteem" of others, the goal of joining the circle rather than one of bettering it. Through claiming that their own bodies were part of the costume, Simon and Marco were not so much seeking honor, demanding respect, or even striving for status, I argue, but rather they sought, with a measure of bravado masking their momentary desperation, to join in.

Children together shape their own economies of dignity, which in turn transform particular goods and experiences into a form of scrip, tokens of value suddenly fraught with meaning. Children's lives can traverse several different economies of dignity—at school, at their after-school program, and in the neighborhood, for example—where different tokens can become salient in the peer culture resident there. And when children—even affluent ones—find themselves without what they need to join the conversation, they perform what I termed "facework" to make up for the omission.

Simon and Marco, for example, knew that Halloween was the official children's holiday in American culture (and as a safely secular holiday it was one that was fully celebrated by their public school, which—not unusually—arranged for costume display, candy distribution, and parades during school time). These boys' facework was to interpret their total nonparticipation—at their young age still problematic—not as their families' choice to opt out but as a different sort of costume, an innovation on the cultural imperative of being scary that had even greater cachet by referring to a popular movie. With this discursive move, they demonstrated their cultural bilingualism, translating their own lives into what would make sense—even more, make dignity—in the social world of the after-school program.

The reach of the economy of dignity does not stop at the school-house door, however. Like Max Berger and his fight for the Game Boy, children bring their consumer emergencies home to their parents, who largely control what their children have and how much it matches what they need. What makes some parents more or less attuned to their children's social milieu and the role particular objects or experiences play in it? How do parents handle their children's consumer desire?

I found that when children came home with their desires turned into needs by the alchemy of dignity, most of the time parents heard them and responded, while only very occasionally parents ignored, resisted, or denied their children's desires. Like Judy Berger, who, as we saw, bought Max his Game Boy despite her extreme reluctance, responsive parents prioritize their children's social belonging. This practice has a long history in American culture, as exemplified by Sinclair Lewis's 1920s antihero George Babbitt. In one telling episode in Lewis's classic novel, Babbitt's wife cautions him against disciplining their son's teenage friends at a party, because "we wouldn't want Ted left out of things, would we?" In reply, however, although "Babbit announced he would be enchanted to have Ted left out of things," he then "hurried in to be polite, lest Ted be left out of things." Babbitt, and Judy Berger, are not alone. In one national survey, about half of parents with children under age thirteen confessed: "While it's often against my better judgment, I sometimes buy my children clothing and things they want because I don't want them to feel different from other kids."

The prospect of feeling "different from other kids" animated many parents' buying practices, but I found parents and children watched for three specific forms of difference, each with varying impact: interactional, personal, and social. Interactional difference includes the momentary variations that arise in conversations, such as whether or not someone has gone skiing, can do a handstand, or owns a set of Heelys, the popular sneakers with wheels built into the sole. Personal difference refers to enduring characteristics adhering to the person, such as facts about his or her family, or individual traits, such as being shy or gifted in music. Social difference stems from social categories such as race, gender, class, sexuality, nationality, and the like. The child's unique configuration of difference, coupled with family resources, shaped how much parents bought, in order to shield, cure, or cultivate. In addition, parents were motivated not just by the prospect of the child's difference from others, but also by their own emotional memories—often their anxious recall—of their experiences of being different as a child. These motivations combined to create parents' relative sensitivity to their child's belonging, leading to which desires parents could ignore and which they could not.

Both affluent and low-income parents were responsive to children's wants, but this did not mean these groups bought in the same way. I found that parents aimed their buying to accomplish different symbolic goals depending on where the parents were on the income ladder. Affluent parents practiced a form of "symbolic deprivation," pointing to particularly meaningful goods or experiences that their child did *not* have as evidence of their own moral restraint and worthiness as parents. Affluent parents often disparaged aloud the need to belong as a form of conformity, and children's desires often contradicted the stated goals of adults, some of whom explicitly sought not just to "keep up with the Joneses" but to be "different from the Joneses." Symbolic deprivation was how affluent parents resolved the contradiction between their normative beliefs and their practices, between their ideals and their material plenty.

On the other end of the class spectrum, most low-income parents implemented a form of "symbolic indulgence," making sure (sometimes at considerable sacrifice) to buy particular goods or experiences for their children, those items or events sure to have the most significant symbolic value for the children's social world. For many low-income parents, symbolic indulgence was the best they could do within their resource constraints, even though their personal experience of the pain of difference often led them to prioritize children's belonging above almost all else. These consumer practices thus comprised the way low-income parents demonstrated their own moral worth and value as parents.

PERSONAL VICE OR SOCIAL ILL? WHAT WE TALK ABOUT WHEN WE TALK ABOUT BUYING

Many of the more popular current explanations of the children's spending boom focus on corporate marketers or personal vices and thus feel less like understanding than judgment. While they portray part of the consumption story, they omit the conceptual tools we need to comprehend Judy Berger's regret that "it is a given you will have a Game Boy," or Simon and Marco's discursive facework to invent a new Halloween costume.

Some commentators explain the consumption boom by looking first to the children, whose consumer desires seem to arouse considerable adult anxiety. Children are often portrayed as "agents of materialism," to use Robert Wuthnow's term, conduits for the commercial culture that Americans regard with mixed feelings. Bloggers by the thousands decry children's seeming addiction to video games, collectibles like Yu-Gi-Oh! cards, or Air Jordans, while in works with titles like *Born to Buy* scholars issue warnings depicting the psychological costs of consumerism. Waggish terms such as "the nag factor" or "pester power" capture the notion of parents subjected to children who know no appropriate limits. Media portrayals feature children as either unwitting dupes to corporate marketing, or avaricious and amoral; in one editorial pledging a series on "how much of parenting has been reduced to fending off requests from children for commercial products," a national newspaper opined that childhood "has been transformed into consumerhood."

Yet, as media critic David Buckingham wrote, there is "at least a degree of irony in adults accusing children of 'consumerism' when their power to consume at all is almost entirely in the hands of adults themselves." Some writers point out that commercialized children surely learn from their materialistic parents, those who enact their own status concerns through their children's toys and wardrobes. On a more fundamental level, a number of scholars have recently argued we should hardly be surprised by the spread of children's consumption, because children's culture mirrors that of adults generally. Widespread concerns about the intensity and extent of children's marketized desires, these analysts contend, reflect more about our misguided need to consider childhood as it never was—a time and place apart from the cares, woes, and temptations of adult life. As childhood expert Daniel Cook has argued, consumption is not separate from childhood, as the profane is distinct from the sacred; children are "always, already embedded in market relations," and the market is "indispensable and unavoidable" in constructing childhoods. Perhaps childhood has turned into consumerhood, then, because adulthood has, too.

Stories about greed, whether in children or adults, certainly have their magnetic appeal—witness the annual journalistic exercise in charting spending excess during the holiday season, leading to articles with headlines like "18 Shopping Bags and 3 Empty Wallets, One Family's Ritual: Daylong Orgy of Buying Christmas Gifts." Yet charges of materialism, with its underlying image of uncontrolled vice and unrestrained desire—as in the hedonism captured by the headline's term "orgy"—seem less to offer answers than to raise questions. Who are those people who just cannot seem to get their spending under control? Why are they driven by desire for the latest doll fad or video game to stand outside stores before dawn, name their children after favorite brands, or go to extreme measures to buy?

WHOSE NEEDS? WHOSE LUXURIES? SPENDING AND INEQUALITY

The morality tales of spending are part of a cultural contest of who can buy and how much. Whether consumers are depicted as the poor and minority "combat consumers," as Elizabeth Chin argued, willing to rob to buy Timberland boots, or the luxury-obsessed wealthy, intent upon owning the largest yacht or the most diverting East Hampton castle, popular representations of materialism or greed are most often portrayals of the vice of Others, mostly for the benefit of an assumed white, middle-class audience.

In families' daily lives, however, inequality and consumption are deeply, mutually implicated, albeit in complex, sometimes counterintuitive ways. Poor families are *not,* as one analyst recently asserted against much evidence, somehow "relatively insulated by their poverty from the consequences if not the temptations of consumer marketing." Indeed, until recently, most research has shown that low-income families spend disproportionately *more* on their children than do wealthier families, suggesting that in times of budget constraints, in many homes children's needs are more fixed, more compelling than those of adults. Marketers have dubbed the children's market "bulletproof," meaning that it is practically impervious to economic dislocations, because parents report being unable to take pride in cutting back on children's expenses.

Talk of spending immediately raises questions of need versus luxury. But even the economist Adam Smith understood that needs are fungible, relative, based on cultural standards. Lauded by free-market celebrants, Smith is less well known for his passages recognizing the primacy of dignity. "By necessaries," he wrote, "I understand not only the commodities which are indispensably necessary for the support of life, but whatever the customs of the country renders it indecent for creditable people, even of the lowest order to do without."

Thus we might say that a family's relative means to spend (inequality), and what a family spends to mean (consumption), are intricately, intimately connected, although not in a simple, linear way. As one shifts and changes, so does the other—and not merely with the stiff formality of figures and numbers, but in the warp and bend of human feeling. Inexorably, inevitably perhaps, the standards of childhood change, with "needs" chased by children and adults from marbles and bicycles to Nintendo Wii and iPods. These shifting standards are met by shifting emotions, the despair of the parent working two jobs to cover what used to be the basics, the dread of the middle-class parent trying to stave off the addictive appeal of the latest fad, the triumph of the taxi driver's daughter when she uses her own money to buy her own PlayStation. While greed or materialism might fuel some of their actions, their intense emotions hint at a deeper mystery, of the meaning of things, of care, and of belonging.

NOT-SO-HIDDEN PERSUADERS

Some researchers have argued that the meaning of things, and hence the urge to buy, stem from the powerful reach of particularly effective corporate marketing. Corporate marketing is so insidious and potent that it can make children desire, and parents desire for their children. There is certainly plenty of solid research into the impact of advertising, demonstrating that corporate marketing is increasingly sophisticated and unfettered, and that children are particularly vulnerable to marketing tactics, as children are believed to be unaware of the advertisers' persuasive intent until about the age of seven. Much of this research is conducted by psychologists, who fabricate "strange situations" involving individual children exposed to ads and then asked about products, and there is a plethora of studies showing children do indeed respond to corporate efforts to convince. A number of scholars have also documented the expansion of campaigns to plumb the psyches of children, the weakening of advertising regulation, and the development of new and even more powerful market tactics to lure buyers, such as the thinly disguised market research among "tweens" involving staged and sponsored "sleep-overs" where girls talk about products. Corporate marketing, this research demonstrates, is targeting children with a gimlet eye.

Given the soaring and pervasive rates of children's media exposure, the attention these scholars pay to corporate actors is undoubtedly warranted: American youth spend more time with media per week (6.4 hours) than they do with their parents (2.3 hours), with friends (2.3 hours), or in school (on an annual basis). We may not yet have reached the moment predicted more than a half century ago by E. B. White in a science-fiction story, when "children early formed the habit of gaining all their images at second hand, by looking at a screen, [and] only what had been touched by electronics was valid and real." At the very least, however, children's lives are increasingly beginning to approach the atomistic existence modeled by the psychology experiments, as more and more they watch TV alone in their rooms.

Yet these arguments rely on a rather weak notion of human behavior, in which people have all the substance of tissue paper, blown this way and that by nothing more than the airwaves, or by their individual vices. Either the corporations are too powerful to resist or parents are too weak to set limits or delay gratification; the answer to exploding consumption is thus either more corporate regulation or more parental responsibility. While these perspectives are commonly argued against one another, they share a common perception: parents *buy* merely because they (or their children) have been successfully *sold*.

CONSUMPTION AS CARE

Other scholars argue that consumption is a social practice, one in which people are communicating meaning to each other through goods, although these experts disagree about just what kind of meaning consumption conveys. Some researchers contend buying for children is driven by parents' efforts to establish their children's socioeconomic status—or, more subtly, to shape their children's class-specific tastes—through their purchases; by parents enacting their class status in the practices they employ to make purchases; or by parents' recognition of the role that consumption plays in signaling the full citizenship available only to those with means. More recently, scholars have explored the intersections of the market and intimacy, arguing that consumption forges "connected lives," in the words of Viviana Zelizer. These researchers expand our notion of why buyers buy beyond the obsession with status, arguing that consumption acts as a symbolic language through which buyers make connections to others. As the British anthropologist Daniel Miller contended, shopping for others can be considered a devotional rite, and commodities "the material culture of love." In this vein, parents buy for children to strengthen emotional bonds that are fraying due to increasing work hours, cultural prescriptions encouraging children's defiance, the high incidence of divorce, or the strains of poverty, among other factors. These scholars contribute a critical observation: the importance of feeling in motivating action, in shaping cultural meaning, in spurring consumption. As the sociologist Sharon Zukin observed, "the things we need to buy are framed by our love for the significant others we buy for."

Yet in focusing on the bridging of consumption, analysts sometimes seem to gloss over how consumption can separate as well, and downplay the very real inequalities embedded in the sheer capacity to spend. In addition, even though people may use commodities as a tool to express their connections, the very system of commodification exerts its own influence on the relationships it mediates, much as a set of tires will drive a car forward or back but not up, say, or sideways. We need not "presume that the realm of commodities debases the realm of sentiment," sociologist Eva Illouz cautioned, but "the vocabulary of emotions is now more exclusively dictated by the market."

Families adjust to new circumstances, and evidence suggests they are indeed adjusting to the commodification of childhood. Arlie Hochschild has analyzed some of the strategies parents use to handle the pressures of overwork and what she calls the "commercialization of intimate life." She points to people using goods to represent their ideal selves ("we'll go camping someday"), to engage in "caring consumption" to avoid family conflict, to revisit the question of just what aspects of family life—birthday parties? photo albums?—are and are not appropriate to pay someone else to do. As Hochschild reports, however, these adaptations have their own impact, just as someone favoring a bad knee can start to feel a twinge in the good one, too. Relationships—between men and women, between parents and children—suffer from the sacrifice of our time, energy, and focus on the twin altars of cultural capitalism: work and shopping. Hochschild warns that such practices serve "to push men and women further into the worlds of workplace and the mall," to decenter family life as the focus of collective rituals, and finally, to "materialize love."

MAKING MEANING: CULTURE AS PROCESS

The realm of emotional meaning, wherein neutral objects and events are transformed into things and experiences that matter to people, is the realm of culture. Culture is often defined as a system of meanings, in the words of Sharon Hays "a social, durable, layered pattern of cognitive and normative systems." Yet perhaps this description makes culture sound a little more ossified, more finished, than people experience. We do not invent culture out of whole cloth, of course, but we do work with what we receive, albeit often unconsciously. We mix and blend meanings across social realms and experiences, bringing one to another in a daily project of individual and collective creativity that nonetheless often serves to reproduce understandings and relationships. As my research focuses on how children and parents make meaning out of things, I emphasize here the movement, the dynamism of culture, by proposing that we think of it as a process.

What is the process of making meaning? Meaning comes from a sort of emotional thinking, so that the way we feel about commodities and experiences colors the way we perceive them. We might conceive of culture, then, as a patterned, collective process by which people attach personal, emotional significance to their world, indeed, as a sort of dynamic, two-way bridge between the social and the psychological. Much of that process is captured in interactions that serve as occasions to reconfirm, and occasionally to reshape, the powerful social asymmetries that order our experience.

In this work, I argue that certain shared cultural notions—powerful ideas about what parents owe their children, about the challenge posed by difference, about the primacy of belonging—make it near-impossible for most American-born parents of varied class and race backgrounds to ignore children's yearnings. To be sure, our trajectories and choices are profoundly shaped by the "organization of human existence," the social institutions, categories, and resources that frame and produce social life. But what makes children yearn, and parents buy, is also in part a cultural story of what we value and what we fear, ideas that are continually made concrete in interactions, rituals, and daily experiences. Taking into account the institutional backdrop, this book tells that cultural story, exploring how consumption expresses care and belonging for children and parents, how social inequality and intolerance can make care and belonging feel scarce or plentiful, and how such feelings shape contemporary childhood.

* * *

CONCLUSION

At the center of the word *belonging* is a synonym for *desire*, as one contemporary novelist recently observed, and these twin ideas explain the particular magic of children's consumer yearnings. In service to these yearnings, I argue, spending on children has exploded, and this trend has been costly for American families. Compared to families of decades ago with or without children, today's families with children work more hours, accumulate more debt, and declare bankruptcy more often. Affluent families lament the sheer quantity of children's stuff but can also mourn the degree to which parent-child relations are mediated through consumer goods. The cost is no less significant for low-income families; research documents the great lengths to which low-income families go to equip their children. Low-income parents take on extra jobs over Christmas, plan birthday gifts and seasonal clothing purchases long in advance, juggle creditors to be able to float expenses, and otherwise strive to meet children's designated needs, protecting their place in the family budget.

There are also other costs to this spending race, beyond the impact on individual children and their families, that we all bear. On a society-wide level, the trend promotes a culture of spending that redefines care and belonging as mediated through the market. Those who want to opt out find it difficult to do so. The cost of raising a child increases, and the impact of income inequality on the distribution of opportunity is intensified. Furthermore, poor children—attending high-poverty schools with an economy of dignity that can contrast sharply with that of some of the more affluent schools—are perhaps enduring what we might call an unequal distribution of sentiment, one in which differences are subject to intense peer discipline of scorn or invisibility. Not only, then, are the opportunities afforded by different contexts for children highly unequal, but so too might be their emotional allowances, suggesting perhaps another cost of commodified childhood: the stratification of feeling. We might consider collectively these expenses of modern spending practices as an invisible tax, a tax that no one collects but one that we all pay, adding to the $300 price tag for the Nintendo Wii, the $90 American Girl doll, or the $165 pair of Air Jordans.

But perhaps most important, the commodification of childhood turns the child into a pipeline of commercial culture, the cause of the ratcheting up of standards, the target of cultural animosity about the costs of rising inequality even as he or she is its primary victim. Who bears the emotional fallout for these trends? Furthermore, who takes on the burden when parents do the "right" thing, eschew consumer culture, ignore their children's entreaties? A hint, perhaps, lies in the identity of who often shoulders the blame for what are really the residual effects of materialism, greed, and the effectiveness of advertising: children. Calling children the conduit of commercial culture is a bit like faulting fish for the water in which they swim.

Children's emotional experience records the impact of consumer capitalism on all of us—the expansion of work time, the expression of love through things, the pressure of increasing inequality, and the diminution of public provisioning, which has withered like a raisin. Could adults' anxiety swirling around children reflect instead worries about our own materialistic culture, our own inability to stem desire, our own failure to connect with others? We could be relegating to children what we fear for ourselves, while all along they just want to belong.

17

Deviance and Liminality

FROM *Something Old, Something Bold: Bridal Showers and Bachelorette Parties*

BETH MONTEMURRO

Some cultural practices are secular rituals, especially those marking passages in the life cycle. The way societies—our own included—recognize and ritualize birth, the onset of puberty (adulthood), marriage, and death are sometimes seen as curious events. The author's term liminality refers to being "neither here nor there" in passing from one status to another, e.g., youth to married person. Liminality provides a moment, an opportunity, for deviant behavior in a socially approved if often embarrassing way. It also reveals the continuing struggle of young women to find greater gender equality, however imperfectly pursued.

DEVIANCE AND LIMINALITY

For some women, the deviant activity consistent at bachelorette parties—going to see strippers, kissing or flirting with strange men, getting intoxicated—was part of the fun. John Lofland (1969) suggested that some deviance is performed for the fun or thrill generated from participating in what he called "the adventurous deviant act." He wrote, "Some kinds of prohibited activities are claimed by some parts of the population to be *in themselves* fun, exciting, and adventurous. More than simply deriving pleasant fearfulness from violating the prohibition per se, there can exist claims that the prohibited activity itself produces a pleasant level of excitation" (Lofland 1969, 109). Drinking was clearly fun for many of the women at bachelorette parties. Brides-to-be were more comfortable engaging in embarrassing and otherwise deviant acts, such as being dressed up in a costume or watching a dance by a stripper, when they had consumed a substance that made them less self-conscious. Dwight Heath suggested that because alcohol is associated with lowered inhibitions, it is sometimes used as an excuse to deviate: "Others who claim to drink, 'just to get drunk' or 'to be totally out of it' subsequently take great pleasure in recounting their outlandish behavior, suggesting that they may . . . have been drinking primarily in order to misbehave while enjoying the temporary suspension of certain social expectations (time-out) that is often accorded to the inebriate" (2000, 171). Though for some women the subsequént hangover was described as the worst part of the party, it was clear that drinking with friends and feeling the effects of alcohol were quite pleasurable. Alcohol is associated with increased sociability and solidarity (Trice 1966), and this heightened feeling of camaraderie was enjoyable for and important to women on bachelorette parties.

Since play is seen as time off or time out from the responsibilities of everyday life and adulthood, the focus on having a good time or giving the bride-to-be a night she will never forget may imply that she sacrifices this type of play when she is married. Play, particularly in the form of binge drinking and having a "girls' night," is associated with youthfulness and a more carefree lifestyle. To some extent, the freedom to do this frequently is something that is given up upon marriage. The idea of going all out for the bachelorette party can be explained in part, then, by the idea that this is the bride's last chance to free herself of urges to do so in the future. As Jamie, aged twenty-eight and engaged, noted, "Your bachelorette party is supposed to be a crazy, uninhibited time, and you're supposed to act like you wouldn't normally act. . . . [I]t's kind of like your free pass for the night. . . . As we become adults, we don't do that, and we can't because we have to get up the next morning. We have to go to work. . . . Like every other night, you really can't because—not because you have a husband at home, but because you have a job or you have kids." For many women this transition from single to married is not merely that but also a symbolic transition from childhood to adulthood. Since we do not have any secular rituals expressly designated to mark this status passage, exactly when this transition is completed is ambiguous. Not only is marriage about the union of two individuals; it also functions as recognition of adulthood. In this sense, the drinking and play of the bachelorette party are opportunities for brides-to-be to act not as children or responsible adults, but somewhere in between.

There is little doubt that the activities engaged in at bachelorette parties are defined as deviant by the participants in this ritual because this is exactly the point of these parties. Although some women called their own behavior "bad" or "naughty," they did so while grinning, seemingly proud of their transgressions because such acts meant they had accomplished the goals of the bachelorette party. However, a couple of women said they felt regret for what happened or described friends who felt guilty about what they did on their bachelorette parties. April, for example, described the aftermath of a friend's bachelorette party in which pictures were taken of the bride-to-be kissing random men. She described her friend's feelings of remorse, saying "When she showed me the photos at work the next week and she had to censor them for her fiancé, you know, I think she felt bad about that. I'm sure there's a lot worse things that happen at bachelorette parties then just kissing a couple of guys because your friends egg you on to do it. I'm sure horrible things happen. But she felt guilty, I think, about that part of it. I think overall she had a good time . . . but I do think she had a little bit of regret."

Most women, however, recognized their behavior as deviant but felt it was excused or legitimated within the context of the bachelorette party. David Matza (1969) argued that all members of society have periods of nonconformity and, as a result, develop justifications or accounts in order to explain why they violate the norms, rules, and laws of society at certain points in their lives. Matza argued that we all "drift" in and out of conformity; yet, we still like to consider ourselves conforming, moral members of society. Since these deviant acts are subject to evaluation and judgment by others, when otherwise rule-following members of society deviate, they account for or defend their rule or norm breaking by using what Sykes and Matza (1957) called "techniques of neutralization." Jamie employed the "denial, of responsibility" technique in her comment above when she called the bachelorette party a "free pass," indicating that because it is the bride's special night, she is not responsible for her actions. One way women employed this technique was by saying that their actions were the result of their friends' pressure or instruction. The friends at the bachelorette party create the task list or scavenger hunt and the bachelorette, as the submissive initiate, knows it is her duty to play along. Pam, for example, was instructed to have two dozen men sign her shirt. When her fiancé saw her shirt after the bachelorette party and asked about it, she responded, "Hey, it wasn't my doing." April, who was quoted above regarding the guilt her friend felt after her bachelorette party, defended her friend, explaining to me that her behavior was not really her fault. She said, "I mean she was forced to wear and do these things, but she's such an easy going person that she just went along with it. . . . She has this group of friends and they do a lot of things together, and I guess a few of them were married and they had gone through this exact same thing, so they were determined to put [this bride] through it all. . . . But it was very familiar and there was a whole set way they had to do all of this." In this case, April attempted to neutralize her friend's deviant behavior by suggesting that she did what she did because her friends pressured her to do so. Related to this, the bachelorette party calls attention to the transitory or liminal status of the bride-to-be at this point in time. Victor Turner argued that liminality is when one is between statuses, and those who experience it "elude or slip through the network of classifications that normally locate states and positions in cultural space. Liminal entities are neither here nor there; they are betwixt and between" (1969, 95). At the bachelorette party the bride-to-be is no longer single but not yet married. She is spoken for but not legally committed. As Tye and Powers suggested, part of the successful bachelorette role is the communal understanding that "while she is available, she is not available" (1998, 58). Because of this special and ambiguous status, the bride-to-be has a degree of freedom that she will not have again.

Erikson (1966) noted that some societies, like ours, sanction this type of behavior, what I call "liminal deviance." He stated, "There are societies which appoint special days or occasions as periods of general license, during which members of the group are permitted (if not expected) to violate rules they have observed during the preceding season and will again observe during the coming season" (Erikson 1966, 27). The bride-to-be is not in a constant state of back and forth during the engagement period, kissing strange men, going to strip clubs, and then being devoted to her fiancé. Rather, she is offered one opportunity during this time to act out feelings of ambivalence or doubt (whether she has them or not). She is given one chance to play and behave as a single woman before returning to her role as a faithful, committed romantic partner. This "special period of license" is when the bride-to-be is both allowed and expected to cross the boundaries of acceptable behavior for a girlfriend, fiancée, or (especially) wife. Thus, the bachelorette party itself, given the liminal status of its central participant, functions as an excuse for deviant and excessive behavior.

STRIPPERS AND SEDUCTION: INTERPRETING THE MEANINGS OF SEX SYMBOLS

The majority of bachelorette parties described (81 percent, or 115) and all parties that I observed included a sexual element or theme. Sex was a major component of the bachelorette party, and some of the women I interviewed questioned the legitimacy of bachelorette parties that omitted it entirely. Much of the deviant behavior at bachelorette parties involved sexualized interaction and play. Brides-to-be danced with strippers. Random men sucked candy pieces that were suggestively attached to brides' shirts. Women carried around giant phallic-shaped novelty items. Why is the bachelorette party sexualized? How can the use of sex symbols and props be interpreted? The association between sex and marriage is certainly a partial explanation. Traditionally, sex was expected to be reserved for marriage, and thus the bachelorette party could be interpreted as a means of socializing women into marriage by giving them sexual advice and showering them with symbols of sexuality so that they are prepared for a sexual relationship with their husbands. However, since the majority of women who marry in contemporary American society are not virgins (Laumann et al. 1994), and since the bachelorette party appears to have emerged in the United States after the sexual revolution of the 1960s, this rationale is insufficient.

A modern explanation would be what I have suggested thus far, that women have dated different men prior to marriage and that many have had more than one sexual partner. Like men have for decades with bachelor parties, they see the bachelorette party as a way to acknowledge the termination of their single life. It is a symbolic means of showing that they are "off the market." Similarly, part of the sexual element comes directly from bachelor parties, from which the bachelorette party is certainly derived. Stereotypes about bachelor parties suggest that they are hyper-sexualized and that men frequent strip clubs or view pornography as a part of their "last night of freedom" (Schultz 1995). Luanne, a bride-to-be in her mid-twenties, expressed this when she stated why she felt sex talk and imagery are involved. She said, "When . . . girls were copying the bachelor party into the bachelorette party, they really were just kind of copying the same thing. It's not that girls are as interested in [sex] when they're just sitting around—not that, I mean shoot, [you] can't get a group of girls together without it coming up eventually, too. But I think . . . we can certainly find other things to talk about. I think it was more copycatting the whole bachelor party thing." Luanne's comments, coupled with an examination of the structure of the bachelorette party, particularly the Women's Bachelor Party or Anything Goes types, suggest that a major reason women include sexual elements is that they are purposefully replicating their image of the bachelor party.

One prominent element of bachelorette parties, the inclusion of a stripper, seems to have been copied from women's perceptions of men's parties. The stereotype of strippers as a part of bachelor parties is certainly dominant in our cultural history. Films depicting bachelor parties, such as *Bachelor Party* (1984) and *Very Bad Things* (1999), include strippers as central elements. However, while strippers were often included in bachelorette parties, and bachelorette parties made up a large portion of patrons of strip clubs like the Hideaway and the Regal Room (Montemurro 2001), women's interactions with and feelings about strippers conveyed ambivalence. In trying to replicate the bachelor party, it seems that some women ignored their own indifference to or even dislike of strippers in order to do what they felt was appropriate for a bachelorette party. Several women admitted that they really did not want to have strippers at their parties or did not care about having strippers but did so because they thought that was what was supposed to be done. Luanne communicated this as she told me about the first bachelorette party she attended. She said, "It almost seemed like we were trying to chase down that novel idea, but weren't really having a good time with it. Like you think you are going into a strip club with a bunch of girls and you're going to hoot and holler and it's going to be great. And we did, but after about thirty minutes it's like, "This is getting boring. Let's go and meet some real men.'"

* * *

The games played at most bachelorette parties were notably different from those at the bridal shower. Even though some of the bridal shower games were laced with sexual innuendo, most were dated and sustained the assumption of the virgin bride. As in the game where the maid of honor records the bride's reactions as she opens her presents, then reads the list back as if it is what she might say on her wedding night, the bride at the shower is sexually naive. Knowing older relatives and married peers introduce her to the adult world with advice or lingerie, communicating their approval of sexual activity within the bounds of marriage. These older family members often tease the bride about her future sexual activity, communicating that they hope it will soon lead to procreation. When the bride-to-be is told that the number of ribbons she breaks when she opens her gifts is equivalent to the number of children she will have, she receives the message that motherhood follows marriage. Simply, the sexualized games at the shower connect sex to marriage and childbearing. In contrast, the games at the bachelorette party assume an opposite identity for the bride-to-be.

* * *

Furthermore, women may have found the sexualized atmosphere of the bachelorette party to be awkward given the cultural ambivalence about women's sexuality in contemporary society. As Susan Douglas articulated in her study of images of women in popular culture, American media have presented conflicting images of girls and women, images that paint them as either innocent or promiscuous, resulting in "schizophrenic [ideas] about women's sexuality" (1995, 15). The women in this study have grown up with a sexual double standard that suggests that men who have multiple sexual partners are to be congratulated while women who do so are to be punished. They also have learned from American culture, through media and other agents of socialization, that men are the sexual aggressors while women should be sexually passive (Spade and Valentine 2004). At parties, engaging in the various tasks positioned the bride-to-be as object more often than aggressor. When women played the Suck for a Buck game or had men remove pieces of candy from necklaces, or when they had men sign their underwear, this placed them as sexual objects, selling or making themselves available for men's pleasure. Rather than representing their sexual confidence or participating in acts that were sexually titillating as a means of celebrating their last night of sexual freedom, instead, some of the bachelorette party games were about offering themselves up one last time to interested men. Some tasks called for brides-to-be to play aggressor by approaching random men and asking for their phone numbers or other items on a scavenger hunt. Thus, it is not surprising that the women's response to exotic dancers and the general sexualized atmosphere of the party was ambivalence because, on one hand, women are told to claim and embrace their sexuality, but, on the other hand, much of the expected sexual expression is based on making themselves available to arouse and entertain men.

The bachelorette party is based on the idea of the non-virgin bride who has had sexual experiences and is acknowledging, even lamenting, the end of her freedom. Yet the sexually experienced woman is not a privileged position in Western society. Leora Tanenbaum (2000) argued as much in her study of female sexual activity. She noted that teenage girls and women face pressure both to have sex and to preserve their reputation as "good girls." Having grown up in the wake of the feminist movement, the women I interviewed received the message that they can do what boys or men do. But in terms of sexuality, when women of this generation listened to such rhetoric, they would quickly be made aware of the consequences of promiscuity (Tanenbaum 2000). Furthermore, women received mixed messages about how they should express this sexual liberation. The bride-to-be at the bachelorette party exemplifies this contradiction with the props she carries, the way she is costumed, and the expectations for her behavior. The party itself is indicative of this incongruity as women play along with a male-defined image of feminine sexuality in terms of the show or performative aspect of bachelorette parties.

* * *

REFERENCES

Douglas, Susan. 1995. *Where the Girls Are: Growing up Female with the Mass Media.* New York: Times Books.

Erikson, Kai T. 1966. *Wayward Puritans: A Study in the Sociology of Deviance.* New York: John Wiley and Sons.

Heath, Dwight B. 2000. *Drinking Occasions: Comparative Perspectives on Alcohol and Culture.* Philadelphia: Brunner/Mazel.

Lofland, John, 1969. *Deviance and Identity.* Englewood Cliffs, NJ: Prentice Hall.

Matza, David. 1969. *Becoming Deviant.* Englewood Cliffs, NJ: Prentice Hall.

Montemurro, Beth. 2001. Strippers and Screamers: The Emergence of Social Control in a Non-Institutionalized Setting. *Journal of Contemporary Ethnography* 30: 275–304.

Schultz, Jason. 1995. Getting off on Feminism. In *To Be Real: Telling the Truth and Changing the Face of Feminism,* edited by Rebecca Walker, 107–126. New York: Anchor Books.

Spade, Joan Z., and Catherine G. Valentine. 2004. Tracing Gender's Mark on Bodies, Sexualities, and Emotions. In *The Kaleidoscope of Gender: Prisms, Patterns, and Possibilities,* edited by Joan Z. Spade and Catherine G. Valentine, 279–285. Belmont, CA: Wadsworth.

Sykes, Gresham, and David Matza. 1957. Techniques of Neutralization: A Theory of Delinquency. *American Sociological Review* 22: 664–670.

Tanenbaum, Leora. 2000. *Slut! Growing up Female with a Bad Reputation.* New York: HarperCollins.

Trice, Harrison. 1966. *Alcoholism in America.* New York: McGraw-Hill.

Turner, Victor. 1969. *The Ritual Process: Structure and Anti-structure.* Repr., New York: Aldine de Gruyter, 1995.

Tye, Diane, and Ann Marie Powers. 1998. Gender, Resistance, and Play: Bachelorette Parties in Atlantic Canada. *Women's Studies International Forum* 21: 551–561.

PART FOUR

SOCIAL INTERACTION AND IDENTITY

18

On Face-Work

ERVING GOFFMAN

Many students find the idea of a "self-presentation" to be manipulative, insincere, and inauthentic. What Goffman's work shows is that we cannot avoid the work of presenting a "face" or identity in social interaction. We can deny that this activity goes on and we can be unaware of what we are doing, but all of us must do this work in order to carry on social interaction. Goffman takes sociology into the deepest realm of social life: our most intimate relations and our most private ideas about who we are.

Every person lives in a world of social encounters, involving him either in face-to-face or mediated contact with other participants. In each of these contacts, he tends to act out what is sometimes called a *line*—that is, a pattern of verbal and nonverbal acts by which he expresses his view of the situation and through this his evaluation of the participants, especially himself. Regardless of whether a person intends to take a line, he will find that he has done so in effect. The other participants will assume that he has more or less willfully taken a stand, so that if he is to deal with their response to him he must take into consideration the impression they have possibly formed of him.

The term *face* may be defined as the positive social value a person effectively claims for himself by the line others assume he has taken during a particular contact. Face is an image of self-delineation in terms of approved social attributes—albeit an image that others may share, as when a person makes a good showing for his profession or religion by making a good showing for himself.

A person tends to experience an immediate emotional response to the face which a contact with others allows him; he cathects his face; his "feelings become attached to it. If the encounter sustains an image of him that he has long taken for granted, he probably will have few feelings about the matter. If events establish a face for him that is better than he might have expected, he is likely to "feel good"; if his ordinary expectations are not fulfilled, one expects that he will "feel bad" or "feel hurt." In general, a persons attachment to a particular face, coupled with the ease with which disconfirming information can be conveyed by himself and others, provides one reason why he finds that participation in any contact with others is a commitment. A person will also have feelings about the face sustained for the other participants, and while these feelings may differ in quantity and direction from those he has for his own face, they constitute an involvement in the face of others that is as immediate and spontaneous as the involvement he has in his own face. One's own face and the face of others are constructs of the same order; it is the rules of the group and the definition of the situation which determine how much feeling one is to have for face and how this feeling is to be distributed among the faces involved.

A person may be said to *have,* or *be in,* or *maintain* face when the line he effectively takes presents an image of him that is internally consistent, that is supported by judgments and evidence conveyed by other participants, and that is confirmed by evidence conveyed through impersonal agencies in the situation. At such times the persons face clearly is something that is not lodged in or on his body, but rather something that is diffusely located in the flow of events in the encounter and becomes manifest only when these events are read and interpreted for the appraisals expressed in them.

The line maintained by and for a person during contact with others tends to be of a legitimate institutionalized kind. During a contact of a particular type, an interactant of known or visible attributes can expect to be sustained in a particular face and can feel that it is morally proper that this should be so. Given his attributes and the conventionalized nature of the encounter, he will find a small choice of lines will be open to him and a small choice of faces will be waiting for him. Further, on the basis of a few known attributes, he is given the responsibility of possessing a vast number of others. His coparticipants are not likely to be conscious of the character of many of these attributes until he acts perceptibly in such a way as to discredit his possession of them; then everyone becomes conscious of these attributes and assumes that he willfully gave a false impression of possessing them.

* * *

A person may be said to *be in wrong face* when information is brought forth in some way about his social worth which cannot be integrated, even with effort, into the line that is being sustained for him. A person may be said to *be out of face* when he participates in a contact with others without having ready a line of the kind participants in such situations are expected to take. The intent of many pranks is to lead a person into showing a wrong face or no face, but there will also be serious occasions, of course, when he will find himself expressively out of touch with the situation.

When a person senses that he is in face, he typically responds with feelings of confidence and assurance. Firm in the line he is taking, he feels that he can hold his head up and openly present himself to others. He feels some security and some relief—as he also can when the others feel he is in wrong face but successfully hide these feelings from him.

When a person is in wrong face or out of face, expressive events are being contributed to the encounter which cannot be readily woven into the expressive fabric of the occasion. Should he sense that he is in wrong face or out of face, he is likely to feel ashamed and inferior because of what has happened to the activity on his account and because of what may happen to his reputation as a participant. Further, he may feel bad because he had relied upon the encounter to support an image of self to which he has become emotional attached and which he now finds threatened. Felt lack of judgmental support from the encounter may take him aback, confuse him, and momentarily incapacitate him as an interactant. His manner and bearing may falter, collapse and crumble. He may become embarassed and chagrined; he may become shamefaced. The feeling, whether warranted or not, that he is perceived in flustered state by others, and that he is presenting no usable line, may add further injuries to his feelings, just as his change from being in wrong face or out of face to being shamefaced can add further disorder to the expressive organization of the situation. Following common usage, I shall employ the term *poise* to refer to the capacity to suppress and conceal any tendency to become shamefaced during encounters with others.

In our Anglo-American society, as in some others, the phrase "to lose face" seems to mean to be in wrong face, to be out of face, or to be shamefaced. The phrase "to save one's face" appears to refer to the process by which the person sustains an impression for others that he has not lost face. Following Chinese usage, one can say that "to give face" is to arrange for another to take a better line than he might otherwise have been able to take, the other thereby gets face given him, this being one way in which he can gain face.

* * *

Just as the member of any group is expected to have self-respect, so also he is expected to sustain a standard of considerateness; he is expected to go to certain lengths to save the feelings and the face of others present, and he is expected to do this willingly and spontaneously because of emotional identification with the others and with their feelings. In consequence, he is disinclined to witness the defacement of others. The person who can witness another's humiliation and unfeelingly retain a cool countenance himself is said in our society to be "heartless," just as he who can unfeelingly participate in his own defacement is thought to be "shameless."

The combined effect of the rule of self-respect and the rule of considerateness is that the person tends to conduct himself during an encounter so as to maintain both his own face and the face of the other participants. This means that the line taken by each participant is usually allowed to prevail, and each participant is allowed to carry off the role he appears to have chosen for himself. A state where everyone temporarily accepts everyone else's line is established. This kind of mutual acceptance seems to be a basic structural feature of interaction, especially the interaction of face-to-face talk. It is typically a "working" acceptance, not a "real" one, since it tends to be based not on agreement of candidly expressed heart-felt evaluations, but upon a willingness to give temporary lip service to judgments with which the participants do not really agree.

The mutual acceptance of lines has an important conservative effect upon encounters. Once the person initially presents a line, he and the others tend to build their later responses upon it, and in a sense become stuck with it. Should the person radically alter his line, or should it become discredited, then confusion results, for the participants will have prepared and committed themselves for actions that are now unsuitable.

Ordinarily, maintenance of face is a condition of interaction, not its objective. Usual objectives, such as gaining face for oneself, giving free expression to one's true beliefs, introducing depreciating information about the others, or solving problems and performing tasks, are typically pursued in such a way as to be consistent with the maintenance of face. To study face-saving is to study the traffic rules of social interaction; one learns about the code the person adheres to in his movement across the paths and designs of others, but not where he is going, or why he wants to get there. One does not even learn why he is ready to follow the code, for a large number of different motives can equally lead him to do so. He may want to save his own face because of his emotional attachment to the image of self which it expresses, because of his pride or honor, because of the power his presumed status allows him to exert over the other participants, and so on. He may want to save the others' face because of his emotional attachment to an image of them, or because he feels that his coparticipants have a moral right to this protection, or because he wants to avoid the hostility that may be directed toward him if they lose their face. He may feel that an assumption has been made that he is the sort of person who shows compassion and sympathy toward others, so that to retain his own face, he may feel obliged to be considerate of the line taken by the other participants.

* * *

THE BASIC KINDS OF FACE-WORK

The Avoidance Process. The surest way for a person to prevent threats to his face is to avoid contacts in which these threats are likely to occur. In all societies one can observe this in the avoidance relationship and in the tendency for certain delicate transactions to be conducted by go-betweens. Similarly, in many societies, members know the value of voluntarily making a gracious withdrawal before an anticipated threat to face has had a chance to occur.

Once the person does chance an encounter, other kinds of avoidance practices come into play. As defensive measures, he keeps off topics and away from activities that would lead to the expression of information that is inconsistent with the line he is maintaining. At opportune moments he will change the top of conversation or the direction of activity. He will often present initially a front of diffidence and composure, suppressing any show of feeling until he has found out what kind of line the others will be ready to support for him. Any claims regarding self may be made with belittling modesty, with strong qualifications, or with a note of unseriousness; by hedging in these ways he will have prepared a self for himself that will not be discredited by exposure, personal failure, or the unanticipated acts of others. And if he does not hedge his claims about self, he will at least attempt to be realistic about them, knowing that otherwise events may discredit him and make him lose face.

Certain protective maneuvers are as common as these defensive ones. The person shows respect and politeness, making sure to extend to others any ceremonial treatment that might be their due. He employs discretion; he leaves unstated facts that might implicitly or explicitly contradict and embarrass the positive claims made by others. He employs circumlocutions and deceptions, phrasing his replies with careful ambiguity so that the others' face is preserved even if their welfare is not. He employs courtesies, making slight modifications of his demands on or appraisals of the others so that they will be able to define the situation as one in which their self-respect is not threatened. In making a belittling demand upon the others, or in imputing uncomplimentary attributes to them, he may employ a joking manner, allowing them to take the line that they are good sports, able to relax from their ordinary standards of pride and honor. And before engaging in a potentially offensive act, he may provide explanations as to why the others ought not to be affronted by it. For example, if he knows that it will be necessary to withdraw from the encounter before it has terminated, he may tell the others in advance that it is necessary for him to leave, so that they will have faces that are prepared for it. But neutralizing the potentially offensive act need not be done verbally; he may wait for a propitious moment or natural break—for example, in conversation, a momentary lull when no one speaker can be affronted—and then leave, in this way using the context instead of his words as a guarantee of inoffensiveness.

When a person fails to prevent an incident, he can still attempt to maintain the fiction that no threat to face has occurred. The most blatant example of this is found where the person acts as if an event that contains a threatening expression has not occurred at all. He may apply this studied nonobservance to his own acts—as when he does not by any outward sign admit that his stomach is rumbling—or to the acts of others, as when he does not "see" that another has stumbled. Social life in mental hospitals owes much to this process; patients employ it in regard to their own peculiarities, and visitors employ it, often with tenuous desperation, in regard to patients. In general, tactful blindness of this kind is applied only to events that, if perceived at all, could be perceived and interpreted only as threats to face.

* * *

Another kind of avoidance occurs when a person loses control of his expressions during an encounter. At such times he may try not so much to overlook the incident as to hide or conceal his activity in some way, thus making it possible for the others to avoid some of the difficulties created by a participant who has not maintained face. Correspondingly, when a person is caught out of face because he had not expected to be thrust into interaction, or because strong feelings have disrupted his expressive mask, the others may protectively turn away from him or his activity for a moment, to give him time to assemble himself.

The Corrective Process. When the participants in an undertaking or encounter fail to prevent the occurrence of an event that is expressively incompatible with the judgments of social worth that are being maintained, and when the event is of the kind that is difficult to overlook, then the participants are likely to give it accredited status as an incident—to ratify it as a threat that deserves direct official attention—and to proceed to try to correct for its effects. At this point one or more participants find themselves in an established state of ritual disequilibrium or disgrace, and an attempt must be made to reestablish a satisfactory ritual state for them. I use the term *ritual* because I am dealing with acts through whose symbolic component the actor shows how worthy he is of respect or how worthy he feels others are of it. The imagery of equilibrium is apt here because the length and intensity of the corrective effort is nicely adapted to the persistence and intensity of the threat. One's face, then, is a sacred thing, and the expressive order required to sustain it is therefore a ritual one.

The sequence of acts set in motion by an acknowledged threat to face, and terminating in the re-establishment of ritual equilibrium, I shall call an *interchange.* Defining a message or move as everything conveyed by an actor during a turn at taking action, one can say that an interchange will involve two or more moves and two or more participants. Obvious examples in our society may be found in the sequence of "Excuse me" and "Certainly," and in the exchange of presents or visits. The interchange seems to be a basic concrete unit of social activity and provides one natural empirical way to study interaction of all kinds. Face-saving practices can be usefully classified according to their position in the natural sequence of moves that comprise this unit. Aside from the event which introduces the need for a corrective interchange, four classic moves seem to be involved.

There is, first, the challenge, by which participants take on the responsibility of calling attention to the misconduct; by implication they suggest that the threatened claims are to stand firm and that the threatening event itself will have to be brought back into line.

The second move consists of the offering, whereby a participant, typically the offender, is given a chance to correct for the offense and reestablish the expressive order. Some classic ways of making this move are available. On the one hand, an attempt can be made to show that what admittedly appeared to be a threatening expression is really a meaningless event, or an unintentional act, or a joke not meant to be taken seriously, or an unavoidable, "understandable" product of extenuating circumstances. On the other hand, the meaning of the event may be granted and effort concentrated on the creator of it. Information may be provided to show that the creator was under the influence of something and not himself, or that he was under the command of somebody else and not acting for himself. When a person claims that an act was meant in jest, he may go on and claim that the self that seemed to lie behind the act was also projected as a joke. When a person suddenly finds that he has demonstrably failed in capacities that the others assumed him to have and to claim for himself—such as the capacity to spell, to perform minor tasks, to talk without malapropisms, and so on—he may quickly add, in a serious or unserious way, that he claims these incapacities as part of his self. The meaning of the threatening incident thus stands, but it can now be incorporated smoothly into the flow of expressive events.

As a supplement to or substitute for the strategy of redefining the offensive act or himself, the offender can follow two other procedures: he can provide compensations to the injured—when it is not his own face that he has threatened; or he can provide punishment, penance, and expiation for himself. These are important moves or phases in the ritual interchange. Even though the offender may fail to prove his innocence, he can suggest through these means that he *is* now a renewed person, a person who has paid for his sin against the expressive order and is once more to be trusted in the judgmental scene. Further, he can show that he does not treat the feelings of the others lightly, and that if their feelings have been injured by him, however innocently he is prepared to pay a price for his action. Thus he assures the others that they can accept his explanations without this acceptance constituting a sign of weakness and a lack of pride on their part. Also, by his treatment of himself, by his self-castigation, he shows that he is clearly aware of the kind of crime he would have committed had the incident been what it first appeared to be, and that he knows the kind of punishment that ought to be accorded to one who would commit such a crime. The suspected person thus shows that he is thoroughly capable of taking the role of the others toward his own activity, that he can still be used as a responsible participant in the ritual process, and that the rules of conduct which he appears to have broken are still sacred, real, and unweakened. An offensive act may arouse anxiety about the ritual code; the offender allays this anxiety by showing that both the code and he as an upholder of it are still in working order.

After the challenge and the offering have been made, the third move can occur: the persons to whom the offering is made can accept it as a satisfactory means of reestablishing the expressive order and the faces supported by this order. Only then can the offender cease the major part of his ritual offering.

In the terminal move of the interchange, the forgiven person conveys a sign of gratitude to those who have given him the indulgence of forgiveness.

The phases of the corrective process—challenge, offering, acceptance, and thanks—provide a model for interpersonal ritual behavior, but a model that may be departed from in significant ways. For example, the offended parties may give the offender a chance to initiate the offering on his own before a challenge is made and before they ratify the offense as an incident. This is a common courtesy, extended on the assumption that the recipient will introduce a self-challenge. Further, when the offended persons accept the corrective offering, the offender may suspect that this has been grudgingly done from tact, and so he may volunteer additional corrective offerings, not allowing the matter to rest until he has received a second or third acceptance of his repeated apology. Or the offended persons may tactfully take over the role of the offender and volunteer excuses for him that will, perforce, be acceptable to the offended persons.

An important departure from the standard corrective cycle occurs when a challenged offender patently refuses to heed the warning and continues with his offending behavior, instead of setting the activity to rights. This move shifts the play back to the challengers. If they countenance the refusal to meet their demands, then it will be plain that their challenge was a bluff and that the bluff has been called. This is an untenable position; a face for themselves cannnot be derived from it, and they are left to bluster. To avoid this fate, some classic moves are open to them. For instance, they can resort to tactless, violent retaliation, destroying either themselves or the person who had refused to heed their warning. Or they can withdraw from the undertaking in a visible huff—righteously indignant, outraged, but confident of ultimate vindication. Both tacks provide a way of denying the offender his status as an interactant, and hence denying the reality of the offensive judgment he has made. Both strategies are ways of salvaging face, but for all concerned the costs are usually high. It is partly to forestall such scenes that an offender is usually quick to offer apologies; he does not want the affronted persons to trap themselves into the obligation to resort to desperate measures.

It is plain that emotions play a part in these cycles of response, as when anguish is expressed because of what one has done to another's face, or anger because of what has been done to one's own. I want to stress that these emotions function as moves, and fit so precisely into the logic of the ritual game that it would seem difficult to understand them without it.[1] In fact, spontaneously expressed feelings are likely to fit into the formal pattern of the ritual interchange more elegantly than consciously designed ones.

---

1. Even when a child demands something and is refused, he is likely to cry and sulk not as an irrational expression of frustration but as a ritual move, conveying that he already has a face to lose and that its loss is not to be permitted lightly. Sympathetic parents may even allow for such display, seeing in these crude strategies the beginnings of a social self.

COOPERATION IN FACE-WORK

When a face has been threatened, face-work must be done, but whether this is initiated and primarily carried through by the person whose face is threatened, or by the offender, or by a mere witness, is often of secondary importance. Lack of effort on the part of one person induces compensative effort from others; a contribution by one person relieves the others of the task. In fact, there are many minor incidents in which the offender and the offended simultaneously attempt to initiate an apology. Resolution of the situation to everyone's apparent satisfaction is the first requirement; correct apportionment of blame is typically a secondary consideration.

Since each participant in an undertaking is concerned, albeit for differing reasons, with saving his own face and the face of the others, then tacit cooperation will naturally arise so that the participants together can attain their shared but differently motivated objectives.

One common type of tacit cooperation in face-saving is the tact exerted in regard to face-work itself. The person not only defends his own face and protects the face of the others, but also acts so as to make it possible and even easy for the others to employ face-work for themselves and him. He helps them to help themselves and him. Social etiquette, for example, warns men against asking for New Year's Eve dates too early in the season, lest the girl find it difficult to provide a gentle excuse for refusing. This second-order tact can be further illustrated by the widespread practice of negative-attribute etiquette. The person who has an unapparent negatively valued attribute often finds it expedient to begin an encounter with an unobtrusive admission of his failing, especially with persons who are uninformed about him. The others are thus warned in advance against making disparaging remarks about his kind of person and are saved from the contradiction of acting in a friendly fashion to a person toward whom they are unwittingly being hostile. This strategy also prevents the others from automatically making assumptions about him which place him in a false position and saves him from painful forbearance or embarrassing remonstrances.

* * *

Another form of tacit cooperation, and one that seems to be much used in many societies, is reciprocal self-denial. Often the person does not have a clear idea of what would be a just or acceptable apportionment of judgments during the occasion, and so he voluntarily deprives or depreciates himself while indulging and complimenting the others, in both cases carrying the judgments safely past what is likely to be just. The favorable judgments about himself he allows to come from the others; the unfavorable judgments of himself are his own contributions. This "after you, Alphonse" technique works, of course, because in depriving himself he can reliably anticipate that the others will compliment or indulge him. Whatever allocation of favors is eventually established, all participants are first given a chance to show that they are not bound or constrained by their own desires and expectations, that they have a properly modest view of themselves, and that they can be counted upon to support the ritual code. Negative bargaining, through which each participant tries to make the terms of trade more favorable to the other side, is another instance; as a form of exchange perhaps it is more widespread than the economist's kind.

A person's performance of face-work, extended by his tacit agreement to help others perform theirs, represents his willingness to abide by the ground rules of social interaction. Here is the hallmark of his socialization as an interactant. If he and the others were not socialized in this way, interaction in most societies and most situations would be a much more hazardous thing for feelings and faces. The person would find it impractical to be oriented to symbolically conveyed appraisals of social worth, or to be possessed of feelings—that is, it would be impractical for him to be a ritually delicate object. And as I shall suggest, if the person were not a ritually delicate object, occasions of talk could not be organized in the way they usually are. It is no wonder that trouble is caused by a person who cannot be relied upon to play the face-saving game.

THE RITUAL ROLES OF THE SELF

So far I have implicitly been using a double definition of self: the self as an image pieced together from the expressive implications of the full flow of events in an undertaking; and the self as a kind of player in a ritual game who copes honorably or dishonorably, diplomatically or undiplomatically, with the judgmental contingencies of the situation. A double mandate is involved. As sacred objects, men are subject to slights and profanation; hence as players of the ritual game they have had to lead themselves into duels, and wait for a round of shots to go wide of the mark before embracing their opponents.

* * *

Further, within limits the person has a right to forgive other participants for affronts to his sacred image. He can forbearantly overlook minor slurs upon his face, and in regard to somewhat greater injuries he is the one person who is in a position to accept apologies on behalf of his sacred self. This is a relatively safe prerogative for the person to have in regard to himself, for it is one that is exercised in the interests of the others or of the undertaking. Interestingly enough, when the person commits a *gaffe* against himself, it is not he who has the license to forgive the event; only the others have that prerogative, and it is a safe prerogative for them to have because they can exercise it only in his interests or in the interests of the undertaking. One finds, then, a system of checks and balances by which each participant tends to be given the right to handle only those matters which he will have little motivation for mishandling.

In short, the rights and obligations of an interactant are designed to prevent him from abusing his role as an object of sacred value.

When a person begins a mediated or immediate encounter, he already stands in some kind of social relationship to the others concerned, and expects to stand in a given relationship to them after the particular encounter ends. This, of course, is one of the ways in which social contacts are geared into the wider society. Much of the activity occurring during an encounter can be understood as an effort on everyone's part to get through the occasion and all the unanticipated and unintentional events that can cast participants in an undesirable light, without disrupting the relationships of the participants. And if relationships are in the process of change, the object will be to bring the encounter to a satisfactory close without altering the expected course of development. This perspective nicely accounts, for example, for the little ceremonies of greeting and farewell which occur when people begin a conversational encounter or depart from one. Greetings provide a way of showing that a relationship is still what it was at the termination of the previous coparticipation and, typically, that this relationship involves sufficient suppression of hostility for the participants temporarily to drop their guards and talk. Farewells sum up the effect of the encounter upon the relationship and show what the participants may expect of one another when they next meet. The enthusiasm of greetings compensates for the weakening of the relationship caused by the absence just terminated, while the enthusiasm of farewells compensates the relationship for the harm that is about to be done to it by separation.

19

The Body and Bathing: Help with Personal Care at Home

JULIA TWIGG

The sociology of the body is a fascinating area of inquiry, whether focused on no-tions of beauty, fitness, health, or infirmity. The body is a significant object of social meaning and personal identity. In this essay, set in England where bathing is more often preferred to showering, the challenges of being an elderly adult in need of as-sistance in the bath is explored with considerable sociological imagination. Young, healthy medical professionals can project a sense of superiority when looking upon the infirm elderly. How can an older person, then, maintain a dignified sense of self in such a situation?

To write about the body is to write about the mundane and the everyday, for that is what the body is: something that is with us always and every-where—both our constant companion and our essence. Nothing could be more mundane or day to day than the processes of body care. These actions punctu-ate our daily lives in the forms of dressing, shaving, showering, combing, wash-ing, eating, drinking, excreting, and sleeping, providing us with a rhythm and pattern to the day. The bodily rhythms provide a basic experiential security in daily life. We are, however, mostly acculturated to ignore these patterns, at least at the level of polite speech. The processes of body care are assumed to be both too private and too trivial for comment, certainly too trivial for traditional academic analysis. They belong with those other aspects of bodily life that we are socialized to pass over in silence. Though such bodily processes form the bedrock of daily life, they are bedrocks assumed, rather than reflected on. So long as they are there, functioning correctly, we have no need to comment.

But for many older people this easeful state of bodily ignorance and tran-scendence is no longer available. Their bodies force themselves into the front of their thoughts, posing a mass of practical problems. The body assumes new prominence by virtue of its inability to do things. Among those things can be the tasks of body care such as washing, showering, and bathing. This chap-ter explores what happens when older people can no longer cope with these aspects of life but need assistance in doing them. In particular, it focuses on the situation of older people living at home receiving help with personal care, typically washing and bathing.

While a discussion of the everyday activities of washing and bathing is, by definition, concerned with micro-processes, these actions are not outside wider discursive concerns. Bathing is located in a wider set of discourses than the simple discussion of hygiene that tends to permeate accounts in the area. In this chapter, I will explore how far the provision of help does indeed draw on these wider discourses and how far it remains located in a narrower set of preoccupations. Help with bathing also entails negotiating the management of the body; it involves touch and nakedness and at times verges on the taboo. I will explore how older people feel about this, and who they prefer to help them in these areas. Before doing so, however, I will discuss briefly the paradoxical neglect of the subject of the body in relation to the support of older people.

THE NEGLECTED BODY OF SOCIAL CARE

Though body care lies at the heart of service provision, this has not been emphasized in accounts of the sector. There are three primary reasons for this: The first derives from a concern within gerontology to resist the dominant discourses of medicine and popular accounts of aging that present it in terms of inevitable bodily decline. The excessive focus on the body is seen as damaging—endorsing ageist stereotypes in which older people are reduced to their aging and sick bodies, which visibly mark them as old. Progressive gerontology by contrast aims to present a more rounded account of age: one that gives due weight to social rather than just bodily elements in the structuring of its experiences. The "political economy" approach, in particular, that has dominated social gerontology in Britain and North America since the 1980s, emphasizes the degree to which old age is the product of social structural factors such as retirement age, pension provision, and ageist assumptions (Phillipson and Walker 1986; Estes and Binney 1989; Arber and Ginn 1991). From this perspective, factors like the differential access to resources or social exclusion primarily determine the social experience of old age not bodily decline. Close, analytic attention to the body from this perspective is thus regarded as a step backwards.

The second reason for the neglect of the body derives from the way in which the field of community care has traditionally been conceptualized within the debate on aging. "Community care" is the term commonly used in Britain and elsewhere for the support of older and disabled people enabling them to live in the community, typically in their own homes, and it is the principal policy objective in most advanced industrial societies.

Community care is not, however, predominantly conceptualized in terms of the body. Partly this is because the dominant professional group in the field is social work, which concentrates on questions of interpersonal and social functioning and whose remit tends to stop short of the body. This territory is traditionally handed over to the care of medicine. As a result, though community care is inherently about the body and its day-to-day problems, this fact is not emphasized in accounts of the sector. The evasion is further compounded by the increasing influence of managerialism in the sector. Managerial discourse, constructed as it is out of the disciplines of economics, business studies, organization, and methods, embodies an abstract and distancing form of theorizing that is far from the messy, dirty realities of bodily life. When community care is discussed, it is done so in a manner that largely dismisses the body, rendering it invisible as a site of concern.

The third reason for neglect comes from work on the body itself. Since the 1980s there has been an explosion of writing in this area (Williams and Bendelow 1998), but its focus has been on younger, sexier, more transgressive bodies. The roots of much of this literature in feminism, queer theory, and cultural studies have not encouraged it to venture into the territory of old age. Indeed, these approaches have displayed a significant degree of ageism in their assumptions about what is interesting and important. More recently, however, new work has begun to address bodily issues in relation to later years (Öberg 1996; Tulle-Winton 2000; Gilleard and Higgs 2000). Some of the best of this work has—belatedly—come out of feminism (Woodward 1991, 1999; Andrews 1999; Furman 1997, 1999). It has been marked by a sense of agency and a desire to emphasize the subjective, meaning-making experiences of people as they engage in the aging process. Often these ideas are linked to concepts of the Third Age.

The Third Age represents a postretirement period of extended middle age in which people who are no longer confined by the labor market and are free from direct responsibility for children can pursue leisure interests, develop aspects of their personalities, and enjoy the fruits of later life. The emergence of this new social space is often linked to theories about identity and selfhood in postmodernity, particularly ones that emphasize self-fashioning. It is open, however, to the familiar critique that such optimistic accounts of the Third Age are only possible by virtue of projecting the negative aspects of aging into a dark Fourth Age, a period of declining health and social loss, sometimes also termed "deep" old age. As Gilliard and Higgs (2000) note, accounts of the Third Age emphasize agency and subjectivity and are described from the perspective of the optimistic self. But accounts of the Fourth Age focus on dependency and are written from the outside. A macro-level perspective dominates this literature. In such accounts, older persons are rarely seen as agents at all but are often presented as the "other."

Physical decline is frequently presented as marking the point of transition between the Third and Fourth Ages, and receiving personal care of a close and intimate kind is a key marker in this transition. In this chapter we focus on just such a personal care situation. In doing so I am thus attempting to extend the analysis in terms of the body to a group who until recently has been excluded from such a perspective. The literature on the body and aging that has emerged of late has tended to focus on the earlier optimistic stage of the Third Age, exploring the ways in which people negotiate issues of bodily aging as they make the transitions from middle to later life. * * *

PERSONAL CARE AS A SOCIAL MARKER

Why is personal care such a marker of social states? The reason lies in the profound social symbolism that relates to the body and its management. This means that receiving help in these areas erodes the personhood and adult status of the subject. Personal care means being helped with precisely those tasks that as adults we do for ourselves: getting washed and dressed, moving, eating, and excreting. However rich we are, these are things that—at least in the modern West—we do for ourselves, typically alone or in the company of intimates. Body care of this type thus marks the boundary of the truly personal and individual in modern life. Having to be helped in these areas transgresses this boundary and undermines adulthood. Only babies and children are helped in this way, and this underwrites the profoundly infantilizing tendencies of "care."

* * *

Personal care also involves nakedness. Nakedness is not, largely, part of ordinary social interaction. It is a special state reserved for certain situations and relationships, and it is a marker of close, typically sexual, intimacy. To be naked in a social situation, as recipients of personal care are, is therefore to be put in a disjunctive context. It is made all the more so by the fact that the nakedness is asymmetrical: the recipient is naked, while the helper is fully clothed. To be naked in this way is to be exposed and vulnerable, and it inevitably creates a power dynamic in which the helper, usually younger and stronger, is clearly the dominant party.

Personal Care and Bathing

Personal care has become an increasingly significant issue for social care agencies across the Western world as a result of widespread social and political policies aimed at supporting frail elders living at home. Home care in Britain and elsewhere is no longer primarily a matter of housework and shopping, but of personal care, in which washing and bathing form an important aspect. Historically, in Britain such help was primarily provided by the community nursing service but is now largely provided within a home care system. This same shift in home care can be detected in other Western welfare systems.

The principal driver behind it has been cost reduction, with the desire to move the provision of home care away from the relatively expensive health care sector where staff are trained and where the provision of personal care is often free to the recipient, into the less expensive social care sector where staff are typically untrained and where recipients are often required to fund their care. The shift has, however, also arisen from concerns about the over-medicalization of older people's lives. Home care services are seen as embodying a potentially more sympathetic and caring approach than that of medically directed ones.

This chapter draws on a study of help with washing and bathing provided to older and disabled people living at home in Britain (Twigg 2000a). The study was based on interviews with recipients, caregivers, and managers. In the research, elders received help with bathing from a variety of sources: the local authority home care service; voluntary sector or for profit agencies; or a specialist voluntary sector bathing service (the last is unusual in Britain). Depending on their income, users either received such help free or were expected to meet some or all of the costs.

The Meanings of Bathing

Within public welfare services, washing and bathing tend to be presented narrowly in terms of a discourse of hygiene and cleanliness. The broader meanings of bathing in terms of luxury, pleasure, and well-being are not emphasized. There are a number of reasons for this: Partly it arises from a narrow concern with health and physical functioning, which is regarded as a particularly legitimate aim for such interventions. Bathing in this context is presented as a concern for hygiene; though in reality, dirtiness has to be extreme before health is genuinely threatened. Partly it comes from long-established political pressures to ensure that the remit of public welfare remains limited in scope and extent; and this is linked to a related puritanism that regards ideas of bodily pleasure in connection with public provision as—at the very least—discordant. * * *

But bathing has much broader meanings. While there is certainly not space here to explore the history of washing and bathing and of the various practices and discourses that have led to its construction (see Twigg 2000a for such a discussion), I will, however, refer briefly here to four recurring strands in that history to suggest some of the ways in which bathing is located in a wider set of discourses than just those of hygiene.

Historically, bathing has long been connected with luxury, pleasure, and to some degree, eroticism. For the Romans, bathing was a social activity associated with relaxation, exercise, conviviality, and pleasure (Yegül 1992). During the Middle Ages it was recurringly presented in connection with images of feasting and courtship (Vigarello 1988). These meanings narrowed by the nineteenth century, when bathing lost its social dimension and became a more private affair, more closely connected with the tasks of getting clean, though the sense of luxury and pleasure that derived from abundant hot water remains (Wilkie 1986; Bushman and Bushman 1988). During the twentieth century, luxurious bathrooms, whether presented in the celebratory imagery of Hollywood or the dreams of real estate promoters, continued to draw on this discourse of pleasure and luxury and only barely suppressed eroticism (Kira 1967).

Bathing is also located in a wider discourse of well-being. Again, this has been so since Roman times, when baths were seen as part of a general regimen of health and well-being. Baths have also been prominent in the alternative medical tradition from hydrotherapy to nature cure, and they remain a central element in the recent revival of spa culture, often in association with diffuse concepts of "Eastern" medicine, which has become a feature of modern Western lifestyles or at least aspirations. Spa treatments are presented as an antidote to stress and other ills of modern living. Through all of this, well-being is the key concept; and the focus is on the experiential body, not the medical body.

The third theme concerns the frequent use of baths and water as markers of social transitions. This is clearest in relation to classic rites of passage, such as Christian baptism, but it also operates in secular contexts like prisons, schools, and hospitals, where people are commonly compelled to have a bath as part of the initiation into the institution, marking their transition from the status of a citizen outside to that of an inmate inside. Individuals also draw on such symbolism in their daily lives, clearly marking out the transitions of the day or week through bodily practices such as bathing and showering. The bedrock of body care punctuates the day, providing a framework of time and of social states in terms of eating and drinking, washing and dressing, and sleeping and rising. No small part of our sense of ontological security is derived from these practices.

Last, bathing also contains darker themes. Baths have been widely used as part of coercive cultures, particularly within institutions. For example, cold plunges, sudden showers, and shockingly cold water have all been used as part of the history of the treatment of the insane. Though the justification for such techniques has often been in terms of shocking the patient back into reason, a clearly coercive, even sadistic, element is also often intensified by the use of machinery or the enforcement of humiliating bodily postures. * * *

THE ADAPTABILITY OF THE OLD

Before exploring what people feel about receiving help, it is worth reflecting briefly on the adaptability of the old. Accounts of older people often present them as inflexible and unable to cope with change. In fact, the changes imposed on people in their later lives are enormous. No amount of jet travel, adaptation to new information technology systems, or learning to appreciate new music can remotely compare with the changes that older people have to learn to become accustomed to on a day-to-day basis. The aged may lose their lifetime companion; may have to move to a new home, town, or region; and may have to learn to live in an institution among random strangers in a collective way that is wholly at odds with their earlier lives and under the auspices of a staff whose background and worldview may be completely alien to them.

In all of this, bodily experiences can be among the most significant: not being able to move freely, to speak clearly, or to manage your bodily functions present major changes in life. Having to receive help with personal care, in particular, breaches some of the most profound of social expectations, requiring people to cope with new situations and new relationships. As we shall see, some of the respondents expressed dismay at what they had to face, but it is testimony to their adaptability that they did indeed manage to cope. The majority approached old age with stoicism, concentrating on the day and trying to make the best of it. Some developed ingenious and innovative ways to circumvent their physical difficulties.

WHAT DOES BATHING MEAN IN THIS CONTEXT?

Within the British tradition, the predominant ways of getting clean have been baths, in the sense of bathtubs, and washing at a basin. This is in contrast to Continental and American traditions where showering established itself much earlier as the main alternative to strip washing at a basin. Showering is now common among younger people in Britain, but is still largely unfamiliar or disliked among this older age group. Few people in the study had showers in their homes. In the context of drafty houses and feeble flows of hot water, showers do not warm the body in the way that hot baths do. One or two respondents of Continental origin did prefer showers, sharing the mainland European view that baths are not an adequate way to clean oneself.

People varied in how important baths were to them. Some respondents had never been great bathers and relied instead on a strip wash. For others, a daily bath was a long-established habit and one that they greatly missed. As Mrs. Fitzgerald (all respondents' names have been changed) explained, she loved bathing and continues to see it as a vital part of the day: "All my life, up in a morning, throw open the bed, into the bathroom—that's the way I lived. . . . It's always been terribly important to me. And that's when I got panic-stricken when I thought I wasn't going to be able to have any baths."

The care people actually received from the bathing service was not always in line with their hopes. Some individuals did indeed have a "proper bath," in the sense of being placed directly under the water, with all the warmth and buoyancy that this could bring. But for many, "bathing" really meant sitting on a board over the bath while the caregiver helped them to wash and poured warm water over their bodies. This was enjoyable, but it was not a proper bath, and many regretted this. Mrs. Kennelly, whose severe Parkinson's meant that she could no longer have a bath, remembered the experience with a sense of nostalgia, "I'd love to be able to get in the bath. Just lay there and splash it over . . . wallow in it. Lovely." Mrs. Bridgeman tells of how wonderful it would be to just once receive a proper bath, "I *long* to get my bum in the water. It would be bliss you know."

The problem was that many recipients did not have sufficient flexibility to get down into the tub or the strength to get up, and very few homes had the kind of expensive equipment that would allow for this. Workers were forbidden by Health and Safety legislation from lifting the clients out of the bath (though sometimes they still performed the task). This meant that many had more in the way of an assisted wash than a bath. By and large, recipients were resigned to these limitations and grateful for what assistance they received, but problems did occasionally arise, particularly if clients rebelled and attempted to preempt the situation by sitting down fully in the bath. In these cases, the caregivers were instructed to tell the person that they would not help them up, but would instead ring for an ambulance. The potential humiliation of this was sufficient to keep most clients in line.

The Experience of Bathing

For some individuals, bathing did remain a pleasurable, even luxurious, experience. Mrs. Fitzgerald, who had most feared the loss, now saw the coming of the bathing service as "the rose of [her] week." Mrs. Napier also relished the experience as something that brings back pleasurable memories of the past, explaining how "we have nice foamy shower gel. . . . It's lovely, like being a baby again." Baths were also a source of pleasure because of the number of aches and pains that many older people suffer from. The warmth and buoyancy of the water restored lightness to limbs that had become heavy, giving back something of the easy, youthful, bodily experience of the past.

Baths also retained their capacity to wash away more than just dirt. For some, they had always been both a source of renewal and a marker of social transitions. As Miss Garfield explained, baths are "part of, sort of washing the day away and all the bothers and troubles, and you're there and it's all very comfortable and nice." But the experience of bathing was inevitably strongly affected by the presence of the caregiver in the room. For most people, bathing is a private affair, a time apart, when individuals can attend to themselves and not worry about others. But the presence of the worker changes that to some degree, disturbing the ease. Their presence in the room inevitably refocuses the event on tasks to be accomplished, rather than a state to be experienced; recipients were no longer free to control the timing of the event as they had been in the past. Workers needed to get the job done, and this sometimes meant that time was now of the essence, not pleasure. This acted to limit the nature of the experience, removing luxury, and centering it instead on cleaning of the client.

Having a worker in the room also removed much of the spontaneity of bathing; it was no longer possible to draw a bath when you simply felt like it. With this also went much of the capacity of baths to act as personal rites of passage or markers of social transitions. Body care still marked out the rhythm of people's days, in the sense of dressing, washing, and eating, but baths now had to be taken at the times they were scheduled; this could mean otherwise "meaningless" times, such as eleven-thirty in the morning, that disrupted rather than underwrote social patterns. For some people this was less disruptive than expected. This was because those who received such bathing assistance were often among the most frail and dependent, people who rarely if ever left the house. For them, the world of conventional timings had become less significant. To quite an extent, they had reordered the pattern of their lives *around* the provision of care. Care-giving had come to operate as a social structure in itself.

The Gaze of Youth

Much of the recent work in gerontology has emphasized the ways in which we are aged by culture—by the meanings that are ascribed to bodily aging, rather than the aging process itself. Gullette (1997) has described the subtle and omnipresent means by which such meanings are conveyed. We inhale this atmosphere daily, imbuing doses of its toxicity wafting from cartoons, billboards, birthday cards, coffee mugs, newspaper articles, fiction, and poetry: "The system is busy at what ever level of literacy or orality or visual impressionability the acculturated subject is comfortable with." Consumer culture, with its emphasis on youth, is particularly saturated with such messages (Featherstone 1991; Gilleard and Higgs 2000).

The dominant theme in all of this work is that old age is constructed as a negative entity and the bodily process of aging is seen in the same light. Aging represents a form of Otherness, on to which culture projects its fear and denial. As Woodward (1991) argues, our cultural categories here are essentially reducible to two, youth and age, set in a hierarchical arrangement. We are not judged by how old we are, but by how young we are not. Aging is a falling away, a failure to be young. Like disabled people, the old are evaluated as "less than." The bodily realities of aging thus create a version of Erving Goffman's spoilt identity, something that people are, at some level, ashamed of and marked in terms of.

We are accustomed to the idea of the medical gaze in the context of professional power, or the phallic gaze in the context of gender relations, but there is also a gaze of youth. It, too, is an exercise of power in which the "other"—in this case older people—are constituted under its searching eye. Nowhere is the gaze of youth more evident than in relation to bathing care. Here the bodies of older people are directly subject to the gaze of younger workers. From the workers' perspective, this sometimes presents them with a shock. Modern culture, though saturated with visual images of young perfect bodies, rarely permits old imperfect ones to be on display. As a result, the way in which the body looks in old age was something that the younger workers were unprepared for. As one worker explained, seeing old people naked was "weird, and I just had to stop myself staring at people, because I hadn't really seen . . . because you don't really see people naked."

At times this element of gaze was itself part of the professional task. Nurses who do bathing work often comment how the activity is useful in assessing the general state of the older person, in terms not only of illness and physical condition but also in a more extensive way. To be bathed is indeed to be made subject to—very directly subject to—the professional gaze. It is indeed a kind of developed, intimate surveillance.

So how did older people feel about this? It was certainly the case that many respondents appeared to have internalized the wider cultural denigration of the bodies of the old. They constituted their own bodies under the gaze of youth, presenting them as something that it might be unattractive, even distasteful, for people to see or handle. As Mrs. Fitzgerald once remarked of the caregiver, "They're so young and beautiful, it must be awful for them to have to handle old, awkward bodies." At the same time, she added that "they're wonderful people. . . . I must say, I mean they must have something inside them because—it's not the sort of thing—I don't know when I was young whether I would have wanted to have looked after old people." For some, the contrast between their aging bodies and the youthful flesh of the workers was painful to see and experience:

> Mrs. Kennelly: I say to them, "I feel sorry for you, getting up in the morning and this is the kind of job you've got to do." You know, not very nice. . . . This young girl, Amanda it was, came in—twenty-eight, beautiful girl. She's very pretty. And there's the ugly lump. Oh dear!

To be caught within the youthful gaze was disturbing, and many of the elders had turned its corrosive force back on themselves, in turn disciplining their own bodies in the course of assisted practice.

* * *

Parts of the Body

The body is a landscape onto which meanings are inscribed. These are not, however, evenly distributed over the body, and certain parts come to be more heavily freighted with significance than other bodily parts. In general, there is a familiar privacy gradient whereby certain parts of the body are deemed more personal and private. Access to them by sight or touch is socially circumscribed and varies according to relationship and situation. * * * Areas of the body such as the upper arms and back are relatively neutral and can be touched by a range of people. Knees and thighs are less so. Breasts and genitals are in general off-limits in all but erotic relations. Touch is also a vector of status and authority with the powerful accorded more leeway to touch than the less powerful. There is a gender dimension, with women more likely to receive touch than men. Within a service provision context, women are more likely to interpret touch from a service provider in a positive way, while men are more inclined to see it negatively, interpreting it as a marker of inferiority and dependency. In addition, men are also more likely to see touch as sexual.

These sensitivities affect the experience of bathing. Receiving hands-on help with soaping, rinsing, and washing is more tolerable in relation to some parts of the body than to others. Arms, legs, feet, and hair are all fine. Matters become more sensitive, however, in relation to what is often termed "down below": the genital and anal areas. In practice nearly everyone in the study could manage to wash these parts themselves, at least with some indirect assistance, and a number of respondents expressed relief that they were able to do so. Having to be washed in these areas was seen as humiliating and embarrassing, yet another twist in the spiral of dependency. Maintaining one's independence in relation to these intimate areas was an important part of self-esteem. Caregivers were also reluctant to involve themselves with these parts of the body, which they, too, regarded with a certain amount of ambivalence. In general, bathing was practically managed in such a way as to limit direct contact in relation to more sensitive bodily parts.

* * *

There was one part of the body that was recurringly mentioned in the interviews by both recipients and workers: this was the back. In the context of bathing and the ambivalent intimacies it creates, the back has a special meaning, coming to stand for the body in general, or at least for an acceptable version of the body, one that has a certain neutrality about it. In the interviews, the back was the only part of the body that was spontaneously named by recipients, and they sometimes talked about the process of bathing as if it were confined to the process of washing the back. The back was also the one part of the body where pleasure in touch was openly acknowledged.

A number of recipients described how much they enjoyed having their backs scrubbed. Expressing pleasure in this form of touching was acceptable. Caregivers agreed with this account. One in particular commented that "they do enjoy it, that you know, a lot of people really, 'Oooh,' you know, 'give my back a good rub.'" In general, expressing pleasure in touch was something that recipients were reluctant to do. It seemed to suggest in their eyes something that was not quite right, an ambivalent element that did not belong in this context of relative strangers and of public provision. Presenting bathing in terms of scrubbing the back was one means of deflecting an otherwise disturbing intimacy onto a relatively neutral and public part of the body.

The back is also significant in the bath encounter in that it is the part of the body that is both offered to the gaze of the worker and also used to shelter more private and sensitive parts. It stands in for the public presentation of the body in the context of an otherwise discordant intimacy. The back also offers a safe setting for the expression of affection and closeness. Putting an arm across the back while giving the recipient a hug fits in easily with the way bathing disposes the body, while at the same time providing a relatively neutral form of physical contact. Touch could thus be used to express closeness, but in a manner that does not transgress social codes.

Bounded Relationships and Access to the Body
Bathing makes for a strange relationship: in one sense intimate and close, involving physical contact, nakedness, and access to the private dimensions of

life; yet in another, it is a meeting of strangers in which the worker is paid to do a job and may never have met the recipient before. The intimacy, moreover, occurs in a context that is forced. It arises from disability, not choice. The closeness is imposed, not sought. As a result there is an inherent discordance in the relationship. It is transgressive of normal social codes, and effort is needed on both sides to define the character of the relationship and to put limits on the nature of its intimacy.

How the relationship was experienced was clearly affected by who the helper was. What were people's preferences in this regard? Did they, for example, prefer to be helped by close relatives? An assumption of this sort is often made, resting on the idea that kinship closeness renders the negotiation of bodily closeness easier. While this can certainly sometimes be so, often it is not. We have evidence from other studies (Parker 1993; Daatland 1990) that suggests that while people may like to receive more neutral forms of help from relatives, personal care is different. In these cases many people prefer the formal service system. The reason is that bodily care threatens the nature of a relationship. In particular it erodes the status of the recipient and with that their identity in the relationship.

What older people fear is that the person that they once were—and in their own eyes still are—will be lost, and that person, by and large, is someone with their clothes on, managing their own bodily functions and relating to their families in a sociable way. We should not thus make any easy assumptions about kinship closeness translating unproblematically into bodily closeness.

Even less do people want friends to perform this activity. It is in the nature of friendship that it rests on equality and reciprocity, and few friendships survive marked change in circumstances when these occur on only one side of a valued relationship. Intimate care represents just such a change. Lawler (1991) notes how nurses experience similar unease if cared for by a friend and colleague. Though recipients wanted the care worker to be "friendly," they were quite clear that this was a different and defined sort of relationship. These were not friends in the full sense of the word. As Mrs. Ostrovski said to me, "Friend is a very big word."

Bath work involves a kind of intimacy, though it is of a different nature from that of kinship or friendship. What recipients want is a bounded intimacy, something that is close, but in a specialized and limited way. For these reasons they preferred someone whom they had got to know in these particular circumstances and where the relationship was defined by them. This is not to say that that it was not close, friendly, or based on a kind of trust. In most cases it was all of these, but the relationship was of a special kind, in which bodily closeness played a part but was defined and limited.

At the same time, recipients disliked the experience of having to deal with strangers. Bathing involves both a literal and a psychic unwrapping of the self. Having to participate in this process repeatedly with strangers was exposing and dispiriting. Recipients wanted the ease that comes with familiarity; they did not want constantly to have to readjust to a new person. But agencies could not always be relied on to send the same person, and indeed the constant staff turnover that is characteristic of low-wage sectors in cities like London meant that it was quite difficult for them to do so. Some recipients subverted the problem by refusing to have a bath if an unfamiliar worker was sent, diverting them into other household tasks rather than facing the unwelcome process of self-disclosure. What recipients wanted, therefore, was someone they knew, who was friendly and sensitive and who would offer emotional support, but who understood the limits of the relationship.

* * *

The recipients also made assumptions about gender. This invariably focuses on who was appropriate to do the care work. Responses varied according to whether the person was a man or woman. In general, women-to-women care was regarded as "natural" and unproblematic. Issues arose, however, in relation to cross-gender tending and, to some extent, in relation to same-sex male tending.

What underpinned this asymmetrical pattern were wider assumptions about the meaning and management of the body. Within Western culture, men's and women's bodies have traditionally been treated differently. Women's bodies tend to be regarded with greater circumspection. Access to them, both physical and visual, is more guarded. They are seen as more private, something that is secluded and hidden. Women's bodies are also often presented as more sexual, indeed often coming to represent the principle of sexuality more widely within culture. Women's bodies are also subject to greater control. There is more constraint over what they may do and express. Men's bodies are, by contrast, presented as more public and neutral in character. They tend to embody active principles rather than the passive ones circumscribed on the female body. They desire, rather than are constituted by the desire of others.

These cultural patterns underwrite responses to bathing help. In general women preferred not to have a male worker, and some expressed their feelings very strongly in this regard, "Oh, no. I wouldn't have a man. No thank you!" This was not universal, and some said that they would not mind. But in practice this situation only rarely arose. The majority of workers are female, as are the clients, and this "naturally" delivers a pattern in accord with dominant values. Most agencies also have a policy against men giving personal care to women in their own homes, partly out of respect for client's assumed preferences and partly to avoid accusations of abuse. Running through attitudes toward male care workers was a set of assumptions about the nature of male sexuality as something that is active and potentially predatory. This is in contrast to the assumptions that are made about women. They are presented as passive or asexual in this context, dominated by the values of maternity, not sexuality.

For men, the experience of receiving cross-gender tending was, by its very nature, different. Men are accustomed to being helped by women from childhood onwards, and many saw such assistance in old age as a natural extension of that. Such care contained no sense of threat. Indeed, for many men the idea of being helped by a woman was pleasant. As one manager remarked: "A lot of the men quite enjoy having a woman. And honestly I think, you know, specially a nice young girl come to help them have a bath, they like it. You know, not in any sort of perverted way, just, just in a you know, they like the attention."

As Mr. Lambert said, provided the women were married—that is where women were accustomed to seeing men naked—there was no difficulty in cross-gender tending. Mr. Wagstaff concurred with this sentiment:

Interviewer: Did you find it embarrassing at first or . . . ?

Mr. Wagstaffe: Well not really. I thought it might be more embarrassing for *them* than for me, but they don't seem to mind a bit.

Interviewer: Why did you think it would be more embarrassing for them?

Mr. Wagstaffe: Well, the first girl I had she was only about eighteen I think. She was a sort of punk, she'd got bright red hair and earrings in her eyebrows. Sort of girl that a person of my age looks at and thinks Gawd Almighty. But she was absolutely sweet, she was a lovely girl. It turns out that they nearly all live with their boyfriends or something, so I don't bother about it now. . . . And young ladies in their early twenties these days are rather different from when I was the same age.

For men, therefore, cross-gender tending contains no sense of threat. The issue is one of managing the encounter in such a way as to avoid embarrassment, in which they had some remaining sense of responsibility for not disturbing the innocence of the young. Even in old age, men experience a residual sense of the power of the phallus.

For men being cared for by men, the assumptions were slightly different. In many cases this occurred without comment or problems. But for some men the idea was unwelcome. Men construct other men as sexually predatory in relation to themselves (Connell 1995). Intimate care by a man raises the possibility of a homosexual encounter, a concern reinforced by ideas that caregiver was not proper work for a man at all.

* * *

CONCLUSION

Throughout this chapter, I have argued that bathing and washing exemplify day-to-day and mundane activities of the old. As a result they have received little in the way of academic attention, often considered too practical and too banal to be of interest. But it is in these ordinary and banal patterns that much of the texture and meaning of life exists. The life of the body is the bedrock on which our existence rests. Tending, caring for, managing our bodies, and using and presenting them in a social life are central to our day-to-day experience, though it is not often brought to the front of our consciousness. Until, that is, some disruption in these taken-for-granted activities forces them and the existential life of the body into conscious consideration. Old age is one such source of disruption. Though we are indeed aged by culture as some theorists suggest, we are also aged by our bodies. The body can impose its own constraints, as we have seen concerning the practical difficulties some people experience in relation to personal care. The ways in which personal care is managed, the meanings it contains, and the discourses that encode it significantly affect how these bodily constraints are experienced.

Among the discourses within which personal care is encoded are those relating to bathing. As we have seen, the official account of service provision presents the activity in a narrow, utilitarian way—as the achievement of adequate standards of hygiene. The discourse of social welfare is a constrained one in which the scope of interventions are limited and in which health and hygiene have a privileged status. But as we have seen, baths and bathing are about more than this. They touch on other matters; their meanings are wider and more diffuse, and the experiences they offer more various. Bathing is part of the experiential life of the body and as such is drawn into a variety of discourses and sets of meanings around pleasure, luxury, eroticism, renewal, initiation, and power. Echoes of these wider meanings reverberate through the experience of bathing in the community. Hearing them enables us to set community care in a broader social and cultural context and thus to rescue it from too narrow a policy context. It also allows us to hear something of the voices of some of the most disabled older people, people whose bodily experiences have received little analytic attention in our overarching focus on the body.

REFERENCES

Andrews, M. 1999. The Seductiveness of Agelessness. *Ageing and Society* 19: 301–18.
Bushman, R. L., and C. L. Bushman. 1988. The Early History of Cleanliness in America. *Journal of American History* 74: 1213–38.
Connell, R. W. 1995. *Masculinities.* Cambridge, U.K.: Polity.
Daatland, S. 1990. What are Families For: On Family Solidarity and Preference for Help. *Ageing and Society* 10: 1–15.
Featherstone, M. 1991. The Body in Consumer Culture. In *The Body: Social Process and Cultural Theory.* Edited by M. Featherstone, M. Hepworth, and B. S. Turner, 170–96. London: Sage.
Furman, F. K. 1997. *Facing the Mirror: Older Women and Beauty Shop Culture.* New York: Routledge.
———. 1999. There Are No Old Venuses: Older Women's Responses to Their Aging Bodies. In *Mother Time: Women, Aging and Ethics.* Edited by M. U. Walker, 7–22. Boulder, Colo.: Rowman & Littlefield.

Gilleard, C., and P. Higgs. 2000. *Culture of Ageing: Self, Citizen and the Body*. London: Prentice Hall.

Gullette, M. M. 1997. *Declining to Decline: Cultural Combat and the Politics of Midlife*. Charlottesville: University Press of Virginia.

Kira, A. 1967. *The Bathroom: Criteria for Design*. New York: Bantam.

Lawler, J. (ed.) 1997. Knowing the Body and Embodiment: Methodologies, Discourses and Nursing. In *The Body in Nursing*. Melbourne, Australia: Churchill Livingstone.

Öberg, P. 1996. The Absent Body: A Social Gerontological Paradox. *Ageing and Society* 16: 701–19.

Parker, G. 1993. *With This Body: Caring and Disability in Marriage*. Buckingham, U.K.: Open University Press.

Phillipson, C., and A. Walker. 1986. *Ageing and Social Policy: A Critical Assessment*. Aldershot, U.K.: Gower.

Tulle-Winton, E. 2000. Old Bodies. In *The Body, Culture and Society*. Edited by P. Hancock, B. Hughes, E. Jagger, K. Patterson, R. Russell, E. Tulle-Winton, and M. Tyler. Buckingham, U.K.: Open University Press.

Twigg, J. 2000a. *Bathing: The Body and Community Care*. London: Routledge.

———. 2000b. Carework as a Form of Bodywork. *Ageing and Society* 20: 389–411.

Vigarello, G. 1988. *Concepts of Cleanliness: Changing Attitudes in France Since the Middle Ages*. Cambridge, U.K.: CUP.

Williams, S. J., and G. Bendelow. 1998. *The Lived Body: Sociological Themes, Embodied Issues*. London: Routledge.

Wilkie, J. S. 1986. Submerged Sensuality: Technology and Perceptions of Bathing. *Journal of Social History* 19: 649–54.

Woodward, K. 1991. *Aging and Its Discontents: Freud and Other Fictions*. Bloomington: Indiana University Press.

Woodward, K. (ed.) 1999. *Figuring Age: Women, Bodies, Generations*. Bloomington: Indiana University Press.

Yegül, F. 1992. *Baths and Bathing in Classical Antiquity*. Cambridge: MIT Press.

20

Women without Class: *Chicas, Cholas,* Trash, and the Presence/Absence of Class Identity

JULIE BETTIE

This essay predates the author's award-winning book by the same title. It tells the complex story of high school females finding and presenting (performing) identities that express different versions of femininity. The author's participant observation study seeks to make these young women, and their gender, more visible objects of study, with a steady eye on social class as being critical to who they are and wish to become. Add to this the dimension of ethnicity, and you have a quintessential analysis of the major dimensions of social inequality as they play out in contemporary youth culture.

A cover story in the San Francisco *Examiner Magazine* (Wagner 1996) on the topic of "wiggas" (which, the article explains, is shorthand for "white niggas") reads, "suburban kidz hip-hop across the color line." The story is about white youth who appropriate hip-hop culture and perform "black" identity. The cover picture is a collage of magazine cutouts showing white kids with blue eyes and blond hair (functioning as a code for racial purity) wearing hip-hop fashion and standing in front of a white picket fence behind which sits a charming two-story house and an apple tree. Although there is a girl pictured on the front cover, girls are absent from the story itself.

In a 1993 episode of the TV talk show *Oprah* on the same topic, several groups of boys, white and black, sat on the stage. The audience was confounded by the white boys in hip-hop style who "grew up in 'the 'hood'" and by the young black man who, as one guest explained, "looks like he walked out of Eddie Bauer," as participants debated what it meant to dress black or dress white. During the course of the hour-long program all parties failed to note that, race and ethnicity aside, these were different versions of *masculinity* and that girls were missing again from this story about "youth." The "urban romanticism" and "masculinist overtones" (McRobbie 1991, 20) of subculture studies, where the supposedly gender-neutral term *youth* actually stands for male, are equally often present in popular culture and news media portrayals of youth. In order to envision themselves as class or racial/ethnic subjects in either site, girls must read themselves as boys.

But beyond the invisibility of gender, there is also a failure to "think class" with much clarity. On the *Oprah* show, as with the magazine cover, the same sets of binaries surface repeatedly: white is middle class is suburban; black is lower class is urban. But a slippage occurs where the class references are dropped out and white stands in for middle, where black stands in for lower, or where suburban stands in for white and urban for black. Class and race signifiers are melded together in such a way that "authentic" black, and sometimes brown, identity is imagined as lower class, urban, and often violent and male as well. These are the overly simplified identity categories offered, but they do not reflect the complexity of life. Middle-class youth of color are missing, for example, as are multiracial/multiethnic identity and small-town or rural poverty. The racial/ethnic and class subject positions offered by the "identity formation material" (McRobbie 1994, 192) of popular culture often do not allow for more nuanced social locations.

The observations I make in this article are based on my ethnographic study of working-class white and Mexican-American girls in their senior year of high school in a small town in California's central valley.

* * *

These were girls who knew from experience in their own families of origin that male wages cannot support families alone and that men cannot be counted on to meet their ideals of intimacy and egalitarianism in relationships. These were girls who saw that the men in their working-class community were often unemployed or underemployed and too often dealt with this hardship by abandoning their obligation and responsibilities to the women in their lives and to the children they helped create. These girls were not holding out for princes.

My title, "Women Without Class," has multiple meanings. Most simply, it reflects my interest in young women from families of modest means and low educational attainment who therefore have little "cultural capital" (Bourdieu 1984) to enable class mobility. The other meanings of the title speak to the theory debates I engage and to which I already have alluded: a second meaning refers to the fact that class analysis and social theory have, until recently perhaps, remained insufficiently transformed by feminist theory, unable to conceptualize women as class subjects. Ignoring women's experience of class results in a profound androcentric bias such that women are routinely invisible as class subjects. In much leftist analysis women are assumed to be without class, as these theorists often seem unable to see the category "working class" unless it is marked white and male. Such biases promote the invisibility of both white women and women of color as class subjects.

Ironically, some versions of feminism have been complicit in constructing women as without either class or racial/ethnic subjectivity. On a third level, then, my title considers debates *within* feminist theory and refers to feminist accounts that, while working as correctives to androcentric biases and class reduction, tend toward gender reductionism, focusing primarily on the differences between boys and girls or women and men and failing to account for gender differences *within* sex categories. Historically such studies have focused on white middle-class girls or women but have failed to define them as such. Thus, they too were perceived and presented not as class or racial/ethnic subjects but only as gendered.

It was with these theory debates and empirical gaps in mind that I set off to explore if and how young women understand class difference. I intended to foreground, while not privileging, class as I examined how gender, color, and ethnicity intersect with and shape class as a lived culture and a subjective identity. The context of the lives of these young women includes a deindustrializing economy, the growth of service-sector occupations held largely by women and men of color and by white women, the related family revolutions of the twentieth century, the elimination of affirmative action, a rise in anti-immigrant sentiment, and changing cultural representations and iconographies of class, race, and gender meanings. These are social forces that render the term *working class* anachronistic even as many of these girls move toward low-wage, low-prestige jobs in their community.

NOTES TOWARD CLASS AS "PERFORMANCE" AND "PERFORMATIVE"

My study was done in a small town of approximately forty thousand people. The high school reflects the town demographically, being about 60 percent white and 40 percent Mexican-American, with other people of color composing less than 2 percent each of the population. Located in California's central valley, the town was built on agriculture and the industries that support it. Approximately 16 percent of the Mexican-American students were Mexican-born, while the remainder were second and third generation. The majority of students at the school, both white and Mexican American, were from working-class families, but the children of middle-class professionals were a present minority. Most of the latter were white, but a handful were Mexican American. Working-class students ranged from "hard-living" to "settled-living" (Howell 1973) in experience. The former term describes lives that are chaotic and unpredictable, characterized by low-paying, unstable occupations, lack of health care benefits, and no home ownership. The latter describes lives that are orderly and predictable, characterized by relatively secure, higher-paying jobs, sometimes health benefits, and sometimes ownership of a modest home.

I "hung out" with girls in classrooms and hallways, during lunch hours, at school dances, sports events, Future Homemakers of America meetings, at a Future Farmers of America hay-bucking contest and similar events, at MEChA meetings (Movimiento Estudiantil Chicano de Aztlán; the Chicano student movement organization), in coffee shops, restaurants, the shopping mall, and the school parking lot, near the bleachers behind the school, at birthday parties, and sometimes sitting cross-legged on the floor of a girl's bedroom, "just talkin'." I spent almost every day at the school during the school year, often returning in the evening to attend an extracurricular event and sometimes on weekends to meet and "kick it" with the girls. I came to know more than sixty girls well (approximately half were white and half Mexican American) and many more as acquaintances. I talked with them about such details of their lives as friendships, dating, partying, clothes, makeup, popular culture, school, family, work, and their hopes and expectations for the future.

Over the course of the school year, I came to know the clique structure, or informal peer hierarchy, at the school, as it was the primary way students understood class and racial/ethnic differences among themselves. Labels and descriptions of each group varied, of course, depending on the social location of the student providing the description. Nonetheless, there was a general mapping that almost all students agreed on and provided easily when asked. Although there were exceptions, the groups were largely race/ethnic and class segregated. Among whites they included "preps" (middle class), "skaters/alternatives" (settled-living), "hicks" (settled-and hard-living), and "smokers/rockers/trash" (hard-living); among Mexican-American students there were "Mexican preps" (middle class and settled- and hard-living), "*las chicas*" (settled-living), and "*cholas/os*" or "hard cores" (hard-living).[1]

Group membership was linked to social roles, including curriculum choices (college prep or vocational track) and extracurricular activities (whether a student was involved in what are considered either college-prep or nonprep activities). These courses and activities combined to shape class futures leading some girls to four-year colleges, some to vocational programs at junior colleges, and some to low-wage jobs directly out of high school. While there is a strong correlation between a girl's class of "origin" (by which I mean her parents' socioeconomic status) and her class performance at school (which includes academic achievement, prep or nonprep activities, and membership in friendship groups and their corresponding style), it is an imperfect one, and there are exceptions in which middle-class girls perform working-class identity and vice versa. In other words, some students were engaged in class "passing" as they chose to perform class identities that were not their "own."

Although clique membership was not entirely determined by class, there was certainly "a polarization of attitudes toward class characteristics," and group categories (such as preps, smokers, *cholas,* etc.) were "embodiment[s] of the middle and working-class[es]" (Eckert 1989, 4–5). On the one hand, embracing and publicly performing a particular class culture mattered more than origins in terms of a student's aspirations, her treatment by teachers and other students, and her class future. On the other hand, class origins did matter significantly, of course, as girls' life chances were shaped by the

1. *Chola/o* describes a Mexican-American street style that sometimes marks identification with gangs, but it also can mark merely racial/ethnic belonging. Moreover, the degree of commitment to a gang exists on a continuum. Nonetheless, *cholas/os*, like *pachucas/os* before them, are often wrongly assumed to engage in criminal behavior (Vigil 1988).

economic and cultural resources provided at home. Because of the imperfect correlation, I came to define students not only as working or middle class in origin but also as working- or middle-class *performers* (and, synonymously, as prep and nonprep students). Girls who were passing, or metaphorically cross-dressing, had to negotiate their "inherited" identity from home with their "chosen" public identity at school. There was a disparity for them between how their and their friends' families looked and talked at home and their own class performances at school. As I came to understand these negotiations of class as cultural (not political) identities, it became useful to conceptualize class as not only a material location but also a performance.

Consequently, I ask: What are the cultural gestures involved in the performance of class? How is class "authenticity" accomplished? And how is it imbued with racial/ethnic and gender meaning? Little attention has been paid to the ways class subjectivity, as a cultural identity, is experienced in relation to the cultural meanings of race/ethnicity, gender, and sexuality.

DISSIDENT FEMININITIES

Because I spent my first few days at the school in a college-preparatory class (one that fulfills a requirement for admission to state universities), the first girls I met were college bound. Later I came to know these girls through the eyes of non-college-prep students as "the preps." They were mostly white but included a handful of Mexican-American girls. Some of the white girls were also known as "the 90210s" after the television show *Beverly Hills 90210* about wealthy high schoolers in Beverly Hills. The preps related easily to what they saw as my "school project." They eagerly volunteered to help me out and were ready and willing to talk at length about themselves and others. Displaying both social and academic skills, they were, in short, "teacher's pets" (Luttrell 1993) or "the rich and populars" (Lesko 1988).

The first day I attended Ms. Parker's business skills class was characteristic of my future visits to nonprep classes. On this particular day, there was a substitute teacher taking her place. These girls appeared different from the girls in the college-prep class: they wore more makeup, tight-fitting clothing, and seemed to have little interest in the classroom curriculum. In fact, the class was out of the teacher's hands. The girls, mostly Mexican American, were happy to have me as a distraction, and one, whom I later came to know as Lorena, said loudly (Lorena was always loud), "Oh, we heard you might be coming. What do you want to know? I'll tell you." Completely ignoring the substitute, who had clearly given up on having any control over the class, they invited me to play cards. I hesitated: "What if Mr. D. (the vice principal) comes by?"

LORENA: Oh he never does, besides (flirtatiously) he *likes* me.
BECKY: He doesn't like me. He's always callin' me into his office for something.
LORENA: He'll just ask me where's the other half of my shirt?

Lorena was referring to her short crop top, fashionable at the moment and against school dress codes because it reveals the midriff. Lorena went on, "That's Mr. H. He's our sub. Don't you think he's attractive? He's from the university too." She called him over to ask a question, and when he arrived, Lorena opened her book and pointed entirely randomly at a paragraph on the page and said coyly, "I don't understand *this*." He tried to respond appropriately by explaining the course material. * * *

The expression of self through one's relationship to and creative use of commodities (both artifacts and the discourses of popular culture) is a central practice in capitalist society. The girls' alternative versions of gender performance were shaped by a nascent knowledge of race and class hierarchies. They were very able to communicate a sense of unfairness, a "structure of feeling" (Williams 1965), where inequalities were felt but not politically articulated. Their struggles were often waged less over explicit political ideologies than over modes of identity expression. In short, among students there existed a symbolic economy of style that was the ground on which class and race relations were played out. A whole array of gender-specific commodities were used as markers of distinction among different groups of girls who performed race/ethnic- and class-specific versions of femininity. Hairstyles, clothes, shoes, and the colors of lip liner, lipstick, and nail polish were key markers used to express group membership as the body became a resource and a site on which difference was inscribed. For example, Lorena and her friends preferred darker colors for lips and nails, in comparison to the preps who either went without or wore clear lip gloss, pastel lip and nail color, or French manicures (the natural look). Each group knew the other's stylistic preferences and was aware that their own style was in opposition. Girls created and maintained symbolic oppositions in which, as Penelope Eckert puts it, "elements of behavior that come to represent one category [are] rejected by the other, and . . . may be exploited by the other category through the development of a clearly opposed element" (1989, 50).

The importance of colors as a tool of distinction became evident when *las chicas* explained that the darker lip color they chose and the lighter colors the preps wore were not simply related to skin color. Lorena explained, "it's not that, 'cause some Mexican girls who look kinda white, they wear real dark lip color" so that no one will mistake them as white. When I mentioned that I rarely saw white girls in dark lipstick, Lisa, a white prep, explained, scoffing and rolling her eyes, "oh there are some, but they're girls who are trying to be hard-core," which meant they were white girls who were performing *chola* identity.

Where middle-class performers experienced an extended adolescence by going to college, working-class performers across race began their adult lives earlier. And where middle-class performing girls (both white and Mexican American) chose academic performance and the praise of teachers and parents as signs of achieving adult status, nonprep girls wore different "badges of dignity" (Sennett and Cobb 1972; MacLeod 1995). For them, expressions of sexuality operated as a sign of adult status and served to reject teachers' and parents' methods of keeping them childlike.

It is too simple to treat the meaning of the expression of what appears as a sexualized version of femininity for working-class girls, and girls of color in particular, as a consequence of competitive heterosexuality and gender-subordinate learning. This fails to explain why girls made the choices they did from a variety of gender performances available to them. Rather, girls were negotiating meanings in a race- and class-stratified society, using commodities targeted at them as girls. They performed different versions of femininity that were integrally linked and inseparable from their class and race performances.

Las chicas, having "chosen" and/or been tracked into non-college-prep courses, were bored with their vocational schooling and often brought heterosexual romance and girl culture into the classroom as a favorite form of distraction, demonstrated in their repeated attempts to "set me up" with subs (which became almost a hazing ritual). But their gender performance and girl culture were not necessarily designed to culminate in a heterosexual relationship. Despite what appeared to be an obsession with heterosexual romance, a "men are dogs" theme was prevalent among them. Some said they didn't want to marry until their thirties if at all, and they resented their boyfriends' infidelities and attempts to police their sexuality by telling them what they should and should not wear. They knew that men should not be counted on to support them and any children they might have, and they desired economic independence. Their girl culture was less about boys than about sharing rituals of traditional femininity as a kind of friendship bonding among girls. Although the overt concern in girl culture may be with boys and romance, girls often set themselves physically apart from boys (McRobbie 1991). Lorena made this clear one day:

> LORENA: Well, when we go out, to the clubs or someplace. We all get a bunch of clothes and makeup and stuff and go to one person's house to get ready. We do each other's hair and makeup and try on each other's clothes. It takes a long time. It's more fun that way. [Thoughtfully, as if it just occurred to her,] sometimes, I think we have more fun getting ready to go out than we do going out. 'Cause when we go out we just *sit* there.
> JULIE BETTIE: So then the clothes and makeup and all aren't for the men, or about getting their attention?
> LORENA: Well, we like to see how many we can *meet*. But, well *you* know I don't fall for their lines. We talk to them, but when they start buggin' then we just go.

In short, *las chicas* had no more or less interest in heterosexual romance than did girls who performed prep or school-sanctioned femininity. Nonetheless, teachers and preps often confused the expression of class and race differences in style and activities among working-class girls as evidence of heterosexual interest. They often failed to perceive girls' class and race performances and unknowingly reproduced the commonsense belief that what is most important about girls, working-class performers in particular, is their girlness. *Las chicas'* style was not taken as a marker of race/ethnic and class distinction but was reduced to gender and sexuality.

In spite of the meanings that working-class girls themselves gave to their gender-specific cultural markers, their performances were always overdetermined by broader cultural meanings that code women in heavy makeup and tight clothes as oversexed—in short, cheap. In other words, class differences are often understood as sexual differences, where "the working class is cast as the bearer of an exaggerated sexuality, against which middle-class respectability is defined" (Ortner 1991, 177). Among women, "clothing and cosmetic differences are taken to be indexes of the differences in sexual morals" between classes (178). Indeed, this is what I observed: middle-class performing prep girls (both white and Mexican American) perceived *las chicas*, as well as working-class performing white girls, as overly sexually active.

But Mexican-American nonprep girls were perceived as even more sexually active than their white counterparts because, although there was no evidence that they were more sexually active, they were more likely to keep their babies if they became pregnant, so there was more often a visible indicator of their sexual activity. And while school personnel at times explained working-class Mexican-American girls' gender performances as a consequence of "their" culture—an assumed real ethnic cultural difference in which women are expected to fulfill traditional roles and/or are victims of machismo and a patriarchal culture—the girls' generational status (according to two meanings) was not taken into account. On the one hand, *las chicas* were a generation of girls located in a historical context of dual-wage families, and they did not describe parents who had traditional roles in mind for their daughters. Moreover, they were second-generation Mexican-Americans, young women with no intention of submitting to traditional gender ideologies.

Class was thus a present social force in the versions of femininity that the girls performed, but it was unarticulated and rendered invisible because it was interpreted (by school personnel, by preps, and at times by working-class girls themselves) as primarily about gender and a difference of sexual morality between good girls and bad girls.

"ACTING WHITE"

Many of the Mexican-American students did have a way to both recognize and displace class simultaneously, at times explaining differences among themselves solely in racial/ethnic terms, such as "acting white" versus acting "the Mexican role." The class coding of these descriptions is revealed when they are pushed only slightly. When I asked Lorena what she meant by "acting white," she gave an animated imitation of a white girl she had met at a Future Business Leaders of America meeting, affecting a stereotypical "valley girl" demeanor and speech pattern: "Ohmigod, like I can't believe I left my cell phone in my car. It was so nice to meet you girls, do keep in touch." Lorena perceived this sentiment as quite disingenuous, since they had just met. Part of working-class girls' interpretation of preps was that they were "fake" and their friendships phony and insincere, always in the interest of social ambition. Lorena went on, "I'm going to play volleyball for Harvard next year." Clearly, "Harvard" was an exaggeration on Lorena's part. But to Lorena any university may as well have been Harvard as it was just as distant a possibility. Erica, a Filipina-American girl who had befriended and been accepted as one of *las chicas*, confided to me, "There's a lot of trashing of white girls really, and Mexican girls who act white." When I asked her what she meant by "acting white," her answer was straightforward: "The preps." "Not the smokers or the hicks?" I asked. "Oh no, never smokers, basically preps."

At some level, the girls knew that they didn't mean white generally but preps specifically (that is, a particular middle-class version of white), but "class" as a way of making distinctions among whites was not easily articulated. The whites most visible to them were those who inflicted the most class injuries, the preps. In fact, working-class whites were often invisible in their talk, unless I asked specifically about them. The most marginalized ones, known as the "smokers," were either unknown to the Mexican-American students or perplexing. As Mariana, a Mexican-American middle-class performer said, almost exasperated, "I mean they're white. They've had the opportunity. What's wrong with them?" Students found it useful or necessary to describe class performances in racial terms such as "acting white" because of the difficulty of coming up with a more apt way to describe class differences in a society in which class discourse as such is absent and because the correlation of race and class (the overrepresentation of people of color among the poor) was a highly visible reality to Mexican-American students.

MIDDLE-CLASS *CHOLAS*

A handful of the girls were third-generation Mexican Americans from professional middle-class families. They had struggled to find their place in this race-class system. They had grown up in white neighborhoods and gone to elementary school with primarily white kids, where, as Rosa explained, "I knew I was different, because I was brown." In junior high, which was less segregated, some of them became *cholas* and were "jumped in" to a gang. When I asked why, Ana explained that she hated her family:

ANA: My mom wanted this picture-perfect family, you know. And I just hated it.
JULIE: What do you mean by a perfect family?

ANA: You know, we had dinner at night together, and everything was just, okay. She was so *happy*. And I hated that. My life was sad, my friends' lives were sad.
JULIE: Why were they sad?
ANA: One friend's mom was on welfare, the other didn't know who her dad was. Everything was wrong in their families.

As she described class differences between herself and her friends, she struggled for the right words to describe it. And as Lorena sought to describe the difference between herself and her friend Ana, she too searched for words: "Well, in junior high she was way down kinda low, she got in with the bad crowd. But in high school she is higher up kinda. I mean not as high as Patricia is (another middle-class performer) but she's not as low as she used to be." Lorena's perception of Ana as high but low was shaped by Ana's crossover style and the sense that she had "earned" her "low" status by performing *chola* identity and gang-banging. In Ana's attempt to understand her place in a social order where color and poverty correlate more often than not, the salience of color was integral to her identity formation. She felt compelled to perform working-class identity at school as a marker of racial/ethnic belonging. As she explained, "the Mexican Mexicans, they aren't worried about whether they're Mexican or not."

Although Ana, Rosa, and Patricia eventually had accepted the cultural capital their parents had to give them and were now college prep and headed to four-year colleges, they were friendly with *las chicas* and still dressed and performed the kind of race-class femininity that *las chicas* did. In this way, they distanced themselves from preps and countered potential accusations of "acting white." In short, their style confounded the race-class equation and was an intentional strategy. By design, they had middle-class aspirations without assimilation to prep, which for them meant white, style. It went beyond image to a set of race politics as they tried to recruit *las chicas* to be a part of MEChA. In fact, when I went along on a bus ride to tour a nearby business school with *las chicas*, I was surprised to find that Ana, Rosa, and Patricia came along. I asked why they had come along since they had already been accepted to four-year schools. Rosa responded, "Because we're with the girls, you know, we have to be supportive, do these things together."

Mexican-American girls' friendships crossed class performance boundaries more often than white girls' did because of a sense of racial alliance that drew them together in relation to white students at school and because the Mexican-American community brought them together in activities outside school. They were also far more pained about divisions among themselves than white girls ever were (an aspect of whiteness that can seem invisible). They felt the need to present a united front, and this was particularly acute among girls who were politicized about their racial/ethnic identity and participated in MEChA. For white girls, competition among them did not threaten them as a racial/ethnic minority community.

WHITE TRASH *CHOLA*

Not surprisingly, white students generally did not explain class differences among themselves in racial terms. Rather, class difference was articulated as individual difference (she's "popular" or she's a "loser") and as differences in group membership and corresponding style (hicks, smokers, preps, etc.). But class meaning was at times bound to racial signifiers in the logic of white students, as it was among Mexican-American students. This was apparent in the way the most marginalized white working-class students, who were at times described by other white students as "white trash," worked hard inter-actionally to clarify that they were not Mexican.[2] In our very first conversation, Tara explained, without any solicitation, "I'm kinda dark, but I'm not Mexican." In our conversation about her boyfriend's middle-class parents, she explained that his mom had "accused me of being Mexican." She explained to me that she was Italian-American, and her color and features did match this self-description.

Similarly, Starr, a white girl who grew up in a Mexican-American neighborhood and went to the largely Mexican-American elementary school in town, also had the sense that some whites, those at the bottom of the heap like herself, were almost brown. We were talking in the lunchroom one day about girls and fights when she told me this story:

> STARR: Well the worst one was back in junior high. All of my friends were Mexican, 'cause I went to London. So I was too.
> JULIE: You were what?
> STARR: Mexican. Well I acted like it, and they thought I was. I wore my hair up high in front you know. And I had an accent. Was in a gang. I banged [gang-banged] red [gang color affiliation].
> JULIE: Were you the only white girl?
> STARR: Yeah.
> JULIE: What happened? Why aren't you friends with them now?
> STARR: We got into a fight. I was in the bowling alley one day with my boyfriend. They came in and called him a piece of white trash. That made me mad and I smacked her. Lucky for her someone called the cops. They came pretty fast.
> JULIE: What did she mean by white trash?
> STARR: Welfare people. He was a rocker. Had long hair, smoked.

This episode ended her *chola* performance, and she was part of the white smoker crowd when I met her. Like most other girls, Starr had told me that girls fight primarily about "guys." But her actual story reveals something different. A boy was central to the story, but the girls were not fighting *over*

---

2. See Bettie 1995 and Wray and Newitz 1997 for explorations of the race and class meanings of the designation "poor white trash."

him. Rather, Starr's *chola* friends were bothered by her association with him, which pointed to her violation of the race-class identity she had been performing as a *chola*. Her friends forced her to make a choice.

Starr's race-class performance was a consequence of the neighborhood in which she grew up, and, like Tara, she had absorbed the commonsense notions that white is middle, that brown is low, and, most interesting, that low may become brown in certain contexts. Not unlike the experience of middle-class *cholas* for whom being middle-class Mexican-American felt too close to being white, Starr's working-class version of whiteness felt too close to being Mexican-American in this geographic context. Girls reported that cross-race friendships were more common in grade school, but in junior high a clear sorting out along racial lines emerged (and along class lines too, although with less awareness). Starr's story is about junior-high girls working to sort out class and color and ethnicity, about the social policing of racial boundaries, and about her move from a brown to a white racial performance (where both remained working class). Not insignificantly, her white performance included a racist discourse by which she distanced herself from Mexican-Americans via derogatory statements about them.

(MIS)USES OF "CLASS": A CAUTION

Class difference was salient, although not articulated as such, *within* these racial/ethnic groups. But in relationships *across* racial/ethnic groups, race often "trumps" class. One way racial/ethnic alliances across class were manifested was in attitudes toward California's Proposition 209 (misleadingly called the California Civil Rights Initiative), passed in 1996, which eliminated state affirmative-action programs, including admissions policies for the state's university systems. To the pleasure of white conservatives, University of California regent Ward Connerly, a black man, became the leading spokesperson and argued for income instead of race as a fairer admission criterion. In this conservative community, all of the white students I spoke to, without exception, supported Proposition 209. Both working- and middle-class white students were easily swayed by the "class instead of race" logic, which both groups interpreted as white instead of brown, where "class" stands in for white, and "race" stands in for brown (and black).

Working-class performers were less concerned with college admission than with job competition, since the decisive moment of whether a student is going on to college had occurred two to three years earlier, when they began the vocational track. Consequently, by their senior year they lacked the coursework for admission to state universities. Although white working-class students experienced a feeling of unfairness in relation to preps regarding educational achievement and college, they lacked a discourse of class that could explain their own and their parents' "failure" and that would allow them to articulate the class antagonism they felt toward middle-class students. In its absence, a discourse of individualism and meritocracy helped render institutionalized class inequality invisible and consequently left white working-class students feeling like individually flawed "losers." * * * Unfortunately, working-class students were less likely to see themselves as victims of class inequality than as victims of "reverse discrimination."

Somewhat curiously, white middle-class students were also swayed by the color-blind class logic of Proposition 209. Preps' sense of racial competition regarded who was and who was not getting into which college. The students of color most visible to them were the handful who sat next to them in college-prep classes. Preps' own class privilege was unapparent to them, so much so that the mass of working-class whites and working-class Mexican Americans were so "othered" as to be invisible. The only Mexican-American students whom preps could imagine going to college seemed to be very much like them in that they were middle-class performers. At times, these college-prep Mexican-American students were resented as "box checkers" who were perceived to be unfairly benefiting from their "minority" status, as middle-class white students constructed themselves as victims of reverse discrimination. These college-prep Mexican-American students were highly visible, to the disadvantage of their vocational-track peers. Since the large body of working-class vocational students were not in the running for college admission anyway, among college-prep students discussing college admissions, *class* was taken as a code for *white*.

And perhaps rightly so. Class inequality is not adequately addressed by eliminating race as an admission criterion since the vast majority of working-class students of all colors had been tracked out two to three years earlier. When liberal education policy attempts to deal with social inequality by trying to get everyone into college, it fails to address the fundamental fact that the global economy needs uneducated, unskilled workers, and workers need living wages.

CONCLUSION

Thinking through class as a performance enables us to acknowledge exceptions to the rule that class origin equals class future and to understand that economic and cultural resources often, but not inevitably, determine class futures. It allows us to explore the experience of negotiating inherited and chosen identities, as, for example, when middle-class students of color felt compelled to perform working-class identities as a marker of racial/ethnic belonging. It helps demonstrate, too, how other axes of identity intersect with and inform class identity and consequently shape class futures. Thinking through class as a performance is useful for understanding exceptions, those who are consciously "passing" (whether it be up or down).

But it is also useful to think of class as performative in the sense that class as cultural identity is an *effect* of social structure. Social actors largely perform the cultural capital that is a consequence of the material and cultural resources to which they have had access. Cultural performances most often reflect one's habitus or unconscious learned dispositions, which are not natural or inherent or prior to the social organization of class inequality but are in fact produced by it. Considering class as performative is consistent with regarding it more as a cultural than a political identity and more as a "sense of place" than as class consciousness in a political, marxist sense. It helps explain why class struggle is often waged more over modes of identity expression than over explicit political ideologies.

REFERENCES

Bettie, Julie. 1995. "Class Dismissed? *Roseanne* and the Changing Face of Working-Class Iconography." *Social Text* 45, vol. 14, no. 4:125–49.

Bourdieu, Pierre. 1984. *Distinction: A Social Critique of the Judgment of Taste.* Cambridge, Mass.: Harvard University Press.

Eckert, Penelope. 1989. *Jocks and Burnouts: Social Categories and Identity in the High School.* New York: Teachers College Press.

Howell, Joseph. 1973. *Hard Living on Clay Street: Portraits of Blue-Collar Families.* Garden City, N.Y.: Anchor.

Lesko, Nancy. 1988. "The Curriculum of the Body: Lessons from a Catholic High School." In *Becoming Feminine: The Politics of Popular Culture*, ed. Leslie G. Roman, Linda K. Christian-Smith, and Elizabeth Ellsworth, 123–42. London: Falmer.

Luttrell, Wendy. 1993. "The Teachers, They All Had Their Pets: Concepts of Gender, Knowledge, and Power." *Signs* 18(3):505–46.

MacLeod, Jay. 1995. *Ain't No Makin' It: Aspirations and Attainment in a Low-Income Neighborhood.* Boulder, Colo.: Westview.

McRobbie, Angela. 1991. *Feminism and Youth Culture.* London: Macmillan.

———. 1994. *Postmodernism and Popular Culture.* London: Routledge.

Ortner, Sherry. 1991. "Preliminary Notes on Class and Culture." In *Recapturing Anthropology: Working in the Present*, ed. Richard G. Fox. Santa Fe, N.M.: School of American Research Press.

Sennett, Richard, and Jonathan Cobb. 1972. *The Hidden Injuries of Class.* New York: Vintage.

Vigil, James Diego. 1988. *Barrio Gangs: Street Life and Identity in Southern California.* Austin: University of Texas Press.

Wagner, Venise. 1996. "Crossover." *San Francisco Examiner Magazine*, November 10, 8–32.

Williams, Raymond. 1965. *Marxism and Literature.* New York: Oxford University Press.

Wray, Matt, and Annalee Newitz, eds. 1997. *White Trash: Race and Class in America.* New York: Routledge.

21

Love and Race Caught in the Public Eye

HEIDI ARDIZZONE AND EARL LEWIS

The tragic consequences of racial prejudice are nowhere more appalling than in love and marriage. This essay chronicles a love story caught up in racism as well as class prejudice and gender discrimination. It challenges the reader to ask, What is the meaning of race? We continue to ask this question, even when we believe it has or should have no meaning in our relationships. This essay also describes a research approach often found in sociology—the use of existing records. Ardizzone and Lewis reminds us that social inquiry is an ongoing process that seldom provides final answers or solid conclusions.

Lovers seek to create a place that they can inhabit together against the obstacles of the world. Marriage promises that they will live in that place forever. What happens, though, when love cannot keep out the world's strictures? What happens when the bond severs, and the nation serves as a witness to marital separation? And what happens when a culture's notions about love and romance come into conflict with the lines dividing races and classes?

In 1925 Alice Beatrice Jones and Leonard "Kip" Rhinelander found themselves painfully trapped in this conflict between love and family, desire and social standing. Their marriage had the trappings of a fairy tale—wealthy New York scion marries humble girl from New Rochelle—yet the events that led to their estrangement provide an unusual window into the nation's attitudes about race, class, and sexuality. Their sensational annulment trial scandalized 1920's America and opened their private life to public scrutiny, amid cultural conflicts over racial definitions, class propriety, proper courtship and sexual behavior, and racial mixing.

As a Rhinelander, Leonard was descended from several of New York's oldest and wealthiest families. Had he followed in the family tradition, Leonard might have attended Columbia University, joined the Rhinelander Real Estate Company, and made his mark on New York society through philanthropy and support of the arts.

By contrast, Alice's parents immigrated in 1891 to the United States from England, where they had both worked as servants. George Jones had had some success in his adopted country; he eventually owned a fleet of taxicabs and several small properties. Alice, her sisters, and their husbands worked primarily as domestics and servants—solid members of the working class.

Despite this pronounced class difference, Alice and Leonard met and began dating in 1921. Their love deepened over the next three years, tested by months and years of separation as Leonard's father tried to keep them apart. Philip Rhinelander's efforts were in vain, however. From 1921 to 1924 the lovers exchanged hundreds of letters and visited when possible. As soon as Leonard turned 21 and received money from a trust fund, he left school and returned to Alice. In the fall of 1924, they quietly married in a civil ceremony at the New Rochelle City Hall.

Had reporters from the *New Rochelle Standard Star* ignored the entry in the City Hall records, the couple might have lived their lives away from the public spotlight. They did not. Someone eventually realized that a Rhinelander had married a local woman, and it was news. And once they discovered who Alice Jones was, it was big news. The first story appeared one month after their wedding, announcing to the world that the son of a Rhinelander had married the daughter of a colored man.

Or had he? Well, at least he had married the daughter of a working-class man, and that was enough to start a tremor of gossip throughout New York. Reporters rushed to sift through the legal documents and contradictory accounts of and by the Joneses and the newlyweds. Despite the confidence of the first announcement, there was confusion for quite some time as to George Jones's—and therefore Alice's—precise racial identity.

Leonard initially stood by his wife during the tumult of national coverage of their cross-class, possibly cross-racial, marriage. But after two weeks, he left her and signed an annulment complaint that his father's lawyers had prepared. The suit charged Alice with misrepresenting her racial identity to her would-be husband. She was black, the document asserted, but had tried to pass as white. She was not the woman Leonard thought she was when he married her.

Our interest in the Rhinelander case began more than 18 years ago, when Earl came across newspaper accounts of the trial in the *Norfolk Journal and Guide*. The story pulsed with the complexities of race and identity in Jim Crow-era America, and he couldn't pull himself away from it. A dozen years later he mentioned the story to Heidi, who began tracking down more information but eventually decided not to incorporate it into her dissertation. Instead, we decided to try a collaborative effort, and Heidi began a series of trips to Westchester County and New York City, tracking trial records, legal documents, and New York newspaper coverage and looking for surviving members of the families involved. We produced an article and quickly turned to writing a book.

Every researcher knows that of the many paths of inquiry planned, some will inevitably lead nowhere. We were, nonetheless, quite surprised to find that, despite repeated inquiries, our research failed to produce an extant copy of the court transcript in the Westchester County courthouses or their archives, or in the appellate courts, newspaper archives, or lawyers' offices. Tantalizing hints of its existence materialized, including an index of testimony and documents from subsequent legal challenges. Unfortunately, none of the courts could produce the transcript.

Without a transcript, we turned to newspaper coverage of the case. We culled pertinent coverage from several dozen national newspapers—black-and white-published—including dailies and tabloids from New York City and neighboring communities. From these sources we recreated the trial, sometimes overlaying numerous accounts of the same event to reconcile discrepancies or omissions. Our ability to do so was aided immensely by several daily newspapers' habit of reproducing each day's court record alongside their summaries, editorials, photographs, and cartoon coverage.

The regional and racial diversity of the sources gave us a more highly textured story than we first imagined, one that enabled us to gauge how the nation responded to its unfolding. Depending on newspapers made us aware not only of the immense popularity of the case but also of how the story reached different audiences with different messages and, to some extent, how the readership responded. Our book became a study of the cultural response to the trial and the issues it raised as much as it was an analysis of the trial itself.

Another path we hoped to pursue lay in finding Alice or Leonard or family members who might have more information about their relationship and lives after the trial. We quickly learned that Leonard had died in 1936, but we had no idea if Alice had remarried, had had children, or still lived. *The New York Times* had no obituary for her, nor did the *New Rochelle Standard Star*. While Alice was listed in city directories until the 1960's, apparently still living in her childhood home, thereafter she either moved or maintained an unlisted address. Local people remembered the case, but no one knew where she was.

One day in New Rochelle, after pursuing several unfruitful leads, Heidi stopped by the local cemetery, where she knew Alice's parents were buried. The office had no record of Alice being buried with her family, but Heidi decided to visit the family plot anyway. As she walked around reading the graves, she literally tripped over a small flat stone lying almost flush with the grass. There was Alice's grave. She had died in 1989.

More so than the absence of a transcript, the inability to interview participants and observers of the events left several still-unanswered questions. (Though more distant Rhinelanders did reply to our inquiries, most family members could not be found or declined to respond.) Most importantly, how did George and Alice define themselves racially? At the beginning of the trial, Alice's lawyers said that Alice "had some colored blood in her veins." Although the lawyers said they had only made the admission "for the purposes of the trial" and were careful never to call her black most Americans understood that having colored ancestry meant she was black, albeit of mixed ancestry.

Her sisters both acknowledged on the witness stand that they were colored, and that they had never denied it. Their mother, Elizabeth, who was white, made a sharp distinction between having colored blood and being black. She was surprised that her husband was considered a Negro in the United States. She believed he was a mulatto but not black. This distinction, of course, contradicted white America's system of popular and legal racial classification, which held that just one drop of black blood made one black. As a rule, Americans made few distinctions between colored and Negro by the 1920s; gradations in mixed blood had given way to absolutes.

The illogic of such definitions did not go unnoticed by many blacks and some whites. Still, George Jones's skin was dark enough that all who saw him agreed that in the American racial lexicon he could not be called white. He claimed only to know that his mother was white and his father had been a subject of the British colonies. But his daughters' appearances were more ambiguous. Interviews with family members, neighbors, and friends did not clarify matters much. They offered conflicting stories of what people thought they were, how they presented themselves, and whether they defined themselves as black, white, colored, or something else entirely.

Whether or not George and Elizabeth thought he was black, the family was clearly considered mixed by most people in their community, and their union threatened settled assumptions in Jim Crow-era America. By the 1920s, prohibitions against interracial marriage existed in more than half of the states. Most of these statutes also tried to define who was black and who was white—most using the one-drop rule, some offering a specific blood quantum (such as anyone with at least one-eighth black ancestry was black).

Although the U.S. Supreme Court had refused in *Plessy* v. *Ferguson* to provide a definition of black and white, it did offer an opinion in 1924 on whether Asian Indians were white. The case in question involved an Indian immigrant, Bhagat Thind, who argued that he was Caucasian and therefore white and therefore eligible for U.S. citizenship, from which Asian immigrants were excluded. The court agreed with him on one count: He was Caucasian. The majority concluded he was not white, however, since the perceptions and beliefs of the average man defined whiteness by pale skin and European ancestry. The *Thind* case made clear that American legal racial categories were socially constructed, not based in scientific racialism. It also highlighted the racial fissure many immigrants like George Jones experienced as they found themselves placed in a different classification in the United States than they had previously occupied.

At the conclusion of our research it had become quite obvious that "passing" did not adequately explain Alice's life. She and her family seemed to live in between the worlds of black and white, a difficult but not unknown act in the age of social and legal segregation. In admitting colored blood but avoiding identification as black, the Jones family raised serious challenges to the meaning of race—social, cultural, and biological.

Alice's admission of colored blood did not solve the ambiguity of her racial identity. In a state that had never made interracial marriages illegal, the primary issue turned on whether Leonard had known she wasn't white when he married her. The question became not was she black or white, but how could he and other white Americans know? Thus, the case continued to expose many of the nation's contradictory definitions of race.

Throughout the trial, reporters carefully scrutinized Alice's deportment, clothing, and appearance. They searched for any detail that might explain who she was and give a fuller hint of her race. They also looked to see if she betrayed any lingering affection for Leonard. The reporters characterized her as "fair" or "slightly tanned" or "dusky" or even "ebony," her skin tone waxing and waning with the tides of evidence and scandal. At perhaps the most memorable point of the trial, Alice, at the request of her lawyer, partially disrobed before the court, baring her breasts, back, and legs. Although no reporters were actually in the judge's chambers when she exposed her body, all were sure she had proven her attorney's point: that Leonard must have known from viewing her body prior to marriage that she was not white.

While she gave a few interviews to the press, Alice never actually testified, never told her story for the court record. She won her case, however. The annulment was denied, and the marriage was upheld. Editors generally agreed that the weight of evidence had been on her side, although some were surprised that Leonard's race and class standing didn't sway the jury. After another round of appeals Leonard disappeared, amidst continued speculation that the two had reunited. In 1930 Leonard resurfaced alone in Nevada, where he won a divorce that was recognized only in that state; they later signed a separation agreement in New York.

According to the terms, Leonard paid Alice a $32,500 lump sum and $3,600 per year for life. In return, Alice forfeited all claims to the Rhinelander estate and agreed not to use the Rhinelander name, nor to lecture or write publicly about her story, pledges she honored the rest of her life. Her parents and Leonard all died during the 1930's, events that recalled the trial for local and New York City newspapers. So did a series of trials between Alice and the Rhinelander heirs over her annuity, which Alice again won. By the time she died, the print media and their readers had forgotten the case and her past notoriety. No one noticed that upon dying, and without speaking, she would get the last word. Her gravestone reads "Alice J. Rhinelander"—a reclamation of her identity as Leonard's wife.

* * *

While Alice got the last word in her own story, we do not expect to do so with our book [*Love on Trial: An American Scandal in Black and White*]. Even now, a previously abandoned research path has reopened. This latest twist came just a few months ago, long after we had turned in the manuscript. We heard from the literary scholar Werner Sollors that one of his former students had obtained a copy of the trial transcript from the New York Bar Association. In March, after an initial report that it did not exist there either, we received a copy of the transcript.

Did finding it change anything? Yes and no. We now have the full texts of Leonard's two letters that no newspaper was willing to print in full due to their explicit sexual nature. So far we have found nothing that would alter either our narrative or our overall analysis of the Rhinelander/Jones case. In fact, we are convinced that the route we took, while more difficult, made for a richer story.

And what about the other paths we could not follow? Will publication of this book prompt Alice's heirs or other Rhinelander family members to tell their story? That would be a fascinating development, indeed. What might we learn about Alice and Leonard's relationship? The Jones family's thoughts about race and their own identity?

Alice's family must have played a role in placing her married name on her gravestone. Perhaps Alice would get the last word once again.

22

Optional Ethnicities: For Whites Only?

MARY C. WATERS

Social status—both positive and negative—is often a matter of choice or accomplishment, what sociologists call achieved status. In other cases status is ascribed, based on features associated with the group with which we are identified or associated, like it or not. Sex, age, visible disabilities, and skin color are important ascribed characteristics in American society. Less visible are national origin and ethnicity. Some people choose to be ethnically identified, usually to benefit from a positive personal identity or the celebration of a proud tradition. Others do not choose an ethnic identity, nor does it always confer benefits. For them, ethnicity is not optional. This essay by Mary Waters may help some students understand a little better what others are saying about the meaning of being Black or Chicano or Asian or American Indian or another nonoptional ethnicity.

ETHNIC IDENTITY FOR WHITES IN THE 1990S

What does it mean to talk about ethnicity as an option for an individual? To argue that an individual has some degree of choice in their ethnic identity flies in the face of the commonsense notion of ethnicity many of us believe in—that one's ethnic identity is a fixed characteristic, reflective of blood ties and given at birth. However, social scientists who study ethnicity have long concluded that while ethnicity is based in a *belief* in a common ancestry, ethnicity is primarily a *social* phenomenon, not a biological one. The belief that members of an ethnic group have that they share a common ancestry may not be a fact. There is a great deal of change in ethnic identities across generations through intermarriage, changing allegiances, and changing social categories. There is also a much larger amount of change in the identities of individuals over their life than is commonly believed. While most people are aware of the phenomenon known as "passing"—people raised as one race who change at some point and claim a different race as their identity—there are similar life course changes in ethnicity that happen all the time and are not given the same degree of attention as "racial passing."

White Americans of European ancestry can be described as having a great deal of choice in terms of their ethnic identities. The two major types of options White Americans can exercise are (1) the option of whether to claim any specific ancestry, or to just be "White" or American, and (2) the choice of which of their European ancestries to choose to include in their description of their own identities. In both cases, the option of choosing how to present your-self on surveys and in everyday social interactions exists for Whites because of social changes and societal conditions that have created a great deal of social mobility, immigrant assimilation, and political and economic power for Whites in the United States. Specifically, the option of being able to not claim any ethnic identity exists for Whites of European background in the United States because they are the majority group—in terms of holding political and social power, as well as being a numerical majority. The option of choosing among different ethnicities in their family backgrounds exists because the degree of discrimination and social distance attached to specific European backgrounds has diminished over time.

The Ethnic Miracle

When European immigration to the United States was sharply curtailed in the late 1920s, a process was set in motion whereby the European ethnic groups already in the United States were for all intents and purposes cut off from any new arrivals. As a result, the composition of the ethnic groups began to age generationally. The proportion of each ethnic group made up of immigrants or the first generation began to gradually decline, and the proportion made up of the children, grandchildren, and eventually greatgrandchildren began to increase. Consequently, by 1990 most European-origin ethnic groups in the United States were composed of a very small number of immigrants, and a very large proportion of people whose link to their ethnic origins in Europe was increasingly remote.

This generational change was accompanied by unprecedented social and economic changes. The very success of the assimilation process these groups experienced makes it difficult to imagine how much the question of the immi-grants' eventual assimilation was an open one at the turn of the century. At the peak of immigration from southern and central Europe there was wide-spread discrimination and hostility against the newcomers by established Americans. Italians, Poles, Greeks, and Jews were called derogatory names, attacked by nativist mobs, and derided in the press. Intermarriage across ethnic lines was very uncommon—castelike in the words of some sociologists (Pagnini and Morgan 1990). The immigrants and their children were residen-tially segregated, occupationally specialized, and generally poor.

After several generations in the United States, the situation has changed a great deal. The success and social mobility of the grandchildren and great-grandchildren of that massive wave of immigrants from Europe has been called "The Ethnic Miracle" (Greeley 1976). These Whites have moved away from the inner-city ethnic ghettos to White middle-class suburban homes. They are doctors, lawyers, entertainers, academics, governors, and Supreme Court jus-tices. But contrary to what some social science theorists and some politicians predicted or hoped for, these middle-class Americans have not completely given up ethnic identity. Instead, they have maintained some connection with their immigrant ancestors' identities—becoming Irish American doctors, Italian American Supreme Court justices, and Greek American presidential candidates. In the tradition of cultural pluralism, successful middle-class Americans in the late twentieth century maintain some degree of identity with their ethnic backgrounds. They have remained "hyphenated Americans." So while social mobility and declining discrimination have created the option of not identifying with any European ancestry, most White Americans continue to report some ethnic background.

* * *

Symbolic Ethnicities for White Americans

What do these ethnic identities mean to people and why do they cling to them rather than just abandoning the tie and calling themselves American? My own field research with suburban Whites in California and Pennsylvania found that later-generation descendants of European origin maintain what are called "symbolic ethnicities." Symbolic ethnicity is a term coined by Herbert Gans (1979) to refer to ethnicity that is individualistic in nature and without real social cost for the individual. These symbolic identifications are essentially leisure time activities, rooted in nuclear family traditions and reinforced by the voluntary enjoyable aspects of being ethnic (Waters 1990). Richard Alba (1990) also found later-generation Whites in Albany, New York, who chose to keep a tie with an ethnic identity because of the enjoyable and voluntary aspects to those identities, along with the feelings of specialness they entailed. An example of symbolic ethnicity is individuals who identify as Irish, for example, on occasions such as Saint Patrick's Day, on family holidays, or for vacations. They do not usually belong to Irish American organizations, live in Irish neighborhoods, work in Irish jobs, or marry other Irish people. The symbolic meaning of being Irish American can be constructed by individuals from mass media images, family traditions, or other intermittent social activities. In other words, for later-generation White ethnics, ethnicity is not something that influences their lives unless they want it to. In the world of work and school and neighborhood, individuals do not have to admit to being ethnic unless they choose to. And for an increasing number of European-origin individuals whose parents and grandparents have intermarried, the ethnicity they claim is largely a matter of personal choice as they sort through all of the possible combinations of groups in their genealogies.

* * *

In responding to the ancestry question, the comparative latitude that White respondents have does not mean that Whites pick and choose ethnicities out of thin air. For the most part people choose an identity that corresponds with some element of their family tree. However, there are many anecdotal instances of people adopting ethnicities when they marry or move to a strongly identified neighborhood or community. For instance Micaela di Leonardo (1984) reported instances of non-Italian women who married into Italian American families and "became Italian." Karen Leonard (1992) describes a community of Mexican American women who married Punjabi immigrants in California. Some of the Punjabi immigrants and their descendants were said to have "become Mexican" when they joined their wives' kin group and social worlds. Alternatively she describes the community acknowledging that Mexican women made the best curry, as they adapted to life with Indian-origin men.

But what do these identities mean to individuals? Surely an identity that is optional in a number of ways—not legally defined on a passport or birth certificate, not socially consequential in terms of societal discrimination in terms of housing or job access, and not economically limiting in terms of blocking opportunities for social mobility—cannot be the same as an identity that results from and is nurtured by societal exclusion and rejection. The choice to have a symbolic ethnicity is an attractive and widespread one despite its lack of demonstrable content, because having a symbolic ethnicity combines individuality with feelings of community. People reported to me that they liked having an ethnic identity because it gave them a uniqueness and a feeling of being special. They often contrasted their own specialness by virtue of their ethnic identities with "bland" American-ness. Being ethnic makes people feel unique and special and not just "vanilla," as one of my respondents put it. * * *

* * *

Symbolic ethnicity is the best of all worlds for these respondents. These White ethnics can claim to be unique and special, while simultaneously finding the community and conformity with others that they also crave. But that "community" is of a type that will not interfere with a persons individuality. It is not as if these people belong to ethnic voluntary organizations or gather as a group in churches or neighborhoods or union halls. They work and reside within the mainstream of American middle-class life, yet they retain the interesting benefits—the "specialness"—of ethnic allegiance, without any of its drawbacks.

* * *

RACE RELATIONS AND SYMBOLIC ETHNICITY

However much symbolic ethnicity is without cost for the individual, there is a cost associated with symbolic ethnicity for the society. That is because symbolic ethnicities of the type described here are confined to White Americans of European origin. Black Americans, Hispanic Americans, Asian Americans, and American Indians do not have the option of a symbolic ethnicity at present in the United States. For all of the ways in which ethnicity does not matter for White Americans, it does matter for non-Whites. Who your ancestors are does affect your choice of spouse, where you live, what job you have, who your friends are, and what your chances are for success in American society, if those ancestors happen not to be from Europe. The reality is that White ethnics have a lot more choice and room for maneuver than they themselves think they do. The situation is very different for members of racial minorities, whose lives are strongly influenced by their race or national origin regardless of how much they may choose not to identify themselves in terms of their ancestries.

When White Americans learn the stories of how their grandparents and great-grandparents triumphed in the United States over adversity, they are usually told in terms of their individual efforts and triumphs. The important role of labor unions and other organized political and economic actors in their social and economic successes are left out of the story in favor of a generational story of individual Americans rising up against communitarian, Old World intolerance and New World resistance. As a result, the "individualized" voluntary, cultural view of ethnicity for Whites is what is remembered.

One important implication of these identities is that they tend to be very individualistic. There is a tendency to view valuing diversity in a pluralist environment as equating all groups. The symbolic ethnic tends to think that all groups are equal; everyone has a background that is their right to celebrate and pass on to their children. This leads to the conclusion that all identities are equal and all identities in some sense are interchangeable—"I'm Italian American, you're Polish American. I'm Irish American, you're African American." The important thing is to treat people as individuals and all equally. However, this assumption ignores the very big difference between an individualistic symbolic ethnic identity and a socially enforced and imposed racial identity.

* * *

When White Americans equate their own symbolic ethnicities with the socially enforced identities of non-White Americans, they obscure the fact that the experiences of Whites and non-Whites have been qualitatively different in the United States and that the current identities of individuals partly reflect that unequal history.

In the next section I describe how relations between Black and White students on college campuses reflect some of these asymmetries in the understanding of what a racial or ethnic identity means. While I focus on Black and White students in the following discussion, you should be aware that the myriad other groups in the United States—Mexican Americans, American Indians, Japanese Americans—all have some degree of social and individual influences on their identities, which reflect the group's social and economic history and present circumstance.

Relations on College Campuses

Both Black and White students face the task of developing their race and eth-nic identities. Sociologists and psychologists note that at the time people leave home and begin to live independently from their parents, often ages eighteen to twenty-two, they report a heightened sense of racial and ethnic identity as they sort through how much of their beliefs and behaviors are idiosyncratic to their families and how much are shared with other people. It is not until one comes in close contact with many people who are different from oneself that individuals realize the ways in which their backgrounds may influence their individual personality. This involves coming into contact with people who are different in terms of their ethnicity, class, religion, region, and race. For White students, the ethnicity they claim is more often than not a symbolic one—with all of the voluntary, enjoyable, and intermittent characteristics I have described above.

Black students at the university are also developing identities through interactions with others who are different from them. Their identity develop-ment is more complicated than that of Whites because of the added element of racial discrimination and racism, along with the "ethnic" developments of finding others who share their background. Thus Black students have the pos-itive attraction of being around other Black students who share some cultural elements, as well as the need to band together with other students in a reac-tive and oppositional way in the face of racist incidents on campus.

Colleges and universities across the country have been increasing diversity among their student bodies in the last few decades. This has led in many cases to strained relations among students from different racial and ethnic back-grounds. The 1980s and 1990s produced a great number of racial incidents and high racial tensions on campuses. While there were a number of racial incidents that were due to bigotry, unlawful behavior, and violent or vicious attacks, much of what happens among students on campuses involves a low level of tension and awkwardness in social interactions.

Many Black students experience racism personally for the first time on campus. The upper-middle-class students from White suburbs were often iso-lated enough that their presence was not threatening to racists in their high schools. Also, their class background was known by their residence and this may have prevented attacks being directed at them. Often Black students at the university who begin talking with other students and recognizing racial slights will remember incidents that happened to them earlier that they might not have thought were related to race.

* * *

Black students do experience a tension and a feeling of being singled out. It is unfair that this is part of their college experience and not that of White students. Dealing with incidents like this, or the ever-present threat of such incidents, is an ongoing developmental task for Black students that takes energy, attention, and strength of character. It should be clearly understood that this is an asymmetry in the "college experience" for Black and White students. It is one of the unfair aspects of life that results from living in a society with ongoing racial prejudice and discrimination. It is also very understandable that it makes some students angry at the unfairness of it all, even if there is no one to blame specifically. * * *

In some sense then, as Blauner (1992) has argued, you can see Black students coming together on campus as both an "ethnic" pull of wanting to be together to share common experiences and community, and a "racial" push of banding together defensively because of perceived rejection and tension from Whites. In this way the ethnic identities of Black students are in some sense similar to, say, Korean students wanting to be together to share experiences. And it is an ethnicity that is generally much stronger than, say, Italian Americans. But for Koreans who come together there is generally a definition of themselves as "different from" Whites. For Blacks reacting to exclusion, there is a tendency for the coming together to involve both being "different from" but also "opposed to" Whites.

The anthropologist John Ogbu (1990) has documented the tendency of minorities in a variety of societies around the world, who have experienced severe blocked mobility for long periods of time, to develop such oppositional identities. An important component of having such an identity is to describe others of your group who do not join in the group solidarity as devaluing and denying their very core identity. This is why it is not common for successful Asians to be accused by others of "acting White" in the United States, but it is quite common for such a term to be used by Blacks and Latinos. The oppositional component of a Black identity also explains how Black people can question whether others are acting "Black enough." On campus, it explains some of the intense pressures felt by Black students who do not make their racial identity central and who choose to hang out primarily with non-Blacks. This pressure from the group, which is partly defining itself by not being White, is exacerbated by the fact that race is a physical marker in American society. No one immediately notices the Jewish students sitting together in the dining hall, or the one Jewish student sitting surrounded by non-Jews, or the Texan sitting with the Californians, but everyone notices the Black student who is or is not at the "Black table" in the cafeteria.

An example of the kinds of misunderstandings that can arise because of different understandings of the meanings and implications of symbolic versus oppositional identities concerns questions students ask one another in the dorms about personal appearances and customs. A very common type of interaction in the dorm concerns questions Whites ask Blacks about their hair. Because Whites tend to know little about Blacks, and Blacks know a lot about Whites, there is a general asymmetry in the level of curiosity people have about one another. Whites, as the numerical majority, have had little contact with Black culture; Blacks, especially those who are in college, have had to develop bicultural skills—knowledge about the social worlds of both Whites and Blacks. Miscommunication and hurt feelings about White students' questions about Black students' hair illustrate this point. One of the things that happens freshman year is that White students are around Black students as they fix their hair. White students are generally quite curious about Black students' hair—they have basic questions such as how often Blacks wash their hair, how they get it straightened or curled, what products they use on their hair, how they comb it, etc. Whites often wonder to themselves whether they should ask these questions. One thought experiment Whites perform is to ask themselves whether a particular question would upset them. Adopting the "do unto others" rule, they ask themselves, "If a Black person was curious about my hair would I get upset?" The answer usually is "No, I would be happy to tell them." Another example is an Italian American student wondering to herself, "Would I be upset if someone asked me about calamari?" The answer is no, so she asks her Black roommate about collard greens, and the roommate explodes with an angry response such as, "Do you think all Black people eat watermelon too?" Note that if this Italian American knew her friend was Trinidadian American and asked about peas and rice the situation would be more similar and would not necessarily ignite underlying tensions.

⁎ ⁎ ⁎ Because Blacks tend to have more knowledge about Whites than vice versa, there is not an even exchange going on, the Black freshman is likely to have fewer basic questions about his White roommate than his White roommate has about him. Because of the differences historically in the group experiences of Blacks and Whites there are some connotations to Black hair that don't exist about White hair. (For instance, is straightening your hair a form of assimilation, do some people distinguish between women having "good hair" and "bad hair" in terms of beauty and how is that related to looking "White"?). Finally, even a Black freshman who cheerfully disregards or is unaware that there are these asymmetries will soon slam into another asymmetry if she willingly answers every innocent question asked of her. In a situation where Blacks make up only 10 percent of the student body, if every non-Black needs to be educated about hair, she will have to explain it to nine other students. As one Black student explained to me, after you've been asked a couple of times about something so personal you begin to feel like you are an attraction in a zoo, that you are at the university for the education of the White students.

Institutional Responses

Our society asks a lot of young people. We ask young people to do something that no one else does as successfully on such a wide scale—that is to live together with people from very different backgrounds, to respect one another, to appreciate one another, and to enjoy and learn from one another. The successes that occur every day in this endeavor are many, and they are too often overlooked. However, the problems and tensions are also real, and they will not vanish on their own. We tend to see pluralism working in the

United States in much the same way some people expect capitalism to work. If you put together people with various interests and abilities and resources, the "invisible hand" of capitalism is supposed to make all the parts work together in an economy for the common good.

There is much to be said for such a model—the invisible hand of the market can solve complicated problems of production and distribution better than any "visible hand" of a state plan. However, we have learned that unequal power relations among the actors in the capitalist marketplace, as well as "externalities" that the market cannot account for, such as long-term pollution, or collusion between corporations, or the exploitation of child labor, means that state regulation is often needed. Pluralism and the relations between groups are very similar. There is a lot to be said for the idea that bringing people who belong to different ethnic or racial groups together in institutions with no interference will have good consequences. Students from different backgrounds will make friends if they share a dorm room or corridor, and there is no need for the institution to do any more than provide the locale. But like capitalism, the invisible hand of pluralism does not do well when power relations and externalities are ignored. When you bring together individuals from groups that are differentially valued in the wider society and provide no guidance, there will be problems. In these cases the "invisible hand" of pluralist relations does not work, and tensions and disagreements can arise without any particular individual or group of individuals being "to blame." On college campuses in the 1990s some of the tensions between students are of this sort. They arise from honest misunderstandings, lack of a common background, and very different experiences of what race and ethnicity mean to the individual.

The implications of symbolic ethnicities for thinking about race relations are subtle but consequential. If your understanding of your own ethnicity and its relationship to society and politics is one of individual choice, it becomes harder to understand the need for programs like affirmative action, which recognize the ongoing need for group struggle and group recognition, in order to bring about social change.* It also is hard for a White college student to understand the need that minority students feel to band together against discrimination. It also is easy, on the individual level, to expect everyone else to be able to turn their ethnicity on and off at will, the way you are able to, without understanding that ongoing discrimination and societal attention to minority status makes that impossible for individuals from minority groups to do. The paradox of symbolic ethnicity is that it depends upon the ultimate goal of a pluralist society, and at the same time makes it more difficult to achieve that ultimate goal. It is dependent upon the concept that all ethnicities mean the same thing, that enjoying the traditions of one's heritage is an option

---

*This point is explored further in my essay "Thinking About Affirmative Action" (Massey 2004). [*Editor's note*].

available to a group or an individual, but that such a heritage should not have any social costs associated with it.

* * * [T]here are many societal issues and involuntary ascriptions associated with non-White identities. The developments necessary for this to change are not individual but societal in nature. Social mobility and declining racial and ethnic sensitivity are closely associated. The legacy and the present reality of discrimination on the basis of race or ethnicity must be overcome before the ideal of a pluralist society, where all heritages are treated equally and are equally available for individuals to choose or discard at will, is realized.

REFERENCES

Alba, Richard D. (1990). *Ethnic Identity: The Transformation of White America.* New Haven: Yale University Press.

Blauner, Robert (1992). "Talking Past Each Other: Black and White Languages of Race." *American Prospect* (summer): 55–64.

di Leonardo, Micaela (1984). *The Varieties of Ethnic Experience: Kinship, Class and Gender Among Italian Americans.* Ithaca, NY: Cornell University Press.

Gans, Herbert (1979). "Symbolic Ethnicity: The Future of Ethnic Groups and Cultures in America." *Ethnic and Racial Studies* 2: 1–20.

Greeley, Andrew H. (1976). "The Ethnic Miracle." *Public Interest* 45 (fall): 20–36.

Leonard, Karen (1992). *Making Ethnic Choices: Califonia's Punjabi Mexican Americans.* Philadelphia: Temple University Press.

Massey, Garth (2004). "Thinking about Affirmative Action: Arguments Supporting Preferential Policies." *Review of Policy Research*, 21 (6): 783–797.

Ogbu, John (1990). "Minority Status and Literacy in Comparative Perspective." *Daedalus* 119: 141–169.

Pagnini, Deanna L., and S. Philip Morgan (1990). "Intermarriage and Social Distance among U.S. Immigrants at the Turn of the Century." *American Journal of Sociology* 96 (2): 405–432.

Waters, Mary C. (1990). *Ethnic Options: Choosing Identities in America.* Berkeley and Los Angeles: University of California Press.

PART FIVE

SOCIAL INEQUALITY AND LABOR

23

Nickel and Dimed:
On (Not) Getting By in America

BARBARA EHRENREICH

Major changes in welfare legislation in 1996 eliminated cash payments to millions of America's poor, requiring them to find employment in order to support themselves and their families. This change in the law, though popular, raised questions for many people, including Barbara Ehrenreich, who had doubts about the "uplifting benefits" of working in the low-wage economy. One of America's most popular sociological writers, Ehrenreich traveled to the heart of the low-wage economy to see firsthand what it has to offer.

At the beginning of June 1998 I leave behind everything that normally soothes the ego and sustains the body—home, career, companion, reputation, ATM card—for a plunge into the low-wage workforce. There, I become another, occupationally much diminished "Barbara Ehrenreich"—depicted on job-application forms as a divorced homemaker whose sole work experience consists of housekeeping in a few private homes. I am terrified, at the beginning, of being unmasked for what I am: a middle-class journalist setting out to explore the world that welfare mothers are entering, at the rate of approximately 50,000 a month, as welfare reform* kicks in. Happily, though, my fears turn out to be entirely unwarranted: during a month of poverty and toil, my name goes unnoticed and for the most part unuttered. In this parallel universe where my father never got out of the mines and I never got through college, I am "baby," "honey," "blondie," and, most commonly, "girl."

My first task is to find a place to live. I figure that if I can earn $7 an hour—which, from the want ads, seems doable—I can afford to spend $500 on rent, or maybe, with severe economies, $600. In the Key West area, where I live, this pretty much confines me to flophouses and trailer homes—like the one, a pleasing fifteen-minute drive from town, that has no air-conditioning, no screens, no fans, no television, and, by way of diversion, only the challenge of evading the landlord's Doberman pinscher. The big problem with this place, though, is the rent, which at $675 a month is well beyond my reach. All right,

---

*On the basis of 1996 federal legislation, states were required to adopt new guidelines for providing social assistance. The most important program providing cash assistance, Aid to Families with Dependent Children (AFDC), was eliminated and replaced by requirements that poor adults work or participate in job training in order to quality for cash assistance. [*Editor's note*].

Key West is expensive. But so is New York City, or the Bay Area, or Jackson Hole, or Telluride, or Boston, or any other place where tourists and the wealthy compete for living space with the people who clean their toilets and fry their hash browns.[1] Still, it is a shock to realize that "trailer trash" has become, for me, a demographic category to aspire to.

So I decide to make the common trade-off between affordability and convenience, and go for a $500-a-month efficiency thirty miles up a two-lane highway from the employment opportunities of Key West, meaning forty-five minutes if there's no road construction and I don't get caught behind some sun-dazed Canadian tourists. I hate the drive, along a roadside studded with white crosses commemorating the more effective head-on collisions, but it's a sweet little place—a cabin, more or less, set in the swampy backyard of the converted mobile home where my landlord, an affable TV repairman, lives with his bartender girlfriend. Anthropologically speaking, a bustling trailer park would be preferable, but here I have a gleaming white floor and a firm mattress, and the few resident bugs are easily vanquished.

Besides, I am not doing this for the anthropology. My aim is nothing so mistily subjective as to "experience poverty" or find out how it "really feels" to be a long-term low-wage worker. I've had enough unchosen encounters with poverty and the world of low-wage work to know it's not a place you want to visit for touristic purposes; it just smells too much like fear. And with all my real-life assets—bank account, IRA, health insurance, multiroom home—waiting indulgently in the background, I am, of course, thoroughly insulated from the terrors that afflict the genuinely poor.

No, this is a purely objective, scientific sort of mission. The humanitarian rationale for welfare reform—as opposed to the more punitive and stingy impulses that may actually have motivated it—is that work will lift poor women out of poverty while simultaneously inflating their self-esteem and hence their future value in the labor market. Thus, whatever the hassles involved in finding child care, transportation, etc., the transition from welfare to work will end happily, in greater prosperity for all. Now there are many problems with this comforting prediction, such as the fact that the economy will inevitably undergo a downturn, eliminating many jobs. Even without a downturn, the influx of a million former welfare recipients into the low-wage labor market could depress wages by as much as 11.9 percent, according to the Economic Policy Institute (EPI) in Washington, D.C.

---

1. According to the Department of Housing and Urban Development, the "fair-market rent" for an efficiency is $551 here in Monroe County, Florida. A comparable rent in the five boroughs of New York City is $704; in San Francisco, $713; and in the heart of Silicon Valley, $808. The fair-market rent for an area is defined as the amount that would be needed to pay rent plus utilities for "privately owned, decent, safe, and sanitary rental housing of a modest (non-luxury) nature with suitable amenities."

But is it really possible to make a living on the kinds of jobs currently available to unskilled people? Mathematically, the answer is no, as can be shown by taking $6 to $7 an hour, perhaps subtracting a dollar or two an hour for child care, multiplying by 160 hours a month, and comparing the result to the prevailing rents. According to the National Coalition for the Homeless, for example, in 1998 it took, on average nationwide, an hourly wage of $8.89 to afford a one-bedroom apartment, and the Preamble Center for Public Policy estimates that the odds against a typical welfare recipient's landing a job at such a "living wage" are about 97 to 1. If these numbers are right, low-wage work is not a solution to poverty and possibly not even to homelessness.

It may seem excessive to put this proposition to an experimental test. As certain family members keep unhelpfully reminding me, the viability of low-wage work could be tested, after a fashion, without ever leaving my study. I could just pay myself $7 an hour for eight hours a day, charge myself for room and board, and total up the numbers after a month. Why leave the people and work that I love? But I am an experimental scientist by training. In that business, you don't just sit at a desk and theorize; you plunge into the everyday chaos of nature, where surprises lurk in the most mundane measurements. Maybe, when I got into it, I would discover some hidden economies in the world of the low-wage worker. After all, if 30 percent of the workforce toils for less than $8 an hour, according to the EPI, they may have found some tricks as yet unknown to me. Maybe—who knows?—I would even be able to detect in myself the bracing psychological effects of getting out of the house, as promised by the welfare wonks at places like the Heritage Foundation. Or, on the other hand, maybe there would be unexpected costs—physical, mental, or financial—to throw off all my calculations. Ideally, I should do this with two small children in tow, that being the welfare average, but mine are grown and no one is willing to lend me theirs for a month-long vacation in penury. So this is not the perfect experiment, just a test of the best possible case: an unencumbered woman, smart and even strong, attempting to live more or less off the land.

On the morning of my first full day of job searching, I take a red pen to the want ads, which are suspiciously numerous. Everyone in Key West's booming "hospitality industry" seems to be looking for someone like me—trainable, flexible, and with suitably humble expectations as to pay. I know I possess certain traits that might be advantageous—I'm white and, I like to think, well-spoken and poised—but I decide on two rules: One, I cannot use any skills derived from my education or usual work—not that there are a lot of want ads for satirical essayists anyway. Two, I have to take the best-paid job that is offered me and of course do my best to hold it[.] * * * In addition, I rule out various occupations for one reason or another: Hotel front-desk clerk, for example, which to my surprise is regarded as unskilled and pays around $7 an hour, gets eliminated because it involves standing in one spot for eight hours a day. Waitressing is similarly something I'd like to avoid, because I remember it leaving me bone tired when I was eighteen, and I'm decades of varicosities and back pain beyond that now. Telemarketing, one of the first refuges of the suddenly indigent, can be dismissed on grounds of personality. This leaves certain supermarket jobs, such as deli clerk, or housekeeping in Key West's thousands of hotel and guest rooms. Housekeeping is especially appealing, for reasons both atavistic and practical: it's what my mother did before I came along, and it can't be too different from what I've been doing part-time, in my own home, all my life.

So I put on what I take to be a respectful-looking outfit of ironed Bermuda shorts and scooped-neck T-shirt and set out for a tour of the local hotels and supermarkets. Best Western, Econo Lodge, and HoJo's all let me fill out application forms, and these are, to my relief, interested in little more than whether I am a legal resident of the United States and have committed any felonies. My next stop is Winn-Dixie, the supermarket, which turns out to have a particularly onerous application process, featuring a fifteen-minute "interview" by computer since, apparently, no human on the premises is deemed capable of representing the corporate point of view. I am conducted to a large room decorated with posters illustrating how to look "professional" (it helps to be white and, if female, permed) and warning of the slick promises that union organizers might try to tempt me with. The interview is multiple choice: Do I have anything, such as child-care problems, that might make it hard for me to get to work on time? Do I think safety on the job is the responsibility of management? Then, popping up cunningly out of the blue: How many dollars' worth of stolen goods have I purchased in the last year? Would I turn in a fellow employee if I caught him stealing? Finally, "Are you an honest person?"

Apparently, I ace the interview, because I am told that all I have to do is show up in some doctor's office tomorrow for a urine test. This seems to be a fairly general rule: if you want to stack Cheerio boxes or vacuum hotel rooms * * * you have to be willing to squat down and pee in front of some health worker (who has no doubt had to do the same thing herself). The wages Winn-Dixie is offering—$6 and a couple of dimes to start with—are not enough, I decide, to compensate for this indignity.[2]

I lunch at Wendy's, where $4.99 gets you unlimited refills at the Mexican part of the Superbar, a comforting surfeit of refried beans and "cheese sauce." A teenage employee, seeing me studying the want ads, kindly offers me an application form, which I fill out, though here, too, the pay is just $6 and change

---

2. According to the *Monthly Labor Review* (November 1996), 28 percent of work sites surveyed in the service industry conduct drug tests (corporate workplaces have much higher rates), and the incidence of testing has risen markedly since the Eighties. The rate of testing is highest in the South (56 percent of work sites polled), with the Midwest in second place (50 percent). The drug most likely to be detected—marijuana, which can be detected in urine for weeks—is also the most innocuous, while heroin and cocaine are generally undetectable three days after use.

an hour. Then it's off for a round of the locally owned inns and guesthouses. At "The Palms," let's call it, a bouncy manager actually takes me around to see the rooms and meet the existing housekeepers, who, I note with satisfaction, look pretty much like me—faded ex-hippie types in shorts with long hair pulled back in braids. Mostly, though, no one speaks to me or even looks at me except to proffer an application form. At my last stop, a palatial B&B, I wait twenty minutes to meet "Max," only to be told that there are no jobs now but there should be one soon, since "nobody lasts more than a couple weeks." (Because none of the people I talked to knew I was a reporter, I have changed their names to protect their privacy and, in some cases perhaps, their jobs.)

Three days go by like this, and, to my chagrin, no one out of the approximately twenty places I've applied calls me for an interview. I had been vain enough to worry about coming across as too educated for the jobs I sought, but no one even seems interested in finding out how overqualified I am. Only later will I realize that the want ads are not a reliable measure of the actual jobs available at any particular time. They are, as I should have guessed from Max's comment, the employers' insurance policy against the relentless turnover of the low-wage work force. Most of the big hotels run ads almost continually, just to build a supply of applicants to replace the current workers as they drift away or are fired, so finding a job is just a matter of being at the right place at the right time and flexible enough to take whatever is being offered that day. This finally happens to me at one of the big discount hotel chains, where I go, as usual, for housekeeping and am sent, instead, to try out as a waitress at the attached "family restaurant," a dismal spot with a counter and about thirty tables that looks out on a parking garage and features such tempting fare as "Pollish [*sic*] sausage and BBQ sauce" on 95-degree days. Phillip, the dapper young West Indian who introduces himself as the manager, interviews me with about as much enthusiasm as if he were a clerk processing me for Medicare, the principal questions being what shifts can I work and when can I start. I mutter something about being woefully out of practice as a waitress, but he's already on to the uniform: I'm to show up tomorrow wearing black slacks and black shoes; he'll provide the rust-colored polo shirt with hearthside embroidered on it, though I might want to wear my own shirt to get to work, ha ha. At the word "tomorrow," something between fear and indignation rises in my chest. I want to say, "Thank you for your time, sir, but this is just an experiment, you know, not my actual life."

So begins my career at the Hearthside, I shall call it, one small profit center within a global discount hotel chain, where for two weeks I work from 2:00 till 10:00 p.m. for $2.43 an hour plus tips.[3] In some futile bid for gentility,

---

3. According to the Fair Labor Standards Act, employers are not required to pay "tipped employees," such as restaurant servers, more than $2.13 an hour in direct wages. However, if the sum of tips plus $2.13 an hour falls below the minimum wage, or $5.15 an hour, the employer is required to make up the difference. This fact was not mentioned by managers or otherwise publicized at either of the restaurants where I worked.

the management has barred employees from using the front door, so my first day I enter through the kitchen, where a red-faced man with shoulder-length blond hair is throwing frozen steaks against the wall and yelling, "Fuck this shit!" "That's just Jack," explains Gail, the wiry middle-aged waitress who is assigned to train me. "He's on the rag again —a condition occasioned, in this instance, by the fact that the cook on the morning shift had forgotten to thaw out the steaks. For the next eight hours, I run after the agile Gail, absorbing bits of instruction along with fragments of personal tragedy. All food must be trayed, and the reason she's so tired today is that she woke up in a cold sweat thinking of her boyfriend, who killed himself recently in an upstate prison. No refills on lemonade. And the reason he was in prison is that a few DUIs caught up with him, that's all, could have happened to anyone. Carry the creamers to the table in a monkey bowl, never in your hand. And after he was gone she spent several months living in her truck, peeing in a plastic pee bottle and reading by candlelight at night, but you can't live in a truck in the summer, since you need to have the windows down, which means anything can get in, from mosquitoes on up.

At least Gail puts to rest any fears I had of appearing overqualified. From the first day on, I find that of all the things I have left behind, such as home and identity, what I miss the most is competence. Not that I have ever felt utterly competent in the writing business, in which one day's success augurs nothing at all for the next. But in my writing life, I at least have some notion of procedure: do the research, make the outline, rough out a draft, etc. As a server, though, I am beset by requests like bees: more iced tea here, ketchup over there, a to-go box for table fourteen, and where are the high chairs, anyway? Of the twenty-seven tables, up to six are usually mine at any time, though on slow afternoons or if Gail is off, I sometimes have the whole place to myself. There is the touch-screen computer-ordering system to master, which is, I suppose, meant to minimize server-cook contact, but in practice requires constant verbal fine-tuning: "That's gravy on the mashed, okay? None on the meatloaf," and so forth—while the cook scowls as if I were inventing these refinements just to torment him. Plus, something I had forgotten in the years since I was eighteen: about a third of a server's job is "side work" that's invisible to customers—sweeping, scrubbing, slicing, refilling, and restocking. If it isn't all done, every little bit of it, you're going to face the 6:00 P.M. dinner rush defenseless and probably go down in flames. I screw up dozens of times at the beginning, sustained in my shame entirely by Gail's support—"It's okay, baby, everyone does that sometime"—because, to my total surprise and despite the scientific detachment I am doing my best to maintain, I care.

The whole thing would be a lot easier if I could just skate through it as Lily Tomlin in one of her waitress skits, but I was raised by the absurd Booker T. Washingtonian precept that says: If you're going to do something, do it well. In fact, "well" isn't good enough by half. Do it better than anyone has ever done it before. Or so said my father, who must have known what he was talking about because he managed to pull himself, and us with him, up from the mile-deep copper mines of Butte to the leafy suburbs of the Northeast, ascending from boilermakers to martinis before booze beat out ambition. As in most endeavors I have encountered in my life, doing it "better than anyone" is not a reasonable goal. Still, when I wake up at 4:00 A.M. in my own cold sweat, I am not thinking about the writing deadlines I'm neglecting; I'm thinking about the table whose order I screwed up so that one of the boys didn't get his kiddie meal until the rest of the family had moved on to their Key Lime pies. That's the other powerful motivation I hadn't expected—the customers, or "patients," as I can't help thinking of them on account of the mysterious vulnerability that seems to have left them temporarily unable to feed themselves. After a few days at the Hearthside, I feel the service ethic kick in like a shot of oxytocin, the nurturance hormone. The plurality of my customers are hardworking locals—truck drivers, construction workers, even housekeepers from the attached hotel—and I want them to have the closest to a "fine dining" experience that the grubby circumstances will allow. No "you guys" for me; everyone over twelve is "sir" or "ma'am." I ply them with iced tea and coffee refills; I return, mid-meal, to inquire how everything is; I doll up their salads with chopped raw mushrooms, summer squash slices, or whatever bits of produce I can find that have survived their sojourn in the cold-storage room mold-free.

* * *

Ten days into it, this is beginning to look like a livable lifestyle. I like Gail, who is "looking at fifty" but moves so fast she can alight in one place and then another without apparently being anywhere between them. I clown around with Lionel, the teenage Haitian busboy, and catch a few fragments of conversation with Joan, the svelte fortyish hostess and militant feminist who is the only one of us who dares to tell Jack to shut the fuck up. I even warm up to Jack when, on a slow night and to make up for a particularly unwarranted attack on my abilities, or so I imagine, he tells me about his glory days as a young man at "coronary school"—or do you say "culinary"?—in Brooklyn, where he dated a knock-out Puerto Rican chick and learned everything there is to know about food. I finish up at 10:00 or 10:30, depending on how much side work I've been able to get done during the shift, and cruise home[.] * * * To bed by 1:30 or 2:00, up at 9:00 or 10:00, read for an hour while my uniform whirls around in the landlord's washing machine, and then it's another eight hours spent following Mao's central instruction, as laid out in the Little Red Book, which was: Serve the people.

I could drift along like this, in some dreamy proletarian idyll, except for two things. One is management. If I have kept this subject on the margins thus far it is because I still flinch to think that I spent all those weeks under the surveillance of men (and later women) whose job it was to monitor my behavior for signs of sloth, theft, drug abuse, or worse. Not that managers and especially "assistant managers" in low-wage settings like this are exactly the class enemy. In the restaurant business, they are mostly former cooks or servers, still capable of pinch-hitting in the kitchen or on the floor, just as in hotels they are likely to be former clerks, and paid a salary of only about $400 a week. But everyone knows they have crossed over to the other side, which is, crudely put, corporate as opposed to human. Cooks want to prepare tasty meals; servers want to serve them graciously; but managers are there for only one reason—to make sure that money is made for some theoretical entity that exists far away in Chicago or New York, if a corporation can be said to have a physical existence at all. Reflecting on her career, Gail tells me ruefully that she had sworn, years ago, never to work for a corporation again. "They don't cut you no slack. You give and you give, and they take."

Managers can sit—for hours at a time if they want—but it's their job to see that no one else ever does, even when there's nothing to do, and this is why, for servers, slow times can be as exhausting as rushes. You start dragging out each little chore, because if the manager on duty catches you in an idle moment, he will give you something far nastier to do. So I wipe, I clean, I consolidate ketchup bottles and recheck the cheesecake supply, even tour the tables to make sure the customer evaluation forms are all standing perkily in their places—wondering all the time how many calories I burn in these strictly theatrical exercises. When, on a particularly dead afternoon, Stu finds me glancing at a *USA Today* a customer has left behind, he assigns me to vacuum the entire floor with the broken vacuum cleaner that has a handle only two feet long, and the only way to do that without incurring orthopedic damage is to proceed from spot to spot on your knees.

On my first Friday at the Hearthside there is a "mandatory meeting for all restaurant employees," which I attend, eager for insight into our overall marketing strategy and the niche (your basic Ohio cuisine with a tropical twist?) we aim to inhabit. But there is no "we" at this meeting. Phillip, our top manager except for an occasional "consultant" sent out by corporate headquarters, opens it with a sneer: "The break room—it's disgusting. Butts in the ashtrays, newspapers lying around, crumbs." This windowless little room, which also houses the time clock for the entire hotel, is where we stash our bags and civilian clothes and take our half-hour meal breaks. But a break room is not a right, he tells us. It can be taken away. We should also know that the lockers in the break room and whatever is in them can be searched at any time. Then comes gossip; there has been gossip; gossip (which seems to mean employees talking among themselves) must stop. Off-duty employees are henceforth barred from eating at the restaurant, because "other servers gather around them and gossip." When Phillip has exhausted his agenda of rebukes, Joan complains about the condition of the ladies' room and I throw in my two bits about the vacuum cleaner. But I don't see any backup coming from my fellow servers, each of whom has subsided into her own personal funk; Gail, my role model, stares sorrowfully at a point six inches from her nose. The meeting ends when Andy, one of the cooks, gets up, muttering about breaking up his day off for this almighty bullshit.

Just four days later we are suddenly summoned into the kitchen at 3:30 P.M., even though there are live tables on the floor. We all—about ten of us—stand around Phillip, who announces grimly that there has been a report of some "drug activity" on the night shift and that, as a result, we are now to be a "drug-free" workplace, meaning that all new hires will be tested, as will possibly current employees on a random basis. I am glad that this part of the kitchen is so dark, because I find myself blushing as hard as if I had been caught toking up in the ladies' room myself: I haven't been treated this way—lined up in the corridor, threatened with locker searches, peppered with carelessly aimed accusations—since junior high school.

* * *

The other problem, in addition to the less-than-nurturing management style, is that this job shows no sign of being financially viable. You might imagine, from a comfortable distance, that people who live, year in and year out, on $6 to $10 an hour have discovered some survival stratagems unknown to the middle class. But no. It's not hard to get my co-workers to talk about their living situations, because housing, in almost every case, is the principal source of disruption in their lives, the first thing they fill you in on when they arrive for their shifts. After a week, I have compiled the following survey:

- Gail is sharing a room in a well-known downtown flophouse for which she and a roommate pay about $250 a week. Her roommate, a male friend, has begun hitting on her, driving her nuts, but the rent would be impossible alone.
- Claude, the Haitian cook, is desperate to get out of the two-room apartment he shares with his girlfriend and two other, unrelated, people. As far as I can determine, the other Haitian men (most of whom only speak Creole) live in similarly crowded situations.
- Annette, a twenty-year-old server who is six months pregnant and has been abandoned by her boyfriend, lives with her mother, a postal clerk.
- Marianne and her boyfriend are paying $ 170 a week for a one-person trailer.
- Jack, who is, at $10 an hour, the wealthiest of us, lives in the trailer he owns, paying only the $400-a-month lot fee.
- The other white cook, Andy, lives on his dry-docked boat, which, as far as I can tell from his loving descriptions, can't be more than twenty feet long. He offers to take me out on it, once it's repaired, but the offer comes with inquiries as to my marital status, so I do not follow up on it.
- Tina and her husband are paying $60 a night for a double room in a Days Inn. This is because they have no car and the Days Inn is within walking distance of the Hearthside. When Marianne, one of the breakfast

servers, is tossed out of her trailer for subletting (which is against the trailer-park rules), she leaves her boyfriend and moves in with Tina and her husband.

■ Joan, who had fooled me with her numerous and tasteful outfits (hostesses wear their own clothes), lives in a van she parks behind a shopping center at night and showers in Tina's motel room. The clothes are from thrift shops.[4]

It strikes me, in my middle-class solipsism, that there is gross improvidence in some of these arrangements. When Gail and I are wrapping silverware in napkins—the only task for which we are permitted to sit—she tells me she is thinking of escaping from her roommate by moving into the Days Inn herself. I am astounded: How can she even think of paying between $40 and $60 a day? But if I was afraid of sounding like a social worker, I come out just sounding like a fool. She squints at me in disbelief, "And where am I supposed to get a month's rent and a month's deposit for an apartment?" I'd been feeling pretty smug about my $500 efficiency, but of course it was made possible only by the $1,300 I had allotted myself for start-up costs when I began my low-wage life: $1,000 for the first month's rent and deposit, $100 for initial groceries and cash in my pocket, $200 stuffed away for emergencies. In poverty, as in certain propositions in physics, starting conditions are everything.

There are no secret economies that nourish the poor; on the contrary, there are a host of special costs. If you can't put up the two months' rent you need to secure an apartment, you end up paying through the nose for a room by the week. If you have only a room, with a hot plate at best, you can't save by cooking up huge lentil stews that can be frozen for the week ahead. You eat fast food, or the hot dogs and styrofoam cups of soup that can be microwaved in a convenience store. If you have no money for health insurance—and the Hearthside's niggardly plan kicks in only after three months—you go without routine care or prescription drugs and end up paying the price.

* * *

My own situation, when I sit down to assess it after two weeks of work, would not be much better if this were my actual life. The seductive thing about waitressing is that you don't have to wait for payday to feel a few bills in your pocket, and my tips usually cover meals and gas, plus something left over to stuff into the kitchen drawer I use as a bank. But as the tourist business slows in the summer heat, I sometimes leave work with only $20 in tips (the gross is

---

4. I could find no statistics on the number of employed people living in cars or vans, but according to the National Coalition for the Homeless's 1997 report "Myths and Facts About Homelessness," nearly one in five homeless people (in twenty-nine cities across the nation) is employed in a full- or part-time job.

higher, but servers share about 15 percent of their tips with the busboys and bartenders). With wages included, this amounts to about the minimum wage of $5.15 an hour. Although the sum in the drawer is piling up, at the present rate of accumulation it will be more than a hundred dollars short of my rent when the end of the month comes around. Nor can I see any expenses to cut. True, I haven't gone the lentil-stew route yet, but that's because I don't have a large cooking pot, pot holders, or a ladle to stir with (which cost about $30 at Kmart, less at thrift stores), not to mention onions, carrots, and the indispensable bay leaf. I do make my lunch almost every day—usually some slow-burning, high-protein combo like frozen chicken patties with melted cheese on top and canned pinto beans on the side. Dinner is at the Hearthside, which offers its employees a choice of BLT, fish sandwich, or hamburger for only $2. The burger lasts longest, especially if it's heaped with gut-puckering jalapeños, but by midnight my stomach is growling again.

So unless I want to start using my car as a residence, I have to find a second, or alternative, job. I call all the hotels where I filled out housekeeping applications weeks ago—the Hyatt, Holiday Inn, Econo Lodge, HoJo's, Best Western, plus a half dozen or so locally run guesthouses. Nothing. Then I start making the rounds again, wasting whole mornings waiting for some assistant manager to show up, even dipping into places so creepy that the front-desk clerk greets you from behind bulletproof glass and sells pints of liquor over the counter. But either someone has exposed my real-life housekeeping habits—which are, shall we say, mellow—or I am at the wrong end of some infallible ethnic equation: most, but by no means all, of the working housekeepers I see on my job searches are African Americans, Spanish-speaking, or immigrants from the Central European post-Communist world, whereas servers are almost invariably white and monolingually English-speaking. When I finally get a positive response, I have been identified once again as server material. Jerry's, which is part of a well-known national family restaurant chain and physically attached here to another budget hotel chain, is ready to use me at once. The prospect is both exciting and terrifying, because, with about the same number of tables and counter seats, Jerry's attracts three or four times the volume of customers as the gloomy old Hearthside.

Picture a fat person's hell, and I don't mean a place with no food. Instead there is everything you might eat if eating had no bodily consequences—cheese fries, chicken-fried steaks, fudge-laden desserts—only here every bite must be paid for, one way or another, in human discomfort. The kitchen is a cavern, a stomach leading to the lower intestine that is the garbage and dish-washing area, from which issue bizarre smells combining the edible and the offal: creamy carrion, pizza barf, and that unique and enigmatic Jerry's scent—citrus fart. The floor is slick with spills, forcing us to walk through the kitchen with tiny steps[.] * * * Sinks everywhere are clogged with scraps of lettuce, decomposing lemon wedges, waterlogged toast crusts. Put your hand down on any counter and you risk being stuck to it by the film of ancient syrup spills, and this is unfortunate, because hands are utensils here, used for scooping up lettuce onto salad plates, lifting out pie slices, and even moving hash browns from one plate to another. The regulation poster in the single unisex restroom admonishes us to wash our hands thoroughly and even offers instructions for doing so, but there is always some vital substance missing— soap, paper towels, toilet paper—and I never find all three at once. You learn to stuff your pockets with napkins before going in there, and too bad about the customers, who must eat, though they don't realize this, almost literally out of our hands.

The break room typifies the whole situation: there is none, because there are no breaks at Jerry's. For six to eight hours in a row, you never sit except to pee. Actually, there are three folding chairs at a table immediately adjacent to the bathroom, but hardly anyone ever sits here, in the very rectum of the gastro-architectural system. Rather, the function of the peritoilet area is to house the ashtrays in which servers and dishwashers leave their cigarettes burning at all times, like votive candles, so that they don't have to waste time lighting up again when they dash back for a puff. Almost everyone smokes as if his or her pulmonary well-being depended on it—the multinational mélange of cooks, the Czech dishwashers, the servers, who are all American natives— creating an atmosphere in which oxygen is only an occasional pollutant. My first morning at Jerry's, when the hypoglycemic shakes set in, I complain to one of my fellow servers that I don't understand how she can go so long without food. "Well, I don't understand how you can go so long without a cigarette," she responds in a tone of reproach—because work is what you do for others; smoking is what you do for yourself. I don't know why the anti-smoking crusaders have never grasped the element of defiant self-nurturance that makes the habit so endearing to its victims—as if, in the American workplace, the only thing people have to call their own is the tumors they are nourishing and the spare moments they devote to feeding them.

Now, the Industrial Revolution is not an easy transition, especially when you have to zip through it in just a couple of days. I have gone from craft work straight into the factory, from the air-conditioned morgue of the Hearth-side directly into the flames. Customers arrive in human waves, sometimes disgorged fifty at a time from their tour buses, peckish and whiny. Instead of two "girls" on the floor at once, there can be as many as six of us running around in our brilliant pink-and-orange Hawaiian shirts.

* * *

I start out with the beautiful, heroic idea of handling the two jobs at once, and for two days I almost do it: the breakfast/lunch shift at Jerry's, which goes till 2:00, arriving at the Hearthside at 2:10, and attempting to hold out until 10:00. In the ten minutes between jobs, I pick up a spicy chicken sandwich at the Wendy's drive-through window, gobble it down in the car, and change from khaki slacks to black, from Hawaiian to rust polo. There is a problem, though. When during the 3:00 to 4:00 P.M. dead time I finally sit down to wrap silver, my flesh seems to bond to the seat. I try to refuel with a purloined cup of soup, as I've seen Gail and Joan do dozens of times, but a manager catches me and hisses "No eating!" though there's not a customer around to be offended by the sight of food making contact with a server's lips. So I tell Gail I'm going to quit, and she hugs me and says she might just follow me to Jerry's herself.

But the chances of this are minuscule. She has left the flophouse and her annoying roommate and is back to living in her beat-up old truck. But guess what? she reports to me excitedly later that evening: Phillip has given her permission to park overnight in the hotel parking lot, as long as she keeps out of sight, and the parking lot should be totally safe, since it's patrolled by a hotel security guard! With the Hearthside offering benefits like that, how could anyone think of leaving?

Gail would have triumphed at Jerry's, I'm sure, but for me it's a crash course in exhaustion management. Years ago, the kindly fry cook who trained me to waitress at a Los Angeles truck stop used to say: Never make an unnecessary trip; if you don't have to walk fast, walk slow; if you don't have to walk, stand. But at Jerry's the effort of distinguishing necessary from unnecessary and urgent from whenever would itself be too much of an energy drain. The only thing to do is to treat each shift as a one-time-only emergency; you've got fifty starving people out there, lying scattered on the battlefield, so get out there and feed them! Forget that you will have to do this again tomorrow, forget that you will have to be alert enough to dodge the drunks on the drive home tonight—just burn, burn, burn! Ideally, at some point you enter what servers call "a rhythm" and psychologists term a "flow state," in which signals pass from the sense organs directly to the muscles, bypassing the cerebral cortex, and a Zen-like emptiness sets in. * * *

But there's another capacity of the neuromuscular system, which is pain. I start tossing back drugstore-brand ibuprofen pills as if they were vitamin C, four before each shift, because an old mouse-related repetitive-stress injury in my upper back has come back to full-spasm strength, thanks to the tray carrying. In my ordinary life, this level of disability might justify a day of ice packs and stretching.

* * *

I make friends, over time, with the other "girls" who work my shift: Nita, the tattooed twenty-something who taunts us by going around saying brightly, "Have we started making money yet?" Ellen, whose teenage son cooks on the graveyard shift and who once managed a restaurant in Massachusetts but won't try out for management here because she prefers being a "common worker" and not "ordering people around." Easy-going fiftyish Lucy, with the raucous laugh, who limps toward the end of the shift because of something that has gone wrong with her leg, the exact nature of which cannot be determined without health insurance. We talk about the usual girl things—men, children, and the sinister allure of Jerry's chocolate peanut-butter cream pie—though no one, I notice, ever brings up anything potentially expensive, like shopping or movies. As at the Hearthside, the only recreation ever referred to is partying, which requires little more than some beer, a joint, and a few close friends. Still, no one here is homeless, or cops to it anyway, thanks usually to a working husband or boyfriend. All in all, we form a reliable mutual-support group: If one of us is feeling sick or overwhelmed, another one will "bev" a table or even carry trays for her. If one of us is off sneaking a cigarette or a pee,[5] the others will do their best to conceal her absence from the enforcers of corporate rationality.

But my saving human connection—my oxytocin receptor, as it were—is George, the nineteen-year-old, fresh-off-the-boat Czech dishwasher. We get to talking when he asks me, tortuously, how much cigarettes cost at Jerry's. I do my best to explain that they cost over a dollar more here than at a regular store and suggest that he just take one from the half-filled packs that are always lying around on the break table. But that would be unthinkable. Except for the one tiny earring signaling his allegiance to some vaguely alternative point of view, George is a perfect straight arrow—crew-cut, hardworking, and hungry for eye contact. "Czech Republic," I ask, "or Slovakia?" and he seems delighted that I know the difference. "Václav Havel," I try. "Velvet Revolution, Frank Zappa!" "Yes, yes, 1989," he says, and I realize we are talking about history.

* * *

I make the decision to move closer to Key West. First, because of the drive. Second and third, also because of the drive: gas is eating up $4 to $5 a day, and although Jerry's is as high-volume as you can get, the tips average only 10 percent, and not just for a newbie like me. Between the base pay of $2.15 an hour and the obligation to share tips with the busboys and dishwashers, we're averaging only about $7.50 an hour. Then there is the $30 I had to spend on the regulation tan slacks worn by Jerry's servers—a setback it could take

---

5. Until April 1998, there was no federally mandated right to bathroom breaks. According to Marc Linder and Ingrid Nygaard, authors of *Void Where Prohibited: Rest Breaks and the Right to Urinate on Company Time* (Cornell University Press, 1997), "The right to rest and void at work is not high on the list of social or political causes supported by professional or executive employees, who enjoy personal workplace liberties that millions of factory workers can only daydream about.... While we were dismayed to discover that workers lacked an acknowledged legal right to void at work, [the workers] were amazed by outsiders' naive belief that their employers would permit them to perform this basic bodily function when necessary.... A factory worker, not allowed a break for six-hour stretches, voided into pads worn inside her uniform; and a kindergarten teacher in a school without aides had to take all twenty children with her to the bathroom and line them up outside the stall door when she voided."

weeks to absorb. (I had combed the town's two downscale department stores hoping for something cheaper but decided in the end that these marked-down Dockers, originally $49, were more likely to survive a daily washing.) Of my fellow servers, everyone who lacks a working husband or boyfriend seems to have a second job: Nita does something at a computer eight hours a day; another welds. Without the forty-five-minute commute, I can picture myself working two jobs and having the time to shower between them.

So I take the $500 deposit I have coming from my landlord, the $400 I have earned toward the next month's rent, plus the $200 reserved for emergencies, and use the $1,100 to pay the rent and deposit on trailer number 46 in the Overseas Trailer Park, a mile from the cluster of budget hotels that constitute Key West's version of an industrial park. Number 46 is about eight feet in width and shaped like a barbell inside, with a narrow region—because of the sink and the stove—separating the bedroom from what might optimistically be called the "living" area, with its two-person table and half-sized couch. The bathroom is so small my knees rub against the shower stall when I sit on the toilet, and you can't just leap out of the bed, you have to climb down to the foot of it in order to find a patch of floor space to stand on. Outside, I am within a few yards of a liquor store, a bar that advertises "free beer tomorrow," a convenience store, and a Burger King—but no supermarket or, alas, laundromat. By reputation, the Overseas park is a nest of crime and crack, and I am hoping at least for some vibrant, multicultural street life. But desolation rules night and day, except for a thin stream of pedestrian traffic heading for their jobs at the Sheraton or 7-Eleven. There are not exactly people here but what amounts to canned labor, being preserved from the heat between shifts.

In line with my reduced living conditions, a new form of ugliness arises at Jerry's. First we are confronted—via an announcement on the computers through which we input orders—with the new rule that the hotel bar is henceforth off-limits to restaurant employees. The culprit, I learn through the grapevine, is the ultra-efficient gal who trained me—another trailer-home dweller and a mother of three. Something had set her off one morning, so she slipped out for a nip and returned to the floor impaired. This mostly hurts Ellen, whose habit it is to free her hair from its rubber band and drop by the bar for a couple of Zins before heading home at the end of the shift, but all of us feel the chill. Then the next day, when I go for straws, for the first time I find the dry-storage room locked. Ted, the portly assistant manager who opens it for me, explains that he caught one of the dishwashers attempting to steal something, and, unfortunately, the miscreant will be with us until a replacement can be found—hence the locked door. I neglect to ask what he had been trying to steal, but Ted tells me who he is—the kid with the buzz cut and the earring [George].

* * *

When my month-long plunge into poverty is almost over, I finally land my dream job—housekeeping. I do this by walking into the personnel office of the only place I figure I might have some credibility, the hotel attached to Jerry's, and confiding urgently that I have to have a second job if I am to pay my rent and, no, it couldn't be front-desk clerk. "All right," the personnel lady fairly spits, "So it's housekeeping," and she marches me back to meet Maria, the housekeeping manager, a tiny, frenetic Hispanic woman who greets me as "babe" and hands me a pamphlet emphasizing the need for a positive attitude. The hours are nine in the morning till whenever, the pay is $6.10 an hour, and there's one week of vacation a year. I don't have to ask about health insurance once I meet Carlotta, the middle-aged African-American woman who will be training me. Carla, as she tells me to call her, is missing all of her top front teeth.

On that first day of housekeeping and last day of my entire project—although I don't yet know it's the last—Carla is in a foul mood. We have been given nineteen rooms to clean, most of them "checkouts," as opposed to "stay-overs," that require the whole enchilada of bed-stripping, vacuuming, and bathroom-scrubbing. When one of the rooms that had been listed as a stay-over turns out to be a checkout, Carla calls Maria to complain, but of course to no avail. "So make up the motherfucker," Carla orders me, and I do the beds while she sloshes around the bathroom. For four hours without a break I strip and remake beds, taking about four and a half minutes per queen-sized bed, which I could get down to three if there were any reason to. We try to avoid vacuuming by picking up the larger specks by hand, but often there is nothing to do but drag the monstrous vacuum cleaner—it weighs about thirty pounds—off our cart and try to wrestle it around the floor. Sometimes Carla hands me the squirt bottle of "BAM" (an acronym for something that begins, ominously, with "butyric"; the rest has been worn off the label) and lets me do the bathrooms. No service ethic challenges me here to new heights of perfor-mance. I just concentrate on removing the pubic hairs from the bathtubs, or at least the dark ones that I can see.

I had looked forward to the breaking-and-entering aspect of cleaning the stay-overs, the chance to examine the secret, physical existence of strangers. But the contents of the rooms are always banal and surprisingly neat—zipped up shaving kits, shoes lined up against the wall (there are no closets), flyers for snorkeling trips, maybe an empty wine bottle or two. It is the TV that keeps us going, from *Jerry* to *Sally* to *Hawaii Five-O* and then on to the soaps. If there's something especially arresting, like "Won't Take No for an Answer" on *Jerry,* we sit down on the edge of a bed and giggle for a moment as if this were a pajama party instead of a terminally dead-end job. The soaps are the best, and Carla turns the volume up full blast so that she won't miss anything from the bathroom or while the vacuum is on. In room 503, Marcia confronts Jeff about Lauren. In 505, Lauren taunts poor cuckolded Marcia. In 511, Helen offers Amanda $10,000 to stop seeing Eric, prompting Carla to emerge from the bathroom to study Amanda's troubled face. "You take it, girl," she advises. "I would for sure."

The tourists' rooms that we clean and, beyond them, the far more expensively appointed interiors in the soaps, begin after a while to merge. We have entered a better world—a world of comfort where every day is a day off, waiting to be filled up with sexual intrigue. We, however, are only gate-crashers in this fantasy, forced to pay for our presence with backaches and perpetual thirst. The mirrors, and there are far too many of them in hotel rooms, contain the kind of person you would normally find pushing a shopping cart down a city street—bedraggled, dressed in a damp hotel polo shirt two sizes too large, and with sweat dribbling down her chin like drool. I am enormously relieved when Carla announces a half-hour meal break, but my appetite fades when I see that the bag of hot-dog rolls she has been carrying around on our cart is not trash salvaged from a checkout but what she has brought for her lunch.

When I request permission to leave at about 3:30, another housekeeper warns me that no one has so far succeeded in combining housekeeping at the hotel with serving at Jerry's: "Some kid did it once for five days, and you're no kid." With that helpful information in mind, I rush back to number 46, down four Advils (the name brand this time), shower, stooping to fit into the stall, and attempt to compose myself for the oncoming shift. So much for what Marx termed the "reproduction of labor power," meaning the things a worker has to do just so she'll be ready to work again. The only unforeseen obstacle to the smooth transition from job to job is that my tan Jerry's slacks, which had looked reasonably clean by 40-watt bulb last night when I handwashed my Hawaiian shirt, prove by daylight to be mottled with ketchup and ranch-dressing stains. I spend most of my hour-long break between jobs attempting to remove the edible portions with a sponge and then drying the slacks over the hood of my car in the sun.

I can do this two-job thing, is my theory, if I can drink enough caffeine and avoid getting distracted by George's ever more obvious suffering.[6]

* * *

I resolve to give him all my tips that night and to hell with the experiment in low-wage money management. At eight, Ellen and I grab a snack together standing at the mephitic end of the kitchen counter, but I can only manage two

6. In 1996, the number of persons holding two or more jobs averaged 7.8 million, or 6.2 percent of the workforce. It was about the same rate for men and for women (6.1 versus 6.2), though the kinds of jobs differ by gender. About two thirds of multiple jobholders work one job full-time and the other part-time. Only a heroic minority—4 percent of men and 2 percent of women—work two full-time jobs simultaneously. (From John F. Stinson Jr., "New Data on Multiple Jobholding Available from the CPS," in the *Monthly Labor Review,* March 1997.)

or three mozzarella sticks and lunch had been a mere handful of Mc-Nuggets. I am not tired at all, I assure myself, though it may be that there is simply no more "I" left to do the tiredness monitoring. What I would see, if I were more alert to the situation, is that the forces of destruction are already massing against me. There is only one cook on duty, a young man named Jesus ("Hay-Sue," that is) and he is new to the job. And there is Joy, who shows up to take over in the middle of the shift, wearing high heels and a long, clingy white dress and fuming as if she'd just been stood up in some cocktail bar.

Then it comes, the perfect storm. Four of my tables fill up at once. Four tables is nothing for me now, but only so long as they are obligingly staggered. As I bev table 27, tables 25, 28, and 24 are watching enviously. As I bev 25, 24 glowers because their bevs haven't even been ordered. Twenty-eight is four yuppyish types, meaning everything on the side and agonizing instructions as to the chicken Caesars. Twenty-five is a middle-aged black couple, who complain, with some justice, that the iced tea isn't fresh and the tabletop is sticky. But table 24 is the meteorological event of the century: ten British tourists who seem to have made the decision to absorb the American experience entirely by mouth. Here everyone has at least two drinks—iced tea and milk shake, Michelob and water (with lemon slice, please)—and a huge promiscuous orgy of breakfast specials, mozz sticks, chicken strips, quesadillas, burgers with cheese and without, sides of hash browns with cheddar, with onions, with gravy, seasoned fries, plain fries, banana splits. Poor Jesus! Poor me! Because when I arrive with their first tray of food—after three prior trips just to refill bevs—Princess Di refuses to eat her chicken strips with her pancake-and-sausage special, since, as she now reveals, the strips were meant to be an appetizer. Maybe the others would have accepted their meals, but Di, who is deep into her third Michelob, insists that everything else go back while they work on their "starters." Meanwhile, the yuppies are waving me down for more decaf and the black couple looks ready to summon the NAACP.

Much of what happened next is lost in the fog of war. Jesus starts going under. The little printer on the counter in front of him is spewing out orders faster than he can rip them off, much less produce the meals. Even the invincible Ellen is ashen from stress. I bring table 24 their reheated main courses, which they immediately reject as either too cold or fossilized by the microwave. When I return to the kitchen with their trays (three trays in three trips), Joy confronts me with arms akimbo: "What is this?" She means the food—the plates of rejected pancakes, hash browns in assorted flavors, toasts, burgers, sausages, eggs. "Uh, scrambled with cheddar," I try, "and that's . . ." "NO," she screams in my face. "Is it a traditional, a super-scramble, an eye-opener?" I pretend to study my check for a clue, but entropy has been up to its tricks, not only on the plates but in my head, and I have to admit that the original order is beyond reconstruction. "You don't know an eye-opener from a traditional?" she demands in outrage. All I know, in fact, is that my legs have lost interest in the current venture and have announced their intention to fold.

I am saved by a yuppie (mercifully not one of mine) who chooses this moment to charge into the kitchen to bellow that his food is twenty-five minutes late. Joy screams at him to get the hell out of her kitchen, please, and then turns on Jesus in a fury, hurling an empty tray across the room for emphasis.

I leave. I don't walk out, I just leave. I don't finish my side work or pick up my credit-card tips, if any, at the cash register or, of course, ask Joy's permission to go. And the surprising thing is that you can walk out without permission, that the door opens, that the thick tropical night air parts to let me pass, that my car is still parked where I left it. There is no vindication in this exit, no fuck-you surge of relief, just an overwhelming, dank sense of failure pressing down on me and the entire parking lot. I had gone into this venture in the spirit of science, to test a mathematical proposition, but somewhere along the line, in the tunnel vision imposed by long shifts and relentless concentration, it became a test of myself, and clearly I have failed. Not only had I flamed out as a housekeeper/server, I had even forgotten to give George my tips, and, for reasons perhaps best known to hardworking, generous people like Gail and Ellen, this hurts. I don't cry, but I am in a position to realize, for the first time in many years, that the tear ducts are still there, and still capable of doing their job.

When I moved out of the trailer park, I gave the key to number 46 to Gail and arranged for my deposit to be transferred to her. She told me that Joan is still living in her van and that Stu had been fired from the Hearthside. I never found out what happened to George.

In one month, I had earned approximately $1,040 and spent $517 on food, gas, toiletries, laundry, phone, and utilities. If I had remained in my $500 efficiency, I would have been able to pay the rent and have $22 left over (which is $78 less than the cash I had in my pocket at the start of the month). During this time I bought no clothing except for the required slacks and no prescription drugs or medical care (I did finally buy some vitamin B to compensate for the lack of vegetables in my diet). Perhaps I could have saved a little on food if I had gotten to a supermarket more often, instead of convenience stores, but it should be noted that I lost almost four pounds in four weeks, on a diet weighted heavily toward burgers and fries.

How former welfare recipients and single mothers will (and do) survive in the low-wage workforce, I cannot imagine. Maybe they will figure out how to condense their lives—including child-raising, laundry, romance, and meals—into the couple of hours between full-time jobs. Maybe they will take up residence in their vehicles, if they have one. All I know is that I couldn't hold two jobs and I couldn't make enough money to live on with one. And I had advantages unthinkable to many of the long-term poor—health, stamina, a working car, and no children to care for and support. Certainly nothing in my experience contradicts the conclusion of Kathryn Edin and Laura Lein, in their recent book *Making Ends Meet: How Single Mothers Survive Welfare and Low-Wage Work*, that low-wage work actually involves more hardship and deprivation than life at the mercy of the welfare state. In the coming months and years, economic conditions for the working poor are bound to worsen, even without the almost inevitable recession. As mentioned earlier, the influx of former welfare recipients into the low-skilled workforce will have a depressing effect on both wages and the number of jobs available. A general economic downturn will only enhance these effects, and the working poor will of course be facing it without the slight, but nonetheless often saving, protection of welfare as a backup.

The thinking behind welfare reform was that even the humblest jobs are morally uplifting and psychologically buoying. In reality they are likely to be fraught with insult and stress. But I did discover one redeeming feature of the most abject low-wage work—the camaraderie of people who are, in almost all cases, far too smart and funny and caring for the work they do and the wages they're paid. The hope, of course, is that someday these people will come to know what they're worth, and take appropriate action.

24

Manifesto of the Communist Party

KARL MARX AND FRIEDRICH ENGELS

Europe in the eighteenth and nineteenth centuries changed dramatically with the onset of in-dustrialization and the phenomenal growth of cities. While some writers saw great promise of abundance and freedom in these changes, the reality for millions of people was increased labor and grinding poverty. Karl Marx (1818–1883) was one of the nineteenth century's most articulate critics of the disparity between possibility and reality. Here he and his collaborator, Friedrich Engels, explain the reasons for this in their pamphlet written for workers.

I. BOURGEOIS AND PROLETARIANS[1]

The history of all hitherto existing society[2] is the history of class struggles.

Freeman and slave, patrician and plebeian, lord and serf, guild-master[3] and journeyman, in a word, oppressor and oppressed, stood in constant opposition to one another, carried on an uninterrupted, now hidden, now open fight, a fight that each time ended, either in a revolutionary re-constitution of society at large, or in the common ruin of the contending classes.

In the earlier epochs of history, we find almost everywhere a complicated arrangement of society into various orders, a manifold gradation of social rank. In ancient Rome we have patricians, knights, plebeians, slaves; in the

---

1. By bourgeoisie is meant the class of modern Capitalists, owners of the means of social production and employers of wage-labour. By proletariat, the class of modern wage-labourers who, having no means of production of their own, are reduced to selling their labour-power in order to live. [*Engels, English edition of 1888*]

2. That is, all *written* history. In 1847, the pre-history of society, the social organisation existing previous to recorded history, was all but unknown. Since then, Haxthausen discovered common ownership of land in Russia, Maurer proved it to be the social foundation from which all Teutonic races started in history, and by and by village communities were found to be, or to have been the primitive form of society everywhere from India to Ireland. The inner organisation of this primitive Communistic society was laid bare, in its typical form, by Morgan's crowning discovery of the true nature of the *gens* and its relation to the *tribe.* With the dissolution of these primaeval communities society begins to be differentiated into separate and finally antagonistic classes. I have attempted to retrace this process of dissolution in: "Der Ursprung der Familie, des Privateigenthums und des Staats" [*The Origin of the Family, Private Property and the State*], 2nd edition, Stuttgart 1886. [*Engels, English edition of 1888*]

3. Guild-master, that is, a full member of a guild, a master within, not a head of a guild. [*Engels, English edition of 1888*]

Middle Ages, feudal lords, vassals, guild-masters, journey-men, apprentices, serfs; in almost all of these classes, again, subordinate gradations.

The modern bourgeois society that has sprouted from the ruins of feudal society has not done away with class antagonisms. It has but established new classes, new conditions of oppression, new forms of struggle in place of the old ones.

Our epoch, the epoch of the bourgeoisie, possesses, however, this distinctive feature: it has simplified the class antagonisms: Society as a whole is more and more splitting up into two great hostile camps, into two great classes directly facing each other: Bourgeoisie and Proletariat.

From the serfs of the Middle Ages sprang the chartered burghers of the earliest towns. From these burgesses the first elements of the bourgeoisie were developed.

The discovery of America, the rounding of the Cape, opened up fresh ground for the rising bourgeoisie. The East-Indian and Chinese markets, the colonisation of America, trade with the colonies, the increase in the means of exchange and in commodities generally, gave to commerce, to navigation, to industry, an impulse never before known, and thereby, to the revolutionary element in the tottering feudal society, a rapid development.

The feudal system of industry, under which industrial production was monopolised by closed guilds, now no longer sufficed for the growing wants of the new markets. The manufacturing system took its place. The guild-masters were pushed on one side by the manufacturing middle class; division of labour between the different corporate guilds vanished in the face of division of labour in each single workshop.

Meantime the markets kept ever growing, the demand ever rising. Even manufacture no longer sufficed. Thereupon, steam and machinery revolutionised industrial production. The place of manufacture was taken by the giant, Modern Industry, the place of the industrial middle class, by industrial millionaires, the leaders of whole industrial armies, the modern bourgeois.

Modern industry has established the world-market, for which the discovery of America paved the way. This market has given an immense development to commerce, to navigation, to communication by land. This development has, in its turn, reacted on the extension of industry; and in proportion as industry, commerce, navigation, railways extended, in the same proportion the bourgeoisie developed, increased its capital, and pushed into the background every class handed down from the Middle Ages.

We see, therefore, how the modern bourgeoisie is itself the product of a long course of development, of a series of revolutions in the modes of production and of exchange.

Each step in the development of the bourgeoisie was accompanied by a corresponding political advance of that class. An oppressed class under the sway of the feudal nobility, an armed and self-governing association in the mediaeval commune;[4] here independent urban republic (as in Italy and Germany), there taxable "third estate" of the monarchy (as in France), afterwards, in the period of manufacture proper, serving either the semi-feudal or the absolute monarchy as a counterpoise against the nobility, and, in fact, corner-stone of the great monarchies in general, the bourgeoisie has at last, since the establishment of Modern Industry and of the world-market, conquered for itself, in the modern representative State, exclusive political sway. The executive of the modem State is but a committee for managing the common affairs of the whole bourgeoisie.

The bourgeoisie, historically, has played a most revolutionary part.

The bourgeoisie, wherever it has got the upper hand, has put an end to all feudal, patriarchal, idyllic relations. It has pitilessly torn asunder the motley feudal ties that bound man to his "natural superiors," and has left remaining no other nexus between man and man than naked self-interest, than callous "cash payment." It has drowned the most heavenly ecstasies of religious fervour, of chivalrous enthusiasm, of philistine sentimentalism, in the icy water of egotistical calculation. It has resolved personal worth into exchange value, and in place of the numberless indefeasible chartered freedoms, has set up that single, unconscionable freedom—Free Trade. In one word, for exploitation, veiled by religious and political illusions, it has substituted naked, shameless, direct, brutal exploitation.

The bourgeoisie has stripped of its halo every occupation hitherto honoured and looked up to with reverent awe. It has converted the physician, the lawyer, the priest, the poet, the man of science, into its paid wage-labourers.

The bourgeoisie has torn away from the family its sentimental veil, and has reduced the family relation to a mere money relation.

The bourgeoisie has disclosed how it came to pass that the brutal display of vigour in the Middle Ages, which Reactionists so much admire, found its fitting complement in the most slothful indolence. It has been the first to show what man's activity can bring about. It has accomplished wonders far surpassing Egyptian pyramids, Roman aqueducts, and Gothic cathedrals; it has conducted expeditions that put in the shade all former Exoduses of nations and crusades.

The bourgeoisie cannot exist without constantly revolutionising the instruments of production, and thereby the relations of production, and with them

---

4. "Commune" was the name taken, in France, by the nascent towns even before they had conquered from their feudal lords and masters local self-government and political rights as the "Third Estate." Generally speaking, for the economical development of the bourgeoisie, England is here taken as the typical country; for its political development, France. [*Engels, English edition of 1888*]

This was the name given their urban communities by the townsmen of Italy and France, after they had purchased or wrested their initial rights of self-government from their feudal lords. [*Engels, Gentian edition of 1890*] the whole relations of society. Conservation of the old modes of production in unaltered form, was, on the contrary, the first condition of existence for all earlier industrial classes. Constant revolutionising of production, uninterrupted disturbance of all social conditions, everlasting uncertainty and agitation distinguish the bourgeois epoch from all earlier ones. All fixed, fast-frozen relations, with their train of ancient and venerable prejudices and opinions, are swept away, all new-formed ones become antiquated before they can ossify. All that is solid melts into air, all that is holy is profaned, and man is at last compelled to face with sober senses, his real conditions of life, and his relations with his kind.

The need of a constantly expanding market for its products chases the bourgeoisie over the whole surface of the globe. It must nestle everywhere, settle everywhere, establish connexions everywhere.

The bourgeoisie has through its exploitation of the world-market given a cosmopolitan character to production and consumption in every country. To the great chagrin of Reactionists, it has drawn from under the feet of industry the national ground on which it stood. All old-established national industries have been destroyed or are daily being destroyed. They are dislodged by new industries, whose introduction becomes a life and death question for all civilised nations, by industries that no longer work up indigenous raw material, but raw material drawn from the remotest zones; industries whose products are consumed, not only at home, but in every quarter of the globe. In place of the old wants, satisfied by the productions of the country, we find new wants, requiring for their satisfaction the products of distant lands and climes. In place of the old local and national seclusion and self-sufficiency, we have intercourse in every direction, universal inter-dependence of nations. And as in material, so also in intellectual production. The intellectual creations of individual nations become common property. National one-sidedness and narrow-mindedness become more and more impossible, and from the numerous national and local literatures, there arises a world literature.

The bourgeoisie, by the rapid improvement of all instruments of production, by the immensely facilitated means of communication, draws all, even the most barbarian, nations into civilisation. The cheap prices of its commodities are the heavy artillery with which it batters down all Chinese walls, with which it forces the barbarians' intensely obstinate hatred of foreigners to capitulate. It compels all nations, on pain of extinction, to adopt the bourgeois mode of production; it compels them to introduce what it calls civilisation into their midst, *i.e.*, to become bourgeois themselves. In one word, it creates a world after its own image.

The bourgeoisie has subjected the country to the rule of the towns. It has created enormous cities, has greatly increased the urban population as compared with the rural, and has thus rescued a considerable part of the population from the idiocy of rural life. Just as it has made the country dependent on the towns, so it has made barbarian and semi-barbarian countries dependent on the civilised ones, nations of peasants on nations of bourgeois, the East on the West.

The bourgeoisie keeps more and more doing away with the scattered state of the population, of the means of production, and of property. It has agglomerated population, centralised means of production, and has concentrated property in a few hands. The necessary consequence of this was political centralisation. Independent, or but loosely connected provinces, with separate interests, laws, governments and systems of taxation, became lumped together into one nation, with one government, one code of laws, one national class-interest, one frontier and one customs-tariff.

The bourgeoisie, during its rule of scarce one hundred years, has created more massive and more colossal productive forces than have all preceding generations together. Subjection of Nature's forces to man, machinery, application of chemistry to industry and agriculture, steam-navigation, railways, electric telegraphs, clearing of whole continents for cultivation, canalisation of rivers, whole populations conjured out of the ground—what earlier century had even a presentiment that such productive forces slumbered in the lap of social labour?

We see then: the means of production and of exchange, on whose foundation the bourgeoisie built itself up, were generated in feudal society. At a certain stage in the development of these means of production and of exchange, the conditions under which feudal society produced and exchanged, the feudal organisation of agriculture and manufacturing industry, in one word, the feudal relations of property became no longer compatible with the already developed productive forces; they became so many fetters. They had to be burst asunder; they were burst asunder.

Into their place stepped free competition, accompanied by a social and political constitution adapted to it, and by the economical and political sway of the bourgeois class.

A similar movement is going on before our own eyes. Modern bourgeois society with its relations of production, of exchange and of property, a society that has conjured up such gigantic means of production and of exchange, is like the sorcerer, who is no longer able to control the powers of the nether world whom he has called up by his spells. For many a decade past the history of industry and commerce is but the history of the revolt of modern productive forces against modern conditions of production, against the property relations that are the conditions for the existence of the bourgeoisie and of its rule. It is enough to mention the commercial crises that by their periodical return put on its trial, each time more threateningly, the existence of the entire bourgeois society. In these crises a great part not only of the existing products, but also of the previously created productive forces, are periodically destroyed. In these crises there breaks out an epidemic that, in all earlier epochs, would have seemed an absurdity—the epidemic of over-production. Society suddenly finds itself put back into a state of momentary barbarism; it

appears as if a famine, a universal war of devastation had cut off the supply
of every means of subsistence; industry and commerce seem to be destroyed;
and why? Because there is too much civilisation, too much means of subsistence, too much industry, too much commerce. The productive forces at the
disposal of society no longer tend to further the development of the conditions
of bourgeois property; on the contrary, they have become too powerful for
these conditions, by which they are fettered, and so soon as they overcome
these fetters, they bring disorder into the whole of bourgeois society, endanger the existence of bourgeois property. The conditions of bourgeois society
are too narrow to comprise the wealth created by them. And how does the
bourgeoisie get over these crises? On the one hand by enforced destruction of
a mass of productive forces; on the other, by the conquest of new markets, and
by the more thorough exploitation of the old ones. That is to say, by paving the
way for more extensive and more destructive crises, and by diminishing the
means whereby crises are prevented.

The weapons with which the bourgeoisie felled feudalism to the ground are
now turned against the bourgeoisie itself.

But not only has the bourgeoisie forged the weapons that bring death to
itself; it has also called into existence the men who are to wield those weapons
the modern working class—the proletarians.

In proportion as the bourgeoisie, *i.e.*, capital, is developed, in the same proportion is the proletariat, the modern working class, developed—a class of
labourers, who live only so long as they find work, and who find work only so
long as their labour increases capital. These labourers, who must sell themselves piece-meal, are a commodity, like even' other article of commerce, and
are consequently exposed to all the vicissitudes of competition, to all the fluctuations of the market.

Owing to the extensive use of machinery and to division of labour, the work
of the proletarians has lost all individual character, and consequently, all
charm for the workman. He becomes an appendage of the machine, and it is
only the most simple, most monotonous, and most easily acquired knack, that
is required of him. Hence, the cost of production of a workman is restricted,
almost entirely, to the means of subsistence that he requires for his maintenance, and for the propagation of his race. But the price of a commodity,
and therefore also of labour,[5] is equal to its cost of production. In proportion,
therefore, as the repulsiveness of the work increases, the wage decreases. Nay
more, in proportion as the use of machinery and division of labour increases,
in the same proportion the burden of toil also increases, whether by prolonga-
tion of the working hours, by increase of the work exacted in a given time or
by increased speed of the machinery, etc.

Modern industry has converted the little workshop of the patriarchal master into the great factory of the industrial capitalist. Masses of labourers,

5. Subsequently Marx pointed out that the worker sells not his labour but his labour power.

crowded into the factory, are organised like soldiers. As privates of the industrial army they are placed under the command of a perfect hierarchy of officers and sergeants. Not only are they slaves of the bourgeois class, and of the bourgeois State; they are daily and hourly enslaved by the machine, by the over-looker, and, above all, by the individual bourgeois manufacturer himself. The more openly this despotism proclaims gain to be its end and aim, the more petty, the more hateful and the more embittering it is.

The less the skill and exertion of strength implied in manual labour, in other words, the more modern industry becomes developed, the more is the labour of men superseded by that of women. Differences of age and sex have no longer any distinctive social validity for the working class. All are instruments of labour, more or less expensive to use, according to their age and sex.

No sooner is the exploitation of the labourer by the manufacturer, so far, at an end, that he receives his wages in cash, than he is set upon by the other portions of the bourgeoisie, the landlord, the shopkeeper, the pawnbroker, etc.

The lower strata of the middle class—the small tradespeople, shopkeepers, and retired tradesmen generally, the handicraftsmen and peasants—all these sink gradually into the proletariat, partly because their diminutive capital does not suffice for the scale on which Modern Industry is carried on, and is swamped in the competition with the large capitalists, partly because their specialised skill is rendered worthless by new methods of production. Thus the proletariat is recruited from all classes of the population.

The proletariat goes through various stages of development. With its birth begins its struggle with the bourgeoisie. At first the contest is carried on by individual labourers, then by the workpeople of a factory, then by the operatives of one trade, in one locality, against the individual bourgeois who directly exploits them. They direct their attacks not against the bourgeois conditions of production, but against the instruments of production themselves; they destroy imported wares that compete with their labour, they smash to pieces machinery, they set factories ablaze, they seek to restore by force the vanished status of the workman of the Middle Ages.

At this stage the labourers still form an incoherent mass scattered over the whole country, and broken up by their mutual competition. If anywhere they unite to form more compact bodies, this is not yet the consequence of their own active union, but of the union of the bourgeoisie, which class, in order to attain its own political ends, is compelled to set the whole proletariat in motion, and is moreover yet, for a time, able to do so. At this stage, therefore, the proletarians do not fight their enemies, but the enemies of their enemies, the remnants of absolute monarchy, the landowners, the non-industrial bourgeois, the petty bourgeoisie. Thus the whole historical movement is concentrated in the hands of the bourgeoisie; every victory so obtained is a victory for the bourgeoisie.

But with the development of industry the proletariat not only increases in number; it becomes concentrated in greater masses, its strength grows, and it feels that strength more. The various interests and conditions of life within the ranks of the proletariat are more and more equalised, in proportion as machinery obliterates all distinctions of labour, and nearly everywhere reduces wages to the same low level. The growing competition among the bourgeois, and the resulting commercial crises, make the wages of the workers ever more fluctuating. The unceasing improvement of machinery, ever more rapidly developing, makes their livelihood more and more precarious; the collisions between individual workmen and individual bourgeois take more and more the character of collisions between two classes. Thereupon the workers begin to form combinations (Trades Unions) against the bourgeois; they club together in order to keep up the rate of wages; they found permanent associations in order to make provision beforehand for these occasional revolts. Here and there the contest breaks out into riots.

Now and then the workers are victorious, but only for a time. The real fruit of their battles lies, not in the immediate result, but in the ever-expanding union of the workers. This union is helped on by the improved means of communication that are created by modern industry and that place the workers of different localities in contact with one another. It was just this contact that was needed to centralise the numerous local struggles, all of the same character, into one national struggle between classes. But every class struggle is a political struggle. And that union, to attain which the burghers of the Middle Ages, with their miserable highways, required centuries, the modern proletarians, thanks to railways, achieve in a few years.

This organisation of the proletarians into a class, and consequently into a political party, is continually being upset again by the competition between the workers themselves. But it ever rises up again, stronger, firmer, mightier. It compels legislative recognition of particular interests of the workers, by taking advantage of the divisions among the bourgeoisie itself. Thus the ten-hours' bill in England was carried.

Altogether collisions between the classes of the old society further, in many ways, the course of development of the proletariat. The bourgeoisie finds itself involved in a constant battle. At first with the aristocracy; later on, with those portions of the bourgeoisie itself, whose interests have become antagonistic to the progress of industry; at all times, with the bourgeoisie of foreign countries. In all these battles it sees itself compelled to appeal to the proletariat, to ask for its help, and thus, to drag it into the political arena. The bourgeoisie itself, therefore, supplies the proletariat with its own elements of political and general education, in other words, it furnishes the proletariat with weapons for fighting the bourgeoisie.

Further, as we have already seen, entire sections of the ruling classes are, by the advance of industry, precipitated into the proletariat, or are at least threatened in their conditions of existence. These also supply the proletariat with fresh elements of enlightenment and progress.

Finally, in times when the class struggle nears the decisive hour, the process of dissolution going on within the ruling class, in fact within the whole range of society, assumes such a violent, glaring character, that a small section of the ruling class cuts itself adrift, and joins the revolutionary class, the class that holds the future in its hands. Just as, therefore, at an earlier period, a section of the nobility went over to the bourgeoisie, so now a portion of the bourgeoisie goes over to the proletariat, and in particular, a portion of the bourgeois ideologists, who have raised themselves to the level of comprehending theoretically the historical movement as a whole.

Of all the classes that stand face to face with the bourgeoisie today, the proletariat alone is a really revolutionary class. The other classes decay and finally disappear in the face of Modern Industry; the proletariat is its special and essential product.

The lower middle class, the small manufacturer, the shopkeeper, the artisan, the peasant, all these fight against the bourgeoisie, to save from extinction their existence as fractions of the middle class. They are therefore not revolutionary, but conservative. Nay more, they are reactionary, for they try to roll back the wheel of history. If by chance they are revolutionary, they are so only in view of their impending transfer into the proletariat, they thus defend not their present, but their future interests, they desert their own standpoint to place themselves at that of the proletariat.

The "dangerous class," the social scum, that passively rotting mass thrown off by the lowest layers of old society, may, here and there, be swept into the movement by a proletarian revolution; its conditions of life, however, prepare it far more for the part of a bribed tool of reactionary intrigue.

In the conditions of the proletariat, those of old society at large are already virtually swamped. The proletarian is without property; his relation to his wife and children has no longer anything in common with the bourgeois family-relations; modern industrial labour, modern subjection to capital, the same in England as in France, in America as in Germany, has stripped him of every trace of national character. Law, morality, religion, are to him so many bourgeois prejudices, behind which lurk in ambush just as many bourgeois interests.

All the preceding classes that got the upper hand, sought to fortify their already acquired status by subjecting society at large to their conditions of appropriation. The proletarians cannot become masters of the productive forces of society, except by abolishing their own previous mode of appropriation, and thereby also every other previous mode of appropriation. They have nothing of their own to secure and to fortify; their mission is to destroy all previous securities for, and insurances of, individual property.

All previous historical movements were movements of minorities, or in the interests of minorities. The proletarian movement is the self-conscious, independent movement of the immense majority, in the interests of the immense majority. The proletariat, the lowest stratum of our present society, cannot stir, cannot raise itself up, without the whole superincumbent strata of official society being sprung into the air.

Though not in substance, yet in form, the struggle of the proletariat with the bourgeoisie is at first a national struggle. The proletariat of each country must, of course, first of all settle matters with its own bourgeoisie.

In depicting the most general phases of the development of the proletariat, we traced the more or less veiled civil war, raging within existing society, up to the point where that war breaks out into open revolution, and where the violent overthrow of the bourgeoisie lays the foundation for the sway of the proletariat.

Hitherto, every form of society has been based, as we have already seen, on the antagonism of oppressing and oppressed classes. But in order to oppress a class, certain conditions must be assured to it under which it can, at least, continue its slavish existence. The serf, in the period of serfdom, raised himself to membership in the commune, just as the petty bourgeois, under the yoke of feudal absolutism, managed to develop into a bourgeois. The modern labourer, on the contrary, instead of rising with the progress of industry, sinks deeper and deeper below the conditions of existence of his own class. He becomes a pauper, and pauperism develops more rapidly than population and wealth. And here it becomes evident, that the bourgeoisie is unfit any longer to be the ruling class in society, and to impose its conditions of existence upon society as an over-riding law. It is unfit to rule because it is incompetent to assure an existence to its slave within his slavery, because it cannot help letting him sink into such a state, that it has to feed him, instead of being fed by him. Society can no longer live under this bourgeoisie, in other words, its existence is no longer compatible with society.

The essential condition for the existence, and for the sway of the bourgeois class, is the formation and augmentation of capital; the condition for capital is wage-labour. Wage-labour rests exclusively on competition between the labourers. The advance of industry, whose involuntary promoter is the bourgeoisie, replaces the isolation of the labourers, due to competition, by their revolutionary combination, due to association. The development of Modern Industry, therefore, cuts from under its feet the very foundation on which the bourgeoisie produces the appropriates products. What the bourgeoisie, therefore, produces, above all, is its own grave-diggers. Its fall and the victory of the proletariat are equally inevitable.

25

Hanging Tongues: A Sociological Encounter
with the Assembly Line

WILLIAM E. THOMPSON

This story may sound familiar to many of you: what looks like a well-paying job and an avenue to the good life turns out to be a mirage, a treadmill, and a trap. By the time we recognize the mirage for what it is, the alternative paths have become blocked by consumer debt and family commitments, creating obstacles that can prove nearly insurmountable.

This qualitative sociological study analyzes the experience of working on a modern assembly line in a large beef plant. It explores and examines a special type of assembly line work which involves the slaughtering and processing of cattle into a variety of products intended for human consumption and other uses.

Working in the beef plant is "dirty work," not only in the literal sense of being drenched with perspiration and beef blood, but also in the figurative sense of performing a low-status, routine, and demeaning job. Although the work is honest and necessary in a society which consumes beef, slaughtering and butchering cattle is generally viewed as an undesirable and repugnant job. In that sense, workers at the beef plant share some of the same experiences as other workers in similarly regarded occupations (for example, ditch-diggers, garbage collectors, and other types of assembly line workers).

* * *

THE SETTING

The setting for the field work was a major beef processing plant in the Midwest. At the time of the study, the plant was the third largest branch of a corporation which operated ten such plants in the United States.

* * *

The beef plant was organizationally separated into two divisions: Slaughter and Processing. This study focused on the Slaughter division in the area of the plant known as the *kill floor*. A dominant feature of the kill floor was the machinery of the assembly line itself. The line was composed of an overhead stainless steel rail which began at the slaughter chute and curved its way around every work station in the plant. Every work station contained specialized machinery for the job performed at that place on the line. Dangling from the rail were hundreds of stainless steel hooks pulled by a motorized chain. Virtually every part of the line and all of the implements (tubs, racks, knives, etc.) were made of stainless steel. The walls were covered with a ceramic tile and the floor was made of sealed cement. There were floor drains located at every work station, so that at the end of each work segment (at breaks, lunch, and shift's end) the entire kill floor could be hosed down and cleaned for the next work period.

Another dominant feature of the kill floor was the smell. Extremely difficult to describe, yet impossible to forget, this smell combined the smells of live cattle, manure, fresh beef blood, and internal organs and their contents. This smell not only permeated the interior of the plant, but was combined on the outside with the smell of smoke from various waste products being burned and could be smelled throughout much of the community. This smell contributed greatly to the general negative feelings about work at the beef plant, as it served as the most distinguishable symbol of the beef plant to the rest of the community. The single most often asked question of me during the research by those outside the beef plant was, "How do you stand the smell?" In typical line workers' fashion, I always responded, "What smell? All I smell at the beef plant is money."

* * *

METHOD

The method of this study was nine weeks of full-time participant observation as outlined by Schatzman and Strauss (1973) and Spradley (1979; 1980). To enter the setting, the researcher went through the standard application process for a summer job. No mention of the research intent was made, though it was made clear that I was a university sociology professor. After initial screening, a thorough physical examination, and a helpful reference from a former student and part-time employee of the plant, the author was hired to work on the *Offal* crew in the Slaughter division of the plant.

* * *

THE WORK

* * * The line speed on the kill floor was 187. That means that 187 head of cattle were slaughtered per hour. At any particular work station, each worker was required to work at that speed. Thus, at my work station, in the period of one hour, 187 beef tongues were mechanically pulled from their hooks; dropped into a large tub filled with water; had to be taken from the tub and hung on a large stainless steel rack full of hooks; branded with a "hot brand" indicating

they had been inspected by a USDA inspector; and then covered with a small plastic bag. The rack was taken to the cooler, replaced with an empty one, and the process began again.

It would be logical to assume that if a person worked at a steady, continuous pace of handling 187 tongues per hour, everything would go smoothly; not so. In addition to hanging, branding, and bagging tongues, the worker at that particular station also cleaned the racks and cleaned out a variety of empty stainless steel tubs used to hold hearts, kidneys, and other beef organs. Thus, in order to be free to clean the tubs when necessary, the "tongue-hanger" had to work at a slightly faster pace than the line moved. Then, upon returning from cleaning the tubs, the worker would be behind the line (*in a hole*) and had to work much faster to catch up with the line. Further, one fifteen-minute break and a thirty-minute lunch break were scheduled for an eight-hour shift. Before the "tongue-hanger" could leave his post for one of these, all tongues were required to be properly disposed of, all tubs washed and stored, and the work area cleaned.

My first two nights on the job, I discovered the consequences of working at the line speed (hanging, branding, and bagging each tongue as it feel in the tub). At the end of the work period when everybody else was leaving the work floor for break or lunch, I was furiously trying to wash all the tubs and clean the work area. Consequently, I missed the entire fifteen-minute break and had only about ten minutes for lunch. By observing other workers, I soon caught on to the system. Rather than attempting to work at a steady pace consistent with the line speed, the norm was to work sporadically at a very frenzied pace, actually running ahead of the line and plucking tongues from the hooks before they got to the station. With practice, I learned to hang two or three tongues at a time, perform all the required tasks, and then take an unscheduled two or three minute break until the line caught up with me. Near break and lunch everybody worked at a frantic pace, got ahead of the line, cleaned the work areas, and even managed to add a couple of minutes to the scheduled break or lunch.

Working ahead of the line seems to have served as more than merely a way of gaining a few minutes of extra break time. It also seemed to take on a symbolic meaning. The company controlled the speed of the line. Seemingly, that took all element of control over the work process away from the workers. * * * However, when the workers refused to work at line speed and actually worked faster than the line, they not only added a few minutes of relaxation from the work while the line caught up, but they symbolically regained an element of control over the pace of their own work.

* * *

COPING

One of the difficulties of work at the beef plant was coping with three aspects of the work: monotony, danger, and dehumanization. While individual workers undoubtedly coped in a variety of ways, some distinguishable patterns emerged.

Monotony

The monotony of the line was almost unbearable. At my work station, a worker would hang, brand, and bag between 1,350 and 1,500 beef tongues in an eight-hour shift. With the exception of the scheduled fifteen-minute break and a thirty-minute lunch period (and sporadic brief gaps in the line), the work was mundane, routine, and continuous. As in most assembly line work, one inevitably drifted into daydreams (e.g., Garson, 1975; King, 1978; Lin-hart, 1981). It was not unusual to look up or down the line and see workers at various stations singing to themselves, tapping their feet to imaginary music, or carrying on conversations with themselves. I found that I could work with virtually no attention paid to the job, with my hands and arms almost automatically performing their tasks. In the meantime, my mind was free to wander over a variety of topics, including taking mental notes. In visiting with other workers, I found that daydreaming was the norm. Some would think about their families, while others fantasized about sexual escapades, fishing, or anything unrelated to the job. One individual who was rebuilding an antique car at home in his spare time would meticulously mentally rehearse the procedures he was going to perform on the car the next day.

Daydreaming was not inconsequential, however. During these periods, items were most likely to be dropped, jobs improperly performed, and accidents incurred. Inattention to detail around moving equipment, stainless steel hooks, and sharp knives invariably leads to dangerous consequences. Although I heard rumors of drug use to help fight the monotony, I never saw any workers take any drugs nor saw any drugs in any workers' possession. It is certainly conceivable that some workers might have taken something to help them escape the reality of the line, but the nature of the work demanded enough attention that such a practice could be ominous.

Danger

The danger of working in the beef plant was well known. Safety was top priority (at least in theory) and management took pride in the fact that only three employee on-the-job deaths had occurred in twelve years. Although deaths were uncommon, serious injuries were not. The beef plant employed over 1,800 people. Approximately three-fourths of those employed had jobs which demanded the use of a knife honed to razor-sharpness. Despite the use of wire-mesh aprons and gloves, serious cuts were almost a daily occurrence. Since workers constantly handled beef blood, danger of infection was ever present. As one walked along the assembly line, a wide assortment of bandages on fingers, hands, arms, necks, and faces could always be seen.

In addition to the problem of cuts, workers who cut meat continuously sometimes suffered muscle and ligament damage to their fingers and hands.

In one severe case, I was told of a woman who worked in processing for several years who had to wear splints on her fingers while away from the job to hold them straight. Otherwise, the muscles in her hand would constrict her fingers into the grip position, as if holding a knife.

* * *

When I spoke with fellow workers about the dangers of working in the plant, I noticed interesting defense mechanisms. * * * After a serious accident, or when telling about an accident or death which occurred in years past, the workers would almost immediately dissociate themselves from the event and its victim. Workers tended to view those who suffered major accidents or death on the job in much the same way that nonvictims of crime often view crime victims as either partially responsible for the event, or at least as very different from themselves (Barlow, 1981). "Only a part-timer," "stupid," "careless" or something similar was used, seemingly to reassure the worker describing the accident that it could not happen to him. The reality of the situation was that virtually all the jobs on the kill floor were dangerous, and any worker could have experienced a serious injury at any time.

* * *

Dehumanization

Perhaps the most devastating aspect of working at the beef plant (worse than the monotony and the danger) was the dehumanizing and demeaning elements of the job. In a sense, the assembly line worker became a part of the assembly line. The assembly line is not a tool used by the worker, but a machine which controls him/her. A tool can only be productive in the hands of somebody skilled in its use, and hence becomes an extension of the person using it. A machine, on the other hand, performs specific tasks, thus its operator becomes an extension of it in the production process. * * * When workers are viewed as mere extensions of the machines with which they work, their human needs become secondary in importance to the smooth mechanical functioning of the production process. In a bureaucratic structure, when "human needs collide with systems needs the individual suffers" (Hummel, 1977: 65).

Workers on the assembly line are seen as interchangeable as the parts of the product on the line itself. An example of one worker's perception of this phenomenon at the beef plant was demonstrated the day after a fatal accident occurred. I asked the men in our crew what the company did in the case of an employee death (I wondered if there was a fund for flowers, or if the shift was given time off to go to the funeral, etc.). One worker's response was: "They drag off the body, take the hard hat and boots and check 'em out to some other poor sucker, and throw him in the guy's place." While employee death on the job was not viewed quite that coldly by the company, the statement fairly accurately summarized the overall result of a fatal accident, and importance of any individual worker to the overall operation of the production process. If accurately summarized the workers' perceptions about management's attitudes toward them.

* * *

Sabotage

It is fairly common knowledge that assemblyline work situations often led to employee sabotage or destruction of the product or equipment used in the production process (Garson, 1975; Balzer, 1976; Shostak, 1980). This is the classic experience of alienation as described by Marx (1964a,b). * * * At the beef plant I quickly learned that there was an art to effective sabotage. Subtlety appeared to be the key. "The art lies in sabotaging in a way that is not immediately discovered," as a Ford worker put it (King, 1978:202). This seemed to hold true at the beef plant as well.

* * *

The greatest factor influencing the handling of beef plant products was its status as a food product intended for human consumption. * * * Though not an explicitly altruistic group, the workers realized that the product would be consumed by people (even family, relatives, and friends), so consequently, they rarely did anything to actually contaminate the product.

Despite formal norms against sabotage, some did occur. It was not uncommon for workers to deliberately cut chunks out of pieces of meat for no reason (or for throwing at other employees). While regulations required that anything that touched the floor had to be put in tubs marked "inedible," the informal procedural norms were otherwise. When something was dropped, one usually looked around to see if an inspector or foreman noticed. If not, the item was quickly picked up and put back on the line.

Several explanations might be offered for this type of occurrence. First, since the company utilized a profit-sharing plan, when workers damaged the product, or had to throw edible pieces into inedible tubs (which sold for pet food at much lower prices), profits were decreased. A decrease in profits to the company ultimately led to decreased dividend checks to employees. Consequently, workers were fairly careful not to actually ruin anything. Second, when something was dropped or mishandled and had to be rerouted to "inedible," it was more time-consuming than if the product had been handled properly and kept on the regular line. In other words, if no inspector noticed, it was easier to let it go through on the line. There was a third, and seemingly more meaningful, explanation for this behavior, however. It was against the rules to do it, it was a challenge to do it, and thus it was fun to do it.

The workers practically made a game out of doing forbidden things simply to see if they could get away with it. * * * New workers were routinely socialized into the subtle art of rulebreaking as approved by the line workers. At my particular work station, it was a fairly common practice for other workers who were covered with beef blood to come over to the tub of swirling water designed to clean the tongues, and as soon as the inspector looked away, wash their hands, arms, and knives in the tub. This procedure was strictly forbidden by the rules. If witnessed by a foreman or inspector, the tub had to be emptied, cleaned, and refilled, and all the tongues in the tub at the time had to be put in the "inedible" tub. All of that would be a time-consuming and costly procedure, yet the workers seemed to absolutely delight in successfully pulling off the act. As Balzer (1976:90) indicates:

> Since a worker often feels that much if not all of what he does is done in places designated by the company, under company control, finding ways to express personal freedom from this institutional regimentation is important.

Thus, artful sabotage served as a symbolic way in which the workers could express a sense of individuality, and hence, self-worth.

THE FINANCIAL TRAP

Given the preceding description and analysis for work at the beef plant, why did people work at such jobs? Obviously, there are a multitude of plausible answers to that question. Without doubt, however, the key is money. The current economic situation, the lack of steady employment opportunities (especially for the untrained and poorly educated), combined with the fact that the beef plant's starting wage exceeded the minimum wage by approximately $5.50 per hour emerge as the most important reasons people went to work there.

Despite the high hourly wage and fringe benefits, however, the monotony, danger, and hard physical work drove many workers away in less than a week. During my study, I observed much worker turnover. Those who stayed displayed an interesting pattern which helps explain why they did not leave. Every member of my work crew answered similarly my questions about why they stayed at the beef plant. Each of them took the job directly after high school, because it was the highest-paying job available. Each of them had intended to work through the summer and then look for a better job in the fall. During that first summer on the job they fell victim to what I label the "financial trap."

The "financial trap" was a spending pattern which demanded the constant weekly income provided by the beef plant job. This scenario was first told to me by an employee who had worked at the plant for over nine years. He began the week after his high school graduation, intending only to work that summer in order to earn enough money to attend college in the fall. After about four weeks' work he purchased a new car. He figured he could pay off the car that summer and still save enough money for tuition. Shortly after the car purchase, he added a new stereo sound system to his debt; next came a motorcycle; then the decision to postpone school for one year in order to continue working at the beef plant and pay off his debts. A few months later he married; within a year purchased a house; had a child; and bought another new car. Nine years later, he was still working at the beef plant, hated every minute of it, but in his own words "could not afford to quit." His case was not unique. Over and over again, I heard stories about the same process of falling into the "financial trap." The youngest and newest of our crew had just graduated high school and took the job for the summer in order to earn enough money to attend welding school the following fall. During my brief tenure at the beef plant, he purchased a new motorcycle, a new stereo, and a house trailer. When I left, he told me he had decided to postpone welding school for one year in order "to get everything paid for." I saw the financial trap closing in on him fast; he did too.

* * *

SUMMARY AND CONCLUSIONS

There are at least three interwoven phenomena in this study which deserve further comment and research.

First is the subtle sense of unity which existed among the line workers. * * * The line both symbolically and literally linked every job, and consequently every worker, to each other. * * * A system of "uncooperative teamwork" seemed to combine simultaneously a feeling of "one-for-all, all-for-one, and every man for himself." Once a line worker made it past the first three or four days on the job which "weeded out" many new workers, his status as a *beefer* was assured and the sense of unity was felt as much by the worker of nine weeks as it was by the veteran of nine years. Because the workers maintained largely secondary relationships, this feeling of unification is not the same as the unity typically found on athletic teams, in fraternities, or among various primary groups. Yet it was a significant social force which bound the workers together and provided a sense of meaning and worth. Although their occupation might not be highly respected by outsiders, they derived mutual self-respect from their sense of belonging.

A second important phenomenon was the various coping methods * * * the beef plant line workers developed and practiced * * * for retaining their humanness. Daydreaming, horseplay and occasional sabotage protected their sense of self. Further, the prevailing attitude among workers that it was "us" against "them" served as a reminder that, while the nature of the job might demand subjugation to bosses, machines, and even beef parts, they were still human beings.

* * *

A third significant finding was that consumer spending patterns among the beefers seemed to "seal their fate" and make leaving the beef plant almost impossible. A reasonable interpretation of the spending patterns of the beefers is that having a high-income/low-status job encourages a person to consume conspicuously. The prevailing attitude seemed to be "I may not have a nice job, but I have a nice home, a nice car, etc." This conspicuous consumption enabled workers to take indirect pride in their occupations. One of the ways of overcoming drudgery and humiliation on the job was to surround oneself with as many desirable material things as possible off the job. These items (cars, boats, motorcycles, etc.) became tangible rewards for the sacrifices endured at work.

The problem, of course, is that the possession of these expensive items required the continual income of a substantial paycheck which most of these men could only obtain by staying at the beef plant. These spending patterns were further complicated by the fact that they were seemingly "contagious." Workers talked to each other on breaks about recent purchases, thus reinforcing the norm of immediate gratification. A common activity of a group of workers on break or lunch was to run to the parking lot to see a fellow worker's new truck, van, car or motorcycle. Even the seemingly more financially conservative were usually caught up in this activity and often could not wait to display their own latest acquisitions. Ironically, as the workers cursed their jobs, these expensive possessions virtually destroyed any chance of leaving them.

Working at the beef plant was indeed "dirty work." It was monotonous, difficult, dangerous, and demeaning. Despite this, the workers at the beef plant worked hard to fulfill employer expectations in order to obtain financial rewards. Through a variety of symbolic techniques, they managed to overcome the many negative aspects of their work and maintain a sense of self-respect about how they earned their living.

REFERENCES

Balzer, Richard (1976). *Clockwork: Life In and Outside an American Factory.* Garden City, NY: Doubleday.

Barlow, Hugh (1981). *Introduction to Criminology.* 2d ed. Boston: Little, Brown.

Garson, Barbara (1975). *All the Livelong Day: The Meaning and Demeaning of Routine Work.* Garden City, NY: Doubleday.

Hummel, Ralph P. (1977). *The Bureaucratic Experience.* New York: St. Martin's Press.

King, Rick (1978). "In the sanding booth at Ford." Pp. 199–205 in John and Erna Perry (eds.), *Social Problems in Today's World.* Boston: Little, Brown.

Linhart, Robert (translated by Margaret Crosland) (1981). *The Assembly Line.* Amherst: University of Massachusetts Press.

Marx, Karl (1964a). *Economic and Philosophical Manuscripts of 1844.* New York: International Publishing (1844).

_____. (1964b). *The Communist Manifesto.* New York: Washington Square Press (1848).

Schatzman, Leonard, and Anselm L. Strauss (1973). *Field Research.* Englewood Cliffs, NJ: Prentice-Hall.

Shostak, Arthur (1980). *Blue Collar Stress.* Reading, MA: Addison-Wesley.

Spradley, James P. (1979). *The Ethnographic Interview.* New York: Holt, Rinehart & Winston.

_____. (1980). *Participant Observation.* New York: Holt, Rinehart & Winston.

26

From *Borderline Americans: Racial Divisions and Labor War in the Arizona Borderlands* *

KATHERINE BENTON-COHEN

The social construction of reality extends to ethnicity in this essay of labor strife and social hierarchy, what Benton-Cohen calls "race making." In presenting a fascinating slice of history, she uncovers one of the roots of "otherness" that became the dominant society's view of persons of Mexican ancestry. Differences, especially ethnic distinctions, are purposeful. As C. Vann Woodward showed in his classic study, The Strange Career of Jim Crow, *they serve to divide a potentially powerful group who might otherwise be able to demand a greater share of what they produce. Instead, being a "true American" with all the status this confers was given to some (whites) and denied others (Mexicans). And with it came different life chances. Benton-Cohen's story also reminds us that, yes, history does seem to repeat itself, especially in the absence of accurate historical knowledge in a time of economic anxiety.*

"Are you an American, or are you not?" This was the question that Harry Wheeler, the sheriff of Cochise County, Arizona, used to determine his targets in one of the most remarkable vigilante actions in U.S. history. It took place in a remote mountain town near the Arizona-Mexico border on July 12, 1917, three months after the United States joined World War I. In the days leading up to the event, Wheeler had appointed more than two thousand temporary deputies, among them miners, foremen, Protestant clergymen, prominent merchants and businessmen, a company doctor, and a Catholic priest. At 4:00 A.M., the deputies—summoned by phone, organized into companies, and identified by white armbands—emerged onto the streets "as if by magic," as the front page of the *New York Times* reported the following day.

The men carried rifles. Some of those firearms were their own, but most, according to reliable sources, came from a company store and from two boxcars of guns and ammunition recently delivered to a mining-company manager. The deputies swarmed through the steep, narrow streets to snatch up fellow residents at home or at work. The targets of the raid were people suspected of participating in or supporting a strike by the Industrial Workers of the World (IWW, or "Wobblies"), a radical union mobilizing against the copper-mining companies of Bisbee, Arizona.

---

*Footnotes and references can be found in Katherine Benton-Cohen's *Borderline Americans*.

Deputies pounded on doors, rounding up men by threat and by force. They captured not just striking miners, but also restaurant owners, carpenters, a lawyer, and a state legislator. Amado Villalovas was buying food for his family when "about ten gunmen all armed came in and told me to get out. I asked them to let me take my groceries home to my family. They dragged me out of the store, hit me and knocked me down." They "pushed me in line and made me go away leaving parcels on the ground." In private homes and boarding-houses, wives and landladies protested and tried to shame the deputies. In the chaos of the roundup, two men—one on each side—were killed. It is astonishing the count was not higher. The *Bisbee Daily Review*, owned by the largest mining company in the area, reported that at 6:30 A.M. "the crash of the musket butts on the pavement stilled the mutterings and murmurs of the trapped 'wobblies' for the rest of the day." In the July sun, a line of nearly two thousand captives snaked along single-file, escorted by armed deputies.

By noon, the men had been marched through town, past the mines, to a suburban baseball field four miles away. Families and neighbors gathered and gaped as deputies weeded through the men and loaded at least 1,186 of them into twenty-three boxcars belonging to the mining-company railroad. The captives were shipped 180 miles into the New Mexico desert. Some, like Villalovas, had families, but the majority were single and childless. Ninety percent were immigrants. Altogether they included men of thirty-four nationalities, but half came from Mexico or the Slavic regions of eastern Europe. An army camp in nearby Columbus, New Mexico—a border town that had been raided by Mexican revolutionary Pancho Villa a year earlier—rescued the deported men from thirst and starvation. Some stayed there as long as three months. Almost none of them ever returned to Bisbee.

The event became known across the country as the Bisbee Deportation. The term aptly characterized the forcible removal of "undesirables" from a town concerned enough about its racial boundaries to call itself a "white man's camp." Public outcry and national headlines eventually forced President Woodrow Wilson to appoint a mediation commission to investigate labor conflicts across the West, but especially in Arizona's copper camps. It was not an easy decision, because Bisbee's largest mine was owned by the Phelps Dodge Corporation, whose vice president, Cleveland W. Dodge, was Wilson's close friend and former college roommate at Princeton. Wilson named as counsel to the commission a young assistant secretary of labor and Harvard law professor named Felix Frankfurter.

The future Supreme Court justice saw in the strikers' struggles nothing less than a "fight for the status of free manhood" by Mexicans and Slavs who "feel they were not treated as men." After his first glimpse of the Arizona mining camps, Frankfurter wrote to a friend: "As I get deeper and deeper into these marooned outposts of the country, . . . far from the intimacies of my own life, it all seems, it all is, part of the whole. The war, the economic and racial conflicts and cross currents that produced it, the industrial anarchies, our

American striving to realize the democratic faith—here." Frankfurter understood that the events unfolding in the Arizona copper camps engaged one of the foundational questions in U.S. history: Who counts as an American?

County sheriff Harry Wheeler might have agreed on the question, but not, perhaps, with Frankfurter's answers. To ask the question Wheeler did—"Are you an American, or are you not?"—was to assume a whole set of answers about who was *not* really an American in his eyes: labor radicals, Mexicans, Slavs, men whom he believed had no roots to family or town. As a patriotic citizen and law enforcement officer, Wheeler saw a strike against a vital war industry as a threat to the nation. He also believed these men threatened the lives and safety of "American women," as he put it. And so Wheeler joined causes with mine managers and foremen, appointed his deputies, and began his roundup.

The story of Cochise County, Arizona, whose citizens elected Harry Wheeler, is part of a larger national saga of race, belonging, and exclusion. In the nineteenth century, the abolition of slavery and the passage of the Fourteenth and the Fifteenth Amendments loosened the racial strictures around U.S. citizenship. But the incorporation of much of northwestern Mexico into the United States after the U.S.-Mexico War in 1848, and, after 1880, the immigration of southern and eastern Europeans, were accompanied by the spread of scientific racism and a fear of radicalism that raised new questions about who qualified as an American. The Bisbee Deportation was one community's answer to those questions, but it was an answer that echoed debates and dilemmas that racked the nation in a time of mass migration, labor struggle, world war, and revolution. As the Deportation lingered in the national spotlight, the men and women of Cochise County found it difficult to avoid the controversy.

County residents had squinted in media glare and succumbed to federal intervention before. Geronimo, the Chiricahua Apache medicine man and resistance leader, ended the nation's Indian Wars when he surrendered at Cochise County's Skeleton Canyon in 1886. Magazines like *Harper's Weekly* kept eastern readers apprised of Geronimo's daring escapes and fascinating encounters with dashing army officers and their Indian scouts. Five years before Geronimo's surrender, the county seat of Tombstone had become infamous, when escalating violence—culminating in the shootout forever associated with the OK Corral—prompted a threat of martial law by President Chester Arthur.

A hundred years later, at the turn of the twenty-first century, the county attracted renewed media attention as the site of the highest number of undocumented migrants apprehended crossing the U.S.-Mexico border. In response, the county became home to several vigilante-type organizations. In 2004, Tombstone gunfight reenactor and newspaper editor Chris Simcox formed the Minutemen Civil Defense Corps, dedicated to monitoring the border and stopping illegal immigration. The group spawned chapters across the nation, and its April 2005 campaign to observe and report undocumented border crossings shot Cochise County bylines across the world, as far away as Great Britain and Australia. Some members believe they are restoring the geographic border between Mexico and the United States—and therefore the strict racial border between Mexican and American—to what it once was. But such a border in fact never existed.

Cochise County changed dramatically between the eras of Wyatt Earp, Geronimo, and Harry Wheeler on the one hand, and the Minutemen on the other. At its height, military occupation during the Apache Wars involved almost one-fifth of the U.S. Army in chasing Geronimo, and in 1917 a "Citizen's Protective League" maintained checkpoints outside Bisbee to stop deportees from returning. These conditions differ in their particulars from the situation in the twenty-first century: the nearly ubiquitous presence of the Border Patrol and National Guard, joined, in uneasy alliance, by groups like the Minutemen. Still, parallels do exist, and comparisons are worth considering. In both periods, state and private forces policed the boundary between those who belong and those who do not—in terms that often invoked race and nation simultaneously. Anti-Chinese campaigns in Tombstone and Bisbee set a precedent for racial exclusion, and the removal in 1886 of the surrendered Chiricahua Apaches—by boxcar—eerily foreshadowed the Bisbee Deportation three decades later. With the Apaches gone, the racial divisions created and reflected in the labor conflicts of the mines could be embedded in fictions about a natural and bright-line border between "America" and "Mexico."

In the twenty-first century the border can be patrolled as if it were a fixed line (though one easily crossed) between firmly established nation-states, but this is possible only because of a long history in which government officials, corporate interests, and local citizens made that border seem natural by establishing "Mexican" and "white American" as the region's only relevant—and totally separate—racial categories.

This place in the middle of nowhere has been surprisingly central to some of the nation's defining controversies. The story of Cochise County offers a tool for understanding the twinned histories of race and nation in the United States. Although many people continue to think of race in black-white terms, this region of the Southwest contained people from around the globe who were forced to grapple with racial categories and definitions. It's atypical in some ways: not every county in the United States—or the West, for that matter—harbored native resistance like that of the Chiricahua Apaches, a shootout like the OK Corral's, or a deportation like Bisbee's. But Cochise County's past offers a window into the ways that race and nation have been linked and unlinked in the nineteenth and twentieth centuries, and how those connections have shaped the lives of everyday people. The personal stories cast in sharp relief the process of race making, which so often seems amorphous and fuzzy.

At the border, "American" was and is simultaneously a local, national, racial, and ideological category. To ask Wheeler's question—"Are you an American, or are you not?"—was scarcely to ponder an abstraction. Not in Apache country, not on an international border, and not, in 1917, during world war abroad *and* the Mexican Revolution just a few miles away. To take the mantle of "American"—or refuse to bestow it on someone else—asserted what you were, but also what you were not.

The men deported from Bisbee on that hot morning were *borderline Americans*, because most were U.S. residents but not citizens (a point carefully considered and recorded in censuses of their camp in New Mexico), but also because, to many local residents, men like the deportees had at best a tenuous claim on whiteness—a concept that even a half-century after the Fourteenth and Fifteenth amendments was still deeply tied to the meaning of U.S. citizenship.

* * *

Treating the whiteness of new European immigrants as inevitable—but not that of Mexicans—erases the complicated racial histories of both groups. The Treaty of Guadalupe Hidalgo of 1848 (which ended the U.S.-Mexico War) and the Gadsden Purchase of 1853 (which included the strip of Mexico that became southern New Mexico and Arizona and that would contain Cochise County) both guaranteed Mexican citizens in those territories the right to U.S. citizenship. Because a 1790 federal law allowed the naturalization only of "white"immigrants, these two treaties thus made Mexicans legally "white." California's and Arizona's first voting laws in the 1850s and 1860s specifically enfranchised "every white male citizen of Mexico" who had "elected to become" a U.S. citizen. It was possible, in other words, to be both white *and* Mexican in the United States.

In the mid-nineteenth century, "Mexican" and "white" were overlapping categories, not opposite poles in a regional racial system. In this world, Apaches were not Americans, but Mexicans might be. These categories were, however, highly contingent on local conditions. During the height of the violence in Tombstone, for instance, many local residents strongly defended Mexicans against American bandits. Building national and racial boundaries required the removal and exclusion of some peoples, and the new inclusion of others. In small irrigated farm and ranch communities, the Apache Wars encouraged close settlement patterns and intermarriage among Mexicans and European Americans. But race relations in places with different economic systems soon became more problematic. Where Mexicans owned ranches and farms, racial categories were blurry and unimportant. But in the industrial copper-mining town of Bisbee, Mexican workers were segregated economically by their lower pay ("Mexican wage") and geographically by new town-planning experiments. To most non-Mexican residents of Bisbee, Mexicans were peon workers or potential public charges, not neighbors or business partners, not co-workers or co-worshipers, and certainly not poten-tial marriage partners.

Eastern and southern Europeans, welcomed as pioneers in the 1880s, had, by the early twentieth century, become objects of suspicion and racially charged commentary. The arrival of growing numbers of new, often unskilled workers from Serbia, Italy, Finland, and elsewhere generated controversy over who qualified as white. Mining officials came to define a white American man as any family breadwinner so long as he was not Mexican. Unmarried European immigrant miners who took wives, bought single-family homes, and raised families found praise as "domestic miners" in the local press, which voiced complaints about single Italian men living in rooming houses "as no white man can." Rural white homesteaders, who had long been hostile to the mining companies, found common ground with mining-town residents in den-igrating new immigrants.

Well before the crackdowns on radicals and the restrictions on immigra-tion of the 1920s, public officials and private boosters were using "American" as a quasi-national, quasi-racial category embodied in married, homeowning "white" men. In the 1920s and 1930s, middle-class white women—often the wives or employees of company officials—took on increasingly public roles in social reform and government programs that defined the population by race. Nationally, the immigration restriction laws of the 1920s stopped the flow of southern and eastern Europeans but allowed Mexican immigration to con-tinue. In a place where racial identities were tightly bound up with national ones, "American" increasingly equaled "white," and so "Mexican" came to mean the opposite of both.

By the 1930s, the line between "Mexican" and "white" was well entrenched, but it was never completely stable. The New Deal and World War II gave workers new tools to dig away at its foundation, the dual-wage system. The New Deal had two faces: one that offered local elites greater power, and another that granted union rights where none had existed before. Thanks to the right to collective bargaining, granted in the National Industrial Recovery Act and the Wagner Act, a new era of unionizing began in Cochise County. A small Mine-Mill local organized in 1933 went on strike at the Copper Queen Mine in 1935. One supervisor told a striker, "in 300 years we will not give you fellows a job again." Another striker was told, "If you want a job you will have to go to a union camp to get it." The men challenged their firing and blacklist-ing by filing a complaint with the National Labor Relations Board. The case ended up in the U.S. Supreme Court, which in 1941 ruled in favor of the strik-ers. The ruling stated that the company could not blacklist the workers and that it owed them back pay. *Phelps Dodge v. National Labor Relations Board* became a major legal precedent in protecting union workers from blacklists. The Supreme Court's decision was written by a justice who knew a great deal about Bisbee labor practices: Felix Frankfurter.

The men who launched the strike had names like Kalastro, Caretto, Curtis, Vaclav, Bateman, Mortenson, and Erkkila. They represented the new, broader definition of "whiteness," and they were not newcomers to Bisbee. One man had first worked for the mine in 1908. Another, Verne Curtis, signed on as an organizer with Mine-Mill, which left the American Federation of Labor for the Congress of Industrial Organizations in 1937, and began aggressively organizing Mexican workers. Curtis went on to help organize Mexican American workers at the Empire Zinc Mine near Silver City, New Mexico. Empire became the site of a 1950 strike made famous by the 1953 film *Salt of the Earth*, which focused on the decision of Mexican American miners' wives to take over the picket line after a court injunction. Although the 1935 Bisbee strike did not address the disparate pay scales of Mexican and "white American" workers, it was one of a series of worker actions against the Arizona copper industry that eventually led to the dismantling of the dual-wage system.

* * *

Unionizing was legal now, but ending the dual-wage system was not an issue that all union members embraced. In the 1930s, the American Federation of Labor and the Congress of Industrial Organizations competed for copper workers, with the former often holding the line against Mexican wage parity. After the federal government ordered Phelps Dodge to dismantle its company union, PD simply reorganized the union as a sympathetic AFL local. As one federal official noted with considerable understatement, "The employment practices of the industries of the Southwest have become so traditional and the Companies . . . have for so long dominated the political as well as the economic life of their communities, that it will be difficult to get them to change their ways."

Mexican Americans fought the dual-wage system by emphasizing that they, too, were Americans. They emphatically denied that "American" and "Mexican" were opposites, or that "American" had to equal "white." White bosses often disagreed. One day in 1936, the Copper Queen smelter in Douglas was short-handed. Carlos Rivera briefly took over as a puncher, traditionally a "whiteman's job." Soon after, Rivera got "bumped off" by a new white worker. When Rivera complained, the foreman said, "I am putting an American in the American job." Rivera replied, "I was born and raised here in the United States of America and . . . [I am] an American." The foreman replied: "I don't care if you were born in China you are still a Mexican and I am putting a whiteman on the job."

Jose Estrada, another experienced smelter worker in Douglas, complained that he was forced to work with the "Mexican gang" doing menial work, even though he had "broken in fifty or sixty Anglos" since he started at the smelter. "I taught them their jobs, but I got the Mexican scale while I was teaching them their work and they got the so-called white scale. The Anglos got approximately $1.52 per day more while I was breaking them in." Estrada emphasized that "I feel I am subjected to discrimination because of my race." Co-worker

Bob Hart asked the boss why Estrada was not promoted to a recent opening, and the boss replied, "Bob, you know how it is. We have to save all of the best jobs for the Americans because they pay more money and that's the rule of the company." Hart clarified for federal investigators that "I understood the term American, as he used it, to mean Anglo-American."

Language was changing. Smelter workers like Jose Chavez used the terms "Latin American" and "of Spanish extraction" to describe themselves, while relating that what they earned was "the so-called Mexican rate." The terms downplayed race, as political leaders did in New Mexico and Texas, where organizations like the League of United Latin American Citizens were arguing that Mexicans were white Caucasians and thus should not be segregated. Burgeoning civil rights efforts in Arizona were doing the same. These terms were also a way for American citizens of Mexican descent to assert their rights in contradistinction to immigrants with Mexican citizenship. Whether claiming whiteness or not, Mexican American workers and their defenders were insisting that people of Mexican descent could be Americans—and skilled workers, for that matter.

Managers continued to blame tradition and the opposition of white workers for the endurance of the dual-wage system, but Phelps Dodge had its own reasons for keeping things the way they were. One manager "frankly admitted" that the company did not want to stir up labor troubles by promoting Mexican miners against white workers' objections. More important, though, the status quo was profitable. In the early 1940s, two federal investigators calculated how much money the company earned by preserving the system. If five thousand miners in Arizona worked for $1.52 less than Anglos in the same jobs (the differential Estrada had used), the dual-wage system saved Arizona copper companies $2,371,200 in wages per year.

New federal tools combined with the activism of ordinary men and women to challenge the dual-wage system as never before. With the aid first of Mine-Mill and, by the middle of World War II, of some AFL locals, Mexican American workers attacked the dual-wage system and their exclusion from high-paying jobs. Their plight was detailed in hundreds of affidavits collected by the Fair Employment Practices Commission (FEPC). In response to black union activist A. Philip Randolph's threat to launch a massive march on Washington in 1941, President Roosevelt created the FEPC to investigate complaints of racial discrimination in the nation's war industries. Although FEPC representatives interviewed copper workers like Carlos Rivera and Jose Estrada across the Southwest who experienced discrimination, pressure to keep good relations with Mexico and foot-dragging by corporate attorneys meant that the FEPC failed to hold a proposed public hearing in El Paso on their findings. The FEPC's concrete accomplishments proved limited, and its institutional dedication to ending discrimination against Mexicans was lukewarm.

* * *

In 1917, the patriotic xenophobia of World War I had blunted the attack against the dual-wage system. But in World War II, racially inclusive rhetoric and manpower shortages combined to open up new opportunities for equal wages and job advancement. In 1942, an Anglo officer in a Bisbee union wrote to an FEPC official, "We know that racial discrimination is greater in the Southwestern part of the country than else where. We feel that racial discrimination is one of the major factors contributing to the man power crisis and must be tackled quickly. Discrimination against minority groups is obviously working on Hitler's side and not ours." In Bisbee, a handful of Mexican workers began working underground, and across the industry Mine-Mill continued to fight the dead-end job classification schemes that had replaced explicit racial job categories as a means of keeping Mexican workers in menial positions. A report on New Year's Day, 1944, warned that it would take "drastic measures . . . to obtain the copper necessary to successfully fight the war." The "drastic measure" was finally to dismantle the racial hierarchy of mine work. The War Production Board and the Nonferrous Metals Commission supported efforts to end racial discrimination in the copper industry. The "Victory Campaigns" conducted that year by union leaders got more AFL locals to cooperate with the Congress of Industrial Organizations, in its efforts to push for an end to racially discriminatory wage scales.

In the years that followed, Mexican Americans made significant advances in the copper industry, tearing down more job barriers and wage differentials, and building powerful unions. They fought even as Mine-Mill, which had Communist allies and members, became a target of continual attack at the height of the Red Scare. By the late 1960s, the United Steelworkers had destroyed Mine-Mill's dominance among southwestern mine workers. A legacy of union organizing centered on racial equality continued, though. The United Steelworkers launched an industry-wide strike in 1967, and intermittent ones regularly followed. By the late 1960s, Mexican American union activism cast increased attention to electoral politics. The union experiences of their parents influenced many young men and women of the "Chicano generation," who came of age in the 1960s and began to launch social movements in college and to run for public office. One of these was Representative Ed Pastor, who replaced Morris Udall, descended from Mormon pioneers, to become Arizona's first Mexican American member of Congress in 1991. In an industry slump in the 1980s, an industry-wide strike led to massive defeat for the unions, however, and more than thirty union locals lost their right to collective bargaining in Phelps Dodge mining towns across the Southwest.

* * *

Cochise County had already entered a new phase—one as unique and typical of the American Southwest as ever. Following a shift from underground to open-pit mining during the 1950s, Bisbee's mines closed in 1975. The Douglas smelter closed in 1987. The county relies mostly on military spending related to Fort Huachuca and on tourist dollars, spent during the 1940s and 1950s at dude ranches, and more recently in Tombstone and in Bisbee, which has become a little Santa Fe resettled by hippies and retirees in the late 1970s. Mexican Americans live in Bisbee, as always, but I have also heard it called the "whitest border town."

RV parks have replaced ranches in Benson, and tract homes surround Sierra Vista, the military town that has sprung up around Fort Huachuca. Most—but not all—of the remaining family ranchers and farmers in the rural parts of the county have been forced to sell out or subdivide, as drought devastates the landscape and their livelihoods. Open range has been carved into ranchettes in some parts of the county, yet some local ranch owners are working with the Bureau of Land Management and environmental organizations to protect open space and endangered species. There is still no Apache reservation in the county, although the place where Cochise is buried is a state park, and the Chiricahua Mountains are a National Monument.

Cascabel, the tiny Mexican American enclave in the northwestern corner of the county, remains accessible only by a fifty-mile dirt road and had no phone service until 1993. Most pioneering Mexican families sold or lost their land, but a few descendants are buying some of it back and are returning to the area. There they find a unique community—resettled in part by social activists (many of them Quakers) involved in Tucson's Sanctuary Movement, which offers protection and support for undocumented immigrants.

Others in the county take a less welcoming view of border-crossers. The biggest story in Cochise County remains the border, which is still—even with an unprecedented amount of enforcement—more permeable than it is concrete. Since 1994, Border Patrol policies have funneled illegal immigration away from cities like San Diego and Nogales, where it is easy to hide among the crowds, and toward the open desert of southern Arizona. By 2000, the number of migrants detained in Arizona was double that of the entire rest of the border *combined*. In 2004, the Border Patrol made 235,648 apprehensions of undocumented immigrants in Cochise County, about double the county's entire permanent population. Numbers were down considerably in subsequent years, but the county remains an epicenter of migration. From Fall 2007 to September 2008, at least 167 people died while traversing the southern Arizona deserts.

The vast majority of border crossers do so with no other intent than to find work or reunite with family. In 2006, the county sheriff estimated that immigrants accounted for only 3 to 4 percent of the county's criminal violations (not counting trespassing and littering). But the scale of the migration and its furtive nature have done serious damage to residents' property and sense of security. Ranchers' fences have been cut; their lands have been covered with trash and clothing abandoned by migrants. Thefts and break-ins are a real fear.

The Border Patrol has become ubiquitous. In October 2001, 699 agents were stationed in Cochise County, and by 2005 there were 909 (to put this into context, note that Bisbee's current population is about six thousand). At one ranch outside Bisbee with more than seven miles of land along the border, fifteen to twenty Border Patrol agents have worked at a time, because dozens of immigrants cross the property almost daily. Border Patrol agents set up checkpoints outside Tombstone and on rural roads across the county. In 2007 three thousand National Guardsmen also served at the Arizona border. Some residents oppose what amounts to a military buildup along the border, while others lament that it is not nearly enough. Some, like the men who created the Minutemen Project, have launched private organizations that monitor the border, build fences, or apprehend migrants. Other groups, alarmed at the number of migrant deaths, have provided water stations and maps for migrants. Bisbee, in a turn from its past as an exclusionary white man's camp, has become a regional haven for pro-immigrant activists. Both sides in the debate over the county's undocumented immigrants see the situation as a crisis.

As the shootout at the OK Corral celebrated its 125th anniversary, then, Cochise County had come full circle from Tombstone's Cowboy era. The Tombstone marshal's office has a federal grant to increase its ability to apprehend lawbreaking immigrants. Nowadays, the National Guard is called out to protect the border from immigrants and drug traffickers, not from white American bandits. The governor who made this decision, Janet Napolitano, is expected to be President Obama's secretary of the Department of Homeland Security, in large part because of her border-enforcement experience. Most residents of the border region would be surprised to hear that the Border Patrol's roots lie in the late nineteenth century, in attempts to find Chinese immigrants. And in the early twenty-first century, the Department of Homeland Security has emphasized the national-security threat posed by people from many nations crossing illegally at the Mexico border. But more than 96 percent of those who cross the southern border illegally are of Mexican descent—everyone else detained there by the Border Patrol is referred to as "OTM" (other than Mexican). This nomenclature reinforces the fiction that the border line is a natural divide between Mexicans and Americans.

What the future holds at the county's and nation's border is hard to say. But in Cochise County, as in the rest of the United States, race and nation have proved difficult to extricate from each other. Over time, the division between "Mexican" and "white" sharpened, but it was a binary distilled from myriad other possible outcomes. Along the way, ideas about race became wrapped up in assumptions about manliness, womanhood, nation, family, work, and class. The collusion of private and public power on the local and state levels bolstered the power of corporate leaders and their allies in defining racial difference, even as individual citizens fought back and formulated their own ideas—for both good and ill. Intellectual discussions of the social origins of race can seem rarefied and theoretical, divorced from lived experience. Cochise County's history demonstrates that the lived experience of race— on the border and elsewhere—has daunting and even tragic power. Yet this history also testifies that realities can change, and this gives us cause for hope.

27

"Getting" and "Making" a Tip

FROM *Dishing It Out: Power and Resistance among Waitresses in a New Jersey Restaurant*

GRETA FOFF PAULES

Waitresses, like many people who provide a service, are highly vulnerable to the whims of the customers who, by their tips, decide their daily earnings. Waitresses structure their encounters with more care than most of us realize. The reason for this is the need to have some power over their work and their livelihood. For those of you who have never been a waiter or waitress, this participant observation study may change forever the way you think about being served and treat those who serve you.

> The waitress can't help feeling a sense of personal failure and public censure when she is "stiffed."
>
> -*William F. Whyte*, "When Workers and Customers Meet"

> They're rude, they're ignorant, they're obnoxious, they're inconsiderate.... Half these people don't deserve to come out and eat, let alone try and tip a waitress.
>
> -*Route [Restaurant] waitress*

The financial and emotional hazards inherent in the tipping system have drawn attention from sociologists, and more recently anthropologists, concerned with the study of work. In general these researchers have concluded that workers who receive gratuities exercise little control over the material outcome of tipping and less over its symbolic implications.

* * *

MAKING A TIP AT ROUTE [RESTAURANT]

A common feature of past research is that the worker's control over the tipping system is evaluated in terms of her efforts to con, coerce, compel, or otherwise manipulate a customer into relinquishing a bigger tip. Because these efforts have for the most part proven futile, the worker has been seen as having little defense against the financial vicissitudes of the tipping system. What these studies have overlooked is that an employee can increase her tip income by controlling the number as well as the size of tips she receives. This oversight has arisen from the tendency of researchers to concentrate narrowly on the relationship between server and served, while failing to take into account the broader organizational context in which this relationship takes place.

Like service workers observed in earlier studies, waitresses at Route strive to boost the amount of individual gratuities by rendering special services and being especially friendly. As one waitress put it, "I'll sell you the world if you're in my station." In general though, waitresses at Route Restaurant seek to boost their tip income, not by increasing the amount of individual gratuities, but by increasing the number of customers they serve. They accomplish this (a) by securing the largest or busiest stations and working the most lucrative shifts; (b) by "turning" their tables quickly; and (c) by controlling the flow of customers within the restaurant.

Technically, stations at Route are assigned on a rotating basis so that all waitresses, including rookies, work fast and slow stations equally. Station assignments are listed on the work schedule that is posted in the office window where it can be examined by all workers on all shifts, precluding the possibility of blatant favoritism or discrimination. Yet a number of methods exist whereby experienced waitresses are able to circumvent the formal rotation system and secure the more lucrative stations for themselves. A waitress can trade assignments with a rookie who is uncertain of her ability to handle a fast station; she can volunteer to take over a large station when a *call-out* necessitates reorganization of station assignments; or she can establish herself as the only waitress capable of handling a particularly large or chaotic station. Changes in station assignments tend not to be formally recorded, so inconsistencies in the rotation system often do not show up on the schedule. Waitresses on the same shift may notice of course that a co-worker has managed to avoid an especially slow station for many days, or has somehow ended up in the busiest station two weekends in a row, but the waitresses' code of noninterference * * * inhibits them from openly objecting to such irregularities.

A waitress can also increase her tip income by working the more lucrative shifts. Because day is the busiest and therefore most profitable shift at Route, it attracts experienced, professional waitresses who are most concerned and best able to maximize their tip earnings. There are exceptions; some competent, senior-ranking waitresses are unable to work during the day due to time constraints of family or second jobs. Others choose not to work during the day despite the potential monetary rewards, because they are unwilling to endure the intensely competitive atmosphere for which day shift is infamous.

The acutely competitive environment that characterizes day shift arises from the aggregate striving of each waitress to maximize her tip income by serving the greatest possible number of customers. Two strategies are enlisted to this end. First, each waitress attempts to *turn* her tables as quickly as possible. Briefly stated, this means she takes the order, delivers the food, clears and resets a table, and begins serving the next party as rapidly as customer lingering and the speed of the kitchen allow. A seven-year veteran of Route describes the strategy and its rewards:

What I do is I prebus my tables. When the people get up and go all I got is glasses and cups, pull off, wipe, set, and I do the table turnover. But see that's from day shift. See the girls on graveyard . . . don't understand the more times you turn that table the more money you make. You could have three tables and still make a hundred dollars. If you turn them tables.

As the waitress indicates, a large part of turning tables involves getting the table cleared and set for the next customer. During a rush, swing and grave waitresses tend to leave dirty tables standing, partly because they are less experienced and therefore less efficient, partly to avoid being given parties, or *sat,* when they are already behind. In contrast, day waitresses assign high priority to keeping their tables cleared and ready for customers. The difference in method reflects increased skill and growing awareness of and concern with money-making strategies.

A waitress can further increase her customer count by controlling the flow of customers within the restaurant. Ideally the hostess or manager running the front house rotates customers among stations, just as stations are rotated among waitresses. Each waitress is given, or *sat,* one party at a time in turn so that all waitresses have comparable customer counts at the close of a shift. When no hostess is on duty, or both she and the manager are detained and customers are waiting to be seated, waitresses will typically seat incoming parties.

Whether or not a formal hostess is on duty, day waitresses are notorious for bypassing the rotation system by racing to the door and directing incoming customers to their own tables. A sense of the urgency with which this strategy is pursued is conveyed in the comment of one five-year veteran, "They'll run you down to get that person at the door, to seat them in their station." The competition for customers is so intense during the day that some waitresses claim they cannot afford to leave the floor (even to use the restroom) lest they return to find a co-worker's station filled at their expense. "In the daytime, honey," remarks an eight-year Route waitress, "in the daytime it's like pulling teeth. You got to stay on the floor to survive. To survive." It is in part because they do not want to lose customers and tips to their co-workers that waitresses do not take formal breaks. Instead, they rest and eat between waiting tables or during lulls in business, returning to the floor intermittently to check on parties in progress and seat customers in their stations.

The fast pace and chaotic nature of restaurant work provide a cover for the waitress's aggressive pursuit of customers, since it is difficult for other servers to monitor closely the allocation of parties in the bustle and confusion of a rush. Still, it is not uncommon for waitresses to grumble to management and co-workers if they notice an obvious imbalance in customer distribution. Here again, the waitress refrains from directly criticizing her fellow servers, voicing her displeasure by commenting on the paucity of customers in her own station, rather than the overabundance of customers in the stations of certain co-waitresses. In response to these grumblings, other waitresses may moderate somewhat their efforts to appropriate new parties, and management may make a special effort to seat the disgruntled server favorably.

A waitress can also exert pressure on the manager or hostess to keep her station filled. She may, for instance, threaten to leave if she is not seated enough customers.

> I said, "Innes [a manager], I'm in [station] one and two. If one and two is not filled at all times from now until three, I'm getting my coat, my pocketbook, and I'm leaving." And one and two was filled, and I made ninety-five dollars.

Alternatively, she can make it more convenient for the manager or hostess to seat her rather than her co-workers, either by keeping her tables open (as described), or by taking extra tables. If customers are waiting to be seated, a waitress may offer to pick up parties in a station that is closed or, occasionally, to pick up parties in another waitress's station. In attempting either strategy, but especially the latter, the waitress must be adept not only at waiting tables, but in interpersonal restaurant politics. Autonomy and possession are of central concern to waitresses, and a waitress who offers to pick up tables outside her station must select her words carefully if she is to avoid being accused of invading her co-workers' territory. Accordingly, she may choose to present her bid for extra parties as an offer to help—the manager, another waitress, the restaurant, customers—rather than as a request.

The waitress who seeks to increase her tip income by maximizing the number of customers she serves may endeavor to cut her losses by refusing to serve parties that have stiffed her in the past. If she is a low-ranking waitress, her refusal is likely to be overturned by the manager. If she is an experienced and valuable waitress, the manager may ask someone else to take the party, assure the waitress he will take care of her (that is, pad the bill and give her the difference), or even pick up the party himself. Though the practice is far from common, a waitress may go so far as to demand a tip from a customer who has been known to stiff in the past.

> This party of two guys come in and they order thirty to forty dollars worth of food . . . and they stiff us. Every time. So Kaddie told them, "If you don't tip us, we're not going to wait on you." They said, "We'll tip you." So Kaddie waited on them, and they tipped her. The next night they came in, I waited on them and they didn't tip me. The third time they came in [the manager] put them in my station and I told [the manager] straight up, "I'm not waiting on them . . ." So he made Hailey pick them up. And they stiffed Hailey. So when they came in the next night . . . [they] said, "Are you going to give us a table?" I said, "You going to tip me? I'm not going to wait on you. You got all that money, you sell all that crack on the streets and you come here and you can't even leave me a couple bucks?" . . . So they left me a dollar. So when they come in Tuesday night, I'm telling them a dollar ain't enough.

The tactics employed by waitresses, and particularly day-shift waitresses, to increase their customer count and thereby boost their tip earnings have earned them a resounding notoriety among their less competitive co-workers. Day (and some swing) waitresses are described as "money hungry," "sneaky little bitches," "self-centered," "aggressive," "backstabbing bitches," and "cut-throats over tables." The following remarks of two Route waitresses, however, indicate that those who employ these tactics see them as defensive, not aggressive measures. A sense of the waitress's preoccupation with autonomy and with protecting what is hers also emerges from these comments.

> You have to be like that. Because if you don't be like that, people step on you. You know, like as far as getting customers. I mean, you know, I'm sorry everybody says I'm greedy. I guess that's why I've survived this long at Route. Cause I am greedy. . . . *I want what's mine,* and if it comes down to me cleaning your table or my table, I'm going to clean my table. Because see I went through all that stage where I would do your table. To be fair. And you would walk home with seventy dollars, and I'd have twenty-five, cause I was being fair all night. (emphasis added)
>
> If the customer comes in the door and I'm there getting that door, don't expect me to cover your backside while you in the back smoking a cigarette and I'm here working for myself. You not out there working for me. . . . When I go to the door and get the customers, when I keep my tables clean and your tables are dirty, and you wonder why you only got one person . . . then that's just tough shit. . . . You're damn right my station is filled. *I'm not here for you.* (emphasis added)

Whether the waitress who keeps her station filled with customers is acting aggressively or defensively, her tactics are effective. It is commonly accepted that determined day waitresses make better money than less competitive coworkers even when working swing or grave. Moreover Nera, the waitress most infamous for her relentless use of "money-hungry" tactics, is at the same time most famous for her consistently high daily takes. While other waitresses jingle change in their aprons, Nera is forced to store wads of bills in her shoes and in paper bags to prevent tips from overflowing her pockets. She claims to make a minimum of five hundred dollars a week in tip earnings; her record for one day's work exceeds two hundred dollars and is undoubtedly the record for the restaurant.

INVERTING THE SYMBOLISM OF TIPPING

It may already be apparent that the waitress views the customer—not as a master to pamper and appease—but as substance to be processed as quickly and in as large a quantity as possible. The difference in perspective is expressed in the objectifying terminology of waitresses: a customer or party is referred to as a *table,* or by table number, as *table five* or simply *five*; serving successive parties at a table is referred to as *turning the table*; taking an order

employees marks them as needy in the eyes of their customers. [One study] reports that among cabdrivers "a forever repeated story is of the annoyed driver, who, after a grueling trip with a Lady Shopper, hands the coin back, telling her, 'Lady, keep your lousy dime. You need it more than I do.'" [Another study reports] a hotel waitress's claim that "if she had served a large family with children for one or two weeks, and then was given a 10p[ence] piece, she would give the money back, saying, 'It's all right, thank you, I've got enough change for my bus fare home.'" In an incident I observed (not at Route), a waitress followed two male customers out of a restaurant calling, "Excuse me! You forgot this!" and holding up the coins they had left as a tip. The customers appeared embarrassed, motioned for her to keep the money, and continued down the sidewalk. The waitress, now standing in the outdoor seating area of the restaurant and observed by curious diners, threw the money after the retreating men and returned to her work. Episodes such as these allow the worker to repudiate openly the evaluation of her financial status that is implied in an offensively small gratuity, and permit her to articulate her own understanding of what a small tip says and about whom. If customers can only afford to leave a dime, or feel a 10p piece is adequate compensation for two weeks' service, they must be very hard up or very ignorant indeed.

In the following incident the waitress interjects a denial of her neediness into an altercation that is not related to tipping, demonstrating that the customer's perception of her financial status is a prominent and persistent concern for her.

> She [a customer] wanted a California Burger with mayonnaise. And when I got the mayonnaise, the mayonnaise had a little brown on it. . . . So this girl said to me, she said, "What the fuck is this you giving me?" And I turned around, I thought, "Maybe she's talking to somebody else in the booth with her." And I turned around and I said, "Excuse me?" She said, "You hear what I said, I said, 'What the fuck are you giving me?'" And I turned around, I said, "I don't know if you're referring your information to *me,*" I said, "but if you're referring your information to *me,*" I said, "I don't *need* your bullshit." I said, "I'm not going to even take it. . . . Furthermore, I could care less if you eat or *don't* eat. . . . And you see this?" And I took her check and I ripped it apart. . . . And I took the California Burger and I says, "You don't have a problem anymore now, right?" She went up to the manager. And she says, "That black waitress"—I says, "Oh. By the way, what is my name? I don't have a name, [using the words] 'that black waitress.' . . . My name happens to be Nera. . . . That's N-E-R-A. . . . And I don't need your bullshit, sweetheart. . . . People like you I can walk on, because you don't know how to talk to human beings." And I said, "I don't need you. I don't need your quarters. I don't need your nickels. I don't need your dimes. So if you want service, be my guest. Don't you *ever* sit in my station, cause I won't wait on you." The manager said, "Nera, please. Would you wait in the back?" I said, "No. I don't take back seats no more for nobody."

In each of these cases, the waitress challenges the customer's definition of the relationship in which tipping occurs. By speaking out, by confronting the customer, she demonstrates that she is not subservient or in fear of losing her job; that she is not compelled by financial need or a sense of social hierarchy to accept abuse from customers; that she does not, in Nera's words, "take back seats no more for nobody." At the same time, she reverses the symbolic force of the low tip, converting a statement on her social status or work skills into a statement on the tipper's cheapness or lack of savoir faire.

28

Upward Mobility Through Sport?

D. STANLEY EITZEN

You can trace the history of twentieth-century immigration in the United States by reading the list of boxers who held the title of Champion of the World. The names of Irish, Jewish, Italian, African American, and Latino boxers record the stirrings of upward mobility for those who shared the boxers' ethnicity or nationality. But the lives of the boxers themselves were often far less successful than a championship title would indicate. And what of sports more generally? In true sociological fashion, Stanley Eitzen shows us that sports may do far less in advancing the life chances of young people than is often assumed.

Typically, Americans believe that sport is a path to upward social mobility. This belief is based on the obvious examples we see as poor boys and men (rarely girls and women) from rural and urban areas, whether white or black, sometimes skyrocket to fame and fortune through success in sports. Sometimes the financial reward has been astounding, such as the high pay that some African American athletes received in recent years. In 1997 Tracy Mc-Grady, an NBA-bound high school star, bypassed college, signed a $12 million deal over 6 years with Adidas. Golfer Tiger Woods in his first year as a professional made $6.82 million in winnings (U.S. and worldwide) and appearance fees plus signed a series of five-year deals with Nike, Titleist, American Express, and Rolex worth $95.2 million. In 1998 Wood's earnings from endorsements totaled $28 million. Boxer Mike Tyson made $75 million in 1996. It is estimated that Michael Jordan made over $100 million in 1998, including salary, endorsements, and income from merchandise and videos. The recent deals for baseball stars, some exceeding $15 million a year for multiyear contracts, further underscores the incredible money given to some individuals for their athletic talents.

But while the possibility of staggering wealth and status through sport is possible, the reality is that dramatic upward mobility through sport is highly improbable. A number of myths, however, combine to lead us to believe that sport is a social mobility escalator.

MYTH: SPORT PROVIDES A FREE EDUCATION

Good high school athletes get college scholarships. These athletic scholarships are especially helpful to poor youth who otherwise would not be able to attend college because of the high costs. The problem with this assumption is that while true for some, very few high school athletes actually receive full scholarships. Football provides the easiest route to a college scholarship because Division I-A colleges have 85 football scholarships, but even this avenue is exceedingly narrow. In Colorado there were 3,481 male high school seniors who played football during the 1994 season. Of these, 31 received full scholarships at Division I-A schools (0.0089 percent).

Second, of all the male varsity athletes at all college levels only about 15 percent to 20 percent have full scholarships. Another 15 percent to 25 percent have partial scholarships, leaving 55 percent to 70 percent of all intercollegiate athletes without any sport related financial assistance. Third, as low as the chances are for men, women athletes have even less chance to receive an athletic scholarship. While women comprise about 52 percent of all college students, they make up only 35 percent of intercollegiate athletes with a similar disproportionate distribution of scholarships. Another reality is that if you are a male athlete in a so-called minor sport (swimming, tennis, golf, gymnastics, cross-country, wrestling), the chances of a full scholarship are virtually nil. The best hope is a partial scholarship, if that, since these sports are underfunded and in danger of elimination at many schools.

MYTH: SPORT LEADS TO A COLLEGE DEGREE

College graduates exceed high school graduates by hundreds of thousands of dollars in lifetime earnings. Since most high school and college athletes will never play at the professional level, the attainment of a college degree is a crucial determinant of upward mobility through sport. The problem is that relatively few male athletes in the big time revenue producing sports, compared to their non-athletic peers, actually receive college degrees. This is especially the case for African American men who are over represented in the revenue producing sports. In 1996, for example, looking at the athletes who entered Division I schools in 1990, only 45 percent of African American football players and 39 percent of African American basketball players had graduated (compared to 56 percent of the general student body).

There are a number of barriers to graduation for male athletes. The demands on their time and energy are enormous even in the off-season. Many athletes, because of these pressures, take easy courses to maintain eligibility but do not lead to graduation. The result is either to delay graduation or to make graduation an unrealistic goal.

Another barrier is that they are recruited for athletic prowess rather than academic ability. Recent data show that football players in big time programs are, on average, more than 200 points behind their non-athletic classmates on SAT test scores. Poorly prepared students are the most likely to take easy courses, cheat on exams, hire surrogate test takers, and otherwise do the minimum.

A third barrier to graduation for male college athletes is themselves, as they may not take advantage of their scholarships to obtain a quality education. This is especially the case for those who perceive their college experience only as preparation for their professional careers in sport. Study for them is necessary only to maintain their eligibility. The goal of a professional career is unrealistic for all but the superstars. The superstars who do make it at the professional level, more likely than not, will have not graduated from college; nor will they go back to finish their degrees when their professional careers are over. This is also because even a successful professional athletic career is limited to a few years, and not many professional athletes are able to translate their success in the pros to success in their post-athletic careers. Such a problem is especially true for African Americans, who often face employment discrimination in the wider society.

MYTH: A SPORTS CAREER IS PROBABLE

A recent survey by the Center for the Study of Sport in Society found that two-thirds of African American males between the ages of 13 and 18 believe that they can earn a living playing professional sports (more than double the proportion of young white males who hold such beliefs). Moreover, African American parents were four times more likely than white parents to believe that their sons are destined for careers as professional athletes.

If these young athletes could play as professionals, the economic rewards are excellent, especially in basketball and baseball. In 1998 the average annual salary for professional basketball was $2.24 million. In baseball the average salary was $1.37 million with 280 of the 774 players on opening day rosters making $1 million or more (of them, 197 exceeded $2 million or more, while 32 of them made $6 million or more). The average salaries for the National Hockey League and National Football League were $892,000 and $795,000, respectively. In football, for example, 19 percent of the players (333 of 1,765) exceeded $1 million in salary. These numbers are inflated by the use of averages, which are skewed by the salaries of the superstars. Use of the median (in which half the players make more and half make less), reveals that the median salary in basketball was $1.4 million; baseball—$500,000; football—$400,000; and hockey—$500,000. Regardless of the measure, the financial allure of a professional sports career is great.

A career in professional sports is nearly impossible to attain because of the fierce competition for so few openings. In an average year there are approximately 1,900,000 American boys playing high school football, basketball, and baseball. Another 68,000 men are playing those sports in college, and 2,490 are participating at the major professional level. In short, one in 27 high school players in these sports will play at the college level, and only one in 736 high school players will play at the major professional level (0.14 percent). In baseball, each year about 120,000 players are eligible for the draft (high school seniors, college seniors, collegians over 21, junior college players, and foreign players). Only about 1,200 (1 percent) are actually drafted, and most of them will never make it to the major leagues. Indeed, only one in ten of those players who sign a professional baseball contract ever play in the major leagues for at least one day.

The same rigorous condensation process occurs in football. About 15,000 players are eligible for the NFL draft each year. Three hundred thirty-six are drafted and about 160 actually make the final roster. Similarly, in basketball and hockey, only about 40 new players are added to the rosters in the NBA and 60 rookies make the NHL each year. In tennis only about 100 men and 100 women make enough money to cover expenses. In golf, of the 165 men eligible for the PGA tour in 1997, their official winnings ranged from $2,066,833 (Tiger Woods) to $10,653 (Chip Beck). The competition among these golfers is fierce. On average, the top 100 golfers on the tour play within 2 strokes of each other for every 18 holes, yet Tiger Woods, the tops in winnings won over $2 million, and the 100th finisher won only $250,000. Below the PGA tour is the Nike Tour where the next best 125 golfers compete. Their winnings were a top of $225,201 to a low of $9,944.

MYTH: SPORT IS A WAY OUT OF POVERTY

Sport appears to be a major way for African Americans to escape the ghetto. African Americans dominate the major professional sports numerically. While only 12 percent of the population, African Americans comprise about 80 percent of the players in professional basketball, about 67 percent of professional football players, and 18 percent of professional baseball players (Latinos also comprise about 17 percent of professional baseball players). Moreover, African Americans dominate the list of the highest moneymakers in sport (salaries, commercial sponsorships). These facts, while true, are illusory.

While African Americans dominate professional basketball, football, and to a lesser extent baseball, they are rarely found in certain sports such as hockey, automobile racing, tennis, golf, bowling, and skiing. Moreover, African Americans are severely under-represented in positions of authority in sport— as head coaches, referees, athletic directors, scouts, general managers, and owners. In the NFL in 1997, for example, where more than two-thirds of the players were African American, only three head coaches and five offensive or defensive coordinators were African American. In that year there were 11 head coaching vacancies filled none by African Americans. The reason for this racial imbalance in hiring, according to white sports columnist for the *Rocky Mountain News* Bob Kravitz is that: "something here stinks, and it stinks a lot like racism."

Second, while the odds of African American males making it as professional athletes are more favorable than is the case for whites (about 1 in 3,500 African American male high school athletes, compared to 1 in 10,000 white male high school athletes) these odds remain slim. Of the 40,000 or so African Americans boys who play high school basketball, only 35 will make the NBA and only 7 will be starters. Referring to the low odds for young African Americans, Harry Edwards, an African American sociologist specializing in the sociology of sport, said with a bit of hyperbole: "Statistically, you have a better chance of getting hit by a meteorite in the next ten years than getting work as an athlete."

Despite these discouraging facts, the myth is alive for poor youth. As noted earlier, two-thirds of African American boys believe they can be professional athletes. Their parents, too, accept this belief (African American parents are four times more likely than white parents to believe that their children will be professional athletes). The film *Hoop Dreams* and Darcey Frey's book *The Last Shot: City Street, Basketball Dreams* document the emphasis that young African American men place on sports as a way up and their ultimate disappointments from sport. For many of them, sport represents their only hope of escape from a life of crime, poverty, and despair. They latch on to the dream of athletic success partly because of the few opportunities for middle-class success. They spend many hours per day developing their speed, strength, jumping height, or "moves" to the virtual exclusion of those abilities that have a greater likelihood of paying off in upward mobility such as reading comprehension, mathematical reasoning, communication skills, and computer literacy.

Sociologist Jay Coakley puts it this way: "My best guess is that less than 3,500 African Americans . . . are making their livings as professional athletes. At the same time (in 1996), there are about 30,015 black physicians and about 30,800 black lawyers currently employed in the U.S. Therefore, there are 20 times more blacks working in these two professions than playing top level professional sports. And physicians and lawyers usually have lifetime earnings far in excess of the earnings of professional athletes, whose playing careers, on average, last less than five years."

Harry Edwards posits that by spending their energies and talents on athletic skills, young African Americans are not pursuing occupations that would help them meet their political and material needs. Thus, because of belief in the "sports as a way up" myth, they remain dependent on whites and white institutions. Salim Muwakkil, an African American political analyst, argues that "If African Americans are to exploit the socio-economic options opened by varied civil rights struggles more fully, blacks must reduce the disproportionate allure of sports in their communities. Black leadership must contextualize athletic success by promoting other avenues to social status, intensifying the struggle for access to those avenues and better educating youth about those pot-holes on the road to the stadium."

John Hoberman in his book *Darwin's Athletes* also challenges the assumption that sport has progressive consequences. The success of African Americans in the highly visible sports gives white Americans a false sense of black progress and interracial harmony. But the social progress of African

Americans in general has little relationship to the apparent integration that they have achieved on the playing fields.

Hoberman also contends that the numerical superiority of African Americans in sport, coupled with their disproportionate under-representation in other professions, reinforces the racist ideology that African Americans, while physically superior to whites, are inferior to them intellectually.

I do not mean to say that African Americans should not seek a career in professional sport. What is harmful is that the odds of success are so slim, making the extraordinary efforts over many years futile and misguided for the vast majority.

MYTH: WOMEN HAVE SPORT AS A VEHICLE

Since the passage of Title IX in 1972 that required schools receiving federal funds to provide equal opportunities for women and men, sports participation by women in high school and college has increased dramatically. In 1973, for example, when 50,000 men received some form of college scholarship for their athletic abilities, women received only 50. Now, women receive about 35 percent of the money allotted for college athletic scholarships (while a dramatic improvement, this should not be equated with gender equality as many would have us believe). This allows many women athletes to attend college who otherwise could not afford it, thus receiving an indirect upward mobility boost.

Upward mobility as a result of being a professional athlete is another matter for women. Women have fewer opportunities than men in professional team sports. Beach volley-ball is a possibility for a few but the rewards are minimal. Two professional women's basketball leagues began in 1997, but the pay was very low compared to men and the leagues were on shaky financial ground (the average salary in the American Basketball League was $80,000). The other option for women is to play in professional leagues in Europe, Australia, and Asia but the pay is relatively low.

Women have more opportunities as professionals in individual sports such as tennis, golf, ice-skating, skiing, bowling, cycling, and track. Ironically, the sports with the greatest monetary rewards for women are those of the middle and upper classes (tennis, golf, and ice skating). These sports are expensive and require considerable individual coaching and access to private facilities.

Ironically, with the passage of Title IX, which increased the participation rates of women so dramatically, there has been a decline in the number and proportion of women as coaches and athletic administrators. In addition to the glaring pay gap between what the coaches of men's teams receive compared to the coaches of women's teams, men who coach women's teams tend to have higher salaries than women coaching women's teams. Women also have fewer opportunities than men as athletic trainers, officials, sports journalists, and other adjunct positions.

MYTH: SPORTS PROVIDES LIFELONG SECURITY

Even when a professional sport career is attained, the probabilities of fame and fortune are limited. Of course, some athletes make incomes from salaries and endorsements that if invested wisely, provide financial security for life. Many professional athletes make relatively low salaries. During the 1996 season, for example, 17 percent of major league baseball players made the minimum salary of $247,500 for veterans and $220,000 for rookies. This is a lot of money, but for these marginal players their careers may not last very long. Indeed, the average length of a professional career in a team sport is about five years. A marginal athlete in individual sports such as golf, tennis, boxing, and bowling, struggle financially. They must cover their travel expenses, health insurance, equipment, and the like with no guaranteed paycheck. The brief career diverts them during their youth from developing other career skills and experiences that would benefit them.

Ex-professional athletes leave sport, on average, when they are in their late 20s or early 30s, at a time when their non-athletic peers have begun to establish themselves in occupations leading toward retirement in 40 years or so. What are the ex-professional athletes to do with their remaining productive years?

Exiting a sports career can be relatively smooth or difficult. Some athletes have planned ahead, preparing for other careers either in sport (coaching, scouting, administering) or some non-sport occupation. Others have not prepared for this abrupt change. They did not graduate from college. They did not spend the off seasons apprenticing non-sport jobs. Exiting the athlete role is difficult for many because they lose: (1) What has been the focus of their being for most of their lives; (2) the primary source of their identities; (3) their physical prowess; (4) the adulation bordering on worship from others; (5) the money and the perquisites of fame; (6) the camaraderie with teammates; (7) the intense "highs" of competition; and (8) for most ex-athletes retirement means a loss of status. As a result of these "losses," many ex-professional athletes have trouble adjusting to life after sport. A study by the NFL Players Association found, that emotional difficulties, divorce, and financial strain were common problems for ex-professional football players. A majority had "permanent injuries" from football.

The allure of sport, however, remains strong and this has at least two negative consequences. First, ghetto youngsters who devote their lives to the pursuit of athletic stardom are, except for the fortunate few, doomed to failure in sport and in the real world where sports skills are essentially irrelevant to occupational placement and advancement. The second negative consequence is more subtle but very important. Sport contributes to the ideology that legitimizes social inequalities and promotes the myth that all it takes is extraordinary effort to succeed. Sport sociologist George H. Sage makes this point forcefully: "Because sport is by nature meritocratic—that is, superior performance brings status and rewards—it provides convincing symbolic support for hegemonic [the dominant] ideology—that ambitious, dedicated, hard working individuals, regardless of social origin, can achieve success and ascend in the social hierarchy, obtaining high status and material rewards, while those who don't move upward simply didn't work hard enough. Because the rags-to-riches athletes are so visible, the social mobility theme is maintained. This reflects the opportunity structure of society in general—the success of a few reproduces the belief in social mobility among the many."

29

The Saints and the Roughnecks

WILLIAM J. CHAMBLISS

Almost every student can identify the "Saints" and "Roughnecks" in their high school, but it requires an astute observer like William Chambliss to show us the hidden implications of this dichotomy in a class-structured society. Social class matters, just as high school social hierarchies matter, because people are treated according to their position, and not necessarily in terms of who they are or what they actually do.

Eight promising young men—children of good, stable, white upper-middle-class families, active in school affairs, good pre-college students—were some of the most delinquent boys at Hanibal High School. While community residents knew that these boys occasionally sowed a few wild oats, they were totally unaware that sowing wild oats completely occupied the daily routine of these young men. The Saints were constantly occupied with truancy, drinking, wild driving, petty theft, and vandalism. Yet no one was officially arrested for any misdeed during the two years I observed them.

This record was particularly surprising in light of my observations during the same two years of another gang of Hanibal High School students, six lower-class white boys known as the Roughnecks. The Roughnecks were constantly in trouble with police and community even though their rate of delinquency was about equal with that of the Saints. What was the cause of this disparity? the result? The following consideration of the activities, social class, and community perceptions of both gangs may provide some answers.

THE SAINTS FROM MONDAY TO FRIDAY

The Saints' principal daily concern was with getting out of school as early as possible. The boys managed to get out of school with minimum danger that they would be accused of playing hookey through an elaborate procedure for obtaining "legitimate" release from class. The most common procedure was for one boy to obtain the release of another by fabricating a meeting of some committee, program, or recognized club. Charles might raise his hand in his 9:00 chemistry class and ask to be excused—a euphemism for going to the bathroom. Charles would go to Ed's math class and inform the teacher that Ed was needed for a 9:30 rehearsal of the drama club play. The math teacher would recognize Ed and Charles as "good students" involved in numerous school activities and would permit Ed to leave at 9:30. Charles would return to his class, and Ed would go to Tom's English class to obtain his release. Tom would engineer Charles's escape. The strategy would continue until as many of the Saints as possible were freed. After a stealthy trip to the car (which had been parked in a strategic spot), the boys were off for a day of fun.

Over the two years I observed the Saints, this pattern was repeated nearly every day. There were variations on the theme, but in one form or another, the boys used this procedure for getting out of class and then off the school grounds. Rarely did all eight of the Saints manage to leave school at the same time. The average number avoiding school on the days I observed them was five.

Having escaped from the concrete corridors the boys usually went either to a pool hall on the other (lower-class) side of town or to a café in the suburbs. Both places were out of the way of people the boys were likely to know (family or school officials), and both provided a source of entertainment. The pool hall entertainment was the generally rough atmosphere, the occasional hustler, the sometimes drunk proprietor and, of course, the game of pool. The café's entertainment was provided by the owner. The boys would "accidentally" knock a glass on the floor or spill cola on the counter—not all the time, but enough to be sporting. They would also bend spoons, put salt in sugar bowls and generally tease whoever was working in the café. The owner had opened the café recently and was dependent on the boys' business which was, in fact, substantial since between the horsing around and the teasing they bought food and drinks.

THE SAINTS ON WEEKENDS

On weekends the automobile was even more critical than during the week, for on weekends the Saints went to Big Town—a large city with a population of over a million 25 miles from Hanibal. Every Friday and Saturday night most of the Saints would meet between 8:00 and 8:30 and would go into Big Town. Big Town activities included drinking heavily in taverns or nightclubs, driving drunkenly through the streets, and committing acts of vandalism and playing pranks.

By midnight on Fridays and Saturdays the Saints were usually thoroughly high, and one or two of them were often so drunk they had to be carried to the cars. Then the boys drove around town, calling obscenities to women and girls; occasionally trying (unsuccessfully so far as I could tell) to pick girls up; and driving recklessly through red lights and at high speeds with their lights out. Occasionally they played "chicken." One boy would climb out the back window of the car and across the roof to the driver's side of the car while the car was moving at high speed (between 40 and 50 miles an hour); then the driver would move over and the boy who had just crawled across the car roof would take the driver's seat.

Searching for "fair game" for a prank was the boy's principal activity after they left the tavern. The boys would drive alongside a foot patrol-man and ask directions to some street. If the policeman leaned on the car in the course of answering the question, the driver would speed away, causing him to lose his balance. The Saints were careful to play this prank only in an area where they were not going to spend much time and where they could quickly disappear around a corner to avoid having their license plate number taken.

Construction sites and road repair areas were the special province of the Saints' mischief. A soon-to-be-repaired hole in the road inevitably invited the Saints to remove lanterns and wooden barricades and put them in the car, leaving the hole unprotected. The boys would find a safe vantage point and wait for an unsuspecting motorist to drive into the hole. Often, though not always, the boys would go up to the motorist and commiserate with him about the dreadful way the city protected its citizenry.

Leaving the scene of the open hole and the motorist, the boys would then go searching for an appropriate place to erect the stolen barricade. An "appropriate place" was often a spot on a highway near a curve in the road where the barricade would not be seen by an oncoming motorist. The boys would wait to watch an unsuspecting motorist attempt to stop and (usually) crash into the wooden barricade. With saintly bearing the boys might offer help and understanding.

A stolen lantern might well find its way onto the back of a police car or hang from a street lamp. Once a lantern served as a prop for a reenactment of the "midnight ride of Paul Revere" until the "play," which was taking place at 2:00 A.M. in the center of a main street of Big Town, was interrupted by a police car several blocks away. The boys ran, leaving the lanterns on the street, and managed to avoid being apprehended.

Abandoned houses, especially if they were located in out-of-the-way places, were fair game for destruction and spontaneous vandalism. The boys would break windows, remove furniture to the yard and tear it apart, urinate on the walls, and scrawl obscenities inside.

Through all the pranks, drinking, and reckless driving the boys managed miraculously to avoid being stopped by police. Only twice in two years was I aware that they had been stopped by a Big Town policeman. Once was for speeding (which they did every time they drove whether they were drunk or sober), and the driver managed to convince the policeman that it was simply an error. The second time they were stopped they had just left a nightclub and were walking through an alley. Aaron stopped to urinate and the boys began making obscene remarks. A foot patrolman came into the alley, lectured the boys and sent them home. Before the boys got to the car one began talking in a loud voice again. The policeman, who had followed them down the alley, arrested this boy for disturbing the peace and took him to the police station where the other Saints gathered. After paying a $5.00 fine, and with the assurance that there would be no permanent record of the arrest, the boy was released.

The boys had a spirit of frivolity and fun about their escapades. They did not view what they were engaged in as "delinquency," though it surely was by any reasonable definition of that word. They simply viewed themselves as having a little fun and who, they would ask, was really hurt by it? The answer had to be no one, although this fact remains one of the most difficult things to explain about the gang's behavior. Unlikely though it seems, in two years of drinking, driving, carousing, and vandalism no one was seriously injured as a result of the Saints' activities.

THE SAINTS IN SCHOOL

The Saints were highly successful in school. The average grade for the group was "B," with two of the boys having close to a straight "A" average. Almost all of the boys were popular and many of them held offices in the school. One of the boys was vice president of the student body one year. Six of the boys played on athletic teams.

At the end of their senior year, the student body selected ten seniors for special recognition as the "school wheels"; four of the ten were Saints. Teachers and school officials saw no problem with any of these boys and anticipated that they would all "make something of themselves."

How the boys managed to maintain this impression is surprising in view of their actual behavior in school. Their technique for covering truancy was so successful that teachers did not even realize that the boys were absent from school much of the time. Occasionally, of course, the system would backfire and then the boy was on his own. A boy who was caught would be most contrite, would plead guilty and ask for mercy. He inevitably got the mercy he sought.

Cheating on examinations was rampant, even to the point of orally communicating answers to exams as well as looking at one another's papers. Since none of the group studied, and since they were primarily dependent on one another for help, it is surprising that grades were so high. Teachers contributed to the deception in their admitted inclination to give these boys (and presumably others like them) the benefit of the doubt. When asked how the boys did in school, and when pressed on specific examinations, teachers might admit that they were disappointed in John's performance, but would quickly add that they "knew that he was capable of doing better," so John was given a higher grade than he had actually earned. How often this happened is impossible to know. During the time that I observed the group, I never saw any of the boys take homework home. Teachers may have been "understanding" very regularly.

One exception to the gang's generally good performance was Jerry, who had a "C" average in his junior year, experienced disaster the next year, and failed to graduate. Jerry had always been a little more nonchalant than the others about the liberties he took in school. Rather than wait for someone to come get him from class, he would offer his own excuse and leave. Although he probably did not miss any more class than most of the others in the group, he did not take the requisite pains to cover his absences. Jerry was the only Saint whom I ever heard talk back to a teacher. Although teachers often called him a "cut up" or a "smart kid," they never referred to him as a troublemaker or as a kid headed for trouble. It seems likely, then, that Jerry's failure his senior year and his mediocre performance his junior year were consequences of his not playing the game the proper way (possibly because he was disturbed by his parents' divorce). His teachers regarded him as "immature" and not quite ready to get out of high school.

THE POLICE AND THE SAINTS

The local police saw the Saints as good boys who were among the leaders of the youth in the community. Rarely, the boys might be stopped in town for speeding or for running a stop sign. When this happened the boys were always polite, contrite and pled for mercy. As in school, they received the mercy they asked for. None ever received a ticket or was taken into the precinct by the local police.

The situation in Big Town, where the boys engaged in most of their delinquency, was only slightly different. The police there did not know the boys at all, although occasionally the boys were stopped by a patrolman. Once they were caught taking a lantern from a construction site. Another time they were stopped for running a stop sign, and on several occasions they were stopped for speeding. Their behavior was as before: contrite, polite and penitent. The urban police, like the local police, accepted their demeanor as sincere. More important, the urban police were convinced that these were good boys just out for a lark.

THE ROUGHNECKS

Hanibal townspeople never perceived the Saints' high level of delinquency. The Saints were good boys who just went in for an occasional prank. After all, they were well dressed, well mannered and had nice cars. The Roughnecks were a different story. Although the two gangs of boys were the same age, and both groups engaged in an equal amount of wild-oat sowing, everyone agreed that the not-so-well-dressed, not-so-well-mannered, not-so-rich boys were heading for trouble. Townspeople would say, "You can see the gang members at the drugstore, night after night, leaning against the storefront (sometimes drunk) or slouching around inside buying cokes, reading magazines, and probably stealing old Mr. Wall blind. When they are outside and girls walk by, even respectable girls, these boys make suggestive remarks. Sometimes their remarks are downright lewd."

From the community's viewpoint, the real indication that these kids were in trouble was that they were constantly involved with the police. Some of them had been picked up for stealing, mostly small stuff, of course, "but still it's stealing small stuff that leads to big time crimes." "Too bad," people said. "Too bad that these boys couldn't behave like the other kids in town; stay out of trouble, be polite to adults, and look to their future."

The community's impression of the degrees to which this group of six boys (ranging in age from 16 to 19) engaged in delinquency was somewhat distorted. In some ways the gang was more delinquent than the community thought; in other ways they were less.

The fighting activities of the group were fairly readily and accurately perceived by almost everyone. At least once a month, the boys would get into some sort of fight, although most fights were scraps between members of the group or involved only one member of the group and some peripheral hanger-on. Only three times in the period of observation did the group fight together: once against a gang from across town, once against two blacks, and once against a group of boys from another school. For the first two fights the group went out "looking for trouble"—and they found it both times. The third fight followed a football game and began spontaneously with an argument on the football field between one of the Roughnecks and a member of the opposition's football team.

Jack has a particular propensity for fighting and was involved in most of the brawls. He was a prime mover of the escalation of arguments into fights.

More serious than fighting, had the community been aware of it, was theft. Although almost everyone was aware that the boys occasionally stole things, they did not realize the extent of the activity. Petty stealing was a frequent event for the Roughnecks. Sometimes they stole as a group and coordinated their efforts; other things they stole in pairs. Rarely did they steal alone.

The thefts ranged from very small things like paperback books, comics, and ballpoint pens to expensive items like watches. The nature of the thefts varied from time to time. The gang would go through a period of systematically lifting items from automobiles or school lockers. Types of thievery varied with the whim of the gang. Some forms of thievery were more profitable than others, but all thefts were for profit, not just thrills.

Roughnecks siphoned gasoline from cars as often as they had access to an automobile, which was not very often. Unlike the Saints, who owned their own cars, the Roughnecks would have to borrow their parents' cars, an event which occurred only eight or nine times a year. The boys claimed to have stolen cars for joy rides from time to time.

Ron committed the most serious of the group's offenses. With an unidentified associate the boy attempted to burglarize a gasoline station. Although this station had been robbed twice previously in the same month, Ron denied any involvement in either of the other thefts. When Ron and his accomplice approached the station, the owner was hiding in the bushes beside the station. He fired both barrels of a double-barreled shotgun at the boys. Ron was severely injured; the other boy ran away and was never caught. Though he remained in critical condition for several months, Ron finally recovered and served six months of the following year in reform school. Upon release from reform school, Ron was put back a grade in school, and began running around with a different gang of boys. The Roughnecks considered the new gang less delinquent than themselves, and during the following year Ron had no more trouble with the police.

The Roughnecks, then, engaged mainly in three types of delinquency: theft, drinking, and fighting. Although community members perceived that this gang of kids was delinquent, they mistakenly believed that their illegal activities were primarily drinking, fighting, and being a nuisance to passersby. Drinking was limited among the gang members, although it did occur, and theft was much more prevalent than anyone realized.

Drinking would doubtless have been more prevalent had the boys had ready access to liquor. Since they rarely had automobiles at their disposal, they could not travel very far, and the bars in town would not serve them. Most of the boys had little money, and this, too, inhibited their purchase of alcohol. Their major source of liquor was a local drunk who would buy them a fifth if they would give him enough extra to buy himself a pint of whiskey or a bottle of wine.

The community's perception of drinking as prevalent stemmed from the fact that it was the most obvious delinquency the boys engaged in. When one of the boys had been drinking, even a casual observer seeing him on the corner would suspect that he was high.

There was a high level of mutual distrust and dislike between the Roughnecks and the police. The boys felt very strongly that the police were unfair and corrupt. Some evidence existed that the boys were correct in their perception.

The main source of the boys' dislike for the police undoubtedly stemmed from the fact that the police would sporadically harass the group. From the standpoint of the boys, these acts of occasional enforcement of the law were whimsical and uncalled for. It made no sense to them, for example, that the police would come to the corner occasionally and threaten them with arrest for loitering when the night before the boys had been out siphoning gasoline from cars and the police had been nowhere in sight. To the boys, the police were stupid on the one hand, for not being where they should have been and catching the boys in a serious offense, and unfair on the other hand, for trumping up "loitering" charges against them.

From the viewpoint of the police, the situation was quite different. They knew, with all the confidence necessary to be a policeman, that these boys were engaged in criminal activities. They knew this partly from occasionally catching them, mostly from circumstantial evidence ("the boys were around when those tires were slashed"), and partly because the police shared the view of the community in general that this was a bad bunch of boys. The best the police could hope to do was to be sensitive to the fact that these boys were engaged in illegal acts and arrest them whenever there was some evidence that they had been involved. Whether or not the boys had in fact committed a particular act in a particular way was not especially important. The police had a broader view: their job was to stamp out these kids' crimes; the tactics were not as important as the end result.

Over the period that the group was under observation, each member was arrested at least once. Several of the boys were arrested a number of times and spent at least one night in jail. While most were never taken to court, two of the boys were sentenced to six months' incarceration in boys' schools.

THE ROUGHNECKS IN SCHOOL

The Roughnecks' behavior in school was not particularly disruptive. During school hours they did not all hang around together, but tended instead to spend most of their time with one or two other members of the gang who were their special buddies. Although every member of the gang attempted to avoid school as much as possible, they were not particularly successful and most of them attended school with surprising regularity. They considered school a burden—something to be gotten through with a minimum of conflict. If they were "bugged" by a particular teacher, it could lead to trouble. One of the boys, Al, once threatened to beat up a teacher and, according to the other boys, the teacher hid under a desk to escape him.

Teachers saw the boys the way the general community did, as heading for trouble, as being uninterested in making something of themselves. Some were also seen as being incapable of meeting the academic standards of the school. Most of the teachers expressed concern for this group of boys and were willing to pass them despite poor performance, in the belief that failing them would only aggravate the problem.

The group of boys had a grade point average just slightly above "C." No one in the group failed either grade, and no one had better than a *"C"* average. They were very consistent in their achievement or, at least, the teachers were consistent in their perception of the boys' achievement.

Two of the boys were good football players. Herb was acknowledged to be the best player in the school and Jack was almost as good. Both boys were criticized for their failure to abide by training rules, for refusing to come to practice as often as they should, and for not playing their best during practice. What they lacked in sportsmanship they made up for in skill, apparently, and played every game no matter how poorly they had performed in practice or how many practice sessions they had missed.

TWO QUESTIONS

Why did the community, the school, and the police react to the Saints as though they were good, upstanding, nondelinquent youths with bright futures but to the Roughnecks as though they were tough, young criminals who were headed for trouble? Why did the Roughnecks and the Saints in fact have quite different careers after high school—careers which, by and large, lived up to the expectations of the community?

The most obvious explanation for the differences in the community's and law enforcement agencies' reactions to the two gangs is that one group of boys was "more delinquent" than the other. Which group was more delinquent? The answer to this question will determine in part how we explain the differential responses to these groups by the members of the community and, particularly, by law enforcement and school officials.

In sheer number of illegal acts, the Saints were the more delinquent. They were truant from school for at least part of the day almost every day of the week. In addition, their drinking and vandalism occurred with surprising regularity. The Roughnecks, in contrast, engaged sporadically in delinquent episodes. While these episodes were frequent, they certainly did not occur on a daily or even a weekly basis.

The difference in frequency of offenses was probably caused by the Roughnecks' inability to obtain liquor and to manipulate legitimate excuses from school. Since the Roughnecks had less money than the Saints, and teachers carefully supervised their school activities, the Roughnecks' hearts may have been as black as the Saints', but their misdeeds were not nearly as frequent.

There are really no clear-cut criteria by which to measure qualitative differences in antisocial behavior. The most important dimension is generally referred to as the "seriousness" of the offenses.

If seriousness encompasses the relative economic costs of delinquent acts, then some assessment can be made. The Roughnecks probably stole an average of about $5.00 worth of goods a week. Some weeks the figure was considerably higher, but these times must be balanced against long periods when almost nothing was stolen.

The Saints were more continuously engaged in delinquency but their acts were not for the most part costly to property. Only their vandalism and occasional theft of gasoline would so qualify. Perhaps once or twice a month they would siphon a tankful of gas. The other costly items were street signs, construction lanterns, and the like. All of these acts combined probably did not quite average $5.00 a week, partly because much of the stolen equipment was abandoned and presumably could be recovered. The difference in cost of stolen property between the two groups was trivial, but the Roughnecks probably had a slightly more expensive set of activities than did the Saints.

Another meaning of seriousness is the potential threat of physical harm to members of the community and to the boys themselves. The Roughnecks were more prone to physical violence; they not only welcomed an opportunity to fight; they went seeking it. In addition, they fought among themselves frequently. Although the fighting never included deadly weapons, it was still a menace, however minor, to the physical safety of those involved.

The Saints never fought. They avoided physical conflict both inside and outside the group. At the same time, though, the Saints frequently endangered their own and other people's lives. They did so almost every time they drove a car, especially if they had been drinking. Sober, their driving was risky; under the influence of alcohol it was horrendous. In addition, the Saints endangered the lives of others with their pranks. Street excavations left unmarked were a very serious hazard.

Evaluating the relative seriousness of the two gangs' activities is difficult. The community reacted as though the behavior of the Roughnecks was a problem, and they reacted as though the behavior of the Saints was not. But the members of the community were ignorant of the array of delinquent acts that characterized the Saints' behavior. Although concerned citizens were unaware of much of the Roughnecks' behavior as well, they were much better informed about the Roughnecks' involvement in delinquency than they were about the Saints'.

VISIBILITY

Differential treatment of the two gangs resulted in part because one gang was infinitely more visible than the other. This differential visibility was a direct function of the economic standing of the families. The Saints had access to automobiles and were able to remove themselves from the sight of the community. In as routine a decision as to where to go to have a milkshake after school, the Saints stayed away from the mainstream of community life. Lacking transportation, the Roughnecks could not make it to the edge of town. The center of town was the only practical place for them to meet since their homes were scattered throughout the town and any noncentral meeting place put an undue hardship on some members. Through necessity the Roughnecks congregated in a crowded area where everyone in the community passed frequently, including teachers and law enforcement officers. They could easily see the Roughnecks hanging around the drugstore.

The Roughnecks, of course, made themselves even more visible by making remarks to passersby and by occasionally getting into fights on the corner. Meanwhile, just as regularly, the Saints were either at the café on one edge of town or in the pool hall at the other edge of town. Without any particular realization that they were making themselves inconspicuous, the Saints were able to hide their time-wasting. Not only were they removed from the mainstream of traffic, but they were almost always inside a building.

On their escapades the Saints were also relatively invisible, since they left Hanibal and traveled to Big Town. Here, too, they were mobile, roaming the city, rarely going to the same area twice.

DEMEANOR

To the notion of visibility must be added the difference in the responses of group members to outside intervention with their activities. If one of the Saints was confronted with an accusing policeman, even if he felt he was truly innocent of a wrongdoing, his demeanor was apologetic and penitent. A Roughneck's attitude was almost the polar opposite. When confronted with a threatening adult authority, even one who tried to be pleasant, the Roughneck's hostility and disdain were clearly observable. Sometimes he might attempt to put up a veneer of respect, but it was thin and was not accepted as sincere by the authority.

School was no different from the community at large. The Saints could manipulate the system by feigning compliance with the school norms. The availability of cars at school meant that once free from the immediate sight of the teacher, the boys could disappear rapidly. And this escape was well enough planned that no administrator or teacher was nearby when the boys left. A Roughneck who wished to escape for a few hours was in a bind. If it were possible to get free from class, downtown was still a mile away, and even if he arrived there, he was still very visible. Truancy for the Roughnecks meant almost certain detection, while the Saints enjoyed almost complete immunity from sanctions.

BIAS

Community members were not aware of the transgressions of the Saints. Even if the Saints had been less discreet, their favorite delinquencies would have been perceived as less serious than those of the Roughnecks.

In the eyes of the police and school officials, a boy who drinks in an alley and stands intoxicated on the street corner is committing a more serious offense than is a boy who drinks to inebriation in a nightclub or a tavern and drives around afterwards in a car. Similarly, a boy who steals a wallet from a store will be viewed as having committed a more serious offense than a boy who steals a lantern from a construction site.

Perceptual bias also operates with respect to the demeanor of the boys in the two groups when they are confronted by adults. It is not simply that adults dislike the posture affected by boys of the Roughneck ilk; more important is the conviction that the posture adopted by the Roughnecks is an indication of their devotion and commitment to deviance as a way of life. The posture becomes a cue, just as the type of the offense is a cue, to the degree to which the known transgressions are indicators of the youths' potential for other problems.

Visibility, demeanor, and bias are surface variables which explain the day-to-day operations of the police. Why do these surface variables operate as they do? Why did the police choose to disregard the Saints' delinquencies while breathing down the backs of the Roughnecks?

The answer lies in the class structure of American society and the control of legal institutions by those at the top of the class structure. Obviously, no representative of the upper class drew up the operational chart for the police which led them to look in the ghettos and on street corners—which led them to see the demeanor of lower-class youth as troublesome and that of upper-middle-class youth as tolerable. Rather, the procedures simply developed from experience—experience with irate and influential upper-middle-class parents insisting that their son's vandalism was simply a prank and his drunkenness only a momentary "sowing of wild oats"—experience with cooperative or indifferent, powerless, lower-class parents who acquiesced to the law's definition of their son's behavior.

ADULT CAREERS OF THE SAINTS AND THE ROUGHNECKS

The community's confidence in the potential of the Saints and the Roughnecks apparently was justified. If anything, the community members underestimated the degree to which these youngsters would turn out "good" or "bad."

Seven of the eight members of the Saints went on to college immediately after high school. Five of the boys graduated from college in four years. The sixth one finished college after two years in the army, and the seventh spent four years in the air force before returning to college and receiving a B.A. degree. Of these seven college graduates, three went on for advanced degrees. One finished law school and is now active in state politics, one finished medical school and is practicing near Hanibal, and one boy is now working for a Ph.D. The other four college graduates entered submanagerial, managerial, or executive training positions with larger firms.

The only Saint who did not complete college was Jerry. Jerry had failed to graduate from high school with the other Saints. During his second senior year, after the other Saints had gone on to college, Jerry began to hang around with what several teachers described as a "rough crowd"—the gang that was heir apparent to the Roughnecks. At the end of his second senior year, when he did graduate from high school, Jerry took a job as a used-car salesman, got married, and quickly had a child. Although he made several abortive attempts to go to college by attending night school, when I last saw him (ten years after high school) Jerry was unemployed and had been living on unemployment for almost a year. His wife worked as a waitress.

Some of the Roughnecks have lived up to community expectations. A number of them were headed for trouble. A few were not.

Jack and Herb were the athletes among the Roughnecks and their athletic prowess paid off handsomely. Both boys received unsolicited athletic scholarships to college. After Herb received his scholarship (near the end of his senior year), he apparently did an about-face. His demeanor became very similar to that of the Saints. Although he remained a member in good standing of the Roughnecks, he stopped participating in most activities and did not hang on the corner as often.

Jack did not change. If anything, he became more prone to fighting. He even made excuses for accepting the scholarship. He told the other gang members that the school had guaranteed him a "C" average if he would come to play football—an idea that seems far-fetched, even in this day of highly competitive recruiting.

During the summer after graduation from high school, Jack attempted suicide by jumping from a tall building. The jump would certainly have killed most people trying it, but Jack survived. He entered college in the fall and played four years of football. He and Herb graduated in four years, and both are teaching and coaching in high schools. They are married and have stable families. If anything, Jack appears to have a more prestigious position in the community than does Herb, though both are well respected and secure in their positions.

Two of the boys never finished high school. Tommy left at the end of his junior year and went to another state. That summer he was arrested and placed on probation on a manslaughter charge. Three years later he was arrested for murder; he pleaded guilty to second-degree murder and is serving a 30-year sentence in the state penitentiary.

Al, the other boy who did not finish high school, also left the state in his senior year. He is serving a life sentence in a state penitentiary for first-degree murder.

Wes is a small-time gambler. He finished high school and "bummed around." After several years he made contact with a bookmaker who employed him as a runner. Later he acquired his own area and has been working it ever since. His position among the bookmakers is almost identical to the position he had in the gang; he is always around but no one is really aware of him. He makes no trouble and he does not get into any. Steady, reliable, capable of keeping his mouth closed, he plays the game by the rules, even though the game is an illegal one.

That leaves only Ron. Some of his former friends reported that they had heard he was "driving a truck up north," but no one could provide any concrete information.

REINFORCEMENT

The community responded to the Roughnecks as boys in trouble, and the boys agreed with that perception. Their pattern of deviancy was reinforced, and breaking away from it became increasingly unlikely. Once the boys acquired an image of themselves as deviants, they selected new friends who affirmed that self-image. As that self-conception became more firmly entrenched, they also became willing to try new and more extreme deviances. With their growing alienation came freer expression of disrespect and hostility for representatives of the legitimate society. This disrespect increased the community's negativism, perpetuating the entire process of commitment to deviance. Lack of a commitment to deviance works the same way. In either case, the process will perpetuate itself unless some event (like a scholarship to college or a sudden failure) external to the established relationship intervenes. For two of the Roughnecks (Herb and Jack), receiving college athletic scholarships created new relations and culminated in a break with the established pattern of deviance. In the case of one of the Saints (Jerry), his parents' divorce and his failing to graduate from high school changed some of his other relations. Being held back in school for a year and losing his place among the Saints had sufficient impact on Jerry to alter his self-image and virtually to assure that he would not go on to college as his peers did. Although the experiments of life can rarely be reversed, it seems likely in view of the behavior of the other boys who did not enjoy this special treatment by the school that Jerry, too, would have "become something" had he graduated as anticipated. For Herb and Jack outside intervention worked to their advantage; for Jerry it was his undoing.

Selective perception and labeling—finding, processing, and punishing some kinds of criminality and not others—means that visible, poor, non-mobile, outspoken, undiplomatic "tough" kids will be noticed, whether their actions are seriously delinquent or not. Other kids, who have established a reputation for being bright (even though underachieving), disciplined, and involved in respectable activities, who are mobile and monied, will be invisible when they deviate from sanctioned activities. They'll sow their wild oats—perhaps even wider and thicker than their lower-class cohorts—but they won't be noticed. When it's time to leave adolescence most will follow the expected path, settling into the ways of the middle class, remembering fondly the delinquent but unnoticed fling of their youth. The Roughnecks and others like them may turn around, too. It is more likely that their noticeable deviance will have been so reinforced by police and community that their lives will be effectively channeled into careers consistent with their adolescent background.

30

The Economic Plight of Inner-City Black Males*

FROM *More than Just Race: Being Black and Poor in the Inner City*

WILLIAM JULIUS WILSON

Reading this essay, you are stepping into a minefield. Fortunately, William Julius Wilson, one of our preeminent sociologists for the past thirty years, has led the way. As a newcomer to sociology you don't know that academic battles have raged, unkind words and accusations have been hurled, character has been impugned, and friends have become enemies over the question Wilson is addressing: Why are so many Black males overrepresented among school dropouts, the unemployed, the incarcerated, and the unwed fathers in this country? Fortunately, we no longer have to rely on an explanation that "blames the victim" by castigating their "culture of poverty" and lack of personal responsibility. Nor do we have to blame "the system" and treat those in distress as if they are puppets or robots on a downward-sloping treadmill. Wilson knows what he is talking about when he looks closely at the structural barriers to success and the many ways opportunity is denied millions of Black males, including many young Black men today. He also knows about the beliefs and attitudes fostered in the inner city and the accepted practices that keep many men from pursuing possibilities that could change their lives. For so long the odds have been against them.

The economic predicament of low-skilled black men in the inner city has reached catastrophic proportions. Americans may not fully understand the dreadful social and economic circumstances that have moved these black males further and further behind the rest of society, but they often fear black males and perceive that they pose a problem for those who live in the city. Elliot Liebow helped expand our understanding of low-skilled black males when he wrote *Tally's Corner: A Study of Street Corner Men* in the mid-1960s. Since then, researchers have paid more attention to this group.

Although many of Liebow's arguments concerning the work experiences and family lives of black men in a Washington DC ghetto are still applicable to contemporary urban communities, the social and economic predicament of low-skilled black males today, especially their rate of joblessness, has become even more severe. Liebow was perhaps the first scholar to demonstrate that an ongoing lack of success in the labor market (ranging from outright

---

*Footnotes and references can be found in William Julius Wilson's *Not Just About Race*. From *More than Just Race: Being Black and Poor in the Inner City*. 2009. W. W. Norton & Company.

unemployment to being trapped in menial jobs) leads to a lessening of self-confidence and, eventually, to feelings of resignation that frequently result in temporary, or even permanent, abandonment of looking for work.

Even when Liebow's men were successful in finding work, the jobs they occupied paid little and were dirty, physically demanding, and uninteresting. This work did not foster respect, build status, or offer opportunity for advancement. "The most important fact [in becoming discouraged from looking for or keeping a job] is that a man who is able and willing to work cannot earn enough to support himself, his wife, and one or more children," declared Liebow. "A man's chances for working regularly are good only if he is willing to work for less than he can live on, sometimes not even then." Because they held the same ideas about work and reward as other Americans, the street-corner men viewed such jobs disdainfully. "He cannot do otherwise," stated Liebow. "He cannot draw from a job those values which other people do not put into it." Unlike today, menial employment was readily available to these men during the 1960s, and they drifted from one undesirable job to the next.

When I analyzed the data collected from the mid-1980s to the mid-1990s by our research team on poverty and joblessness among black males in inner-city Chicago neighborhoods, I was repeatedly reminded of Liebow's book. Although the job prospects for low-skilled black men were bleak when Liebow conducted his field research in the early 1960s, they were even worse in the last quarter of the twentieth century, when even menial jobs in the service sector were difficult for low-skilled black males to find. That situation persists today.

THE ROLE OF STRUCTURAL FACTORS

Although African American men continue to confront racial barriers in the labor market, many inner-city black males have also been victimized by other structural factors, such as the decreased relative demand for low-skilled labor. The propagation of new technologies is displacing untrained workers and rewarding those with specialized, technical training, while globalization of the economy is increasingly pitting low-skilled workers in the United States against their counterparts around the world, including laborers in countries such as China, India, and Bangladesh who can be employed for substantially lower wages. This decreasing relative demand in the United States for low-skilled labor means that untrained workers face the growing threat of eroding wages and job displacement.

Over the past several decades, African Americans have experienced sharp job losses in the manufacturing sector. Indeed, as John Schmitt and Ben Zipperer point out, "the share of black workers in manufacturing has actually been falling more rapidly than the overall share of manufacturing employment. From the end of the 1970s through the early 1990s, African Americans were just as likely as workers from other racial and ethnic groups to have manufacturing jobs. Since the early 1990s, however, black workers have lost considerable ground in manufacturing. By 2007, blacks were about 15 percent less likely than other workers to have a job in manufacturing." The dwindling proportion of African American workers in manufacturing is important because manufacturing jobs, especially those in the auto industry, have been a significant source of better-paid employment for black Americans since World War II.

The relative decline of black workers in manufacturing parallels their decreasing involvement in unions. From 1983 to 2007 the proportion of all African American workers who were either in unions or represented by a union at their employment site dropped considerably, from 31.7 to 15.7 percent. In 2007, African American workers were still more likely to be unionized (15.7 percent) than whites (13.5) and Hispanics (10.8). Nonetheless, this reduction (down 16 percentage points) over that time span was greater than that for whites (down 8.9 percentage points) and Hispanics (down 13.4). The lack of union representation renders workers more vulnerable in the workplace, especially to cuts in wages and benefits.

Because they tend to be educated in poorly performing public schools, low-skilled black males often enter the job market lacking some of the basic tools that would help them confront changes in their employment prospects. Such schools have rigid district bureaucracies, poor morale among teachers and school principals, low expectations for students, and negative ideologies that justify poor student performance. Inner-city schools fall well below more advantaged suburban schools in science and math resources, and they lack teachers with appropriate preparation in these subjects. As a result, students from these schools tend to have poor reading and math skills, important tools for competing in the globalized labor market. Few thoughtful observers of public education would disagree with the view that the poor employment prospects of low-skilled black males are in no small measure related to their public-education experiences.

Their lack of education, which contributes to joblessness, is certainly related to their risk of incarceration. As Bruce Western so brilliantly revealed in his important book *Punishment and Inequality in America*, following the collapse of the low-skilled urban labor markets and the creation of jobless ghettos in our nation's inner cities, incarceration grew among those with the highest rates of joblessness. "By the early 2000s," states Western, "the chances of imprisonment were more closely linked to race and school failure than at any time in the previous twenty years." Between 1979 and 1999, the risk of imprisonment for less educated men nearly doubled. Indeed, a significant proportion of black men who have been in prison are high school dropouts. "Among [black] male high school dropouts the risk of imprisonment [has] increased to 60 percent, establishing incarceration as a normal stopping point on the route to midlife."

However, Western's research also revealed that national cultural shifts in values and attitudes contributed to a political context associated with a resurgent Republican Party that focused on punitive "solutions" and worsened the plight of low-skilled black men. This more penal approach to crime was reinforced during Bill Clinton's administration. Indeed, rates of incarceration soared even during periods when the overall crime rate had declined. "The growth in violence among the ghetto poor through the 1960s and 1970s stoked fears of white voters and lurked in the rhetoric of law and order," states Western. "Crime, however, did not drive the rise in imprisonment directly, but formed the background for a new style of politics and punishment. As joblessness and low wages became enduring features of the less skilled inner-city economy, the effects of a punitive criminal justice system concentrated on the most disadvantaged." Western estimates that as many as 30 percent of all civilian young adult black males ages sixteen to thirty-four are ex-offenders. In short, cultural shifts in attitudes toward crime and punishment created structural circumstances—a more punitive criminal justice system—that have had a powerful impact on low-skilled black males.

* * *

For inner-city black male workers, the problems created by these structural factors have been aggravated by employers' negative attitudes toward black men as workers. A representative sample of Chicago-area employers by my research team in the late 1980s clearly reveals employer bias against black males. A substantial majority of employers considered inner-city black males to be uneducated, uncooperative, unstable, or dishonest. For example, a suburban drug store manager made the following comment:

> It's unfortunate but, in my business I think overall [black men] tend to be known to be dishonest. I think that's too bad but that's the image they have. (*Interviewer*: So you think it's an image problem?) *Respondent*: An image problem of being dishonest men and lazy. They're known to be lazy. They are [laughs]. I hate to tell you, but. It's all an image though. Whether they are or not. I don't know, but, it's an image that is perceived, (*Interviewer*: I see. How do you think that image was developed?) *Respondent*: Go look in the jails [laughs].

The president of an inner-city manufacturing firm expressed a different reservation about employing black males from certain ghetto neighborhoods:

> If somebody gave me their address, uh, Cabrini Green I might unavoidably have some concerns. (*Interviewer*: What would your concerns be?) *Respondent*: That the poor guy probably would be frequently unable to get to work and . . . I probably would watch him more carefully even if it wasn't fair, than I would with somebody else. I know what I should do though is recognize that here's a guy that is trying to get out of his situation and probably will work harder than somebody else who's already out of there and he might be the best one around here. But I think I would have to struggle accepting that premise at the beginning.

The prevalence of such attitudes, combined with the physical and social isolation of minorities living in inner-city areas of concentrated poverty, severely limits the access that poor black men have to informal job networks (the casual networks of people or acquaintances who can pass along information about employment prospects). This is a notable problem for black males, especially considering that many low-skilled employees first learn about their jobs through an acquaintance or were recommended by someone associated with the company. Research suggests that only a small percentage of low-skilled employees are hired through advertised job openings or cold calls. The importance of knowing someone who knows the boss can be seen by another employer's comments to our interviewer:

> All of a sudden, they take a look at a guy, and unless he's got an in, the reason why I hired this black kid the last time is cause my neighbor said to me, yeah I used him for a few [days], he's good, and I said, you know what, I'm going to take a chance. But it was a recommendation. But other than that, I've got a walk-in, and, who knows? And I think that for the most part, a guy sees a black man, he's a bit hesitant.

These attitudes are classic examples of what social scientists call statistical discrimination: employers make generalizations about inner-city, black male workers and reach decisions based on those assumptions without reviewing the qualifications of an individual applicant. The net effect is that many inner-city, black male applicants are never given the opportunity to prove themselves. Although some of these men scorn entry-level jobs because of the poor working conditions and low wages, many others would readily accept such employment. And although statistical discrimination contains some elements of class bias against poor, inner-city workers, it is clearly a racially motivated practice. It is a frustrating and disturbing fact that inner-city black males are effectively screened out of employment far more often than their Hispanic or white peers who apply for the same jobs. A number of other studies have documented employer bias against black males. For example, research by Devah Pager revealed that a white applicant with a felony conviction was more likely to receive a callback or job offer than was a black applicant with a clean record.

* * *

Forced to turn to the low-wage service sector for employment, inner-city black males—including a significant number of ex-offenders—have to compete, often unsuccessfully, with a growing number of female and immigrant workers. If these men complain or otherwise manifest their dissatisfaction, they seem even more unattractive to employers and therefore encounter even greater discrimination when they search for employment. Because the feelings that many inner-city black males express about their jobs and job prospects reflect their plummeting position in a changing economy, it is important to link these attitudes and other cultural traits with the opportunity structure— that is, the spectrum of life chances available to them in society at large.

Many people would agree that both the structural factors and the national cultural factors discussed earlier have had a very large impact on the experiences of low-skilled black males. But no such consensus exists with respect to the role of cultural factors that have emerged in inner-city ghetto neighborhoods in shaping and directing the lives of young black men.

THE ROLE OF CULTURAL FACTORS

Throughout this discussion I have suggested that cultural factors must be brought to bear if we are to explain economic and social outcomes for racial groups. The exploration of the cultural dimension must do three things: (1) provide a compelling reason for including cultural factors in a comprehensive discussion of race and poverty, (2) show the relationship between cultural analysis and structural analysis, and (3) determine the extent to which cultural factors operate independently to contribute to or reinforce poverty and racial inequality. However, the evidence for the influence of cultural factors on the social and economic circumstances of low-skilled black males is far less compelling than structural arguments, in part because of a dearth of research in this area.

According to Orlando Patterson of Harvard University, since the mid-1960s a strong bias against cultural explanations for human behavior has led social scientists and policy analysts to ignore different groups' distinctive cultural attributes in favor of an emphasis on structural factors to account for the behavior and social outcomes of its members. So instead of looking at attitudes, norms, values, habits, and worldviews (all indications of cultural orientations), we focus on joblessness, low socioeconomic status, and underperforming public schools—in short, structural factors.

Patterson revisited the role of culture and raised several questions that might be better addressed when cultural elements are considered in conjunction with structural and historical explanations. Patterson asks, "Why do so many young unemployed black men have children—several of them—which they have no resources or intention to support? And why . . . do they murder each other at nine times the rate of white youths?" And, he adds, why do young black males turn their backs on low-wage jobs that immigrants are happy to fill? Referring to research conducted by UCLA sociologist Roger Waldinger, Patterson states that such jobs enable the chronically unemployed to enter the labor market and obtain basic work skills that they can later use in securing better jobs. But he also notes that those who accepted the low-paying jobs in Waldinger's study were mostly immigrants.

To help answer his own questions about the behavior of young black men in the ghetto, Patterson refers to anecdotal evidence collected several years ago by one of his former students. He states that the student visited her former high school to discover why "almost all the black girls graduated and went to college whereas nearly all the black boys either failed to graduate or did not go on to college." Her distressing finding was that all of the black boys were fully aware of the consequences of failing to graduate from high school and go on to college. (They indignantly exclaimed, "We're not stupid!"). So, Patterson wonders, why were they flunking out? The candid answer that these young men gave to his former student was their preference for what some call the "cool-pose culture" of young black men, which they found too fulfilling to give up. "For these young men, it was almost like a drug, hanging out on the street after school, shopping and dressing sharply, sexual conquests, party drugs, hip-hop music and culture."

Patterson maintains that cool-pose culture blatantly promotes the most anomalous models of behavior in urban, lower-class neighborhoods, featuring gangsta rap, predatory sexuality, and irresponsible fathering. "It is reasonable to conclude," he states, "that among a large number of urban, Afro-American lower-class young men, these models are now fully normative and that men act in accordance with them whenever they can." For example, Patterson argues that black male pride has become increasingly defined in terms of the impregnation of women. However, this trend is not unique to the current generation of young black males, he notes. Several decades ago the sociologist Lee Rainwater uncovered a similar pattern. Not only did a majority of the inner-city, young black male respondents he interviewed state that they were indifferent to the fact that their girlfriends were pregnant, but some even expressed the proud belief that getting a girl pregnant proves you're a man. The fact that Elijah Anderson and others discovered identical models decades later suggests the possibility of a pattern of cultural transmission—that is, the attitudes and behaviors valorizing a kind of "footloose fatherhood" have been passed down to younger generations. A counterargument—one that does not assume cultural transmission—could also be posed: young black men in roughly similar structural positions in different generations developed similar cultural responses.

Patterson argues that a thoughtful cultural explanation of the self-defeating behavior of poor, young black men could not only speak to the immediate relationship of their attitudes, behavior, and undesirable outcomes, but also examine their brutalized past, perhaps over generations, to investigate the origins and changing nature of these views and practices. Patterson maintains that we cannot understand the behavior of young black men without deeply examining their collective past.

I believe that Patterson tends to downplay the importance of immediate socioeconomic factors: if there is indeed a cool-pose culture, it is reasonable to assume that it is partly related to employment failures and disillusionment with the poorly performing public schools and possibly has its roots in the special social circumstances fostered by pre-1960s legal segregation. But

I fully concur with Patterson's view that cultural explanations that include historical context should be part of our attempt to fully account for behavior that is so contradictory to mainstream ideas of how work and family should fit into a man's life.

In her ethnographic research—that is, work using evidence gathered through field observation and through extended, often repeated, interviews— Katherine Newman reveals that young, low-wage workers in New York City's Harlem neighborhood not only adhere to mainstream values regarding work, but also tend to accept low-skilled, low-wage, often dead-end jobs. In his impressive study of how young, inner-city black men perceive opportunity and mobility in the United States, Alford Young found that although some men associated social mobility with the economic opportunity structure, including race- and class-based discrimination, all of his respondents shared the view that individuals are largely accountable for their failure to advance in society.

The research conducted by my team in Chicago provides only mixed evidence for a subculture of defeatism. Consistent with Liebow's findings in *Tally's Corner,* the ethnographic research in our study revealed that many young black males had experienced repeated failures in their job search, had given up hope, and therefore no longer bothered to look for work. * * * [O]ur research pointed to negative employer attitudes and actions toward low-skilled black males as powerful influences in this cycle. Our ethnographic research suggested that repeated failure results in resignation and the development of cultural attitudes that discourage the pursuit of steady employment in the formal labor market.

On the other hand, data from our large, random survey of black residents in the inner city revealed that despite the overwhelming joblessness and poverty around them, black residents in ghetto neighborhoods, consistent with the findings of Alford Young, spoke unambiguously in support of basic American values concerning individual initiative. For example, nearly all of the black people we questioned felt that plain hard work is either very important or somewhat important for getting ahead. In addition, in a series of open-ended interviews conducted by members of our research team, participants overwhelmingly endorsed the dominant American belief system concerning poverty. The views of some of these individuals—who lived in some of the most destitute neighborhoods in America—were particularly revealing. A substantial majority agreed that America is a land of opportunity where anybody can get ahead, and that individuals get pretty much what they deserve.

The response of a thirty-four-year-old black male, a resident in a ghetto area of the South Side of Chicago where 29 percent of the population was destitute (i.e., with incomes 75 percent below the poverty line) was typical: "Everybody get pretty much what they deserve because if everybody wants to do better they got to go out there and try. If they don't try, they won't make it." Another black male who was residing in an equally impoverished South Side neighborhood stated, "For some it's a land of opportunity, but you can't just let opportunity come knock on your door, you just got to go ahead and work for it. You got to go out and get it for yourself." Although their support of this abstract American ideal was not always consistent with their perceptions and descriptions of the social barriers that impeded the social progress of their neighbors and friends, these endorsements stand in strong contrast to the subculture of defeatism. Nonetheless, I should note that there is frequently a gap between what people state in the abstract and what they perceive to be possible for themselves given their own situations. In other words, it should not be surprising if some residents support the abstract American ideal of individual initiative and still feel that they cannot get ahead, because of factors beyond their control.

The inconsistency between what people say in the abstract and what they believe applies to them may be seen in other ways. Jennifer Hochschild's analysis of national survey data reveals that poor blacks tend to acknowledge the importance of discrimination when they respond to national surveys, but they are not likely to feel that it affects them personally. Often, discrimination is the least mentioned factor among other important forces that black people select when asked what determines their chances in life. Thus, among poor blacks, structural factors such as discrimination and declining job opportunities "do not register as major impediments to achieving their goals. Deficient motivation and individual effort do." The emphasis that poor blacks place on the importance of personal attributes over structural factors for success in America should not come as a surprise. As Hochschild astutely points out, "poor African Americans are usually badly educated and not widely traveled, so they are unlikely to see structural patterns underlying individual actions and situations. Thus even if (or because) the American dream fails as a description of American society, it is a highly seductive prescription for succeeding in that society to those who cannot see the underlying flaw." To repeat, the evidence for a subculture of defeatism is mixed. Nonetheless, until more compelling studies are produced, it remains an important hypothesis for research.

* * *

Sandra Smith provides a compelling and nuanced cultural analysis of other factors that contribute to the complex and often difficult world of work inhabited by low-skilled blacks. Smith conducted in-depth interviews with 105 black men and women in Michigan between the ages of twenty and forty who had no more than a high school education so that she could examine the informal personal networks of low-skilled black job holders and job seekers.

Smith's data provide new information to help explain why informal job networks among blacks were less useful in helping job seekers find employment in the formal economy. She found that distrust on the part of black job holders and the defensive individualism typical of black job seekers profoundly affected the use of job referrals in the search for employment. She points out that the neighborhoods of the black poor are "characterized by chronic poverty and a history of exploitation" and tend to feed the inclination to distrust, "inhibiting the development of mutually beneficial cooperative relationships such as those that facilitate the job-matching process." The cooperation between job seekers and job holders is thwarted by a lack of mutual trust. Thus, low-skilled black job seekers are frequently unable to use their friendships, acquaintances, and family ties—their informal network—to gain employment. Black job holders were reluctant to refer their relatives and friends for jobs because they feared that their own reputations with employers could be jeopardized if the work of the people they recommended was substandard.

* * *

CONCLUSION

The disproportionate number of low-skilled black males in this country is one of the legacies of historical segregation and discrimination. However, aside from the effects of current segregation and discrimination, including those caused by employer bias, I highlighted a number of impersonal economic forces that have contributed to the incredibly high jobless rate of low-skilled black males and their correspondingly low incomes. These forces include the decreased relative demand for low-skilled labor caused by the computer revolution, the globalization of economic activity, the declining manufacturing sector, and the growth of service industries in which most of the new jobs for workers with limited skills and education are concentrated.

I noted that the shift to service industries has created a new set of problems for low-skilled black males because those industries feature jobs that require workers to serve and relate to consumers. Why are such requirements a problem for black men? Simply because employers believe that women and recent immigrants of both genders are better suited than black males, especially those with prison records, for such jobs. This image has been created partly by cultural shifts in national attitudes that reflected concerns about the growth of violence in the ghettos through the 1960s and '70s. In the eyes of many Americans, black males symbolized this violence. Cries for "law and order" resulted in a more punitive criminal justice system and a dramatic increase in black male incarceration.

Cultural arguments have been advanced to explain the social and economic woes of low-skilled black males, but the evidence is mixed. For example, a number of studies have associated black joblessness with high reservation wages, the lowest wages that a worker is willing to accept. Nonetheless, one of the more compelling studies found no significant relationship between the reservation wages of black men and the duration of joblessness. The findings in an important recent study, however, clearly suggest that chronic poverty and exploitation in poor black neighborhoods tend to feed inclinations to distrust. These cultural traits undermine the development of cooperative relationships that are so vital in informal job networks. Black workers in the inner city tend to be less willing to recommend friends and relatives for jobs that become available. Thus, the structural problem of employer job discrimination and the cultural inclination to distrust combine to severely handicap low-skilled, black male workers, especially those with prison records.

31

Uses of the Underclass in America

HERBERT J. GANS

This essay is vintage sociology, taking what everyone thinks they know and turning it on its head. Gans shows how the lives and work of the so-called "undeserving poor" benefit the nonpoor in ways most Americans seldom recognize. "Poverty is good for you," is another way to express Gans's message, "as long as you are not among the poor." This essay also shows how functional analysis, often accused of being conservative, can be a critical perspective.

I. INTRODUCTION

Poverty, like any other social phenomenon, can be analyzed in terms of the *causes* which initiate and perpetuate it, but once it exists, it can also be studied in terms of the consequences or *functions* which follow. These functions can be both *positive* and *negative*, adaptive and destructive, depending on their nature and the people and interests affected.

Poverty has many negative functions (or dysfunctions), most for the poor themselves, but also for the nonpoor. Among those of most concern to both populations, perhaps the major one is that a small but visible proportion of poor people is involved in activities which threaten their physical safety, for example street crime, or which deviate from important norms claimed to be "mainstream," such as failing to work, bearing children in adolescence and out of wedlock, and being "dependent" on welfare. In times of high unemployment, illegal and even legal immigrants are added to this list for endangering the job opportunities of native-born Americans.

Furthermore, many better-off Americans believe that the number of poor people who behave in these ways is far larger than it actually is. More important, many think that poor people act as they do because of moral shortcomings that express themselves in lawlessness or in the rejection of mainstream norms. Like many other sociologists, however, I argue that the behavior patterns which concern the more fortunate classes are *poverty-related*, because they are, and have historically been, associated with poverty. * * * They are in fact caused by poverty, although a variety of other causes must also be at work since most poor people are not involved in any of these activities.

* * *

Because their criminal or disapproved behavior is ascribed to moral short-comings, the poor people who resort to it are often classified as unworthy or *undeserving*. For example, even though the failure of poor young men (or women) to work may be the effect of a lack of jobs, they are frequently accused of laziness, and then judged undeserving. Likewise, even though poor young mothers may decide not to marry the fathers of their children, because they, being jobless, cannot support them, the women are still accused of violating conventional familial norms, and also judged undeserving. Moreover, once judged to be undeserving, poor people are then no longer thought to be deserving of public aid that is financially sufficient and secure enough to help them escape poverty.

Judgments of the poor as undeserving are not based on evidence, but derive from a stereotype, even if, like most others, it is a stereotype with a "kernel of truth" (e.g., the monopolization of street crime by the poor). Furthermore, it is a very old stereotype; Cicero already described the needy of Rome as criminals. By the middle of the sixteenth century, complicated laws to distinguish between the deserving and undeserving were in existence. However, the term undeserving poor was first used regularly in England in the 1830s, at the time of the institution of the Poor Law.[1]

In America, a series of other, more specific, terms were borrowed or invented, with new ones replacing old ones as conditions and fashions changed. Such terms have included *beggar*, *pauper*, the *dangerous class*, *rabble*, *vagabond* and *vagrant*, and so on, which the United States borrowed from Europe. America also invented its own terms, including *shiftless*, *tramp*, and *feeble-minded*, and in the late twentieth century, terms like *hard-core*, *drifter*, *culturally deprived*—and most recently, *underclass*.[2] Nonetheless, in terms of its popular uses and the people to whom it is applied, the term underclass differs little from its predecessors.[3]

---

1. However, the *Oxford English Dictionary*, compiled by J. A. Simpson and E. S. Weiner (New York: Oxford University Press, 1989), 19: 996, already has a 1647 reference to beggars as undeserving, and the adjective itself was earlier used to refer to nonpoor people, for example, by Shakespeare.

2. These terms were often, but not exclusively, applied to the poor "races" who arrived in the nineteenth and early twentieth century from Ireland, Germany, and later, Eastern and Southern Europe. They have also been applied, during and after slavery, to Blacks. Nonetheless, the functions to be discussed in this article are consequences of poverty, not of race, even though a disproportionate rate of those "selected" to be poor have always been darker-skinned than the more fortunate classes.

3. The popular definition of underclass must be distinguished from Gunnar Myrdal's initial scholarly one, which viewed the underclass as a stratum driven to the margins or out of the labor force by what are today called the postindustrial and global economies. Gunnar Myrdal, *Challenge to Affluence* (New York: Pantheon Books, 1963), 10 and passim. Myrdal's definition viewed the underclass as victims of economic change, and said nothing about its moral state.

It is not difficult to understand why people, poor and more fortunate, are fearful of street crime committed by poor people, and even why the jobless poor and welfare recipients, like paupers before them, may be perceived as economic threats for not working and drawing on public funds, at least in bad economic times. Also, one can understand why other forms of poverty-related behavior, such as the early sexual activity of poor youngsters and the dramatic number of poor single-parent families are viewed as moral threats, since they violate norms thought to uphold the two-parent nuclear family and related normative bases of the social order. However, there would seem to be no inherent reason for exaggerating these threats, for example, in the case of welfare recipients who obtain only a tiny proportion of governmental expenditures, or more generally, by stereotyping poor people as undeserving without evidence of what they have and have not done, and why.

One reason, if not the only one, for the exaggeration and the stereotyping, and for the continued attractiveness of the concept of the undeserving poor itself, is that undeservingness has a number of *positive* functions for the better-off population. Some of these functions, or uses, are positive for everyone who is not poor, but most are positive only for some people, interest groups, and institutions, ranging from moderate income to wealthy ones. Needless to say, that undeservingness has uses for some people does not justify it; the existence of functions just helps to explain why it persists.

My notion of function, or empirically observable adaptive consequence, is adapted from the classic conceptual scheme of Robert K. Merton. My analysis will concentrate on those positive functions which Merton conceptualized as *latent*, which are unrecognized and/or unintended, but with the proviso that the functions which are identified as latent would probably not be abolished once they were widely recognized. Positive functions are, after all, also benefits, and people are not necessarily ready to give up benefits, including unintended ones, even if they become aware of them.

* * *

II. FUNCTIONS OF THE UNDESERVING POOR[4]

I will discuss five sets of positive functions: microsocial, economic, normative-cultural, political, and macrosocial, which I divide into 13 specific functions, although the sets are arbitrarily chosen and interrelated, and I could add many more functions. The functions are not listed in order of importance, for such a listing is not possible without empirical research on the various beneficiaries of undeservingness.

---

4. For brevity's sake, I will hereafter refer to the undeserving poor instead of the poor-labeled undeserving, but I always mean the latter.

Two Microsocial Functions

1. *Risk reduction.* Perhaps the primary use of the idea of the undeserving poor, primary because it takes place at the microsocial scale of everyday life, is that it distances the labeled from those who label them. By stigmatizing people as undeserving, labelers protect themselves from the responsibility of having to associate with them, or even to treat them like moral equals, which reduces the risk of being hurt or angered by them. Risk reduction is a way of dealing with actual or imagined threats to physical safety, for example from people who might be muggers, or cultural threats attributed to poor youngsters or normative ones imagined to come from welfare recipients. All pejorative labels and stereotypes serve this function, which may help to explain why there are so many such labels.

2. *Scapegoating and displacement.* By being thought undeserving, the stigmatized poor can be blamed for virtually any shortcoming of everyday life which can be credibly ascribed to them—violations of the laws of logic or social causation notwithstanding. Faulting the undeserving poor can also support the desire for revenge and punishment. In a society in which punishment is reserved for legislative, judicial, and penal institutions, *feelings* of revenge and punitiveness toward the undeserving poor supply at least some emotional satisfaction.

Since labeling poor people undeserving opens the door for nearly unlimited scapegoating, the labeled are also available to serve what I call the displacement function. Being too weak to object, the stigmatized poor can be accused of having caused social problems which they did not actually cause and can serve as cathartic objects on which better-off people can unload their own problems, as well as those of the economy, the polity, or of any other institutions, for the shortcomings of which the poor can be blamed.

Whether societywide changes in the work ethic are displaced on to "shiftlessness," or economic stagnation on to "welfare dependency," the poor can be declared undeserving for what ails the more affluent. This may also help to explain why the national concern with poor Black unmarried mothers, although usually ascribed to the data presented in the 1965 Moynihan Report, did not gather steam until the beginning of the decline of the economy in the mid-1970s. Similarly, the furor about poor "babies having babies" waited for the awareness of rising adolescent sexual activity among the better-off classes in the 1980s—at which point rates of adolescent pregnancy among the poor had already declined. But when the country became ambivalent about the desirability of abortions, the issue was displaced on the poor by making it almost impossible for them to obtain abortions.

Many years ago, James Baldwin, writing in *The Fire Next Time*, illustrated the displacement function in racial terms, arguing that, as Andrew Hacker put it, Whites "need the 'nigger' because it is the 'nigger' within themselves that they cannot tolerate. Whatever it is that Whites feel 'nigger' signifies about Blacks—lust and laziness, stupidity or squalor, in fact exists within themselves. * * * By creating such a creature, Whites are able to say that because only members of the Black race can carry that taint, it follows that none of its attributes will be found in White people.[5]

Three Economic Functions

3. *Economic banishment and the reserve army of labor.* People who have successfully been labeled as undeserving can be banished from the formal labor market. If young people are designated "school dropouts," for example; they can also be thought to lack the needed work habits, such as proper adherence to the work ethic, and may not be offered jobs to begin with. Often, they are effectively banished from the labor market before entering it because employers imagine them to be poor workers simply because they are young, male, and Black. Many ex-convicts are declared unemployable in similar fashion, and some become recidivists because they have no other choice but to go back to their criminal occupations.

Banishing the undeserving also makes room for immigrant workers, who may work for lower wages, are more deferential, and are more easily exploitable by being threatened with deportation. In addition, banishment helps to reduce the official jobless rate, a sometimes useful political function, especially if the banished drop so completely out of the labor force that they are not even available to be counted as "discouraged workers."

The economic banishment function is in many ways a replacement for the old reserve army of labor function, which played itself out when the undeserving poor could be hired as strikebreakers, as defense workers in the case of sudden wartime economic mobilization, as "hypothetical workers," who by their very presence could be used to depress the wages of other workers, or to put pressure on the unions not to make wage and other demands. Today, however, with a plentiful supply of immigrants, as well as of a constantly growing number of banished workers who are becoming surplus labor, a reserve army is less rarely needed—and when needed, can be recruited from sources other than the undeserving poor.

* * *

4. *Supplying illegal goods.* The undeserving poor who are banished from other jobs remain eligible for work in the manufacture and sale of illegal goods, including drugs. Although it is estimated that 80 percent of all illegal drugs are sold to Whites who are not poor, the sellers are often people banished from the formal labor market. Other suppliers of illegal goods include the illegal immigrants, considered undeserving in many American communities, who work for garment industry sweatshops manufacturing clothing under illegal conditions.

---

5. Hacker is paraphrasing Baldwin. Andrew Hacker, *Two Nations: Black and White, Separate, Hostile, Unequal* (New York: Scribner, 1992), 61.

5. *Job creation.* Perhaps the most important economic function of the unde-serving poor today is that their mere presence creates jobs for the better-off population, including professional ones. Since the undeserving poor are thought to be dangerous or improperly socialized, their behavior either has to be modified so that they act in socially approved ways, or they have to be iso-lated from the deserving sectors of society. The larger the number of people who are declared undeserving, the larger also the number of people needed to modify and isolate as well as control, guard, and care for them. Among these are the social workers, teachers, trainers, mentors, psychiatrists, doc-tors and their support staffs in juvenile training centers, "special" schools, drug treatment centers, and penal behavior modification institutions, as well as the police, prosecutors, defense attorneys, judges, court officers, probation personnel and others who constitute the criminal courts, and the guards and others who run the prisons.

Jobs created by the presence of undeserving poor also include the mas-sive bureaucracy of professionals, investigators, and clerks who administer welfare. Other jobs go to the officials who seek out poor fathers for child sup-port monies they may or may not have, as well as the welfare office personnel needed to take recipients in violation of welfare rules off the rolls, and those needed to put them back on the rolls when they reapply. In fact, one can argue that some of the rules for supervising, controlling, and punishing the unde-serving poor are more effective at performing the latent function of creating clerical and professional jobs for the better-off population than the manifest function of achieving their official goals.

More jobs are created in the social sciences and in journalism for conduct-ing research about the undeserving poor and producing popular books, arti-cles, and TV documentaries for the more fortunate who want to learn about them. The "job chain" should also be extended to the teachers and others who train those who serve, control, and study the undeserving poor.

In addition, the undeserving poor make jobs for what I call the salvation industries, religious, civil, or medical, which also try to modify the behavior of those stigmatized as undeserving. Not all such jobs are paid, for the undeserv-ing poor also provide occasional targets for charity and thus offer volunteer jobs for those providing it—and paid jobs for the professional fundraisers who obtain most of the charitable funds these days. Among the most visible volun-teers are the members of "café" and "high" society who organize and contrib-ute to these benefits.

Three Normative Functions

6. *Moral legitimation.* Undeservingness justifies the category of deserving-ness and thus supplies moral and political legitimacy, almost by definition, to the institutions and social structures that include the deserving and exclude the undeserving. Of these structures, the most important is undoubtedly the class hierarchy, for the existence of an undeserving class or stratum legitimates

the deserving classes, if not necessarily all of their class-related behavior. The alleged immorality of the undeserving also gives a moral flavor to, and justification for, the class hierarchy, which may help to explain why upward mobility itself is so praiseworthy.

7. *Norm reinforcement.* By violating, or being imagined as violating, a number of mainstream behavioral patterns and values, the undeserving poor help to reaffirm and reinforce the virtues of these patterns—and to do so visibly, since the violations by the undeserving are highly publicized. As Emile Durkheim pointed out nearly a century ago, norm violations and their punishments also provide an opportunity for preserving and reaffirming the norms. This is not insignificant, for norms sometimes disparaged as "motherhood" values gain new moral power when they are violated, and their violators are stigmatized.

If the undeserving poor can be imagined to be lazy, they help to reaffirm the Protestant work ethic; if poor single-parent families are publicly condemned, the two-parent family is once more legitimated as ideal. In the 1960s, middle-class morality was sometimes criticized as culturally parochial and therefore inappropriate for the poor, but since the 1980s, mainstream values have once more been regarded as vital sources of behavioral guidance for them.

Enforcing the norms also contributes further to preserving them in another way, for one of the standard punishments of the undeserving poor for misbehaving—as well as standard obligation in exchange for help—is practicing the mainstream norms, including those that the members of the mainstream may only be preaching, and that might die out if the poor were not required to incorporate them in their behavior. Old work rules that can no longer be enforced in the rest of the economy can be maintained in the regulations for workfare; old-fashioned austerity and thrift are built into the consumption patterns expected of welfare recipients. Economists like to argue that if the poor want to be deserving, they should take any kind of job, regardless of its low pay or demeaning character, reflecting a work ethic which economists themselves have never practiced.

Similarly, welfare recipients may be removed from the rolls if they are found to be living with a man—but the social worker who removes them has every right to cohabit and not lose his or her job. In most states, welfare recipients must observe rules of housecleaning and child care that middle-class people are free to ignore without being punished. While there are many norms and laws governing child care, only the poor are monitored to see if they obey these. Should they use more physical punishment on their children than social workers consider desirable, they can be charged with child neglect or abuse and can lose their children to foster care.[6]

---

6. Poor immigrants who still practice old-country discipline norms are particularly vulnerable to being accused of child abuse.

The fact is that the defenders of such widely preached norms as hard work, thrift, monogamy, and moderation need people who can be accused, accurately or not, of being lazy, spendthrift, promiscuous, and immoderate. One reason that welfare recipients are a ready target for punitive legislation is that politicians, and most likely some of their constituents, imagine them to be enjoying leisure and an active sex life at public expense. Whether or not very many poor people actually behave in the ways that are judged undeserving is irrelevant if they can be imagined as doing so. Once imagining and stereotyping are allowed to take over, then judgments of undeservingness can be made without much concern for empirical accuracy. For example, in the 1990s, the idea that young men from poor single-parent families were highly likely to commit street crimes became so universal that the news media no longer needed to quote experts to affirm the accuracy of the charge.

Actually, most of the time most of the poor are as law abiding and observant of mainstream norms as are other Americans. Sometimes they are even more observant; thus the proportion of welfare recipients who cheat is always far below the percentage of taxpayers who do so. Moreover, survey after survey has shown that the poor, including many street criminals and drug sellers, want to hold respectable jobs like everyone else, hope someday to live in the suburbs, and generally aspire to the same American dream as most moderate and middle-income Americans.[7]

8. *Supplying popular culture villains.* The undeserving poor have played a long-term role in supplying American popular culture with villains, allowing the producers of the culture both to reinforce further mainstream norms and to satisfy audience demands for revenge, notably by showing that crime and other norm violations do not pay. Street criminals are shown dead or alive in the hands of the police on local television news virtually every day, and more dramatically so in the crime and action movies and television series.

For many years before and after World War II, the criminal characters in Hollywood movies were often poor immigrants, frequently of Sicilian origin. Then they were complemented for some decades by communist spies and other Cold War enemies who were not poor, but even before the end of the Cold War, they were being replaced by Black and Hispanic drug dealers and gang leaders.

At the same time, however, the popular culture industry has also supplied music and other materials offering marketable cultural and political protest which does not reinforce mainstream norms, or at least not directly. Some of the creators and performers come from poor neighborhoods, however, and it may be that some rap music becomes commercially successful by displacing on ghetto musicians the cultural and political protest of record buyers from more affluent classes.

7. See Mark R. Rank, *Living on the Edge: The Realities of Welfare in America* (New York: Columbia University Press, 1994), 93.

Three Political Functions

9. *Institutional scapegoating.* The scapegoating of the undeserving poor mentioned in Function 2 above also extends to institutions which mistreat them. As a result, some of the responsibility for the existence of poverty, slum unemployment, poor schools, and the like is taken off the shoulders of elected and appointed officials who are supposed to deal with these problems. For example, to the extent that educational experts decide that the children of the poor are learning disabled or that they are culturally or genetically inferior in intelligence, attempts to improve the schools can be put off or watered down.

To put it another way, the availability of institutional scapegoats both personalizes and exonerates social systems. The alleged laziness of the jobless and the anger aimed at beggars take the heat off the failure of the economy and the imagined derelictions of slum dwellers and the homeless, off the housing industry. In effect, the undeserving poor are blamed both for their poverty and also for the absence of "political will" among the citizenry to do anything about it.

10. *Conservative power shifting.* Once poor people are declared undeserving they also lose their political legitimacy and whatever little political influence they had before they were stigmatized. Some cannot vote, and many do not choose to vote or mobilize because they know politicians do not listen to their demands. Elected officials might ignore them even if they voted or mobilized because these officials and the larger polity cannot easily satisfy their demands for economic and other kinds of justice.[8] As a result, the political system is able to pay additional attention to the demands of more affluent constituents. It can therefore shift to the "right."

The same shift to the right also takes place ideologically. Although injustices of poverty help justify the existence of liberals and the more radical left the undeserving poor themselves provide justification and opportunities for conservatives to attack their ideological enemies on their left. When liberals can be accused of favoring criminals over victims, their accusers can launch and legitimate incursions on the civil liberties and rights of the undeserving poor, and concurrently on the liberties and rights of defenders of the poor. Moreover, the undeservingness of the poor can be used to justify attacks on the welfare state. Charles Murray understood the essence of this ideological function when he argued that welfare and other welfare state legislation for the poor only increased the number of poor people.[9]

---

8. In addition, the undeserving poor make a dangerous constituency. Politicians who say kind words about them or who act to represent their interests are likely to be attacked for their words and actions. Jesse Jackson was hardly the first national politician to be criticized for being too favorable to the poor.

9. Charles Murray, *Losing Ground: American Social Policy, 1950–1980* (New York: Basic Books, 1984).

11. *Spatial purification.* Stigmatized populations are often used, deliberately or not, to stigmatize the areas in which they live, making such areas eligible for various kinds of purification. As a result, "underclass areas" can be torn down and their inhabitants moved to make room for more affluent residents or higher taxpayers.

However, such areas can also be used to isolate stigmatized poor people and facilities by selecting them as locations for homeless shelters, halfway houses for the mentally ill or for ex-convicts, drug treatment facilities, and even garbage dumps, which have been forced out of middle- and working-class areas following NIMBY (not in my backyard) protests. Drug dealers and other sellers of illegal goods also find a haven in areas stigmatized as underclass areas, partly because these supply some customers, but also because police protection in such areas is usually minimal enough to allow illegal activities without significant interference from the law. In fact, municipalities would face major economic and political obstacles to their operations without stigmatized areas in which stigmatized people and activities can be located.

Two Macrosocial Functions

12. *Reproduction of stigma and the stigmatized.* For centuries now, undeservingness has given rise to policies and agencies which are manifestly set up to help the poor economically and otherwise to become deserving, but which actually prevent the undeserving poor from being freed of their stigma, and which also manage, unwittingly, to see to it that their children face the same obstacles. In some instances, this process works so speedily that the children of the stigmatized face "anticipatory stigmatization," among them the children of welfare recipients who are frequently predicted to be unable to learn, to work, and to remain on the right side of the law even before they have been weaned.

If this outcome were planned deliberately, one could argue that politically and culturally dominant groups are reluctant to give up an easily accessible and always available scapegoat. In actuality, however, the reproduction function results unwittingly from other intended and seemingly popular practices. For example, the so-called War on Drugs, which has unsuccessfully sought to keep hard drugs out of the United States, but has meanwhile done little to provide drug treatment to addicts who want it, thereby aids the continuation of addiction, street crime, and a guaranteed prison population, not to mention the various disasters that visit the families of addicts and help to keep them poor.

The other major source of reproducing stigma and the stigmatized is the routine activities of the organizations which service welfare recipients, the homeless, and other stigmatized poor, and end up mistreating them. For one thing, such agencies, whether they exist to supply employment to the poor or to help the homeless, are almost certain to be underfunded because of the powerlessness of their clientele. No organization has ever had the funds or power to buy, build, or rehabilitate housing for the homeless in sufficient number. Typically, they have been able to fund or carry out small demonstration projects.

In addition, organizations which serve stigmatized people often attract less well-trained and qualified staff than those with high-status clients, and if the clients are deemed undeserving, competence may become even less important in choosing staff. Then too, helping organizations generally reflect the societal stratification hierarchy, which means that organizations with poor, low-status clients frequently treat them as undeserving. If they also fear some of their clients, they may not only withhold help, but attack the clients on a preemptive strike basis. Last but not least, the agencies that serve the undeserving poor are bureaucracies which operate by rules and regulations that routinize the work, encourage the stability and growth of the organizations, and serve the needs of their staffs before those of their clients.

When these factors are combined, as they often are, and become cumulative, as they often do, it should not be surprising that the organizations cut off escape routes from poverty not only for the clients, but in doing so, also make sure that some of their children remain poor as well.

13. *Extermination of the surplus.* In earlier times, when the living standards of all poor people were at or below subsistence, many died at an earlier age than the better off, thus performing the set of functions for the latter forever associated with Thomas Malthus. Standards of living, even for the very poor, have risen considerably in the last century, but even today, morbidity and mortality rates remain much higher among the poor than among moderate-income people. To put it another way, various social forces combine to do away with some of the people who have become surplus labor and are no longer needed by the economy.

Several of the killing illnesses and pathologies of the poor change over time; currently, they include AIDS, tuberculosis, hypertension, heart attacks, and cancer, as well as psychosis, substance abuse, street crime, injury and death during participation in the drug trade and other underworld activities, and intraclass homicide resulting from neighborhood conflicts over turf and "respect." Whether the poor people whose only problem is being unfairly stereotyped and stigmatized as undeserving die earlier than other poor people is not known.

Moreover, these rates can be expected to remain high or even to rise as rates of unemployment—and of banishment from the labor force—rise, especially for the least skilled. Even the better-off jobless created by the downsizing of the 1990s blame themselves for their unemployment if they cannot eventually find new jobs, become depressed, and in some instances begin the same process of being extruded permanently from the labor market experienced by the least skilled of the jobless.

* * *

The early departure of poor people from an economy and society which do not need them is useful for those who remain. Since the more fortunate classes have already developed a purposive blindness to the structural causes of unemployment and to the poverty-related causes of pathology and crime that follow, those who benefit from the current job erosion and the possible extermination of the surplus labor may not admit it consciously either. Nonetheless, those left over to compete for scarce jobs and other resources will have a somewhat easier time in the competition, thus assigning undeservingness a final positive function for the more fortunate members of society.

III. CONCLUSION

I have described thirteen of the more important functions of the undeserving poor, enough to support my argument that both the idea of the undeserving poor and the stigmas with which some poor people are thus labeled may persist in part because they are useful in a variety of ways to the people who are not poor.

This analysis does not imply that undeservingness will or should persist. Whether it *will* persist is going to be determined by what happens to poverty in America. If it declines, poverty-related crime should also decline, and then fewer poor people will probably be described as undeserving. If poverty worsens, so will poverty-related crime, as well as the stereotyping and stigmatization of the poor, and any worsening of the country's economy is likely to add to the kinds and numbers of undeserving poor, if only because they make convenient and powerless scapegoats.

The functions that the undeserving poor play cannot, by themselves, perpetuate either poverty or undeservingness, for as I noted earlier, functions are not causes. For example, if huge numbers of additional unskilled workers should be needed, as they were for the World War II war effort, the undeserving poor will be welcomed back into the labor force, at least temporarily. Of course, institutions often try to survive once they have lost both their reasons for existence and their functions. Since the end of the Cold War, parts of the military-industrial establishment both in the United States and Russia have been campaigning for the maintenance of some Cold War forces and weapons to guarantee their own futures, but these establishments also supply jobs to their national economies, and in the United States, for the constituents of elected officials. Likewise, some of the institutions and interest groups that benefit from the existence of undeservingness, or from controlling the undeserving poor, may try to maintain undeservingness and its stigma. They may not even need to, for if Emile Durkheim was right, the decline of undeservingness would lead to the criminalization, or at least stigmatization, of new behavior patterns.

Whether applying the label of undeservingness to the poor *should* persist is a normative question which ought to be answered in the negative. Although people have a right to judge each other, that right does not extend to judging large numbers of people as a single group, with one common moral fault, or to stereotyping them without evidence either about their behavior or their values. Even if a case could be made for judging large cohorts of people as undeserving, these judgments should be distributed up and down the socio-economic hierarchy, requiring Americans also to consider whether and how people in the working, middle, and upper classes are undeserving.

The same equality should extend to the punishment of crimes. Today, many Americans and courts still treat white-collar and upper-class criminals more leniently than poor ones. The public excuse given is that the street crime of the undeserving poor involves violence and thus injury or death, but as many students of white-collar and corporate crime have pointed out, these also hurt and kill people, and often in larger numbers, even if they do so less directly and perhaps less violently.

Changes also need to be made in the American conception of deviance, which like that of other countries, conflates people whose behavior is *different* with those whose behavior is socially *harmful.* Bearing children without marriage is a long-standing tradition among the poor. Born of necessity rather than preference, it is a poverty-related practice, but it is not, by itself, harmful, or at least not until it can be shown that either the children—or the moral sensibilities of the people who oppose illegitimacy—are significantly hurt. Poor single-parent families are hardly desirable, but as the lack of condemnation of more affluent single-parent families should suggest, the major problem of such families is not the number of parents, actual or surrogate, in the family, but its poverty.

Finally, because many of the poor are stereotyped unjustly as undeserving, scholars, writers, journalists, and others should launch a systematic and public effort to deconstruct and delegitimate the notion of the undeserving poor. This effort, which is necessary to help make effective antipoverty programs politically acceptable again, should place the following five ideas on the public agenda and encourage discussion as well as dissemination of available research.

The five ideas, all discussed earlier in this article, are that (1) the criminal and deviant behavior among the poor is largely poverty related rather than the product of free choice based on distinctive values; (2) the undeservingness of the poor is an ancient stereotype, and like all stereotypes, it vastly exaggerates the actual dangers that stem from the poor; (3) poverty-related deviance is not necessarily harmful just because it does not accord with mainstream norms; (4) the notion of undeservingness survives in part because of the positive functions it has for the better-off population; and (5) the only certain way to eliminate both this notion and the functions is to eliminate poverty.[10]

10. A fuller discussion of policy proposals * * * appear[s] in my * * * book, *Ending the War against the Poor.*

PART SIX

SOCIAL CONTROL AND ORGANIZATIONAL POWER

32

From the Panopticon* to Disney World
CLIFFORD D. SHEARING AND PHILLIP C. STENNING

*To live in a modern society is to know and live within a vast array of invisible struc-
tures designed to ensure orderly behavior. Other structures are quite visible but not
recognized: actual physical barriers, corridors, and messages directing us to come,
go, turn, stop, be silent, not smoke, wear a shirt and shoes, and so forth. We conform
to control systems with our own consent or what Shearing and Stenning call "structured compliance." Disney World is not the only place where this occurs, but it offers
a good illustration for your own investigations.*

One of the most distinctive features of that quintessentially American
playground known as Disney World is the way it seeks to combine a
sense of comfortable—even nostalgic—familiarity with an air of innovative
technological advance. Mingled with the fantasies of one's childhood are the
dreams of a better future. Next to the Magic Kingdom is the Epcot Center. As
well as providing for a great escape, Disney World claims also to be a design
for better living. And what impresses most about this place is that it seems to
run like clockwork.

Yet the Disney order is no accidental by-product. Rather, it is a designed-in
feature that provides—to the eye that is looking for it, but not to the casual
visitor—an exemplar of modern private corporate policing. Along with the
rest of the scenery of which it forms a discreet part, it too is recognizable as a
design for the future.

We invite you to come with us on a guided tour of this modern police facility in which discipline and control are, like many of the characters one sees
about, in costume.

The fun begins the moment the visitor enters Disney World. As one arrives
by car one is greeted by a series of smiling young people who, with the aid of
clearly visible road markings, direct one to one's parking spot, remind one to
lock one's car and to remember its location and then direct one to await the
rubber-wheeled train that will convey visitors away from the parking lot. At
the boarding location one is directed to stand safely behind guard rails and to
board the train in an orderly fashion. While climbing on board one is reminded

---

*Jeremy Bentham (1748–1832) coined this term to describe a futuristic prison where nothing
could be done outside the view of the custodial staff. [*Editor's note*].

to remember the name of the parking area and the row number in which one is parked (for instance, "Donald Duck, 1"). Once on the train one is encouraged to protect oneself from injury by keeping one's body within the bounds of the carriage and to do the same for children in one's care. Before disembarking one is told how to get from the train back to the monorail platform and where to wait for the train to the parking lot on one's return. At each transition from one stage of one's journey to the next, one is wished a happy day and a "good time" at Disney World (this begins as one drives in and is directed by road signs to tune one's car radio to the Disney radio network).

As one moves towards the monorail platform the directions one has just received are reinforced by physical barriers (that make it difficult to take a wrong turn), pavement markings, signs and more cheerful Disney employees who, like their counterparts in other locations, convey the message that Disney World is a "fun place" designed for one's comfort and pleasure. On approaching the monorail platform one is met by enthusiastic attendants who quickly and efficiently organize the mass of people moving onto it into corrals designed to accommodate enough people to fill one compartment on the monorail. In assigning people to these corrals the attendants ensure that groups visiting Disney World together remain together. Access to the edge of the platform is prevented by a gate which is opened once the monorail has arrived and disembarked the arriving passengers on the other side of the platform. If there is a delay of more than a minute or two in waiting for the next monorail one is kept informed of the reason for the delay and the progress the expected train is making towards the station.

Once aboard and the automatic doors of the monorail have closed, one is welcomed aboard, told to remain seated and "for one's own safety" to stay away from open windows. The monorail takes a circuitous route to one of the two Disney locations (the Epcot Center or the Magic Kingdom) during which time a friendly disembodied voice introduces one briefly to the pleasure of the world one is about to enter and the methods of transport available between its various locations. As the monorail slows towards its destination one is told how to disembark once the automatic doors open and how to move from the station to the entrance gates, and reminded to take one's possessions with one and to take care of oneself, and children in one's care, on disembarking. Once again these instructions are reinforced, in a variety of ways, as one moves towards the gates.

It will be apparent from the above that Disney Productions is able to handle large crowds of visitors in a most orderly fashion. Potential trouble is anticipated and prevented. Opportunities for disorder are minimized by constant instruction, by physical barriers which severely limit the choice of action available and by the surveillance of omnipresent employees who detect and rectify the slightest deviation.

The vehicles that carry people between locations are an important component of the system of physical barriers. Throughout Disney World vehicles are used as barriers. This is particularly apparent in the Epcot Center, . . . where many exhibits are accessible only via special vehicles which automatically secure one once they begin moving.

Control strategies are embedded in both environmental features and structural relations. In both cases control structures and activities have other functions which are highlighted so that the control function is overshadowed. Nonetheless, control is pervasive. For example, virtually every pool, fountain, and flower garden serves both as an aesthetic object and to direct visitors away from, or towards, particular locations. Similarly, every Disney Productions employee, while visibly and primarily engaged in other functions, is also engaged in the maintenance of order. This integration of functions is real and not simply an appearance: beauty *is* created, safety *is* protected, employees *are* helpful. The effect is, however, to embed the control function into the "woodwork" where its presence is unnoticed but its effects are ever present.

A critical consequence of this process of embedding control in other structures is that control becomes consensual. It is effected with the willing cooperation of those being controlled so that the controlled become, as Foucault (1977) has observed, the source of their own control. Thus, for example, the batching that keeps families together provides for family unity while at the same time ensuring that parents will be available to control their children. By seeking a definition of order within Disney World that can convincingly be presented as being in the interest of visitors, order maintenance is established as a voluntary activity which allows coercion to be reduced to a minimum. Thus, adult visitors willingly submit to a variety of devices that increase the flow of consumers through Disney World, such as being corralled on the monorail platform, so as to ensure the safety of their children. Furthermore, while doing so they gratefully acknowledge the concern Disney Productions has for their family, thereby legitimating its authority, not only in the particular situation in question, but in others as well. Thus, while profit ultimately underlies the order Disney Productions seeks to maintain, it is pursued in conjunction with other objectives that will encourage the willing compliance of visitors in maintaining Disney profits. This approach to profit making, which seeks a coincidence of corporate and individual interests (employee and consumer alike), extends beyond the control function and reflects a business philosophy to be applied to all corporate operations (Peters and Waterman, 1982).

The coercive edge of Disney's control system is seldom far from the surface, however, and becomes visible the moment the Disney-visitor consensus breaks down, that is, when a visitor attempts to exercise a choice that is incompatible with the Disney order. It is apparent in the physical barriers that forcefully prevent certain activities as well as in the action of employees who detect breaches of order. This can be illustrated by an incident that occurred during a visit to Disney World by Shearing and his daughter, during the course of which she developed a blister on her heel. To avoid further irritation she removed her shoes and proceeded to walk barefooted. They had not progressed ten yards before they were approached by a very personable security guard dressed as a Bahamian police officer, with white pith helmet and white gloves that perfectly suited the theme of the area they were moving through (so that he, at first, appeared more like a scenic prop than a security person), who informed them that walking barefoot was, "for the safety of visitors," not permitted. When informed that, given the blister, the safety of this visitor was likely to be better secured by remaining barefooted, at least on the walkways, they were informed that their safety and how best to protect it was a matter for Disney Productions to determine while they were on Disney property and that unless they complied he would be compelled to escort them out of Disney World. Shearing's daughter, on learning that failure to comply with the security guard's instruction would deprive her of the pleasures of Disney World, quickly decided that she would prefer to further injure her heel and remain on Disney property. As this example illustrates, the source of Disney Productions' power rests both in the physical coercion it can bring to bear and in its capacity to induce cooperation by depriving visitors of a resource that they value.

The effectiveness of the power that control of a "fun place" has is vividly illustrated by the incredible queues of visitors who patiently wait, sometimes for hours, for admission to exhibits. These queues not only call into question the common knowledge that queueing is a quintessentially English pastime (if Disney World is any indication Americans are at least as good, if not better, at it), but provide evidence of the considerable inconvenience that people can be persuaded to tolerate so long as they believe that their best interests require it. While the source of this perception is the image of Disney World that the visitor brings to it, it is, interestingly, reinforced through the queueing process itself. In many exhibits queues are structured so that one is brought close to the entrance at several points, thus periodically giving one a glimpse of the fun to come while at the same time encouraging one that the wait will soon be over.

Visitor participation in the production of order within Disney World goes beyond the more obvious control examples we have noted so far. An important aspect of the order Disney Productions attempts to maintain is a particular image of Disney World and the American industrialists who sponsor its exhibits (General Electric, Kodak, Kraft Foods, etc.). Considerable care is taken to ensure that every feature of Disney World reflects a positive view of the American Way, especially its use of, and reliance on, technology. Visitors are, for example, exposed to an almost constant stream of directions by employees, robots in human form and disembodied recorded voices (the use of recorded messages and robots permits precise control over the content and tone of the directions given) that convey the desired message. Disney World acts as a giant magnet attracting millions of Americans and visitors from other lands who pay to learn of the wonders of American capitalism.

Visitors are encouraged to participate in the production of the Disney image while they are in Disney World and to take it home with them so that they can reproduce it for their families and friends. One way this is done is through the "Picture Spots," marked with signposts, to be found throughout Disney World, that provide direction with respect to the images to capture on film (with cameras that one can borrow free of charge) for the slide shows and photo albums to be prepared "back home." Each spot provides views which exclude anything unsightly (such as garbage containers) so as to ensure that the visual images visitors take away of Disney World will properly capture Disney's order. A related technique is the Disney characters who wander through the complex to provide "photo opportunities" for young children. These characters apparently never talk to visitors, and the reason for this is presumably so that their media-based images will not be spoiled.

As we have hinted throughout this discussion, training is a pervasive feature of the control system of Disney Productions. It is not, however, the redemptive soul-training of the carceral project but an ever-present flow of directions for, and definitions of, order directed at every visitor. Unlike carceral training, these messages do not require detailed knowledge of the individual. They are, on the contrary, for anyone and everyone. Messages are, nonetheless, often conveyed to single individuals or small groups of friends and relatives. For example, in some of the newer exhibits, the vehicles that take one through swivel and turn so that one's gaze can be precisely directed. Similarly, each seat is fitted with individual sets of speakers that talk directly to one, thus permitting a seductive sense of intimacy while simultaneously imparting a uniform message.

In summary, within Disney World control is embedded, preventative, subtle, cooperative and apparently non-coercive and consensual. It focuses on categories, requires no knowledge of the individual and employs pervasive surveillance. Thus, although disciplinary', it is distinctively non-carceral. Its order is instrumental and determined by the interests of Disney Productions rather than moral and absolute. As anyone who has visited Disney World knows, it is extraordinarily effective.

While this new instrumental discipline is rapidly becoming a dominant force in social control it is as different from the Orwellian totalitarian nightmare as it is from the carceral regime. Surveillance is pervasive but it is the antithesis of the blatant control of the Orwellian State: its source is not government and its vehicle is not Big Brother. The order of instrumental discipline is not the unitary order of a central State but diffuse and separate orders defined by private authorities responsible for the feudal-like domains of Disney World, condominium estates, commercial complexes and the like. Within contemporary discipline, control is as fine-grained as Orwell imagined but its features are very different. It is thus, paradoxically, not to Orwell's socialist-inspired Utopia that we must look for a picture of contemporary control but to the capitalist-inspired disciplinary model conceived of by Huxley, who, in his *Brave New World*, painted a picture of consensually based control that bears a striking resemblance to the disciplinary control of Disney World and other corporate control systems. Within Huxley's imaginary world people are seduced into conformity by the pleasures offered by the drug "soma" rather than coerced into compliance by threat of Big Brother, just as people are today seduced to conform by the pleasures of consuming the goods that corporate power has to offer.

The contrasts between morally based justice and instrumental control, carceral punishment and corporate control, the Panopticon and Disney World and Orwell's and Huxley's visions is succinctly captured by the novelist Beryl Bainbridge's (1984) observations about a recent journey she made retracing J. B. Priestley's (1933) celebrated trip around Britain. She notes how during his travels in 1933 the center of the cities and towns he visited were defined by either a church or a center of government (depicting the coalition between Church and State in the production of order that characterizes morally based regimes).

During her more recent trip one of the changes that struck her most forcibly was the transformation that had taken place in the center of cities and towns. These were now identified not by churches or town halls, but by shopping centers, often vaulted glass-roofed structures that she found reminiscent of the cathedrals they had replaced both in their awe-inspiring architecture and in the hush that she found they sometimes created. What was worshipped in these contemporary cathedrals, she noted, was not an absolute moral order but something much more mundane: people were "worshipping shopping" and through it, we would add, the private authorities, the order and corporate power their worship makes possible.

REFERENCES

Bainbridge, B. (1984). Television interview with Robert Fulford on "Realities" Global Television, Toronto, October.

Foucault, M. (1977). *Discipline and Punish: The Birth of the Prison.* New York: Vintage.

Peters, T. J. and Waterman, R. H. (1982). *In Search of Excellence.* New York: Warner Books.

Priestley, J. B. (1934). *English Journey: Being a Rambling but Truthful Account of What One Man Saw and Heard and Felt and Thought during a Journey through England Autumn of the Year 1933.* London: Heinemann and Gollancz.

33

From *Total Confinement: Madness and Reason in the Maximum Security Prison*

LORNA A. RHODES

For millennia human societies have used ostracism and social exclusion as punishment for extreme violations of social norms. In the more than sixty maximum security prisons in the United States today "control units" isolate society's rejected members, rendering them nearly invisible. Building on the work of Max Weber (author of reading 40), critical sociologists have questioned the apparent irrationality of our technically rational systems, nowhere more in evidence than in modern prisons. The author draws on portraits of inmates she met during months of observation in one prison in order to explore the effects of intensive confinement on both prisoners and the staff who regulate their confinement.

> I don't know if you can get your point across except by bringing the public in and sticking them in one of those little cages for a week or two.
>
> Jeremy Roland,* Control Unit Prisoner

Waiting on my side of a visiting booth in a maximum security unit, I am looking through a clear, thick plastic window into a small, bare room identical to the one in which I am sitting. But unlike the ordinary wooden door I just closed behind me, the door into the room on the other side is solid steel with a small hinged slot, or cuffport, at waist height. As it opens, two blue-uniformed officers hand in a dark-haired young man in a white jumpsuit, hands cuffed behind his back. The door closes behind him with a heavy clank. In one smooth motion the prisoner takes a step inside and backs his hands through the cuffport so that one of the officers can free them from the cuffs.

After Jeremy Roland settles onto the metal stool on his side of the window and I place my tape recorder microphone up against the small speaker in the wall on my side, he tells me that he knows this situation would seem odd to an outsider. "Seeing someone come in here with handcuffs and backing up to the door probably seems very strange to you, but I've been doing it for a few years now. It's like putting on your shoes and walking out of your house." But his grandmother will be coming soon for what he knows will be the last time, and he is sorry that he will have to meet her in one of these booths. He doesn't want her to see him here under maximum custody restrictions. "I still get

---

*All names given for prisoners in this book are pseudonyms.

embarrassed in front of visitors and being handcuffed. Not so much embarrassed as I am ashamed. . . . I'm gonna have a real hard time with it." I notice that the window between us is covered with smudges right at eye level where previous visitors have tried to press their hands together through the plastic pane.

Jeremy has a life sentence. He came to prison at twenty after his third "strike"; his worst offense was an assault during a robbery in which no one was killed. "Everything that was most important to me then is least important to me now," he says. "And everything that was least important is most important to me now. [My third strike] woke me up. I wish it had happened ten years ago. I wish so much. But it's too late. They've thrown away the key." He talks about the other prisoners who are here with him on this unit where he is confined to a solitary cell for twenty-three hours a day. Some seem to be deranged, "sick individuals" who "make everyone miserable, day in and day out" by pounding on their sinks and doors. It seems to him that no sooner does one leave than another takes his place. Others are murderers who have done "brutal things"—"I know some horrible people [who] commit horrible crimes. . . . You've got some pretty bad prisoners in here, just awful."

Once he gets past the "little trouble" that brought him to this unit, Jeremy likely will do his time in the "general population," where the vast majority of prisoners live. But like many who live or work in prisons, he frames his description of his environment with two figures who, like book-ends, mark the limits of comprehension: one "sick" and the other "bad."

Jeremy is typical of many prisoners and staff in his description of the disturbing—but far from uniform—effects of intensive confinement. My introduction to a prisoner Jeremy would have called "sick" occurred one day during the first year of our project when I visited a psychiatric unit for seriously mentally ill inmates. A small group of staff took me to the end of a long cell-lined hallway. Thomas Vincent had lived there for several years, and his delusions, odd behavior, and attacks on staff had diminished in response to the care he received. But his sentence expired the next day, and two days earlier his condition had deteriorated dramatically. Now, he was "locked down" in his small room behind his heavy door with its small window. He had destroyed most of his property, including his clothes, and had wrapped his naked body in threads unraveled from a sheet. Before I quickly glanced away, I saw his frightened eyes and the gleam of dozens of white strings wound around his tense body. He looked as though he wanted to jump out of his skin.

One of the unit's counselors was rather awkwardly cradling a pair of shoes, which he held up in front of the window so that Vincent could see them. Setting them carefully on the floor in front of the cell, he explained to me that he wanted to reassure the prisoner that the things that had been removed from his cell were still available. After we had walked back down the tier, we gathered in a little knot near the unit's control booth. The staff explained that they could not, of course, keep Vincent where he was, and they had no obligation other than to let him go from the gate of their prison into the surrounding semi-rural landscape. They had scheduled a commitment hearing with a state hospital and planned to argue that his psychosis and history of assault made him a danger to both himself and others. What, I asked, if that doesn't work? Then they would drive him to a nearby city and drop him off outside the emergency room of a public hospital.

A prison mental health worker described the facility that Vincent seems reluctant to leave as a "black box within a black box" into which the public and even other prisons want men like him to disappear. Vincent may well have arrived there from another maximum security setting, psychotic and banging on his cell like the inmates Jeremy described. Now he had nowhere to go, no reason to step into those shoes outside his door.

During that same first year I went for the first time into the kind of maximum security unit in which I interviewed Roland. The unit had a circular design, with a control booth in the center and rows of cells around the periphery. Standing next to the control booth with the two prison workers who were escorting me, at first I barely noticed the man exercising in a small indoor yard in front of the tiers. The prisoner, Jamal Nelson, was facing the wall and swinging his arms out in gradually widening circles, an exercise that made sense given the lack of any exercise equipment in the little space. But gradually we became aware that he was calmly and rhythmically swinging one arm closer and closer to the wall, a bloodstain spreading as his hand hit the concrete. "Let's go," said one of my companions sharply, "before we give him any more attention." As we left, I saw that two officers had moved quickly into the yard to stop him.

The "box" of the prison presents a smooth surface to the outside world, which is of course how it works as a place of disappearance. But inside, it has distinct internal separations. The two prisoners I have just described were in the different, though equally controlled, environments designated for the system's "problem children." Vincent had a diagnosis of chronic mental illness; the staff of the treatment unit felt he needed attention in the form of medication, reassurance, and, they hoped, some sort of continuing treatment. Nelson was considered disturbed, though more ambiguously; those keeping him felt that he was playing for "attention" and that attention was harmful to him. They believed that he needed to be maintained—maybe permanently—in a condition offering the barest of human contact.

Maximum security prisons have in common extreme forms of control that go well beyond that effected by ordinary prison discipline. Confined to these units are the prisoners called—in the shorthand of psychiatry—the "mad" and the "bad." At the heart of this book is the paradox represented in my sketches of Vincent and Nelson: the tighter control becomes, the more problematic are the effects it precipitates. Often situations like these are approached in terms of whether and how individuals choose their own behavior. To what extent are these men in control of themselves? Are these strange behaviors signs of underlying disturbances—"madness" in one of its many forms—in those subjected to intensive confinement? Or are they willful, character-based attempts to exert a minimal, if counterproductive, resistance? A second way to frame these questions, however, is to shift to the level of the institutional mechanisms of control. What assumptions about dangerousness, self-control, and individual choice are contained in, and signaled by, measures of extreme confinement? What conundrums are encountered both by those who are the object of these measures and by those who enforce them? These questions point us less toward the inmate as a disturbed individual and more toward his position in and his responses to the social world formed around him by the conditions in which he is held.

Reflecting on the path that sent him to prison, Roland says that he has "made some mistakes in [his] life, some bad choices" for which he deserves punishment, though he protests that the punishment itself is excessive. He mourns the rational actor he could have been and wants to be now. "So here I sit," he says sadly. Vincent clearly cannot make rational choices and has been given a kind of partial exemption, but he is in a larger context that has abandoned him. Nelson's strange act is ambiguous; is it a calculated bid for attention? He has lived in a control unit for years without a resolution to this question. Within the larger issue of control, then, we find that the behavior of these prisoners is understood in terms of their capacity to reason, an understanding that in turn determines where they live and the attitudes they encounter in prison staff. Both the "horrible" prisoners described by Roland and the "attention-seeking" Nelson, as well as Roland himself, are being treated as rational actors. They are believed capable of choosing not to be where they are. Vincent, on the other hand, is treated as irrational and therefore unable to control his behavior.

The issue of whether and how prisoners make rational decisions is embedded in a larger question: what of the institution itself? The kind of control exercised in these maximum security settings is technologically sophisticated and planned down to the smallest detail. The myriad elements of housing design, placement, and daily routine shaping these prisoners' situations rest on the assumption that rational practices underlie the operation of "the system." But what, really, is this rationality of the system? Perhaps—as suggested by the history of modern forms of punishment—it lies in an institutional regime of order designed to contain and correct the disordered products of society. Perhaps, as many prison workers and some prisoners believe, it arises "naturally" from the connection between the project of containment and our innate capacity to reason. Punishment, in this view, simply aligns human nature with laws that reflect that nature back to us. But perhaps the institution carries a secret: that it is, under these surface appearances, profoundly irrational. Roland's sentence, with its wastefulness of life and incredible cost, Vincent's impending ejection, delusional and assaultive, to "the streets," the interpretation offered for Nelson's self-destruction—all suggest that the "system" itself may be mad. These prisoners are entangled in institutional contradictions within which they become—and suffer for becoming—the extremes and exceptions that mark the limits of the rational.

* * *

Finally, the contemporary prison has developed a new technology—in the form of the control prison—for the creation of a potentially absolute social exclusion. Historically, and in many prison systems in the United States, this exclusion is correlated with and profoundly linked to race. The current proliferation and expansion of the technology suggests that it is being enlisted to manage other projects of separation and isolation as well. When these projects of exclusion are framed in entirely individualistic and non-rehabilitative terms, they confront us with disturbing questions about what it means to be a human—a social—being. I believe this is the issue most deeply at stake in the contemporary prison. I approach it here, not at the level of national policy where it has been well described, but at the level of local practice where it is enacted in daily assertions of authority and resistance.

A former prisoner writes, "Most Americans remain ignorant . . . that they live in a country that holds hostage behind bars another populous country of their fellow citizens." In this other country there is tremendous variation among prisoners and among the environments in which they live. One reason I began with my conversation with Jeremy Roland is that although he was a maximum custody inmate at the time, he represents the many inmates who pass through that status quickly and whose lives in prison do not revolve around the kind of difficulties that I describe in this book. The term "general population" is used in prisons to refer to the ordinary conditions under which most prisoners live and to which Roland would return.

General population inmates are not personally restrained and move about the prison (at specific times) to jobs and other activities. They eat together in large dining halls, share two- to four-man cells in crowded living units, and exercise in large communal yards. A prisoner living in general population writes of Stateville in Illinois:

> If you expect the usual tale of constant violence, brutal guards, gang rapes, daily escape efforts, turmoil . . . you will be deeply disappointed. Prison life . . . is not a daily round of threats, fights, plots, and "shanks" (prison-made knives)—though you have to be constantly careful to avoid situations or behavior that might lead to violence. . . . For me, and many like me in prison, violence is not the major problem; the major problem is monotony. . . . boredom, time-slowing boredom, interrupted by occasional bursts of fear and anger, is the governing reality of life in prison.*

---

*Morris, Norval. "The Contemporary Prison: 1965—Present." In *The Oxford History of the Prison: The Practice of Punishment in Western Society*, ed. Norval Morris and David J. Rothman. Oxford: Oxford University Press, 1998.

For the purpose of understanding the contexts I describe here, the most important feature of general population is that it requires prisoners to manage themselves in groups within a complex, overcrowded system. Assignment to special maximum security units occurs in a larger context of pressures for conformity, jam-packed quarters, intergroup tensions, and various kinds of victimization. Large living units can be dangerous for prisoners with psychiatric problems or other vulnerabilities; even fairly minor aberrant behavior may cause an inmate to be rejected or injured by his peers. Once confined to a special unit, some inmates regard general population as a sort of Promised Land where they can have access to their property, sit in the sun, yard with other inmates (in prison, "yard" is a verb as well as a noun). Others, however, find the intense social life on regular living units more deadly than a lonely special-unit cell. Both prisoners and staff negotiate an environment in which the difficult, boring, or dangerous conditions of the prison as a whole are in ongoing tension with—and the only alternative to—the isolation and stasis of intensive confinement.

CONTROLLING TROUBLES

> These people are taught we're the *enemy,* that this is the worst of the worst.
>
> Control Unit Inmate, of Officers

> He is definitely a very dangerous person, capable of probably doing anything that he has ever been accused of, whether founded or unfounded. He is very dangerous, very smart.
>
> Control Unit Officer, of an Inmate

The control unit sits alone on the prison grounds, built partly underground and surrounded by its own razor-wire fence. My companion, a quiet man who works in a different section of the prison, leads the way through the double gate in the fence, through a set of heavy metal doors, along a clean, bright hallway, and past several small offices. Finally we emerge into the circular interior. A glassed-in control booth sits in its center, slightly elevated, a row of video monitors visible above the booth officer's head. Around the perimeter are two tiers of tightly secured cells. Each has a narrow window on its outside wall, frosted to prevent prisoners from seeing out. Looking down a tier, one sees rows of cells with their steel doors, small windows and cuffports hinged to open outward. The interior space of the unit is divided into sections of these cells—called "pods"—separated from one another and from the control booth by shatterproof clear walls and locked doors. This clean, shadowless interior, almost devoid of natural light, gives the fleeting impression that it is empty except for the uniformed staff working the booth.

An officer takes us for a brief and gingerly walk along one of the tiers, where we can see through the little windows into the 8 x 10 cells. Most of the prisoners wear only their underwear. Some sleep on their concrete beds, or simply lie on them staring into space; others pace restlessly back and forth. Some gaze at us silently; others yell up and down the tiers to one another. Echoing in the hard-edged interior, their shouts are a blur of rage-saturated sound. The atmosphere is dense as an inmate calls out to us from his cell. He's got a "nine mil" in his cell, he says through the window, and he's gonna kill himself if they don't let him out. The officer asks him what he means. He raises a clenched fist and waves his muscled, tattooed arm in our faces: *This* is my nine mil. The noise around us escalates, though I can't make out the words. My companions explain that this man's neighbors are egging him on. Eventually, they say, he will do something to himself because, the officer tells me, "The guy next to him will talk him into it."

On our way into the unit we walked past big carts stacked with plastic meal trays. Since the inmates are not allowed to have anything sharp, all the food is soft or bite-size; today each tray has a grapefruit cut into quarters. Two officers deliver lunch to each pod, carrying the trays to the inmates one at a time. One officer opens the cuffport and stands carefully to one side while the other, who is dressed in a waterproof jumpsuit, quickly pushes in the tray. The officers stay clear because sometimes inmates stab them through the opening or hurl feces or urine at them. On the upper tier of cells one door has been covered with plastic to keep the man inside from throwing as the officers walk by.

Like all control prisons, this one is based on a "lockdown" system that keeps prisoners in their cells twenty-three or more hours a day. Booth officers operate a twenty-four-hour computerized system that runs the unit's mechanized doors and gates, trains video monitors into every corner of the building, and makes it possible to listen in on cells and tiers. An inmate can leave his cell only under escort after allowing himself to be cuffed through the cuffport. The two officers who bring him out may add leg and waist chains, or a tether that hooks onto his cuffs. One on each side, they lead him to a brief shower or to solitary exercise in a small, walled-in yard. An ad from a correctional trade journal reflects the concerns of those who design these units. Offering the "highest reliability," it promises a seamless electronic control that works in tandem with architecture to completely encompass the space of the prison. Each panel of the illustration shows an aspect of this control: the centralized system that manages the internal doors, the tight, possibly electrified perimeter, the computer screen that can display not only the space itself but the history and photograph of every inmate, and the impressive electronics. Thus the prisoner who is controlled by visible and routinized forms of bodily restraint is also contained within a pervasive and efficient surveillance. The intent is to ensure that all "complexities" remain in the hands of management; in reality, as we have just glimpsed and as the ad itself seems to acknowledge, this focus on control occurs in the face of "possibilities" that challenge the order imposed by these technologies.

The United States has over sixty maximum security prisons like this one. They have many names: maximum security units, supermaximum prisons, special housing units, or intensive management units (the term in Washington State). I will use the generic "control prison" or "control unit." Control prisons are freestanding institutions, while control units, which are more common, are special sections of larger prisons. These facilities are routinely described by correctional officials and in the press as housing "the worst of the worst" and thus serving as "prisons within prisons."

THE "WORST OF THE WORST"

> You either deal with it or you don't deal with it. . . . I feel I could act like a fool and do crazy shit and talk shit to them all the time and smash my TV and break up the cell. People get pretty determined sometimes. You can tear the toilet off the wall if you're strong enough.
>
> Control Unit Prisoner

> It's the end of the line for inmates who threaten the security of the staff, the security of the institution. This is basically the end of the line and this is where you will go and you will be [here] until you can get a straight behavior.
>
> Control Unit Administrator

> HEARING OFFICER: Why are you still in the [control unit]?
> PRISONER: Because I refuse to submit.

Control units are in a complex relationship to a larger institutional system for which they serve both practical and symbolic purposes. In some cases of misbehavior a prisoner undergoes a fairly brief—if thoroughly unpleasant—period of segregation followed by an uneventful reintegration into the general population. But many ambiguities attend the issue of "misbehavior." The placement of mentally ill inmates in control units and the development in some cases—whether the prisoner is regarded as mentally ill or not—of ongoing patterns of throwing and violence raise questions about the relationship between the ratcheting up of measures of control and a decreasing ability on the part of the prisoner to control himself. In addition, particularly out-of-control prisoners who are kept in these units until the end of their sentences emerge directly into their communities. This raises troubling questions about what purpose such control really serves.

Those outside prisons assume that "the worst of the worst" refers to prisoners who have committed particularly heinous crimes. Control units do contain a greater proportion of prisoners with violent histories, younger prisoners with juvenile records, and, of course, prisoners who have harmed other inmates or prison staff. But others are in intensive confinement for their own protection or because they have accumulated a prescribed number of infractions. Mentally ill, disturbed, or persistently defiant inmates continue to accumulate sanctions while in maximum custody, thus adding to their time. Some prisoners may be placed in isolation preemptively, and some are kept there indefinitely regardless of their behavior.

These differences among prisoners raise the question of what it means to "get a straight behavior," as the administrator quoted above said in defense of his unit. Those who manage these units offer arguments based on their own accountability as well as the inmates'. A control unit administrator explained, "We try our best and we're professional. We make the inmates accountable and so we keep them [here, in the control unit] for a long time . . . [because when we recommend release] we have to deal with the inmate in a revolving door process." Some argue bluntly for a primarily punitive and deterrent effect. The warden of a large facility in Minnesota, for example, said in response to inmate interviewers, "[Special housing units] serve a punitive purpose. . . . They exist to deter people from acting out. I'm not going to apologize for that." These comments point to fundamental issues that attended imprisonment since the early 1800s: Is its purpose punishment, with or without a presumed deterrent effect? Or is it—perhaps instead, perhaps also—intended to change behavior.

* * *

The passage of those with diagnosed psychiatric conditions into prisons is connected to events that have occurred in the larger society over the past thirty years. Most important is the deinstitutionalization of public psychiatric hospitals in the 1970s and early '80s, which shifted many who would have been hospitalized into prison as the asylum of last resort. Ironically, the institutionalization of patients, which the closure of the hospitals and the laws against involuntary hospitalization were intended to avoid, returns in full force in prisons. A prison administrator expressed the feelings of many who find themselves on the receiving end of this change, "These decisions [by the courts] are so irresponsible. I don't think mentally ill inmates should ever get to a prison situation." Despite these objections, prison officials and administrators find themselves legally and practically required to provide an approximation of the treatment that used to be the province of state hospitals.

The net slung across the receiving unit to catch those with serious mental illness is the first step in a process that resembles the intake procedures of a psychiatric facility. But it would be a mistake to make too much of this resemblance. In fact, almost all the men who pour into the wide mouth of the prison are tumbled together as they disperse through the system. The vast majority go on into living units at this and other prisons, sorted roughly according to their prior history of violence. Most of these men never or rarely receive infractions and live in general population units with a degree of autonomy. But over time, some will have difficulty accommodating to crowded and regimented conditions and will precipitate out of these units on the basis of their behavior. These are the inmates who accumulate infractions and—as though falling through a sieve—are sorted into control units and into special units for the mentally ill.

The word "ding" is used by prison staff and inmates to mean "crazy." It is often used in ways that seem synonymous with "mentally ill" but, as with the term "crazy," its range is wider than any psychiatric diagnosis. To be a ding, or to ding out or become dingy means to exhibit crazy behavior—behavior that doesn't make sense. Talking to oneself, refusing to wash, mania, general strangeness of demeanor—all are dingy. The extent to which the "ding jacket" (prison term for label) is felt to be disparaging varies, with both inmates and staff making casual references like "This is the ding wing." An officer with whom I discussed the disturbing symptoms of a friend asked in a completely matter-of-fact way, "Is she dingy?" At other times, however, "ding" is highly pejorative. Control unit inmates speak with disgust of "these crazy dings they've got in here." Prison workers do not use the word in formal contexts or when talking to outsiders.

* * *

In the control unit, just to one side of the door, built-in concrete benches form a rough circle. I am here with other visitors, including a consulting psychiatrist and the social worker, nurse, and resident psychiatrist who work in the prison's mental health unit. The big space is noisy: doors clang and officers shout back and forth as they pass out lunch trays. The keys and cuffs on the officers' belts clank and jangle as they walk by, ignoring our little gathering.

One person in our circle is the prisoner we have come to see, a middle-aged man in an orange jumpsuit named William Kramer. His long hair and full beard are matted, hiding his face as he slumps slightly forward and gazes down at the floor through his grimy, tightly clasped hands. The visiting psychiatrist, much younger, sits close to him on the bench. He leans forward and clasps his own hands in front of him, mirroring the posture of the prisoner. Slowly, as though he could easily sit there for the rest of the day, he asks Kramer if it is all right to talk in front of so many people. The prisoner nods yes, never raising his eyes from the floor. Softly the psychiatrist asks, "How can we be helpful?"

Kramer's voice is so small in the big noisy space that we make out only part of his words as he begins talking, haltingly at first. He tells the psychiatrist that he comes from a large family; we catch something about spacecraft mixed into what he says. There is a long, generous pause. "I like to work with my hands," he adds. The doctor picks up on this, and asks him about his work as a carpenter. The prisoner begins to talk more easily, a little louder, about the jobs he used to do.

Then the psychiatrist reaches out and gently takes Kramer's hands in his. He turns them over, delicately stroking the palms and touching the long, curling nails. "What do you think people should know about [you]?" he asks. Kramer is silent, but it is a not a tense silence. "It's been tough for you," the psychiatrist continues. The prisoner nods. "This isolation has sort of set in," he offers. The doctor waits, adjusting his posture slightly to mirror the signs of a slight increase in animation. The prisoner continues, "It [isolation] makes a person upset, and it's like you're diseased because you're upset. It's kind of a circle." His eyes suddenly fill with tears. "You certainly do get depressed."

Kramer is quiet now. The doctor says gently, "You've been all by yourself way too much, for far too long. We'll keep checking in with you about how we are doing [with you]. We'll work with you about how fast you want to be with people." The resident psychiatrist, a silent observer until now, turns to the prisoner and adds, "I'll bring in some nail clippers tomorrow and cut your nails for you. Let's just hope they won't fire me for it!"

Later, the visiting psychiatrist ends his consultation with some advice for the staff. "He's lonely and terrified that he's lost his mind. Anchor everything in the real world, play cards with him. He's interesting; there's a brightness in there that's still alive. That's what makes it hard. He knows what he has lost."

William Kramer was sent to prison from a country jail where he had been confined in isolation for two years. Charged with gradually moving him from the control unit into their facility, these mental health workers had already begun the process by removing his handcuffs. "Yesterday," says one, "we were afraid that we'd never get him off maximum security. We just had to observe him and act on faith [that he would not become violent], because he was mute. But we did it, and he is like a new person. He was sad and grateful when the cuffs came off. . . . He seems less afraid he's in a death camp now." Even after studying the huge stack of records that arrived with him, the staff are baffled by his case. "This sort of situation shouldn't be happening," one says angrily. "This demonstrates our system's clumsiness."

The task of these workers is well symbolized by the circle they form as they listen to Kramer: to encircle him with a rough approximation of psychiatric and social service. They are charged with easing his symptoms of paranoia, depression, and delusion, while recognizing that, as he says, these are related in "kind of a circle" to the treatment—or lack thereof—that he has already received. They also try, though the extent to which this is their charge is unclear, to protect him from the prison itself. We can see that the situation is tenuous. Kramer may strike out in fear and confusion, bringing down again the full weight of custody. They have no control over how he came to them and little more over where he will go when he leaves. And conditions are not conducive to their professional and personal inclination toward listening and care taking. As they take in what has happened to Kramer, the visiting psychiatrist offers sympathy for them, too. The resident psychiatrist may suspect that he won't be fired for slipping nail clippers into his pocket, but his remark points to his position as an outsider who is not fully aligned with custodial concerns.

One African American inmate, Stephen Tillich, had been in and out of control units for several years and described himself as mired in legal troubles, grievances against the corrections department, and multiple symptoms. He was in a control unit when he talked of his increasingly disturbed perception of his environment:

> I have a lot of fatigue and abnormal sleep patterns. . . . The lighting [here] can be either poor or extremely light—the rays . . . just come in and hit you. I have hallucinations. I see things that is on the wall . . . that there is no explanation for. I know it might be a figment of my imagination, I don't know. Sometimes I see faces coming past my window when I am lying on my bed. Sometimes I see things on the walls. . . . Sometimes I hear voices. . . . My speech, my talk, my voice, it has all been changed, you know? This [prison] affects every aspect of my life. . . . There is no hope for my future, no matter how hard I try to just be patient, be humble. . . . There is nobody to talk to . . . and vent my frustration and as a result, sometimes I am violent. Pound on the walls. Yell and scream.

The perceptual world of a control unit—and to some extent of any prison unit—includes flat, steady, artificial light, a built environment of harsh angles and flat planes, sudden noise and echoing voices that can't quite be made out, constant surveillance, and utter dependence on others for basic physical needs. This world is similar to that described by people experiencing certain extreme states of mind. Paranoia about the cameras and being watched is common, as is the "peopling" of the isolating spaces with animals, people, and spirits. Other routine aspects of the physical environment—such as building maintenance or nighttime deliveries of medication—may also be disturbing. Tillich is in poor physical health, and the airlessness, smell, and mysterious activities of the unit create in him a sense of ominous strangeness whose meaning hovers just out of reach.

* * *

Kramer and Tillich both show signs of physical deterioration and neglect. Tillich speaks of length of the difficulty of keeping up his hygiene and the negative effects of confinement on his skin and hair. Kramer's long nails and matted hair are vivid evidence of his entombment. Their fragile bodies are not just evidence of poor hygiene; they also represent a descent into a radical otherness. As with throwing, the connection between failure to maintain the body and abject social status sets up a downward spiral of which Tillich, at least, seems well aware. In screening we saw men who, even as they emerged from shackles and were tumbled together into prison, washed their hands, changed their clothes, and emerged looking, in the main, neat and self-possessed. Kramer and Tillich, unable to "maintain," have precipitated out of this process. Their long months in isolation suggest that when both the mind and body of the prisoner become disheveled—no longer giving evidence of the self-regulation that stands in for social order—it is increasingly difficult for him to be imagined in anything less than permanent quarantine.

The staff who reach out to Kramer challenge his isolation and in doing so they make the dual gesture that creates the foundation for mental health units. On one hand, they draw him toward them, encircling him and offering attention, touch, and the understanding that his situation is a human one, a mistake, and not merely his just deserts as a criminal. On the other, they begin a process of sense making that will enfold him in a new—or at least a modified—identity. This reentry into language simultaneously distances as it draws him in. With it he becomes someone who "has" a condition, someone whose depression, bipolar disease, or schizophrenia places him in relation to the norm—however remote normal may seem in an environment where everyone is defined as deviant—and explains his behavior.

34

The Rise and Fall of Mass Rail Transit

FROM *Building American Cities: The Urban Real Estate Game*

JOE R. FEAGIN AND ROBERT PARKER

There are more automobiles than people in Los Angeles. Is this a consequence of the preferences and choices of individual consumers, a reflection of the so-called American love affair with the automobile, or is it the result of structured choices? The authors show that farsighted corporations found common cause in organizing transportation to suit their interests, and the romance of Americans and their cars began a new chapter.

Most U.S. cities have become *multinucleated,* with major commercial, industrial, and residential areas no longer closely linked to or dependent upon the downtown center. Decentralization has become characteristic of our cities from coast to coast. Essential to decentralization has been the development and regular extension of an automobile-dominated transportation system serving businesses and the general citizenry, but mostly paid for by rank-and-file taxpayers. With and without citizen consent, corporate capitalists, industrialists and developers, and allied political officials have made key decisions fundamentally shaping the type of transportation system upon which all Americans now depend.

THE AUTO-OIL-RUBBER INDUSTRIAL COMPLEX

The auto-oil-rubber industrial complex has long been central to both the general economy and the urban transportation system in the United States. Automobile and auto-related industries provide a large proportion, sometimes estimated at one-sixth, of all jobs, although this proportion may be decreasing with the decline and stagnation in the auto industry over the last two decades. An estimated one-quarter to one-half of the land in central cities is used for the movement, storage, selling, and parking of automobiles, trucks, and buses. The expanding production of automobiles and trucks has been coordinated with the expansion of highways and freeways and has facilitated the bulging suburbanization around today's cities.

Because of the dominance of autos and trucks in the U.S. transportation system, the traditional social scientists * * * have typically viewed that transportation system as preordained by the American "love" for the automobile. For example, in a recent book on Los Angeles, historian Scott Bottles argues that "America's present urban transportation system largely reflects choices made by the public itself"; the public freely chose the automobile as a "liberating and democratic technology." Conventional explanations for auto-centered patterns focus on the response of a market system to these consumers. Auto-linked technologies are discussed as though they force human decisions: Thus "the city dweller, especially in recent times, has been a victim of the technological changes that have been wrought in transportation systems." * * * [T]raditional ecologists and other social scientists view the complexity and shape of cities as largely determined by technological developments in transportation—a reasonable view—but these technologies are not carefully examined in terms of their economic contexts, histories, and possible technological alternatives. For example, unlike the United States, numerous capitalist countries in Europe, including prosperous West Germany, have a mixed rail transit/automobile transport system. There interurban and intraurban rail transit remains very important. For this reason, the U.S. system cannot be assumed to be simply the result of "free" consumer choices in a market context. The capitalistic history and decision-making contexts that resulted in the positioning of automobiles at the heart of the U.S. transportation system must be examined.

EARLY MASS RAIL TRANSIT

Rural and urban Americans have not always been so dependent on automobiles for interurban and intraurban transport. In the years between the 1880s and the 1940s many cities had significant mass transit systems. By 1890 electric trolleys were in general use. Indeed, electric trolley routes, elevated railroads, and subways facilitated the first urban expansion and decentralization. Some investor-owned rail transit companies extended their trolley lines beyond existing urbanized areas out into the countryside in an attempt to profit from the land speculation along the rail lines. Glenn Yago has documented how transit owners and real estate speculators worked together to ensure the spatial and economic development of cities by private enterprise. Transit companies were a significant force in urban sprawl. The suburban spread of Los Angeles, for example, got its initial push from the expansion of trolley rail lines. Not initially laid out as an automobile city, this sprawling metropolis developed along streetcar tracks; only later was the streetcar network displaced by automobiles.

The reorganization and disruption of mass rail transit that took place in the early 1900s did not result just from the challenge of improved automobile technology. Rather, capitalist entrepreneurs and private corporations seeking profits reorganized and consolidated existing rail transit systems. Electrification of horse-drawn streetcars increased investment costs and stimulated concentration of ownership in larger "transit trusts" of landowning, finance, and utility entrepreneurs. Mergers of old transit firms and the assembly of new companies were commonplace, and there was much speculation in transit company stock. Yago has provided evidence on the corrupt accounting practices, over-extension of lines for real estate speculation, and overcapitalization which led to the bankruptcy of more than one-third of the private urban transit companies during the period 1916–1923. Sometimes the capitalists involved in the transit companies were too eager for profits. "These actions in turn," Charles Cheape notes, "drained funds, discouraged additional investment, and contributed significantly to the collapse and reorganization of many transit systems shortly after World War I and again in the 1930s."

Ironically, one consequence of the so-called "progressive" political reform movement in cities in the first decades of the twentieth century was that supervision of rail transit systems was often placed in the hands of business-dominated regulatory commissions, many of whose members were committed to the interests of corporate America (for example, transit stock manipulation for profit), rather than to the welfare of the general public. In numerous cases the extraordinary profits made by rail transit entrepreneurs, together with their ties to corrupt politicians, created a negative public image—which in turn made the public less enthusiastic about new tax-supported subsidies and fare hikes for the troubled rail transit systems. Moreover, as the profits of many of the private transit firms declined, public authorities in some cities, including Boston and New York, were forced to take over the transit lines from the poorly managed private companies in response to citizen pressure for mass transportation. This fact suggests that there has long been popular *demand* for publicly owned rail transit that is reliable, convenient, and inexpensive. Indeed, during the period 1910–1930 a *majority* of Americans either could not afford, because of modest incomes, or could not use, because of age or handicap, an automobile.

A CORPORATE PLAN TO KILL MASS TRANSIT?

By the late 1910s and 1920s the ascension of the U.S. auto-oil-rubber industrial complex brought new corporate strategies to expand automobile markets and secure government subsidies for road infrastructure. Mass rail transit hindered the profit-oriented interests of this car-centered industrial complex, whose executives became involved not only in pressuring governments to subsidize roads but also in the buying up of mass transit lines. For example, in the early 1920s, Los Angeles had the largest and most effective trolley car system in the United States. Utilizing more than a thousand miles of track, the system transported millions of people yearly. During World War II, the streetcars ran 2,800 scheduled runs a day. But by the end of that war, the trolleys were disappearing. And their demise had little to do with consumer choice. As news analyst Harry Reasoner has observed, it "was largely a result of a criminal conspiracy":

> The way it worked was that General Motors, Firestone Tire and Standard Oil of California and some other companies, depending on the location of the target,

would arrange financing for an outfit called National City Lines, which cozied up to city councils and county commissioners and bought up transit systems like L.A.'s. Then they would junk or sell the electric cars and pry up the rails for scrap and beautiful, modern buses would be substituted, buses made by General Motors and running on Firestone Tires and burning Standard's gas.

Within a month after the trolley system in Los Angeles was purchased, 237 new buses arrived. It is important to realize that, for all the financial and management problems created by the private owners of the rail transit firms, the old transit systems were still popular. In the year prior to the takeover, the Los Angeles electric lines made $1.5 million in profits and carried more than 200 million passengers. The logic behind the corporate takeover plan was clear. The auto-related firms acted because a trolley car can carry the passengers of several dozen automobiles.

During the 1930s GM created a holding company through which it and other auto-related companies channeled money to buy up electric transit systems in 45 cities from New York to Los Angeles. As researcher Bradford Snell has outlined it, the process had three stages. First, General Motors (GM) helped the Greyhound corporation displace long-distance passenger transportation from railroads to buses. Then GM and other auto-related companies bought up and dismantled numerous local electric transit systems, replacing them with the GM-built buses. Moreover, in the late 1940s, GM was convicted in a Chicago federal court of having conspired to destroy electric transit and to convert trolley systems to diesel buses, whose production GM monopolized. William Dixon, the man who put together the criminal conspiracy case for the federal government, argued that individual corporate executives should be sent to jail. Instead, each received a trivial $1 fine. The corporations were assessed a modest $5,000 penalty, the maximum under the law. In spite of this conviction, GM continued to play a role in converting electric transit systems to diesel buses. And these diesel buses provided more expensive mass transit: "The diesel bus, as engineered by GM, has a shorter life expectancy, higher operating costs, and lower overall productivity than electric buses. GM has thus made the bus economically noncompetitive with the car also." One source of public discontent with mass transit was this inferiority of the new diesel buses compared to the rail transit cars that had been displaced without any consultation with consumers. Not surprisingly, between 1936 and 1955 the number of operating trolley cars in the United States dropped from about 40,000 to 5,000.

In a lengthy report GM officials have argued that electric transit systems were already in trouble when GM began intervening. As noted above, some poorly managed transit systems were declining already, and some had begun to convert partially to buses before GM's vigorous action. So from GM's viewpoint, the corporations direct intervention only accelerated the process. This point has been accented by Bottles, who shows that GM did not single-handedly destroy the streetcar systems in Los Angeles. These privately controlled systems were providing a lesser quality of service before GM became involved. The profit milking and corruption of the private streetcar firms in Los Angeles were not idiosyncratic but were common for privately owned mass transport in numerous cities.

Also important in destroying mass transit was the new and aggressive multimillion-dollar marketing of automobiles and trucks by General Motors and other automobile companies across the United States. And the automobile companies and their advertisers were not the only powerful actors involved in killing off numerous mass transit systems. Bankers and public officials also played a role. Yago notes that "after World War II, banks sold bankrupt and obsolete transit systems throughout the country at prices that bore no relation to the systems' real values." Often favoring the auto interests, local banks and other financial institutions tried to limit government bond issues that could be used to finance new equipment and refurbish the remaining rail transit systems.

Because of successful lobbying by executives from the auto-oil-rubber complex, and their own acceptance of a motorization perspective, most government officials increasingly backed street and highway construction. They cooperated with the auto industry in eliminating many mass transit systems. Increased governmental support for auto and truck transportation systems has meant systematic disinvestment in mass transit systems. Over the several decades since World War II, governmental mass transit subsidies have been small compared with highway subsidies. This decline has hurt low-and moderate-income people the most. Less public transit since World War II has meant increased commuting time in large cities where people are dependent on the automobile, which is especially troublesome for moderate-income workers who may not be able to afford a reliable car; less mass transit has also meant increased consumer expenditures for automobiles and gasoline. Auto expansion has frustrated the development of much mass transit because growing street congestion slows down buses and trolleys, further reducing their ridership. As a result, governmental funding for public rail transit has been cut, again chasing away riders who dislike poorly maintained equipment. And fares have been increased. Riders who can use automobiles do so. And the downward spiral has continued to the point of extinction of most public rail transit systems.

Mass transit was allowed to decline by the business-oriented government officials in most cities. Consumer desires were only partly responsible for this. Consumers did discover the freedom of movement of autos, and even in cities with excellent rail transit systems many prefer the auto for at least some types of travel. But consumers make their choices *from the alternatives available*. With no real rail transportation alternative to the automobile in most urban areas, consumers turned to it as a necessity. Ironically, as the auto and truck congestion of the cities has mounted between the 1950s and the 1980s, more and more citizens, and not a few business leaders, have called for new mass transit systems for their cities.

* * *

MASS TRANSIT IN OTHER CAPITALISTIC COUNTRIES

Comparative research on U.S. and German transportation systems by Yago has demonstrated the importance of looking at corporate power and economic structure. Mass rail transport developed in Germany before 1900. In the 1870s and 1880s the German national and local governments became interested in mass transit; at that time the coal, steel, iron, chemical, and electrical manufacturing companies were dominant in German capitalism. Interestingly, corporate executives in these industries supported the development of rail transportation; by 1900 the national and local governments had subsidized and institutionalized intraurban and interurban rail transport systems, which served the transport needs not only of the citizenry but also of the dominant coal, steel, chemical, and electrical industries. These industries also supplied equipment and supplies for the rail networks. In contrast, in the United States early transport companies were involved in manipulation and land speculation; transit service was rarely the central goal of the early rail transit firms. In contrast to Germany, dominance of U.S. industry by a major economic concentration did not come to the United States until after 1900, and when it did come, the auto-oil-rubber industrial complex was dominant. There was no other integrated industrial complex to contest this dominance of the auto-related firms, and governmental intervention was directed at support of motorization and the automobile. In Germany governmental intervention for mass rail transit had preceded this dominance of the motorization lobby. This suggests that the *timing* of the implementation of technological innovations in relation to corporate development is critical to their dominance, or lack of dominance, in cities and societies.

Interestingly, it was the Nazi interest in motorization and militarization in the 1930s that sharply increased the role of auto and truck transport in Germany. Adolf Hitler worked hard to motorize the military and the society. After World War II, the German auto lobby increased in power, and an auto transport system was placed alongside the rail transport system. However, the West German government and people have maintained a strong commitment to both systems; and the OPEC-generated oil crises of the 1970s brought an unparalleled revival of mass transit in Germany, whereas in the United States there was a more modest revival. The reason for the dramatic contrast between the two countries was that Germany had retained a rail passenger transport system, one that is still viable and energy conserving to the present day.

35

Size Does Count, at Least for French Fries: Minnesota's Straight River

FROM *Water Follies: Groundwater Pumping and the Fate of America's Fresh Waters*

ROBERT GLENNON

When most of us make a decision, we usually think about how the decision will affect us. But the sociological perspective urges us to look beyond ourselves to what are called the manifest and latent functions and the dysfunctions of social actions. That is, as sociologists we seek to anticipate and recognize unintended consequences. With growing awareness of human threats to the natural environment, one branch of sociology traces the chain of human activities to realms normally examined by the physical and biological sciences, and in so doing has expanded the sociological perspective to include global ecology. In this chapter from the author's book, Water Follies, *a seemingly benign decision by McDonald's to make its French fries "consumer friendly" sets off a chain reaction of social and environmental change far beyond whatever discussions might have been held in the boardroom of the corporation.*

> I wish to make it clear to you, there is not sufficient water to irrigate all the lands which could be irrigated.
>
> —John Wesley Powell (1893)

Ray Kroc, the founder of McDonalds, revolutionized the french fry in the 1950s. It was not mere marketing prowess that allowed him to do so. It was science. He discovered that potatoes vary widely in their water content. A potato that contains too much water will become soggy when fried. Kroc actually sent employees armed with hydrometers into the potato fields of his suppliers to ensure that the potatoes contained the optimum percentage of water. A freshly harvested potato typically consists of 80 percent water. The french frying process essentially removes most of that water and replaces it with fat. The high fat content makes french fries unhealthy, but it also makes them delicious. The typical American consumes thirty pounds of french fries a year, a 700 percent increase since the 1950s, when Ray Kroc began to mass-produce french fries. According to Eric Schlosser, author of *Fast Food Nation*, "French fries have become the most widely sold foodservice item in the United States." Frozen french fries have also nudged aside fresh potatoes, called "table stock" by the food industry, in the at-home diets of many Americans. Potato manufacturers have thoughtfully nurtured our enjoyment of convenience foods by packaging french fries to suit our every whim for a fry of a certain size, shape, or flavoring. The freezer section of a Safeway supermarket is likely to carry some twelve different types of Ore-Ida french fries: shoestring, crinkles, twirls, crispers, fajita-seasoned, zesties, country style, tater tots, hash browns (country and southern style), potatoes O'Brien, and, of course, plain old french fries.

Any baking potato will suffice to make french fries, though the fast-food industry prefers Burbank russet potatoes, a variety that is mealy or starchy, not waxy. When ready for processing, the potatoes are washed, steam-peeled, sliced, and blanched, all of which ensures that the inside will have a fluffy texture. After quick drying, the potatoes are deep-fried for thirty seconds to produce a crisp shell. These steps usually occur at a processing plant located close to the potato fields to save on transportation costs. The fries are then frozen and shipped to a warehouse, which delivers them to retail outlets as needed. The fries remain frozen until the moment of service. At this point, they are deep-fried again for approximately three minutes.

Some potato species that we cultivate today were gathered and cultivated in the Peruvian and Bolivian Andes of South America for thousands of years before the first European explorations. Potatoes first reached North America from England in the early 1600s. The Irish potato blight in the 1840s taught the lesson that cross-fertilization and new cultivars ward off insects and fungi that attack potatoes. In the United States, the intense cultivation of Burbank russets has required growers to use large quantities of insecticides, pesticides, and herbicides to protect the single cultivar. One recent study found that babies in the Red River Valley in North Dakota, a major potato farming region, had low birth weights and a high incidence of birth defects, conditions blamed on the local use of herbicides and other agricultural chemicals.

The potato industry has recently fallen on hard times. To break even, a potato farmer must receive about $5 per hundred pounds. In 1996–97, potato prices fell to $1.50 per hundredweight. By 2001, the prices had declined to $1 per hundred pounds. Most small producers have left the business, and the process of consolidation has resulted in a small number of corporate farms, each growing thousands of acres of potatoes. As large as these farms are, the farmers are still beholden to the processors, who, in turn, must answer to the fast-food chains. In the business of potato farming, a very small number of buyers wield extraordinary power over a large number of sellers.

The advent of the fast-food industry and the converging technologies that made it possible have created American consumers who expect the same uniformity in their food products that they find in their vehicles, shoes, or notebook paper. In the past, fast-food french fries came in small waxed paper bags. The small bags would not stand up, so they often tipped over and spilled the fries, making a bit of a mess. For marketing reasons, in 1988, McDonald's began to offer consumers "super-sized" meals with larger portions of fries now served in rectangular boxes with flat bottoms. They were a huge hit.

French fries are a tremendously competitive component of the fast-food industry. The hook that keeps customers coming back to a particular franchise is not only the taste of the french fries but also their appearance. According to Dean John Gardner of the University of Missouri Agricultural Extension program, the fast-food industry decided that the french fry, to appeal aesthetically to consumers, had to be a certain length. It needed to jut out of the super-size box by just the right amount, so that the consumer can grasp the potato between index finger and thumb and dip it in ketchup.

Ron Offutt grew up on his family's 240-acre farm in Moorhead, Minnesota. After graduation from college in 1964, he began to expand his family's potato growing operation. He recognized that the sandy soil of central Minnesota would provide an ideal medium for growing potatoes if the lands were irrigated. The R. D. Offutt Company now farms 200,000 acres of land in eleven states, with 66,000 acres in potatoes, making Ron the country's largest potato grower. His farms annually produce 2.9 billion pounds of potatoes.

As Ron's farming operation expanded, he needed a lot of tractors, so he acquired a John Deere franchise. Soon, RDO Equipment Co. became the nation's largest John Deere agricultural retailer *and* its largest construction equipment dealer, with forty-six stores in ten states. Ron also realized, in the 1970s, that it would be useful to own a french fry processing plant. So he bought one. In 1980, he completed construction of another processing plant in Park Rapids, Minnesota. He has since added two more processing facilities. Today, R. D. Offutt Company serves as the umbrella for a vast, vertically integrated agribusiness enterprise. Dean Gardner describes R. D. Offutt Company as "a classic, commercial success story for the production of an industrial potato for french fries." Industrial, he suggests, because the length and size of the potato is a critical part of the marketing. A uniform-length fry requires a uniform potato, which requires irrigation.

Until rather recently, many farms in the United States were "dryland farmed," meaning that the farmers had no system of irrigation. Their fortunes varied with the precipitation that Mother Nature provided, from flood to drought, in any given growing season. Many farmers, especially in the Midwest and the East, have come to realize that an occasional supplemental irrigation produces greater yields per acre and larger crops. Irrigation also enables farmers to apply fertilizers or pesticides to their fields through water-soluble solutions.

Americans' love affair with processed foods caused potato farmers to shift from dryland to irrigation farming. The problem with dryland potatoes is that their size, shape, and texture depend heavily on seasonal weather patterns. During the growing season, potatoes need constant moisture or they will have knobs and odd shapes. A misshapen or knobby potato is perfectly edible, but it is not an acceptable potato for the fast-food industry, at least in the United States. According to a potato processing executive, "American consumers were spoiled by the McDonald's of the world. They haven't made that mistake in Japan, where the specifications for potatoes are more reasonable. More of the potato gets used there than here." In Minnesota, potato farmers irrigate their fields because the two big suppliers for fast-food restaurants—Frito-Lay and Simplot—will contract only with potato growers who irrigate their fields in order to obtain potatoes with a uniform length, appearance, and color.

The R. D. Offutt Company farm near Park Rapids, Minnesota, in the Straight River basin, grows about 7,500 acres of Burbank russet potatoes, mostly for french fries, though also for tater tots, hash browns, and potato wedges. During the four-week harvesting season, potatoes are sent to the Lamb Weston/ RDO Frozen processing plant in Park Rapids, which is a joint venture between Lamb-Weston Foods Corp. (a major supplier to McDonald's) and R. D. Offutt Company. The plant immediately processes some potatoes but stores the rest for up to eleven months. Storing potatoes creates two problems for processors. Most American consumers understand the first problem: they occasionally purchase a bag of potatoes, which they store under the sink and promptly forget. When finally discovered, the potatoes have become soft and flabby through dehydration and are suitable only for a child's science project. Once harvested, a potato begins to lose moisture to the air. To combat this problem, growers and processors store potatoes in a 95 percent humidity environment to prevent the loss of weight, which can be as much as 30 percent, or nearly one-third of the cash value.

Minnesota potato growers and processors face an additional problem. Most of us have enjoyed a summertime glass of iced tea with moisture on the outside of the glass. As we may remember from our own science classes, the cold glass chills the air immediately around it, and because the chilled air cannot hold the same amount of moisture as warmer air elsewhere in the room, water vapor condenses on the outside of the glass. The differential in temperature that produces condensation poses a problem for potato storage. The moisture in the high-humidity storage facility eventually condenses, which usually occurs on the facility's inside walls in a place with winters as cold as Minnesota. As moisture forms on the walls and ceiling of the plant, it begins to drip onto the potatoes, which, if wet, will eventually rot.

The humidity and temperature of stored potatoes are not important to the typical consumer who buys a large bag of potatoes, stores them in the garage or attic during the wintertime, and eats them over a six- or eight-month period. But humidity and temperature *are* critical for the fast-food industry. When a potato is stored at a cool temperature, its carbohydrates naturally turn to sugars. When baked, the potato will be somewhat sweeter from the sugars that caramelize during baking. If this potato is used for french fries, the caramelized sugar produces a brown color that is aesthetically unacceptable. As Larry Monico, director of operations for the R. D. Offutt farm in Park Rapids has explained, "We as Americans, or somebody, has decided that french fries should be white in color and not brown. If you made french fries out of potatoes that have been stored at a cold temperature, they would be brown in color like shoe leather. Not that they would taste bad, or anything else, but they are undesirable to us as consumers." Consequently, processors must use water to store potatoes at a precise temperature and humidity.

The Lamb Weston/RDO Frozen storage facility in Park Rapids, Minnesota, has a capacity of 26.5 million pounds of potatoes. They must store the entire crop so that there is not more than a one degree Fahrenheit difference between any two potatoes in the entire building. Otherwise, when fried, they might be slightly different colors. According to Larry Monico, "McDonald's won't accept french fries that aren't all white, and so, therefore, we have to keep the temperature constant so that they will all fry to the same color." To achieve the required uniform humidity and temperature, the inside walls are entirely separated from the exterior walls by an air space or cavity that creates an envelope separating the potato storage area from the exterior walls. A separate furnace heats the cavity to a certain temperature and prevents the outside air from affecting the temperature and the humidity at which the potatoes are stored. A computer-controlled system regulates the temperature and humidity in the storage area.

The Straight River in north-central Minnesota, about 180 miles northwest of the Twin Cities, is quite deep and meanders, contrary to its name, in a series of S turns. Typical of rivers and streams in the upper Midwest, the Straight River flows through glacial outwash. As a consequence of the sandy soil, the surface and groundwater are very closely connected hydrologically. At the end of Minnesota's legendary winters, snowmelt rapidly recharges substantial quantities of water to shallow aquifers that, in turn, quickly transmit the water to the river.

In the past, local farmers eked out a living by dryland farming corn and small grains such as wheat, barley, and oats. The sandy soil made farming a marginal economic enterprise. The genius of Ron Offutt was to realize the region's potential for growing potatoes, if the lands were irrigated. The uniform texture of the sandy soils, aided by the application of water, provided an ideal medium for producing the uniform potatoes demanded by the fast-food industry. The threat to the Straight River comes from this shift from dryland to irrigated farming and from changes in the technology of irrigation.

Airplane passengers regularly query flight attendants about conspicuous green circles that dot the landscape of the Great Plains from North Dakota to Texas and that contrast dramatically with the arid land surrounding them. The circles are produced by center-pivot irrigation systems. In a center-pivot system, a well drilled in the center of a quarter-section (160 acres) attaches by a swivel to aluminum pipes suspended six or eight feet off the ground, which are supported by A-frame towers with tandem wheels on the base. A hydraulic drive or a diesel or electric motor supplies power that slowly pivots the pipes and towers in a circle around the well. The resulting irrigation-water pattern produces a perfect circle easily seen from 35,000 feet. Unlike older forms of row irrigation, center-pivot systems allow farmers to tailor precisely the frequency and amount of water applied in order to achieve better yields. Modern center-point systems reduce evaporation loss by using low pressure with specially designed nozzles that produce larger droplets aimed toward the ground and that can achieve an efficiency of 90 percent. Older systems relied on high pressure to spray fine mists of water into the air. Much of the water evaporated before it ever reached the ground.

Center-pivot irrigation has transformed the Straight River basin; in the 1940s, there were only five irrigation wells in the area. By 1998, farmers had drilled seventy center-pivot irrigation systems within two miles of the river, and they now pump almost 3 billion gallons of groundwater each growing season. Groundwater adjacent to the Straight River irrigates the potatoes and provides water for processing.

Beneath and immediately adjacent to the Straight River, the glacial out-wash constitutes a shallow, quite permeable aquifer. Below this aquifer lies a confining layer of glacial till, a mixture of clay and other relatively impermeable sediments, and below that lies a deeper aquifer from deposits during earlier glacial periods. The confining layer retards but does not completely block water moving between the shallow and deep aquifers. Pumping from the deep aquifer will increase recharge from the shallow aquifer to the deep aquifer and, depending on the location of the well, may also reduce discharge from the shallow aquifer to the Straight River. One thing is certain: groundwater pumping from the *shallow* aquifer reduces discharge from the aquifer to the Straight River.

Hydrologists are confident about this conclusion for a quite surprising reason. All water bodies contain radioactive isotopes, the product of either natural geologic processes or atomic fallout from nuclear bomb tests that stopped in the 1950s. Because isotopes have differing half-lives, the law of radioactive decay allows hydrologists to calculate the length of time that it takes for precipitation to infiltrate the ground and to discharge to a stream. It turns out that 95 percent of the water in the Straight River comes from discharge from the shallow aquifer. As of 1988, about half the irrigation wells pumped water from the shallow aquifer and the other half from the deeper aquifer.

One of Minnesota's most productive trout fishing streams, the Straight River contains brown trout that can weigh up to nine pounds. Although brown trout are not as sensitive to water temperatures as other trout species, they still require cold, clear water. Reduced flow in the Straight River produces higher ambient water temperatures that threaten the brown trout. A 1994 U.S. Geological Survey (USGS) report identified three factors that degrade the Straight River's trout habitat: (1) a decrease in stream flow from groundwater withdrawals for irrigation that reduces discharge from the aquifer to the stream; (2) higher-temperature irrigation water that percolates into the groundwater system and then discharges to the river; and (3) the introduction of agricultural chemicals to the river when irrigation water percolates into the ground and then discharges into the river. According to the USGS, the river's flow typically decreased during the summer, "possibly as a result of groundwater withdrawal for irrigation." Compared to farms in the West, Minnesota farmers use only a small amount of groundwater—approximately twelve inches per acre per year. Even this modest amount of pumping has the potential, according to the USGS, to reduce the Straight River's flow by as much as 34 percent during the irrigation season. This reduction in flow would increase the water temperature and might adversely affect the brown trout.

The USGS also found an increase in nitrate concentrations in the shallow aquifer along the Straight River. Farmers typically apply 235 pounds per acre of nitrogen fertilizer to grow Burbank russets. Biochemical processes convert organic nitrogen into inorganic nitrate that dissolves in water and leaches into the aquifer. Although the number of documented cases of human illness caused by nitrate-contaminated groundwater is small, the potential health hazards pose a significant environmental concern. A 1994 USGS study found that 6 percent of 600 groundwater samples from shallow wells in the Midwest had nitrate levels that exceeded the U.S. Environmental Protection Agency drinking water limit.

In the mid-1990s, Lamb Weston/RDO Frozen proposed a $60 million expansion of the potato processing plant at Park Rapids. The Minnesota chapter of Trout Unlimited, the Minnesota Center for Environmental Advocacy, and the Headwaters Chapter of the Audubon Society filed a lawsuit to prevent the state of Minnesota from issuing the necessary permits for the plant. The environmental groups feared that the plant's increased groundwater pumping would reduce Straight River flows and that the plant's effluent would adversely affect water quality. The lawsuit ultimately was settled when Lamb Weston/RDO Frozen agreed to change its operations in significant ways. First, it funded monitoring and other data collection efforts. Lamb Weston/ RDO Frozen donated in excess of $300,000 to the Minnesota Department of Natural Resources (DNR) to help fund a comprehensive watershed study and a hydrologic model that could predict changes in river flow from groundwater pumping. Between 1996 and 1998, DNR placed a moratorium on issuing new water appropriation permits in order to conduct its study, but the resulting model was not precise enough to provide sufficiently accurate data to predict the impact of specific wells on the river. Lamb Weston/RDO Frozen also capped wells located at the processing plant and drilled two new ones, at a cost of $100,000, about a mile north of the plant in an area that hydrologists determined would not affect the Straight River. The company made these changes solely for the possible benefit of the Straight River. To get the water from the new wells to the processing plant, it built an $80,000 pipeline. Lamb Weston/RDO Frozen also upgraded the wastewater treatment facilities, at a cost of $14 million, and uses the effluent from the treatment plant to irrigate nearby crops.

After DNR lifted its moratorium, Lamb Weston/RDO Frozen ultimately obtained the necessary permits and expanded the plant, which is an enormous operation. Each day, seventy-five semitrailer truckloads of potatoes arrive for processing. Each year, the plant receives almost one billion pounds of potatoes and produces approximately 540 million pounds of french fries. It takes two pounds of potatoes to make one pound of french fries that are acceptable to the plant's largest customer—McDonald's. The plant uses 600 million gallons per year of groundwater in its washing, peeling, and storing operations. It's a lot of water, but R. D. Offutt Company's potato farming and processing businesses employ approximately 600 people and generate $11 million in annual payroll, which has a huge impact in rural Minnesota.

For the moment, the Straight River trout population is in no danger. However, a tall stack of groundwater permit applications waits to be processed by DNR. A large increase in irrigation for potatoes, with new wells being drilled in the deeper aquifer, would change the equilibrium. A 1999 Minnesota DNR study concluded: "Potential expansion in potato farming and irrigation could put the Straight River trout population at further risk of thermal impact and eventually raise water temperatures beyond their threshold of survival." Increased pumping from the deeper aquifer would increase recharge from the shallow aquifer, thus reducing discharge from the shallow aquifer to the river. Lower flows would mean higher ambient water temperatures and less dilution of nitrates that contaminate the river. One long-term answer, of course, is for us, as American consumers, to accept french fries that have slightly different colors, or minor discolorations, or even ones that are not long enough to stick out from a super-size carton.

PART SEVEN

SOCIAL INSTITUTIONS

36

Police Accounts of Normal Force

JENNIFER HUNT

There are several ways to read this article. On the one hand, it instructs us about police behavior and how police officers do their work. Another is to see the way bureaucracies and formal procedures are contradicted by informal norms and group consensus. A third reading, and the one Jennifer Hunt intends, dissects the social construction of the reality in which police officers make sense of their work and their actions. The accounts police provide for their actions "normalize" an unpredictable and complex world. As you read this essay, think how you, too, normalize events in your everyday world and what this means for those with whom you interact.

The police are required to handle a variety of peacekeeping and law enforcement tasks including settling disputes, removing drunks from the street, aiding the sick, controlling crowds, and pursuing criminals. What unifies these diverse activities is the possibility that their resolution might require the use of force. Indeed, the capacity to use force stands at the core of the police mandate.

The bulk of the sociological literature on the use of force by police is concerned with analyzing the objective causes of "excessive" force. Some social scientists, for example, suggest that the incidence of extra-legal force correlates with characteristics of individual officers—in particular, their authoritarianism, age, or length of service. Others emphasize the relevance of the behavior and characteristics of the target population, including demeanor, sex, race, and class. Still others investigate the legal and organizational roots of force. They are concerned with how formal rules and/or subcultural norms may influence the police officer's decision to employ force.

Although representing diverse perspectives, these approaches share a similar underlying orientation to use of force by police. First, they all specify, in advance of study, formal or legal definitions of permissible force, definitions of permissible force, definitions that are then used to identify deviations legally classifiable as brutal or "excessive." This procedure disregards the understandings and standards police officers actively employ in using and evaluating force in the course of their work. Second, these studies are primarily concerned with identifying the objective conditions held to determine "excessive" force defined in this way. As a result, they minimize the active role of consciousness in police decisions to use force, tending to depict such decisions as mere passive responses to external determinants.

In contrast, sociologists working within the symbolic interactionist tradition have displayed particular interest in the police officer's own assessment of what constitutes necessary force. This research has varied in how such assessments are conceptualized. Rubinstein (1973; 302) for example, suggests that police use force instrumentally to control persons whom they perceive as presenting a physical threat. In contrast, Van Maanen (1978) explores how police, in reacting to others, are highly attentive to symbolic violation of their authority, dispensing harsh treatment to categories of persons who commit such violations.

The following research departs from and seeks to extend the symbolic interactionist concern with police officers' own assessments of the use of force. It explores how police themselves classify and evaluate acts of force as either legal, normal, or excessive. Legal force is that coercion necessary to subdue, control, and restrain a suspect in order to take him into custody. Although force not accountable in legal terms is technically labelled excessive by the courts and the public, the police perceive many forms of illegal force as normal. Normal force involves coercive acts that specific "cops" on specific occasions formulate as necessary, appropriate, reasonable, or understandable. Although not always legitimated or admired, normal force is depicted as a necessary or natural response of normal police to particular situational exigencies.

Most officers are expected to use both legal and normal force as a matter of course in policing the streets. In contrast, excessive force or brutality exceeds even working police notions of normal force. These are acts of coercion that cannot be explained by the routine police accounting practices ordinarily used to justify or excuse force. Brutality is viewed as illegal, illegitimate, and often immoral violence, but the police draw the lines in extremely different ways and at different points than do either the court system or the public.

These processes of assessing and accounting for the use of force, with special reference to the critical distinction between normal and excessive force as drawn by the police, will be explored in what follows. The study begins by examining how rookie police learn on the street to use and account for force in a manner that contradicts what they were taught at the academy. It then considers "normal force" and the accounting processes whereby police discrimi-natively judge when and how much force is appropriate in specific situations and incidents. It concludes with a discussion of excessive force and peer reactions to those who use it frequently.

The article is based on approximately eighteen months of participant observation in a major urban police department referred to as the Metro City P.D. I attended the police academy with male and female recruits and later rode with individual officers in one-person cars on evening and night shifts in high-crime districts.[1] The female officers described in this research were among the first 100 women assigned to the ranks of uniformed patrol as a result of a discrimination suit filed by the Justice Department and a police-woman plaintiff.

LEARNING TO USE NORMAL FORCE

The police phrase "it's not done on the street the way that it's taught at the academy" underscores the perceived contradiction between the formal world of the police academy and the informal world of the street. This contradiction permeates the police officer's construction of his world, particularly his view of the rational and moral use of force.

In the formal world of the police academy, the recruit learns to account for force by reference to legality. He or she is issued the regulation instruments and trained to use them to subdue, control, and restrain a suspect. If threatened with great bodily harm, the officer learns that he can justifiably use deadly force and fire his revolver. Yet the recruit is taught that he cannot use his baton, jack, or gun unnecessarily to torture, maim, or kill a suspect.

When recruits leave the formal world of the academy and are assigned to patrol a district, they are introduced to an informal world in which police recognize normal as well as legal and brutal force. Through observation and instruction, rookies gradually learn to apply force and account for its use in terms familiar to the street cop. First, rookies learn to adjust their arsenals to conform to street standards. They are encouraged to buy the more powerful weapons worn by veteran colleagues as these colleagues point out the inadequacy of a wooden baton or compare their convoy jacks to vibrators. They quickly discover that their department-issued equipment marks them as new recruits. At any rate, within a few weeks, most rookies have dispensed with the wooden baton and convoy jack and substituted them with the more powerful plastic nightstick and flat-headed slapjack.[2]

Through experience and informal instruction, the rookie also learns the street use of these weapons. In school, for example, recruits are taught to avoid hitting a person on the head or neck because it could cause lethal damage. On the street, in contrast, police conclude that they must hit wherever it causes the most damage in order to incapacitate the suspect before they themselves are harmed. New officers also learn that they will earn the respect of their veteran coworkers not by observing legal niceties in using force, but by being "aggressive" and using whatever force is necessary in a given situation.

---

1. Nonetheless masculine pronouns are generally used to refer to the police in this article, because the Metro P.D. remained dominated by men numerically, in style and in tone.

2. Some officers also substitute a large heavy-duty flashlight for the nightstick. If used correctly, the flashlight can inflict more damage than the baton and is less likely to break when applied to the head or other parts of the body.

Peer approval helps neutralize the guilt and confusion that rookies often experience when they begin to use force to assert their authority. One female officer, for example, learned she was the object of a brutality suit while listening to the news on television. At first, she felt so mortified that she hesitated to go to work and face her peers. In fact, male colleagues greeted her with a standing ovation and commented, "You can use our urinal now." In their view, any aggressive police officer regularly using normal force might eventually face a brutality suit or civilian complaint. Such accusations confirm the officer's status as a "street cop" rather than an "inside man" who doesn't engage in "real police work."

Whereas male rookies are assumed to be competent dispensers of force unless proven otherwise, women are believed to be physically weak, naturally passive, and emotionally vulnerable. Women officers are assumed to be reluctant to use physical force and are viewed as incompetent "street cops" until they prove otherwise. As a result, women rookies encounter special problems in learning to use normal force in the process of becoming recognized as "real street cops." It becomes crucial for women officers to create or exploit opportunities to display their physical abilities in order to overcome sexual bias and obtain full acceptance from coworkers. As a result, women rookies are encouraged informally to act more aggressively and to display more machismo than male rookies. Consider the following incident where a young female officer reflects upon her use of force during a domestic disturbance:

> And when I get there, if goddamn, there isn't a disturbance going on. So Tom comes, the guy that I went to back up. The male talks to him. I take the female and talk to her. And the drunk (cop) comes and the sergeant comes and another guy comes. So while we think we have everything settled, and we have the guy calmed down, he turns around and says to his sister, no less, that's who it is, "Give me the keys to my car!" And with that, she rips them out of her pocket and throws them at him. Now, he goes nuts. He goes into a Kung fu stance and says he's gonna kill her. The drunk cop says, "Yo, knock it off!" and goes to grab him and the guy punches him. So Mike (the drunk cop) goes down. Tommy goes to grab him and is wrestling with him. And all the cops are trying to get in there. So I ran in with my stick and I stick the guy in the head. But I just missed Tommy's face and opened him (the suspect) up. So all of a sudden everybody's grabbin' him and I'm realizing that if we get him down, he won't hurt anybody. So I pushed the sergeant out of the way and I got my stick under the guy's legs and I pulled his legs out from under him and I yelled, "Tommy, take him down." I pulled his legs and he went down and I sat on him. So Tommy says, "Well, cuff him." And I says, "I can't find my goddamned cuffs." I molested my body trying to get my cuffs. . . .
>
> So, when I [finally] get my cuffs, we cuff him. And we're sitting there talking. And Tommy, he has no regard for me whatsoever. . . . The guy's opened up and he bled all over Tommy's shirt. And I turned around and said, "Tommy, look at your

shirt. There's blood all over your shirt." He said, "Who the hell almost clobbered me?" I said, "I'm sorry Tom, that was me." He said, "You're the one that opened him up? And I said, "Yeh. I'm sorry, I didn't mean to get so close to you." . . .

So when the sergeant came out he said, "And you, what do you mean telling me to get outta the way." He said, "Do you know you pushed me outta your way." . . . And I said, "I didn't want you to get hurt . . . and I was afraid he was gonna kick one of you." And he says, "I still can't believe you pushed me outta your way. You were like a little dynamo." And I found after that I got respect from the sergeant. He doesn't realize it but he treated me differently after that.

Her colleagues' reactions provided informal instruction in the use of normal force, confirming that her actions under these circumstances were reasonable and even praiseworthy.

For a street cop, it is often a graver error to use too little force and develop a "shaky" reputation than it is to use too much force and be told to calm down. Thus officers, particularly rookies, who do not back up their partners in appropriate ways or who hesitate to use force in circumstances where it is deemed necessary are informally instructed regarding their aberrant ways. If the problematic incident is relatively insignificant and his general reputation is good, a rookie who "freezes" one time is given a second chance before becoming generally known as an untrustworthy partner. However, such incidents become the subject of degrading gossip, gossip that pressures the officer either to use force as expected or risk isolation. Such talk also informs rookies about the general boundaries of legal and normal force.

For example, female rookie was accused of "freezing" in an incident that came to be referred to as a "Mexican standoff." A pedestrian had complained that "something funny is going on in the drugstore." The officer walked into the pharmacy, where she found an armed man committing a robbery. Although he turned his weapon on her when she entered the premises, she still pulled out her gun and pointed it at him. When he ordered her to drop it, claiming that his partner was behind her with a revolver at her head, she refused and told him to drop his. He refused, and the stalemate continued until a sergeant entered the drugstore and ordered the suspect to drop his gun.

Initially, the female officer thought she had acted appropriately and even heroically. She soon discovered, however, that her hesitation to shoot had brought into question her competence with some of her fellow officers. Although many veterans claimed that "she had a lot a balls" to take her gun out at all when the suspect already had a gun on her, most contended "she shoulda shot him." Other policeman confirmed that she committed a "rookie mistake"; she had failed to notice a "lookout" standing outside the store and hence had been unprepared for an armed confrontation. Her sergeant and lieutenant, moreover, even insisted that she had acted in a cowardly manner, despite her reputation as a "gung-ho cop," and cited the incident as evidence of the general inadequacy of policewomen.

In the weeks that followed, this officer became increasingly depressed and angry. She was particularly outraged when she learned that she would not receive a commendation, although such awards were commonly made for "gun pinches" of this nature. Several months later, the officer vehemently expressed the wish that she had killed the suspect and vowed that next time she would "shoot first and ask questions later." The negative sanctions of supervisors and colleagues clearly encouraged her to adopt an attitude favorable to using force with less restraint in future situations.

Reprimand, gossip, and avoidance constitute the primary means by which police try to change or control the behavior of coworkers perceived as unreliable or cowardly. Formal accusations, however, are discouraged regardless of the seriousness of the misconduct. One male rookie, for example, earned a reputation for cowardice after he allegedly had to be "dragged" out of the car during an "assist officer." Even then, he apparently refused to help the officers in trouble. Although no formal charges were filed, everyone in the district was warned to avoid working with this officer.

Indeed, to initiate formal charges against a coworker may discredit the accuser. In one incident a male rookie, although discouraged by veteran officers and even his district captain, filed charges of cowardice against a female rookie. The rookie gained the support of two supervisors and succeeded in having the case heard before the Board of Inquiry. During the trial he claimed the woman officer failed to aid him in arresting a man who presented physical resistance and had a knife on his person. In rebuttal, the woman testified that she perceived no need to participate in a physical confrontation because she saw no knife and the policeman was hitting the suspect. In spite of conflicting testimony, she was found guilty of "Neglect of Duty." Although most veterans thought the woman was "flaky" and doubted her competence, they also felt the male rookie had exaggerated his story. Moreover, they were outraged that he filed formal charges and he quickly found himself ostracized.

At the same time that male and female rookies are commended for using force under appropriate circumstances, they are reprimanded if their participation in force is viewed as excessive or inappropriate. In this way, rookies are instructed that although many acts of coercion are accepted and even demanded, not everything goes. They thereby learn to distinguish between normal and brutal force. In the following incident, for example, a policewoman describes how she instructed a less experienced officer that her behavior was unreasonable and should be checked. Here, the new officer is chastised for misreading interactional cues and overreacting to minor affronts when treating a crazy person involved in a minor dispute as if he were a serious felon.

> But like I said, when I first heard about it (another fight) I'd wondered if Mary had provoked it any because we'd gone on a disturbance and it was a drunk black guy who called to complain that the kid who lived upstairs keeps walking through his apartment. The kid to me looks wacky. He's talking crazy. He's

saying they shoulda sent men. What are you women going to do. Going on and on. And to me it was a bullshit job. But Mary turns around and says, "We don't have to take that from him. Let's lock him up." I said, "Mary forget it." And the kid has numchuck sticks on him and when he turned his back . . . he had them in his back pocket. So, as he's pulling away saying you're scared, like a little kid, I turned around and said, "I've got your sticks." And I go away. Mary . . . so Mary was . . . I looked at her and she was so disappointed in me . . . like I'd turned chicken on her. So I tried to explain to her, I said, "Mary, all we have is disorderly conduct. That's a summary offense. That's bullshit." I said, "Did you want to get hurt for a summary offense?" I said, "The guy was drunk who called to complain. It wasn't even a legit complaint." I said, "It's just . . . You've got to use discretion. If you think I'm chicken think of the times when a 'man with a gun' comes over the air and I'm the first car there." I said, "When it's worth it, I'll do anything. When it's not worth it, I'll back off." And I think she tries to temper herself some because Collette and her, they finally had a talk about why they hated each other. And Collette said to her, "I think you're too physical. I think you look for fights." And I think maybe Mary hearing it twice, once from me and once from Collette, might start to think that maybe she does provoke. Instead of going up . . . I always go up to them friendly and then if they act shitty I get shitty.

In summary, when rookies leave the academy, they begin to familiarize themselves with street weapons and to gain some sense of what kinds of behavior constitute too little or too much force. They also begin to develop an understanding of street standards for using and judging appropriate and necessary force. By listening to and observing colleagues at work and by experiencing a variety of problematic interactions with the public, newcomers become cognizant of the occasions and circumstances in which to use various degrees and kinds of force. But at the same time, they are learning not only when and how to use force, but also a series of accounting practices to justify and to legitimate as "normal" (and sometimes to condemn) these acts of coercion. Normal force is thus the product of the police officers' accounting practices for describing what happened in ways that prefigure or anticipate the conclusion that it was in some sense justified or excusable and hence "normal." It is to a consideration of the ways in which officers learn to provide such accounts for normal force that I now turn.

ACCOUNTING FOR NORMAL FORCE

Police routinely normalize the use of force by two types of accounts: excuses and justifications. Excuses deny full responsibility for an act of force but acknowledge its inappropriateness. Acts of force become excusable when they are depicted as the natural outcome of strong, even uncontrollable emotions normally arising in certain routine sorts of police activities. Through such accounts, officers excuse force by asserting that it is a "natural," "human" reaction to certain extreme, emotionally trying situations. Justifications accept responsibility for the coercive act in question but deny that the act was wrongful or blameworthy.

Police justify force through two analytically distinct kinds of accounts: situational and abstract. In the former, the officer represents force as a response in some specific situation needed to restore immediate control or to reestablish the local order of power in the face of a threat to police authority. In contrast, abstract accounts justify force as a morally appropriate response to certain categories of crime and criminals who symbolize a threat to the moral order. As an account, abstract justification does not highlight processes of interactional provocation and threats to immediate control, but rather legitimates force as a means of obtaining some higher moral purpose, particularly the punishment of heinous offenders.

None of these accounts are mutually exclusive, and are often combined in justifying and excusing the use of force in any specific instance. For example, police consider it justifiable to use force to regain control of someone who has challenged an officers authority. However, an officer may also excuse his behavior as an "overreaction," claiming he "snapped out" and lost control, and hence used more force or different kinds of force than were required to regain control. Mixed accounts involving situational and abstract justifications of force are also frequent: force may be depicted as necessary to regain control when an officer is physically assaulted; but at the same time it may also be justified as punishment appropriate to the kind of morally unworthy person who would challenge an officer's authority.

EXCUSES AND NORMAL FORCE

Excuses are accounts in which police deny full responsibility for an act but recognize its inappropriateness. Excuses therefore constitute socially approved vocabularies for relieving responsibility when conduct is questionable. Police most often excuse morally problematic force by referring to emotional or physiological states that are precipitated by some circumstances of routine patrol work. These circumstances include shootouts, violent fights, pursuits, and instances in which a police officer mistakenly comes close to killing an unarmed person.

Policework in these circumstances can generate intense excitement in which the officer experiences the "combat high" and "adrenaline rush" familiar to the combat soldier. Foot and car pursuits not only bring on feelings of danger and excitement from the chase, but also a challenge to official authority. As one patrolman commented about a suspect: "Yeh, he got tuned up (beaten) . . . you always tune them up after a car chase." Another officer normalized the use of force after a pursuit in these terms:

> It's my feeling that violence inevitably occurs after a pursuit. . . . The adrenaline
> . . . and the insult involved when someone flees increases with every foot of the

pursuit. I know the two or three times that I felt I lost control of myself . . . was when someone would run on me. The further 1 had to chase the guy the madder I got. . . . The funny thing is the reason for the pursuit could have been for something as minor as a traffic violation or a kid you're chasing who just turned on a fire hydrant. It always ends in violence. You feel obligated to hit or kick the guy just for running.

Police officers also excuse force when it follows an experience of helplessness and confusion that has culminated in a temporary loss of emotional control. This emotional combination occurs most frequently when an officer comes to the brink of using lethal force, drawing a gun and perhaps firing, only to learn there were no "real" grounds for this action. The officer may then "snap out" and hit the suspect. In one such incident, for example, two policemen picked up a complainant who positively identified a suspect as a man who just tried to shoot him. Just as the officers approached the suspect, he suddenly reached for his back pocket for what the officers assumed to be a gun. One officer was close enough to jump the suspect before he pulled his hand from his pocket. As it turned out, the suspect had no weapon, having dropped it several feet away. Although he was unarmed and under control, the suspect was punched and kicked out of anger and frustration by the officer who had almost shot him.

Note that in both these circumstances—pursuit and near-miss mistaken shootings—officers would concede that the ensuing force is inappropriate and unjustifiable when considered abstractly. But although abstractly wrong, the use of force on such occasions is presented as a normal, human reaction to an extreme situation. Although not every officer might react violently in such circumstances, it is understandable and expected that some will.

SITUATIONAL JUSTIFICATIONS

Officers also justify force as normal by reference to interactional situations in which an officer's authority is physically or symbolically threatened. In such accounts, the use of force is justified instrumentally—as a means of regaining immediate control in a situation where that control has become tenuous. Here, the officer depicts his primary intent for using force as a need to reestablish immediate control in a problematic encounter, and only incidentally as hurting or punishing the offender.

Few officers will hesitate to assault a suspect who physically threatens or attacks them. In one case, an officer was punched in the face by a prisoner he had just apprehended for allegedly attempting to shoot a friend. The incident occurred in the stationhouse and several policemen observed the exchange. Immediately, one officer hit the prisoner in the jaw and the rest immediately joined the brawl.

Violations of an officer's property such as his car or hat may signify a more symbolic assault on the officer's authority and self, thus justifying a forceful response to maintain control. Indeed, in the police view, almost any person who verbally challenges a police officer is appropriately subject to force. In the following extract, a female officer accounts in these ways for a colleague's use of force against an escaping prisoner:

> And so Susan gets on the scene (of the fight). They cuff one of the girls, and she throws her in the back seat of the car. She climbs over the back seat, jumps out of the car with cuffs on and starts running up the stairs. Susan and Jane are trying to cuff the other girl and all of a sudden Susan looks up and sees her cuffs running away. She (Jane) said Susan turned into an animal. Susan runs up the steps grabs the girl by the legs. Drags her down the five steps. Puts her in the car. Kicks her in the car. Jane goes in the car and calls her every name she can think of and waves her stick in her face.[3]

On rare occasions, women officers encounter special problems in these regards. Although most suspects view women in the same way as policemen, some seem less inclined to accord female officers de facto and symbolic control in street encounters, and on a few occasions seem determined to provoke direct confrontations with such officers, explicitly denying their formal authority and attempting none too subtly to sexualize the encounter. Women officers, then, might use force as a resource for rectifying such insults and for establishing control over such partially sexualized interactions.

* * *

ABSTRACT JUSTIFICATIONS

Police also justify the use of extreme force against certain categories of morally reprehensible persons. In this case, force is not presented as an instrumental means to regain control that has been symbolically or physically threatened. Instead, it is justified as an appropriate response to particularly heinous offenders. Categories of such offenders include: cop haters who have gained notoriety as persistent police antagonizers; cop killers or any person who has attempted seriously to harm a police officer; sexual deviants who prey on children and "moral women"; child abusers; and junkies and other "scum" who inhabit the street. The more morally reprehensible the act is judged, the more likely the police are to depict any violence directed toward its perpetrator as justifiable. Thus a man who exposes himself to children in a playground is less likely to experience police assault than one who rapes or sexually molests a child.

---

3. Note that this account employs both the justifications of reestablishing real and symbolic control, and the excuse of emotionally snapping out in response to this symbolic challenge and to the resulting pursuit.

"Clean" criminals, such as high level mafiosi, white-collar criminals, and professional burglars, are rarely subject to abstract force. Nor are perpetrators of violent and nonviolent street crimes who prey on adult males, prostitutes, and other categories of persons who belong on the street.[4] Similarly, the "psycho" or demented person is perceived as so mentally deranged that he is not responsible for his acts and hence does not merit abstract, punitive force.

Police justify abstract force by invoking a higher moral purpose that legitimates the violation of commonly recognized standards. In one case, for example, a nun was raped by a 17-year-old male adolescent. When the police apprehended the suspect, he was severely beaten and his penis put in an electrical outlet to teach him a lesson. The story of the event was told to me by a police officer who, despite the fact that he rarely supported the use of extra-legal force, depicted this treatment as legitimate. Indeed, when I asked if he would have participated had he been present, he responded, "I'm Catholic. I would have participated."

EXCESSIVE FORCE AND PEER RESPONSES

Although police routinely excuse and justify many incidents where they or their coworkers have used extreme force against a citizen or suspect, this does not mean that on any and every occasion the officer using such force is exonerated. Indeed, the concept of normal force is useful because it suggests that there are specific circumstances under which police officers will not condone the use of force by themselves or colleagues as reasonable and acceptable. Thus, officer-recognized conceptions of normal force are subject to restrictions of the following kinds:

(1) Police recognize and honor some rough equation between the behavior of the suspect and the harmfulness of the force to which it is subject. There are limits, therefore, to the degree of force that is acceptable in particular circumstances. In the following incident, for example, an officer reflects on a situation in which a "symbolic assailant" (Skolnick, 1975: 45) was mistakenly subject to more force than he "deserved" and almost killed:

> One time Bill Johnson and I, I have more respect for him than any other policeman. . . . He and I, we weren't particularly brutal. If the guy deserved it, he got it. It's generally the attitude that does it. We had a particularly rude drunk one day. He was really rude and spit on you and he did all this stuff and we even had to cuff him lying down on the hard stretcher, like you would do an epileptic. . . . We were really mad at this guy. So, what you normally do with drunks is you take them to the district cell. . . . So we were really mad. We said let's just give

4. The categories of persons who merit violence are not unique to the police. Prisoners, criminals, and hospital personnel appear to draw similar distinctions between morally unworthy persons; on the latter, see Sudnow (1967: 105).

him one or two shots. . . . slamming on the brakes and having him roll. But we didn't use our heads. He's screaming and hollering "You lousy cops" and we slammed on the brakes and we didn't use our heads and we heard the stretcher go nnnnnnBam and then nothing. We heard nothing and we realized we had put this man in with his head to the front so when we slammed on the brakes this stretcher. . . . I guess it can roll four foot. Well, it was his head that had hit the front of it and we heard no sounds and my God, I've never been so scared. Me and Bill we thought we killed him. So I'm saying "Bill, what are we gonna do? How are we gonna explain this one." The guy's still saying nothing. So, we went to Madison Street and parked. It's a really lonely area. And we unlocked the wagon and peeked in. We know he's in there. We were so scared and we look in and there's not a sound and we see blood coming in front of the wagon and think "Oh my God we killed this man. What am I gonna do? What am I gonna tell my family?" And to make a long story short, he was just knocked out. But boy was I scared. From then on we learned, feet first.

(2) Although it is considered normal and natural to become emotional and angry in highly charged, taut encounters, officers nonetheless prefer to minimize the harmful consequences of the use of force. As a result, officers usually acknowledge that emotional reactions that might lead to extreme force should be controlled and limited by coworkers if at all possible. In the following account, for example, an officer justified the use of force as a legitimate means to regain situational control when physically challenged. Nonetheless, he expressed gratitude to his partner for stopping him from doing serious harm when he "snapped out" and lost control:

Well, I wasn't sure if she was a girl until I put my hand on her shoulder and realized it was a woman's shoulder. I was trying to stop her. But it happened when she suddenly kicked me in the balls. Then everything inside of me exploded and I grabbed her and pushed her against the car and started pressing her backwards and kept pressing her backwards. All of a sudden something clicked inside of me because I noticed her eyes changed and her body caved in and she looked frightened because she knew that I was gonna kill her. And I stopped. I think I stopped because Susan was on the scene. She must have said something. But anyway she (Susan) told me later that I should calm down. And I snapped at her and told her to mind her own business because she didn't know what happened. The girl kicked me in the balls. But she was right about it. I mean it was getting to me. I'd never hit a woman before.

(3) Similarly, even in cases where suspects are seen as deserving some violent punishment, this force should not be used randomly and without control. Thus, in the following incident, an officer who "snapped out" and began to be a child abuser clearly regarded his partner's attempt to stop the beating reasonable.

We get a call "meet complainant" and I drive up and there's a lady standing out in front of the house and she's saying, "Listen officer, I don't know what the story is but the neighbors in there. They're screaming and hollering and there's kicking going on in there and I can't take it. I can't sleep. There's too much noise." Nothing unusual about that. Just a typical day in the district. So the next thing you do is knock on the door and tell them to please keep the noise down or whatever you do. You say to yourself it's probably a boy friend-girl friend fight. So I knock on the door and a lady answers just completely hysterical. And I say, "Listen, I don't know what's going on in here," but then I hear this, just this screeching. You know. And I figure well I'm just going to find out what's going on so I just go past the lady and what's happening is that the husband had. . . . The kid was being potty trained and the way they were potty training this kid, this two-year-old boy, was that the boyfriend of this girl would pick up this kid and he would sit him down on top of the stove. It was their method of potty training. Well, first of all you think of your own kids. I mean afterwards you do. I mean I've never been this mad in my whole life. You see this little two-year-old boy seated on top of the stove with rings around it being absolutely scalding hot. And he's saying "I'll teach you to go." . . . It just triggered something. An uncontrollable. . . . It's just probably the most violent I ever got. Well you just grab that guy. You hit him ten, fifteen times . . . you don't know how many. You just get so mad. And I remember my partner eventually came in and grabbed me and said, "Don't worry about it. We got him. We got him." And we cuffed him and we took him down. Yeah that was bad.

Learning these sorts of restrictions on the use of normal force and these informal practices of peer control are important processes in the socialization of newcomers. This socialization proceeds both through ongoing observation and experience and, on occasion, through explicit instruction. For example, one veteran officer advised a rookie, "The only reason to go in on a pursuit is not to get the perpetrator but to pull the cop who gets there first offa the guy before he kills him."

It is against this background that patrol officers identify excessive force and the existence of violence-prone peers. Some officers become known for recurrently committing acts of coercion that exceed working notions of normal force and that cannot be excused or justified with routine accounting practices. In contrast to the officer who makes a "rookie mistake" and uses excessive force from inexperience, the brutal cop does not honor the practices of normal force. Such an officer is also not effectively held in check by routine means of peer control. As a result, more drastic measures must be taken to prevent him from endangering the public and his colleagues.

One rookie gained a reputation for brutality from frequent involvement in "unnecessary" fights. One such incident was particularly noteworthy: Answering a call on a demented male with a weapon, he came upon a large man pacing the sidewalk carrying a lead pipe. The officer got out of the patrol car and yelled in a belligerant tone of voice, "What the fuck are you doing creep?" At this point "the creep" attacked the officer and tried to take away his gun. A policewoman arrived on the scene, joined the fight, called an assist, and rescued the patrolman. Although no one was hurt, colleagues felt the incident was provoked by the officer who aggressively approached a known crazy person who should have been assumed to be unpredictable and nonresponsible.

When colleagues first began to doubt this officer's competence, he was informally instructed to moderate his behavior by veteran and even rookie partners. When his behavior persisted, confrontations with fellow officers became explosive. When peers were unable to check his behavior, complaints were made to superiors. Officially, colleagues indicated they did not want to work with him because of "personality problems." Informally, however, supervisors were informed of the nature of his provocative and dangerous behavior. The sergeant responded by putting the rookie in a wagon with a responsible partner whom he thought might succeed in controlling him. When this strategy proved unsuccessful, he was eventually transferred to the subway unit. Such transfers to "punishment districts," isolated posts, "inside units," or the subway are typical means of handling police officers deemed dangerous and out of control.

As this discussion indicates, the internal control of an exceptionally or inappropriately violent police officer is largely informal. With the exception of civilian complaints and brutality suits, the behavior of such officers rarely becomes the subject of formal police documents. However, their reputations are often well known throughout the department and the rumors about their indiscretions educate rookies about how the line between normal force and brutality is drawn among working police officers.

It takes more than one incident of excessively violent behavior for a police officer to attain a brutal reputation. The violent officer is usually involved in numerous acts of aggressive behavior that are not accountable as normal force either because of their frequency or because of their substance. However, once identified as "brutal," a "head beater," and so on, an officer's use of force will be condemned by peers in circumstances in which competent officers would be given the benefit of the doubt. For example, one officer gained national notoriety during a federal investigation into a suspicious shooting. Allegedly, a local resident had thrown an axe at the patrol wagon. According to available accounts, the police pursued the suspect inside a house and the officer in question shot him in the head. Although witnesses claimed the victim was unarmed, the officer stated that he fired in self-defense. The suspect reportedly attacked him with a metal pipe. This policeman had an established reputation for being "good with his hands," and many colleagues assumed he had brutally shot an unarmed man in the aftermath of a pursuit.

CONCLUSION

The organization of policework reflects a poignant moral dilemma: for a variety of reasons, society mandates to the police the right to use force but provides little direction as to its proper use in specific, "real life" situations. Thus, the police, as officers of the law, must be prepared to use force under circumstances in which its rationale is often morally, legally, and practically ambiguous. This fact explains some otherwise puzzling aspects of police training and socialization.

The police academy provides a semblance of socialization for its recruits by teaching formal rules for using force. It is a semblance of socialization because it treats the use of force as capable of rationalization within the moral and legal conventions of the civilian world. The academy also, paradoxically, trains recruits in the use of tools of violence with potential for going far beyond the limitations of action imposed by those conventions. Consequently, the full socialization of a police officer takes place outside the academy as the officer moves from its idealizations to the practicalities of the street. This movement involves several phases: (1) a decisive, practical separation from the formal world established within the academy; (2) the cultivation of a working distinction between what is formally permissible and what is practically and informally required of the "street cop"; and (3) the demonstration of competence in using and accounting for routine street practices that are morally and legally problematic for those not working the street.

The original dilemma surrounding the use of force persists throughout the socialization process, but is increasingly dealt with by employing accounts provided by the police community that reduce and neutralize the moral tension. The experienced "street cop" becomes an expert at using techniques of neutralization to characterize the use of force on the streets, at judging its use by others, and at evaluating the necessity for using force by standards those techniques provide. Use of these techniques also reinforces the radical separation of the formal and informal worlds of policework, duplicating within the context of the organization itself the distinction between members and outsiders. This guarantees that members will be able to distinguish between those who can and cannot be trusted to use force and to understand the conditions under which its use is reasonable.

As accounts neutralizing the use of force, justifications and excuses both serve—though each in a different way—to manage the tension inherent in situations fraught with moral insecurity. They conventionalize but do not reform situations that are inherently charged and morally ambiguous. In this way they simultaneously preserve the self-image of police as agents of the conventional order, provide ways in which individual officers can resolve their personal doubts as to the moral status of their action and those of their colleagues, and reinforce the solidarity of the police community.

REFERENCES

Emerson, R. M. (1969). *Judging Delinquents: Context and Process in Juvenile Court.* Chicago: Aldine.

Rubinstein, J. (1973). *City Police.* New York: Ballantine.

Skolnick, J. (1975). *Justice Without Trial.* New York: John Wiley.

Sudnow, D. (1967). *Passing On: The Social Organization of Dying.* Englewood Cliffs, NJ: Prentice-Hall.

Van Maanen, J. (1978). "The asshole," in P. K. Manning and J. Van Maanen (eds.) *Policing: A View From the Street.* Santa Monica, CA: Goodyear.

37

Love, Arranged Marriage, and the Indian Social Structure

GIRI RAJ GUPTA

For most of you, the idea of marrying someone you do not love borders on the ab-surd or abusive. In many societies, however, arranged marriages are common and result in lasting and satisfying bonds between husband and wife. Marital success is dependent not only on how partners feel toward one another. The social supports for their partnership and family are critical. In India's Hindu and Muslim societies, the family not only plays a major role in arranging a marriage but in making the marriage a success.

Marriage is an immemorial institution which, in some form, is found every-where. Mating patterns are closely associated with marriage, more so with the social structure. It's not the institution of marriage itself, but the insti-tutionalization of mating patterns which determine the nature of family rela-tionships in a society. Primitive societies present a wide array of practices rang-ing from marriage by capture to mutual love and elopement. Yet, the people who marry through customary practice are those who are eligible, who con-sciously followed the established norms, and who did the kind of things they were supposed to do. The main purpose of marriage is to establish a family, to produce children, and to further the family's economic and social position. Per-haps, there are some transcendental goals too. Generally, women hope for kind and vigorous providers and protectors and men for faithful mothers and good housekeepers; both undoubtedly hope for mutual devotion and affection too. Irrespective of the various ways of instituting marriage, most marriages seem to have these common goals.

There are few works commenting on mating patterns in India. Though some monographs on tribal and rural India have treated the subject, nev-ertheless, serious sociological attention has only infrequently been given. The present paper attempts to explain the variables as a part of the cultural system which help in promotion and sustenance of the arranged marriage, particularly in the Hindu society in India. In addition, the paper also criti-cally analyzes the present-day mating patterns which relate to precaution-ary controls working against the potentially disintegrative forces of change; especially those endangering family unity, religious structure, and the strati-fication system.

ROMANTIC LOVE VERSUS CONJUGAL LOVE

One is intrigued by the cultural pattern in India where the family is characterized by arranged marriage. Infatuation as well as romantic love, though, is
reported quite in abundance in the literature, sacred books, and scriptures,
yet is not thought to be an element in prospective marital alliance (see Meyer
1953: 322–39).

Sanskrit or Hindi terms like *sneh* (affection) and *prem* or *muhbbat* carry two
different meanings. *Sneh* is nonsensual love, while *prem* is a generic term con-
noting love with god, people, nation, family, [neighbor], and, of course, lover
or beloved. In fact, there is a hierarchy of relationships. In Urdu literature,
concepts like *ishque ruharti* (love with the spirit), *ishque majazi* (love with the
supreme being), and *ishque haqiqi* (love with the lover or beloved) are commonly referred to love relationships. Interestingly, the humans supposedly
reach the highest goal of being in love with god through the love they cher-
ish among humans. Great love stories in mythology and history illustrate the
emotion, as opposed to reason, which characterize the thoughts and acts of
persons in love. The quality of the emotions may be characterized best by
the altruistic expressions of a person for the person in love. Most people in
India do not go around singing of their love as one might imagine after watching Indian movies and dramatic performances. Even the proximity, intimacy,
freedom, and permissiveness characterized in such media are rarely commonplace in the reality of the day-to-day life. In general, to verbalize and
manifest romantic expressions of love is looked upon as a product of poets' or
novelists' fantasies. Yet, at least theoretically, to be in love with someone is a
highly cherished ideal.

In one of the most ancient scriptures, Rgveda, it was wished that a person's life be of a hundred-year duration. The Hindu sages in their theory of
pu-rusharthas suggested four aims of life: *dharma*, righteousness, which provides a link between animal and god in man; *artha*, acquisitive instinct in man,
enjoyment of wealth and its manifestations; *kama*, instinctive and emotional
life of man and the satisfaction of sex drives and aesthetic urges; and *moksha*,
the end of life and the realization of an inner spirituality in man (see Kapadia
1966: 25).

The Hindu scriptures written during 200 B.C. to A.D. 900 mention eight
modes of acquiring a wife known as Brahma, Daiva, Arsha, Prajapatya, Asura,
Gandharva, Rakshasa, and Paisacha. Only the first four are known as *dharmya*,
that is, according to religion. An exchange of gifts between the subjects' families marks the wedding ceremony, but no dowry is paid. In the Asura form
payment of the bride price is the main element, while Rakshasa and Paisacha, respectively, pertain to the abduction and seduction of a girl when she is
unconscious. The Gandharva marriage refers to a marriage by mutual choice.
The Hindu lawgivers differ in their opinions and interpretations of this kind
of marriage; some called it the best mode of marriage, while others viewed it

stigmatic on religious and moral grounds. However, there is no reliable data to support or justify the popularity of any one of these modes of marriage. The first four kinds pertain to arranged marriages in which the parental couple ritually gives away the daughter to a suitable person, and this ideal continues to be maintained in the Hindu society. Opposed to these are four others, three of which were objected to by the scriptwriters in the past and viewed as illegal today, though nevertheless, they happen. The Gandharva mode, though opposed to the accepted norm, is nearest to what may be variously termed as "free-choice," "romantic," or "love" marriage. Yet through the ages Hindu revivalism and other socioreligious and economic factors discredited the importance of Gandharva marriage.

Diversified sects of Muslims and Christians view marriage as a civil contract as opposed to a sacrament. However, marriages are arranged most often with the consent of the subjects. The Muslims, at least theoretically, permit polygamy according to Islamic law; however, they prefer monogamy. As opposed to Hindu and Christian communities it is customary that the boy's party initiates a marriage proposal (see Kapadia 1966: 209–14; Kurian 1974: 357–58, 1975).

Most Indian marriages are arranged, although sometimes opinions of the partners are consulted, and in cases of adults, their opinions are seriously considered. Another aspect of this pattern is that individuals come to believe that their life mate is predestined, their fate is preordained, they are "right for each other," they are helpless as far as choice is concerned and therefore must succumb to the celestial forces of the universe. That the entire syndrome, typical for the society, represents a complex set of forces working around and upon the individual to get married to a person whom one is destined to love. It is also believed to be good and desirable that critical issues like the choosing of a life partner should be handled by responsible persons of family and kin group. However, it is generally possible that persons in love could marry if related prohibitions have been effectively observed.

Generally, love is considered a weak basis for marriage because its presence may overshadow suitable qualities in spouses. Therefore, arranged marriages result from more or less intense care given to the selection of suitable partners so that the family ideals, companionship, and co-parenthood can grow, leading to love. Ernest Van Den Haag writes about the United States:

> A hundred years ago, there was every reason to marry young—though middle-class people seldom did. The unmarried state had heavy disadvantages for both sexes. Custom did not permit girls to be educated, to work, or to have social, let alone sexual, freedom. . . . And, though less restricted than girls shackled to their families, single men often led a grim and uncomfortable life. A wife was nearly indispensable, if only to darn socks, sew, cook, clean, take care of her man. (1973: 181)

Goode views romantic love paradoxically, and calls it the antithesis of "conjugal love," because marriage is not based upon it, actually a couple strives to seek it within the marital bond (1959: 40). The latter, presumably, protect the couple against the harmful effects of individualism, freedom, and untoward personality growth. It may be worthwhile here to analyze the structural conditions under which mating relationships occur and to see how they relate to various values and goals in Indian society.

A study conducted in 1968, on 240 families in Kerala, a state which has the highest literacy rate in India, reveals that practical consideration in the selection of mates rather than free-choice or romantic love becomes the basis of marriage. In order of importance, the study reports that the major qualities among the girls considered important are: good character, obedience, ability to manage home, good cook, should take active part in social and political affairs, educated, religious, depending entirely on husband for major decisions, fair complexion, good companion with similar intellectual interests, and beauty (Kurian 1974: 335). Among the boy's qualities, his appearance, charm, and romantic manifestation do not count much, while the social and economic status of his family, education, and earning potential overshadow his personal qualities (Kurian 1974: 355; see also Ross 1961: 259).

The Kerala study further illustrates some interesting trends, such as: that only 59 percent of the respondents thought that meeting the prospective wife before marriage contributes to marital happiness. The parental preferences about the nature of choice of spouse of their children showed that 5.8 percent wanted to arrange the marriage without consulting sons and daughters, while 75.6 percent wanted to arrange the marriage with the consent of sons and daughters, 17.3 percent were willing to allow free choice to their children with their approval, and only 1.3 percent will allow freedom of choice without parental interference (Kurian 1974: 358). In fact, what Srinivas observed over three decades ago in Mysore was that "romantic love as a basis of marriage is still not very deep or widely spread in the family mores of India today," has not yet changed much (see Srinivas 1942: 60).

The dilemma of a boy who had fallen in love with a girl from a lower caste is reported from a study of Bangalore, a city of about a million people:

> My love affair has caused me great trouble, for my intense love of the girl and the devotion to my parents cannot be reconciled. My parents don't like our engagement, and I cannot displease them, but on the other hand I cannot give up my girl who has done so much for me. She is responsible for progress and the bright future which everyone says is ahead of me. The problem is my greatest headache at the present time. (Ross 1961: 269)

During my own fieldwork during 1963–67, in Awan, a community of about three thousand people in Rajasthan state, having extensive and frequent urban contacts, it took me no time to figure out that a question inquiring about "romantic" or "love" marriage would be futile, because people simply laughed it away. Parental opinion was reinforced by several other considerations. One man, a community elite, remarked:

> Young people do not know what love is; they are, if at all, infatuated which is very transitory and does not entail considerations of good marital life. If my son marries, I wish to see that the girl is well-raised, obedient, preserves the family traditions, ready to bear the hardships with us, and to nurse us in our old age.

Love, a premarital manifestation, is thus thought to be a disruptive element in upsetting the firmly established close ties in the family, a transference of loyalty from the family of orientation to a person, and a loss of allegiance of a person, leaving the family and kin group in disdain for personal goals.

Continued loyalty of the individual to the family of orientation and kin group is the most cherished ideal in the Indian family system. To preserve this ideal, certainly the simplest recourse is child marriage or adolescent marriage. The child is betrothed, married, and most often placed in a job and generally provides the deference demanded by the elders. Though this pattern does not give much opportunity to the individual to act freely in matrimonial affairs, it maintains a close link of the couple with the father's household which requires much physical, social, and emotional care throughout the family cycle and particularly in old age. The relationships in the extended joint family are all-important.

The Hindu scriptural texts prescribe that a person should go through *grahstaslirama* (a stage of householder's life) which includes procreation of children. The status system gives high prestige to the parents of large families. Kinship and religious values stress the need for a male heir. Large families provide security, both in economic and social terms, for the old and the destitute and the ill in a country where old-age pensions, disability, sickness benefits, and unemployment as well as medical insurance are either nonexistent or inadequate. When a family has several children, their marriages have to be spaced for economic as well as social reasons, which in turn necessitates early marriages.

Similar to other indigenous civilizations, a high value is placed upon chastity, especially female virginity in its ideal form. Love as play or premarital activity is not encouraged. Rather, elders consider it as their most important duty to supervise nubile girls. Marriage is an ideal, a duty, and a social responsibility usually preceded by highly ritualized ceremonial and festive events illustrating gradual involvement, especially of the female preparatory to the initiation of her marital role. Interestingly, all these ritual activities are role oriented (such as contributing to the long and prosperous life of the prospective husband) rather than person oriented (such as taking vows for the success of a person who is in love). This is one of those most pertinent factors which infuses longevity to the marital bond. The upper caste ideal that a girl could be ritually married only once in her lifetime and destined to marry the same person in lives to come continues to determine explicit and categorical aversion among girls to premarital interactions with strangers. Paradoxically, though, there is an implicit assumption that a person's marriage to a person of the opposite sex is governed by supreme celestial forces; in actual practice, mundane realities usually settle a marriage.

The early marriage of the person does not permit much personal independence and is further linked with another structural pattern in which the kinship rules define a class (caste, subcaste, regional group) of eligible future spouses. In other words, in the interest of homogamy and sanctity of the kin group, marriage should occur early. Thus, this would eliminate the chances of an unmarried adult to disregard a link with his or her kin group and caste. Problems arise at times when a person goes across the narrow limits of a group, often losing his chances of obtaining the usual support from the family, the kin group, and the caste. However, transgressions of basic family norms by an individual which may cause loss of identity, rejection, and an aggravated departure from the value system are rare. Often it is circumventing rather than contradicting the system which provides clues to change. Under such a pattern, elders negotiate and arrange marriages of their children and dependents with a likelihood of minimum generational conflict reinforcing greater chances of family unity. Adolescent physical and social segregation is marked by a greater emphasis on the learning of discrete sex roles idealizing, at least theoretically, parental roles.

As found in Western cultures, the youth culture frees the individual from family attachments thus permitting the individual to fall in love; and love becomes a substitute for the interlocking of kinship roles. The structural isolation of the Western family also frees the married partners' affective inclinations, that they are able to love one another (Parsons 1949: 187–89). Such a pattern is absent in the Indian family system.

Contrary to this, in India, marriage of a boy indirectly strengthens his bonds with the family of orientation. It is one of the major crises which marks his adulthood and defines his responsibilities towards his parents and the kin group. His faith and sentimental involvement in the family of orientation is an acknowledgment of the usual obligations incurred in his raising and training. A pervasive philosophy of individualism appears to be spreading and suggests a trend toward free mate choices, equality for women, equal divorce rights, and taking up of traditionally known ritually inferior but lucrative occupations; this militantly asserts the importance of the welfare of the person over any considerations of the continuity of the group. The trend toward conjugal family systems, widespread as it is, is generally confined to the urbanized regions (Gore 1958; Kapur 1970). Moreover, these changes where they appear on one hand, are viewed as social problems and as symptoms of the breakdown of time-honored ways; on the other, they are looked at as indicators of personal achievement, individual fulfilment, and family prestige.

SOCIALIZATION

The cultural pattern demands that a child in India cannot isolate himself from his parents, siblings, and other members of the extended family.

The maturation process is rarely fraught with problems or turmoil associated with parent and adolescent children as they all learn to play new roles and feel new feelings. A child's expanding world gradually gives a mature sense of responsibilities to share in most of the important decisions in his life cycle. Covert parent-child conflict is shadowed by affection and sentimental ties helping the adolescents to achieve desirable balance between rebellion and conformity, individual wishes and feelings of the parents. Occasionally, this causes some problems. Since parents make decisions about most significant aspects of the family, including the marriage of their children, passive, indifferent, and sometimes negative feelings develop in the children as they seek to be dependent on other members of the family.

The family in India is known for its cohesive function, especially providing for the emotional needs of its members. Most often, this function is effectively performed by the extended kin group which, in fact, is a segment of the caste or subcaste. Adults, as well as children, must have love and security in order to maintain emotional stability under the stresses of life and in order to meet the emotional demands made upon them by the crises. In addition to providing the positive emotional needs of its members by personal sacrifices done by the members on a regular basis throughout the life cycle of the family, it also provides a safe outlet for negative feelings. Conflicts arising from interpersonal relations are generally handled by the older members, and care is taken by them to ensure that roles and responsibilities are clearly defined. Conflicts are resolved and mitigated by a general concern in the group favoring the emotional satisfaction of the individual. A person throughout his adolescence is never isolated from the family. Thus, not only generations, but extended and local units of kin groups are forced into a more intensive relationship. The affectional ties are solidified by mutual care, help in crisis situations, and assistance provided. This often destroys negative feelings. Several rituals, rites, and ceremonial occasions reinforce the unity of the family (Dube 1955: 131–58; Gupta 1974: 104–16). In general, a person substantially invests his emotions and feelings in his family and kin group, denial of which may be hazardous to his psyche. Such a deep involvement of the individual causes his emotional dependence on the family and acceptance to its wishes in most of the crucial decisions and events in his life, including marriage.

PREMARITAL INTERACTION AND MATE SELECTION

India is perhaps the only subcontinent which provides a wide variety of mate selection processes from an open to a very closed system, from marriage by capture in the primitives to the arranged marriage among Hindus and Muslims. Moreover, rules prohibiting certain classes of persons from marrying one another also vary, such as three to four clan avoidance rules in central and northern parts to preferential cross-cousin or maternal uncle and niece marriages in the south. In other words, rules regarding the definition of incest or areas of potential mates vary substantially. Most people in the Northern states, for example, prohibit marriage between persons of similarly named clans and extend this rule to several other related clans, such as of mothers clan, mother's mother clan, and father's mother clan. The people bearing these clan names may be living several hundred miles away * * * but are usually thought to be related. From this point of view, then, the ideal mate for any person could also be a stranger, an outsider, but an individual related to him in distant terms. * * * A person living across a state belonging to one's caste has a greater chance of being an eligible for a prospective mate than a person belonging to some other caste living next door. Caste is thus an extended kin group and, at least theoretically, membership in which is related through various kinds of kinship ties. Marriage alliances within the *jati* (caste or subcaste) reinforce kinship and family ties and cause a sort of evolution of the class system. Class generally determines future marital alliances within the caste. The resources assessed by a family in seeking a marital alliance from another family play a crucial role in determining the decision about the alliance. The voices of the significant members of the family are crucial in making a marriage since newlywed couples are barely into adulthood and have neither the material nor psychological resources to start a household of their own. Later in their married life when they have resources, they may still consider the opinions of the significant members because the disadvantages of not adhering to such opinions are greater than the annoyances of living together.

A SOCIOLOGICAL PARADIGM OF ARRANGED MARRIAGES

Recent research on the changing aspects of the family in India (Collver 1963; Conklin 1974; Desai 1964; Gore 1965; Gould 1968; Gupta 1974; Hooja 1968; Kapur 1970; Kurian 1961, 1974; Orenstein 1959, 1961, 1966; Ross 1961; Shah 1974; Singer 1968) suggests that there has been little change in the joint family system in India, which is a vanguard of the arranged marriage.

The above discussion gives us to understand that what is needed in our approach to arranged marriage is a frame of reference which is more fully on the sociological level. As a step toward this goal, a general theoretical approach to the arranged marriage or "conjugal love" relationship has been formulated which, it is believed, takes account of the historical, cultural, and psychological levels, and brings into central focus the sociological level. The following tentative theoretical formulation is proposed only as a first attempt to outline what sociological factors are generally responsible to the growth of "conjugal love" as opposed to "romantic love." By any conservative estimate, love marriages occur in only less than 1 percent of the population.

1. It is important to note that arranged marriages are closely associated with "closed systems" wherein the hierarchies are very intricate and more than one factor such as historical origins, ritual positions, occupational affiliations, and social distance determinants play significant roles in defining the in-group and the out-group, particularly in marital alliances. In such systems, group identity is marked by strong senses of esoteric values, and such values are preserved and reinforced by attributes which distinguish a group in rank and its interaction with others. That is, most proximate ties of the individuals ought to be within their own group.

2. Continuity and unity of the extended family is well-preserved since all the significant members of the family share the mate-selection decision make-up which involves several persons who are supposedly known to have experience and qualifications to find a better choice as against the free choice of the subject. Obviously, this leads to lower age at marriage and, in turn, strengthens the predominance of the family over the individual choice.

3. Any possible problems emerging from a couple's functioning in marital life become problems for the whole family. Advice and counseling from the members of the extended family to improve the couple's relationship, weathering life's storms, or even sharing in crises are reinforced by the shared responsibilities. This is also partly responsible for denouncing the idea of divorce and forces working against it. This is not to say that this, in fact, resolves all the conflicts in marriage.

4. As long as the social system is unable to develop a value system to promote individualism, economic security outside the family system, and a value system which advances the ideals of nuclear family, the individuals in such a system continue to demand support from the family which, in turn, would lead to reemphasizing the importance of arranged marriage. Forces of modernization supporting the "romantic ideal" would continue to find partial support in such a system as long as the sources of moral and material support for the individual are based in the extended/joint family system.

5. It is difficult to assume that arranged marriage is related to the low status of a woman since man is also a party to it. If the concept of "free choice" is applicable to either sex, perhaps it will not support the ideal of arranged marriage. Apparently, an individual who opts for free choice or a "love marriage" is likely to dissociate from his/her family, kin group, caste, and possibly community, which he/she cannot afford unless he/she has been ensured tremendous support from sources other than these conventional institutions.

6. Arranged marriages, in general, irrespective of caste or class categories, help in maintaining closer ties with several generations. Families in such a system are an insurance for the old and the orthodox, a

recluse for the devout and the defiant, a haven for the invalid and the insipid.

7. The demographic situation in India, as in most developing societies, is also a contributing factor, among others, to the early arranged marriages. After independence, India has made many advancements in science, technology, and medicine. * * * life expectancy, which was 29 years in 1947, is now 54 years. However, the vicious circle of early child marriage, early pregnancy, high mortality rate, and replacement of the population are closely interwoven to ensure society from extinction. While the value system notoriously maintains this chain-work, the declining mortality rate further accentuates early marriages to shelve off the economic burden of the family by spacing weddings. The family protects and insulates from ruining itself by arranging marriages as early as possible and for using its resources for status aggrandizement.

Since the changes in Indian society often present a welter of traditional and modern, conventional as well as prestige and [glamor]-oriented marital role models with significant changes in the value system, it is quite probable that in the long run, "romantic ideal" will pervade the system. Whether such changes will be a part of a continuum, that is, revitalization of the mythological past or acceptance of the ideals of the modern West, preserving tenacity and positive elements of its own against the swaggering forces of change, has yet to be seen.

REFERENCES

Chekki, D. A. (1968). Mate selection, age at marriage and propinquity among the Lingayats of India. *Journal of Marriage and the Family*, 30 (November): 707–11.

Collver, A. (1963). The family cycle in India and the United States. *American Sociological Review*, 28: 86–96.

Conklin, G. H. (1974). The extended family as an independent factor in social change: A case from India. *Journal of Marriage and Family*, 36 (November): 798–804.

Cormack, M. (1953). *The Hindu woman.* New York: Bureau of Publications, Columbia University.

Desai, I. P. (1964). *Some aspects of family in Mahuva.* Bombay: Asia Publishing House.

Dube, S. C. (1955). *Indian village.* New York: Cornell University Press.

Goode, W. J. (1959). The theoretical importance of love. *American Sociological Review*, 24: 38–47.

_____. (1963). *World revolution and family patterns.* New York: Free Press.

Gore, M. S. (1968). *Urbanization and family change.* Bombay: Popular Prakashan.

Gupta, G. R. (1974). *Marriage, religion and society: Pattern of change in an Indian village.* New York: Halsted Press.

Hate, C. A. (1970). Raising the age at marriage. *The Indian Journal of Social Work*, 30: 303–09.

Hooja, S. (1968). Dowry system among the Hindus in North India: A case study. *The Indian Journal of Social Work,* 38: 411–26.

Kapadia, K. M. (1966). *Marriage and family in India,* 3rd ed. London: Oxford University Press.

Kapur, P. (1970). *Marriage and the working woman in India.* Delhi: Vikas Publications.

Karve, I. (1965). *Kinship organization in India.* Bombay: Asia Publishing House.

Klass, M. (1966). Marriage rules in Bengal. *American Anthropologist,* 68: 951–70.

Kurian, G. (1961). *The Indian family in transition.* The Hague: Mouton.

———. (1974). Modern trends in mate selection and marriage with special reference to Kerala. In G. Kurian, Ed., *The Family in India—A Regional View* (pp. 351–67). The Hague: Mouton.

———. (1975). Structural changes in the family in Kerala, India. In T. R. Williams, ed., *Psychological Anthropology.* The Hague: Mouton.

Madan, T. N. (1965). *Family and kinship: A study of the Pandits of rural Kashmir.* New York: Asia Publishing House.

Mandelbaum, D. G. (1970). *Society in India,* vol. I & II. Berkeley: University of California Press.

Meyer, J. J. (1953). *Sexual life in ancient India.* New York: Barnes & Noble.

Orenstein, H. (1959). The recent history of the extended family in India. *Social Problems,* 8: 341–50.

———. (1961). The recent history of family in India. *Social Problems,* 8 (Spring): 341–50.

———. (1966). The Hindu joint family: The norms and the numbers. *Pacific Affairs,* 39 (Fall-Winter): 314–25.

Parsons, T. (1949). *Essays in sociological theory.* Glencoe, Illinois: Free Press.

Ross, A. D. (1961). *The Hindu family in its urban setting.* Toronto: University of Toronto Press.

Shah, A. M. (1974). *The household dimension of family in India.* Berkeley: University of California Press.

Singer, M. (1968). The Indian joint family in modern industry. In M. Singer & B. S. Cohn, Eds., *Structure and change in Indian society.* Chicago: Aldine Publishing Co.

Srinivas, M. N. (1942). *Marriage and family in Mysore.* Bombay: New Book Co.

Van Den Haag, E. (1973). Love or marriage. In M. E. Lasswell & Thomas E. Lasswell, Eds., *Love, marriage and family: A developmental approach* (pp. 181–86). Glenview, Illinois: Scott, Foresman and Co.

Vatuk, S. (1972). *Kinship and urbanization.* Berkeley: University of California Press.

38

The Radical Idea of Marrying for Love*

FROM *Marriage, a History*

STEPHANIE COONTZ

As Peter Berger discussed in reading 1, what everyone knows is often not actually the case. Social historian Stephanie Coontz, in the best sociological fashion, explains with insight and humor how marital bonding and long-term partnerships have only recently been the responsibility of "so strong yet transient an emotion" as love. Author of the very popular The Way We Never Were *and other books, Coontz's historical and anthropological evidence provides some welcome understanding of marital patterns that may seem inappropriate, unnatural, or even immoral to those of us raised to believe there is one person with whom we can forever be happy. Record numbers of young people today are delaying marriage, and many who will never marry will be parents and have long-term monogamous relationships. Perhaps the Western version of love and marriage is changing, and those who embrace it can find guidance with Coontz's sociological insight.*

George Bernard Shaw described marriage as an institution that brings together two people "under the influence of the most violent, most insane, most delusive, and most transient of passions. They are required to swear that they will remain in that excited, abnormal, and exhausting condition continuously until death do them part."

Shaw's comment was amusing when he wrote it at the beginning of the twentieth century, and it still makes us smile today, because it pokes fun at the unrealistic expectations that spring from a dearly held cultural ideal—that marriage should be based on intense, profound love and a couple should maintain their ardor until death do them part. But for thousands of years the joke would have fallen flat.

For most of history it was inconceivable that people would choose their mates on the basis of something as fragile and irrational as love and then focus all their sexual, intimate, and altruistic desires on the resulting marriage. In fact, many historians, sociologists, and anthropologists used to think romantic love was a recent Western invention. This is not true. People have always fallen in love, and throughout the ages many couples have loved each other deeply.

---

*Footnotes and references can be found in Stephanie Coontz's *Marriage, a History*.

But only rarely in history has love been seen as the main reason for getting married. When someone did advocate such a strange belief, it was no laughing matter. Instead, it was considered a serious threat to social order.

In some cultures and times, true love was actually thought to be incompatible with marriage. Plato believed love was a wonderful emotion that led men to behave honorably. But the Greek philosopher was referring not to the love of women, "such as the meaner men feel," but to the love of one man for another.

Other societies considered it good if love developed after marriage or thought love should be factored in along with the more serious considerations involved in choosing a mate. But even when past societies did welcome or encourage married love, they kept it on a short leash. Couples were not to put their feelings for each other above more important commitments, such as their ties to parents, siblings, cousins, neighbors, or God.

In ancient India, falling in love before marriage was seen as a disruptive, almost antisocial act. The Greeks thought lovesickness was a type of insanity, a view that was adopted by medieval commentators in Europe. In the Middle Ages the French defined love as a "derangement of the mind" that could be cured by sexual intercourse, either with the loved one or with a different partner. This cure assumed, as Oscar Wilde once put it, that the quickest way to conquer yearning and temptation was to yield immediately and move on to more important matters.

In China, excessive love between husband and wife was seen as a threat to the solidarity of the extended family. Parents could force a son to divorce his wife if her behavior or work habits didn't please them, whether or not he loved her. They could also require him to take a concubine if his wife did not produce a son. If a son's romantic attachment to his wife rivaled his parents' claims on the couple's time and labor, the parents might even send her back to her parents. In the Chinese language the term *love* did not traditionally apply to feelings between husband and wife. It was used to describe an illicit, socially disapproved relationship. In the 1920s a group of intellectuals invented a new word for love between spouses because they thought such a radical new idea required its own special label.

In Europe, during the twelfth and thirteenth centuries, adultery became idealized as the highest form of love among the aristocracy. According to the Countess of Champagne, it was impossible for true love to "exert its powers between two people who are married to each other."

In twelfth-century France, Andreas Capellanus, chaplain to Countess Marie of Troyes, wrote a treatise on the principles of courtly love. The first rule was that "marriage is no real excuse for not loving." But he meant loving someone outside the marriage. As late as the eighteenth century the French essayist Montaigne wrote that any man who was in love with his wife was a man so dull that no one else could love him.

Courtly love probably loomed larger in literature than in real life. But for centuries, noblemen and kings fell in love with courtesans rather than the wives they married for political reasons. Queens and noblewomen had to be more discreet than their husbands, but they too looked beyond marriage for love and intimacy.

This sharp distinction between love and marriage was common among the lower and middle classes as well. Many of the songs and stories popular among peasants in medieval Europe mocked married love.

The most famous love affair of the Middle Ages was that of Peter Abelard, a well-known theologian in France, and Héloïse, the brilliant niece of a fellow churchman at Notre Dame. The two eloped without marrying, and she bore him a child. In an attempt to save his career but still placate Héloïse's furious uncle, Abelard proposed they marry in secret. This would mean that Héloïse would not be living in sin, while Abelard could still pursue his church ambitions. But Heloise resisted the idea, arguing that marriage would not only harm his career but also undermine their love.

LOVE, IN AND OUT OF MARRIAGE

"Nothing Is More Impure Than to Love One's Wife as if She Were a Mistress"

Even in societies that esteemed married love, couples were expected to keep it under strict control. In many cultures, public displays of love between husband and wife were considered unseemly. A Roman was expelled from the Senate because he had kissed his wife in front of his daughter. Plutarch conceded that the punishment was somewhat extreme but pointed out that everyone knew that it was "disgraceful" to kiss one's wife in front of others.

Some Greek and Roman philosophers even said that a man who loved his wife with "excessive" ardor was "an adulterer." Many centuries later Catholic and Protestant theologians argued that husbands and wives who loved each other too much were committing the sin of idolatry. Theologians chided wives who used endearing nicknames for their husbands, because such familiarity on a wife's part undermined the husband's authority and the awe that his wife should feel for him. Although medieval Muslim thinkers were more approving of sexual passion between husband and wife than were Christian theologians, they also insisted that too much intimacy between husband and wife weakened a believer's devotion to God. And, like their European counterparts, secular writers in the Islamic world believed that love thrived best outside marriage.

Many cultures still frown on placing love at the center of marriage. In Africa, the Fulbe people of northern Cameroon do not see love as a legitimate emotion, especially within marriage. One observer reports that in conversations with their neighbors, Fulbe women "vehemently deny emotional attachment to a husband." In many peasant and working-class communities, too much love between husband and wife is seen as disruptive because it encourages the couple to withdraw from the wider web of dependence that makes the society work.

As a result, men and women often relate to each other in public, even after marriage, through the conventions of a war between the sexes, disguising the fondness they may really feel. They describe their marital behavior, no matter how exemplary it may actually be, in terms of convenience, compulsion, or self-interest rather than love or sentiment. In Cockney rhyming slang, the term for *wife* is *trouble and strife*.

Whether it is valued or not, love is rarely seen as the main ingredient for marital success. Among the Taita of Kenya, recognition and approval of married love are widespread. An eighty-year-old man recalled that his fourth wife "was the wife of my heart. . . . I could look at her and no words would pass, just a smile." In this society, where men often take several wives, women speak wistfully about how wonderful it is to be a "love wife." But only a small percentage of Taita women experience this luxury, because a Taita man normally marries a love wife only after he has accumulated a few more practical wives.

In many cultures, love has been seen as a desirable outcome of marriage but not as a good reason for getting married in the first place. The Hindu tradition celebrates love and sexuality in marriage, but love and sexual attraction are not considered valid reasons for marriage. "First we marry, then we'll fall in love" is the formula. As recently as 1975, a survey of college students in the Indian state of Karnataka found that only 18 percent "strongly" approved of marriages made on the basis of love, while 32 percent completely disapproved.

Similarly, in early modern Europe most people believed that love developed after marriage. Moralists of the sixteenth and seventeenth centuries argued that if a husband and wife each had a good character, they would probably come to love each other. But they insisted that youths be guided by their families in choosing spouses who were worth learning to love. It was up to parents and other relatives to make sure that the woman had a dowry or the man had a good yearly income. Such capital, it was thought, would certainly help love flower.

"[I]t Made Me Really Sick, Just as I Have Formerly Been When in Love with My Wife"

I don't believe that people of the past had more control over their hearts than we do today or that they were incapable of the deep love so many individuals now hope to achieve in marriage. But love in marriage was seen as a bonus, not as a necessity. The great Roman statesman Cicero exchanged many loving letters with his wife, Terentia, during their thirty-year marriage. But that didn't stop him from divorcing her when she was no longer able to support him in the style to which he had become accustomed.

Sometimes people didn't have to make such hard choices. In seventeenth-century America, Anne Bradstreet was the favorite child of an indulgent father who gave her the kind of education usually reserved for elite boys. He later arranged her marriage to a cherished childhood friend who eventually became the governor of Massachusetts. Combining love, duty, material security, and marriage was not the strain for her that it was for many men and women of that era. Anne wrote love poems to her husband that completely ignored the injunction of Puritan ministers not to place one's spouse too high in one's affections. "If ever two were one," she wrote him, "then surely we; if ever man were loved by wife, then thee. . . . I prize thy love more than whole mines of gold, or all the riches that the East doth hold; my love is such that rivers cannot quench, nor ought but love from thee, give recompense."

The famous seventeenth-century English diarist Samuel Pepys chose to marry for love rather than profit. But he was not as lucky as Anne. After hearing a particularly stirring piece of music, Pepys recorded that it "did wrap up my soul so that it made me really sick, just as I have formerly been when in love with my wife." Pepys would later disinherit a nephew for marrying under the influence of so strong yet transient an emotion.

There were always youngsters who resisted the pressures of parents, kin, and neighbors to marry for practical reasons rather than love, but most accepted or even welcomed the interference of parents and others in arranging their marriages. A common saying in early modern Europe was "He who marries for love has good nights and bad days." Nowadays a bitter wife or husband might ask, "Whatever possessed me to think I loved you enough to marry you?" Through most of the past, he or she was more likely to have asked, "Whatever possessed me to marry you just because I loved you?"

"Happily Ever After"

Through most of the past, individuals hoped to find love, or at least "tranquil affection," in marriage. But nowhere did they have the same recipe for marital happiness that prevails in most contemporary Western countries. Today there is general agreement on what it takes for a couple to live "happily ever after." First, they must love each other deeply and choose each other unswayed by outside pressure. From then on, each must make the partner the top priority in life, putting that relationship above any and all competing ties. A husband and wife, we believe, owe their highest obligations and deepest loyalties to each other and the children they raise. Parents and in-laws should not be allowed to interfere in the marriage. Married couples should be best friends, sharing their most intimate feelings and secrets. They should express affection openly but also talk candidly about problems. And of course they should be sexually faithful to each other.

This package of expectations about love, marriage, and sex, however, is extremely rare. When we look at the historical record around the world, the customs of modern America and Western Europe appear exotic and exceptional.

Leo Tolstoy once remarked that all happy families are alike, while every unhappy family is unhappy in its own way. But the more I study the history of marriage, the more I think the opposite is true. Most unhappy marriages in history share common patterns, leaving their tear-stained—and sometimes bloodstained—records across the ages. But each happy, successful marriage seems to be happy in its own way. And for most of human history, successful marriages have not been happy in *our* way.

A woman in ancient China might bring one or more of her sisters to her husband's home as backup wives. Eskimo couples often had cospousal arrangements, in which each partner had sexual relations with the other's spouse. In Tibet and parts of India, Kashmir, and Nepal, a woman may be married to two or more brothers, all of whom share sexual access to her.

In modern America, such practices are the stuff of trash TV: "I caught my sister in bed with my husband"; "My parents brought their lovers into our home"; "My wife slept with my brother"; "It broke my heart to share my husband with another woman." In other cultures, individuals often find such practices normal and comforting. The children of Eskimo cospouses felt that they shared a special bond, and society viewed them as siblings. Among Tibetan brothers who share the same wife, sexual jealousy is rare.

In some cultures, cowives see one another as allies rather than rivals. In Botswana women add an interesting wrinkle to the old European saying "Woman's work is never done." There they say: "Without cowives, a woman's work is never done." A researcher who worked with the Cheyenne Indians of the United States in the 1930s and 1940s told of a chief who tried to get rid of two of his three wives. All three women defied him, saying that if he sent two of them away, he would have to give away the third as well.

Even when societies celebrated the love between husband and wife as a pleasant by-product of marriage, people rarely had a high regard for marital intimacy. Chinese commentators on marriage discouraged a wife from confiding in her husband or telling him about her day. A good wife did not bother her husband with news of her own activities and feelings but treated him "like a guest," no matter how long they had been married. A husband who demonstrated open affection for his wife, even at home, was seen as having a weak character.

In the early eighteenth century, American lovers often said they looked for "candor" in each other. But they were not talking about the soul-baring intimacy idealized by modern Americans, and they certainly did not believe that couples should talk frankly about their grievances. Instead candor meant fairness, kindliness, and good temper. People wanted a spouse who did *not* pry too deeply. The ideal mate, wrote U.S. President John Adams in his diary, was willing "to palliate faults and Mistakes, to put the best Construction upon Words and Action, and to forgive Injuries."

Modern marital advice books invariably tell husbands and wives to put each other first. But in many societies, marriage ranks very low in the hierarchy of meaningful relationships. People's strongest loyalties and emotional connections may be reserved for members of their birth families. On the North American plains in the 1930s, a Kiowa Indian woman commented to a researcher that "a woman can always get another husband, but she has only one brother." In China it was said that "you have only one family, but you can always get another wife." In Christian texts prior to the seventeenth century, the word *love* usually referred to feelings toward God or neighbors rather than toward a spouse.

In Confucian philosophy, the two strongest relationships in family life are between father and son and between elder brother and younger brother, not between husband and wife. In thirteenth-century China the bond between father and son was so much stronger than the bond between husband and wife that legal commentators insisted a couple do nothing if the patriarch of the household raped his son's wife. In one case, although the judge was sure that a woman's rape accusation against her father-in-law was true, he ordered the young man to give up his sentimental desire "to grow old together" with his wife. Loyalty to parents was paramount, and therefore the son should send his wife back to her own father, who could then marry her to someone else. Sons were sometimes ordered beaten for siding with their wives against their father. No wonder that for 1,700 years women in one Chinese province guarded a secret language that they used to commiserate with each other about the griefs of marriage.

In many societies of the past, sexual loyalty was not a high priority. The expectation of mutual fidelity is a rather recent invention. Numerous cultures have allowed husbands to seek sexual gratification outside marriage. Less frequently, but often enough to challenge common preconceptions, wives have also been allowed to do this without threatening the marriage. In a study of 109 societies, anthropologists found that only 48 forbade extramarital sex to both husbands and wives.

When a woman has sex with someone other than her husband and he doesn't object, anthropologists have traditionally called it wife loaning. When a man does it, they call it male privilege. But in some societies the choice to switch partners rests with the woman. Among the Dogon of West Africa, young married women publicly pursued extramarital relationships with the encouragement of their mothers. Among the Rukuba of Nigeria, a wife can take a lover at the time of her first marriage. This relationship is so embedded in accepted custom that the lover has the right, later in life, to ask his former mistress to marry her daughter to his son.

Among the Eskimo of northern Alaska, as I noted earlier, husbands and wives, with mutual consent, established comarriages with other couples. Some anthropologists believe cospouse relationships were a more socially acceptable outlet for sexual attraction than was marriage itself. Expressing open jealousy about the sexual relationships involved was considered boorish.

Such different notions of marital rights and obligations made divorce and remarriage less emotionally volatile for the Eskimo than it is for most modern Americans. In fact, the Eskimo believed that a remarried person's partner had an obligation to allow the former spouse, as well as any children of that union, the right to fish, hunt, and gather in the new spouse's territory.

Several small-scale societies in South America have sexual and marital norms that are especially startling for Europeans and North Americans. In these groups, people believe that any man who has sex with a woman during her pregnancy contributes part of his biological substance to the child. The husband is recognized as the primary father, but the woman's lover or lovers also have paternal responsibilities, including the obligation to share food with the woman and her child in the future. During the 1990s researchers taking life histories of elderly Bari women in Venezuela found that most had taken lovers during at least one of their pregnancies. Their husbands were usually aware and did not object. When a woman gave birth, she would name all the men she had slept with since learning she was pregnant, and a woman attending the birth would tell each of these men: "You have a child."

In Europe and the United States today such an arrangement would be a surefire recipe for jealousy, bitter breakups, and very mixed-up kids. But among the Bari people this practice was in the best interests of the child. The secondary fathers were expected to provide the child with fish and game, with the result that a child with a secondary father was twice as likely to live to the age of fifteen as a brother or sister without such a father.

Few other societies have incorporated extramarital relationships so successfully into marriage and child rearing. But all these examples of differing marital and sexual norms make it difficult to claim there is some universal model for the success or happiness of a marriage.

About two centuries ago Western Europe and North America developed a whole set of new values about the way to organize marriage and sexuality, and many of these values are now spreading across the globe. In this Western model, people expect marriage to satisfy more of their psychological and social needs than ever before. Marriage is supposed to be free of the coercion, violence, and gender inequalities that were tolerated in the past. Individuals want marriage to meet most of their needs for intimacy and affection and all their needs for sex.

Never before in history had societies thought that such a set of high expectations about marriage was either realistic or desirable. Although many Europeans and Americans found tremendous joy in building their relationships around these values, the adoption of these unprecedented goals for marriage had unanticipated and revolutionary consequences that have since come to threaten the stability of the entire institution.

39

Domestic Networks

FROM *All Our Kin: Strategies for Survival in a Black Community*

CAROL B. STACK

How far do family ties and responsibilities extend? For many African-American families they extend beyond parents and children to cousins, aunts, uncles, and even fictive kin. Decades of discrimination and institutional racism have left many people with few resources of their own to draw on in times of need, and so helping relationships have remained a critical feature of the extended family. Linking ethnicity, class, and gender, Carol Stack reminds us of the strength and resilience of the human community.

In The Flats the responsibility for providing food, care, clothing, and shelter and for socializing children within domestic networks may be spread over several households. Which household a given individual belongs to is not a particularly meaningful question, as we have seen that daily domestic organization depends on several things: where people sleep, where they eat, and where they offer their time and money. Although those who eat together and contribute toward the rent are generally considered by Flats residents to form minimal domestic units, household changes rarely affect the exchanges and daily dependencies of those who take part in common activity.

The residence patterns and cooperative organization of people linked in domestic networks demonstrate the stability and collective power of family life in The Flats. Michael Lee grew up in The Flats and now has a job in Chicago. On a visit to The Flats, Michael described the residence and domestic organization of his kin. "Most of my kin in The Flats lived right here on Cricket Street, numbers sixteen, eighteen, and twenty-two, in these three apartment buildings joined together. My mama decided it would be best for me and my three brothers and sister to be on Cricket Street too. My daddy's mother had a small apartment in this building, her sister had one in the basement, and another brother and his family took a larger apartment upstairs. My uncle was really good to us. He got us things we wanted and he controlled us. All the women kept the younger kids together during the day. They cooked together too. It was good living."

Yvonne Diamond, a forty-year-old Chicago woman, moved to The Flats from Chicago with her four children. Soon afterwards they were evicted. "The landlord said he was going to build a parking lot there, but he never did. The old place is still standing and has folks in it today. My husband's mother and father took me and the kids in and watched over them while I had my baby. We stayed on after my husband's mother died, and my husband joined us when he got a job in The Flats."

When families or individuals in The Flats are evicted, other kinsmen usually take them in. Households in The Flats expand or contract with the loss of a job, a death in the family, the beginning or end of a sexual partnership, or the end of a friendship. Welfare workers, researchers, and landlords have long known that the poor must move frequently. What is much less understood is the relationship between residence and domestic organization in the black community.

The spectrum of economic and legal pressures that act upon ghetto residents, requiring them to move—unemployment, welfare requirements, housing shortages, high rents, eviction—are clear-cut examples of external pressures affecting the daily lives of the poor. Flats residents are evicted from their dwellings by landlords who want to raise rents, tear the building down, or rid themselves of tenants who complain about rats, roaches, and the plumbing. Houses get condemned by the city on landlords' requests so that they can force tenants to move. After an eviction, a landlord can rent to a family in such great need of housing that they will not complain for a while.

Poor housing conditions and unenforced housing standards coupled with overcrowding, unemployment, and poverty produce hazardous living conditions and residence changes. "Our whole family had to move when the gas lines sprung a leak in our apartment and my son set the place on fire by accident," Sam Summer told me. "The place belonged to my sister-in-law's grandfather. We had been living there with my mother, my brother's eight children, and our eight children. My father lived in the basement apartment 'cause he and my mother were separated. After the fire burned the whole place down, we all moved to two places down the street near my cousin's house."

When people are unable to pay their rent because they have been temporarily "cut off aid," because the welfare office is suspicious of their eligibility, because they gave their rent money to a kinsman to help him through a crisis or illness, or because they were laid off from their job, they receive eviction notices almost immediately. Lydia Watson describes a chain of events starting with the welfare office stopping her sister's welfare checks, leading to an eviction, co-residence, overcrowding, and eventually murder. Lydia sadly related the story to me. "My oldest sister was cut off aid the day her husband got out of jail. She and her husband and their three children were evicted from their apartment and they came to live with us. We were in crowded conditions already. I had my son, my other sister was there with her two kids, and my mother was about going crazy. My mother put my sister's husband out 'cause she found out he was a dope addict. He came back one night soon after that and murdered my sister. After my sister's death my mother couldn't face living in Chicago any longer. One of my other sisters who had been adopted and raised by my mother's paternal grandmother visited us and persuaded us to move to The Flats, where she was staying. All of us moved there—my mother, my two sisters and their children, my two baby sisters, and my dead sister's children. My sister who had been staying in The Flats found us a house across the street from her own."

Overcrowded dwellings and the impossibility of finding adequate housing in The Flats have many long-term consequences regarding where and with whom children live. Terence Platt described where and with whom his kin lived when he was a child. "My brother stayed with my aunt, my mother's sister, and her husband until he was ten, 'cause he was the oldest in our family and we didn't have enough room—but he stayed with us most every weekend. Finally my aunt moved into the house behind ours with her husband, her brother, and my brother; my sisters and brothers and I lived up front with my mother and her old man."

KIN-STRUCTURED LOCAL NETWORKS

The material and cultural support needed to absorb, sustain, and socialize community members in The Flats is provided by networks of cooperating kinsmen. Local coalitions formed from these networks of kin and friends are mobilized within domestic networks; domestic organization is diffused over many kin-based households which themselves have elastic boundaries.

People in The Flats are immersed in a domestic web of a large number of kin and friends whom they can count on. From a social viewpoint, relationships within the community are "organized on the model of kin relationships." * * * Kin-constructs such as the perception of parenthood, the culturally determined criteria which affect the shape of personal kindreds, and the idiom of kinship, prescribe kin who can be recruited into domestic networks.

There are similarities in function between domestic networks and domestic groups which [one scholar] characterizes as "workshops of social reproduction." Both domains include three generations of members linked collaterally or otherwise. Kinship, jural and affectional bonds, and economic factors affect the composition of both domains and residential alignments within them. There are two striking differences between domestic networks and domestic groups. Domestic networks are not visible groups, because they do not have an obvious nucleus or defined boundary. But since a primary focus of domestic networks is child-care arrangements, the cooperation of a cluster of adult females is apparent. Participants in domestic networks are recruited from personal kindreds and friendships, but the personnel changes with fluctuating economic needs, changing life styles, and vacillating personal relationships.

In some loosely and complexly structured cognatic systems, kin-structured local networks (not groups) emerge. Localized coalitions of persons drawn from personal kindreds can be organized as networks of kinsmen. Goodenough * * * correctly points out that anthropologists frequently describe "localized kin groups," but rarely describe kin-structured local groups. * * *

The localized, kin-based, cooperative coalitions of people described in this chapter are organized as kin-structured domestic networks. For brevity, I refer to them as domestic networks.

* * *

GENEROSITY AND POVERTY

The combination of arbitrary and repressive economic forces and social behavior, modified by successive generations of poverty, make it almost impossible for people to break out of poverty. There is no way for those families poor enough to receive welfare to acquire any surplus cash which can be saved for emergencies or for acquiring adequate appliances or a home or a car. In contrast to the middle class, who are pressured to spend and save, the poor are not even permitted to establish an equity.

The following examples from Magnolia and Calvin Waters' life illustrates the ways in which the poor are prohibited from acquiring any surplus which might enable them to change their economic condition or life style.

In 1971 Magnolia's uncle died in Mississippi and left an unexpected inheritance of $1,500 to Magnolia and Calvin Waters. The cash came from a small run-down farm which Magnolia's uncle sold shortly before he died. It was the first time in their lives that Magnolia or Calvin ever had a cash reserve. Their first hope was to buy a home and use the money as a down payment.

Calvin had retired from his job as a seasonal laborer the year before and the family was on welfare. AFDC alloted the family $100 per month for rent. The housing that the family had been able to obtain over the years for their nine children at $100 or less was always small, roach infested, with poor plumbing and heating. The family was frequently evicted. Landlords complained about the noise and often observed an average of ten to fifteen children playing in the household. Magnolia and Calvin never even anticipated that they would be able to buy a home.

Three days after they received the check, news of its arrival spread throughout their domestic network. One niece borrowed $25 from Magnolia so that her phone would not be turned off. Within a week the welfare office knew about the money. Magnolia's children were immediately cut off welfare, including medical coverage and food stamps. Magnolia was told that she would not receive a welfare grant for her children until the money was used up, and she was given a minimum of four months in which to spend the money. The first surplus the family ever acquired was effectively taken from them.

During the weeks following the arrival of the money, Magnolia and Calvin's obligations to the needs of kin remained the same, but their ability to meet these needs had temporarily increased. When another uncle became very ill in the South, Magnolia and her older sister, Augusta, were called to sit by his side. Magnolia bought round-trip train tickets for both of them and for her three youngest children. When the uncle died, Magnolia bought round-trip train tickets so that she and Augusta could attend the funeral. Soon after his death, Augusta's first "old man" died in The Flats and he had no kin to pay for the burial. Augusta asked Magnolia to help pay for digging the grave. Magnolia was unable to refuse. Another sister's rent was two months overdue and Magnolia feared that she would get evicted. This sister was seriously ill and had no source of income. Magnolia paid her rent.

Winter was cold and Magnolia's children and grandchildren began staying home from school because they did not have warm winter coats and adequate shoes or boots. Magnolia and Calvin decided to buy coats, hats, and shoes for all of the children (at least fifteen). Magnolia also bought a winter coat for herself and Calvin bought himself a pair of sturdy shoes.

Within a month and a half, all of the money was gone. The money was channeled into the hands of the same individuals who ordinarily participate in daily domestic exchanges, but the premiums were temporarily higher. All of the money was quickly spent for necessary, compelling reasons.

Thus random fluctuations in the meager flow of available cash and goods tend to be of considerable importance to the poor. A late welfare check, sudden sickness, robbery, and other unexpected losses cannot be overcome with a cash reserve like more well-to-do families hold for emergencies. Increases in cash are either taken quickly from the poor by the welfare agencies or dissipated through the kin network.

Those living in poverty have little or no chance to escape from the economic situation into which they were born. Nor do they have the power to control the expansion or contraction of welfare benefits * * * or of employment opportunities, both of which have a momentous effect on their daily lives. In times of need, the only predictable resources that can be drawn upon are their own children and parents, and the fund of kin and friends obligated to them.

40

From *The Protestant Ethic and the Spirit of Capitalism*

MAX WEBER

Why did capitalism (and industrialization) emerge in Western Europe rather than in ancient China, Egypt, or India? All had sufficient knowledge and resources. What made the difference? In this classic study, Max Weber (1864–1920) presents his famous thesis about the connection between early Protestant beliefs and the emergence of industrial capitalism. His view of the fate of the Protestant ethic is, to many people, prophetic for the twentieth and twenty-first centuries. A contemporary of Émile Durkheim, Weber began writing soon after the death of Karl Marx. Weber is one of sociology's founders.

In the title of this study is used the somewhat pretentious phrase, the *spirit* of capitalism. What is to be understood by it? The attempt to give anything like a definition of it brings out certain difficulties which are in the very nature of this type of investigation.

If any object can be found to which this term can be applied with any understandable meaning, it can only be an historical individual, i.e. a complex of elements associated in historical reality which we unite into a conceptual whole from the standpoint of their cultural significance.*

* * *

"Remember, that *time* is money. He that can earn ten shillings a day by his labour, and goes abroad, or sits idle, one half of that day, though he spends but sixpence during his diversion or idleness, ought not to reckon *that* the only expense; he has really spent, or rather thrown away, five shillings besides.

* * *

"Remember, that money is of the prolific, generating nature. Money can beget money, and its offspring can beget more, and so on. Five shillings turned is six, turned again it is seven and threepence, and so on, till it becomes a hundred pounds. The more there is of it, the more it produces every turning, so

---

*This is what Weber calls an "ideal type" concept that has become a commonly used feature of sociology. [*Editor's note*].

that the profits rise quicker and quicker. He that kills a breedingsow, destroys all her offspring to the thousandth generation. He that murders a crown, destroys all that it might have produced, even scores of pounds.

* * *

"For six pounds a year you may have the use of one hundred pounds, provided you are a man of known prudence and honesty.

"He that spends a groat a day idly, spends idly above six pounds a year, which is the price for the use of one hundred pounds.

"He that wastes idly a groat's worth of his time per day, one day with another, wastes the privilege of using one hundred pounds each day.

"He that idly loses five shillings' worth of time, loses five shillings, and might as prudently throw five shillings into the sea.

"He that loses five shillings, not only loses that sum, but all the advantage that might be made by turning it in dealing, which by the time that a young man becomes old, will amount to a considerable sum of money."

It is Benjamin Franklin who preaches to us in these [preceding paragraphs].

* * *

That it is the spirit of capitalism which here speaks in characteristic fashion, no one will doubt, however little we may wish to claim that everything which could be understood as pertaining to that spirit is contained in it. Let us pause a moment to consider this passage, the philosophy of which Kürnberger sums up in the words, "They make tallow out of cattle and money out of men." The peculiarity of this philosophy of avarice appears to be the ideal of the honest man of recognized credit, and above all the idea of a duty of the individual toward the increase of his capital, which is assumed as an end in itself. Truly what is here preached is not simply a means of making one's way in the world, but a peculiar ethic. The infraction of its rules is treated not as foolishness but as forgetfulness of duty. That is the essence of the matter. It is not mere business astuteness, that sort of thing is common enough, it is an ethos: *This* is the quality which interests us.

* * *

And in truth this peculiar idea, so familiar to us to-day, but in reality so little a matter of course, of one's duty in a calling, is what is most characteristic of the social ethic of capitalistic culture, and is in a sense the fundamental basis of it. It is an obligation which the individual is supposed to feel and does feel towards the content of his professional activity, no matter in what it consists, in particular no matter whether it appears on the surface as a utilization of his personal powers, or only of his material possessions (as capital).

* * *

Thus the capitalism of today, which has come to dominate economic life, educates and selects the economic subjects which it needs through a process of economic survival of the fittest. But here one can easily see the limits of the concept of selection as a means of historical explanation. In order that a manner of life so well adapted to the peculiarities of capitalism could be selected at all, i.e. should come to dominate others, it had to originate somewhere, and not in isolated individuals alone, but as a way of life common to whole groups of men. This origin is what really needs explanation. Concerning the doctrine of the more naïve historical materialism,[†] that such ideas originate as a reflection or superstructure of economic situations. * * * At this point it will suffice for our purpose to call attention to the fact that without doubt, in the country of Benjamin Franklin's birth (Massachusetts), the spirit of capitalism (in the sense we have attached to it) was present before the capitalistic order. There were complaints of a peculiarly calculating sort of profit-seeking in New England, as distinguished from other parts of America, as early as 1632. It is further undoubted that capitalism remained far less developed in some of the neighbouring colonies, the later Southern States of the United States of America, in spite of the fact that these latter were founded by large capitalists for business motives.

* * *

To be sure the capitalistic form of an enterprise and the spirit in which it is run generally stand in some sort of adequate relationship to each other, but not in one of necessary interdependence. Nevertheless, we provisionally use the expression spirit of (modern) capitalism to describe that attitude which seeks profit rationally and systematically in the manner which we have illustrated by the example of Benjamin Franklin. This, however, is justified by the historical fact that that attitude of mind has on the one hand found its most suitable expression in capitalistic enterprise, while on the other the enterprise has derived its most suitable motive force from the spirit of capitalism.

* * *

It will be our task to find out whose intellectual child the particular concrete form of rational thought was, from which the idea of a calling and the devotion to labour in the calling has grown, which is, as we have seen, so irrational from the standpoint of pure * * * self-interest, but which has been and still is one of the most characteristic elements of our capitalistic culture. We are here particularly interested in the origin of precisely the irrational element which lies in this, as in every conception of a calling.

[†]Weber is critiquing Marx's idea of historical materialism. [*Editor's note*].

LUTHER'S CONCEPTION OF THE CALLING

* * *

Now it is unmistakable that even in the German word *Beruf,* and perhaps still more clearly in the English *calling,* a religious conception, that of a task set by God, is at least suggested. * * * And if we trace the history of the word through the civilized languages, it appears that neither the predominantly Catholic peoples nor those of classical antiquity have possessed any expression of similar connotation for what we know as a calling (in the sense of a life-task, a definite field in which to work), while one has existed for all predominantly Protestant peoples.

* * *

Like the meaning of the word, the idea is new, a product of the Reformation. * * * It is true that certain suggestions of the positive valuation of routine activity in the world, which is contained in this conception of the calling, had already existed in the Middle Ages, and even in late Hellenistic antiquity. We shall speak of that later. But at least one thing was unquestionably new: the valuation of the fulfilment of duty in worldly affairs as the highest form which the moral activity of the individual could assume. This it was which inevitably gave every-day worldly activity a religious significance, and which first created the conception of a calling in this sense. The conception of the calling thus brings out that central dogma of all Protestant denominations. * * * The only way of living acceptably to God was not to surpass worldly morality in monastic asceticism, but solely through the fulfilment of the obligations imposed upon the individual by his position in the world. That was his calling.

Luther developed the conception in the course of the first decade of his activity as a reformer.

* * *

[L]abour in a calling appears to him as the outward expression of brotherly love. This he proves by the observation that the division of labour forces every individual to work for others. * * * [T]he fulfilment of worldly duties is under all circumstances the only way to live acceptably to God. It and it alone is the will of God, and hence every legitimate calling has exactly the same worth in the sight of God.

* * *

ASCETICISM AND THE SPIRIT OF CAPITALISM

[I]f that God, whose hand the Puritan sees in all the occurrences of life, shows one of His elect a chance of profit, he must do it with a purpose. Hence the faithful Christian must follow the call by taking advantage of the opportunity. "If

God show you a way in which you may lawfully get more than in another way (without wrong to your soul or to any other), if you refuse this, and choose the less gainful way, you cross one of the ends of your calling, and you refuse to be God's steward, and to accept His gifts and use them for Him when He requireth it: you may labour to be rich for God, though not for the flesh and sin."[‡]

* * *

Wealth is thus bad ethically only in so far as it is a temptation to idleness and sinful enjoyment of life, and its acquisition is bad only when it is with the purpose of later living merrily and without care. But as a performance of duty in a calling it is not only morally permissible, but actually enjoined. The parable of the servant who was rejected because he did not increase the talent which was entrusted to him seemed to say so directly. To wish to be poor was, it was often argued, the same as wishing to be unhealthy; it is objectionable as a glorification of works and derogatory to the glory of God. Especially begging, on the part of one able to work, is not only the sin of slothfulness, but a violation of the duty of brotherly love according to the Apostle's own word.

The emphasis on the ascetic importance of a fixed calling provided an ethical justification of the modern specialized division of labour. In a similar way the providential interpretation of profit-making justified the activities of the business man. * * * But, on the other hand, it has the highest ethical appreciation of the sober, middle-class, self-made man. "God blesseth His trade" is a stock remark about those good men who had successfully followed the divine hints.

* * *

Let us now try to clarify the points in which the Puritan idea of the calling and the premium it placed upon ascetic conduct was bound directly to influence the development of a capitalistic way of life. As we have seen, this asceticism turned with all its force against one thing: the spontaneous enjoyment of life and all it had to offer.

* * *

As against this the Puritans upheld their decisive characteristic, the principle of ascetic conduct. For otherwise the Puritan aversion to sport, even for the Quakers, was by no means simply one of principle. Sport was accepted if it served a rational purpose, that of recreation necessary for physical efficiency. But as a means for the spontaneous expression of undisciplined impulses, it was under suspicion; and in so far as it became purely a means of enjoyment, or awakened pride, raw instincts or the irrational gambling instinct, it was of course strictly condemned. Impulsive enjoyment of life, which leads away both from work in a calling and from religion, was as such the enemy.

* * *

[‡]Richard Baxter, Nonconformist (Puritan) scholar, 1615–1691. [*Editor's note*].

436 ■ MAX WEBER

Man is only a trustee of the goods which have come to him through God's grace. He must, like the servant in the parable, give an account of every penny entrusted to him, and it is at least hazardous to spend any of it for a purpose which does not serve the glory of God but only one's own enjoyment. What person, who keeps his eyes open, has not met representatives of this viewpoint even in the present? The idea of a man's duty to his possessions, to which he subordinates himself as an obedient steward, or even as an acquisitive machine, bears with chilling weight on his life. The greater the possessions the heavier, if the ascetic attitude toward life stands the test, the feeling of responsibility for them, for holding them undiminished for the glory of God and increasing them by restless effort. The origin of this type of life also extends in certain roots, like so many aspects of the spirit of capitalism, back into the Middle Ages. But it was in the ethic of ascetic Protestantism that it first found a consistent ethical foundation. Its significance for the development of capitalism is obvious.

This worldly Protestant asceticism, as we may recapitulate up to this point, acted powerfully against the spontaneous enjoyment of possessions; it restricted consumption, especially of luxuries. On the other hand, it had the psychological effect of freeing the acquisition of goods from the inhibitions of traditionalistic ethics. It broke the bonds of the impulse of acquisition in that it not only legalized it, but (in the sense discussed) looked upon it as directly willed by God. The campaign against the temptations of the flesh, and the dependence on external things, was, as besides the Puritans the great Quaker apologist Barclay expressly says, not a struggle against the rational acquisition, but against the irrational use of wealth.

* * *

On the side of the production of private wealth, asceticism condemned both dishonesty and impulsive avarice. What was condemned as covetousness, Mammonism, etc., was the pursuit of riches for their own sake. For wealth in itself was a temptation. But here asceticism was the power "which ever seeks the good but ever creates evil"; what was evil in its sense was possession and its temptations. For, in conformity with the Old Testament and in analogy to the ethical valuation of good works, asceticism looked upon the pursuit of wealth as an end in itself as highly reprehensible; but the attainment of it as a fruit of labour in a calling was a sign of God's blessing. And even more important: the religious valuation of restless, continuous, systematic work in a worldly calling, as the highest means to asceticism, and at the same time the surest and most evident proof of rebirth and genuine faith, must have been the most powerful conceivable lever for the expansion of that attitude toward life which we have here called the spirit of capitalism.

When the limitation of consumption is combined with this release of acquisitive activity, the inevitable practical result is obvious: accumulation of capital through ascetic compulsion to save. The restraints which were imposed upon the consumption of wealth naturally served to increase it by making possible the productive investment of capital.

* * *

As far as the influence of the Puritan outlook extended, under all circumstances—and this is, of course, much more important than the mere encouragement of capital accumulation—it favoured the development of a rational bourgeois economic life; it was the most important, and above all the only consistent influence in the development of that life. It stood at the cradle of the modern economic man.

* * *

THE SPIRIT OF CAPITALISM TODAY

At present under our individualistic political, legal, and economic institutions, with the forms of organization and general structure which are peculiar to our economic order, this spirit of capitalism might be understandable, as has been said, purely as a result of adaptation. The capitalistic system so needs this devotion to the calling of making money, it is an attitude toward material goods which is so well suited to that system, so intimately bound up with the conditions of survival in the economic struggle for existence, that there can today no longer be any question of a necessary connection of that acquisitive manner of life with any single *Weltanschauung*. In fact, it no longer needs the support of any religious forces, and feels the attempts of religion to influence economic life, in so far as they can still be felt at all, to be as much an unjustified interference as its regulation by the State. In such circumstances men's commercial and social interests do tend to determine their opinions and attitudes. Whoever does not adapt his manner of life to the conditions of capitalistic success must go under, or at least cannot rise. But these are phenomena of a time in which modern capitalism has become dominant and has become emancipated from its old supports.

The Puritan wanted to work in a calling; we are forced to do so. For when asceticism was carried out of monastic cells into everyday life, and began to dominate worldly morality, it did its part in building the tremendous cosmos of the modern economic order. This order is now bound to the technical and economic conditions of machine production which to-day determine the lives of all the individuals who are born into this mechanism, not only those directly concerned with economic acquisition, with irresistible force. Perhaps it will so determine them until the last ton of fossilized coal is burnt. In Baxter's view the care for external goods should only lie on the shoulders of the "saint like a light cloak, which can be thrown aside at any moment." But fate decreed that the cloak should become an iron cage.

Since asceticism undertook to remodel the world and to work out its ideals in the world, material goods have gained an increasing and finally an inexorable power over the lives of men as at no previous period in history. To-day the spirit of religious asceticism—whether finally, who knows?—has escaped from the cage. But victorious capitalism, since it rests on mechanical foundations, needs its [asceticism's] support no longer. The rosy blush of its laughing heir, the Enlightenment, seems also to be irretrievably fading, and the idea of duty in one's calling prowls about in our lives like the ghost of dead religious beliefs. Where the fulfilment of the calling cannot directly be related to the highest spiritual and cultural values, or when, on the other hand, it need not be felt simply as economic compulsion, the individual generally abandons the attempt to justify it at all. In the field of its highest development, in the United States, the pursuit of wealth, stripped of its religious and ethical meaning, tends to become associated with purely mundane passions, which often actually give it the character of sport.

No one knows who will live in this cage in the future, or whether at the end of this tremendous development entirely new prophets will arise, or there will be a great rebirth of old ideas and ideals, or, if neither, mechanized petrification, embellished with a sort of convulsive self-importance. For of the last stage of this cultural development, it might well be truly said: "Specialists without spirit, sensualists without heart; this nullity imagines that it has attained a level of civilization never before achieved."

41

The Emotional Geography of Work and Family Life

FROM *The Time Bind: When Work Becomes Home and Home Becomes Work*

ARLIE RUSSELL HOCHSCHILD

In the past two decades Americans who are employed full-time are working more and more hours, despite their support for "family values" and a belief that parents need to spend more time with their children. The apparent contradiction is addressed by Arlie Hochschild in this essay that preceded her book The Time Bind. *On the basis of fieldwork with many working parents, she provides an analysis of how people manage both their time and emotions. This leads to some interesting insights about the possible future of work and family.*

Over the last two decades, American workers have increasingly divided into a majority who work too many hours and a minority with no work at all. This split hurts families at both extremes, but I focus here on the growing scarcity of time among the long-hours majority. For many of them, a speed-up at the office and factory has marginalized life at home, so that the very term "work-family balance" seems to them a bland slogan with little bearing on real life. In this chapter, I describe the speed-up and review a range of cultural responses to it, including "family-friendly reforms" such as flextime, job sharing, part time work and parental leave. Why, I ask, do people not resist the speed-up more than they do? When offered these reforms, why don't more take advantage of them? Drawing upon my ongoing research in an American Fortune 500 company, I argue that a company's "family-friendly" policy goes only as deep as the "emotional geography" of the workplace and home, the drawn and redrawn boundaries between the sacred and the profane. I show how ways of talking about time (for example, separating "quality" from "quantity" time) become code words to describe that emotional geography. * * *

A WORK-FAMILY SPEED-UP

Three factors are creating the current speedup in work and family life in the United States. (By the term "family," I refer to committed unmarried couples, same-sex couples, single mothers, two-job couples and wage-earner-housewife couples. My focus is on all families who raise children.) First of all, increasing numbers of mothers now work outside the home. In 1950, 22 per cent of American mothers of children eighteen and under worked for pay; in 1991, 67 per cent did. Half of the mothers of children age one year and younger work for pay.

Second, they work in jobs which generally lack flexibility. The very model of "a job" and "career" has been based, for the most part, on the model of a traditional man whose wife cared for the children at home. Third, over the last 20 years, both women and men have increased their hours of work. In her book *The Overworked American*, the economist Juliet Schor argues that over the last two decades American workers have added an extra 164 hours to their year's work—an extra month of work a year. Compared to 20 years ago, workers take fewer unpaid absences, and even fewer *paid* ones. Over the last decade, vacations have shortened by 14 per cent. The number of families eating evening meals together has dropped by 10 per cent. Counting overtime and commuting time, a 1992 national sample of men averaged 48.8 hours of work, and women, 41.7. Among young parents, close to half now work more than 8 hours a day. Compared to the 1970s, mothers take less time off for the birth of a child and are more likely to work through the summer. They are more likely to work continuously until they retire at age 65. Thus, whether they have children or not, women increasingly fit the profile of year-round, lifelong paid workers, a profile that has long characterized men. Meanwhile, male workers have not reduced their hours but, instead, expanded them.

Not all working parents with more free time will spend it at home tending children or elderly relatives. Nor, needless to say, if parents do spend time at home, will all their children find them kind, helpful and fun. But without a chance for more time at home, the issue of using it well does not arise at all.

COOL MODERN, TRADITIONAL, WARM MODERN STANCES TOWARD THE SPEED-UP

Do the speed-up people think the speed-up is a problem? Does anybody else? If so, what cultural stances toward gender equity, family life and capitalism underlie the practical solutions they favor? If we explore recent writing on the hurried life of a working parent, we can discern three stances toward it.

One is a *cool modern* stance, according to which the speed-up has become "normal," even fashionable. Decline in time at home does not "marginalize" family life, proponents say, it makes it different, even better. Like many other popular self-help books addressed to the busy working mother, *The Superwoman Syndrome*, by Marjorie Schaevitz, offers busy mothers tips on how to fend off appeals for help from neighbors, relatives, friends, and how to stop feeling guilty about their mothering. It instructs the mother how to frugally measure out minutes of "quality time" for her children and abandons as hopeless the project of getting men more involved at home. Such books call for no changes in the workplace, no changes in the culture and no change in men. The solution to rationalization at work is rationalization at home. Tacitly such books accept the corrosive effects of global capitalism on family life and on the very notion of what people need to be happy and fulfilled.

A second stance toward the work-family speed-up is traditional in that it calls for women's return to the home, or quasi-traditional in that it acquiesces to a secondary role, a lower rank "mommy track," for women at work. Those who take this sort of stance acknowledge the speed-up as a problem but deny the fact that most women now have to work, want to work, and embrace the concept of gender equity. They essentialize different male and female "natures," and notions of time, for men and women—"industrial" time for men, and "family" time for women.

A third warm modern stance is both humane (the speed-up is a problem) and egalitarian (equity at home and work is a goal). Those who take this approach question the terms of employment—both through a nationwide program of worksharing, (as in Germany), a shorter working week, and through company-based family friendly reforms. What are these family-friendly reforms?

- flextime; a workday with flexible starting and quitting times, but usually 40 hours of work and the opportunity to "bank" hours at one time and reclaim them later;
- flexplace; home-based work, such as telecommuting;
- regular or permanent part-time; less than full-time work with full- or pro-rated benefits and promotional opportunities in proportion to one's skill and contribution;
- job sharing; two people voluntarily sharing one job with benefits and salary pro-rated;
- compressed working week; four 10-hour days with 3 days off, or three 12-hour days with 4 days off;
- paid parental leave;
- family obligations as a consideration in the allocation of shift work and required overtime.

Together, worksharing and this range of family-friendly reforms could spread work, increase worker control over hours, and create a "warm modern" world for women to be equal within. As political goals in America over the last 50 years, worksharing and a shorter working week have "died and gone to heaven" where they live on as Utopian ideals. In the 1990s, family-friendly reforms are the lesser offering on the capitalist bargaining table. But are companies in fact offering these reforms? Are working parents pressing for them?

The news is good and bad. Recent nationwide studies suggest that more and more American companies offer their workers family-friendly alternative work schedules. According to one recent study, 88 per cent of 188 companies surveyed offer part-time work, 77 per cent offer flextime of some sort, 48 per cent offer job-sharing, 35 per cent offer some form of flexplace, and 20 per cent offer a compressed working week. (But in most companies, the interested worker must seek and receive the approval of a supervisor or department head. Moreover, most policies do not apply to lower-level workers whose conditions of work are covered by union contracts.)

But even if offered, regardless of need, few workers actually take advantage of the reforms. One study of 384 companies noted that only nine companies reported even one father who took an official unpaid leave at the birth of his child. Few are on temporary or permanent part-time. Still fewer share a job.

* * *

INSIDE A FORTUNE 500 COMPANY

Why, when the opportunity presents itself, do so few working parents take it? To find out, 1 set about interviewing managers, and clerical and factory workers in a large manufacturing company in the northeastern United States— which I shall call, simply, the Company. I chose to study this Company because of its reputation as an especially progressive company. Over the last 15 years, for example, the Company devoted millions of dollars to informing workers of its family-friendly policies, hiring staff to train managers to implement them, making showcase promotions of workers who take extended maternity leaves or who work part-time. If change is to occur anywhere, I reasoned, it was likely to be within this Company.

But the first thing I discovered was that even in this enlightened Company, few young parents or workers tending elderly relatives took advantage of the chance to work more flexible or shorter hours. Among the 26,000 employees, the average working week ranged from 45 to 55 hours. Managers and factory workers often worked 50 or 60 hours a week while clerical workers tended to work a more normal, 40-hour, week. Everyone agreed the Company was a "pretty workaholic place." Moreover, for the last 5 years, hours of work had increased.

EXPLANATIONS THAT DON'T WORK

Perhaps workers shy away from applying for leaves or shortening their hours because they can't afford to earn less. This certainly explains why many young parents continue to work long hours. But it doesn't explain why the wealthiest workers, the managers and professionals, are among the least interested in additional time off. Even among the Company's factory workers, who in 1993 averaged between eleven and twelve dollars an hour, and who routinely competed for optional overtime, two 40-hour-a-week paychecks with no overtime work were quite enough to support the family. A substantial number said they could get by on one paycheck if they sold one of their cars, put in a vegetable garden and cut down on "extras." Yet, the overwhelming majority did not want to.

Perhaps, then, employees shied away from using flexible or shorter hour schedules because they were afraid of having their names higher on the list of workers who might be laid off in a period of economic downturn. Through the 1980s, a third of America's largest companies experienced some layoffs, though this did not happen to managers or clerical workers at this company.

By union contract, production workers were assured that layoffs, should they occur, would be made according to seniority and not according to any other criteria—such as how many hours an employee had worked. Yet, the workaholism went on. Employees in the most profitable sectors of the Company showed no greater tendency to ask for shorter or more flexible hours for family reasons than employees in the least profitable sectors.

Is it, then, that workers who could afford shorter hours didn't *know* about the Company's family-friendly policies? No. All of the 130 working parents I spoke with had heard about alternative schedules and knew where they could find out more.

Perhaps the explanation lies not with the workers but with their managers. Managers responsible for implementing family-friendly policies may be openly or covertly undermining them. Even though Company policy allowed flexibility, the head of a division could, for reasons of production, openly refuse a worker permission to go part-time or to job-share, which some did. For example, when asked about his views on flextime, the head of the engineering division of the Company replied flatly, "My policy on flextime is that there is no flextime." Other apparently permissive division heads had supervisors who were tough on this issue "for them." Thus, there seemed to be some truth to this explanation for why so few workers stepped forward.

But even managers known to be cooperative had few employees asking for alternative schedules. Perhaps, then, workers ask for time off, but do so "off the books." To some extent, this "off the books" hypothesis did hold, especially for new fathers who may take a few days to a week of sick leave for the birth of a baby instead of filing for "parental leave," which they feared would mark them as unserious workers.

Even counting informal leaves, most women managers returned to full-time 40- to 55-hour work schedules fairly soon after their 6 weeks of paid maternity leave. Across ranks, most women secretaries returned after 6 months; most women production workers returned after 6 weeks. Most new fathers took a few days off at most. Thus, even "off the books," working parents used very little of the opportunity to spend more time at home.

Far more important than all these factors seemed to be a company "speed-up" in response to global competition. In the early years of the 1990s, workers each year spoke of working longer hours than they had the year before, a trend seen nationwide. When asked why, they explained that the Company was trying to "reduce costs," in part by asking employees to do more than they were doing before.

But the sheer existence of a company speed-up doesn't explain why employees weren't trying to actively resist it, why there wasn't much back-talk. Parents were eager to tell me how their families came first, how they were clear about that. (National polls show that next to a belief in God, Americans most strongly believe in "the family.") But, practices that might express this belief—such as sharing breakfast and dinner—were shifting in the opposite direction. In the minds of many parents of young children, warm modern intentions seemed curiously, casually, fused with cool modern ideas and practices. In some ways, those within the work-family speed-up don't seem to want to slow down. . . .

WORK AND FAMILY AS EMOTIONAL CULTURES

Through its family-friendly reforms, the Company had earned a national reputation as a desirable family-friendly employer. But at the same time, it wasn't inconvenienced by having to arrange alternate schedules for very many employees. One can understand how this might benefit a company. But how about the working parents?

For the answer, we may need a better grasp of the emotional cultures, and the relative "draw" of work and family. Instead of thinking of the workplace or the family as unyielding thing-like structures, Anthony Giddens suggests that we see structures as fluid and changeable. "Structuration," Giddens, [author of *New Rules of Sociological Method*] tells us, is the "dynamic process whereby structures come into being." For structures to change, there must be changes in what people do. But in doing what they do, people unconsciously draw on resources, and depend on larger conditions to develop the skills they use to change what they do.

With this starting point, then, let us note that structures come with—and also "are"—emotional cultures. A change in structure requires a change in emotional culture. What we lack, so far, is a vocabulary for describing this culture, and what follows is a crude attempt to create one. An emotional culture is a set of rituals, beliefs about feelings and rules governing feeling which induce emotional focus, and even a sense of the "sacred." This sense of the sacred selects and favors some social bonds over others. It selects and reselects relationships into a core or periphery of family life.

Thus, families have a more or less *sacred core* of private rituals and shared meanings. In some families what is most sacred is sexuality and marital communication (back rubs, pillow talk, sex), and in other families the "sacred" is reserved for parental bonds (bedtime cuddles with children, bathtime, meals, parental talk about children). In addition, families have secondary zones of less important daily, weekly, seasonal rituals which back up the core rituals. They also have a profane outer layer, in which members might describe themselves as "doing nothing in particular"—doing chores, watching television, sleeping. The character and boundaries of the sacred and profane aspects of family life are in the eye of the beholder. "Strong families" with "thick ties" can base their sense of the sacred on very different animating ideas and practices. Families also differ widely on how much one member's sense of the sacred matches another's and on how much it is the occasion for expressing harmony or conflict. Furthermore, families creatively adapt to new circumstances by ritualizing new activities—for example, couples in commuter marriages may "ritualize" the phone call or the daily e-mail exchange. Couples with "too much time together" may de-ritualize meals, sex, or family events. Furthermore, families have different structures of sacredness. Some have thick actual cores and thin peripheries, others have a porous core and extensive peripheral time in which people just "hang out." But in each case, emotional culture shapes the experience of family life.

Emotional cultures stand back-to-back with ideas about time. In the context of the work—family speed-up, many people speak of actively "managing time, finding time, making time, guarding time, or fighting for time." Less do they speak of simply "having" or "not having" time. In their attempt to take a more active grip on their schedules, many working parents turn a telephone answering machine on at dinner, turn down work assignments and social engagements, and actively fight to defend "family time."

One's talk about time is itself a verbal practice that does or doesn't reaffirm the ritual core of family life. In the core of family life, we may speak more of living in the moment. Because a sacred activity is an end in itself, and not a means to an end, the topic of time is less likely to arise. If it does, one speaks of "enjoying time," or "devoting time." With the work-family speed-up, the term "quality time" has arisen, as in "I need more quality time with my daughter," a term referring to freedom from distraction, time spent in an attitude of intense focus. In general, we try to "make" time for core family life because we feel it matters more.

In the intermediate and peripheral zones of family life, we may speak of "having time on our hands, wasting or killing time." In the new lexicon, we speak of "quantity time." In general, we feel we can give up peripheral time, because it matters less. More hotly contested is the time to participate in a child's school events, help at the school auction, buy a birthday gift for a baby-sitter, or call an elderly neighbor.

With a decline in this periphery, the threads of reciprocity in the community and neighborhood grow weaker. By forcing families to cut out what is "least important," the speed-up thins out and weakens ties that bind it to society. Thus, under the press of the "speed-up," families are forced to give up their periphery ties with neighbors, distant relatives, bonds sustained by "extra time." The speed-up privatizes the family. The "neighborhood goes to work," where it serves the emotional interests of the workplace. Where are one's friends? At work.

Although the family in modern society is separated from the workplace, its emotional culture is ecologically linked to and drawn from it. Both the family and workplace are also linked to supportive realms. For the family, this often includes the neighborhood, the church, the school. For the workplace, this includes the pub, the golf club, the commuter van friendship network. A loss of supportive structure around the family may result in a gain for the workplace, and vice versa. Insofar as the "periphery" of family life protected its ritual core, to a certain degree for working parents these ties are not so peripheral at all.

A gender pattern is clear. Because most women now must and for the most part want to work outside the home, they are performing family rituals less. At the same time, men are not doing them very much more. Together, these two facts result in a net loss in ritual life at home.

At the same time, at some workplaces, an alternative cultural magnet is drawing on the human need for a center, a ritual core. As family life becomes deritualized, in certain sectors of the economy, the engineers of corporate cultures are re-ritualizing the workplace. Thus, the contraction of emotional culture at home is linked to a socially engineered expansion of emotional culture at work.

WORK LIKE A FAMILY, AND FAMILY, FOR SOME, LIKE WORK

At a certain point, change in enough personal stories can be described as a change in culture, and I believe many families at the Company are coming to this turning point now. Pulled toward work by one set of forces and propelled from the family by another set of forces, a growing number of workers are unwittingly altering the twin cultures of work and family. As the cultural shield surrounding work has grown stronger, the supportive cultural shield surrounding the family has weakened. Fewer neighborhood "consultants" talk to one when trouble arises at home, and for some, they are more to help out with problems at work.

* * *

THE MODEL OF FAMILY AS A HAVEN IN A HEARTLESS WORLD[1]

When I entered the field, I assumed that working parents would *want* more time at home. I imagined that they experienced home as a place where they could relax, feel emotionally sheltered and appreciated for who they "really are." I imagined home to feel to the weary worker like the place where he or

---

1. This refers to Christopher Lasch's examination of the American family in his book *Haven in a Heartless World*. [*Editor's note*].

she could take off a uniform, put on a bathrobe, have a beer, exhale—a picture summed up in the image of the worker coming in the door saying, "Hi honey, I'm home!." To be sure, home life has its emergencies and strains but I imagined that home was the place people thought about when they thought about rest, safety and appreciation. Given this, they would want to maximize time at home, especially time with their children. I also assumed that these working parents would not feel particularly relaxed, safe or appreciated at work, at least not more so than at home, and especially not factory workers.

When I interviewed workers at the Company, however, a picture emerged which partly belied this model of family life. For example, one 30-year-old factory shift supervisor, a remarried mother of two, described her return home after work in this way:

> I walk in the door and the minute I turn the key in the lock my oldest daughter is there. Granted she needs somebody to talk to about her day. The baby is still up . . . she should have been in bed two hours ago and that upsets me. The oldest comes right up to the door and complains about anything her father said or did during the evening. She talks about her job. My husband is in the other room hollering to my daughter, "Tracy, I don't ever get no time to talk to your mother because you're always monopolizing her time first before I even get a chance!" They all come at me at once.

The unarbitrated quarrels, the dirty dishes, and the urgency of other people's demands she finds at home contrast with her account of going to work:

> I usually come to work early just to get away from the house. I go to be there at a quarter after the hour and people are there waiting. We sit. We talk. We joke. I let them know what is going on, who has to be where, what changes I have made for the shift that day. We sit there and chitchat for five or ten minutes. There is laughing. There is joking. There is fun. They aren't putting me down for any reason. Everything is done in humour and fun from beginning to end. It can get stressful, though, when a machine malfunctions and you can't get the production out.

Another 38-year-old working mother of two, also a factory worker, had this to say:

> My husband is a great help (with caring for their son). But as far as doing housework, or even taking the baby when I'm at home, no. When I'm home, our son becomes my job. He figures he works five days a week, he's not going to come home and clean. But he doesn't stop to think that I work seven days a week. . . . Why should I have to come home and do the housework without help from anybody else? My husband and I have been through this over and over again. Even if he would pack up the kitchen table and stack the dishes for me when I'm at

work, that would make a big difference. He does nothing. On his weekends off, I have to provide a sitter for the baby so he can go fishing. When I have my day off, I have the baby all day long. He'll help out if I'm not here . . . the minute I'm here he lets me do the work.

To this working mother, her family was not a haven, a zone of relief and relaxation. It was a workplace. More than that, she could only get relief from this domestic workplace by going to the factory. As she continued:

I take a lot of overtime. The more I get out of the house, the better I am. It's a terrible thing to say, but that's the way I feel!

I assumed that work would feel to workers like a place in which one could be fired at the whim of a profit-hungry employer, while in the family, for all its hassles, one was safe. Based as it is on the impersonal mechanism of supply and demand, profit and loss, work would feel insecure, like being in "a jungle." In fact, many workers I interviewed had worked for the Company for 20 years or more. But they were on their second or third marriages. To these employed, *work* was their rock, their major source of security, while they were receiving their "pink slips" at home.

To be sure, most workers *wanted* to base their sense of stability at home, and many did. But I was also struck by the loyalty many felt toward the Company and a loyalty *they felt* coming from it, despite what might seem like evidence to the contrary—the speed-up, the restructuring. When problems arose at work, many workers felt they could go to their supervisors or to a human resources worker and resolve it. If one division of the Company was doing poorly, the Company might "de-hire" workers within that division and rehire in a more prosperous division. This happened to one female engineer, very much upsetting her, but her response to it was telling:

I have done very well in the Company for twelve years, and I thought my boss thought very highly of me. He'd said as much. So when our division went down and several of us were de-hired, we were told to look for another position within the Company *or* outside. I thought, "Oh my God, *outside!*" I was stunned! Later, in the new division it was like a remarriage. . . . I wondered if I could love again.

Work was not always "there for you," but increasingly "home," as they had known it, wasn't either. As one woman recounted, "One day my husband came home and told me, 'I've fallen in love with a woman at work. . . . I want a divorce.'"

Finally, the model of family-as-haven led me to assume that the individual would feel most known and appreciated at home and least so at work. Work might be where they felt unappreciated, "a cog in the machine"—an image brought to mind by the Charlie Chaplin classic film on factory life, *Modern Times.*

But the factory is no longer the archetypical workplace and, sadly, many workers felt more appreciated for what they were doing at work than for what they were doing at home. For example, when I asked one 40-year-old technician whether he felt more appreciated at home or at work, he said:

> I love my family. I put my family first . . . but I'm not sure I feel more appreciated by them (laughs). My 14-year-old son doesn't talk too much to anyone when he gets home from school. He's a brooder. I don't know-how good I've been as a father . . . we fix cars together on Saturday. My wife works opposite shifts to what I work, so we don't see each other except on weekends. We need more time together—need to get out to the lake more. I don't know. . . .

This worker seemed to feel better about his skill repairing machines in the factory than his way of relating to his son. This is not as unusual as it might seem. In a large-scale study, Arthur Emlen found that 59 per cent of employees rated their family performance "good or unusually good" while 86 per cent gave a similar rating to their performance on the job.

This overall cultural shift may account for why many workers are going along with the work-family speed-up and not joining the resistance against it. A 1993 nationally representative study of 3400 workers conducted by the Families and Work Institute reflects two quite contradictory findings. On one hand, the study reports that 80 per cent of workers feel their jobs require "working very hard" and 42 per cent "often feel used up by the end of the work day." On the other hand, when workers are asked to compare how much time and energy they *actually* devoted to their family, their job or career and themselves, with how much time they would *like* to devote to each, there was little difference. Workers estimate that they actually spend 43 per cent of their time and energy on family and friends, 37 per cent on job or career, and 20 per cent on themselves. But they *want* to spend just about what they *are* spending—47 per cent on family and friends, 30 per cent on the job, and 23 per cent on themselves. Thus, the workers I spoke to who were "giving" in to the work-family speed-up may be typical of a wider trend.

CAUSAL MECHANISMS

Three sets of factors may exacerbate this reversal of family and work cultures; trends in the family, trends at work, and a cultural consumerism which reinforces trends in the family and work.

First, half of marriages in America end in divorce—the highest divorce rate in the world. Because of the greater complexity of family life, the emotional skills of parenting, woefully underestimated to begin with, are more important than ever before. Many workers spoke with feeling about strained relationships with stepchildren and ex-wives or husbands. New in scope, too, are the numbers of working wives who work "two shifts," one at home and one at work, and face their husband's resistance to helping fully with the load at home—a strain that often leaves both spouses feeling unappreciated.

Second, another set of factors apply at work. Many corporations have emotionally engineered for top and upper middle managers a world of friendly ritual and positive reinforcement. New corporate cultures call for "valuing the individual" and honoring the "internal customer" (so that requests made by employees within the Company are honored as highly as those by customers outside the Company). Human relations employees give seminars on human problems at work. High-performance teams, based on co-operation between relative equals who "manage themselves," tend to foster intense relations at work. The Company frequently gives out awards for outstanding work at award ceremonies. Compliments run freely. The halls are hung with new plaques praising one or another worker on recent accomplishments. Recognition luncheons, department gatherings and informal birthday remembrances are common. Career planning sessions with one's supervisor, team meetings to talk over "modeling, work relations, and mentoring" with co-workers all verge on, even as they borrow from, psychotherapy. For all its aggravation and tensions, the workplace is where quite a few workers feel appreciated, honored, and where they have real friends. By contrast, at home there are fewer "award ceremonies" and little helpful feedback about mistakes.

In addition, courtship and mate selection, earlier more or less confined to the home-based community, may be moving into the sphere of work. The later age for marriage, the higher proportion of unmarried people, and the high divorce rate all create an ever-replenishing courtship pool at work. The gender desegregation of the workplace, and the lengthened working day also provide opportunity for people to meet and develop romantic or quasi-romantic ties. At the factory, romance may develop in the lunchroom, pub, or parking lot; and for upper management levels, at conferences, in "fantasy settings" in hotels and dimly lit restaurants.

In a previous era, an undetermined number of men escaped the house for the pub, the fishing hole, and often the office. A common pattern, to quote from the title of an article by Jean Duncombe and Dennis Marsden, was that of "workaholic men" and "whining women." Now that women compose 45 percent of the American labor force and come home to a "second shift" of work at home, some women are escaping into work too—and as they do so, altering the cultures of work and home.

Forces pulling workers out of family life and into the workplace are set into perpetual motion by consumerism. Consumerism acts as a mechanism which maintains the emotional reversal of work and family. Exposed to advertisements, workers expand their material "needs." To buy what they now "need," they need money. To earn money, they work longer hours. Being away from home so many hours, they make up for their absence at home with gifts which cost money. They "materialize" love. And so the cycle continues.

Once work begins to become a more compelling arena of appreciation than home, a self-fulfilling prophecy takes hold. For, if workers flee into work from the tensions at home, tensions at home often grow worse. The worse the tensions at home, the firmer the grip of the workplace on the worker's human needs, and hence the escalation of the entire syndrome.

If more workers conceive of work as a haven, it is overwhelmingly in some sense *against their wishes*. Most workers in this and other studies say they value family life above all. Work is what they do. Family is why they live. So, I believe the logic I have described proceeds despite, not because of, the powerful intentions and deepest wishes of those in its grip.

MODELS OF FAMILY AND WORK IN THE FLIGHT PLAN OF CAPITALISM

To sum up, for some people work may be becoming more like family, and family life more like work. Instead of the model of the *family* as haven from work, more of us fit the model of *work* as haven from home. In this model, the tired parent leaves a world of unresolved quarrels, unwashed laundry and dirty dishes for the atmosphere of engineered cheer, appreciation and harmony at work. It is at work that one drops the job of *working* on relating to a brooding adolescent, an obstreperous toddler, rivaling siblings or a retreating spouse. At last, beyond the emotional shield of work, one says not, "Hi honey, I'm home," but "Hi fellas, I'm here!" For those who fit this model, the ritual core of family life is not simply smaller, it is less of a ritual core.

How extensive is this trend? I suspect it is a slight tendency in the lives of many working parents, and the basic reality for a small but growing minority. This trend holds for some people more than others and in some parts of society more than in others. Certain trends—such as the growth of the contingency labor force[2]—may increase the importance of the family, and tend toward reinstalling the model of family as haven, and work as "heartless world." A growing rate of unemployment might be associated with yet a third "double-negative" model according to which neither home nor work are emotional bases, but rather the gang at the pub, or on the street.

But the sense of sacred that we presume to be reliably attached to home may be more vulnerable than we might wish.

Most working parents more deeply want, or want to want, a fourth, "double-positive" model of work-family balance. In the end, these four patterns are unevenly spread over the class structure—the "haven in a heartless world" more at the top, the "double-negative" more at the bottom, the "reverse-haven" emerging in the middle.

---

2. The contingency labor force is those employees who work on a short-term contractual basis or are hired as temporary workers. [*Editor's note*].

Each pattern of work and family life is to be seen somewhere in the flight plan of late capitalism. For, capitalist competition is not simply a matter of market expansion around the globe, but of local geographies of emotion at home. The challenge, as I see it, is to understand the close links between economic trends, emotional geographies, and pockets of cultural resistance. For it is in those pockets that we can look for "warm modern" answers.

42

The McDonald's System

FROM *The McDonaldization of Society*

GEORGE RITZER

McDonald's has become a buzzword not only for fast food but for a way of organizing activities, calculated to maximize efficiency by minimizing opportunities for error. For some this is wonderful, but for others this is lifeless and without joy, despite the images that appear in McDonald's commercials. Ultimately, it may not be as efficient as it seems.

THE DIMENSIONS OF MCDONALDIZATION: FROM DRIVE-THROUGHS TO UNCOMFORTABLE SEATS

Even if some domains are able to resist McDonaldization, this book intends to demonstrate that many other aspects of society are being, or will be, McDonaldized. This raises the issue of why the McDonald's model has proven so irresistible. Four basic and alluring dimensions lie at the heart of the success of the McDonald's model and, more generally, of the process of McDonaldization.

First, McDonald's offers *efficiency*. That is, the McDonald's system offers us the optimum method for getting from one point to another. Most generally, this means that McDonald's proffers the best available means of getting us from a state of being hungry to a state of being full. * * * Other institutions, fashioned on the McDonald's model, offer us similar efficiency in losing weight, lubricating our cars, filling eyeglass prescriptions, or completing income tax forms. In a fast-paced society in which both parents are likely to work, or where there may be only a single parent, efficiently satisfying the hunger and many other needs of people is very attractive. In a highly mobile society in which people are rushing, usually by car, from one spot to another, the efficiency of a fast-food meal, perhaps without leaving one's car while passing by the drive-through window, often proves impossible to resist. The fast-food model offers us, or at least appears to offer us, an efficient method for satisfying many of our needs.

Second, McDonald's offers us food and service that can be easily *quantified* and *calculated*. In effect, McDonald's seems to offer us "more bang for the buck." (One of its recent innovations, in response to the growth of other fast-food franchises, is to proffer "value meals" at discounted prices.) We often feel that we are getting a *lot* of food for a modest amount of money. Quantity has become equivalent to quality; a lot of something means it must be good.

As two observers of contemporary American culture put it, "As a culture, we tend to believe—deeply—that in general 'bigger is better.'" Thus, we order the *Quarter Pounder*, the *Big* Mac, the *large* fries. We can quantify all of these things and feel that we are getting a lot of food, and, in return, we appear to be shelling out only a nominal sum of money. This calculus, of course, ignores an important point: the mushrooming of fast-food outlets, and the spread of the model to many other businesses, indicates that our calculation is illusory and it is the owners who are getting the best of the deal.

There is another kind of calculation involved in the success of McDonald's—a calculation involving time. People often, at least implicitly, calculate how much time it will take them to drive to McDonald's, eat their food, and return home and then compare that interval to the amount of time required to prepare the food at home. They often conclude, rightly or wrongly, that it will take less time to go and eat at the fast-food restaurant than to eat at home. This time calculation is a key factor in the success of Domino's and other home-delivery franchises, because to patronize them people do not even need to leave their homes. To take another notable example, Lens Crafters promises us "Glasses fast, glasses in one hour." Some McDonaldized institutions have come to combine the emphases on time and money. Domino's promises pizza delivery in one-half hour, *or* the pizza is free. Pizza Hut will serve us a personal pan pizza in five minutes, or it, too, will be free.

Third, McDonald's offers us *predictability*. We know that the Egg McMuffin we eat in New York will be, for all intents and purposes, identical to those we have eaten in Chicago and Los Angeles. We also know that the one we order next week or next year will be identical to the one we eat today. There is great comfort in knowing that McDonald's offers no surprises, that the food we eat at one time or in one place will be identical to the food we eat at another time or in another place. We know that the next Egg McMuffin we eat will not be awful, but we also know that it will not be exceptionally delicious. The success of the McDonald's model indicates that many people have come to prefer a world in which there are no surprises.

Fourth and finally, *control*, especially through the *substitution of non-human for human technology*, is exerted over the human beings who enter the world of McDonald's. The humans who work in fast-food restaurants are trained to do a very limited number of things in precisely the way they are told to do them. Managers and inspectors make sure that workers toe the line. The human beings who eat in fast-food restaurants are also controlled, albeit (usually) more subtly and indirectly. Lines, limited menus, few options, and uncomfortable seats all lead diners to do what the management wishes them to do—eat quickly and leave. Further, the drive-through (and in some cases walk-through) window leads diners to first leave and then eat rapidly. This attribute has most recently been extended by the Domino's model, according to which customers are expected to *never* come, yet still eat speedily.

McDonald's also controls people by using nonhuman technology to replace human workers. Human workers, no matter how well they are programmed and controlled, can foul up the operation of the system. A slow or indolent worker can make the preparation and delivery of a Big Mac inefficient. A worker who refuses to follow the rules can leave the pickles or special sauce off a hamburger, thereby making for unpredictability. And a distracted worker can put too few fries in the box, making an order of large fries seem awfully skimpy. For these and other reasons, McDonald's is compelled to steadily replace human beings with nonhuman technologies, such as the soft-drink dispenser that shuts itself off when the glass is full, the french-fry machine that rings when the fries are crisp, the preprogrammed cash register that eliminates the need for the cashier to calculate prices and amounts, and, perhaps at some future time, the robot capable of making hamburgers. (Experimental robots of this type already exist.) All of these technologies permit greater control over the human beings involved in the fast-food restaurant. The result is that McDonald's is able to reassure customers about the nature of the employee to be encountered and the nature of the service to be obtained.

In sum, McDonald's (and the McDonald's model) has succeeded because it offers the consumer efficiency and predictability, and because it seems to offer the diner a lot of food for little money and a slight expenditure of effort. It has also flourished because it has been able to exert greater control through non-human technologies over both employees and customers, leading them to behave the way the organization wishes them to. The substitution of non-human for human technologies has also allowed the fast-food restaurant to deliver its fare increasingly more efficiently and predictably. Thus, there are good, solid reasons why McDonald's has succeeded so phenomenally and why the process of McDonaldization continues unabated.

A CRITIQUE OF MCDONALDIZATION: THE IRRATIONALITY OF RATIONALITY

There is a downside to all of this. We can think of efficiency, predictability, calculability, and control through nonhuman technology as the basic components of a *rational* system. However, as we shall see in later chapters, rational systems often spawn irrationalities. The downside of McDonaldization will be dealt with most systematically under the heading of the *irrationality of rationality*. Another way of saying this is that rational systems serve to deny human reason; rational systems can be unreasonable.

For example, the fast-food restaurant is often a dehumanizing setting in which to eat or work. People lining up for a burger, or waiting in the drive-through line, often feel as if they are dining on an assembly line, and those who prepare the burgers often appear to be working on a burger assembly line. Assembly lines are hardly human settings in which to eat, and they have been shown to be inhuman settings in which to work. As we will see, dehumanization is only one of many ways in which the highly rationalized fast-food restaurant is extremely irrational.

Of course, the criticisms of the irrationality of the fast-food restaurant will be extended to all facets of our McDonaldizing world. This extension has recently been underscored and legitimated at the opening of Euro Disneyland outside Paris. A French socialist politician acknowledged the link between Disney and McDonald's as well as their common negative effects when he said that Euro Disney will "bombard France with uprooted creations that are to culture what fast food is to gastronomy."

Such critiques lead to a question: Is the headlong rush toward McDonaldization around the world advantageous or not? There are great gains to be made from McDonaldization, some of which will be discussed below. But there are also great costs and enormous risks, which this book will focus on. Ultimately, we must ask whether the creation of these rationalized systems creates an even greater number of irrationalities. At the minimum, we need to be aware of the costs associated with McDonaldization. McDonald's and other purveyors of the fast-food model spend billions of dollars each year outlining the benefits to be derived from their system. However, the critics of the system have few outlets for their ideas. There are no commercials on Saturday morning between cartoons warning children of the dangers associated with fast-food restaurants. Although few children are likely to read this book, it is aimed, at least in part, at their parents (or parents-to-be) in the hope that it will serve as a caution that might be passed on to their children.

A legitimate question may be raised about this analysis: Is this critique of McDonaldization animated by a romanticization of the past and an impossible desire to return to a world that no longer exists? For some critics, this is certainly the case. They remember the time when life was slower, less efficient, had more surprises, when people were freer, and when one was more likely to deal with a human being than a robot or a computer. Although they have a point, these critics have undoubtedly exaggerated the positive aspects of a world before McDonalds, and they have certainly tended to forget the liabilities associated with such a world. More importantly, they do not seem to realize that we are *not* returning to such a world. The increase in the number of people, the acceleration in technological change, the increasing pace of life—all this and more make it impossible to go back to a nonrationalized world, if it ever existed, of home-cooked meals, traditional restaurant dinners, high-quality foods, meals loaded with surprises, and restaurants populated only by workers free to fully express their creativity.

While one basis for a critique of McDonaldization is the past, another is the future. The future in this sense is what people have the potential to be if they are unfettered by the constraints of rational systems. This critique holds that people have the potential to be far more thoughtful, skillful, creative, and well-rounded than they now are, yet they are unable to express this potential because of the constraints of a rationalized world. If the world were less rationalized, or even derationalized, people would be better able to live up to their human potential. This critique is based not on what people were like in the past, but on what they could be like in the future, if only the constraints of McDonaldized systems were eliminated, or at least eased substantially. The criticisms to be put forth in this book are animated by the latter, future-oriented perspective rather than by a romanticization of the past and a desire to return to it.

THE ADVANTAGES OF MCDONALDIZATION : FROM THE CAJUN BAYOU TO SUBURBIA

Much of this book will focus on the negative side of McDonald's and McDonaldization. At this point it is important, however, to balance this view by mentioning some of the benefits of these systems and processes. The economic columnist, Robert Samuelson, for example, is a strong supporter of McDonald's and confesses to "openly worship McDonald's." He thinks of it as "the greatest restaurant chain in history." (However, Samuelson does recognize that there are those who "can't stand the food and regard McDonald's as the embodiment of all that is vulgar in American mass culture.")

Let me enumerate some of the advantages of the fast-food restaurant as well as other elements of our McDonaldized society:

- The fast-food restaurant has expanded the alternatives available to consumers. For example, more people now have ready access to Italian, Mexican, Chinese, and Cajun foods. A McDonaldized society is, in this sense, more egalitarian.
- The salad bar, which many fast-food restaurants and supermarkets now offer, enables people to make salads the way they want them.
- Microwave ovens and microwavable foods enable us to have dinner in minutes or even seconds.
- For those with a wide range of shopping needs, supermarkets and shopping malls are very efficient sites. Home shopping networks allow us to shop even more efficiently without ever leaving home.
- Today's high-tech, for-profit hospitals are likely to provide higher-quality medical care than their predecessors.
- We can receive almost instantaneous medical attention at our local, drive-in "McDoctors."
- Computerized phone systems (and "voice mail") allow people to do things that were impossible before, such as obtain a bank balance in the middle of the night or hear a report on what went on in their child's class during the day and what homework assignments were made. Similarly, automated bank teller machines allow people to obtain money any time of the day or night.

- Package tours permit large numbers of people to visit countries that they would otherwise not visit.
- Diet centers like Nutri/System allow people to lose weight in a carefully regulated and controlled system.
- The 24-second clock in professional basketball has enabled outstanding athletes such as Michael Jordan to more fully demonstrate their extraordinary talents.
- Recreational vehicles let the modern camper avoid excessive heat, rain, insects, and the like.
- Suburban tract houses have permitted large numbers of people to afford single-family homes.

CONCLUSION

The previous list gives the reader a sense not only of the advantages of McDonaldization but also of the range of phenomena that will be discussed under that heading throughout this book. In fact, such a wide range of phenomena will be discussed under the heading of McDonaldization that one is led to wonder: What isn't McDonaldized? Is McDonaldization the equivalent of modernity? Is everything contemporary McDonaldized?

While much of the world has been McDonaldized, it is possible to identify at least three aspects of contemporary society that have largely escaped McDonaldization. First, there are phenomena traceable to an earlier, "premodern" age that continue to exist within the modern world. A good example is the Mom and Pop grocery store. Second, there are recent creations that have come into existence, at least in part, as a reaction against McDonaldization. A good example is the boom in bed and breakfasts (B&Bs), which offer rooms in private homes with personalized attention and a homemade breakfast from the proprietor. People who are fed up with McDonaldized motel rooms in Holiday Inn or Motel 6 can instead stay in so-called B&Bs. Finally, some analysts believe that we have moved into a new, "postmodern" society and that aspects of that society are less rational than their predecessors. Thus, for example, in a postmodern society we witness the destruction of "modern" high-rise housing projects and their replacement with smaller, more livable communities. Thus, although it is ubiquitous, McDonaldization is *not* simply another term for contemporary society. There *is* more to the contemporary world than McDonaldization.

In discussing McDonaldization, we are *not* dealing with an all-or-nothing process. Things are not either McDonaldized or not McDonaldized. There are degrees of McDonaldization; it is a continuum. Some phenomena have been heavily McDonaldized, others moderately McDonaldized, and some only slightly McDonaldized. There are some phenomena that may have escaped McDonaldization completely. Fast-food restaurants, for example, have been heavily McDonaldized, universities moderately McDonaldized, and the Mom and Pop grocers mentioned earlier only slightly McDonaldized. It is difficult to think of social phenomena that have escaped McDonaldization totally, but I suppose there is local enterprise in Fiji that has been untouched by this process. In this context, McDonaldization thus represents a process—a process by which more and more social phenomena are being McDonaldized to an increasing degree.

Overall, the central thesis is that McDonald's represents a monumentally important development and the process that it has helped spawn, McDonaldization, is engulfing more and more sectors of society and areas of the world. It has yielded a number of benefits to society, but it also entails a considerable number of costs and risks.

Although the focus is on McDonald's and McDonaldization, it is important to realize that this system has important precursors in our recent history. * * * That is, McDonaldization is not something completely new, but rather its success has been based on its ability to bring together a series of earlier innovations. Among the most important precursors to McDonaldization are bureaucracy, scientific management, the assembly line, and the original McDonald brothers' hamburger stand.

43

Religious Community and American Individualism

FROM *Habits of the Heart: Individualism and Commitment in American Life*

ROBERT N. BELLAH, RICHARD MADSEN, WILLIAM M. SULLIVAN,
ANN SWIDLER, AND STEVEN M. TIPTON

Belief in God and regular church attendance are higher in the United States than in any other industrialized country. Americans are also very independent-minded and pride themselves on this. In this selection from one of sociology's most widely read studies, the authors explore the apparent contradiction between participating in a community of believers and deciding for oneself what to believe.

Religion is one of the most important of the many ways in which Americans "get involved" in the life of their community and society. Americans give more money and donate more time to religious bodies and religiously associated organizations than to all other voluntary associations put together. Some 40 percent of Americans attend religious services at least once a week (a much greater number than would be found in Western Europe or even Canada) and religious membership is around 60 percent of the total population.

In our research, we were interested in religion not in isolation but as part of the texture of private and public life in the United States. Although we seldom asked specifically about religion, time and again in our conversations, religion emerged as important to the people we were interviewing, as the national statistics just quoted would lead one to expect.

For some, religion is primarily a private matter having to do with family and local congregation. For others, it is private in one sense but also a primary vehicle for the expression of national and even global concerns. Though Americans overwhelmingly accept the doctrine of the separation of church and state, most of them believe, as they always have, that religion has an important role to play in the public realm.

* * *

THE LOCAL CONGREGATION [INVOLVEMENT AND INDEPENDENCE]

We may begin a closer examination of how religion operates in the lives of those to whom we talked by looking at the local congregation, which traditionally has a certain priority. The local church is a community of worship that contains within itself, in small, so to speak, the features of the larger church, and in some Protestant traditions can exist autonomously. The church as a community of worship is an adaptation of the Jewish synagogue. Both Jews and Christians view their communities as existing in a covenant relationship with God, and the Sabbath worship around which religious life centers is a celebration of that covenant. Worship calls to mind the story of the relationship of the community with God: how God brought his chosen people out of Egypt or gave his only begotten son for the salvation of mankind. Worship also reiterates the obligations that the community has undertaken, including the biblical insistence on justice and righteousness, and on love of God and neighbor, as well as the promises God has made that make it possible for the community to hope for the future. Though worship has its special times and places, especially on the Sabbath in the house of the Lord, it functions as a model or pattern for the whole of life. Through reminding the people of their relationship to God, it establishes patterns of character and virtue that should operate in economic and political life as well as in the context of worship. The community maintains itself as a community of memory, and the various religious traditions have somewhat different memories.

The very freedom, openness, and pluralism of American religious life makes this traditional pattern hard for Americans to understand. For one thing, the traditional pattern assumes a certain priority of the religious community over the individual. The community exists before the individual is born and will continue after his or her death. The relationship of the individual to God is ultimately personal, but it is mediated by the whole pattern of community life. There is a givenness about the community and the tradition. They are not normally a matter of individual choice.

For Americans, the traditional relationship between the individual and the religious community is to some degree reversed. On the basis of our interviews, we are not surprised to learn that a 1978 Gallup poll found that 80 percent of Americans agreed that "an individual should arrive at his or her own religious beliefs independent of any churches or synagogues." From the traditional point of view, this is a strange statement—it is precisely within church or synagogue that one comes to one's religious beliefs—but to many Americans it is the Gallup finding that is normal.

Nan Pfautz, raised in a strict Baptist church, is now an active member of a Presbyterian congregation near San Jose. Her church membership gives her a sense of community involvement, of engagement with issues at once social and moral. She speaks of her "commitment" to the church, so that being a member means being willing to give time, money, and care to the community it embodies and to its wider purposes. Yet, like many Americans, she feels that her personal relationship to God transcends her involvement in any particular church. Indeed, she speaks with humorous disdain of "churchy people" such as those who condemn others for violations of external norms. She says, "I believe I have a commitment to God which is beyond church. I felt my relationship with God was O.K. when I wasn't with the church."

For Nan, the church's value is primarily an ethical one. "Church to me is a community, and it's an organization that I belong to. They do an awful lot of good." Her obligations to the church come from the fact that she has chosen to join it, and "just like any organization that you belong to, it shouldn't be just to have another piece of paper in your wallet." As with the Kiwanis or any other organization, "you have a responsibility to do something or don't be there," to devote time and money, and especially to "care about the people." It is this caring community, above all, that the church represents. "I really love my church and what they have done for me, and what they do for other people, and the community that's there." Conceived as an association of loving individuals, the church acquires its value from "the caring about people. What I like about my church is its community."

* * *

In talking to Art Townsend, the pastor of Nan's church, we found views quite consonant with hers. Art is not unaware of the church as a community of memory, though he is as apt to tell a story from the Maharishi or a Zen Buddhist text as from the New Testament. But what excites him are the individuals themselves: "The church is really a part of me and I am a part of the church, and my shift professionally has gone from 'how can I please them and make them like me so that I can keep my job and get a promotion' to 'how can I love them, how can I help these beautiful, special people to experience how absolutely wonderful they are.'" It is the self—both his and those of others—that must be the source of all religious meaning. In Art's optimistic vision, human beings need to learn to "lighten up" as "one of the steps to enlightenment." His job in turn is to "help them take the scales from their eyes and experience and see their magnificence." Difficulties between people are misunderstandings among selves who are ultimately in harmony. If a couple who are angry or disappointed or bored with each other really share their feelings, "you get into a deeper level, and what happens is that feelings draw together, and you actually, literally feel the feeling the same way the other person feels it. And when you do, there is a shift, there is a zing, and it is like the two become one."

For Art Townsend, God becomes the guarantee of what he has "experienced in my life, that there is nothing that happens to me that is not for the fulfillment of my higher self." His cheery mysticism eliminates any real possibility of sin, evil, or damnation, since "if I thought God were such a being that he would waste a human soul on the basis of its mistakes, that would be a little limiting." In consonance with this primarily expressive individualist ethos, Art's philosophy is remarkably upbeat. Tragedy and sacrifice are not what they seem. "Problems become the playground of consciousness" and are to be welcomed as opportunities for growth.

Such a view can justify high levels of social activism, and Art Townsend's church engages in a wide variety of activities, volunteering as a congregation to care for Vietnamese refugee families, supporting broader understanding of the homosexual minority, and visiting the sick or distressed in the congregation. A member such as Nan Pfautz carries her sense of responsibility further, participating through the church in a range of activities from environmental protection to fighting multinational corporations marketing infant formula in the Third World. But it is clear for her, as for Art Townsend, that the ultimate meaning of the church is an expressive-individualist one. Its value is as a loving community in which individuals can experience the joy of belonging. As the church secretary says, "Certainly all the things that we do involve caring about people in a loving manner, at least I hope that we do." She puts it succinctly when she says, "For the most part, I think this community is a safe place for a lot of people."

Art Townsend's Presbyterian church would be viewed as theologically liberal. A look at a nearby conservative church brings out many differences but also many similarities. Pastor Larry Beckett describes his church as independent, conservative, and evangelical, and as neither liberal nor fundamentalist. At first glance, this conservative evangelical church is more clearly a community of memory than Art Townsend's. Larry Beckett indicates that its central beliefs are the divinity of Christ and the authority of scripture. A great deal of time is given to the study and exposition of scripture. Larry even gave a brief course on New Testament Greek so that the original text would be to some degree available to the congregation. While Larry insists that the great commandment to love God and one's neighbor is the essence of biblical teaching, his church tries to follow the specific commandments as much as possible. It is, for example, strongly against divorce because of Jesus' injunction (Matt. 19:6) against putting asunder what God has joined together. The firm insistence on belief in God and in the divinity of Christ, the importance of Christ as a model for how to act, and the attempt to apply specific biblical injunctions as far as possible provide the members of this church with a structure of external authority that might make the members of Art Townsend's congregation uneasy. Not so different socially and occupationally from the nearby Presbyterian church, and subject to many of the same insecurities and tensions, the members of this evangelical church have found a faith that is secure and unchanging. As Larry Beckett says, "God doesn't change. The values don't change. Jesus Christ doesn't change. In fact, the Bible says He is the same yesterday, today and forever. Everything in life is always changing, but God doesn't change."

* * *

For Larry Beckett and the members of his congregation, biblical Christianity provides an alternative to the utilitarian individualist values of this world. But that alternative, appealing precisely because it is "real clear," does not go very far in helping them understand their connection to the world or the society in which they live. The Bible provides unambiguous moral answers about "the essential issues—love, obedience, faith, hope," so that "killing or, say, murdering is never right. Or adultery. A relationship outside of your marriage is never right. The Bible says that real simple." To "follow the Scriptures and the words of Jesus" provides a clear, but narrow, morality centered on family and personal life. One must personally, as an individual, resist temptation and put the good of others ahead of one's own. Christian love applies to one-to-one relationships—I may not cheat my neighbor, or exploit him, or sell him something I know he can't afford. But outside this sphere of personal morality, the evangelical church has little to say about wider social commitments. Indeed, the sect draws together those who have found a personal relationship to Christ into a special loving community, and while it urgently seeks to have everyone make the same commitment, it separates its members off from attachment to the wider society. Morality becomes personal, not social; private, not public.

Both Larry Beckett's conservative church and Art Townsend's liberal one stress stable, loving relationships, in which the intention to care outweighs the flux of momentary feelings, as the ideal pattern in marriage, family, and work relationships. Thus both attempt to counter the more exploitative tendencies of utilitarian individualism. But in both cases, their sense of religious community has trouble moving beyond an individualistic morality. In Art Townsend's faith, a distinctively religious vision has been absorbed into the categories of contemporary psychology. No autonomous standard of good and evil survives outside the needs of individual psyches for growth. Community and attachment come not from the demands of a tradition, but from the empathetic sharing of feelings among therapeutically attuned selves.

Larry Beckett's evangelical church, in contrast, maintains a vision of the concrete moral commitments that bind church members. But the bonds of loyalty, help, and responsibility remain oriented to the exclusive sect of those who are "real" Christians. Direct reliance on the Bible provides a second language with which to resist the temptations of the "world," but the almost exclusive concentration on the Bible, especially the New Testament, with no larger memory of how Christians have coped with the world historically, diminishes the capacity of their second language to deal adequately with current social reality. There is even a tendency visible in many evangelical circles to thin the biblical language of sin and redemption to an idea of Jesus as the friend who helps us find happiness and self-fulfillment. The emphasis on love, so evident within the community, is not shared with the world, except through missionary outreach.

There are thousands of local churches in the United States, representing an enormous range of variation in doctrine and worship. Yet most define themselves as communities of personal support. A recent study suggests that what Catholics look for does not differ from the concerns of the various types of Protestants we have been discussing. When asked the direction the church should take in future years, the two things that a national sample of Catholics most asked for were "personal and accessible priests" and "warmer, more personal parishes." The salience of these needs for personal intimacy in American religious life suggests why the local church, like other voluntary communities, indeed like the contemporary family, is so fragile, requires so much energy to keep it going, and has so faint a hold on commitment when such needs are not met.

RELIGIOUS INDIVIDUALISM

Religious individualism, evident in these examples of church religion, goes very deep in the United States. Even in seventeenth-century Massachusetts, a personal experience of salvation was a prerequisite for acceptance as a church member. It is true that when Anne Hutchinson began to draw her own theological conclusions from her religious experiences and teach them to others, conclusions that differed from those of the established ministry, she was tried and banished from Massachusetts. But through the peculiarly American phenomenon of revivalism, the emphasis on personal experience would eventually override all efforts at church discipline. Already in the eighteenth century, it was possible for individuals to find the form of religion that best suited their inclinations. By the nineteenth century, religious bodies had to compete in a consumers' market and grew or declined in terms of changing patterns of individual religious taste. But religious individualism in the United States could not be contained within the churches, however diverse they were. We have noted the presence of individuals who found their own way in religion even in the eighteenth century. Thomas Jefferson said, "I am a sect myself," and Thomas Paine, "My mind is my church." Many of the most influential figures in nineteenth-century American culture could find a home in none of the existing religious bodies, though they were attracted to the religious teachings of several traditions. One thinks of Ralph Waldo Emerson, Henry David Thoreau, and Walt Whitman.

Many of these nineteenth-century figures were attracted to a vague pantheistic mysticism that tended to identify the divine with a higher self. In recent times, what had been a pattern confined to the cultural elite has spread to significant sections of the educated middle class. Tim Eichelberger, a young Campaign for Economic Democracy activist in Southern California, is typical of many religious individualists when he says, "I feel religious in a way. I have no denomination or anything like that." In 1971, when he was seventeen, he became interested in Buddhism. What attracted him was the capacity of Buddhism to allow him to "transcend" his situation: "I was always into change and growth and changing what you were sort of born into and I was always interested in not having that control me. I wanted to define my own self." His religious interest involved the practice of yoga and a serious interest in leading a nonviolent life. "I was into this religious purity and I wanted the earth around me to be pure, nonviolence, nonconflict. Harmony. Harmony with the earth. Man living in harmony with the earth; men living in harmony with each other." His certainty about nonviolence eventually broke down when he had to acknowledge his rage after being rejected in a love relationship. Coming to terms with his anger made him see that struggle is a part of life. Eventually, he found that involvement in CED gave an expression to his ideals as well as his understanding of life as a struggle. His political concern with helping people attain "self-respect, self-determination, self-realization" continues his older religious concern to define his own self. But neither his religion nor his politics transcend an individualism in which "self-realization" is the highest aspiration.

That radical religious individualism can find its own institutional form is suggested by the story of Cassie Cromwell, a suburban San Diego volunteer a generation older than Eichelberger, who came to her own religious views in adolescence when she joined the Unitarian church. She sums up her beliefs succinctly: "I am a pantheist. I believe in the 'holiness' of the earth and all other living things. We are a product of this life system and are inextricably linked to all parts of it. By treating other living things disrespectfully, we are disrespectful of ourselves. Our very survival depends on the air 'god,' the water, sun, etc." Not surprisingly, she has been especially concerned with working for ecological causes. Like Eichelberger, she began with a benign view of life and then had to modify it. "I used to believe that man was basically good," her statement of her philosophy continues. "I didn't believe in evil. I still don't know what evil is but see greed, ignorance, insensitivity to other people and other living things, and irresponsibility." Unlike most of those to whom we talked, Cassie is willing to make value judgments about religion and is openly critical of Christianity. She believes that "the Christian idea of the superiority of man makes it so difficult to have a proper concern for the environment. Because only man has a soul, everything on the earth can be killed and transformed for the benefit of man. That's not right."

Commoner among religious individualists than criticism of religious beliefs is criticism of institutional religion, or the church as such. "Hypocrisy" is one of the most frequent charges against organized religion. Churchgoers do not practice what they preach. Either they are not loving enough or they do not practice the moral injunctions they espouse. As one person said, "It's not religion or the church you go to that's going to save you." Rather it is your "personal relationship" with God. Christ will "come into your heart" if you ask, without any church at all.

In the cases of Tim Eichelberger and Cassie Cromwell, we can see how mystical beliefs can provide an opening for involvement in the world. Nonetheless, the links are tenuous and to some extent fortuitous. Both had to modify their more cosmic flights in order to take account of evil and aggression and work for the causes they believe in. The CED provides a focus for Eichelberger's activities, as the ecology movement does for Cassie. But their fundamental views were formed outside those contexts and their relation to the respective groups, even Cassie's longstanding connection with the Unitarians, remains one of convenience. As social ideals, neither "self-realization" nor the "life system" provide practical guidance. Indeed, although both Tim and Cassie value "harmony with the earth," they lack a notion of nature form which any clear social norms could be derived. Rather, the tendency in American nature pantheism is to construct the world somehow out of the self. * * * If the mystical quest is pursued far enough, it may take on new forms of self-discipline, committed practice, and community, as in the case of serious practitioners of Zen Buddhism. But more usually the languages of Eastern spirituality and American naturalistic pantheism are employed by people not connected with any particular religious practice or community.

INTERNAL AND EXTERNAL RELIGION

Radically individualistic religion, particularly when it takes the form of a belief in cosmic selfhood, may seem to be in a different world from conservative or fundamentalist religion. Yet these are the two poles that organize much of American religious life. To the first, God is simply the self magnified; to the second, God confronts man from outside the universe. One seeks a self that is finally identical with the world; the other seeks an external God who will provide order in the world. Both value personal religious experience as the basis of their belief. Shifts from one pole to the other are not as rare as one might think.

Sheila Larson is, in part, trying to find a center in herself after liberating herself from an oppressively conformist early family life. * * * The two experiences that define her faith took a similar form. One occurred just before she was about to undergo major surgery. God spoke to her to reassure her that all would be well, but the voice was her own. The other experience occurred when, as a nurse, she was caring for a dying woman whose husband was not able to handle the situation. Taking over care in the final hours, Sheila had the experience that "if she looked in the mirror" she "would see Jesus Christ." Tim Eichelberger's mystical beliefs and the "nonrestrictive" nature of his yoga practices allowed him to "transcend" his family and ethnic culture and define a self free of external constraint.

Conversely, cosmic mysticism may seem too threatening and undefined, and in reaction a religion of external authority may be chosen. Larry Beckett was attracted to Hinduism and Buddhism in his counter-cultural stage, but found them just too amorphous. The clarity and authority that he found in the New Testament provided him with the structure that till then had been lacking in his life.

Howard Crossland, a scientist and a member of Larry Beckett's congregation * * *, finds a similar security in his religion. He tends to view his Christianity as a matter of facts rather than emotion: "Because I have the Bible to study, it's not really relying on your emotions. There are certain facts presented and you accept the facts." Not surprisingly, Crossland is concerned about his own self-control and respects self-control in others. He never went through a countercultural phase, but he does have memories of a father who drank too much—an example of what can happen when control gets lost. In his marriage, in relation to his children, and with the several people who work under him, Crossland tries to be considerate and put the good of others ahead of his own. As he sees it, he is able to do that because of the help of God and His church: "From the help of other members of the congregation and with the help of the Holy Spirit, well, first of all you accept God, and then He gives you help to do good to your fellowman, to refrain from immorality, to refrain from illegal things."

Ruth Levy, [an] Atlanta therapist * * *, comments on what she calls "born-again Jews," who are in many ways similar to born-again Christians. They come from assimilated families who haven't kept kosher in three generations, yet "incredibly, they do stuff that my grandparents may not even have done." What these born-again Jews are doing is "instilling structure, discipline, and meaning." They have found that "to be free to do anything you want isn't enough. There isn't anything you want to do."

Since these two types of religion, or two ways of being religious, are deeply interrelated, if our analysis is correct, some of the obvious contrasts between them turn out to be not quite what they seem. It is true that the first style emphasizes inner freedom and the second outer control, but we cannot say that the first is therefore liberating and the second authoritarian, or that the first is individualistic and the second collectivist. It is true that the first involves a kind of radical individualism that tends to elevate the self to a cosmic principle, whereas the second emphasizes external authorities and injunctions. But the first sees the true self as benevolent and harmonious with nature and other humans and so as incompatible with narrow self-seeking. And the second finds in external authority and regulation something profoundly freeing: a protection against the chaos of internal and external demands, and the basis for a genuine personal autonomy. Thus, though they mean somewhat different things by freedom and individuality, both hold these as central values. And while the first is clearly more focussed on expressive freedom, the second in its own way also allows important opportunities for expressive freedom in intensely participatory religious services and through emphasis on love and caring. Finally, though conservative religion does indeed have a potential for authoritarianism, particularly where a magnetic preacher gathers inordinate power in his own hands, so does extreme religious individualism. Where a guru or other religious teacher is thought to have the secret of perfect personal liberation, he or she may gain excessive power over adherents.

44

From *Amish Society*

JOHN A. HOSTETLER

One of the most basic sociological truths is that people seek to organize their lives, families, and communities in order to become the kind of people they most admire. This is especially true for the Amish, who see their own beliefs as tied to the maintenance of their communities. In this study you can see how beliefs dictate a way of living, while at the same time a pattern of social structure upholds and reinforces the beliefs that dominate the society.

Small communities, with their distinctive character—where life is stable and intensely human—are disappearing. Some have vanished from the face of the earth, others are dying slowly, but all have undergone change as they have come into contact with an expanding machine civilization. The merging of diverse peoples into a common mass has produced tension among members of the minorities and the majority alike.

The Old Order Amish, who arrived on American shores in colonial times, have survived in the modern world in distinctive, viable, small communities. They have resisted the homogenization process more successfully than others. In planting and harvest time one can see their bearded men working the fields with horses and their women hanging out the laundry in neat rows to dry. Many American people have seen Amish families, with the men wearing broad-brimmed black hats and the women in bonnets and long dresses, in railway depots or bus terminals. Although the Amish have lived with industrialized America for over two and a half centuries, they have moderated its influence on their personal lives, their families, communities, and their values.

The Amish are often perceived by other Americans to be relics of the past who live an austere, inflexible life dedicated to inconvenient and archaic customs. They are seen as renouncing both modern conveniences and the American dream of success and progress. But most people have no quarrel with the Amish for doing things the old-fashioned way. Their conscientious objection was tolerated in wartime, for after all, they are meticulous farmers who practice the virtues of work and thrift.

In recent years the status of the Amish in the minds of most Americans has shifted toward a more favorable position. This change can scarcely be attributed to anything the Amish have done; rather, it is the result of changes in the way Americans perceive their minority groups. A century ago, hardly anyone knew the Amish existed. A half-century ago they were viewed as an obscure sect living by ridiculous customs, as stubborn people who resisted education and exploited the labor of their children. Today the Amish are the unwilling objects of a thriving tourist industry on the eastern seaboard. They are revered as hard-working, thrifty people with enormous agrarian stamina, and by some, as islands of sanity in a culture gripped by commercialism and technology run wild.

In the academic community several models have been advanced for understanding Amish society. Social scientists, like other Americans, have been influenced by the upward push of an advancing civilization and changes in the social discourse between the dominant society and its minorities. University teachers have traditionally taught their students to think of the Amish people as one of many old-world cultural islands left over in the modern world.

* * *

The Amish are a church, a community, a spiritual union, a conservative branch of Christianity, a religion, a community whose members practice simple and austere living, a familistic entrepreneuring system, and an adaptive human community. In this chapter several models will be discussed in terms of their usefulness and limitations as avenues for understanding Amish society as a whole. By models I mean structured concepts currently used by anthropologists to characterize whole societies. The serious reader will want to transcend the scientific orientation and ask, What is the meaning of the Amish system? What, if anything, is it trying to say to us?

A COMMONWEALTH

The Amish are in some ways a little commonwealth, for their members claim to be ruled by the law of love and redemption. The bonds that unite them are many. Their beliefs, however, do not permit them solely to occupy and defend a particular territory. They are highly sensitive in caring for their own. They will move to other lands when circumstances force them to do so.

Commonwealth implies a place, a province, which means any part of a national domain that geographically and socially is sufficiently unified to have a true consciousness of its unity. Its inhabitants feel comfortable with their own ideas and customs, and the "place" possesses a sense of distinction from other parts of the country. Members of a commonwealth are not footloose. They have a sense of productivity and accountability in a province where "the general welfare" is accepted as a day-to-day reality. Commonwealth has come to have an archaic meaning in today's world, because when groups and institutions become too large, the sense of commonwealth or the common good is lost. Thus it is little wonder that the most recent dictionaries of the American English language render the meaning of commonwealth as "obsolescent." In reality, the Amish are in part a commonwealth. There is, however, no provision for outcasts.

It may be argued that the Amish have retained elements of wholesome provincialism, a saving power to which the world in the future will need more and more to appeal. Provincialism need not turn to ancient narrowness and ignorance, confines from which many have sought to escape. A sense of province or commonwealth, with its cherished love of people and self-conscious dignity, is a necessary basis for relating to the wider world community. Respect for locality, place, custom, and local idealism can go a long way toward checking the monstrous growth of consolidation in the nation and thus help to save human freedom and individual dignity.

A SECTARIAN SOCIETY

Sociologists tend to classify the Amish as a sectarian society. Several European scholars have compared the social structure of "sect" and "church" types of religious institutions. The established church was viewed as hierarchic and conservative. It appealed to the ruling classes, administered grace to all people in a territorial domain, and served as an agency of social control. The sect was egalitarian. Essentially a voluntary religious protest movement, its members separated themselves from others on the basis of beliefs, practices, and institutions. The sects rejected the authority of the established religious organizations and their leaders. The strains between sect and church were viewed as a dialectic principle at work within Christianity. The use of an ideal type helped to clarify particular characteristics of the sectarian groups. The Anabaptists, for example, were described as small, voluntary groupings attempting to model their lives after the spirit of the Sermon on the Mount (Matt. 5, 6, 7) while also exercising the power to exclude and discipline members. Absolute separation from all other religious loyalties was required. All members were considered equal, and none were to take oaths, participate in war, or take part in worldly government.

Sects have employed various techniques of isolation for maintaining separateness. Today the extreme mobility of modern life brings people together in multiple contexts. The spatial metaphors of separation (i.e., valley, region, sector, etc.) are fast becoming obsolete. Nevertheless, modern sectarians turn to psychic insularity and contexts that protect them from mainstream values and competing systems. Members of the sect remain segregated in various degrees, chiefly by finding a group whose philosophy of history contradicts the existing values so drastically that the group sustains itself for a generation or more. To the onlooker, sectarianism, like monasticism, may appear to serve as a shelter from the complications of an overly complex society. For its participants, it provides authentic ways of realizing new forms of service and humility as well as protection from mainstream culture.

Sectarians, it is claimed, put their faith first by ordering their lives in keeping with it. The established churches compromise their faith with other interests and with the demands of the surrounding environment. Sectarians are pervasively religious in that they practice their beliefs in everyday life. Sects are often considered marginal or odd groups of alienated people with fanatic ideas. Yet the sects have had an immense influence in shaping the course of history. The British sociologist Bryan Wilson has observed that sects are "self-conscious attempts by men to construct their own societies, not merely as political entities with constitutions, but as groups with a firm set of values and mores, of which they are conscious." The growth of religious toleration in America has resulted in the development of religious pluralism in a manner that has not been realized in Europe. Wilson, who has characterized modern Christian sects into several types, classes the Amish as *introversionist* rather than *conversionist* or *reformist.* "Salvation is to be found in the community of those who withdraw from involvement in the affairs of mankind." The Amish recognize the evil circumstance of man, attempt to moderate its influence upon them, and retreat into a community to experience, cultivate, and preserve the attributes of God in ethical relationships.

The sectarian model lends itself to a historical, religious context. As a model, it offers some insight into the proliferation of groups with a negative orientation during a specific time period. Today there are many types of movements that did not exist in the early stages of industrialization. Sects may lose their spontaneity in a variety of ways. While the model may teach us something of how sects originate and grow from a protest movement to a separate religious entity, it does not provide us with a knowledge of the dynamics of the group. The Amish, for example, are not sectarians in the sense that they demand that others conform to their practices. Nor do they claim to base all actions on holy writ. They are not in conflict with the dominant culture in the same way, or with the same intensity, as are a number of sects such as the "apocalyptic" or "manipulationist" types.

Many sectarian societies, including the Amish, make little or no attempt to communicate their message. They recognize instinctively that authentic communication would mean greater literacy, education, and sophistication, and this would mean the beginning of the end. "The contribution of the sect to the larger society is," according to Martin Marty, "made best through the sympathetic observer who carries with him a picture of the advantages or particularity and assertiveness back to the world of dialogical complexity." In the Amish case, the message of the sectarian society is exemplary. A way of living is more important than communicating it in words. The ultimate message is the life. An Amish person will have no doubt about his basic convictions, his view of the meaning and purpose of life, but he cannot explain it except through the conduct of his life.

A FOLK SOCIETY

Anthropologists, who have compared societies all over the world, have tended to call semi-isolated peoples "folk societies," "primitives," or merely "simple societies." These societies constitute an altogether different type in contrast to the industrialized, or so-called civilized, societies. The "folk society," as conceptualized by Robert Redfield, is a small, isolated, traditional, simple, homogeneous society in which oral communication and conventionalized ways are important factors in integrating the whole of life. In such an ideal-type society, shared practical knowledge is more important than science, custom is valued more than critical knowledge, and associations are personal and emotional rather than abstract and categoric.

Folk societies are uncomfortable with the idea of change. Young people do what the old people did when they were young. Members communicate intimately with one another, not only by word of mouth but also through custom and symbols that reflect a strong sense of belonging to one another. A folk society is *Gemeinschaft*-like,[1] there is a strong sense of "we-ness." Leadership is personal rather than institutionalized. There are no gross economic inequalities. Mutual aid is characteristic of the society's members. The goals of life are never stated as matters of doctrine, but neither are they questioned. They are implied by the acts that constitute living in a small society. Custom tends to become sacred. Behavior is strongly patterned, and acts as well as cultural objects are given symbolic meaning that is often pervasively religious. Religion is diffuse and all-pervasive. In the typical folk society, planting and harvesting are as sacred in their own ways as singing and praying.

The significance of the Amish as an intimate, face-to-face primary group has long been recognized. Charles P. Loomis was the first to conceptualize the character of the Amish. In his construction of a scale he contrasted the Amish as a familistic *Gemeinschaf*-type system with highly rational social systems of the *Gesellschaft*-type in contemporary civilization.

The folk model lends itself well to understanding the tradition-directed character of Amish society. The heavy weight of tradition can scarcely be explained in any other way. The Amish, for example, have retained many of the customs and small-scale technologies that were common in rural society in the nineteenth century. Through a process of syncretism, Amish religious values have been fused with an earlier period of simple country living when everyone farmed with horses and on a scale where family members could work together. The Amish exist as a folk or "little" community in a rural subculture within the modern state, as distinguished from the primitive or peasant types described in anthropological literature. Several aspects of Redfield's folk-society model and features of the Toennies-Loomis *Gemeinscliaft* aid us in understanding the parameters of Amish society. They are *distinctiveness, smallness of scale, homogeneous culture patterns*, and the *strain toward self-sufficiency*.

Distinctiveness. The Amish people are highly visible. The outsider who drives through an Amish settlement cannot help but recognize them by their

---

1. The German term *Gemeinschaft* is often translated as "community." Ferdinand Toen-nies's classic work, *Gemeinschaft und Gesellschaft* provided sociology with this concept which is contrasted to urban, modern and industrialized society (*Gesellschaft*).

clothing, farm homes, furnishings, fields, and other material traits of culture. Although they speak perfect English with outsiders, they speak a dialect of German among themselves.

Amish life is distinctive in that religion and custom blend into a way of life. The two are inseparable. The core values of the community are religious beliefs. Not only do the members worship a deity they understand through the revelation of Jesus Christ and the Bible, but their patterned behavior has a religious dimension. A distinctive way of life permeates daily life, agriculture, and the application of energy to economic ends. Their beliefs determine their conceptions of the self, the universe, and man's place in it. The Amish world view recognizes a certain spiritual worth and dignity in the universe in its natural form. Religious considerations determine hours of work and the daily, weekly, seasonal, and yearly rituals associated with life experience. Occupation, the means and destinations of travel, and choice of friends and mate are determined by religious considerations. Religious and work attitudes are not far distant from each other. The universe includes the divine, and Amish society itself is considered divine insofar as the Amish recognize themselves as "a chosen people of God." The Amish do not seek to master nature or to work against the elements, but try to work with them. The affinity between Amish society and nature in the form of land, terrain, and vegetation is expressed in various degrees of intensity.

Religion is highly patterned, so one may properly speak of the Amish as a tradition-directed group. Though allusions to the Bible play an important role in determining their outlook on the world, and on life after death, these beliefs have been fused with several centuries of struggling to survive in community. Out of intense religious experience, societal conflict, and intimate agrarian experience, a mentality has developed that prefers the old rather than the new. While the principle seems to apply especially to religion, it has also become a charter for social behavior. "The old is the best, and the new is of the devil," has become a prevalent mode of thought. By living in closed communities where custom and a strong sense of togetherness prevail, the Amish have formed an integrated way of life and a folklike culture. Continuity of conformity and custom is assured and the needs of the individual from birth to death are met within an integrated and shared system of meanings. Oral tradition, custom, and conventionality play an important part in maintaining the group as a functioning whole. To the participant, religion and custom are inseparable. Commitment and culture are combined to produce a stable human existence.

These are some of the qualities of the little Amish community that make it distinctive. "Where the community begins and where it ends is apparent. The distinctiveness is apparent to the outside observer and is expressed in the group consciousness of the people of the community." The Amish community is in some aspects a functional part of modern society but is a distinctive subculture within it.

PART EIGHT

SOCIAL CHANGE

45

A More Perfect Union

BARACK OBAMA

When Barack Obama delivered this speech in March 2008, it was hailed as the most important statement about race in America since Dr. Martin Luther King's "I Have a Dream" speech in 1963. When he delivered this speech during the presidential campaign, Mr. Obama was in the midst of a public opinion tempest over remarks his longtime pastor Jeremiah Wright delivered. These remarks, castigating the government, to quote Jeff Weiss of the Dallas Morning News, *were "a cultural lightning bolt illuminating a chasm between the races, followed by thunderous arguments."* As he explained in his* Dreams from My Father *(and resembling the social form of the stranger in reading 4), President Obama came to understand himself as a black man in America when he worked as a community organizer in Chicago and married Michelle Robinson. In this speech he foresees social change in urging the nation to move beyond racial divides, as many of the Millennial Generation seem to have done.*

"We the people, in order to form a more perfect union . . ."—221 years ago, in a hall that still stands across the street, a group of men gathered and, with these simple words, launched America's improbable experiment in democracy. Farmers and scholars, statesmen and patriots who had traveled across an ocean to escape tyranny and persecution finally made real their declaration of independence at a Philadelphia convention that lasted through the spring of 1787.

The document they produced was eventually signed but ultimately unfinished. It was stained by this nation's original sin of slavery, a question that divided the colonies and brought the convention to a stalemate until the founders chose to allow the slave trade to continue for at least twenty more years, and to leave any final resolution to future generations.

Of course, the answer to the slavery question was already embedded within our Constitution—a Constitution that had at its very core the ideal of equal citizenship under the law; a Constitution that promised its people liberty and justice and a union that could be and should be perfected over time.

---

*Jeffrey Weiss, "Sermon Highlights Deep Racial Divide: Distrust of Government Often Preached in the Pulpit, Shared in Pews." *Dallas Morning News* (April 11, 2008): B1.

And yet words on a parchment would not be enough to deliver slaves from bondage, or provide men and women of every color and creed their full rights and obligations as citizens of the United States. What would be needed were Americans in successive generations who were willing to do their part—through protests and struggles, on the streets and in the courts, through a civil war and civil disobedience, and always at great risk—to narrow that gap between the promise of our ideals and the reality of their time.

This was one of the tasks we set forth at the beginning of this presidential campaign—to continue the long march of those who came before us, a march for a more just, more equal, more free, more caring and more prosperous America. I chose to run for president at this moment in history because I believe deeply that we cannot solve the challenges of our time unless we solve them together, unless we perfect our union by understanding that we may have different stories, but we hold common hopes; that we may not look the same and we may not have come from the same place, but we all want to move in the same direction—toward a better future for our children and our grandchildren.

This belief comes from my unyielding faith in the decency and generosity of the American people. But it also comes from my own story.

I am the son of a black man from Kenya and a white woman from Kansas. I was raised with the help of a white grandfather who survived a Depression to serve in Patton's army during World War II and a white grandmother who worked on a bomber assembly line at Fort Leavenworth while he was overseas. I've gone to some of the best schools in America and lived in one of the world's poorest nations. I am married to a black American who carries within her the blood of slaves and slave owners—an inheritance we pass on to our two precious daughters. I have brothers, sisters, nieces, nephews, uncles, and cousins of every race and every hue, scattered across three continents, and for as long as I live, I will never forget that in no other country on Earth is my story even possible.

It's a story that hasn't made me the most conventional of candidates. But it is a story that has seared into my genetic makeup the idea that this nation is more than the sum of its parts—that out of many, we are truly one.

Throughout the first year of this campaign, against all predictions to the contrary, we saw how hungry the American people were for this message of unity. Despite the temptation to view my candidacy through a purely racial lens, we won commanding victories in states with some of the whitest populations in the country. In South Carolina, where the Confederate flag still flies, we built a powerful coalition of African Americans and white Americans.

This is not to say that race has not been an issue in this campaign. At various stages in the campaign, some commentators have deemed me either "too black" or "not black enough." We saw racial tensions bubble to the surface during the week before the South Carolina primary. The press has scoured every single exit poll for the latest evidence of racial polarization, not just in terms of white and black, but black and brown as well.

And yet, it has only been in the last couple of weeks that the discussion of race in this campaign has taken a particularly divisive turn.

On one end of the spectrum, we've heard the implication that my candidacy is somehow an exercise in affirmative action; that it's based solely on the desire of wide-eyed liberals to purchase racial reconciliation on the cheap. On the other end, we've heard my former pastor, Jeremiah Wright,[1] use incendiary language to express views that have the potential not only to widen the racial divide, but views that denigrate both the greatness and the goodness of our nation, and that rightly offend white and black alike.

I have already condemned, in unequivocal terms, the statements of Reverend Wright that have caused such controversy and, in some cases, pain. For some, nagging questions remain. Did I know him to be an occasionally fierce critic of American domestic and foreign policy? Of course. Did I ever hear him make remarks that could be considered controversial while I sat in the church? Yes. Did I strongly disagree with many of his political views? Absolutely—just as I'm sure many of you have heard remarks from your pastors, priests, or rabbis with which you strongly disagreed.

But the remarks that have caused this recent firestorm weren't simply controversial. They weren't simply a religious leader's efforts to speak out against perceived injustice. Instead, they expressed a profoundly distorted view of this country—a view that sees white racism as endemic, and that elevates what is wrong with America above all that we know is right with America; a view that sees the conflicts in the Middle East as rooted primarily in the actions of stalwart allies like Israel, instead of emanating from the perverse and hateful ideologies of radical Islam.

As such, Reverend Wright's comments were not only wrong but divisive, divisive at a time when we need unity; racially charged at a time when we need to come together to solve a set of monumental problems—two wars, a terrorist threat, a falling economy, a chronic health care crisis and potentially devastating climate change—problems that are neither black or white or Latino or Asian, but rather problems that confront us all.

Given my background, my politics, and my professed values and ideals, there will no doubt be those for whom my statements of condemnation are not enough. Why associate myself with Reverend Wright in the first place, they may ask? Why not join another church? And I confess that if all that I knew of Reverend Wright were the snippets of those sermons that have run in an endless loop on the television sets and YouTube, or if Trinity United Church of Christ conformed to the caricatures being peddled by some commentators, there is no doubt that I would react in much the same way.

---

1. The Reverend Jeremiah Wright was the pastor at the Trinity United Church of Christ from 1972 to 2008. [*Editor's note*].

But the truth is, that isn't all that I know of the man. The man I met more than twenty years ago is a man who helped introduce me to my Christian faith, a man who spoke to me about our obligations to love one another, to care for the sick, and lift up the poor. He is a man who served his country as a United States Marine; who has studied and lectured at some of the finest universities and seminaries in the country, and who for over thirty years has led a church that serves the community by doing God's work here on Earth—by housing the homeless, ministering to the needy, providing day care services and scholarships and prison ministries, and reaching out to those suffering from HIV/AIDS.

In my first book, *Dreams From My Father*, I describe the experience of my first service at Trinity:

> People began to shout, to rise from their seats and clap and cry out, a forceful wind carrying the reverend's voice up into the rafters. And in that single note— hope!—I heard something else: At the foot of that cross, inside the thousands of churches across the city, I imagined the stories of ordinary black people merging with the stories of David and Goliath, Moses and Pharaoh, the Christians in the lion's den, Ezekiel's field of dry bones. Those stories—of survival and freedom and hope—became our stories, my story. The blood that spilled was our blood, the tears our tears, until this black church, on this bright day, seemed once more a vessel carrying the story of a people into future generations and into a larger world. Our trials and triumphs became at once unique and universal, black and more than black. In chronicling our journey, the stories and songs gave us a meaning to reclaim memories that we didn't need to feel shame about—memories that all people might study and cherish, and with which we could start to rebuild.

That has been my experience at Trinity. Like other predominantly black churches across the country, Trinity embodies the black community in its entirety—the doctor and the welfare mom, the model student and the former gang-banger. Like other black churches, Trinity's services are full of raucous laughter and sometimes bawdy humor. They are full of dancing and clapping and screaming and shouting that may seem jarring to the untrained ear. The church contains in full the kindness and cruelty, the fierce intelligence and the shocking ignorance, the struggles and successes, the love and, yes, the bitterness and biases that make up the black experience in America.

And this helps explain, perhaps, my relationship with Reverend Wright. As imperfect as he may be, he has been like family to me. He strengthened my faith, officiated my wedding, and baptized my children. Not once in my conversations with him have I heard him talk about any ethnic group in derogatory terms, or treat whites with whom he interacted with anything but courtesy and respect. He contains within him the contradictions—the good and the bad—of the community that he has served diligently for so many years.

I can no more disown him than I can disown the black community. I can no more disown him than I can disown my white grandmother—a woman who helped raise me, a woman who sacrificed again and again for me, a woman who loves me as much as she loves anything in this world, but a woman who once confessed her fear of black men who passed her by on the street, and who on more than one occasion has uttered racial or ethnic stereotypes that made me cringe.

These people are a part of me. And they are part of America, this country that I love.

Some will see this as an attempt to justify or excuse comments that are simply inexcusable. I can assure you it is not. I suppose the politically safe thing to do would be to move on from this episode and just hope that it fades into the woodwork. We can dismiss Reverend Wright as a crank or a demagogue, just as some have dismissed Geraldine Ferraro,[2] in the aftermath of her recent statements, as harboring some deep-seated bias.

But race is an issue that I believe this nation cannot afford to ignore right now. We would be making the same mistake that Reverend Wright made in his offending sermons about America—to simplify and stereotype and amplify the negative to the point that it distorts reality.

The fact is that the comments that have been made and the issues that have surfaced over the last few weeks reflect the complexities of race in this country that we've never really worked through—a part of our union that we have not yet made perfect. And if we walk away now, if we simply retreat into our respective corners, we will never be able to come together and solve challenges like health care or education or the need to find good jobs for every American.

Understanding this reality requires a reminder of how we arrived at this point. As William Faulkner once wrote, "The past isn't dead and buried. In fact, it isn't even past." We do not need to recite here the history of racial injustice in this country. But we do need to remind ourselves that so many of the disparities that exist between the African American community and the larger American community today can be traced directly to inequalities passed on from an earlier generation that suffered under the brutal legacy of slavery and Jim Crow.

Segregated schools were and are inferior schools; we still haven't fixed them, fifty years after *Brown v. Board of Education*. And the inferior education they provided, then and now, helps explain the pervasive achievement gap between today's black and white students.

Legalized discrimination—where blacks were prevented, often through violence, from owning property, or loans were not granted to African American

2. Geraldine Ferraro was U.S. representative from New York from 1978 to 1985. In 1984 she was selected by the Democratic Party as presidential candidate Walter Mondale's running mate. [*Editor's note*].

business owners, or black homeowners could not access FHA mortgages, or blacks were excluded from unions or the police force or the fire department— meant that black families could not amass any meaningful wealth to bequeath to future generations. That history helps explain the wealth and income gap between blacks and whites, and the concentrated pockets of poverty that persist in so many of today's urban and rural communities.

A lack of economic opportunity among black men, and the shame and frustration that came from not being able to provide for one's family contributed to the erosion of black families—a problem that welfare policies for many years may have worsened. And the lack of basic services in so many urban black neighborhoods—parks for kids to play in, police walking the beat, regular garbage pickup, building code enforcement—all helped create a cycle of violence, blight, and neglect that continues to haunt us.

This is the reality in which Reverend Wright and other African Americans of his generation grew up. They came of age in the late '50s and early '60s, a time when segregation was still the law of the land and opportunity was systematically constricted. What's remarkable is not how many failed in the face of discrimination, but how many men and women overcame the odds; how many were able to make a way out of no way, for those like me who would come after them.

For all those who scratched and clawed their way to get a piece of the American Dream, there were many who didn't make it—those who were ultimately defeated, in one way or another, by discrimination. That legacy of defeat was passed on to future generations—those young men and, increasingly, young women who we see standing on street corners or languishing in our prisons, without hope or prospects for the future. Even for those blacks who did make it, questions of race and racism continue to define their worldview in fundamental ways. For the men and women of Reverend Wright's generation, the memories of humiliation and doubt and fear have not gone away; nor has the anger and the bitterness of those years. That anger may not get expressed in public, in front of white co-workers or white friends. But it does find voice in the barbershop or the beauty shop or around the kitchen table. At times, that anger is exploited by politicians, to gin up votes along racial lines, or to make up for a politician's own failings.

And occasionally it finds voice in the church on Sunday morning, in the pulpit and in the pews. The fact that so many people are surprised to hear that anger in some of Reverend Wright's sermons simply reminds us of the old truism that the most segregated hour of American life occurs on Sunday morning. That anger is not always productive; indeed, all too often it distracts attention from solving real problems; it keeps us from squarely facing our own complicity within the African American community in our condition, and prevents the African American community from forging the alliances it needs to bring about real change. But the anger is real; it is powerful. And to simply wish it away, to condemn it without understanding its roots, only serves to widen the chasm of misunderstanding that exists between the races.

In fact, a similar anger exists within segments of the white community. Most working- and middle-class white Americans don't feel that they have been particularly privileged by their race. Their experience is the immigrant experience—as far as they're concerned, no one handed them anything. They built it from scratch. They've worked hard all their lives, many times only to see their jobs shipped overseas or their pensions dumped after a lifetime of labor. They are anxious about their futures, and they feel their dreams slipping away. And in an era of stagnant wages and global competition, opportunity comes to be seen as a zero sum game, in which your dreams come at my expense. So when they are told to bus their children to a school across town; when they hear an African American is getting an advantage in landing a good job or a spot in a good college because of an injustice that they themselves never committed; when they're told that their fears about crime in urban neighborhoods are somehow prejudiced, resentment builds over time.

Like the anger within the black community, these resentments aren't always expressed in polite company. But they have helped shape the political landscape for at least a generation. Anger over welfare and affirmative action helped forge the Reagan Coalition. Politicians routinely exploited fears of crime for their own electoral ends. Talk show hosts and conservative commentators built entire careers unmasking bogus claims of racism while dismissing legitimate discussions of racial injustice and inequality as mere political correctness or reverse racism.

Just as black anger often proved counterproductive, so have these white resentments distracted attention from the real culprits of the middle-class squeeze—a corporate culture rife with inside dealing, questionable accounting practices and short-term greed; a Washington dominated by lobbyists and special interests; economic policies that favor the few over the many. And yet, to wish away the resentments of white Americans, to label them as misguided or even racist, without recognizing they are grounded in legitimate concerns—this too widens the racial divide and blocks the path to understanding.

This is where we are right now. It's a racial stalemate we've been stuck in for years. Contrary to the claims of some of my critics, black and white, I have never been so naïve as to believe that we can get beyond our racial divisions in a single election cycle, or with a single candidacy—particularly a candidacy as imperfect as my own.

But I have asserted a firm conviction—a conviction rooted in my faith in God and my faith in the American people—that, working together, we can move beyond some of our old racial wounds, and that in fact we have no choice if we are to continue on the path of a more perfect union.

For the African American community, that path means embracing the burdens of our past without becoming victims of our past. It means continuing to insist on a full measure of justice in every aspect of American life. But it also means binding our particular grievances—for better health care and better schools and better jobs—to the larger aspirations of all Americans: the white woman struggling to break the glass ceiling, the white man who has been laid off, the immigrant trying to feed his family. And it means taking full responsibility for our own lives—by demanding more from our fathers, and spending more time with our children, and reading to them, and teaching them that while they may face challenges and discrimination in their own lives, they must never succumb to despair or cynicism; they must always believe that they can write their own destiny.

Ironically, this quintessentially American—and yes, conservative—notion of self-help found frequent expression in Reverend Wright's sermons. But what my former pastor too often failed to understand is that embarking on a program of self-help also requires a belief that society can change.

The profound mistake of Reverend Wright's sermons is not that he spoke about racism in our society. It's that he spoke as if our society was static; as if no progress had been made; as if this country—a country that has made it possible for one of his own members to run for the highest office in the land and build a coalition of white and black, Latino and Asian, rich and poor, young and old—is still irrevocably bound to a tragic past. But what we know—what we have seen—is that America can change. That is the true genius of this nation. What we have already achieved gives us hope—the audacity to hope—for what we can and must achieve tomorrow.

In the white community, the path to a more perfect union means acknowledging that what ails the African American community does not just exist in the minds of black people; that the legacy of discrimination—and current incidents of discrimination, while less overt than in the past—are real and must be addressed, not just with words, but with deeds, by investing in our schools and our communities; by enforcing our civil rights laws and ensuring fairness in our criminal justice system; by providing this generation with ladders of opportunity that were unavailable for previous generations. It requires all Americans to realize that your dreams do not have to come at the expense of my dreams; that investing in the health, welfare, and education of black and brown and white children will ultimately help all of America prosper.

In the end, then, what is called for is nothing more and nothing less than what all the world's great religions demand—that we do unto others as we would have them do unto us. Let us be our brother's keeper, scripture tells us. Let us be our sister's keeper. Let us find that common stake we all have in one another, and let our politics reflect that spirit as well.

For we have a choice in this country. We can accept a politics that breeds division and conflict and cynicism. We can tackle race only as spectacle—as we did in the O. J. trial—or in the wake of tragedy—as we did in the aftermath of Katrina—or as fodder for the nightly news. We can play Reverend Wright's sermons on every channel, every day and talk about them from now until the election, and make the only question in this campaign whether or not the American people think that I somehow believe or sympathize with his most offensive words. We can pounce on some gaffe by a Hillary supporter as evidence that she's playing the race card, or we can speculate on whether white men will all flock to John McCain in the general election regardless of his policies.[3]

We can do that.

But if we do, I can tell you that in the next election, we'll be talking about some other distraction. And then another one. And then another one. And nothing will change.

That is one option. Or, at this moment, in this election, we can come together and say, "Not this time." This time, we want to talk about the crumbling schools that are stealing the future of black children and white children and Asian children and Hispanic children and Native American children. This time, we want to reject the cynicism that tells us that these kids can't learn; that those kids who don't look like us are somebody else's problem. The children of America are not those kids, they are our kids, and we will not let them fall behind in a 21st-century economy. Not this time.

This time we want to talk about how the lines in the emergency room are filled with whites and blacks and Hispanics who do not have health care, who don't have the power on their own to overcome the special interests in Washington, but who can take them on if we do it together.

This time, we want to talk about the shuttered mills that once provided a decent life for men and women of every race, and the homes for sale that once belonged to Americans from every religion, every region, every walk of life. This time, we want to talk about the fact that the real problem is not that someone who doesn't look like you might take your job; it's that the corporation you work for will ship it overseas for nothing more than a profit.

This time, we want to talk about the men and women of every color and creed who serve together and fight together and bleed together under the same proud flag. We want to talk about how to bring them home from a war that should have never been authorized and should have never been waged. And we want to talk about how we'll show our patriotism by caring for them and their families, and giving them the benefits that they have earned.

I would not be running for president if I didn't believe with all my heart that this is what the vast majority of Americans want for this country. This union may never be perfect, but generation after generation has shown that it can always be perfected. And today, whenever I find myself feeling doubtful or cynical about this possibility, what gives me the most hope is the next generation—the young people whose attitudes and beliefs and openness to change have already made history in this election.

---

3. Hillary Clinton, senator from New York, was running against Barack Obama in the 2008 Democratic primary. John McCain became the Republican Party nominee that year, losing to Barack Obama in the presidential election. [*Editor's note*].

There is one story in particularly that I'd like to leave you with today—a story I told when I had the great honor of speaking on Dr. King's birthday at his home church, Ebenezer Baptist, in Atlanta.

There is a young, 23-year-old white woman named Ashley Baia who organized for our campaign in Florence, South Carolina. She had been working to organize a mostly African American community since the beginning of this campaign, and one day she was at a round table discussion where everyone went around telling their story and why they were there.

And Ashley said that when she was nine years old, her mother got cancer. And because she had to miss days of work, she was let go and lost her health care. They had to file for bankruptcy, and that's when Ashley decided that she had to do something to help her mom.

She knew that food was one of their most expensive costs, and so Ashley convinced her mother that what she really liked and really wanted to eat more than anything else was mustard and relish sandwiches—because that was the cheapest way to eat. That's the mind of a nine-year-old.

She did this for a year until her mom got better. So she told everyone at the round table that the reason she joined our campaign was so that she could help the millions of other children in the country who want and need to help their parents, too.

Now, Ashley might have made a different choice. Perhaps somebody told her along the way that the source of her mother's problems were blacks who were on welfare and too lazy to work, or Hispanics who were coming into the country illegally. But she didn't. She sought out allies in her fight against injustice.

Anyway, Ashley finishes her story and then goes around the room and asks everyone else why they're supporting the campaign. They all have different stories and different reasons. Many bring up a specific issue. And finally they come to this elderly black man who's been sitting there quietly the entire time. And Ashley asks him why he's there. And he does not bring up a specific issue. He does not say health care or the economy. He does not say education or the war. He does not say that he was there because of Barack Obama. He simply says to everyone in the room, "I am here because of Ashley."

"I'm here because of Ashley." By itself, that single moment of recognition between that young white girl and that old black man is not enough. It is not enough to give health care to the sick, or jobs to the jobless, or education to our children.

But it is where we start. It is where our union grows stronger. And as so many generations have come to realize over the course of the 221 years since a band of patriots signed that document right here in Philadelphia, that is where the perfection begins.

46

Job on the Line

WILLIAM M. ADLER

Two women share the same job. For decades Molly James performs the work in Paterson, New Jersey; then Balbina Duque Granados does it in Matamoros, Mexico. Molly James is laid off; Balbina Duque Granados struggles to make ends meet. The global transformation of work benefits consumers with lower prices and a wider range of products. It brings industry to formerly agrarian countries and changes them forever. But the unrecorded costs are considerable. In this highly personal account we are able to see many of the negative features of globalization. The challenge of globalization in the years ahead will be to address these often-hidden costs.

At 3 o'clock on a warm June afternoon, the second of two wash-up bells rings for the final time. Mollie James stands hunched over the sink as she rinses her hands with industrial soap alongside her co-workers. She first came to work here, on the assembly line at Universal Manufacturing Company in Paterson, New Jersey, a few years after the factory opened in 1951. She was the first woman at the factory to run a stamping machine, the first to laminate steel. She was among the first female union stewards and among the first African American stewards; hers was a self-assured presence any grievant would want on their side. And now, after 34 years on the line—nearly two-thirds of her life—she is the last to go.

At the end of every other shift for more than three decades, Mollie and her fellow employees beat a quick path to the plant parking lot. On this day there is less sense of hurry. There are still children to feed, clothes to wash, bills to pay, errands to run, other jobs to race to. But as she and the others leave the washroom, no one seems pressed to leave. All about the plant entrance, and out in the lot, people stand in small clusters, like mourners at their own wake, talking, laughing, hugging, crying. Almost always Mollie James is outgoing and outspoken, her voice loud and assertive, her smile nicely lighted. At 59 she is a strong woman, her strength forged from a life of hard work and sacrifice, and faith in God. She is not one to betray her emotions, but this day is different. Her bearing has turned to reserve, her normally quick eyes dull and watery. Her working life is over, and that is the only life she has ever known.

Universal had always turned a tidy profit. Its signature product, ballasts that regulate the current in fluorescent lights, attracted attention only when the ballast failed—causing the light fixture to hum or flicker. In the mid-1980s, however, the locally owned company was twice swept up in the gale winds of Wall Streets merger mania. Twice within eight months Universal was sold, both times to firms headed by disciples of Michael Milken, the Street's reigning evil genius. Not long after the second sale, to a Los Angeles-based electrical components conglomerate called MagneTek, Inc., movers began pulling up the plant's massive machinery, much of which had been bolted to the floor when the factory opened.

Mollie had sensed what was happening in January 1989, the morning she came to work and noticed the hole in the floor. It wasn't a hole, really, in the sense of an opening; it was more of a void: a great yawning space of discolored concrete where just the afternoon before had sat a steel-stamping machine, a hulking piece of American industrial might. Before long, more holes appeared, each tracing the outline of the base of another machine, like chalk around a sidewalk corpse.

Now, on the last day, when there is no one left to say goodbye to, Mollie slumps behind the wheel of her rusting 1977 Dodge Charger and follows the procession out of the lot. It is not far, three miles or so, from the plant in Paterson's industrial Bunker Hill neighborhood to the three-story, three-family house she owns on the near East Side. Upon pulling into her customary space in the driveway, Mollie sits in the car a good long while, letting the heat of the summer afternoon settle her. By the time she fits the key into the back-door lock and begins climbing the three flights of stairs to her bedroom, she has stopped crying.

The machine that Mollie used to stamp steel for three decades makes its way south, past factories that Universal opened in Mississippi and Arkansas during the 1960s and 1970s to take advantage of cheaper labor and taxes, before arriving in Matamoros, Mexico, a booming border city just across the Rio Grande from Brownsville, Texas. On a blindingly blue morning, MagneTek executives from "corporate" in L.A. arrive for the gala ribbon cutting of the first MagneTek plant here. Plant manager Chuck Peeples, an affable Arkansas expatriate, leads the officials on a tour of the gleaming factory. Outfitted in natty going-native panama hats emblazoned with the company's royal-blue capital-M "power" logo, the MagneTek honchos parade past equipment ripped from the shopworn floor in Paterson, machinery now operated by a young, almost entirely female workforce. These women, primarily in their teens and 20s, have come north to Matamoros in search of work and a better future than the bleakness promised in the jobless farming towns of the interior.

Balbina Duque Granados found a job at MagneTek in 1993, after leaving her family's home in a picturesque but poor mountain village of central Mexico. Just out of her teens, she has an easy, dimpled smile and long black hair worn in a ponytail. With its comparatively low wages, endless supply of labor, lack of regulation, and proximity to the United States, Matamoros is a magnet for *maquiladoras,* the foreign-owned assembly plants that wed First World engineering with Third World working conditions. Balbina's probationary pay is slightly less than $26 a week, or about 65 cents an hour. It is difficult work, winding coils, repetitive and tiring and mind numbing, but it is a job she is thrilled to have—her "answered prayer." And although Balbina doesn't know it, it is not just any job. It is Mollie's job.

The job in which Mollie James once took great pride, the job that both fostered and repaid her loyalty by enabling her to rise above humble beginnings and provide for her family—that job does not now pay Balbina Duque a wage sufficient to live on. Embedded in that central fact, and in the intersecting lives and fates of the two women who held that single job, is a broader story about the fundamental changes currently remaking the economy—the ways in which "free trade" harms democracy, undermines stable businesses and communities, and exploits workers on both sides of the border, both ends of the global assembly line.

At a few minutes before 2 o'clock on a cold, pitch-black morning in November 1950, Mollie and her father, Lorenzo Brown, waited anxiously on the platform of the ornate World War I-era train station in Richmond, Virginia. The Browns were from Cartersville, 45 miles west, in the rolling farmland of central Virginia. Mollie was headed to Penn Station in Newark, New Jersey, to meet her fiance, Sam James, who would take her home, to Paterson, to her new life. She was dressed in her finest: a new navy-blue suit, new shoes, new hairdo. She carried nearly everything she owned in a half-dozen sky-blue suitcases her father had given her for the trip.

Mollie was traveling alone, but the "colored" train cars of the Silver Meteor, and indeed those of the other great northbound coaches—the Champion, the Florida Sunbeam, the Silver Comet—were full of Mollie Browns: black southerners crossing the Mason-Dixon Line, heading for the promised land. Mollies intended was waiting at the station in his new, yellow, two-door Ford to take her to Paterson, a city of 140,000 residents some 15 miles west of New York City. Sam drove her home to the one-room apartment he rented for $20 a week above the flat where his sister and brother-in-law lived. Although the accommodations were far from luxurious—Mollie and Sam shared a kitchen and bath with other upstairs tenants—her new life seemed as bright as Sam's shiny car.

Paterson at precisely the middle of the 20th century was absolutely humming, filled with vibrant neighborhoods, a bustling downtown retail and cultural district, and above all, factories small and large, producing everything from textiles to machine tools to electrical components. "There were so many places to work, I could have five jobs in the same day," Mollie recalled years later. "And if I didn't like one, I could leave and get another, sure."

Mollie's new hometown was born of entrepreneurial dreamers and schemers. The city had been founded on the 16th anniversary of the Declaration of Independence, July 4, 1792, not as a municipality but as a business: the home of the country's first industrial corporation, the Society for Useful Manufactures. The grand plans of the society and its guiding light, Alexander

Hamilton, ultimately failed, but Paterson established itself as a cradle of American industry. The city became renowned for its textile mills—silk, especially—and later for the union-busting tactics of its mill owners. During the 19th century, textile manufacturers in Paterson were responsible for what were probably the nation's first runaway shops, opening "annexes" in rural Pennsylvania to take advantage of workers who could be subjected to longer hours for half the wages paid in New Jersey. In 1913, the Industrial Workers of the World mobilized Paterson's 25,000 employees to walk away from their looms, effectively nailing shut the nation's silk-manufacturing center. Able to rely on their nonunion factories, mill owners refused to negotiate; starved into submission, the strikers were forced to return to work with neither gains in wages nor improved working conditions.

By the time the 19-year-old Mollie Brown arrived in Paterson, the economy was booming. Unemployment was low, wages high. In her first few years in town, Mollie ran through several jobs. "You'd just catch the bus and go from factory to factory and see who was hiring." Among her stops was a low-slung cement building in northeast Paterson. The sign out front said Universal Manufacturing Co. The owner himself, a gregarious man named Archie Sergy, showed her through the plant, explaining that the company made a part for fluorescent lights called a ballast. "They showed me how it was made, the whole assembly line. I learned there's a lot to it, a *very* lot." The starting salary was 90 cents an hour, but the company was about to implement a second shift, from 3 p.m. to midnight, that would pay an extra dime an hour. Those hours were ideal for Mollie. She and Sam had three children under the age of five and another on the way, and if she were to work nights and he days, the couple could care for the children without hiring a sitter. She accepted the job. "I hope you'll be here a long time," Sergy told her. "I hope we'll all be here a long time!"

By the early 1960s, Universal employed a workforce of some 1,200. Archie Sergy and his top managers continued to demonstrate a sincere interest in the welfare of their employees. "They never treated you as inferior, regardless of whether you cleaned the toilets or whatever your job was," Mollie says. "They'd walk up and down the line and talk to us, joke with us, sometimes have their sandwiches with us right there on the line. * * * If you needed a home loan, they'd give it to you, and you could make arrangements to pay it back."

Sergy saw the world as an industrialist, not a financier, and he maintained a steely-eyed focus on quality and customer service to the degree that it probably hurt profit margins. But his company was no social service agency; it venerated the bottom line as much as any self-respecting capitalist enterprise. Mollie and her co-workers enjoyed good wages and job security in large part because they belonged to Teamsters Local 945, which bargained for higher pay and better benefits. In 1963, determined to insulate Universal from threats of work stoppage, Sergy followed the tradition established by the early Paterson silk makers: He opened an annex, a Universal factory in the Deep South. The new plant was located in rural Mississippi, providing Sergy with a low-wage workforce as well as an ever-present threat of plant closing to quiet employees in Paterson.

That same year, strapped for operating capital and lacking a successor, Sergy also succumbed to the lure of Wall Street: He sold Universal to a New York–based conglomerate. Sergy remained as titular head of Universal, but outsiders controlled the economic destiny of the women and men who toiled there. This was most evidently revealed when Sergy announced to the employees in April 1968, seven months before his death, that the parent company itself had been swallowed whole by *another* conglomerate. "We're all working for a company out of Chicago," he said. "Who they are I have no idea."

Whether those who held the purse strings were faceless financiers from New York or Chicago or Los Angeles didn't matter much to Mollie James. Owners came and went, and the principal visible sign of each transition was a new company name on the payroll checks. So when word spread in early 1986 that an outfit called MagneTek was the new owner, Mollie took the news calmly. Surely some things would change—managers in, managers out, maybe—but she had no reason to question her job security. Although the company had added a second Southern plant, in Arkansas, Paterson was still the flagship. Mollie came to work for Universal—and stayed—because of the peace of mind that came from a secure job: a job she could raise a family on, buy a house, a car, borrow money against, count on for the future.

But right away Mollie could tell the future was darkening. Like the earlier owners, MagneTek was a faraway, far-flung holding company, but the previous management's hands-off, don't fix-it-if-it-ain't-broke page was missing from its corporate manual. "It started the day our name disappeared from the building," she says. "Poof, no more Universal."

By the end of 1988, not only had Universal's name vanished from the plant; its machines, too, were disappearing, torn from the floor like trees from their roots. "The movers came at night, like thieves, sometimes just taking one piece at a time," Mollie recalls. "We'd come in in the mornings and there'd be another hole in the floor."

The machinery had been used to make a large specialty ballast known as the HID, or High Intensity Discharge, the kind used in thousand-watt fixtures installed in outdoor stadiums. Paterson was the lone Universal plant manufacturing the HID; making its precision-wound coils required different training and equipment than the garden-variety 40-watt fluorescent ballast the two Southern plants pumped out by the tens of thousands daily.

If Paterson's workers were more sophisticated, they were also more costly. Mollie earned $7.91 an hour, 75 cents more than she would have earned in Mississippi and almost a dollar more than in Arkansas. But if the wages down South were low, they were not low enough. They were not the cheapest possible wages. They weren't as low as workers earned in Mexico, where the prevailing pay at the maquiladoras was less than $8 a day. And so, in the early months of 1988, the machines began disappearing, bound ultimately for Matamoros. "All we kept hearing was how good a job we were doing," Mollie says, "that we had nothing to worry about, that we'd always have work in Paterson."

The nightly bus to Matamoros would not roll through the depot nearest Balbina Duque's village until 9:15. It was only mid-morning, just a couple of hours since she'd said her goodbyes to the family, since she'd pressed her lips for the last time to her baby son's cheek and handed him to her mother. It was only mid-morning, and already Balbina could feel the tropical sun on her face, could feel her funds dwindling fast. She had started with 200 pesos, the equivalent of about $65, and now that she'd paid a man nearly $20 to taxi her the hour from Monte Bello, her mountain village—a place of clean and clear air, brilliant high-desert flowers, and almost surrealistically bright light—to the bus station in town, and now that she'd bought a couple of tamales from a sidewalk vendor and a one-way ticket to the border for $30, Balbina was down to less than $15.

Balbina had turned 20 only weeks earlier. She was leaving for Matamoros, 400 miles north, to look for work in the maquiladoras. She was torn about going, especially about having to leave behind her 18-month-old son, Iban. "If there were work here," Balbina said in Spanish during a visit home some years later, "everyone would stay."

There was nothing to keep them at home. Balbina's village comprised maybe 1,000 people living in a couple of hundred pastel-colored homes with thatched roofs. There was neither running water nor electricity. Much of Balbina's day was spent filling and refilling a water bucket from a central well down a hill and carrying it back on her head to use for bathing, laundry, washing dishes, cooking, and drinking. A typical day might require 24 trips to the well, a chore that claimed three to four hours beginning at first light.

The interminable, grueling days were not for Balbina. Monte Bello felt like a sentence from which she needed to escape. It was a place for "people too old to work or too young to work," she said. "For me there was nothing. If you do not work in the fields there is nothing else to do." She decided she would celebrate her 20th birthday with her family, and then, as soon as she had saved enough for the bus fare, would take off for the border, where the maquiladoras favor young women for their nimble fingers and compliant minds, and where a job in a *maquila* trumps any other employment options.

It was dark when Balbina finally boarded the bus. Heading north, through a vast valley of corn, Highway 85 was flat as a tortilla. With two seats to herself, Balbina was able to curl into a comfortable enough position, and sleep came at once. When the bus pulled into Matamoros at dawn, she had to rouse herself from a dream about her son. Meeting her at the central station on Canales Avenue was a distant aunt, who escorted her to a small dwelling in the liltingly named *Colonia Vista Hemwsa*—Beautiful View. But there was little beauty in the *colonia*; it was wedged between a pungent, milky-white irrigation canal and the Finsa park, the massive industrial park where MagneTek and other foreign-owned maquiladoras employed most of the working-age residents of Vista Hermosa.

One morning, the second Friday of 1993, Balbina and her younger sister, Elsa, caught a ride downtown to the headquarters of the big maquiladora workers' union, the SJOI—the Spanish acronym for the Union of Industrial Workers and Day Laborers. Four times weekly, waves of several thousand applicants washed up at dawn at the SJOI offices, the de facto employment agency for the maquilas. All nonsalaried workers applied through its central hiring hall, women on Mondays and Fridays, men on Tuesdays and Thursdays.

It was not yet 7 o'clock, and Balbina and Elsa had already been in line for an hour, a line that snaked through the three-story building, past the armed guard at the door, and stretched outside for more than a block. By eight, they had squeezed and elbowed and prodded their way inside the assembly hall, a room roughly the size and ambience of a drafty old high-school gymnasium. Mounted fans whirred overhead, efficiently distributing the rank air and grime into all corners.

At 8:30, with no conspicuous signal that the cattle call was on the verge of starting, there was a near stampede toward the makeshift elevated stage at the front quadrant of the room. The entire room seemed like an aquarium, one rear corner of which had suddenly been tipped, causing its entire contents to flow into its diagonal. For the next few hours, Balbina, Elsa, and 1,600 other hopefuls would be crammed nose to shoulder, as close to the stage as possible, like groupies at a rock concert.

At 8:40, three union officials emerged from the anteroom beside the stage. Through a two-way mirror, they had been keeping an eye on the surging crowd while their clerks matched the day's maquila employment needs with the application forms on file. All morning long, the fax machines and phones in the union headquarters had been ringing with the day's specifications from the companies. One maquila, for instance, asked for 91 applicants, all of whom should be 16 (the legal minimum age) or older, with a secondary-school education and without "scheduling problems"—code for childless. All the maquilas favor youth, and some, MagneTek for one, insist on it. "*No may-ores de 27 años*"—None older than 27—the company's director of industrial relations instructed in a faxed letter to the union. Women in their late teens and early 20s are considered in the prime of their working lives; a 31-year-old is unlikely to be hired, and a 35-year-old is considered a relic.

When the tally of the day's employment needs was deemed complete, the officials stepped onto the stage, and into the bedlam. Between them and the spirited throng were three steps cordoned by a thin chain, a flimsy plywood railing, and a bouncer the size of an offensive lineman, whose sartorial taste ran to late Elvis: a white shirt unbuttoned nearly the length of his heroic torso, a gold medallion dangling to his midsection, and a formidable, gleaming pompadour crowning a Frigidaire face and muttonchop sideburns.

Following a call to order on a tinny public-address system, a woman unceremoniously announced the day's available jobs. "We're calling workers for Deltronicos," she said, referring to the GM car-radio subsidiary, and then read a list of 50 names. The "lucky ones," as one disappointed applicant called them, made their way through a pair of swinging doors, where a fleet of old Loadstar school buses waited to transport them to the Finsa park for a job interview and medical screening with their prospective employer. If their luck held, they would then be hired for a 30-day probationary period at lower, "training" wages before attaining full-employee status.

The drill was repeated for each maquila until the day's hiring needs were met. Neither Balbina nor Elsa were among the lucky ones, but they knew that few are chosen on the first go-round; some they met had endured several months of twice-weekly trips to the hall. Each Monday and Friday over the next few weeks the Duques returned faithfully. In March, Balbina's prayers were finally answered. She was assigned to a third-shift coil-winding job at MagneTek. All she knew about the job was that her sister-in-law once worked in the same plant, a low-lying white building no more than 75 yards from her tiny house. What she did not know was that Mollie James once held that very job.

Balbina started work at MagneTek the same year President Clinton signed the North American Free Trade Agreement, designed in large part to hasten the spread of maquiladoras. The trade deal enables companies to take advantage of 700,000 workers at 1,800 plants all along the border in ways that would not be tolerated in the United States. When MagneTek first set up shop in Matamoros, employees worked six-day weeks in a stifling, poorly ventilated plant; speaking on the line or going to the bathroom was grounds for suspension.

Although the company has improved working conditions in the last few years, sexual harassment and discrimination remain a constant of factory life. Many female employees at MagneTek have firsthand stories to tell about sexism on the job. "When new girls come in," says a 31-year-old MagneTek retiree who asked not to be identified, "a supervisor gives them the eye and asks them to go for a walk." Balbina says she received similar propositions when she started work at Plant 1. "My supervisor asked if I wanted to work more overtime. I told him I did, but that I wouldn't go to a hotel with him to get it."

The other constant of factory life is low wages. Even when she works an eight-hour overtime shift, as she usually does two or three times a week, Balbina finds it impossible to make ends meet on a MagneTek salary. "*No al-cance,*" she says. It doesn't reach. For years she surmounted her weekly shortfall by pooling her income and expenses with Elsa. The sisters lived, like nearly all of their co-workers, "*en montón*"—in a heap: two adults and five children in two small rooms, the kitchen in front, the bedroom in the rear. Their shared three-family flat was a cement structure 45 feet by 15 feet by 10 feet high. Its corrugated metal roof doubled as the ceiling. Their were cinder-block walls between the three units that stopped about a foot short of the ceiling, making for a pungent stew of sound and aroma when all three families were home.

The shadeless yard—of mud or dust, depending on the season—was fenced by chicken wire and a rickety gate, and served as an extension of the kitchen. The residents shared a clothesline, an outhouse, and a single spigot—the lone source of water. Balbina believes the water flowed from an open canal running near plants in the industrial park that manufacture pesticides or use toxic solvents. The water had to be boiled, of course; sometimes there was propane to do so, sometimes not.

The neighborhood, Vista Hermosa, exists in a commercial and municipal twilight zone. It sprang up to serve the maquiladoras, not the residents. There are several high-priced convenience stores in the colonia, but no full-fledged grocers, no place to buy meat. Nor is there a pharmacy or medical clinic. There is no police presence, and vandalism and petty theft are rampant. There is one school, an overcrowded kindergarten. Older students catch the same bus to school that drops off first-shift workers at the industrial park. "You have to adapt to the maquilas' routine," says a neighbor with school-age children, "because they're not going to adapt to ours."

The city mostly shuns residents because of the high cost and low return of providing them with services. "They have no money," says Andres Cuellar, the city historian of Matamoros, "so no city official accepts responsibility." But a former mayor offers a different explanation: Federal policy prevents the city from taxing the maquilas to improve the colonias. "We insisted before the federal government that we don't have the financial means to support the maquilas' growth," says Fernando Montemayor Lozano, mayor from 1987 until 1989. "Besides the salaries paid to Mexican workers, the maquiladora contribution is practically zero here." It was not until 1991 that running water was piped into the neighborhood (but not as yet into houses), and only in 1993 were the first houses wired for electricity. The roads remain unpaved and deeply rutted. Nor does the city provide trash pickup; Balbina and her neighbors burn their garbage in a nearby ditch.

Vista Hermosa breeds disease like it does mosquitoes. The lack of septic and sewage lines, potable water, and sanitation services puts the neighborhood at great risk for all manner of illnesses, from intestinal parasites to tuberculosis. But the gravest, most frightening threat comes not from the neighborhood, but from beyond the chain-link fence around the Finsa park. The fence, less than a football field away from Balbina's house, may divide the First and Third worlds, but it also unites them under a single toxic cloud. When the maquilas illegally dump toxic waste into irrigation canals, when a hot north wind blows the acrid smell of *chapapote*—pitch—from the Magne-Tek plant over its workers' homes, when runoff from a pesticide plant spills into a ditch, when chemical spills or leaks or explosions or fires erupt in the air, it doesn't take a Sierra Club member to understand the environmental wasteland the maquilas have created.

Nor does it take an epidemiologist to question the cause of an outbreak of anencephaly—babies born with either incomplete or missing brains and skulls. In one 36-hour period in the spring of 1991, three babies were born without brains at a single hospital across the river in Brownsville. Doctors soon learned of dozens of other anencephalic births in Brownsville and Matamoros. From 1989 to 1991, the rate of such defects for Brownsville was 10 times the U.S. average, or about 30 anencephalic births per 10,000 births. During the same years, there were 68 cases in Matamoros and 81 in Reynosa, a maquila site upriver.

Many who have studied the outbreak suspect it was due to industrial pollution unchecked by regulatory agencies in both countries. "These were atrocities committed by two uncaring governments," says Dr. Margaret Diaz, the occupational health specialist in Brownsville who detected the anencephaly cluster. "They are the product of years of neglect."

In a lawsuit filed in 1993, families of 28 children born with anencephaly or spina bifida—an incomplete closure of the spinal cord—blamed the outbreak on contamination from the Matamoros maquilas. The families sued 40 maquilas, including MagneTek, charging that the companies negligently handled "toxic compounds" and that the birth defects occurred after "exposure to toxins present in the local environment." The companies steadfastly denied wrongdoing, but internal memoranda documented that some plants released toxic emissions into the air in quantities impermissible in the United States. And trash sifted from the Matamoros city dump established that the maquilas were burning their industrial waste there, rather than disposing of it in the United States, as required by law. One videotape made by an investigator for the families portrays the charred but clearly visible remains of a MagneTek rapid-start ballast. The companies eventually paid a total of $17 million to the stricken families and cleaned up their worst excesses.

Although MagneTek and other companies insist they are improving conditions both inside and outside their plants, wages remain at poverty levels. Rolando Gonzalez Barron, a maquila owner and former president of the Matamoros Maquila Association, points to an advertising supplement in the *Brownsville Herald* lauding companies for their financial contributions to Matamoros schools. "Take 'Adopt-a-School,'" he says. "We put sewerage and bathrooms in schools where little girls had to do their necessities outside."

What about paying a living wage so that the parents of those little girls could afford indoor plumbing themselves? "Yes," Gonzalez replies, "housing needs to be developed, but our main goal is to create value for our customers."

What about your employees? What is your obligation to them? "If a worker is not eating," Gonzalez says, sounding every bit the farmer discussing a plow horse, "he's not going to work for you. We need to meet at least the basic needs."

But the basic needs—"eating, housing, clothing," as Gonzalez puts it—are unmet, and the evidence is as obvious and irrefutable as the colonia in MagneTek's backyard, where Balbina and her neighbors wrestle every single day with ferociously difficult decisions: Should I work overtime or huddle with my children to keep them warm? Buy meat or medicine? Pay the light bill or the gas bill? She makes those decisions based on a daily salary of 58 pesos, the equivalent of $7.43. That's an hourly wage of 92 cents—roughly the same starting wage Mollie James earned nearly half a century before. And Balbina often makes those decisions after working a grueling double shift—from 3:30 in the afternoon until six the following morning, after which she arrives home in time to fix breakfast for her children, accompany her oldest to school, and squeeze in a few hours of sleep before heading back to the plant in the afternoon.

No alcance. It doesn't reach. Over and over one hears this. *No alcance,* but we make it reach. They make it reach by taking odd jobs, or by scavenging for recyclables at the Matamoros city dump—an otherworldly metropolis of its own covering 50 acres—or peddling wares in the plant during breaks and shift changes. "It's prohibited," Balbina says, "but the company looks the other way and almost everybody does it." There are the ubiquitous Avon ladies, as well as sellers of homemade candy, tamales and gorditas, clothes, marijuana. And some sell their bodies, living *la doble vida*—the double life of coil-winder by day and prostitute by night.

Balbina has yet to resort to a second job. Instead, she works overtime as often as possible and recently moved into a government-subsized house; it is more comfortable than the one she shared with her sister, but it is hers only as long as she keeps her job. She is 29, an advanced age for a maquiladora worker. She lives with her boyfriend, a fellow MagneTek employee, and they stagger their shifts so that one provides child care while the other is working. Still, even the small necessities remain out of reach. "I need a lock for the door," Balbina says one afternoon. "I don't need it now, but soon I will."

Why not now?

"There is nothing worth locking now," she replies.

Mollie James never again found full-time work. She received a severance payment, after taxes, of $3,171.66—about $93 for each of the 34 years she worked. She collected unemployment benefits for six months and then enrolled in a computer-repair school, receiving a certificate of completion and numerous don't-call-us responses to job inquiries. Late last year, at the age of 68, she took a part-time job as an attendant at a nursing home. For the remainder of her income, she depends on Social Security and the rent she collects from the three-family house she owns, as well as a monthly pension of $71.23 from her Teamsters local. "That's nothing," she says. "That doesn't even pay your telephone bill. It's gone before you know it."

Although Paterson is a tenacious city, it seems defined by what is gone. Its last heyday was during and after World War II, when entrepreneurs like Archie Sergy and migrants like Mollie James helped sustain the city as a proud symbol of industrial might. But the old factory district near the Great Falls has been in ruins for decades, and although a number of the ancient brick mills have been splendidly restored—as a museum, a hospital clinic, and housing for artists—Paterson today is thought of as one of those discarded American places, a city so squalid, so defeated, that few people who do not live or work in Paterson venture there.

Mollie James has spent a half-century in Paterson. She married and divorced there, raised four children, bought a house. She sank deep roots, and would like nothing better than to see the seeds of renewal take sprout, but she is fed up with high taxes, crime, the unstable economy. Like many "up-South" blacks of retirement age, she thinks often about going home, to rural central Virginia, to the land she left as a teenager. She still owns her childhood home amid three wooded acres.

During a trip back home not long ago, Mollie visited the cemetery where her parents are buried. It is where she wishes to be buried as well. "They better not put me in no dirt up there in New Jersey," she says. "Bring me back home, brother."

Balbina, too, dreams of returning to her ancestral home, to the quiet and clear air of Monte Bello, where she could raise her children in a calm, safe place. But there is no work around Monte Bello for her, no future there for her children. She is more concerned with the immediate future of her job. In the last couple of years, MagneTek closed the two old Universal plants in Arkansas and Mississippi and transferred the bulk of those operations not to Malamoros, but 60 miles upriver to Reynosa, where the union is even weaker, the wages lower still. Now the talk in Matamoros is that the company will once again use the threat of a move, as it did first in Paterson and then in the Southern plants, as a lever for lower wages.

Balbina scoffs at the notion of transferring to Reynosa if the company relocates her job there. "What if they were to move again?" she asks. "Maybe to Juárez or Tijuana? What then? Do I chase my job all over the world?"

47

Grassroots Activism: Mothers
of East Los Angeles

MARY PARDO

This retrospective on community activism in East Los Angeles shows how places and individuals are changed when people make their voices heard. Mary Pardo's life-history approach allows us to hear the voices of the women who worked on behalf of their families and communities. Despite obstacles of gender, class, ethnicity, and personal inexperience, they organized and confronted the powerful forces of the city and state. This is democracy in action.

THE COMMUNITY CONTEXT:
EAST LOS ANGELES RESISTING SIEGE

In 1984, the state of California commissioned a public relations firm to assess the political difficulties facing the construction of energy-producing waste incinerators. The report provided a "personality profile" of those residents most likely to organize effective opposition to projects:

> middle and upper socioeconomic strata possess better resources to effectuate their opposition. Middle and higher socioeconomic strata neighborhoods should not fall within the one-mile and five-mile radii of the proposed site. Conversely, older people, people with a high school education or less are least likely to oppose a facility.[1]

The state accordingly placed the [toxic waste incinerator] plant in Commerce, a predominantly Mexican American, low-income community. This pattern holds throughout the state and the country: three out of five Afro-Americans and Latinos live near toxic waste sites, and three of the five largest hazardous waste landfills are in communities with at least 80 percent minority populations.

Similarly, in March 1985, when the state sought a site for the first state prison in Los Angeles County, Governor Deukmejian resolved to place the 1,700-inmate institution in East Los Angeles, within a mile of the long-established Boyle Heights neighborhood and within two miles of thirty-four

---

1. Cerrell Associates, Inc., "Political Difficulties Facing Waste-to-Energy Conversion Plant Siting," Report Prepared for California Waste Management Board, Slate of California (Los Angeles, 1984): 43.

schools. Furthermore, violating convention, the state bid on the expensive parcel of industrially zoned land without compiling an environmental impact report or providing a public community hearing. * * *

In spring 1986, after much pressure from the 56th assembly district office and the community, the Department of Corrections agreed to hold a public information meeting, which was attended by over 700 Boyle Heights residents. From this moment on, Vigil observed, "the tables turned, the community mobilized, and the residents began calling the political representatives and requesting their presence at hearings and meetings."[2] By summer 1986, the community was well aware of the prison site proposal. Over two thousand people, carrying placards proclaiming "No Prison in ELA," marched from Resurrection Church in Boyle Heights to the 3rd Street bridge linking East Los Angeles with the rapidly expanding downtown Los Angeles. This march marked the beginning of one of the largest grassroots coalitions to emerge from the Latino community in the last decade.

Prominent among the coalition's groups is "Mothers of East Los Angeles," a loosely knit group of over 400 Mexican American women. MELA initially coalesced to oppose the state prison construction but has since organized opposition to several other projects detrimental to the quality of life in the central city. Its second large target is a toxic waste incinerator proposed for Vernon, a small city adjacent to East Los Angeles. This incinerator would worsen the already debilitating air quality of the entire county and set a precedent dangerous for other communities throughout California. When MELA took up the fight against the toxic waste incinerator, it became more than a single-issue group and began working with environmental groups around the state. As a result of the community struggle, AB58 (Roybal-Allard), which provides all Californians with the minimum protection of an environmental impact report before the construction of hazardous waste incinerators, was signed into law. But the law's effectiveness relies on a watchful community network. Since its emergence, "Mothers of East Los Angeles" has become centrally important to just such a network of grassroots activists including a select number of Catholic priests and two Mexican American political representatives. Furthermore, the group's very formation, and its continued spirit and activism, fly in the face of the conventional political science beliefs regarding political participation.

Predictions by the "experts" attribute the low formal political participation (i.e., voting) of Mexican American people in the U.S. to a set of cultural "retardants" including primary kinship systems, fatalism, religious traditionalism traditional cultural values, and mother country attachment. The core activists in MELA may appear to fit this description, as well as the state-commissioned profile of residents least likely to oppose toxic waste incinerator projects.

2. James Vigil, Jr., field representative for Assemblywoman Gloria Molina, 1984–1986, Personal Interview, Whittier, Calif., 27 September 1989.

All the women live in a low-income community. Furthermore, they identify themselves as active and committed participants in the Catholic Church; they claim an ethnic identity—Mexican American; their ages range from forty to sixty; and they have attained at most high school educations. However, these women fail to conform to the predicted political apathy. Instead, they have transformed social identity—ethnic identity, class identity, and gender identity—into an impetus as well [as] a basis for activism. And, in transforming their existing social networks into grassroots political networks, they have also transformed themselves.

TRANSFORMATION AS A DOMINANT THEME

From the life histories of the group's core activists and from my own field notes, I have selected excerpts that tell two representative stories. One is a narrative of the events that led to community mobilization in East Los Angeles. The other is a story of transformation, the process of creating new and better relationships that empower people to unite and achieve common goals.

First, women have transformed organizing experiences and social networks arising from gender-related responsibilities into political resources. When I asked the women about the first community, not necessarily "political," involvement they could recall, they discussed experiences that predated the formation of MELA. Juana Gutiérrez explained:

> Well, it didn't start with the prison, you know. It started when my kids went to school. I started by joining the Parents Club and we worked on different problems here in the area. Like the people who come to the parks to sell drugs to the kids. I got the neighbors to have meetings. I would go knock at the doors, house to house. And I told them that we should stick together with the Neighborhood Watch for the community and for the kids.

Erlinda Robles similarly recalled:

> I wanted my kids to go to Catholic school and from the time my oldest one went there, I was there every day. I used to take my two little ones with me and I helped one way or another. I used to question things they did. And the other mothers would just watch me. Later, they would ask me, "Why do you do that? They are going to take it out on your kids." I'd say, "They better not." And before you knew it, we had a big group of mothers that were very involved.

Part of a mother's "traditional" responsibility includes overseeing her child's progress in school, interacting with school staff, and supporting school activities. In these processes, women meet other mothers and begin developing a network of acquaintanceships and friendships based on mutual concern for the welfare of their children.

Although the women in MELA carried the greatest burden of participating in school activities, Erlinda Robles also spoke of strategies they used to draw men into the enterprise and into the networks:

> At the beginning, the priests used to say who the president of the mothers guild would be; they used to pick urn. But, we wanted elections, so we got elections. Then we wanted the fathers to be involved, and the nuns suggested that a father should be president and a mother would be secretary or be involved there [at the school site].

Of course, this comment piqued my curiosity, so I asked how the mothers agreed on the nuns' suggestion. The answer was simple and instructive:

> At the time we thought it was a "natural" way to get the fathers involved because they weren't involved; it was just the mothers. Everybody [the women] agreed on them [the fathers] being president because they worked all day and they couldn't be involved in a lot of daily activities like food sales and whatever. During the week, a steering committee of mothers planned the group's activities. But now that I think about it, a woman could have done the job just as well!

So women got men into the group by giving them a position they could manage. The men may have held the title of "president," but they were not making day-to-day decisions about work, nor were they dictating the direction of the group. Erlinda Robles laughed as she recalled an occasion when the president insisted, against the wishes of the women, on scheduling a parents' group fundraiser—a breakfast—on Mother's Day. On that morning, only the president and his wife were present to prepare breakfast. This should alert researchers against measuring power and influence by looking solely at who holds titles.

Each of the cofounders had a history of working with groups arising out of the responsibilities usually assumed by "mothers"—the education of children and the safety of the surrounding community. From these groups, they gained valuable experiences and networks that facilitated the formation of "Mothers of East Los Angeles." Juana Gutiérrez explained how preexisting networks progressively expanded community support:

> You know nobody knew about the plan to build a prison in this community until Assemblywoman Gloria Molina told me. Martha Molina called me and said, "You know what is happening in your area? The governor wants to put a prison in Boyle Heights!" So, I called a Neighborhood Watch meeting at my house and we got fifteen people together. Then, Father John started informing his people at the Church and that is when the group of two to three hundred started showing up for every march on the bridge.

MELA effectively linked up preexisting networks into a viable grassroots coalition.

Second, the process of activism also transformed previously "invisible" women, making them not only visible but the center of public attention. From a conventional perspective, political activism assumes a kind of gender neutrality. This means that anyone can participate, but men are the expected key actors. In accordance with this pattern, in winter 1986 an informal group of concerned businessmen in the community began lobbying and testifying against the prison at hearings in Sacramento. Working in conjunction with Assemblywoman Molina, they made many trips to Sacramento at their own expense. Residents who did not have the income to travel were unable to join them. Finally, Molina, commonly recognized as a forceful advocate for Lati-nas and the community, asked Frank Villalobos, an urban planner in the group, why there were no women coming up to speak in Sacramento against the prison. As he phrased it, "I was getting some heat from her because no women were going up there."

In response to this comment, Veronica Gutiérrez, a law student who lived in the community, agreed to accompany him on the next trip to Sacramento. He also mentioned the comment to Father John Moretta at Resurrection Catholic Parish. Meanwhile, representatives of the business sector of the community and of the 56th assembly district office were continuing to compile arguments and supportive data against the East Los Angeles prison site. Frank Villalobos stated one of the pressing problems:

> We felt that the Senators whom we prepared all this for didn't even acknowledge that we existed. They kept calling it the "downtown" site, and they argued that there was no opposition in the community. So, I told Father Moretta, what we have to do is demonstrate that there is a link (proximity) between the Boyle Heights community and the prison.

The next juncture illustrates how perceptions of gender-specific behavior set in motion a sequence of events that brought women into the political limelight. Father Moretta decided to ask all the women to meet after mass. He told them about the prison site and called for their support. When I asked him about his rationale for selecting the women, he replied:

> I felt so strongly about the issue, and I knew in my heart what a terrible offense this was to the people. So, I was afraid that once we got into a demonstration situation we had to be very careful. I thought the women would be cooler and calmer than the men. The bottom line is that the men came anyway. The first times out the majority were women. Then they began to invite their husbands and their children, but originally it was just women.

Father Moretta also named the group. Quite moved by a film, *The Official Story*, about the courageous Argentine women who demonstrated for the return of their children who disappeared during a repressive right-wing military dictatorship, he transformed the name "Las Madres de la Plaza de Mayo" into "Mothers of East Los Angeles."

However, Aurora Castillo, one of the cofounders of the group, modified my emphasis on the predominance of women:

> Of course the fathers work. We also have many, many grandmothers. And all this IS with the support of the fathers. They make the placards and the posters; they do the security and carry the signs; and they come to the marches when they can.

Although women played a key role in the mobilization, they emphasized the group's broad base of active supporters as well as the other organizations in the "Coalition Against the Prison." Their intent was to counter any notion that MELA was composed exclusively of women or mothers and to stress the "inclusiveness" of the group. All the women who assumed lead roles in the group had long histories of volunteer work in the Boyle Heights community; but formation of the group brought them out of the "private" margins and into "public" light.

Third, the women in "Mothers of East L.A." have transformed the definition of "mother" to include militant political opposition to state-proposed projects they see as adverse to the quality of life in the community. Explaining how she discovered the issue, Aurora Castillo said,

> You know if one of your children's safety is jeopardized, the mother turns into a lioness. That's why Father John got the mothers. We have to have a well-organized, strong group of mothers to protect the community and oppose things that are detrimental to us. You know the governor is in the wrong and the mothers are in the right. After all, the mothers have to be right. Mothers are for the children's interest, not for self-interest; the governor is for his own political interest.

The women also have expanded the boundaries of "motherhood" to include social and political community activism and redefined the word to include women who are not biological "mothers." At one meeting a young Latina expressed her solidarity with the group and, almost apologetically, qualified herself as a "resident," not a "mother," of East Los Angeles. Erlinda Robles replied:

> When you are fighting for a better life for children and "doing" for them, isn't that what mothers do? So we're all mothers. You don't have to have children to be a "mother."

* * *

Fourth, the story of MELA also shows the transformation of class and ethnic identity. Aurora Castillo told of an incident that illustrated her growing knowledge of the relationship of East Los Angeles to other communities and the basis necessary for coalition building:

> And do you know we have been approached by other groups? [She lowers her voice in emphasis.] You know that Pacific Palisades group asked for our backing. But what they did, they sent their powerful lobbyist that they pay thousands of dollars to get our support against the drilling in Pacific Palisades. So what we did was tell them to send their grassroots people, not their lobbyist. We're suspicious. We don't want to talk to a high-salaried lobbyist; we are humble people. We did our own lobbying. In one week we went to Sacramento twice.

The contrast between the often tedious and labor-intensive work of mobilizing people at the "grassroots" level and the paid work of a "high salaried lobbyist" represents a point of pride and integrity, not a deficiency or a source of shame. If the two groups were to construct a coalition, they must communicate on equal terms.

The women of MELA combine a willingness to assert opposition with a critical assessment of their own weaknesses. At one community meeting, for example, representatives of several oil companies attempted to gain support for placement of an oil pipeline through the center of East Los Angeles. The exchange between the women in the audience and the oil representative was heated, as women alternated asking questions about the chosen route for the pipeline:

> "Is it going through Cielito Lindo [Reagan's ranch]?" The oil representative answered, "No." Another woman stood up and asked, "Why not place it along the coastline?" Without thinking of the implications, the representative responded, "Oh, no! If it burst, it would endanger the marine life." The woman retorted, "You value the marine life more than human beings?" His face reddened with anger and the hearing disintegrated into angry chanting.

The proposal was quickly defeated. But Aurora Castillo acknowledged that it was not solely their opposition that brought about the defeat:

> We won because the westside was opposed to it, so we united with them. You know there are a lot of attorneys who live there and they also questioned the representative. Believe me, no way is justice blind. . . . We just don't want all this garbage thrown at us because we are low-income and Mexican American. We are lucky now that we have good representatives, which we didn't have before.

Throughout their life histories, the women refer to the disruptive effects of land use decisions made in the 1950s. As longtime residents, all but one share the experience of losing a home and relocating to make way for a freeway.

* * *

The freeways that cut through communities and disrupted neighborhoods are now a concrete reminder of shared injustice, of the vulnerability of the community in the 1950s. The community's social and political history thus informs perceptions of its current predicament; however, today's activists emphasize not the powerlessness of the community but the change in status and progression toward political empowerment.

Fifth, the core activists typically tell stories illustrating personal change and a new sense of entitlement to speak for the community. They have transformed the unspoken sentiments of individuals into a collective community voice. Lucy Ramos related her initial apprehensions:

> I was afraid to get involved. I didn't know what was going to come out of this and I hesitated at first. Right after we started, Father John came up to me and told me, "I want you to be a spokesperson." I said, "Oh no, I don't know what I am going to say." I was nervous. I am surprised I didn't have a nervous breakdown then. Every time we used to get in front of the TV cameras and even interviews like this, I used to sit there and I could feel myself shaking. But as time went on, I started getting used to it.
>
> And this is what I have noticed with a lot of them. They were afraid to speak up and say anything. Now, with this prison issue, a lot of them have come out and come forward and given their opinions. Everybody used to be real "quietlike."

She also related a situation that brought all her fears to a climax, which she confronted and resolved as follows:

> When I first started working with the coalition, Channel 13 called me up and said they wanted to interview me and I said OK. Then I started getting nervous. So I called Father John and told him, "You better get over here right away." He said, "Don't worry, don't worry, you can handle it by yourself." Then Channel 13 called me back and said they were going to interview another person, someone I had never heard of, and asked if it was OK if he came to my house. And I said OK again. Then I began thinking, what if this guy is for the prison? What am I going to do? And 1 was so nervous and I thought, I know what I am going to do!

Since the meeting was taking place in her home, she reasoned that she was entitled to order any troublemakers out of her domain:

> If this man tells me anything, I am just going to chase him out of my house. That is what I am going to do! All these thoughts were going through my head. Then Channel 13 walk into my house followed by six men I had never met. And I thought, Oh, my God, what did I get myself into? I kept saying to myself, if they get smart with me I am throwing them ALL out.

At this point her tone expressed a sense of resolve. In fact, the situation turned out to be neither confrontational nor threatening, as the "other men" were also members of the coalition. This woman confronted an anxiety-laden situation by relying on her sense of control within her home and family—a quite "traditional" source of authority for women—and transforming that control into the courage to express a political position before a potential audience all over one of the largest metropolitan areas in the nation.

People living in Third World countries as well as in minority communities in the United States face an increasingly degraded environment. Recognizing the threat to the well-being of their families, residents have mobilized at the neighborhood level to fight for "quality of life" issues. The common notion that environmental well-being is of concern solely to white middle-class and upper-class residents ignores the specific way working-class neighborhoods suffer from the fallout of the city "growth machine" geared for profit.

In Los Angeles, the culmination of postwar urban renewal policies, the growing Pacific Rim trade surplus and investment, and low-wage international labor migration from Third World countries are creating potentially volatile conditions. Literally palatial financial buildings swallow up the space previously occupied by modest, low-cost housing. Increasing density and development not matched by investment in social programs, services, and infrastructure erode the quality of life, beginning in the core of the city. Latinos, the majority of whom live close to the center of the city, must confront the distilled social consequences of development focused solely on profit. The Mexican American community in East Los Angeles, much like other minority working-class communities, has been a repository for prisons instead of new schools, hazardous industries instead of safe work sites, and one of the largest concentrations of freeway interchanges in the country, which transports much wealth past the community. And the concerns of residents in East Los Angeles may provide lessons for other minority as well as middle-class communities. Increasing environmental pollution resulting from inadequate waste disposal plans and an out-of-control "need" for penal institutions to contain the casualties created by the growing bipolar distribution of wages may not be limited to the Southwest. These conditions set the stage for new conflicts and new opportunities, to transform old relationships into coalitions that can challenge state agendas and create new community visions.

Mexican American women living east of downtown Los Angeles exemplify the tendency of women to enter into environmental struggles in defense of their community. Women have a rich historical legacy of community activism, partly reconstructed over the last two decades in social histories of women who contested other "quality of life issues," from the price of bread to "Demon Rum" (often representing domestic violence).

But something new is also happening. The issues "traditionally" addressed by women—health, housing, sanitation, and the urban environment—have moved to center stage as capitalist urbanization progresses. Environmental issues now fuel the fires of many political campaigns and drive citizens beyond the rather restricted, perfunctory political act of voting. Instances of political mobilization at the grassroots level, where women often play a central role, allow us to "see" abstract concepts like participatory democracy and social change as dynamic processes.

* * *

The work "Mothers of East Los Angeles" do to mobilize the community demonstrates that people's political involvement cannot be predicted by their cultural characteristics. These women have defied stereotypes of apathy and used ethnic, gender, and class identity as an impetus, a strength, a vehicle for political activism. They have expanded their—and our—understanding of the complexities of a political system, and they have reaffirmed the possibility of "doing something."

They also generously share the lessons they have learned. One of the women in "Mothers of East Los Angeles" told me, as I hesitated to set up an interview with another woman I hadn't yet met in person,

> You know, nothing ventured nothing lost. You should have seen how timid we were the first time we went to a public hearing. Now, forget it, I walk right up and make myself heard and that's what you have to do.

48

Industry-Driven Activism*

EDWARD WALKER

Political sociologist Edward Walker directs our attention to perhaps one of the most important changes in the political process of the last hundred years: the unlimited and currently anonymous funding* by corporations, wealthy individuals, and unions to back or oppose political candidates. For example, David and Charles Koch, billionaire owners and investors (much of it in fossil fuels), organized Americans for Prosperity, an organization that paid for eighty public events aimed at opposing cap-and-trade legislation, 300 events opposing health-care reform, and, according to Jane Mayer writing in The New Yorker, *worked to "educate, fund, and organize Tea Party protesters."** Social movements have long been recognized as forces for social change in a political system that respects the will of "the people," especially when citizens take the time and trouble to be heard. The question Walker raises concerns the authenticity of their voice, when "grassroots methods can be used, ironically, to increase political inequalities."*

The contentious summer of 2009 raised questions about what we really mean by "grassroots" political advocacy. Many pundits asked aloud whether a number of ostensibly spontaneous, citizen-driven protest events were instead mere "Astroturf"—top-down, industry-funded events. As late summer set in, legislators were met with furious outbursts as they convened town hall meetings on health reform. Activists shouted about government takeovers of healthcare and the dangers of socialism, and politicians stared down an angry and apparently motivated cadre of voters. But, as *The New York Times* reported, some of these seemingly self-motivated citizens were, in fact, called to action by well-heeled groups like former House Majority Leader Dick Armey's FreedomWorks.

---

*Since Teddy Roosevelt's presidency Congress and the courts have restricted campaign financing in order to have a more level playing field among candidates. The 2010 U.S. Supreme Court ruling in *Citizens United v. Federal Election Commission* effectively ended all restrictions on the basis of the First Amendment (freedom of speech). As a consequence, the 2010 midterm elections saw tens of millions of dollars from wealthy individuals and corporations going to candidates without public attribution or a way to identify the funding source.

**Jane Mayer. "Covert Operations." *New Yorker* (August 30, 2010): 45–55.

While direct industry support for the most vocal of the town hall protestors is uncertain, health industries—insurers, in particular—were galvanized by the healthcare reform efforts of the Obama Administration to activate their employees and other stakeholders as issue advocates or "citizen lobbyists." It's no surprise that these companies would come out strongly against ideas like a public option, but it's noteworthy that they've used innovative means and advanced communications technologies to encourage individuals and community groups at the grassroots level to supplement the industry's clout.

As an illustration, consider how America's Health Insurance Plans (AHIP), the leading trade association for nearly 1,300 insurance firms (covering more than 200 million Americans), took action during the reform debates last year. On the one hand, they distributed a "Town Hall Tips" memo to health plan employees, encouraging their attendance at the meetings and asking them to make their message as personal as possible. ("Personal anecdotes are a very compelling way to make your point. In addition. . . speak to the positive impact your company has on the local community.") But, according to Beth Leonard, the AHIP's director of grassroots outreach efforts, these meetings, even during their peak, accounted for a mere 10% of the organization's efforts to mobilize resistance to the public option and support for mandated individual coverage. The remaining 90 percent of AHIP's grassroots mobilization efforts (and others like them) was made up of a large arsenal of tactics for mobilizing stakeholder groups: from television advertisements that encourage calls to representatives to spinning off semiautonomous citizen groups that help build support for their cause.

Campaigns like these are lowering the costs of participation for many citizens and should make us reconsider the way we think about the relationships among corporations, citizens, and government.

MOBILIZING STRATEGIES

Elite advocates use a number of overlapping strategies to activate targeted citizens in the political process, depending upon which groups or citizens are targeted and what the ultimate goal is. In the recent health reform debate, there's evidence of a diverse set of strategies at work, and each comes with its own set of advantages and limitations.

Activate consumers

Efforts to mobilize consumers are hardly unprecedented in corporate mobilization. Pharmaceutical companies have been particularly active in this arena, given that for many of their consumers, access to their products may literally be a matter of life and death. But even when it's not, drug manufacturers and trade groups like PhRMA are busy getting the public to join their cause. PhRMA has developed state-level patient coalitions as part of a long-term political strategy. They take what many call a "grasstops" strategy, in which they work with the leaders of existing voluntary associations in order to build upon those groups' infrastructure and legitimacy. As management scholar Michael Lord reports, pharmaceuticals have also become active in tapping into pre-existing patient and medical advocacy networks. "Who better," Lord asks, "to help defend pharmaceutical companies' need to protect their patents and pricing so that they can afford to invest in R&D to generate the next round of useful therapies and (hopefully) cures?"

Pharmaceuticals aren't the only ones taking a consumer-based strategy. In response to proposed reforms, an association of employer benefits programs recently started the website Savemyflexplan.org, which encourages flex plan enrollees to write their representatives in opposition. Insurance firm Humana contacted their senior Medicare Advantage enrollees with mailings warning them that if reform legislation is enacted, "millions of seniors and disabled individuals could lose many of [their] benefits and services." And AHIP sounded the alarm that these new regulations could cause seniors to face increases in premiums, reduced benefits, or even the loss of their plan altogether, despite evidence that reductions in Advantage plan overpayments are not likely to jeopardize seniors' access to quality care.

Activate employees

There's a growing sentiment in the public affairs offices of many prominent businesses that employees can be a company's strongest advocates. They also represent a large and often well-informed constituency, although the interests of management and employees may not always line up perfectly. When they do, it's a fine line to walk between encouraging employees to voice their independent concerns to their representatives and paying employees to lobby, which is against the law in states like California. Like other sorts of elite public affairs campaigns, there are advantages to lowering the perceived costs of participation, but drawbacks to crafting an overly standardized message. This subject became the topic of considerable debate when insurers Wellpoint and UnitedHealth Group were accused of helping employees call or write their representatives on company time. As business scholar Gerry Keim puts it, even employees with "different ideological lenses will see common ground when discussing issues that affect job growth and business opportunities."

Build a third party organization

If the goal is to activate broad-based groups beyond those who produce or consume an industry's goods and services, organizations may find it effective to build a coalition or third party organization that invites citizen participation. These are often targeted at those who hold ideological beliefs congruent with an industry's political position. Although certain groups hide their industry ties (or have only indirect ties), there's a trend toward increasing disclosure of industry support in order to mitigate potential criticisms.

AHIP's Campaign for the American Solution represents a prominent example. They invite citizens to write their representatives to express support for mandatory coverage and the preservation of the employer-based insurance system. Similarly, the Coalition to Protect Patients' Rights supports the participation of citizens who share their forceful opposition to the public insurance option, arguing that it could "drive health insurance companies out of business." These campaigns in the health arena follow similar efforts by non-health organizations like America's Power Army (coal), the National Smokers' Alliance (tobacco), and, more recently, Hands Off the Internet (telecom).

Advertise

Advocacy advertisements are another prominent way to gain public and legislative support. AHIP's predecessor, the Health Insurance Association of America, gained notoriety for their influential "Harry & Louise" ad campaign in 1994, which played a role in turning public sentiment against then-President Clinton's health reform proposal. Ads today often provide a web link or a toll-free number (like AHIP's) that will patch callers directly through to their representative, typically after suggesting a set of talking points. (A draw-back of this method is that, research shows, Congressional staffers find phone calls much less effective in shaping legislation than in-person visits.)

These efforts are often tied to other forms of lobbying facilitated by professional firms that assist in building broader public support. My own research on these paid public affairs or "grassroots lobbying" firms shows that health-related interests in multiple industries represent a significant share of lobbyists' clients and that the firms help build community coalitions, collect signatures for petitions, target particular demographic groups for activism, and coordinate public events like demonstrations.

Astroturf

This term is often used broadly to refer to any sort of mobilization that supports an industry's issue position, but those involved in public affairs typically restrict this label to legal or ethical violations like forging or doctoring letters to representatives or willfully deceiving participants. Because this strategy is risky—beyond its legal ramifications, it is considered unacceptable by the major professional associations for public affairs—it's exceedingly rare for organizations to take this route. On the other hand, there's evidence that, when stakes are high, certain groups can't resist the temptation. In the fall of 2009, in fact, Reps. Waxman (D-Calif.) and Markey (D-Mass.) held hearings to evaluate the influence of Astroturf campaigns on energy and health policy after forged letters to a Congressional representative from community groups supporting "clean coal" were discovered.

Such allegations are at the root of the cynicism about industry mobilization. But protest events nearly always have outside sponsors or patrons that help organizers get things off the ground. So, despite appearances, there may not be much difference between what groups like FreedomWorks do and what organizers of all stripes do every day. Indeed, a spokesman for Armey's group pointed out to the press, "We hold up this concept that grassroots needs to be 100 percent spontaneous: 50 people showing up spontaneously at the same place at the same time. But there always needs to be some kind of organization. . .we provide the organizational backbone."

The dividing line between "grassroots" and "Astroturf" may be more of a political Rorschach test than a precisely measurable concept. But, in any case, changing relationships between companies and the public—especially in the health domain—are leading more and more industries to institute grassroots mobilization programs.

WHY GO GRASSROOTS?

Imagining how health interests like pharmaceuticals, insurance firms, hospitals, and producers of medical products try to pressure lawmakers conjures up images of Washington lobbyists in expensive suits making lavish contributions to politicians' re-election campaigns. Indeed, the nonpartisan Center for Responsive Politics estimates that these industries have contributed nearly $5 million to federal representatives since 2007 alone, with influential representative and Senate Finance Committee Chair Max Baucus receiving an estimated $450,000. As sizable as these donations are, however, they aren't the whole story.

What are all too often overlooked, once again, are those indirect tactics that go beyond contributions and insider lobbying. We tend to think of grassroots tactics like canvassing, mass letter-writing, building community coalitions, and protest as weapons of the weak, in that those who are kept out of a government or organization's decision-making processes are forced to adopt strategies that fall outside of traditional avenues of influence. Why, then, would powerful interests like health insurers and pharmaceuticals find it worthwhile to go grassroots?

Part of the answer speaks directly to questions of power and influence. In certain situations or for certain debates, these seemingly powerful organizations are, in fact, relatively weak or poorly positioned. Evidence suggests that organized advocates resort to these techniques when the existing political configuration advantages their opponents and can only be offset by expanding the audience of supporters will help correct that imbalance. Given the stakes in health care reform and the fact that the initial energy seemed to be on the side of reformers, the mobilization efforts of the industry are thus not surprising. (Conversely, if a corporation or industry can get what it wants without mobilizing the public, it's more likely to keep things under wraps.)

As institutions without voluntary "members," health insurers, pharmaceutical companies, hospitals, and medical device manufacturers face challenges in influencing public opinion and shaping public policy. Organizational research shows that these tactics not only build public support for certain approaches, they help companies "put a human face" on issues, personalizing matters for elite decision-makers.

Edward Grefe, a guru of the field who teaches courses in lobbying the public, proudly cites the work of famed community organizer Saul Alinsky as a source of inspiration for "the new corporate activism." He writes, "in the 1960s and 1970s, it was the activists who established grassroots movements for the promotion of laws affecting civil rights, women's rights, environmental protections, and consumers' rights. Now, activists are paving the way for corporate and association grassroots movements to follow."

IMPACTS OF INDUSTRY-DRIVEN ACTIVISM

We still don't know if all of this investment really pays off. While public affairs campaigns represent only one of many factors influencing any political decision-maker, political scientist Kenneth Goldstein found that during President Clinton's effort to overhaul health care in 1993–4, health interests were highly effective in micro-targeting influential citizens within particular legislative districts (especially those thought to be swayable votes), shaping legislators' perceptions of public attitudes. People who take the time to contact their representative are showing how serious they are about the issue, even if they're only repeating a set of talking points.

But a further challenge is a well-known chicken-or-egg problem: it's unclear whether mass contacting efforts lead a representative to vote a certain way, or if letters and emails are more likely to be sent to legislators who already agree with the cause (canceling out the apparent "effect" of citizen letter-writing). A field experiment by communications researcher Daniel Bergan supports the former. Bergan found that, other things being equal, those New Hampshire legislators randomly assigned for contact by two advocacy groups supporting tobacco-free workplace legislation were significantly more likely to support the legislation. However, given the state's citizen legislature, it's hard to know whether the same effect could be expected in more professionalized legislatures or on issues other than tobacco.

Researchers are only beginning to scratch the surface in identifying and quantifying the influence of top-down grassroots campaigns, so it is difficult to know how they will ultimately shape health reform. Political recruiters don't like to waste time or money, so they target their efforts at would-be activists who they know are most likely to say "yes" to their participation request (these tend to be the more educated, wealthy, and politically active, according to work by political scientist Henry Brady and colleagues). And, although they can generate a lot of noise, representatives may see right through stacks of boilerplate form letters. Despite these uncertainties, what *is* clear is that corporations and trade groups have learned how to harness the power of public input, and they're doing it in increasingly sophisticated ways.

BROADER IMPLICATIONS AND QUESTIONS

Industry-driven mobilization occurred on a broad scale during the health reform debate and helped those with a financial or professional stake in reform to voice their opinions in the political sphere. While we tend not to think of grassroots recruitment as well-suited to powerful institutional actors, evidence suggests that it is widespread and is encouraging greater civic and political participation—despite the use of selective targeting—while also expanding the influence of elite organizations.

Professional public affairs campaigns are, under current law, regulated neither by lobbying restrictions nor rules about campaign finance. There may be valid reasons for this: industry and civic groups tend to share the belief that required disclosures of grassroots spending would be a violation of their rights under the First Amendment. In fact, it isn't only corporate interests that object to new regulation; resistance to mandated grassroots spending disclosure has brought together surprising bedfellows, from the Traditional Values Coalition to the ACLU, the Sierra Club, and the National Right to Life Committee.

First Amendment concerns also swelled after 2009 calls from Democrats to investigate insurer Humana for allegedly violating federal restrictions on the use of Medicare dollars to distribute political messages. Republicans responded by denouncing this as a gag order and suggested that the restriction "threatens the integrity of our democracy." In mid-October Medicare administrators eased off, claiming that the original message was merely a legal reminder to insurers. This debate reinforces a major point. As a society, we haven't yet come to terms with the rightful place of industry efforts to use the public as a mediator in political battles. There are two main reasons. First, citizens participate in these campaigns through their own free will, not due to coercion, and are generally (although not always) well-informed and in full agreement with the issue position of the sponsoring organization. But second, elite organizations often possess superior resources for influencing public debate, meaning that grassroots methods can be used, ironically, to increase political inequalities.

Reformers are thinking long and hard about whether paid public mobilization should be regulated in the same fashion as traditional lobbying. Some note that such regulations would face serious legal hurdles related to freedom of speech protections for advocates both large and small, for- and non-profit. They also worry, justifiably, that increased disclosure will hardly be a panacea, as resources devoted to subsidizing citizen activism may simply be reallocated to other means of cultivating influence. On the other side, leaders of non-partisan advocacy groups (such as the president of the American League of Lobbyists) have said that such efforts represent a form of paid lobbying and should be regulated in the same fashion. Those in favor of regulation contend that the additional paperwork required of advocacy organizations would be a small price to pay for knowing the extent to which industries are shaping participation and policy.

Despite these political uncertainties, industry-driven grassroots campaigns are deeply entwined with broader changes in American civic and political life. Civil society underwent considerable changes in the 1970s and 80s, as the field of political and civic organizations in the U.S. experienced staggering growth. My own research has shown that this expansion had a significant influence on the founding of firms that provide grassroots mobilization services to elite clients, suggesting that professionalized civic and business groups turned to these firms for help in generating activism. It appears that the expansion of industry-driven public participation reflects a society in which civic and political ties are increasingly indirect and, perhaps as importantly, mediated by communications technologies like email, texting, and social networking websites.

These realities must be tempered by the understanding that much of our civic landscape remains unchanged. Even though it's tempting to conclude that face-to-face recruitment into political activity has been replaced by tele-vised advocacy advertisements, targeted phone calls to likely activists, or mass-emailed "action alerts," there's little evidence to date that such cam-paigns are displacing the efforts of traditional community organizations or civic groups. In fact, many of these industry campaigns cooperate with com-munity groups when it makes strategic sense to do so, and many public affairs professionals have career or personal ties to local civic organizations.

In the end, the growth of industry efforts to mobilize public participation—whether on health reform or on any other issue—is both shaping and shaped by our changing civic life and the social capital that sustains it. It also reminds us that sometimes even established insiders benefit by taking an outsider strategy.

49

The Cuban Diet

BILL MCKIBBIN

Invention born of necessity might explain what is happening throughout the United States. There is an emerging social movement around food: what is grown, how it is grown, and by whom it is grown, processed, transported, and marketed. Michael Pollan (reading 12) gives voice to this, as do many others who promote food coops, farmers markets, organic farms, and locally produced food. With the continuing U.S. embargo, coupled with the disappearance of support by the Soviet Union following its collapse, Cuba's people faced many crises, not the least of which was the provision of food. Their response, definitely born of necessity, looks very much like the social movement about food now growing in the United States.

The pictures hanging in Havana's Museum of the Revolution document the rise (or, depending on your perspective, the fall) of Cuba in the years after Castro's revolt, in 1959. On my visit there last summer, I walked through gallery after gallery, gazing upon the stock images of socialist glory: "anti-imperialist volunteers" fighting in Angola, Cuban boxers winning Olympic medals, five patients at a time undergoing eye surgery using a "method created by Soviet academician Fyodorov." Mostly, though, I saw pictures of farm equipment. "Manual operation is replaced by mechanized processes," read the caption under a picture of some heavy Marxist metal cruising a vast field. Another caption boasted that by 1990, seven bulk sugar terminals had been built, each with a shipping capacity of 75,000 tons a day. In true Soviet style, the Cubans were demonstrating a deeply held (and to our eyes now almost kitschy) socialist belief that salvation lay in the size of harvests, in the number of tractors, and in the glorious heroic machinery that would straighten the tired backs of an oppressed peasantry—and so I learned that day that within thirty years of the people's uprising, the sugarcane industry alone employed 2,850 sugarcane lifting machines, 12,278 tractors, 29,857 carts, and 4,277 combines.

Such was communism. But then I turned a corner and the pictures changed. The sharply focused shots of combines and Olympians now were muddied, as if Cubans had forgotten how to print photos or, as was more likely the case, had run short of darkroom chemicals. I had reached the gallery of the "Special Period." That is to say, I had reached the point in Cuban history where everything came undone. With the sudden collapse of the Soviet Union, Cuba fell off a cliff of its own. All those carts and combines had been the products of an insane "economics" underwritten by the Eastern bloc for ideological purposes. Castro spent three decades growing sugar and shipping it to Russia and East Germany, both of which paid a price well above the world level, and both of which sent the ships back to Havana filled with wheat, rice, and more tractors. When all that disappeared, literally almost overnight, Cuba had nowhere to turn. The United States, Cuba's closest neighbor, enforced a strict trade embargo (which it strengthened in 1992, and again in 1996) and Cuba had next to no foreign exchange with anyone else—certainly the new Russia no longer wanted to pay a premium on Cuban sugar for the simple glory of supporting a tropical version of its Leninist past.

In other words, Cuba became an island. Not just a real island, surrounded by water, but something much rarer: an island outside the international economic system, a moon base whose supply ships had suddenly stopped coming. There were other deeply isolated places on the planet—North Korea, say, or Burma—but not many. And so most observers waited impatiently for the country to collapse. No island is an island, after all, not in a global world. The *New York Times* ran a story in its Sunday magazine titled "The Last Days of Castro's Cuba"; in its editorial column, the paper opined that "the Cuban dictator has painted himself into his own corner. Fidel Castro's reign deserves to end in homegrown failure." Without oil, even public transportation shut down—for many, going to work meant a two-hour bike trip. Television shut off early in the evening to save electricity; movie theaters went dark. People tried to improvise their ways around shortages. "For drinking glasses we'd get beer bottles and cut the necks off with wire," one professor told me. "We didn't have razor blades, till someone in the city came up with a way to resharpen old ones."

But it's hard to improvise food. So much of what Cubans had eaten had come straight from Eastern Europe, and most of the rest was grown industrial-style on big state farms. All those combines needed fuel and spare parts, and all those big rows of grain and vegetables needed pesticides and fertilizer—none of which were available. In 1989, according to the United Nations Food and Agriculture Organization, the average Cuban was eating 3,000 calories per day. Four years later that figure had fallen to 1,900. It was as if they suddenly had to skip one meal a day, every day, week after month after year. The host of one cooking show on the shortened TV schedule urged Cubans to fry up "steaks" made from grapefruit peels covered in bread crumbs. "I lost twenty pounds myself," said Fernando Funes, a government agronomist.

Now, just by looking across the table, I saw that Fernando Funes had since gained the twenty pounds back. In fact, he had a little paunch, as do many Cuban men of a certain age. What happened was simple, if unexpected. Cuba had learned to stop exporting sugar and instead started growing its own food again, growing it on small private farms and thousands of pocket-sized urban market gardens—and, lacking chemicals and fertilizers, much of that food became de facto organic. Somehow, the combination worked. Cubans have as much food as they did before the Soviet Union collapsed. They're still short of meat, and the milk supply remains a real problem, but their caloric intake has returned to normal—they've gotten that meal back.

In so doing they have created what may be the world's largest working model of a semi-sustainable agriculture, one that doesn't rely nearly as heavily as the rest of the world does on oil, on chemicals, on shipping vast quantities of food back and forth. They import some of their food from abroad—a certain amount of rice from Vietnam, even some apples and beef and such from the United States. But mostly they grow their own, and with less ecological disruption than in most places. In recent years organic farmers have visited the island in increasing numbers and celebrated its accomplishment. As early as 1999 the Swedish parliament awarded the Organic Farming Group its Right Livelihood Award, often styled the "alternative Nobel," and Peter Rosset, the former executive director of the American advocacy group Food First, heralded the "potentially enormous implications" of Cuba's new agricultural system.

The island's success may not carry any larger lesson. Cuban agriculture isn't economically competitive with the industrial farming exemplified by a massive food producer across the Caribbean, mostly because it is highly labor-intensive. Moreover, Cuba is a one-party police state filled with political prisons, which may have some slight effect on its ability to mobilize its people—in any case, hardly an "advantage" one would want to emulate elsewhere.

There's always at least the possibility, however, that larger sections of the world might be in for "Special Periods" of their own. Climate change, or the end of cheap oil, or the depletion of irrigation water, or the chaos of really widespread terrorism, or some other malign force might begin to make us pay more attention to the absolute bottom-line question of how we get our dinner (a question that only a very few people, for a very short period of time, have ever been able to ignore). No one's predicting a collapse like the one Cuba endured—probably no modern economy has ever undergone such a shock. But if things got gradually harder? After all, our planet is an island, too. It's somehow useful to know that someone has already run the experiment.

Villa Alamar was a planned community built outside Havana at the height of the Soviet glory days; its crumbling, precast-concrete apartments would look at home (though less mildewed) in Ljubljana or Omsk. Even the names there speak of the past: a central square, for instance, is called Parque Hanoi. But right next to the Parque Hanoi is the Vivero Organopónico Alamar.

Organopónico is the Cuban term for any urban garden. (It seems that before the special period began, the country had a few demonstration hydroponic gardens, much bragged about in official propaganda and quickly abandoned when the crisis hit. The high-tech-sounding name stuck, however, recycled to reflect the new, humbler reality.) There are thousands of *organopónicos* in Cuba, more than 200 in the Havana area alone, but the Vivero Organopónico

Alamar is especially beautiful: a few acres of vegetables attached to a shady yard packed with potted plants for sale, birds in wicker cages, a cafeteria, and a small market where a steady line of local people come to buy tomatoes, lettuce, oregano, potatoes—twenty-five crops were listed on the blackboard the day I visited—for their supper. Sixty-four people farm this tiny spread. Their chief is Miguel Salcines López, a tall, middle-aged, intense, and quite delightful man.

"This land was slated for a hospital and sports complex," he said, leading me quickly through his tiny empire. "But when the food crisis came, the government decided this was more important," and they let Salcines begin his cooperative. "I was an agronomic engineer before that," he said. "I was fat, a functionary. I was a bureaucrat." Now he is not. Most of his farm is what we would call organic—indeed, Salcines showed off a pyramidal minigreenhouse in which he raises seedlings, in the belief that its shape "focuses energy." Magnets on his irrigation lines, he believes, help "reduce the surface tension" of the water—give him a ponytail and he'd fit right in at the Marin farmers' market. Taking a more "traditional" organic approach, Salcines has also planted basil and marigolds at the row ends to attract beneficial insects, and he rotates sweet potato through the rows every few plantings to cleanse the soil; he's even got neem trees to supply natural pesticides. But Salcines is not obsessive even about organicity. Like gardeners everywhere, he has trouble with potato bugs, and he doesn't hesitate to use man-made pesticide to fight them. He doesn't use artificial fertilizer, both because it is expensive and because he doesn't need it—indeed, the garden makes money selling its own compost, produced with the help of millions of worms ("California Reds") in a long series of shaded trenches.

While we ate rice and beans and salad and a little chicken, Salcines laid out the finances of his cooperative farm. For the last six months, he said, the government demanded that the *organopónico* produce 835,000 pesos' worth of food. They actually produced more than a million pesos' worth. Writing quickly on a piece of scrap paper, Salcines predicted that the profit for the whole year would be 393,000 pesos. Half of that he would reinvest in enlarging the farm; the rest would go into a profit-sharing plan. It's not an immense sum when divided among sixty-four workers—about $150—but for Cuban workers this is considered a good job indeed. A blackboard above the lunch line reminded employees what their monthly share of the profit would be: depending on how long they'd been at the farm, and how well they produced, they would get 291 pesos this month, almost doubling their base salary. The people worked hard, and if they didn't their colleagues didn't tolerate them.

What is happening at the Vivero Organopónico Alamar certainly isn't unfettered capitalism, but it's not exactly collective farming either. Mostly it's incredibly productive—sixty-four people earn a reasonable living on this small site, and the surrounding neighbors get an awful lot of their diet from its carefully tended rows. You see the same kind of production all over the city—every formerly vacant lot in Havana seems to be a small farm. The city grew 300,000 tons of food last year, nearly its entire vegetable supply and more than a token amount of its rice and meat, said Egidio Páez Medina, who oversees the *organopónicos* from a small office on a highway at the edge of town. "Tens of thousands of people are employed. And they get good money, as much as a thousand pesos a month. When I'm done with this job I'm going to start farming myself—my pay will double." On average, Páez said, each square meter of urban farm produces five kilograms of food a year. That's a lot. (And it's not just cabbage and spinach; each farm also seems to have at least one row of spearmint, an essential ingredient for the mojito.)

So Cuba—happy healthy miracle. Of course, Human Rights Watch, in its most recent report, notes that the government "restricts nearly all avenues of political dissent," "severely curtails basic rights to free expression," and that "the government's intolerance of dissenting voices intensified considerably in 2003." It's as if you went to Whole Foods and noticed a guy over by the soymilk with a truncheon. Cuba is a weird political system all its own, one that's been headed by the same guy for forty-five years. And the nature of that system, and that guy, had something to do with the way the country responded to its crisis.

For one thing, Castro's Cuba was so rigidly (and unproductively) socialist that simply by slightly loosening the screws on free enterprise it was able to liberate all kinds of pent-up energy. Philip Peters, a Cuba analyst at the conservative Lexington Institute, has documented how the country redistributed as much as two thirds of state lands to cooperatives and individual farmers and, as with the *organopónico* in Alamar, let them sell their surplus above a certain quota. There's no obvious name for this system. It's a lot like sharecropping, and it shares certain key features with, say, serfdom, not to mention high feudalism. It is not free in any of the ways we use the word—who the hell wants to say thank you to the government for "allowing" you to sell your "surplus"? But it's also different from monolithic state communism.

In 1995, as the program geared up, the markets were selling 390 million pounds of produce; sales volume tripled in the next three years. Now the markets bustle, stacked deep with shiny heaps of bananas and dried beans, mangos and tomatoes. But the prices, though they've dropped over the years, are still beyond the reach of the poorest Cubans. And the government, which still sells every citizen a basic monthly food ration for just a few pesos, has also tried to reregulate some of the trade at the farmers' markets, fearing they were creating a two-tier system. "It's not reform like you've seen in China, where they're devolving a lot of economic decision making out to the private sector," Peters said. "They made a decision to graft some market mechanisms onto what remains a fairly statist model. It could work better. But it has worked."

Fidel Castro, as even his fiercest opponents would admit, has almost from the day he took power spent lavishly on the country's educational system. Cuba's ratio of teachers to students is akin to Sweden's; people who want to go to college go to college. Which turns out to be important, because farming, especially organic farming, especially when you're not used to doing it, is no simple task. You don't just tear down the fence around the vacant lot and hand someone a hoe, quoting him some Maoist couplet about the inevitable victory of the worker. The soil's no good at first, the bugs can't wait to attack. You need information to make a go of it. To a very large extent, the rise of Cuba's semi-organic agriculture is almost as much an invention of science and technology as the high-input tractor farming it replaced, which is another thing that makes this story so odd.

* * *

One afternoon, near an *organopónico* in central Havana, I knocked on the door of a small two-room office, the local Center for Reproduction of Entomophages and Entomopathogens. There are 280 such offices spread around the country, each manned by one or two agronomists. Here, Jorge Padrón, a heavyset and earnest fellow, was working with an ancient Soviet refrigerator and autoclave (the writing on the gauges was in Cyrillic) and perhaps three hundred glass beakers with cotton gauze stoppers. Farmers and backyard gardeners from around the district would bring him sick plants, and he'd look at them under the microscope and tell them what to do. Perhaps he'd hand them a test tube full of a *trichoderma* fungus, which he'd grown on a medium of residue from sugarcane processing, and tell them to germinate the seed in a dilute solution; maybe he'd pull a vial of some natural bacteria—*verticillium lecanii* or *beauveria bassiana*—from a rusty coffee can. "It is easier to use chemicals. You see some trouble in your tomatoes, and chemicals take care of it right away," he said. Over the long run, though, thinking about the whole system yields real benefits. "Our work is really about preparing the fields so plants will be stronger. But it works." It is the reverse, that is, of the Green Revolution that spread across the globe in the 1960s, an industrialization of the food system that relied on irrigation, oil (both for shipping and fertilization), and the massive application of chemicals to counter every problem.

The localized application of research practiced in Cuba has fallen by the wayside in countries where corporate agriculture holds sway. I remember visiting a man in New Hampshire who was raising organic apples for his cider mill. Apples are host to a wide variety of pests and blights, and if you want advice about what chemical to spray on them, the local agricultural extension agent has one pamphlet after another with the answers, at least in part, because pesticide companies like Monsanto fund huge amounts of the research that goes on at the land-grant universities. But no one could tell my poor orchardist anything about how to organically control the pests on his apples, even though there must have been a huge body of such knowledge once upon a time, and he ended up relying on a beautifully illustrated volume published in the 1890s. In Cuba, however, all the equivalents of Texas A&M or the University of Nebraska are filled with students looking at antagonist fungi, lion-ant production for sweet potato weevil control, how to intercrop tomatoes and sesame to control the tobacco whitefly, how much yield grows when you mix green beans and cassava in the same rows (60 percent), what happens to plantain production when you cut back on the fertilizer and substitute a natural bacterium called *A. chroococcum* (it stays the same), how much you can reduce fertilizer on potatoes if you grow a rotation of jack beans to fix nitrogen (75 percent), and on and on and on. "At first we had all kinds of problems," said a Japanese-Cuban organoponicist named Olga Oye Gómez, who grows two acres of specialty crops that Cubans are only now starting to eat: broccoli, cauliflower, and the like. "We lost lots of harvests. But the engineers came and showed us the right biopesticides. Every year we get a little better."

Not every problem requires a Ph.D. I visited Olga's farm in midsummer, when her rows were under siege from slugs, a problem for which the Cuban solution is the same as in my own New England tomato patch: a saucer full of beer. In fact, since the pressure is always on to reduce the use of expensive techniques, there's a premium on old-fashioned answers. Consider the question of how you plow a field when the tractor that you used to use requires oil you can't afford and spare parts you can't obtain. Cuba—which in the 1980s had more tractors per hectare than California, according to Nilda Pérez— suddenly found itself relying on the very oxen it once had scorned as emblems of its peasant past. There were perhaps 50,000 teams of the animals left in Cuba in 1990, and maybe that many farmers who still knew how to use them. "None of the large state farms or even the mechanized cooperatives had the necessary infrastructure to incorporate animal traction," wrote Arcadio Ríos, of the Agricultural Mechanization Research Institute, in a volume titled *Sustainable Agriculture and Resistance.* "Pasture and feed production did not exist on site; and at first there were problems of feed transportation." Veterinarians were not up on their oxen therapy.

But that changed. Rios's institute developed a new multi-plow for plowing, barrowing, riding, and tilling, specially designed not "to invert the top-soil layer" and decrease fertility. Harness shops were set up to start producing reins and yokes, and the number of blacksmith shops quintupled. The ministry of agriculture stopped slaughtering oxen for food, and "essentially all the bulls in good physical condition were selected and delivered to cooperative and state farms." Oxen demonstrations were held across the country. (The socialist love of exact statistics has not waned, so it can be said that in 1997 alone, 2,344 oxen events took place, drawing 64,279 participants.) By the millennium there were 400,000 oxen teams plying the country's fields. And one big result, according to a score of Ph.D. theses, is a dramatic reduction in soil compaction, as hooves replaced tires. "Across the country we see dry soils turning healthier, loamier," Professor Pérez said. Soon an ambitious young Cuban will be able to get a master's degree in oxen management.

One question is: How resilient is the new Cuban agriculture? Despite ever tougher restrictions on U.S. travel and remittances from relatives, the country has managed to patch together a pretty robust tourist industry in recent years: Havana's private restaurants fill nightly with Canadians and Germans. The government's investment in the pharmaceutical industry appears to be paying off, too, and now people who are fed by ox teams are producing genetically engineered medicines at some of the world's more advanced labs. Foreign exchange is beginning to flow once more; already many of the bicycles in the streets have been replaced by buses and motorbikes and Renaults. Cuba is still the most unconsumer place I've ever been—there's even less to buy than in the old Soviet Union—but sooner or later Castro will die. What then?

Most of the farmers and agronomists I interviewed professed conviction that the agricultural changes ran so deep they would never be eroded. Pérez, however, did allow that there were a lot of younger oxen drivers who yearned to return to the cockpits of big tractors, and according to news reports some of the country's genetic engineers are trying to clone White Udder herself from leftover tissue. If Cuba simply opens to the world economy—if Castro gets his professed wish and the U.S. embargo simply disappears, replaced by a free-trade regime—it's very hard to see how the sustainable farming would survive for long. We use pesticides and fertilizers because they make for incredibly cheap food. None of that dipping the seedling roots in some *bacillus* solution, or creeping along the tomato rows looking for aphids, or taking the oxen off to be shoed. Our industrial agriculture—at least as heavily subsidized by Washington as Cuba's farming once was subsidized by Moscow—simply overwhelms its neighbors.

* * *

You can also ask the question in reverse, though: Does the Cuban experiment mean anything for the rest of the world? An agronomist would call the country's farming "low-input," the reverse of the Green Revolution model, with its reliance on irrigation, oil, and chemistry. If we're running out of water in lots of places (the water table beneath China and India's grain-growing plains is reportedly dropping by meters every year), and if the oil and natural gas used to make fertilizer and run our megafarms are changing the climate (or running out), and if the pesticides are poisoning farmers and killing other organisms, and if everything at the Stop & Shop has traveled across a continent to get there and tastes pretty much like crap, might there be some real future for low-input farming for the rest of us? Or are its yields simply too low? Would we all starve without the supermarket and the corporate farm?

* * *

[S]trict organic agriculture isn't what the Cubans practice (remember those pesticides for the potato bugs). "If you're going to grow irrigated rice, you'll almost always need some fertilizer," said Jules Pretty, a professor at the University of Essex's Department of Biological Sciences, who has looked at sustainable agriculture in fields around the world. "The problem is being judicious and careful." It's very clear, he added, "that Cuba is not an anomaly. All around the world small-scale successes are being scaled up to regional level." Farmers in northeast Thailand, for instance, suffered when their rice markets disappeared in the Asian financial crisis of the late 1990s. "They'd borrowed money to invest in 'modern agriculture,' but they couldn't get the price they needed. A movement emerged, farmers saying, 'Maybe we should just concentrate on local markets, and not grow for Bangkok, not for other countries.' They've started using a wide range of sustainability approaches—polyculture, tree crops and agroforestry, fish ponds. One hundred and fifty thousand farmers have made the shift in the last three years."

Almost certainly, he said, such schemes are as productive as the monocultures they replaced. "Rice production goes down, but the production of all sorts of other things, like leafy vegetables, goes up." And simply cutting way down on the costs of pesticides turns many bankrupt peasants solvent. "The farmer field schools began in Indonesia, with rice growers showing one another how to manage their paddies to look after beneficial insects," just the kinds of predators the Cubans were growing in their low-tech labs. "There's been a huge decrease in costs and not much of a change in yields."

And what about the heartlands of industrial agriculture, the U.S. plains, for instance? "So much depends on how you measure efficiency," Pretty said. "You don't get something for nothing." Cheap fertilizer and pesticide displace more expensive labor and knowledge—that's why 219 American farms have gone under every day for the last fifty years and yet we're producing ever more grain and a loaf of bread might as well be free. On the other hand, there are those bereft Midwest counties. And the plumes of pesticide poison spreading through groundwater. And the dead zone in the Gulf of Mexico into which the tide of nitrogen washes each planting season. And the cloud of carbon dioxide that puffs out from the top of the fertilizer factories. If you took those things seriously, you might decide that having one percent of your population farming was not such a wondrous feat after all.

The American model of agriculture is pretty much what people mean when they talk about the Green Revolution: high-yielding crop varieties, planted in large monocultures, bathed in the nurturing flow of petrochemicals, often supported by government subsidy, designed to offer low-priced food in sufficient quantity to feed billions. Despite its friendly moniker, many environmentalists and development activists around the planet have grown to despair about everything the Green Revolution stands for. Like Pretty, they propose a lowercase greener counterrevolution: endlessly diverse, employing the insights of ecology instead of the brute force of chemistry, designed to feed people but also keep them on the land. And they have some allies even in the rich countries—that's who fills the stalls at the farmers' markets blooming across North America.

But those farmers' markets are still a minuscule leaf on the giant stalk of corporate agribusiness, and it's not clear that, for all the paeans to the savor of a local tomato, they'll ever amount to much more. Such efforts are easily co-opted—when organic produce started to take off, for instance, industrial growers soon took over much of the business, planting endless monoculture rows of organic lettuce that in every respect, save the lack of pesticides, mirrored all the flaws of conventional agriculture. (By some calculations, the average bite of organic food at your supermarket has traveled even farther than the 1,500-mile journey taken by the average bite of conventional produce.) That is to say, in a world where we're eager for the lowest possible price, it's extremely difficult to do anything unconventional on a scale large enough to matter.

And it might be just as hard in Cuba were Cuba free. I mean, would Salcines be able to pay sixty-four people to man his farm or would he have to replace most of them with chemicals? If he didn't, would his customers pay higher prices for his produce or would they prefer lower-cost lettuce arriving from California's Imperial Valley? Would he be able to hold on to his land or would there be some more profitable use for it? For that matter, would many people want to work on his farm if they had a real range of options? In a free political system, would the power of, say, pesticide suppliers endanger the government subsidy for producing predatory insects in local labs? Would Cuba not, in a matter of several growing seasons, look a lot like the rest of the world? Does an *organopónico* depend on a fixed ballot?

There's clearly something inherently destructive about an authoritarian society—it's soul-destroying, if nothing else. Although many of the Cubans I met were in some sense proud of having stood up to the Yanquis for four decades, Cuba was not an overwhelmingly happy place. Weary, I'd say. Waiting for a more normal place in the world. And poor, much too poor. Is it also possible, though, that there's something inherently destructive about a globalized free-market society—that the eternal race for efficiency, when raised to a planetary scale, damages the environment, and perhaps the community, and perhaps even the taste of a carrot? Is it possible that markets, at least for food, may work better when they're smaller and more isolated? The next few decades may be about answering that question. It's already been engaged in Europe, where people are really debating subsidies for small farmers, and whether or not they want the next, genetically modified, stage of the Green Revolution, and how much it's worth paying for Slow Food. It's been engaged in parts of the Third World, where in India peasants threw out the country's most aggressive free-marketeers in the last election, sensing that the shape of their lives was under assault. Not everyone is happy with the set of possibilities that the multinational corporate world provides. People are beginning to feel around for other choices. The world isn't going to look like Cuba—Cuba won't look like Cuba once Cubans have some say in the matter. But it may not necessarily look like Nebraska either.

* * *

CREDITS

William Adler: "Job on the Line" from Mother Jones, March/April 2000, pp. 41–47, 86–87, © 2000, Foundation for National Progress. Reprinted by permission.

Elijah Anderson: "The Code of the Street" from *The Atlantic Monthly* (May 1994), pp. 81–94. reprinted by permission of the author.

Heidi Ardizzone and Earl Lewis: "Love and Race Caught in the Public Eye" from *Chronicle of Higher Education*, June 8, 2001, pp. B7–9. Reprinted by permission of the authors.

Robert Bellah, et al.: From *Habits of the Heart: Individualism and Commitment to American Life*, pp. 225–237. Copyright © 1985, 1996 by the Regents of the University of California. Reprinted by permission of the University of California Press.

Katherine Benton-Cohen: Reprinted by permission of the publisher. From, *Borderline Americans: Racial Division and Labor War in the Arizona Borderland*s by Katherine Benton-Cohen, pp. 1–9, 267–274, Cambridge, Mass.: Harvard University Press, Copyright © 2009 by the President and Fellows of Harvard College.

Peter Berger: From *An Invitation to Sociology* by Peter Berger, copyright © 1963 by Peter L. Berger. Used by permission of Doubleday, a division of Random House, Inc.

Joel Best: From *Damned Lies and Statistics: Untangling Numbers from the Media, Politicians, and Activists*, pp. 1–7, 161–171. Copyright © 2001, the Regents of the University of California. Reprinted by permission of the University of California Press.

Julie Bettie: From "Women Without Class: Chicas, Cholas, Trash, and the Presence/Absence of Class Identity," *Signs*, Vol. 26, No. 1. Copyright © 2000, The University of Chicago Press. Reprinted by permission.

Allan Brandt: "Racism and Research: The Case of the Tuskegee Syphilis Study" from *The Hastings Center Report* (December 1978), pp. 21–29. Reprinted by permission of the publisher.

Michael Burawoy: From "Public Sociologies: Contradiction, Dilemmas and Possibilities" from *Social Forces*, Vol. 82, No. 4. Copyright © 2004 by the University of North Carolina Press. Used by permission of the publisher. www.uncpress.unc.edu.